GEORGIA HANDBOOK

GEORGIA HANDBOOK

INCLUDING ATLANTA, SAVANNAH, AND THE BLUE RIDGE MOUNTAINS

THIRD EDITION

KAP STANN

GEORGIA HANDBOOK
THIRD EDITION

Published by
Moon Publications, Inc.
P.O. Box 3040
Chico, California 95927-3040, USA

Printed by
Colorcraft

Please send all comments, corrections, additions, amendments, and critiques to:

GEORGIA HANDBOOK
MOON TRAVEL HANDBOOKS
P.O. BOX 3040
CHICO, CA 95927-3040, USA
e-mail: travel@moon.com
www.moon.com

Printing History
1st edition—1995
3rd edition—May 1999

5 4 3 2 1 0

ISBN: 1-56691-150-8
ISSN: 1078-7267

Editor: Jeannie Trizzino
Map Editor: Jeannie Trizzino
Production & Design: Karen McKinley, David Hurst
Cartography: Brian Bardwell and Bob Race
Index: Sondra Nation

Front cover photo: Savannah, Georgia © William Blake/Picturesque, 1999

All illustrations by Bob Race unless otherwise noted.

Distributed in the United States and Canada by Publishers Group West

Printed in China

Although the author and publisher have made every effort to ensure that the information was correct at the time of going to press, the author and publisher do not assume and hereby disclaim any liability to any party for any loss or damage caused by errors, omissions, or any potential travel disruption due to labor or financial difficulty, whether such errors or omissions result from negligence, accident, or any other cause.

In memory of my parents

CONTENTS

SPECIAL TOPICS

MAPS

MAP SYMBOLS

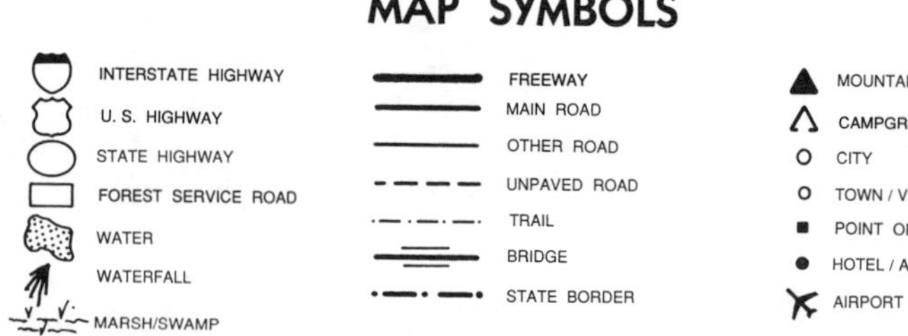

INTERSTATE HIGHWAY
U. S. HIGHWAY
STATE HIGHWAY
FOREST SERVICE ROAD
WATER
WATERFALL
MARSH/SWAMP
FREEWAY
MAIN ROAD
OTHER ROAD
UNPAVED ROAD
TRAIL
BRIDGE
STATE BORDER
MOUNTAIN
CAMPGROUND
CITY
TOWN / VILLAGE
POINT OF INTEREST
HOTEL / ACCOMMODATION
AIRPORT

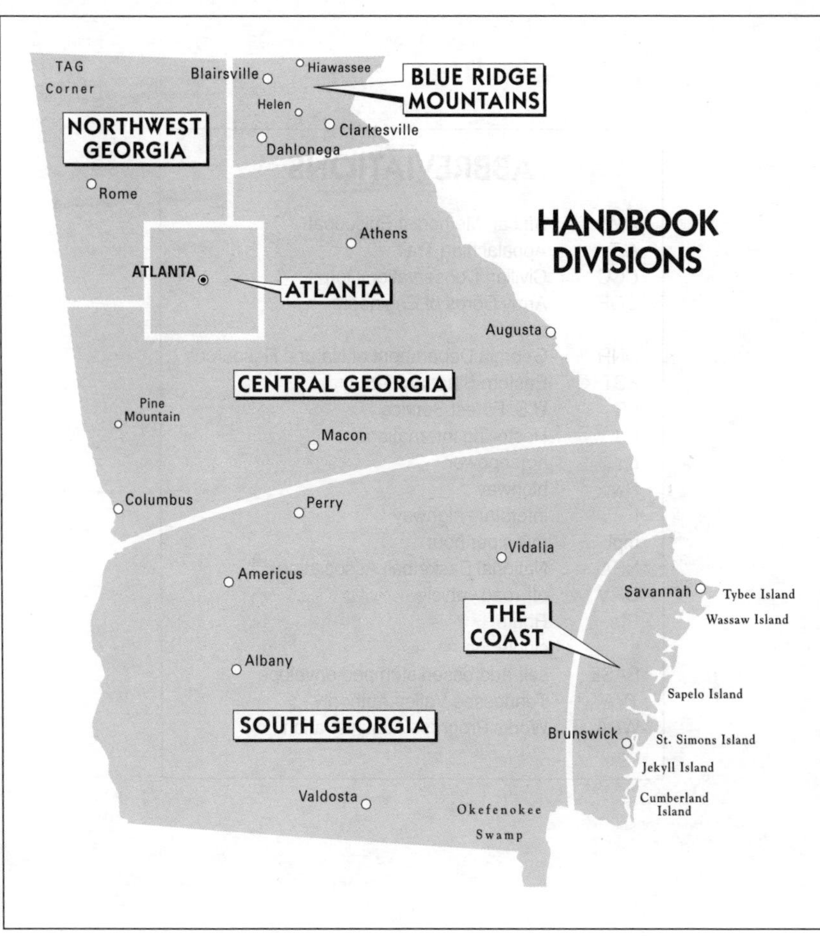
HANDBOOK DIVISIONS
TAG Corner
Blairsville
Hiawassee
BLUE RIDGE MOUNTAINS
Helen
Clarkesville
Dahlonega
NORTHWEST GEORGIA
Rome
Athens
ATLANTA
ATLANTA
Augusta
CENTRAL GEORGIA
Pine Mountain
Macon
Columbus
Perry
Vidalia
Americus
Savannah
Tybee Island
Wassaw Island
THE COAST
Albany
Sapelo Island
SOUTH GEORGIA
Brunswick
St. Simons Island
Jekyll Island
Valdosta
Okefenokee Swamp
Cumberland Island

ABBREVIATIONS

AME	African Methodist Episcopal
A.T.	Appalachian Trail
CCC	Civilian Conservation Corps
COE	Army Corps of Engineers
d	double
DNR	Georgia Department of Natural Resources
EST	Eastern Standard Time
FS	U.S. Forest Service
H.I.	Hostelling International
hp	horsepower
Hwy.	highway
I	interstate highway
mph	miles per hour
NBA	National Basketball Association
ORV	off-road vehicle
Rte.	Route
s	single
SASE	self-addressed stamped envelope
TVA	Tennessee Valley Authority
WPA	Works Progress Administration

ACKNOWLEDGMENTS

Without the contributions of so many generous Georgians, this guide would not be nearly so much fun to research. For wonderful Southern hospitality, thanks go particularly to cousins Bill and Carrie, Sulphur Creek *scappares* Diana and Frank, and old friends Joel and Alison. Thanks also to Belle for her crisp Yankee tips, to Dave for a mean Tom Collins, to Kathy for the trip to the alligator farm, to Joel for the boardwalk tour, to Stanley for the beautiful storm, and to the Kinslands of the Hometown Bookstore for reuniting us with Pup.

For inspiration I owe debts of gratitude to St. EOM, Howard Finster, Thelma's Kitchen, Daddy Dz, Flannery O'Connor, Bull Sluice, the Giant Goober, Br'er Rabbit, shrimp-and-grits, Johnny Mercer, James Brown, Jittery Joe's, JB's BBQ, and the Fruitcake Capital of the World.

This guide could not have been completed without research assistance provided by the Georgia Department of Industry, Trade, and Tourism's Chandler Haydon and ITT's dedicated regional representatives, along with such outstanding local representatives as Ruth Sykes, Karen McNeely, Kathy Ansley, and Jenny Stacey. Many thanks also to Kim Hatcher of Georgia State Parks and Historic Sites, and to colleagues in adventure travel Sonie Green and Michael Gowen.

My most tremendous thanks go to my expert navigator Cory, to my buddy Sally, and to LTR for late-night takeout chicken on deadline.

IS THIS BOOK OUT OF DATE?

Since this book went to press, some hotels, motels, restaurants, and attractions listed herein may have closed, changed hands, or raised their prices. Prices listed inside should be considered approximations; they're not guaranteed by the author or publisher. If you spot errors or omissions of any kind in the text or maps, please let us know. Also, if you have noteworthy experiences in Georgia—good or bad—particularly with any of the establishments listed in this book, please pass them along to us for subsequent updated editions. We'd appreciate hearing from you!

Address all correspondence to:
Georgia Handbook
Moon Publications
P.O. Box 3040
Chico, CA 95927 U.S.A.
e-mail: travel@moon.com

KATHY PETERSON

INTRODUCTION

THE LAND

From the air, Georgia resembles a giant green apron, with a ring of mountains at its neck and a waistband dividing the upper plateau from the wide skirt of the coastal plain. Two mighty Appalachian rivers string along its sides and define the state's territory; the Savannah River forms the border with South Carolina to the east, and the Chattahoochee River separates Georgia from Alabama to the west. In the north, Georgia shares a mountainous border with Tennessee and North Carolina; to the south lies Florida. To the southeast, a cool hundred miles of Atlantic coastline is fringed with islands as wild now as before the days of states and borders.

The 59,265-square-mile state blossoms to the surface with the lush seasonal landscapes the Southeast is famous for: colorful mountain forests and meadows, acres of cotton fields and peach orchards, and evergreen stands of Georgia pine. With this classic southeastern country, it's no wonder the region produced a culture so deeply rooted to the land. And Georgia, largest state east of the Mississippi, has more of that land than anybody.

Appalachian Mountains

Georgia's rugged northern terrain comprises a compact set of three geological subregions, all part of the Appalachian Mountain Range: the **Blue Ridge Province** in the east, the steep **Cumberland Plateau** in the west, and the **Ridge-and-Valley** region in between.

The crashing together of continental plates some 300 million years ago sent these southern Appalachians towering as high as the Rockies, but since then their once bare jagged peaks have eroded to well-worn mountaintops covered with forest. The softer central region eroded even further, creating the V-shaped Great Valley between the two rounded ranges.

This high valley cut a natural route both for the railroad tracks that put Atlanta on the map in 1843, and for the invading Union army of William Tecumseh Sherman that burnt it to the ground 21 years later. Now the modern trail of the interstate highway slices through it, bisecting the state and carrying winter-weary Midwesterners to warm southern beaches.

West of the valley, the long, linear mesas of the dry Cumberland Plateau sit on a bed of sandstone, shale, and limestone at the intersection of three states—Georgia, Alabama, and Tennessee. Isolated until relatively recently by its stark geography (the northwest tip of the state for many years was accessible only from neighboring states), the area attracts adventurers for hang gliding, spelunking (Ellison's Cave is the deepest east of the Mississippi), and wandering through fantastic boulder formations (follow the directive of signs on barns throughout the mountains and See Rock City!).

East of the valley lies the Blue Ridge Province. Here the famous Blue Ridge Mountains and the Cohuttas (a continuation of the Smoky Mountain Range) create a landscape of knobby peaks, narrow "gaps," and streaming waterfalls in moist coves. The state's highest point is here; 4,784-foot **Mt. Enotah** is better known by its nickname "Brasstown Bald" because of its grassy crest surrounded by tall forest. A Cherokee story rivaling that of Noah's Ark ascribes mythological status to the mountain. It was here, the story goes, that the People's giant canoe came to rest after the Great Flood. Such "balds" can be found throughout the Blue Ridge, and botanists are at a loss to explain what caused them. Some speculate that lightning-set fires, localized insect infestations, or prehistoric tribes cleared the grounds.

The discovery of a gold belt that runs from the Carolinas through North Georgia started the nation's first gold rush in Dahlonega ("precious yellow color" in Cherokee), sending thousands of prospectors to Georgia's Blue Ridge in search of fortune. After the boom went bust, spent miners turned back to farming and logging. Today, abandoned mines, pioneer cabins, gristmills, and covered bridges recall that earlier era. You'll still see an occasional horse-drawn or mule-driven plow, but most land once farmed, logged, or strip-mined has since returned to second-growth wilderness, now protected as a national forest. (Virgin forest was rare even when colonists arrived; the natives customarily cleared land for hunting grounds.)

From along the divide of Georgia's Blue Ridge, waters rush to either the Atlantic (via the Savannah River) or the Gulf of Mexico (via the Chattahoochee River or the Tennessee River farther north). River runners are drawn to the region's challenging whitewater, in particular the "Wild and Scenic" Chattooga River. The awesome Tallulah Gorge, placid high-country lakes, many panoramic waterfalls, and trout streams by the dozens add to the region's allure.

But trekkers know North Georgia best as the foot of the 2,036-mile Appalachian Trail. Claimed to be the oldest and longest continually marked footpath in the world, the A.T. crosses through 14 states and eight national parks between Springer Mountain, Georgia, and Mount Katahdin, Maine. Georgia's 83-mile stretch is less congested, and often more rugged, than the trail farther north.

Piedmont Plateau

The high shelf of rolling foothills and broad valleys that lies between the steep Appalachians and the flat coastal plain is the Piedmont Plateau. From the Italian word meaning "foot of the mountain," the Piedmont was so named by European settlers who noted the region's resemblance to southern Europe. Comprising 31% of the state's area, this region also holds nearly all of Georgia's major cities, including Macon, Augusta, Columbus, Athens, and the capital city of Atlanta.

With only one natural boundary at the banks of the Chattahoochee River, Atlanta expands outward, not upward, so while skyscrapers fill downtown, the rest of town spreads out through thick woods. This sprawl, the lack of natural landmarks visible over the trees, and long, winding routes can make metro Atlanta a challenge for newcomers to navigate without a good map.

Stone Mountain is a dramatic vantage point overlooking the city. This 1,683-foot-tall dome east of town—the largest piece of exposed granite in the eastern U.S.—rises in stark contrast to the forested hills all around. Table-flat exfoliated slabs, some as big as a house, lie at its base like huge shingles, and the dense, dry surface harbors an enclave of desert plant species. The rare geological outcropping is matched by an equally unusual relief carving on its face; three Confederate leaders on horseback represent the South's version of Mount Rushmore. Smaller granite outcroppings sprinkled around the Piedmont are less celebrated locally as ge-

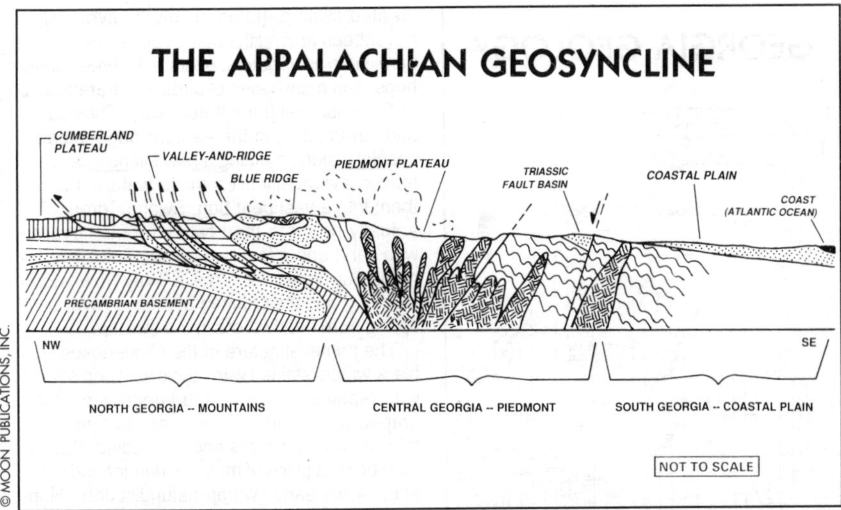

ological wonders than as the source of swimming holes in abandoned quarries.

As you move south, the cooler, rolling uplands around Atlanta and Athens begin to heat up and smooth out. **Pine Mountain,** north of Columbus, is the southernmost contour on the widening lowland plateau.

The Fall Line

The narrow band where the Piedmont meets the coastal plain marks the "fall line," the coastline of an earlier geological era. Along this line, Appalachian rivers spill from upland to lowland in a long run of waterfalls and rapids, below which smooth waters flow to the sea. Recognizing the potential for water power and transportation, early Europeans ventured upriver from the Atlantic coast and settled wherever rivers crossed the fall line. Augusta was founded on the Savannah River in 1735, Macon on the Ocmulgee River in 1825, and Columbus on the Chattahoochee in 1828. Likewise, you can map the fall line along the eastern seaboard by simply connecting the dots of major inland cities, from Columbus, Georgia, clear north through Washington, D.C.

Coastal Plain

Though Georgia is the seventh-fastest-growing state in the nation, you wouldn't know it to look at the rural coastal plain region covering the entire southern half of the state. Since colonial times, this pastoral plantation country has been Georgia's prime agricultural region. Today's top five cash crops—peanuts (Georgia's the number one peanut-growing state in the nation), tobacco, corn, cotton, and soybeans—thrive here along with the state's signature crops of peaches and pecans.

Two significant subregions create contrasting terrain. Antebellum plantations flourished here in the **Black Belt,** a fertile crescent of rich, dark soil running through the middle of the state and dipping into its southwestern corner. The sandier soils of the southeastern interior hold the **pine barrens** that support the state's logging, paper, and pulp industries (more than half the state is owned by lumber and pulpwood companies).

Rivers stained red from iron-rich clay drain the region. The Ocmulgee and Oconee meet near Lumber City to form the ocean-bound Altamaha River; the Chattahoochee and Flint Rivers meet at Lake Seminole. With all the respective forks and tributaries of each, no wonder the original residents of these plains were dubbed "Creeks."

Several naturalist nuggets are hidden within this vast interior. **Providence Canyon** (south

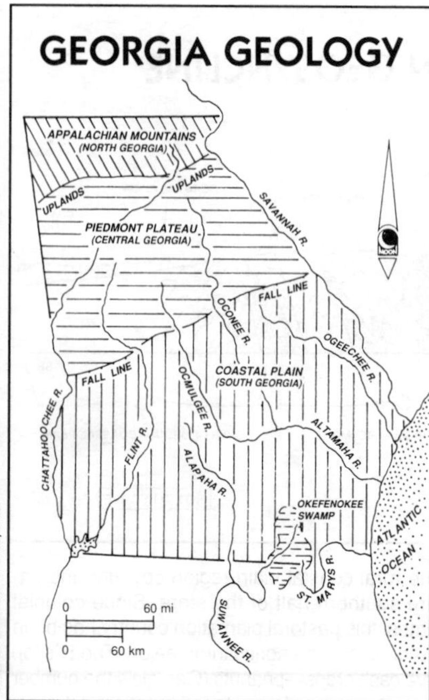

of Columbus), affectionately considered the Little Grand Canyon, features dramatically striped red-to-white walls that drop without warning from its flat, forested rim. **Sand dunes** along the Flint River (south of Albany) attest to the region's origins as an ancient seabed—you can still find prehistoric sharks' teeth among the dunes. Along the wild banks of the isolated Ocmulgee, densely packed 18-foot-high **canebrakes** resemble a forest of fishing poles. Wilder still are the region's scattered **swamps,** placid refuges for distinct varieties of plants and animals.

Okefenokee Swamp

Named from the Seminole term *ecunnau finocau,* meaning "earth trembling," the Okefenokee Swamp in Georgia's southeast pocket is the largest wildlife refuge in the eastern United States. According to Seminole legend, the swamp was created after a dispute between the beavers and the People; the angry beavers broke their dams to flood the area and then abandoned the newly created swamp. (Interestingly, beavers have never been among the many species that thrive here, such as alligators, otters, wild turkeys, wild hogs, and many types of birds and waterfowl.)

Scientists tell it a different way. They say a sudden uplifting in the eastern ridge isolated coastal waters, creating a new inland sea. Vegetation eventually filled these waters, turning them into a vast peat bog. Swamp "ground" is actually no more than twisted roots covered with sand and a few feet of leaf mold. The famous Suwannee River (as in "Way Down upon the . . . ") and the crooked St. Marys River both spring from headwaters in the swamp.

The primeval nature of the Okefenokee—its black waters stained with tannic acid and strewn with reptiles, its dark knob-kneed cypresses draped with Spanish moss—encourages folktales of swamp haunts and foreboding. But "far from being a place of mystery, danger and menace," wrote early swamp naturalist John Hopkins, the Okefenokee is rather "a haven of peace and a refuge from the greater hazards of the outside world."

Atlantic Coast

Georgia's Atlantic coast is actually made up of three separate coasts: the sandy seaward beaches of the dozen or so **barrier islands** farthest east, the **mainland coast** to the west, and the wide **tidal marshlands** that flow between them. From Savannah in the north to St. Marys at the Florida border, 100 miles of semitropical shore is largely preserved in its natural state.

Georgia's marshlands, measuring five to ten miles across, are the most extensive and productive on the eastern seaboard. Where a visitor sees largely a serene panorama of soft grasses, shrimp boats, and oyster beds, underwater the marsh busily churns out more food and energy per square mile than any other ecosystem.

Of the barrier islands, which buffer the marsh and mainland from harsh coastal storms, only four are bridged and developed as resorts (Tybee, St. Simons, Sea Island, and Jekyll). The rest are permanently protected sanctuaries accessible only by boat to a limited number of visitors. Shell middens (circular mounds of discarded oyster shells), ruins of Sea Island Cotton plantations, and wild horses descended from those left by the Spanish in the 17th century attest to the long and varied history of these beautiful palmetto islands.

About 17 miles east of Sapelo Island, in waters 50-70 feet deep, lies **Gray's Reef,** a national marine sanctuary and one of the largest "live-bottom" reefs off the southeastern coast. Its limestone outcroppings attract a wide variety of plant and animal life, not to mention divers and anglers.

CLIMATE

The only thing dry about Georgia is a county that doesn't sell liquor; the rest of the state is well-watered, downright lush. Road shoulders soften with saturation; hydrants occasionally explode to release pressure from too much water. But unlike other wet places where it's always raining (Seattle comes to mind), southeastern skies are mostly clear. The land just has a way of hanging on to moisture. Of course, the region has drier spells too, but what Georgians consider land ravaged by drought would look like a rainforest out west.

Rainfall averages 50 inches a year, varying from 70 inches in the extreme northeast mountain region to 45 inches around the fall line. In summer, daily afternoon thundershowers typically douse the day's heat for a few minutes, until the sun returns and turns the water to steam. In winter, snow falls in North Georgia's mountains—seven to ten inches worth supports the East's southernmost ski run in Sky Valley—and sometimes as far south as Atlanta.

The southeastern U.S. averages mild, comfortable temperatures in the 60-70° F range most of the year, without the harsh winters and freezing temperatures typical farther north. Summers, however, are decidedly subtropical, with high humidity and temperatures that can reach uncomfortable highs in the 90s (°F) most days in July and August.

Temperatures year-round stay cooler in the mountains and warmer at the coast, so, predictably, people seek refuge by the coast in winter and in the mountains in summer. City folk complain how much more insufferable South Georgia feels in comparison to the Piedmont uplands, but the difference may appear slight to sweltering visitors (see **Health and Safety** in the On the Road chapter for tropical precautions).

Travel Seasons

If you have to choose just one season, either spring or fall would be a good choice. Seasonal colors—whether spring flowers or autumn leaves—are spectacular and the climate is at its most comfortable.

Early spring (mid-March through mid-April) brings rain, and temperatures can fluctuate from the 50s to 80s (°F). Many flowering trees and wildflowers bloom during March and April. Late spring (mid-April through May) turns summery, with consistently warm and dry days.

Subtropical southeastern summers are often maligned for their heat and humidity, but where else can you experience those hot summer nights? And summer's what those verandas, porch swings, and mint juleps are all about. It starts heating up in June, and July and August are scorching. Flatlanders flee to cooler temperatures in North Georgia. Early September can be just as hot, but somehow with the summer crowds gone, it just feels cooler.

From mid-September to mid-October Georgia experiences delightfully warm and clear "Indian summer." By the third week in October, temperatures begin to drop; fall colors generally peak around this time too. Temperatures fall faster in

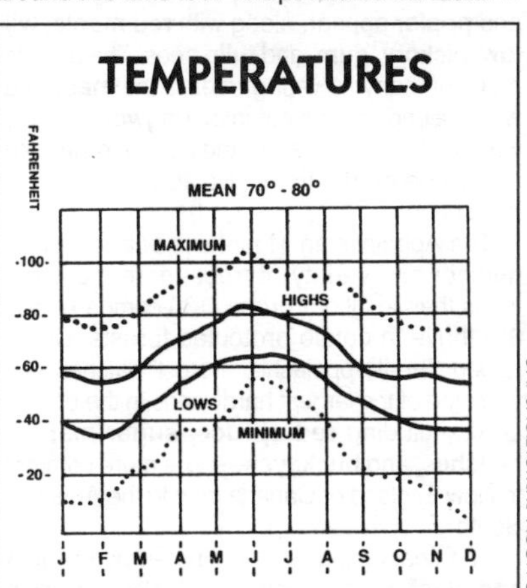

November. Then the winter chill sets in, reaching its frostiest between December and February and usually continuing through to early March. Because many flatlanders are apprehensive about driving in unfamiliarly icy conditions, visitors have the scenic snowy mountains to themselves in winter. Of course, many travelers aim for warm southern beaches in winter.

FLORA

A spectacular abundance of plants covers the South with lush green growth. Each of more than 1,400 species of trees, shrubs, wildflowers, and herbs has its own story to tell, woven into the natural and cultural history of the Southeast. The brief summary that follows of necessity outlines broad features and a few specifics; for more, ask any Southerner. The South's rural heritage has produced a culture finely tuned to the natural environment; most residents can describe in detail the particular characteristics and uses of area plants as though they were members of the family.

Trees

Georgia is trees: hardwoods and softwoods, deciduous and coniferous, flowering varieties, and species used for industry, agriculture, and art. The prevalent **pine, cedar, oak, elm, sycamore,** and **poplar** appear, along with **red maple, willow, hickory, gum,** and **tulip** trees. The most famous of many flowering trees is the **magnolia,** which, along with the common **dogwood** (pink or white), blooms in March and April. **Chinaberry** and **crape myrtle** trees also add flowers to the landscape.

The Appalachian Mountains beat all for the number and variety of trees; here more tree types than in all of Europe (130 compared with 85) thrive in dense protected forests. Undisturbed "Great Appalachian Forest" patches shelter some of the largest hardwoods in the eastern U.S., including **red spruce, sugar maples, beeches,** and **buckeyes**—trees more common to New England or Canada than to the American South.

The coastal plain is dominated by **longleaf and slash pine,** which once fueled a tremendous turpentine business and still support a lumber, pulp, and paper industry. **Live oaks** here and on the coast support the misnomered **Spanish moss;** neither moss nor Spanish, this epiphyte—a plant that gets all its nutrients from the air—is a distant relative of the pineapple family. The short, fat **saw palmetto** covers the coast with its large, fan-shaped fronds. **Bald cypress** looms over the swamps with branchless trunks below a thick canopy, and knobby "knees" of roots that protrude above the water's surface.

Forests reveal the regional history as clearly as rings in a tree. You can accurately date the evolution of a long-abandoned farm or clear-cut by observing a predictable second-growth succession. In a year, broom sedge and short pines begin to mask manmade marks; after 30 years such broadleaf varieties as oaks and hickories have returned. The Southeast has a very forgiving nature—ample moisture, ample space, and ample time heal most everything.

Flowers

One of the South's most magificent traits is an abundance of lusciously flowering plants. About 1,500 varieties of trees, shrubs, herbs, and wild-

KAREN McKINLEY

buckeye

flowers ensure blooms in all but the coldest months. From when the first white **serviceberry** blooms in early March till the last yellow **witch hazel** petal falls in December, the southeastern woods bloom naturally into a wild garden.

Besides towering magnolias and the delicate dogwood trees so closely associated with the South, two common flowering shrubs grow into flowering thickets as high as trees: **mountain laurel** and **rhododendron** reach heights of 30 feet, surrounding visitors with their delicate white blossoms. Miles of fruit orchards bloom in spring in the state's fruit-producing midsection, including the unusual Southern **pawpaw** and famous Georgia **peaches** (whose pink blooms peak in late March). Homey flower gardens are often decorated with such old-fashioned favorites as **snapdragons, sweet peas, candy tuft, larkspur, love-in-a-mist,** and **azaleas.**

The most compelling feature of a Southern garden, however, is not its beauty but its fragrance. Sweet **honeysuckle,** hot **gardenia,** and whispery scents of draped **wisteria** are among hundreds of languorous scents that grace Georgia's air; gardeners design "fragrance gardens" especially to tickle the olfactory nerves.

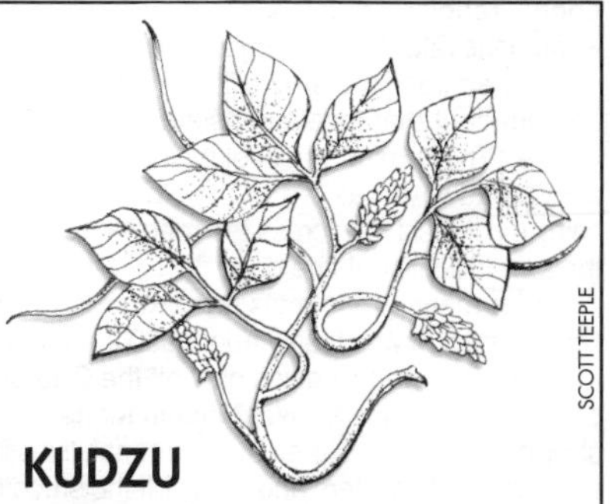
SCOTT TEEPLE

KUDZU

Any interstate traveler is bound to notice the unstoppable vine that seems to shroud whole forests along Georgia's highways like a hexed storybook kingdom. The devilish weed is kudzu (KUD-zoo), a vine of the genus Pueraria. Imported from Japan to the South earlier this century for erosion control, it has overstepped its boundaries. With no natural predators, kudzu thrives like a scourge, often overpowering the naturally varied landscape. It inspired James Dickey to devote a poem to the "green, mindless, unkillable ghosts" of kudzu, in which he writes "In Georgia, the legend says/That you must close your windows/At night to keep it out of the house."

The Japanese turn the plant's hardiness to their advantage. Some pull root fibers to weave into valued cloth, or reduce the roots to powder as a thickener and a botanical medicine for digestive disorders. Others simply grab a handful and throw it into a pot, steaming fresh kudzu shoots, deep-frying kudzu leaves (in tempura batter), or pickling kudzu greens and flowers (served seasoned with soy sauce, miso, or salt).

Grasses

Regional ecology (and even regional culture) can be defined by a single distinctive grass. South Georgia's **Wiregrass** region takes its name from the wiry stalks that inhabit the pine barrens, and locals embrace the name to describe the particular folk heritage of the region. Out on the coast, the productive estuarine ecology—and economy—revolves around the marshland's smooth **cordgrass** *(Spartina alterniflora)* that shelters the complex food chain. The beaches, meanwhile, are stabilized by **sea oats** *(Uniola paniculata),* a grass so critical to the local environment that it's protected by law.

FAUNA

Mammals

The **white-tailed deer,** the favorite game of southeastern natives, is now Georgia's most abundant large mammal. **Black bears, wild hogs, feral horses** (thought to be descended from those left by the departing Spanish in the 17th century), and an occasional endangered **Florida panther** (also called puma or cougar) round out the larger resident animals. **Otters, minks, bobcats, coyotes, foxes,** and **beavers** can also be found. Many homeowners encourage **bats** to move into specially constructed bat boxes as a natural alternative to electric "bug-zappers"—one bat may eat thousands of mosquitoes in a single night. But what you see the most around the state are **opossums, rac-**

coons, rabbits, squirrels (the gray variety, that is; humans rarely see Georgia's flying squirrels), and **armadillos.** The armadillos in particular are so abundant that locals consider them "weed wildlife." The common sight of their lifeless shells along roadways has led to the Southern joke: "Why did the chicken cross the road?—To show the armadillo it could be done."

As for marine mammals, the extremely rare **right whale,** of which only about 350 are known to exist in the world, calves only off the Georgia coast. The endangered **West Indian manatee,** a slow-moving seal-shaped sea mammal, lives in shallow coastal waters and feeds off the smooth cordgrass of the saltmarshes. Beachgoers readily see **dolphins** swimming close to shore.

Reptiles and Amphibians

American alligators—largest, oldest, and most famous of Georgia's reptiles—can grow to a length of nearly 20 feet and inhabit rivers, swamps, and marshes in South Georgia. Once on the brink of extinction, alligators are now strictly protected; campgrounds around their favorite habitat, the Okefenokee Swamp, close at dusk to prevent poaching. Thirteen species of **lizards** live in Georgia, as does a rare amphibian; the **lungless salamander** is not only lungless but blind as well, inhabiting the pitch-black depths of Appalachian caves.

Freshwater turtles (locally called "snappers," "cooters," or "tappins") include 150-pound alligator snapping turtles, softshell varieties, and box turtles. Of the five species of **sea turtles** found in Georgia (all threatened or endangered), the **loggerhead** is most common, nesting on all barrier islands. Georgia's **Caretta Project** uses volunteers to monitor nesting grounds to protect the eggs from predators. The critically endangered **Kemp's ridley sea turtles,** as well as the **green, leatherback,** and **hawksbill** varieties, swim in Georgia waters but nest elsewhere.

Of 42 types of **snakes** found in Georgia, six are venomous: the **copperhead, cottonmouth, coral snake,** and three **rattlesnake** varieties, including the **eastern diamondback** *(Crotalus adamanteus).* Diamondbacks reach lengths of eight feet, making them the largest and most dangerous snakes in the region. They inhabit the southern coastal plain, and though diurnal (active during the day), they avoid going out in temperatures over 85° F and remain relatively inactive through the winter. Pit vipers (the subfamily of snakes to which rattlers belong) are potent symbols in Southern culture, as their abundance in the Bible Belt might lead you to presume. Periodic "rattlesnake roundups" inspire local festivals, and the Primitive Baptist sect demonstrates its faith by snake-handling.

The largest of Georgia's nonvenomous snakes (which include water snakes, coachwhips, corn, rat, and pine snakes) is the farmer's favorite, the **king snake.** It'll grow longer than a man is tall and feeds on rodents and other small animals.

Birds

Georgia is a birder's paradise. It's in a transition zone between northern and southern bird habitats, and its statewide wetlands shelter migratory species along the eastern flyway. Birders can spot more than 350 species of birds at different seasons. Around the state you'll see—or hear—the **mockingbird, brown thrasher, towhee, cardinal, bluejay, catbird, robin, crow, ruby-throated hummingbird,** and several species of **wren, thrush, warbler,** and **woodpecker** (most notably the endangered red-cockaded variety of "Woody Woodpecker" fame).

Purple martins adopt "martins' gourd" birdhouses (carved from large gourds), which hang throughout the Southeast to entice the insect-eating birds to roost. Scavenger **buzzards** feast on roadkill and barely budge for cars; predatory **owls** and **hawks** compete with snakes for rodents. Hunters track **wild turkey, dove,** and **quail**—whole resorts in southwestern Georgia are devoted to quail hunting.

LOUISE FOOTE

armadillo

A spectacular variety of birds appear in dramatic settings in the Okefenokee Swamp; look for **ospreys, egrets, herons,** endangered **woodstorks,** plenty of **waterfowl,** and the occasional **bald eagle** (the state's nesting program should eventually boost eagle sightings).

Fish

Though North Georgia may be famous for its mountain **trout,** plenty of other freshwater varieties breed here, such as **bream, pike, sunfish,** and **black bass.** In Middle Georgia, add **catfish** and **carp;** farther south still you'll find **redfish, bass, mullet, drum, shad,** and **mackerel** in the rivers of the coastal plain.

In estuarine marshlands, shellfish such as **shrimp, blue crabs,** and tidewater **oysters** support a commercial fishery valued at $20 million a year. Saltwater species inhabiting Georgia's Atlantic coast include **spotted sea trout, flounder, Southern stingray,** and various species of **shark.** Beachcombers can discover **sponges, corals,** and colorful purple and tangerine **sea whips,** alongside **clams, horseshoe crabs, sea cucumbers,** and **sand dollars.**

ENVIRONMENTAL ISSUES

Many natural habitats such as woodlands and wetlands, mountain coves, wild swamps, and shifting islands are vanishing throughout the Southeast. But in Georgia, many of the most pristine examples of these strange and wondrous ecosystems are steadfastly protected, accessible only to limited numbers of adventurers.

Georgia was among the first states in the nation to pass legislation protecting its tidal marshlands, which are the most extensive and productive of any on the East Coast. And North Georgia's Appalachian woodlands fall largely under the protection of the 727,000-acre Chattahoochee National Forest—though local environmentalists keep a close eye on federal foresters. Similarly, the exotic Okefenokee Swamp shelters one of the largest wildlife refuges in the nation, and only 300 visitors a day are allowed onto majestic Cumberland Island. Overall, the state's environmental record surpasses that of many Southern states, yet Georgia confronts many of the same challenges as its neighbors.

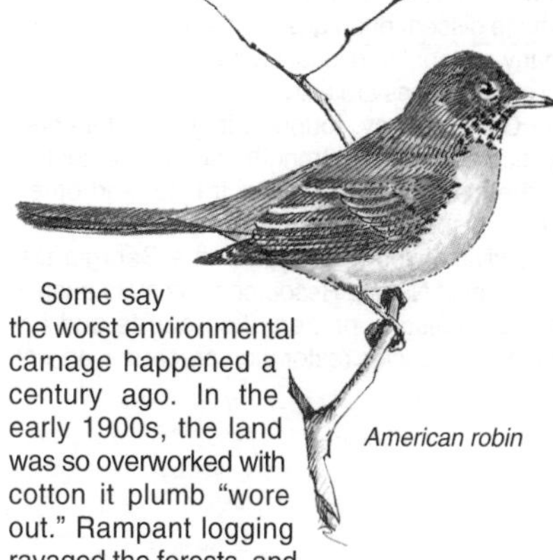

American robin

Some say the worst environmental carnage happened a century ago. In the early 1900s, the land was so overworked with cotton it plumb "wore out." Rampant logging ravaged the forests, and strip-mining for gold brought down the hills. Gradually, persistent second-growth and conscientious preservation restored much of the land, but nevertheless the landscape has been unalterably changed by dammed rivers, drained swamps, and clear-cut logging. Luckily, the southeastern environment has a very forgiving nature—it has to.

Today, a major industrial threat to Georgia's environment comes from pulp and paper manufacturing. Yet the industry is such a critical part of the state's economy that many legislators are tempted to look the other way when influential pulp and paper companies flagrantly exceed EPA standards for dioxin emissions. Besides the noxious odors and emissions from paper mills, warm wastewater entering rivers and estuaries attracts marine animals, exposing them to pollution and the lethal propeller blades of boats they would otherwise avoid.

Military bases (particularly the nuclear-powered Trident submarine base near Cumberland Island, of all places) and nuclear-energy plants (the most notorious offender is on the South Carolina side of the Savannah River) contribute to making Georgia a big producer of hazardous wastes, unfortunately not ameliorated by state spending on waste management. Elsewhere around the state, reckless development in fragile areas creates additional ecological danger zones.

As is true nationwide and particularly insidious in the South, environmental hazards disproportionately hit impoverished minority communities, whose dissent often goes unheard. Fortunately, many national and local environmental advocacy organizations are active in Georgia. The Georgia Conservancy, founded in 1967, deserves particular credit for strengthening the protection of the state's most pristine, fragile, and otherwise indispensable natural areas. Environmental activists work closely with the Georgia Department of Natural Resources, the state agency that administers preservation efforts and endangered species restoration programs, as well as maintaining state parks, historic sites, and wildlife management areas.

But perhaps the biggest friend to Georgia's environment is a Southern sense of stewardship and a citizenry predisposed to be naturally suspicious of ardent developers, moneymen, or commercial zeal of any kind. Whether this spirit can predominate over the competing tradition of patronage that has allowed key industries to have their way with the land is yet to be determined. Beloved bonds to the land and a way of life hang in the balance.

eastern diamondback rattlesnake

HISTORY

Near the intersection of two busy country highways in North Georgia sits an unusual rectangular mound in a fenced field. What's most unusual is not the mound itself (though such mounds throughout the state are the cause of much curiosity and speculation), but the fact that this ancient aboriginal earthwork is topped like a cake with a lacy white latticework gazebo. Together these two cultural symbols enclose the entire human history of Georgia like two neat bookends.

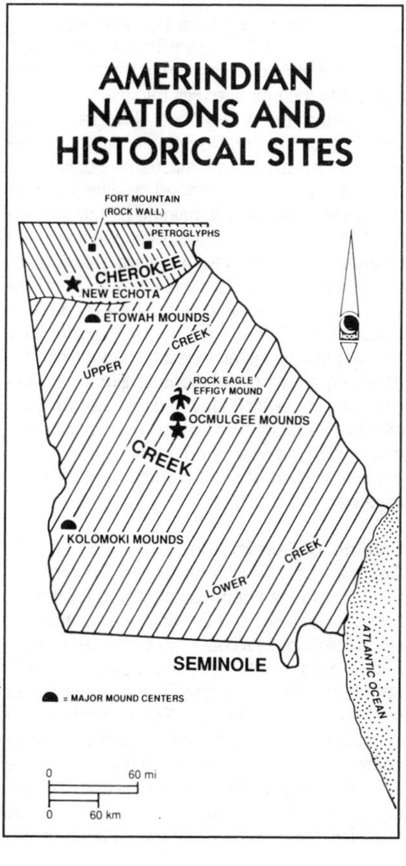

AMERINDIAN NATIONS AND HISTORICAL SITES

= MAJOR MOUND CENTERS

FIRST INHABITANTS

Georgia's aboriginal mounds are so integrated into the character of the Southeast that it's hard not to see them as natural miniature mesas dotting the landscape. Yet they were constructed with extraordinary human effort; basketful by basketful, heaps of earth were shaped into high mounds up to three stories tall, by communities that flourished in this region 2,000 years ago. For these ancient civilizations, such earthworks—hundreds of which remain visible throughout Georgia today—served as ceremonial grounds, tombs, or residence platforms for high-status individuals.

Many historians assert that three of the four most interesting archaeological sites east of the Rocky Mountains are in Georgia. All three are aboriginal earthworks: Ocmulgee Mounds near Macon, Kolomoki Mounds in southwest Georgia, and Etowah Mounds in northwest Georgia (the latter considered among the most important finds in all of North America).

Excavations reveal artifacts dating back 10,000 years. You'll hear the term **Paleo-Indian** to describe these earliest relics, preserved from when nomadic hunters—descendants of Asian groups that migrated across the Bering Straits to North America 50,000 years ago—stalked woolly mammoths and giant sloths. Hunter-gatherers of the subsequent **Archaic** period (9000-1000 B.C.) left the first traces of crop cultivation, traded with far-off tribes, and created the earliest pottery in North America at Stallings Island in the Savannah River, near Augusta, and on coastal islands.

The **Woodland** period (1000 B.C.-A.D. 900) saw fully realized villages and croplands, accompanied by an increasingly sophisticated civilization. Pottery was graced with decoratively stamped designs. An impressive trade network stretched from the gulf and ocean to the Great Lakes. Amazingly elaborate religious ceremonies also came into being, and the first mounds were built. The earliest mounds were cone-shaped gravesites—tribal leaders were buried with sacrificed relatives or attendants and accompanied by such "grave goods" as pottery, jewelry, and decorated sheets of mica. Yet Georgia's most astounding earthworks from this period do not fit that pattern. At Kolomoki Mounds near Blakely, the 56-foot-high mound is rectangular, resembling an Aztec temple, and was valued primarily as a ceremonial platform. And the Rock Eagle effigy mound near Eatonton takes the shape (when viewed from above) of a bird of prey—likely an eagle, which held a high place in native mythology—constructed from heaped rocks, not earth.

The **Mississippian** period, beginning about A.D. 900, brought the highest cultural achievements in the Southeast (or, some argue, in all of North America). About this time, Mississippians migrated east, displaced the Woodland peoples, and developed centralized chiefdoms. They built large villages around a central plaza, thatched huts served as dwellings, and earth-lodges hosted community meetings. Competitions were held on ball fields in the plaza; spectators sat on raised earthen "bleachers." The flat-topped earthen mounds served as sacred grounds; elaborate temple rites accompanied an increasingly complex set of religious beliefs. Artifacts also reveal Mesoamerican influences, likely borrowed from traveling Aztec traders.

The Mississippians farmed extensively, primarily "the three sisters"—corn, beans, and squash—which remain staples of Southern cooking to this day (and also have ancient ties to Mesoamerica). Hunting and gathering of abundant natural food sources continued to supplement agriculture.

Ocmulgee Mounds, preserved as a national monument, allows visitors to enter a restored earth lodge and view huge mounds from this period. Etowah's sacred grounds near Cartersville (an hour and some north of Atlanta) display impressive ceremonial mounds and some of the finest examples of early (and Mesoamerican-influenced) southeastern art.

After 300 years, this mound-building culture disappeared. Surrounding native populations adopted the sites and some traits of the Mississippians, creating an amalgamated culture (called "Lamar") that flourished up until the Europeans arrived in the 17th century. Of the subsequent subgroups that survived widespread annihilation from European-borne diseases, the Cherokee and Creek Confederacy dominated the region that became Georgia. Chickasaw and Choctaw groups were also present, and later the Seminoles broke off from the Creek.

While each aboriginal tradition distinguished itself in many significant ways, all shared certain common characteristics, particularly those that sprang naturally from adaptation to the climate, the land, and its resources—a heritage that continues to differentiate the American South from the rest of the country today.

EUROPEAN EXPLORATION AND SETTLEMENT

In 1540, Spanish explorer Hernando de Soto marched through Georgia with 600 horses and an army of 900 soldiers, in search of gold to rival that of the Inca empire. His hapless pursuit led him through every region in Georgia—an invader's package tour. De Soto encountered (brutally, in most cases) the Timucuan in South Georgia, the Guale (pronounced "Wallie") on the coast, the Creek and remaining Lamar moundbuilders in the central Piedmont, and finally the Cherokee in North Georgia. Here gold was indeed underfoot—in a rich vein that would go unexploited for three more centuries—yet de Soto passed it by. Though his golden dream never materialized, he left an indelible mark on history, exposing native populations to European diseases against which they had no natural immunity. Whole tribes were wiped out; up to three-quarters of the estimated southeastern native population died of such common diseases as influenza and smallpox.

Battling for Domination

Georgia's coastal islands staged the competition for European domination of North America: French, Spanish, and British forces battled for control of Georgia's coast for hundreds of years. French Huguenots first came ashore in 1562, but within a few years the Spanish pushed out the temporary shelters of French traders and constructed a string of forts ("presidios") up the coast. Missionaries followed in the wake of the armies, setting up farming villages and attempting to convert the natives to Christianity. These presidios endured for more than a century, despite the ever-threatening presence of the English and French, rebellious Creeks, and pirates of every stripe. The missionaries finally abandoned the islands in 1686, leaving groves of orange, lemon, fig, and olive trees that still grace the islands. Some say the wild horses on Cumberland Island descended from the stables of the early missions.

The Thirteenth and Final Colony

In 1733, British General James Oglethorpe arrived on the bluffs of the Savannah River to found the southernmost English colony there. He named it after King George II, who sanctioned the effort as a buffer community between the British settlement of "Charles Towne" to the north and Spanish strongholds to the south. This 13th and last of the British colonies was first envisioned as a utopian enterprise, a socially philanthropic experiment in which Oglethorpe offered those jailed for excessive debt a chance for a new life if they would come people the new colony (and relieve England of the burdens of a cripplingly harsh social policy). European Protestants and other persecuted religious refugees soon expanded the scope of this mission, and some adventurers also tagged along.

Oglethorpe mapped out the new town of Savannah—to exacting 18th-century British specifications still evident today—with the cooperation of local Yamasee chief Tomo-chi-chi. The close relationship between Oglethorpe and Tomo-chi-chi (aided by Mary Musgrove, a mixed-race interpreter and negotiator) culminated in a trip together back to England, where the British royal court doted on the befeathered "American savage."

The original Georgia Trustees (the investors who oversaw the colony) dreamed of creating a silk industry in Savannah, yet silk never took hold the way cotton did. They also hoped to impose a strict set of moral and commercial rules on the colonists, but these fared no better and soon proved impossible to maintain. The prohibition of alcohol and restrictions on land sales were the first to go. Lastly went their prohibition of slavery.

Oglethorpe believed that slavery contradicted the colony's purpose to "relieve the distressed," and asserted: "Give in, and we shall occasion the misery of thousands in Africa." More critical historians claim that his humanitarian sentiments were likely of secondary importance to considerations of pure military necessity; as his frontier position demanded a strong defense, he wanted only settlers who could also be soldiers (and armed slaves could rebel). Economic pressures from slaveholding neighbors in South Carolina led to the repeal of the prohibition against slavery 16 years after the founding of the colony.

SCOTT TEEPLE

James Edward Oglethorpe

To secure Georgia's position against the Spanish, Oglethorpe established forts along the 100-mile coast of "Debatable Land" between Savannah and Spain's northernmost outpost at St. Augustine in what is now northern Florida. Skirmishes between the two powers shifted advantages back and forth for years, until an ambush in 1742 in a remote island marsh decided which European power would control American shores.

In the Battle of Bloody Marsh on St. Simons Island, the British ambushed and repelled the invading Spanish. Though a relatively minor engagement, it unnerved the retreating Spanish enough to finally abandon their ambitions for expansion north, and ultimately to relinquish their final hold on North America. Thus this skirmish, fought in a sandy marsh on one of Georgia's remote Sea Islands, became one of the most decisive battles in the history of the world.

The American Revolution

As the newest colony and one begun by British philanthropy, Georgia remained steadfastly loyalist, and was the only colony not represented in the first Continental Congress. Yet in 1776, Georgia joined the rest in declaring independence. Two years later, British forces attacked the coast and captured Savannah, and by the end of 1779, every important town in Georgia had fallen under British control. With British occupation supported by many local Tories, the fighting took on a civil character. England's eventual withdrawal from Georgia brought about widespread confusion and disorganization in government, as well as many disputes over contested private property. (Later generations, remembering their grandparents' vivid accounts of the local turbulence, resolved to staunchly defend the land during the Civil War.)

ANTEBELLUM GEORGIA

"King Cotton"

Once Eli Whitney invented the cotton gin in Georgia in 1793 (dissenters say Catherine Greene did the inventing, yet named her farm mechanic Whitney as a more credible male inventor), cotton production soared. Georgia's annual cotton production rocketed from 1,000 bales in about 1790 to 20,000 bales 10 years later, doubling the next decade, and peaking at 701,000 bales by the advent of the Civil War. Slavery, a dying institution before the cotton gin, was revived as a cheap labor source to fuel this increased production. The plantation system arose, as one historian put it, as a "kind of agribusiness whose machines were human beings."

Slaveholding planters established their dominion. Sufficient free time enabled the planter class to advance its education and engage in a complex social and political life. Even at the height of the plantation system, the members of this oligarchy exercised power out of all proportion to their number. In 1860, the overwhelming majority of farms in the state—31,000—consisted of no more than 100 acres, most all of which functioned without slave labor. By contrast, there were fewer than 1,000 "plantation-size" farms of more than a thousand acres—where the money, power, and slaves were concentrated. Which is to say—contrary to what *Gone with the Wind* may lead people to believe—the overwhelming majority of the cotton-producing population was steadfastly middle class, with interests far removed from those at the top of the plantation hierarchy. Widening class divisions ultimately shaped Southern politics for many generations.

Only certain geographical regions supported large-scale slaveholding plantations. On the coast, large plantations flourished with rice crops as well as a high-quality strand of cotton known as "Sea Island Cotton." The remainder of the large cotton-producing plantations were in a fertile crescent across the middle of the state and down into southwest Georgia. Called the "Black Belt" for its rich dark soil, the region's name could also describe its demographics. Despite the revolutionary changes that swept through the South in the intervening century, the legacy of slavery continues to influence population patterns. Historically slaveless regions, such as northern Georgia, have fewer African-American residents to this day.

Yet not all blacks in the South before the Civil War were slaves. From colonial times on, slaves who bought their freedom, escaped, or were manumitted (released from slavery) joined African immigrants (many of whom were former slaves from Haiti) in free black communities in Georgia's cities. Though small in number (in 1860, Savannah's free black population of 3,000 was the largest in the state), such settlements were highly significant. Though their liberties were restricted, free blacks enjoyed basic rights denied to slaves, such as the ability to forge family bonds, operate businesses, exercise leadership in public life, and carry on traditions lost in the African diaspora. A few managed to amass wealth and hand down their enhanced social position through generations. Of this quiet black elite, a few even owned slaves. Well-off or not, free man or slave, many Southern blacks (and whites) fought for the abolition of slavery and risked their lives and livelihoods to escape slavery or help others escape.

Expansionism

In the early 1800s, the federal government blew the lid off the Yazoo Land Frauds, a scandal in which corrupt politicians and speculators conspired to sell 50 million acres of Georgia territory for their personal gain (and 'twasn't theirs to sell anyhow). As part of the bargain struck with the federal government to extricate the state from the mess, Georgia lost its vaguely mapped western territory to what became Alabama and Mississippi. The new boundary was set at the eastern bank of the Chattahoochee River. Yet the misappropriation would ultimately unleash a series of events with unforeseen consequences far more dire.

The Georgia legislature agreed to cede the fraudulently sold territories back to the U.S. government, *but only if* federal troops would remove Native Americans from what remained of the territory Georgia claimed as its own. Well, Georgia ceded the land but the feds declared that as a sovereign power, the natives could not be evicted. Georgia perceived this turn of events as an encroachment on the original agreement, and the ensuing wrangling over where "states' rights" ended and federal jurisdiction began in this economically motivated and racially charged debate was to foreshadow the coming of civil war. On this earlier score, however, Georgia emerged victorious.

While various treaties (at best questionable, if not outright fraudulent) slipped lands out from under the Creeks, the highly organized Cherokee resisted any bullying to move them from their ancestral homelands. To bolster their defense, they officially established the Cherokee Nation, centered in North Georgia. In 1827, the Cherokee chartered a constitution of representative government based on the U.S. Constitution, and declared New Echota as their capital. One of their most extraordinary cultural achievements around this time was the creation of a syllabary (phonetic alphabet) of the Cherokee language; the printing press that produced a bilingual newspaper in English and Cherokee is among many artifacts on display in New Echota today.

Gold Rush

What sealed the fate of the Cherokee was the discovery of gold. In 1829, a white man hunting on Cherokee territory spied on the ground what looked to him "like the yellow of an egg." It turned out to be part of a rich gold belt that signaled the first major gold rush in U.S. history, sending thousands of prospectors into North Georgia. The center of the gold boom was Dahlonega, named for the Cherokee word for yellow, the largest of several North Georgia towns that retain their gold-rush character.

In 1838, President Andrew Jackson sent troops to evict the Cherokee from the newly exposed gold country. Pulled from their homes and rounded up into jails, the Cherokee (along with dozens of other native groups from throughout the Southeast) were exiled to Oklahoma on a torturous forced march that became known as the Trail of Tears.

CIVIL WAR

The Civil War was the single most defining historical event in the South, or, as many historians assert, in the whole nation. Much of that history was written across the face of Georgia: the Atlanta Campaign, battle and blaze, Sherman's March to the Sea—these and other events that decided the fate of the Confederacy have been memorialized in landmarks across the state, and were implanted into the American imagination by Margaret Mitchell's classic Civil War novel *Gone with the Wind.* Though more than a century has passed, the Civil War lives on in the regional collective memory as if fought in this lifetime. Even the term "Civil War" can generate debate, as it describes the Union position—that of a single nation torn apart, rather than two separate opponents. To the South it was the "War between the States," a term still heard occasionally today.

From Secession to Bloodshed

The Southern states, dependent on an agricultural slave economy, developed social and political systems dramatically different from those in the industrialized (but still slaveholding) states of the north. The escalating national debate over the legal status of slavery in western territories highlighted these differences, fueling an animosity that sparked secession. Starting in 1860, 11 southern states voted to form their own Confederate States of America.

Yet the South was never monolithic. Many Georgians opposed secession, and others supported it only reluctantly. Views on slavery ran a similar gamut. Foremost in the minds of many

PAST AS PRESENT

In 1886, Atlanta journalist Henry Grady traveled to New York to deliver a dinner speech on the "New South." When asked what he intended to say, Grady responded: "I have thought of a thousand things to say; 500 of which if I say they will murder me when I get back home, and the other 500 of which will get me murdered at the banquet." His predicament is one with which even contemporary writers of Southern history can sympathize.

No other part of America lives so intimately with its past as the South, nor is a sense of personal and regional history as acute in any American as in a Southerner. The region's peculiar history, and its retelling, best exemplifies how history is more a matter of selective interpretation than the mere recitation of facts. And in the South, interpretations vary. *Widely.*

The South claims at least three histories: the most familiar one, the textbook kind written by Northerners, is different from white Southern history, which in turn is distinct from a history of the black experience in the South. For the traveler, these complex realities mix with one's own observations to fascinate even the historically impaired. Few places in the U.S. can engage you like the South in red-hot debate on events that happened 150 years ago.

Confederate victory fields, African-American heritage sites, and Native American historical sites make some of the South's most interesting stops because they tell stories often omitted from the mainstream history books. Read the spin on federal brochures about Southern historic sites for a sense of the fine line writers must walk to please Northern editors without offending local sensibilities.

This guide attempts to address a few major points and relate some of the untold stories (for further reading, see the **Booklist**). Yet travelers to the South should keep in mind what one 88-year-old former slave told the WPA: "I know folks think the books tell the truth, but they shore don't." Discover for yourself.

nonslaveholding Southerners—from whose ranks the majority of soldiers rose—was the notion of states' rights: the idea that the United States was a federation, rather than a republic, and states could withdraw their membership if the Union no longer served their needs. Georgia Governor Joseph E. Brown, in fact, so opposed centralized government that in the midst of the war, he threatened to secede from the *Confederacy.*

While slavery served as the initial point of contention, early on President Abraham Lincoln focused exclusively on preserving the Union and insisted abolition was not at issue. Yet no matter what the politicians and armies proclaimed as their purpose, slaves recognized the war as heralding the long-awaited end of bondage. As Union General William T. Sherman described in one encounter with a slave, "He said he'd been looking for 'the Angel of the Lord' ever since he was knee-high, and though we professed to be fighting for the Union, he supposed that slavery was the cause, and that our success was to be his freedom."

Early in the war, the only action in Georgia was on the coast. Georgia's governor first ex-[illegible]d federal troops from Savannah's coastal Fort Pulaski even before Georgia officially seceded. One of the first Union moves was to take the fort back. Here the Union troops, besides monitoring a blockade of the Savannah River (none too effectively, according to accounts of successful blockade runners), waited out most of the war until the action caught up to them. To hear a Southerner tell the story, the languid troops often passed the time playing baseball; to this day locals host period-costumed ball games at the fort annually in honor of the ball-playing Yankees. Federal troops also occupied the Sea Islands, making the isolated refuges a sanctuary for escaping slaves.

Farther down the coast, the port city of Darien was burnt to the ground by the famous all-black regiment, the 54th Massachusetts (scenes recounted in the film *Glory*), despite the objections of the troop commander. Upon later insisting that his men be considered for real warfare rather than such punitive actions, the regiment received and accepted an assignment so challenging it resulted in the death of the commander and most of the regiment.

Elsewhere in Georgia, as yet untouched by war, Georgia's munitions plants in Augusta, Macon, Columbus, and Athens churned out Confederate army supplies, which were then transported through Atlanta's railroad network. Naturally enough, Atlanta soon became the Union's major target.

The Atlanta Campaign

Sherman rightly theorized that a crushing blow to Atlanta would cripple the entire Confederacy. With that plan in mind, Union troops headed south from Chattanooga, Tennessee, in the fall of 1863, only to be stopped at Chickamauga Creek. A Confederate victory at high cost, the Battle of Chickamauga was remembered as the two bloodiest days of the war, with 35,000 casualties. A national park now commemorates the site.

The next spring Sherman's troops plowed through northwest Georgia, following the railroad lines and engaging the Confederate army three times before being repelled outside of Atlanta at Kennesaw Mountain on June 27, 1864. Surrounding the city, Sherman fought four more battles for its control. Atlanta finally surrendered on September 2, 1864. Sherman ordered the city burned, and the resulting fire destroyed 90% of Atlanta's 4,000 buildings, leaving only smoldering chimneys, nicknamed "Sherman's sentinels."

NATIONAL ARCHIVES

Union Gen. William Tecumseh Sherman coined the phrase "war is hell."

Sherman's March to the Sea

After torching Atlanta, Sherman led an army of 60,000 on a march designed to "make Georgia howl." His army cut a 60-mile-wide swath through the Georgia countryside—burning houses, crops, and whole towns in his path—a routing which by Sherman's own estimation caused more than a million dollars' damage. At Georgia's Confederate capital in Milledgeville, Sherman's officers paused to stage a mock session of the Georgia legislature, and lit boxes of Confederate money to fuel fires to boil coffee. As it happened, into the encampment straggled a few emaciated Union soldiers who had escaped the P.O.W. camp at Andersonville (now a national cemetery). When Sherman learned of the horrible conditions there, he swept through the rest of Georgia with an increased vengeance.

Upon reaching Savannah on December 22, 1864, Sherman was reportedly so impressed by the beauty of the town that he spared it and offered it to President Lincoln as a Christmas gift. "I beg to present you," he wrote, "the city of Savannah, with 150 heavy guns and plenty of ammunition; also about 25,000 bales of cotton." Still reeling from Sherman, Georgia surrendered its armies to Union General Wilson after his army charged through Columbus in April 1865.

Sherman's March, unprecedented for destroying nonmilitary targets (private property largely occupied by women, children, and slaves, as most all white men had left to fight), left a legacy of animosity among landowners. For blacks, Sherman represented liberation, and tens of thousands of freed slaves picked up to follow the army. Once he reached Savannah, Sherman sought to rid the army of responsibility for these masses, and conferred with local leaders of the free black community before issuing his famous Field Order #15.

This order set aside the barrier islands and the coastal mainland "low country" of Georgia and South Carolina exclusively for former slaves. On this new homeland, Sherman decreed, each freed man would be allotted "40 acres and a

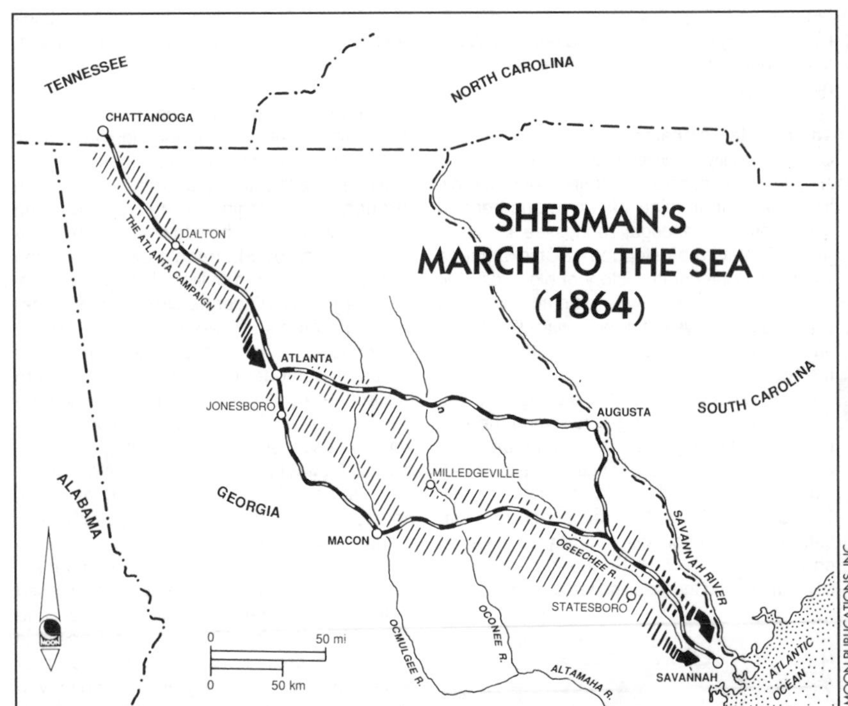

mule" to start a life independent of the plantations. Yet the promptly proclaimed Black Republic on "Sherman's Reservation" was short-lived; federal legislation during Reconstruction rescinded Sherman's decree and returned property to former landowners. The liberated slaves were left with "nothing but freedom"—landless, powerless, and impoverished.

The most scrutinized, mythologized, and controversial event in U.S. history, the Civil War took the sacrifice of 620,000 lives to transform the founding principle of U.S. democracy—that "all men are created equal"—from abstract theory to a practical reality. Unfortunately, for many that promise remains unfulfilled. As contemporary historian Barbara Fields asserts, "If some citizens live in houses and others live on the streets, the Civil War is not over—and regrettably, it can still be lost."

RECONSTRUCTION AND THE "NEW SOUTH"

After the war, Georgia's economic, political, and social systems lay in shambles: the smoldering ruins of Sherman's March stood as a visual symbol of widespread demoralization, confusion, and grief over shattered families, the dead, missing, and maimed. Farms lay fallow, with an agrarian depression on the way. Into this scene marched victorious Yankee troops to impose a mandatory "reconstructed" system of society, labor, and government. Though Georgia moved through this tumultuous time with less strife than in neighboring states (Georgia's higher proportion of white unionists smoothed the transition), its effect was like a second colonization, this time by the North.

Many Southern whites considered Reconstruction the worst of evils, characterized by opportunists bent on exploiting the defeated South. Northerners who arrived by the trainload with tapestry duffels were derided as "carpetbaggers" and their local collaborators as "scalawags." To blacks, Reconstruction transformed slaves to free citizens, guaranteeing the right to vote, hold office, and otherwise engage in an unprecedented interracial democracy. In any case, Reconstruction didn't last long: after five or six frustrating years, the federal government opted out of the region's internecine struggles, leaving the door open for the return of white supremacy in Georgia in 1871. Reconstruction's libertarian goals didn't meaningfully resurface until the modern civil rights movement.

In the decades that followed, entrenched patterns and new realities confronted each other like opposing continental plates—sometimes realignment was painstakingly slow and deliberate, at other times so violent that deep dark fissures cracked the unstable surface. Throughout the South, segregation was institutionalized by "Jim Crow" laws, originally instigated by disputes over passenger seating on the very railroads that brought modernization to the South. "White" and "Colored" signs led to separate—not equal—train cars, waiting rooms, bathrooms, and water fountains. Schools, restaurants, and neighborhoods needed no signs to announce their exclusivity. Voting restrictions effectively denied voting rights to blacks. Worst of all, the outrageous Ku Klux Klan (said to be named after the sound of a gun being loaded) waged horrifying violence against blacks while the entire judicial system—local, state, and federal—turned the other way, strengthening the emerging apartheid.

The Atlanta Compromise

Atlanta, however, began to distinguish itself as the socially and racially progressive capital of the New South. The International Cotton States Exposition, held in Atlanta in 1895, provided an early platform for enlightened voices. At that forum, local journalist Henry Grady promoted the "New South" as eager to compete on the national economic scene, and black educator Booker T. Washington shared the stage. Though many considered Washington's conciliatory message too undemanding (local civil rights leader and co-founder of the National Association for the Advancement of Colored People [NAACP] W.E.B. DuBois dubbed it the "Atlanta Compromise"), it nevertheless initiated a vital dialogue between blacks and the white power structure.

Throughout the state, expanding rail networks, manufacturing, and industry replaced the plantation economy, and the old agricultural system was replaced by sharecropping, in which tenant farmers worked the land for a share of the crop. Post-Civil War changes in the social order raised the voice of the yeomanry, the class of peasant farmers who ushered in the Populist movement of the 1890s. Although Populism constituted the largest agrarian political revolt in American history and was a force to be reckoned with, Populists never assumed control in Georgia.

Georgia's small, pioneering farm communities of the late 19th and early 20th centuries—often nostalgically recalled in Georgia's cultural history—were happily self-sufficient until the arrival of the boll weevil in 1914. This insect infestation wiped out the cotton crop the South had grown singularly dependent upon, sending many poor farming families north in search of jobs. Blacks in particular left in such numbers that the period is remembered by African-Americans as the "Great Migration." After this devastating blow, the region was hit harder still by the nationwide economic collapse of the Great Depression in 1929.

Recovery was slow; the regional economy remained stagnant for decades. Yet despite the hardships of the early 20th century, Southern culture made tremendous strides forward during this period, propelling dramatic new literary and musical movements.

World War II brought economic opportunity to the struggling region. Georgia's major military bases were commissioned and many Southerners—black and white—enlisted in the armed forces. Military service offered "more than a job" to African-American soldiers in particular. Since the Civil War, when the 54th Massachusetts regiment refused pay until its wages were made equal with those of white soldiers, the military found itself strangely ahead of the times—often less discriminatory than the civilian society (North

DIXIE FLAG FLAP

While the Confederate flag may symbolize only Southern pride and independence to many Southern whites, it has understandably become a symbol inextricably linked with slavery and white supremacy. The debate has deadlocked since 1992, when civil-rights advocates first persuaded then-Governor Zell Miller to propose replacing the state's current "stars and bars" state flag—adopted in 1956 as a protest over court-ordered racial integration—with the pre-1956 design adopted in 1879. Many consider the former flag equally unacceptable, considering the tenor of the times, and call for either a return to the original Georgia flag of 1799 or the creation of a wholly new design. Facing an uphill battle from traditionalists in both the legislature and electorate, the flag controversy still waves. In the meantime, some city buildings have decided not to wait for an official pronouncement and have independently removed the state flag from display.

the pre-1956 state flag

the current state flag, bearing the controversial Confederate "stars and bars"

or South). After WW II, Southern soldiers carried back to the South broadened visions of a more equal society, ushering in the following era of revolutionary change.

Civil Rights

Explosive strife and violence characterized the civil rights era of the 1960s in the South, yet once more Georgia was spared the greatest wrath of the times—thanks again to Atlanta's favored position in the vanguard of white-and-black alliance and progressive social justice. Martin Luther King, Jr., was born in Atlanta in 1929 and raised in the city's comfortable black middle class. Here he preached at his family's Ebenezer Baptist Church and later founded the Southern Christian Leadership Conference in the church basement.

In 1963, Atlanta Mayor Ivan Allen, Jr., testified in Washington in support of federal civil rights legislation, the only Southern mayor to do so. And early on, pragmatic white business leaders—such as Coca-Cola magnate Robert Woodruff and *Atlanta Constitution* editor Ralph McGill—aligned with the African-American elite and political advocates such as Dr. King, ensuring a relatively progressive slate of city leaders who brought their influence to bear on statewide politics.

Elsewhere around the state, one of the hardest-fought civil rights battles centered on reform of Georgia's educational system. In Albany, the first attempt to integrate the schools brought a violent mob scene that Dr. King attempted to reconcile peaceably. In January 1961, Charlayne Hunter (now Hunter-Gault, one-time *MacNeil-Lehrer News Hour* reporter) walked into the University of Georgia in Athens, becoming the first African-American to integrate the state institution.

Another battle was waged in the courts in an effort to overturn the state's unjust voting laws. Before the historic Supreme Court decision in *Baker vs. Carr* mandated "one man, one vote," a county unit system accorded nearly equal electoral weight to all counties regardless of population, offsetting more numerous liberal, black, and urban votes in favor of rural conservatives. The 1962 decision marked the turning point for post-Reconstruction Southern politics by dissolving the county unit system.

In 1964, Jimmy Carter won the governorship, replacing race-baiting Lester Maddox. As governor, Carter established a reputation for his humanitarian ideals—a reputation that would help catapult the peanut farmer from Plains into national politics in 1976, when he was elected 39th president of the United States.

In 1973, Atlanta elected Maynard Jackson the first African-American mayor of a major Southern city. Jackson set and enforced strict quotas for minority contracts and representation (though the term "minority" doesn't really fit in a city two-thirds African-American), widening professional opportunities and prompting a retromigration of African-Americans leaving shrinking economic opportunities in the urban North. After serving the maximum mayoral term, Jackson was succeeded by former United Nations ambassador Andy Young, who brought an international perspective to Atlanta's City Hall. Young was in turn succeeded by Jackson again, who continued as before to preside over Atlanta's burgeoning economy. Booming during the 1980s, Atlanta's unstoppable momentum continues to drive the state's healthy economy today.

The South Rises Again

Now a new chapter for the state begins. The 1996 Summer Games in Georgia represented a global affirmation of everything the state's promoters have been putting forward for years. Won on Atlanta's reputation for racial harmony (a

THE MAN FROM PLAINS

JIMMY CARTER NATIONAL HISTORIC SITE

From peanut farmer in Plains, to governor of Georgia, to 39th president of the United States, Jimmy Carter rose from humble South Georgia roots to take over the nation's highest office in 1977. While his Southern manner was much caricatured by the national press (the brown cardigan of his fireside chats, Brother Billy, the Playboy "lust in my heart" interview), Carter was one of the country's most sincere humanitarian leaders, as evidenced by the successful Camp David accords, Panama Canal treaties, and his human-rights and energy policies.

Since 1980, when his reelection bid failed, Carter has continued his commitment to civil rights and humanitarian causes: monitoring free elections worldwide, mediating overseas disputes, constructing low-income housing with the Georgia-based organization Habitat for Humanity, and leading the Atlanta Project (an innovative public-private partnership dedicated to eradicating poverty in the inner city). It's been said, without exaggeration, that Carter is the only man ever to use the U.S. presidency as the stepping stone to greater public service.

The Carter Library in Atlanta displays testaments to his administration's successes (including, by the way, the original brown cardigan), while many exhibits in the Jimmy Carter Visitor Center and throughout the town of Plains tell a more personal side of the story of President Carter (who still resides in town).

message hand-carried by the globally respected Andy Young), this modern platform will redefine the state for the century to come.

GOVERNMENT AND ECONOMY

Georgia's 56 senators and 180 representatives comprise the state legislature, which meets in the state capitol each January to begin a 40-day legislative session. Since its founding as the 13th British colony, Georgia's capital has shifted several times—from its original location in Savannah to Augusta, Louisville, Milledgeville, and finally Atlanta in 1877. The state's governors are elected to four-year terms; a maximum of two terms may be served consecutively.

Georgia has the largest number of counties (139) in any state besides Texas, a significant statistic in local politics, history, and culture. Georgians identify themselves more often by county than by city or region (and often identify destinations the same way, which can confuse travelers who tend not to navigate by county lines).

The state has historically voted so solidly Democratic that party nomination has often been tantamount to general election, creating a tradition of hotly contested primaries and anticlimactic elections (by state law, voting in a party primary is not limited to members of that party). Though around 60% of Georgia's voters remain registered Democrats today, conservative "Dixiecrats" are now an endangered species. Former Speaker of the House Newt Gingrich of Marietta could perhaps be credited with molding a new breed of Republican converts.

The 1998 election brought significant biracial trends to the political arena. A powerful turnout of African-American voters delivered Democratic victories in Georgia's gubernatorial election and throughout the South. Roy E. Barnes was elected governor despite falling short of the 40% of the white vote usually considered necessary for a Democratic victory, which analysts predict will spell a heightened sensitivity to the concerns of blacks within the party.

In Georgia's second Congressional district, a significant crossover of whites voting for an African-American candidate was considered responsible for the reelection of Rep. Sanford Bishop, Jr., whose rural constituents appeared particularly grateful for his fight to preserve Federal price supports for peanuts in 1996. As Camilla farmer James Lee Adams, Jr. told the *New York Times,* "I think most of us have gotten beyond the white and black issue; we prefer to focus on the green." Yet Bishop's victory is sure to be used as artillery by foes of racial majority redistricting policies built on the premise that whites are unwilling to vote for black candidates.

Economy

Service industries comprise nearly three-fourths of Georgia's gross state product, but manufacturing is the single most important activity and largest employer, accounting for 20% of the gross state product. Georgia is the nation's leading textile producer; agribusiness and mining also contribute to Georgia's economic base, and tourism brought in an all-time high of $16 billion in 1997.

Georgia leads the nation as the largest producer of peanuts and pecans, ranks second in poultry sales, and third in peaches. In order, the state's biggest cash crops are peanuts, tobacco, corn, cotton, and soybeans.

Atlanta—the undisputed commercial, transportation, and financial capital of the state and region—is home to such global concerns as Coca-Cola, Delta Air Lines, Lockheed, United Parcel Service, Georgia-Pacific, and Cable News Network. Redefining its historical position as a transportation hub, Atlanta operates Hartsfield International Airport, the largest passenger terminal complex in the world. The city's business reputation brought in half a million new jobs during the 1980s, in 1991 Atlanta was named "America's Best City for Business" by *Fortune* magazine, and convention business in the capital doubled between 1985 and 1995.

THE PEOPLE

Georgia's 1990 census lists a population of 6,478,216; the figure now exceeds 7.5 million. During the 1980s, when Atlanta's economy boomed, the state's population surged 19%. Atlanta dominates the state's urban centers with a metropolitan-region population of 3.4 million and a central-city population numbering 425,000 (city per-capita statistics can vary widely depending on which of these two figures is used). Four other Georgia cities hold populations over 100,000: Columbus, Savannah, Macon, and Albany. The state's population is 71% white, 27% black, and two percent Latin, Asian, and other. Atlanta attracts the widest range of ethnic diversity, though recently, immigrant groups have begun moving beyond the urban area.

All that being said, here's the real information: Georgians are what make a trip to Georgia so memorable. Southern hospitality, a strong sense of place, an oral-history tradition, and the leisurely pace of a semitropical region all combine in friendly residents who greatly enrich the most casual encounter. And of all the Southern states, Georgia is the most accessible, by virtue of its gateway capital. Scenes on a bus, a question asked of a ranger, an inquiry about local history made at a roadside stand—such moments may wind up as the best stories of your trip. So given that a trip begins with its people, here's a brief look at where those people came from, and how they all ended up being the Georgians of today.

ABORIGINAL HERITAGE

Long before the Civil War defined the geo-cultural region known as "the South," aboriginal nations developed a regionally distinctive culture in the American Southeast (see also **History**, above). Today's Southerners hold similarities with these ancient traditions as a natural consequence of shared land-use patterns, climate, and natural resources, but also directly from practices passed down from natives to European settlers. In turn, settlers passed on Euro-

THE CHEROKEE STORY OF CREATION

In the beginning, when people and animals shared a common language, all living things dwelled above the sky. But after a while the creatures became so crowded, someone wondered if they might find more room in the ocean below. The little water beetle went down to investigate. Finding no firm place to land, he dove into the water and brought up mud. The mud grew and spread into the circular island of earth (later fastened to the sky with four giant ropes at each cardinal direction).

The great buzzard flew all over the earth to see if the land was yet dry enough to live on. When he reached Cherokee Country he was very tired, and his giant wings flapped against the ground. Wherever his wings struck the earth a valley appeared, and mountains formed whenever his wings turned back up again. The heart of Cherokee Country is full of mountains to this day.

The Cherokee believe in another world below the earth; high mountain streams form the trails to this underworld, and the doorways are mountaintop springs. The world below experiences seasons opposite from those on earth, evidenced by the fact that springwaters are always cooler than the mountain summer air and warmer than winter's air.

When the animals and plants were first made, the Great One instructed them to stay awake for seven nights, and while they all tried, as time went on many dropped off to sleep. On the seventh night only the owl and panther and one or two others remained awake. To these animals the Great One gave the power to see at night and prey on those that had fallen asleep, which thereafter always will sleep after the sun goes down. Of the trees, only the cedar, pine, spruce, holly, and laurel were awake to the end, and to them it was given that they always stay green while the others shall lose their leaves every winter.

See Cherokee Publications in the **Booklist** for more Cherokee myths.

pean traditions to natives, prompting colonists to dub the five major southeastern nations—the Creek, Cherokee, Seminole, Chickasaw, and Choctaw—the "Five Civilized Tribes." All of these groups were present in Georgia at the time of European settlement, as were other tribes who were wiped out by European-borne diseases. Yet the region was overwhelmingly dominated by the Creek Confederacy and, in the mountain region, the Cherokee. As well as can be approximated, the state's native population before colonization numbered about 10,000.

Local historian Sam Lawton likes to point out how similar the customs of the native southeasterners were to our own. "They'd start the day with a cup of a strong black caffeinated beverage," he explained, "then the town council would meet to discuss the affairs of the day." Their principal crops of corn, squash, and beans—all staples of Southern cooking today—as well as techniques for their cultivation and preparation, were handed down to Europeans. Their main meal consisted of "sofkee," now served throughout the Southeast as hominy grits. The natives engaged in serious sports competitions and enthusiastically celebrated the harvest. The use of native plants as sources of food and medicine also became woven into the fiber of Southern culture, as did a rich folklore.

Yet much was unique to aboriginal traditions. Their matrilineal society organized marriage, child-raising customs, and other social structures around women. (Early women's suffrage advocates pointed to the freedoms and rights accorded Cherokee women to advance their cause.) And the European practice of land ownership was entirely foreign to the natives, who lived on more communal terms.

Their belief structure centered around three worlds: the earth, the "sky vault," and the Under World. The earth where they lived, the native southeasterners believed, was an island resting on a large sea. Above the sky vault was the Upper World, which represented perfection; here earth creatures lived, but in greater sizes than on earth. The Under World below represented chaos and disorder; its features were inverted from the earth world. For example, when it was summer on earth, it was winter below, and vice versa—springs that felt cold in summer and warm in winter affirmed this belief. (See **The Cherokee Story of Creation.**)

The Creek Confederacy, a dozen distinctive groups sharing the same Muskogean linguistic roots and similar characteristics, came together in a centralized government based in Ocmulgee, at the site of the ancient temple mounds. The Upper Creeks lived centrally on the Piedmont, the Lower Creeks in South Georgia. The Europeans named them for their riverine culture along Georgia's many waterways.

The Yamacraw, who first negotiated with the British to permit Georgia's first European settlement in Savannah, were an "outlawed" tribe of the Creek. Similarly, the Seminoles broke away from the Creeks ("Seminole" means "runaway" in the Creek language), some say over disputes about slavery. Seminoles particularly welcomed escaping slaves, leading to the Seminole Wars of 1816 and 1825, when federal troops fought to return escaped slaves to plantations. The majority of Seminoles were pushed south into Florida, and their descendants and culture reflect African influences to this day.

The Cherokee, distinguished by their Iroquoian language and highland culture, lived in the Appalachian mountains of Georgia, Tennessee, and North Carolina, and established the capital of the Cherokee Nation in Georgia's New Echota in 1828. Their advanced culture and government, which included a written Cherokee language and a representative government and Constitution modeled on that of the U.S., did not protect them from a forced "removal" once gold was discovered within their territory. The Five Civilized Tribes were exiled to designated Indian territory in Oklahoma in 1838 along the tragic Trail of Tears; of 16,000 forced migrants, 4,000 died. Their banishment effectively ended their land-based southeastern traditions, and forced them to adapt to new conditions out west. Southeastern reservations are home to small groups whose ancestors managed to escape the removal. Other individuals and families remain scattered throughout the population or have assimilated into Anglo culture. Many Georgians claim to have Indian blood, primarily those in former Cherokee territory. And a glance at a state map reveals many names of Native American origin, such as Chattahoochee, Dahlonega, Oconee, and Ossobaw. Native American cultural events, including powwows, native crafts demonstrations, and the like, are held at aboriginal historic sites throughout the state.

EUROPEAN HERITAGE

The Georgia colony was originally settled by the British and Protestants fleeing religious persecution in continental Europe, notably Germans and Moravians. A Jewish community led by German Jews consisted mostly of Sephardic families originally from Spain and Portugal who had escaped the Inquisition. Soon Highland Scots and Irish Catholics joined this mix (as well as religious minorities; see **Religion,** below), yet the dominant influence continued to be from Anglo-Saxon Protestants, Scotch, and Irish.

Today, Anglo-Saxon traditions have been most keenly retained by Appalachian mountaineers. In acknowledgment of Scotch and Irish heritage, Scottish Highland Games continue to be celebrated throughout the state (Atlanta and Savannah hold the largest Games), and Savannah celebrates St. Patrick's Day for a full week.

Appalachian Folk Culture

As heirs of one of the oldest and most culturally rich folk cultures of the United States, the Appalachian Southern Highlanders carry on 19th-century traditions in the mountains of North Georgia and neighboring states. In fact, North Georgians hold more in common with fellow mountaineers three states removed than with flatlanders in their own state. Always known for being a breed apart, the mountaineers have cultivated a reputation for fierce independence—a characteristic that may stretch back more than three centuries. Many Southern Highlanders descend from groups in disputed borderlands between Scotland and England, where constant feuding that lasted for generations forced residents to develop adaptive resilience and self-sufficiency. America's Southern Appalachian frontier, populated by the Cherokee when the first immigrants arrived to settle the wilderness in the 1750s, re-created familiar strife.

The isolation of mountain communities meant that old folkways that had long died out elsewhere were carried on over time, and many continue today. Though the old-timers who depended on traditional skills and crafts to survive are the last of a breed, younger generations have picked up many of these traditions to preserve their cultural heritage. A national revival of interest in Appalachian folkways has also contributed to the effort to celebrate this distinctive culture.

Unique arts and crafts, music, and a rich set of folk beliefs are among the highlights of Appalachian culture. Pottery from Georgia clay, basketry from native vines, and whittled carvings from Appalachian hardwoods are local specialties, along with weavings and quilts in traditional patterns. Each craft has its own cultural significance and history.

Bluegrass music emanates from the Appalachians, and foot-stompin' festivals, dance halls, and concerts in North Georgia continue this tradition. Old-time mountain music evokes Elizabethan influences, and old ballads passed down through generations are often accompanied by dulcimer. Language also reveals this heritage; the term *reckon* was used by Chaucer before it became a term synonymous with the Southern Highlands.

AFRICAN HERITAGE

The gruesome slave trade that brought captured Africans to North America (95% were taken to the Caribbean or Latin America) operated mainly from Africa's west coast in a region stretching from Senegal to Angola, principally the central "Gold Coast" region (now Ghana, Togo, Benin, and Nigeria). In Georgia, Africans from the Gambia River and Sierra Leone's rice-cultivation areas were valued workers for coastal rice plantations, bringing the specific traditions of the Wolof and Mandinka nations to the low country. Sea Islanders are believed to descend from Angolans, called "Gullah" for short; their fellow Africans thought the Gullah possessed a certain mysticism.

Many former Haitian slaves resettled in Savannah around the time Santo Domingo slaves rebelled in 1804, lending the coast a distinctive Creole nature. This influence may date back even further, to the time of the Revolutionary War, when the French brought an all-Haitian unit to fight the British in Savannah—historians speculate that some wounded soldiers stayed and were assimilated.

Communities of "Free Men of Color" had existed in Georgia's cities from colonial times on. The communities were composed of some African immigrants and many former slaves who either bought their freedom or were released from slavery (manumitted). Escaping slaves sought refuge in backcountry swamps, caves, or in the islands. Many escaped to Native American villages—the Seminoles were particularly welcoming, and Seminole culture reflects the African influences of these "Black Indians" to this day.

Vestiges of African culture managed to survive, despite the slavery system's determination to repress it. African-influenced traditions are now considered inextricably Southern—including the commonplace "swept lawns" (sweeping a dirt apron around humble homes as practiced in West Africa) and the indispensable okra (an African vegetable transported to America by slaves). The folklore of trickster Br'er Rabbit and other such "slave tales" (first recorded by Georgia's Joel Chandler Harris) have become emblematic of Southern storytelling. And the wedding ritual of "jumping the broom" (in which the bride and groom hold hands and jump backward over a broom) has distinct American roots—the ritual got started in slavery time to sanctify a slave marriage not legally recognized by white overseers.

KAP STANN

a young fisherman at the marsh

Today's African-American Georgians celebrate their ethnic heritage in many ways. Martin Luther King Day in January, Black History Month throughout February, Juneteenth (the June 15 abolition anniversary), and Kwanzaa (December's seven-day Afrocentric fest of thanksgiving) are American-born celebrations that bring out African, Afro-Haitian, Caribbean, and distinctly Southern traditions.

Geechee Folk Culture

A rich slice of African culture endures on the Sea Islands off the Georgia and Carolina coast. These remote islands harbor a fascinating history. Once they served as sanctuaries for escaping slaves; later they were left to slaves when plantation owners fled during the Civil War; and at war's end they became part of a black republic after Union General William T. Sherman reserved the islands for newly freed slaves. Here self-sufficient communities have lived for generations outside the traffic of white society and commerce. In their isolation they have managed to meld old African traditions and beliefs with their American experience. Islanders developed a distinct dialect called Gullah (for "Angola"), a combination of American, West Indian, English, and African languages, still a commonly heard accent on the coast today.

Gullah communities at the mouth of Georgia's Ogeechee River led to the local name "Geechee" to describe the people and their dialect. As in the Appalachian folk culture, the true practitioners of this heritage are of such advanced age that the culture is in decline. Younger generations called to the mainland for education, jobs, or other opportunities, combined with inevitable 20th-century intrusion and exposure, leave to question the future of these largely self-governed communities.

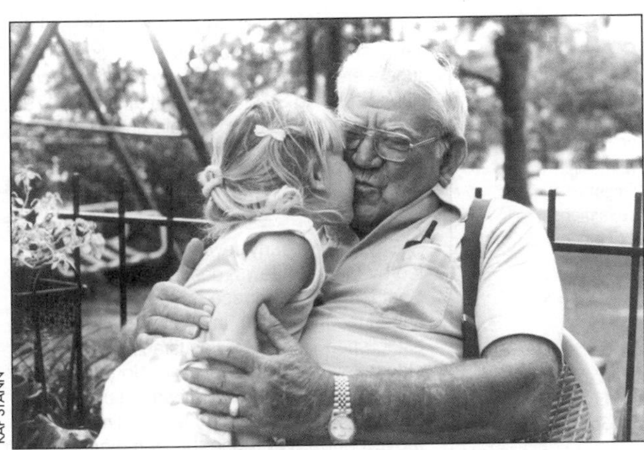

KAP STANN

Uncle Willie "getting some sugar" from grandniece Corinne.

The Gullah historically practiced folk religion that combined threads of Islam, Afro-Christianity, and voodoo influences from the Caribbean (also called "hoodoo"). In this tradition, conjure doctors use magic and "conjure bags" of plant roots believed to possess special powers, or "mojoes" (charms), to protect or malign.

Geechee folklore tells stories of "haunts" (spirits of the dead, pronounced "haints"), "hags" (disembodied spirits of living witches), and "plat-eyes" (evil shape-shifting spirits, commonly with one big eye hanging out in front). When such forces troubled the lives of the living, root doctors or conjure doctors were called in to subdue the spirits. Other island legends are rooted in American history: one tale tells of groups of Africans in chains "walking back to Africa," a mythological ending for slaves who chose drowning over bondage.

SOUTHERN CULTURE TODAY

A Patchwork Quilt

Today's Southern culture borrows from all these beginnings to create a patchwork quilt of Southern traditions. A scrap from the Cherokee, another from the Yoruba, yet another from the Spanish Inquisition or the Irish Sea; all were laced together with a common history and compelling natural environment to produce the rich cultural fabric of the region today. Here oral traditions, social manners, customs, beliefs, and folklore impress visitors with the importance of "traditional" values of family, church, and community.

Americans tend to overstate differences between the races, and many outlanders commonly consider that gap wider in the South. On the contrary, in some sense, Southern whites and blacks have more in common with each other as fellow Southerners than they have with their racial counterparts in other regions.

Besides, it's a misperception to believe that White is White, Black is Black, and Red is Red. Though many exceptionally stable families in the South can trace consistent bloodlines back for centuries, for many others the color line was substantially blurred by intermarriage or by exploitation of slaves by masters. The late Alex Haley, who traced his Southern lineage back to Africa in *Roots,* writes in his final work of his grandmother, the product of an elective biracial relationship, to make the point that if you look back far enough, we're all, in the most real sense, brothers and sisters.

Religion

"The South is by a long way the most simply and sincerely religious country I ever was in," said Victorian rationalist Sir William Archer. "It is not, like Ireland, a priest-ridden country; it is not, like England, a country in which the strength of religion lies in its social prestige; it is not, like Scotland, a country steeped in theology. But it is a country in which religion is a very large factor in life, and God is very real and personal."

SCRIPTURE CAKE

$4^1/2$ c. I Kings 4:22 (flour)
1 c. Judges 5:25 (butter)
2 c. Jeremiah 6:20 (sugar)
2 c. Samuel 30:12 (raisins)
2 c. Nahum 3:12 (figs)
2 c. Numbers 17:8 (almonds)
2 T. I Samuel 14:25 (honey)
1 pinch Leviticus 2:13 (salt)
6 Jeremiah 17:11 (eggs)
$^1/2$ c. Judges 4:19 (milk)
2 T. Amos 4:5 (leaven)

Season to taste with II Chronicles 9:9 (spices); mix like a fruit cake and bake at 350° F.
(Thanks to Jenny Rogers of Southside Baptist Church, Columbus.)

Today religion continues to make up an important facet of Southern culture. People who recall the Carter administration remember how the new Southern president astonished Washington with casual references to his strong religious beliefs and by constantly offering blessings and prayers at public occasions. In this way, Jimmy Carter represented many Southerners, whose lives are filled with church picnics, revivals, homecomings, Sunday clothes, Sunday dinners, fire and brimstone, and Vacation Bible School. The literature and moral code of Southerners are woven with Biblical quotes and themes of faith and grace, damnation, and redemption. Though overwhelmingly Protestant—and predominantly Southern Baptist at that—Georgia's religious tradition draws from spiritual roots as deep and varied as its people.

The first nonindigenous religion practiced on Georgia's shores was Catholicism, brought to coastal Georgia by Spanish missionaries in 1566. For more than a century, the Jesuits and Franciscan priests worked to convert the natives to Christianity, until finally abandoning the effort along with the missions.

Groups fleeing religious persecution were among Georgia's original settlers in the early 1700s. European Protestants, Jews, Quakers, and Puritans all found religious freedom here. Yet this freedom was selective: Roman Catholics were originally banned from the colony when it was founded in 1733, for fear they'd act as spies for the encroaching Spanish or French. The fears subsided (but not before a group of Cajuns were made so unwelcome that they continued south to St. Marys to settle), and by 1792 Savannah had its own Catholic chapel. A major religion was founded in the new colony: John Wesley established the Methodist church in 1738, and also taught the world's first Sunday school here.

Savannah's early Jewish community, though led by German Jews, descended largely from Spanish or Portuguese families who had escaped the Inquisition. In 1735, Savannah Jews established Temple Mikvah Israel, now the third-oldest Jewish congregation in North America. Threatened by occasional Spanish successes at coastal battles, many of these original families moved north, yet those that remained (or returned after British victory) formed a strong Jewish community that continues today. In Atlanta, a new Jewish museum tells the story of the capital's Jewish community. Elsewhere in Georgia, "circuit" rabbis administer to scattered Jewish populations, holding monthly or bimonthly services in the venerable rural tradition of Southern circuit preachers.

When slavery was introduced in Georgia, slaves often attended Christian church services segregated in the upper "slave gallery." As exceptions to this, several early churches organized expressly for Africans are now honored as landmarks in the African-American community: the congregation of Augusta's Springfield Baptist Church dates from 1733, and Savannah's First African Baptist Church dates from 1788. After emancipation, former slaves formed many churches, predominately Baptist, but the two strongest black churches up north, the African Methodist Episcopal (AME) and African Methodist Episcopal Zion also gained a strong following in the New South. Not simply places of worship, these churches provided a critical social structure for communities cut off from full participation in the social, political, and economic life of the broader society.

The 1960s civil rights movement inspired many African-Americans to rediscover African religious traditions, notably Islam. Malcolm X's mentor, Nation of Islam leader Elijah Mohammed, was born Robert Poole in Georgia's Washington County. Today traditional Islamic customs are practiced in homes and mosques in

Atlanta and elsewhere by Muslims of many races.

At the fringes of the dominant Protestant sects, the Primitive Baptists continue to prove their devotion by handling poisonous snakes. Foot washing is also among the ritual practices of these "Hardshell" Baptists, who are most often found in isolated mountain communities.

Visitors are welcome at the restaurant and craft shop operated by a traditional Mennonite community in Montezuma (southeast of Macon), where the Plain People continue Amish-like customs (though, unlike the Amish, they do not forsake such modern conveniences as electricity and automobiles).

Conduct and Dress

In Atlanta, for the most part anything goes for casual dress, but if you're doing business, visiting churches, or attending social dinners, more formal rules apply (jackets and ties for men, commensurate formality for women). In the rest of the state, visitors may draw unwelcome negative attention by appearing too casual (cut-off shorts, overpatched jeans, or anything sloppy or revealing). A posted dress code at one military museum, for example, forbids sleeveless shirts, rubber thongs, too-short skirts and shorts (though a researcher was admitted without meeting two of these conditions). Clean and Tidy are strong social-class indicators, and held in Germanically high esteem. Outward manifestations of neatness extend to keeping cars clean and trimming lawns to stubble (homeowners may be ticketed and fined for even lightly overgrown lawns).

Unfamiliar cultural traits may frustrate visitors unless they can likewise adapt. As in every near-tropical climate, time moves more slowly here (except perhaps in bustling Atlanta); vacationers would be wise to adopt the local pace or at least be patient with it. Also be aware that many well-meaning Southerners hate to say no (it's considered impolite to be too direct), so to be hospitable they may appear to agree to something they have no intention of seeing through.

Photo etiquette also demands a certain cultural sensitivity. Many photographers will no doubt be attracted to the kind of dramatic back-country scenes you can see only in the South—lean-to shacks, ancient country stores with homemade signs, and grizzled portraits—yet visitors need to exercise standard rules of courtesy. Always ask before taking pictures of people, particularly in run-down areas, and don't always expect a positive response. Locals are extremely sensitive about how the national press tends to portray Southerners as "hillbillies" or hicks, and see nothing scenic in perpetuating stereotypes.

Perhaps Georgia-born writer Roy Blount, Jr. spoke for many Southerners when he observed during Clinton's Presidential campaign in 1992 how "New York columnists toss around the term 'cracker' pretty loosely, and now Bubba is taking over as an ethnic term. There's no other ethnic group you could use such a slur about so loosely."

Language

The Southern dialect enlivens the speech of Georgians, from the barely perceptible Atlanta "y'all" to the lengthening lyricism of a coastal drawl. Even in a short time, a visitor traveling through different regions can perceive local variations in speech patterns.

Regional vocabulary, idioms, and manners of speech also spice up the local language. Mountain valleys, summits, and waterfalls become "coves," "knobs," and "cataracts." If you're "fixin' to" buy liquor, find a "package store"; if you want it to go, ask for a "go cup." Folks don't die, they "pass."

Formal addresses of "sir" and "ma'am" are in constant use. Southerners appreciate when visitors adopt such conventions, though non-Southerners aren't expected to be as polite as locals. Also abiding by more conservative rules of address, it's generally considered polite not to address people by their first names unless specifically invited to. As with titles, names tend to be long and inclusive; for example, a building named for a popular politician in Atlanta uses his entire name and nickname—The James H. ("Sloppy") Floyd Building. You'll find the mark of politeness in local newspapers, where second references to names are preceded by a title (Mr. This or Mrs. That instead of simply This or That), and readers are requested to "*please* turn to page X."

In matters of usage, possessive apostrophes have been somehow dispensed with—take for example the coastal place names St. Catherines, St. Simons, and St. Marys. If you used the apostrophe you'd be regarded as another punctuation-crazy outlander.

Windsor Hotel, Americus

ON THE ROAD

SIGHTSEEING HIGHLIGHTS

Most trips to Georgia start rightly in **Atlanta,** and even if you're eager to explore the backcountry, take the opportunity to discover the capital's own wild side. Spend your days visiting the **King Memorial,** wander galleries at the **High Museum,** and explore the city's homier east side neighborhoods. All night, every night, bicultural blues resonate from corner joints till close to dawn (when the Majestic Diner serves flapjacks to worn-out crowds). For a Southern-classic flip side (particularly if your Deep South trip is restricted to Atlanta), **"shoot the 'Hootch"** on a lazy float down the Chattahoochee River, cheer on the **Atlanta Braves,** and order soulful skillet-fried chicken, hush puppies, and a home-brew Coke at **Son's Place** for a delicious taste of the region. Tour fancy houses and sip iced tea from crystal glasses. See the **Swan House** at the Atlanta History Center and drive through **Buckhead's** wide lanes of Gothic mansions for that Old Money feeling.

From Atlanta, you can jump back a few centuries on a trip to coastal **Savannah.** Stay in historic inns overlooking trim English squares designed in the early 1700s. Crack "low country" oysters at seafood festivals, catch the continuous block party at the riverfront, and enjoy the city's seaward sophistication and colonial grace. Drive (or bike) out to nearby beaches to swim near dolphins and explore scenic marshlands; head down the old Atlantic Coast Highway past abandoned rice plantations to remote fishing villages for "fleet-fresh" shrimp and shellfish. For one of the best adventures in the U.S., ferry out to **Cumberland Island,** where spectacular subtropical flora and fauna come together with an exotic history on an island dotted with native shell mounds, Spanish missions, English forts, and antebellum cotton plantations. Bridged "Golden Isles" resorts provide more easily accessible glimpses of this same rich terrain, best seen from the rambling veranda of the historical **Jekyll Island Club Hotel.** Adventurers boat out to de-

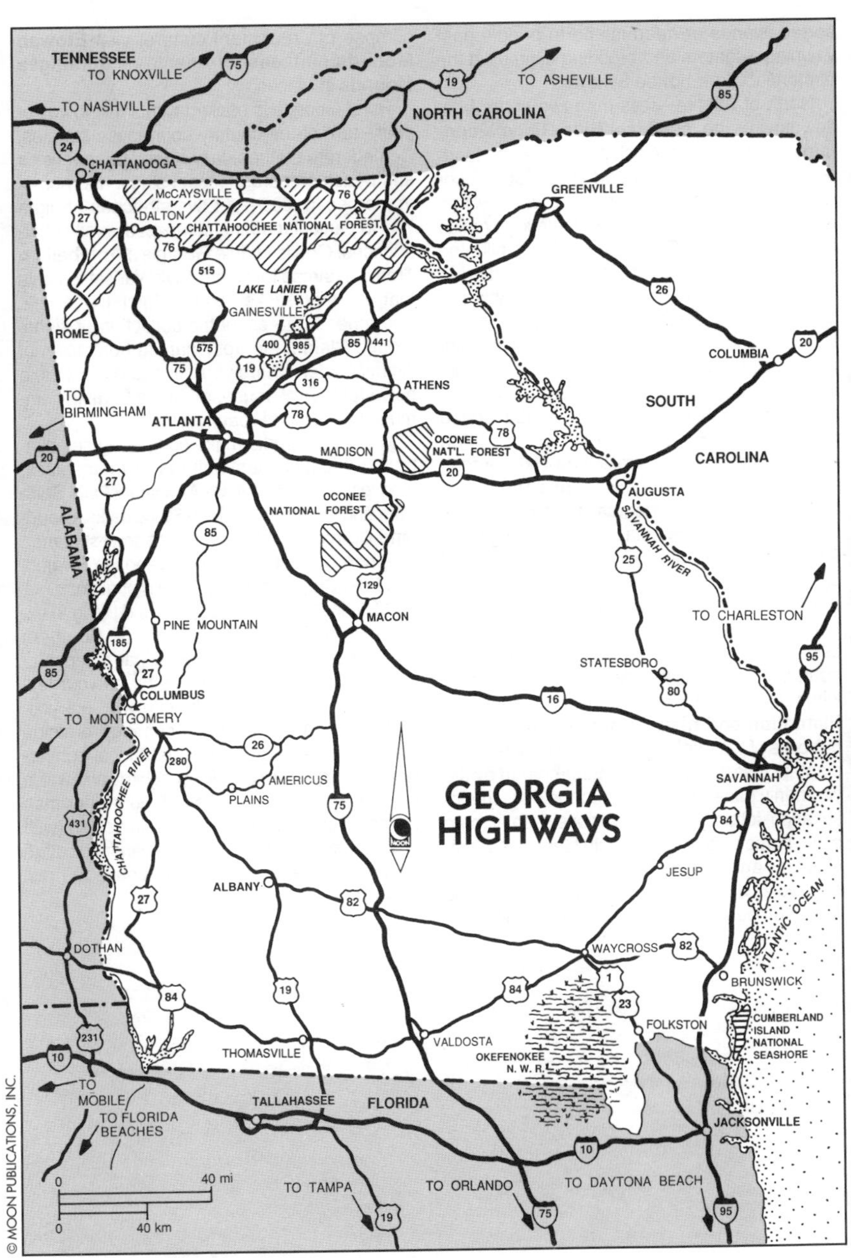
GEORGIA HIGHWAYS
TENNESSEE
TO KNOXVILLE
TO NASHVILLE
CHATTANOOGA
TO ASHEVILLE
NORTH CAROLINA
McCAYSVILLE
DALTON
CHATTAHOOCHEE NATIONAL FOREST
LAKE LANIER
GAINESVILLE
GREENVILLE
ROME
COLUMBIA
ATHENS
SOUTH
CAROLINA
TO BIRMINGHAM
ATLANTA
OCONEE NAT'L. FOREST
MADISON
AUGUSTA
OCONEE NATIONAL FOREST
SAVANNAH RIVER
ALABAMA
MACON
TO CHARLESTON
PINE MOUNTAIN
STATESBORO
COLUMBUS
TO MONTGOMERY
AMERICUS
PLAINS
SAVANNAH
CHATTAHOOCHEE RIVER
JESUP
ALBANY
ATLANTIC OCEAN
DOTHAN
WAYCROSS
BRUNSWICK
CUMBERLAND ISLAND NATIONAL SEASHORE
FOLKSTON
VALDOSTA
THOMASVILLE
OKEFENOKEE N. W. R.
TO MOBILE
TALLAHASSEE
FLORIDA
JACKSONVILLE
TO FLORIDA BEACHES
TO TAMPA
TO ORLANDO
TO DAYTONA BEACH
0
40 mi
0
40 km
MOON
75
19
85
24
76
27
515
575
400
985
441
26
20
316
78
25
129
185
16
95
80
280
431
84
82
1
23
231
10

serted islands or head inland to paddle past yawning alligators and brooding cypress in the primordial **Okefenokee Swamp.**

North of Atlanta—less than two hours from downtown—the legendary **Blue Ridge Mountains** shelter an Appalachian culture and landscape with incredible opportunities for outdoor recreation. Daring rafters ride through *Deliverance*-like wilderness on the white-knuckle rapids of the **Chattooga River,** and trekkers hike the world-famous **Appalachian Trail** starting in North Georgia. Enjoy the Southern Highlands' fiddle-pickin', quilt-stitchin', wood-whittlin' mountaineers—inheritors of America's finest and oldest folk culture. Quaint country towns highlight the region's gold-rush history; see the **Dahlonega** gold museum and descend into abandoned mines nearby. Bavarian affectations in **Helen** come complete with a rollicking Oktoberfest, and popular music festivals in **Blue Ridge** and **Hiawassee** feature bluegrass twang. Or simply squirrel away to the solace of Blue Ridge waterfalls, creekside camps, hideaway cabins, and country inns.

Bask in the South's rich cultural heritage throughout Georgia—hear the lyrical drawl, the tall tales, the fascinating history, and experience boundless *hospitality*—forces that manage to withstand national homogenizing influences. **Plantation and historic home tours** provide glimpses of the rarefied antebellum lifestyle of the planter class, glimpses far outnumbered by the yeomanly cane-grinding, syrup-making, sheep-shearing, tobaccy-spittin' traditions seen at more down-home restorations (South Georgia's **Westville** and **Agrirama** are two of the best) and celebrated local festivals (follow all signs to a "Pig Jig" barbecue or mule parade). For a powerful glimpse of an ancient culture, visit **Etowah Mounds** northeast of Atlanta or **Ocmulgee Mounds** in Macon.

Rural Georgia is packed with small-town appeal—turn-of-the-century courthouse squares, Confederate statues, lazy rivers, peanut fields and peach orchards, gospel sings, and homemade pecan pies—yet two stretches of highway in particular offer a compact diversity of attractions. One is Middle Georgia's **Antebellum Trail,** so-named for its pre-Civil War settlements that Sherman sacked on his March to the Sea. The other is the eccentric collection of sights around **Plains,** the aptly named hometown of Jimmy Carter, where you'll find funky folk art, a powerful P.O.W. museum, and a farming commune with a world-reaching vision.

Many state parks make compelling self-contained vacation destinations in themselves; among the best to visit are **Amicalola Falls State Park** and the rest of the Blue Ridge parks, **Cloudland Canyon** tucked into the northwest corner, **Stephen C. Foster** at the Okefenokee Swamp, and **FDR State Park** atop Pine Mountain.

While it's tempting to bop around trying to experience the whole spectrum, true Southern style means sticking around to get a sense of a place. Try exploring only as far as your feet (or trail bike, raft, or sea kayak) will take you, stopping at a potluck homecoming, roadside stand, or bait shop to engage in local conversation. Or stay still; listen for songbirds and watch the grass grow. If you make it no farther than the porch swing of a single lakeside cabin (with your line strung out in hopes of a pan-fried catfish dinner), you've found Georgia. Leave the rest for your next trip.

OUTDOOR RECREATION

Georgia's beautifully varied natural environment—mountains, coast, woods, rivers, and swamps—combined with a mostly mild climate makes the state a fantastic place for all kinds of outdoor recreation. And Georgians—with their gung-ho enthusiasm for sport—take full advantage of it. While national forest and refuge lands, wonderful state parks, and the "Big" lakes throughout the state are all top draws, two regions in particular offer an exceptional variety of creative recreation.

Adventurers flock to North Georgia for scenic whitewater runs (some of the best in the country), mettle-testing long-distance hiking, rock climbing, hang gliding, caving, biking, paddling, and even skiing (Sky Valley is the southernmost ski run in the eastern U.S.). Campers and naturalists can appreciate the extraordinary wildlife and seasonal Appalachian variety at close range.

APPALACHIAN TRAIL

MAINE TO GEORGIA

The coast, naturally, offers the widest selection of water sports. Boaters sail past shrimpers in the intracoastal waterway's marshlands; paddlers head out to deserted barrier islands; swimmers join dolphins in gentle ocean waters; divers explore a marine sanctuary and sunken battleships. Sea fishing is as popular on the coast as freshwater fishing is elsewhere in Georgia.

The uncommon picks? Try the incomparable adventure of paddling through the Okefenokee Swamp, overnight horseback trips into Blue Ridge wilds, and mountain biking along old jeep trails and shell roads on Georgia's subtropical islands.

NATIONAL PARKLANDS

Chattahoochee-Oconee National Forest

The Chattahoochee-Oconee National Forest covers 859,000 acres of prime Georgia woodland. The Chattahoochee section encompasses most of North Georgia; the Oconee parcel shelters a Piedmont forest in central Georgia (north of Macon). Forest Service (FS) campgrounds throughout both units vary from primitive isolated sites to more developed recreation area camps. The forest's 300 miles of trails include three extraordinary long-distance trails through the Blue Ridge Mountains, offering hikers and backpackers the chance to delve deep into the woods, days and weeks away from civilization. The most famous, the **Appalachian Trail** (A.T.), begins in North Georgia and runs 2,036 miles to Maine along the spine of the Appalachian Mountains. The 50-mile **Benton MacKaye Trail,** named for the founder of the A.T., runs laterally across north-central Georgia from the Tennessee line to its junction with the Appalachian Trail. And the 30-mile **William Bartram Trail,** named for the 18th-century naturalist who pioneered the route, runs through the most dense and remote corner of Georgia's Blue Ridge.

Among the other trails in the national forest, some have been specially designed to accommodate mountain bikes, horses, off-road vehicles, or people with disabilities.

In the forest you'll also find swimming holes and lakeshore beaches, rock-climbing routes, and thousands of acres of boating lakes and fine fishing streams. Visit any ranger station for recreation area directories and trail maps, or write to the central office for more information: U.S. Forest Service, 1755 Cleveland Hwy., Gainesville, GA 30501, tel. (404) 536-0541 (reach the "leaf watch" newsline at 404-536-1310).

Cumberland Island National Seashore

At Georgia's southern coast, Cumberland Island National Seashore preserves the pristine natural environment of this spectacular subtropical barrier island—home to wild horses, bobcats, and wild turkeys, and a breeding area for the loggerhead sea turtle and even the rare right whale. A maximum of 300 visitors a day is allowed on the island, which is accessible only by boat. A National Park Service concessionaire operates a daily ferry from St. Marys; make reservations far in advance for summers, tel. (912) 882-4335.

Okefenokee Swamp

The Okefenokee Swamp National Wildlife Refuge provides a serene sanctuary for alligators, softshell turtles, black bears, and many other animal species, which can best be seen by boat (rentals available). Canoeists can explore the exotic deep swamp wilderness on day or overnight trips (up to five days). The U.S. Fish and Wildlife Service, tel. (912) 496-7836, administers the refuge, which covers most of the swamp. (A state park administers another swamp "entrance," and a private attraction occupies the third major access point.)

Other National Park Service Sites

The National Park Service (NPS) maintains other diverse attractions in Georgia, including the scenic Chattahoochee River corridor (see **Lakes and Rivers,** below), Ocmulgee National Monument (ancient aboriginal temple grounds outside of Macon), the Chickamauga Battlefield (in the state's northwest corner), and Martin Luther King National Historic Park in downtown Atlanta—an offbeat place to find khaki-clad rangers wearing mountie hats.

Entrance Fees

Policies and fees vary among the differing federal agencies (National Forest Service, National Park Service, U.S. Fish and Wildlife Service), but generally, admission prices apply to developed areas only, and fall within a range of either $1-3 per person or $2-10 per vehicle. A **Golden Eagle Pass,** available for $25 at national park sites, entitles you to free admission to all federally operated outdoor recreation areas for one calendar year. For free lifetime access, travelers 62 years and older can receive a **Golden Age Passport,** and travelers who are blind or disabled may request a **Golden Access Passport.** Or buy a **Park Pass** from certain NPS-administered sites for unlimited entry to that site for one calendar year ($10-15). For general information, contact the **National Park Service** Southeast Regional Office, tel. (404) 331-5187.

STATE PARKS

Georgia's outstanding state parks are excellent destinations for a range of recreational activities, particularly water sports. Of 46 park sites, most are perched on a lake or river, with facilities for swimming (pools or imported sand beaches, with bathhouses), fishing, and boating (often including boat rental). Some, such as Little Ocmulgee State Park, rank as full-scale resorts, complete with an 18-hole golf course, tennis courts, lodging, and dining, in addition to the above attractions. All but four of the parks allow camping—see **Accommodations and Food,** below.

Nearly all parks maintain well-marked **hiking trails** that vary from short nature trails to longer ones suitable for day hiking or overnight backpacking. **Amicalola Falls** and **Black Rock Mountain** state parks are backpacker favorites. Many of the parks are at or near historical sites, and most are in beautiful rural country surrounded by local color—scenic old mills, covered bridges, and the like.

The mountain parks and sites are considered among the state's best, popular year-round for scenic seasonal beauty, but especially valued in fall for the colorful foliage and in summer for relatively cooler temperatures. Among all the state parks, **Unicoi** and **Vogel**—the Blue Ridge parks with lakes—draw the biggest crowds.

The park system designs an impressive slate of activities to augment natural attractions. Beyond such customary activities as guided nature hikes, evening campfire programs, and wildlife shows, the program list includes canoe trips, backpacking trips, catfish "rodeos," and cultural festivals (Appalachian crafts workshops, mountain music concerts, and Cherokee Homecomings), most free with the modest parking fee.

Parks charge a $2 per car parking fee (except Wednesdays, which are free). Your $2 gets you a **ParkPass** good for any state park on the day of purchase. A $25 annual **Georgia ParkPass** entitles holders to unlimited use of all sites (discounts for seniors and disabled veterans); it's available at any park office. For a 16-page "Special Events" schedule, a *Great Georgia Getaways* brochure (listing facilities at all state properties), or general information, contact the **Georgia**

KAP STANN

a quiet moment at Delano Lake in Roosevelt State Park near Warm Springs

Department of Natural Resources, State Parks and Historic Sites, 205 Butler St. SE, Atlanta, GA 30334 (enclose a business-size SASE for speediest reply); tel. (404) 656-3530. The park system maintains a centralized toll-free reservation number outside Atlanta: (800) 864-7275 (in metro Atlanta call 770-389-7275).

The most famous of Georgia's state parklands, **Stone Mountain Park** outside Atlanta, operates independently of the state park system. Admission is $6 per car every day.

LAKES AND RIVERS

Whether you visit the lakes, rivers, swamps, marshes, or ocean, a trip on Georgia's waterways is a trip to the best of the Southeast. Every floating conveyance imaginable—inner tubes, kayaks, canoes, rafts, speedboats, houseboats, and pontoon boats—can be found carrying people through the state's well-watered natural areas, from clear, spring-fed North Georgia streams and clay-stained central watersheds to daring South Georgia black water.

The "Big" Lakes

In a state where a personal motorboat is often considered as indispensable as a personal automobile, most locals head to one of Georgia's 26 so-called "Big" lakes, whose shores are a mix of developed recreation areas (with beaches and campgrounds) and remote fishing holes. As these lakes were created by river impoundment (either for reservoirs or hydroelectric power), they are administered by either the state utility company or the Army Corps of Engineers. The most-visited lakes—largely by virtue of their proximity to Atlanta—are **Lake Sidney Lanier** (casually considered Atlanta's "beach") and **Allatoona Lake** (Red Top Mountain State Park is situated on a peninsula jutting out into the lake). Other popular lakes are the impoundments along the Savannah River north of Augusta, and those on the Chattahoochee River at the Alabama border. For maps and recreation directories to Lakes Oconee, Sinclair, Burton, Rabun, Seed, Tallulah Falls, Tugaloo, and Oliver (among others), contact the **Georgia Power Company,** Land Department, Box 4545, Atlanta, GA 30302, tel. (404) 526-2396. For Lakes Allatoona, Carters, Lanier, George, West Point, and Seminole, contact the **U.S. Army Corps of Engineers,** tel. (404) 331-4834. (Or find branch offices around dams for more information.)

Rivers

Fortunately, the wide local appeal of the lakes leaves rivers to those interested in remote backcountry adventure. The wildest ride is down the **Chattooga River**—federally designated as "Wild and Scenic"—where some of the most hazardous whitewater runs in the country cut through the wooded wilderness and gorges made famous in the movie *Deliverance.* Rafting companies licensed by the Forest Service lead excursions down the Chattooga's Class III and IV stretches, which both include individual rapids rated up to Class VI. Yet the TVA-managed **Ocoee River,** right across the Tennessee border, was selected as the site of the 1996 Olympic whitewater canoeing competition because of its compact stretch of rapids. River-running on the Ocoee is organized by a consortium of outfitters.

Although wild water receives the most publicity, paddlers also enjoy discovering Georgia's calmer rivers, which flow gracefully for long distances through semiwilderness, with only a few bridges and a fish camp now and then to punctuate the solitude. The usually placid waters occasionally stir up into manageable rapids—an ideal testing ground for beginners.

The **Chattahoochee River National Recreation Area** preserves a 48-mile stretch of wooded river corridor, bringing leisurely rafting and backcountry hiking within easy reach of downtown Atlanta. The **Altamaha, Ogeechee,** and **Alapaha Rivers** attract paddlers to South Georgia's scenic backcountry, as do the two black-water rivers that emanate from the Okefenokee Swamp: the **Suwannee River** and the **St. Marys River.** And the swamp itself is a paddler's paradise.

FISHING AND HUNTING

Fishing

To say fishing is a popular pastime in Georgia is putting it mildly—it's more like a religion or a local art form. One of the best ways to animate a conversation in the South is to ask where to find good fishing in these parts—but you'd better know a thing or two about bait before you ask, and don't expect anyone to divulge secret fishing holes. Fishing reports can be found in every major newspaper in the region, bait shops are as plentiful as markets, and there's even a call-in fishing program on radio station WNIV-AM in Atlanta.

The 26 Big lakes alone (see **Lakes and Rivers,** above) cover 398,219 acres. Add to that 3,000 acres of state park lakes, as well as rivers and private ponds, and you have a bounty of bass, bream, carp, catfish, crappie, perch, shad, trout, walleye, pike, and sunfish. North Georgia's many trout streams are among the most prized in the Southeast.

Nonresidents 16 years or older must obtain a valid Georgia fishing license, available for $24 a year from more than 2,000 license dealers, usually found at sporting goods stores and hardware stores, marinas, and park concessions. Short-term licenses are also available: $7 a week or $3.50 a day. Additionally, an annual trout stamp ($13) is required to fish for trout, possess trout, or even just to fish in designated trout waters. All annual fishing licenses are valid from April 1 until March 31 of the following year.

The state's **Department of Natural Resources,** Wildlife Resources (tel. 770-918-6400), publishes several brochures on fishing areas and regulations, including a North Georgia trout-stream map and guide. For information on possession limits, length limits, seasons, and other policies, contact the fisheries section at 2123 U.S. Hwy. 278 SE, Social Circle, GA 30279, tel. (770) 918-6418 or (800) ASK-FISH (800-274-3474), or see the Web site www.georgia.org/dnr/wild/.

The state's Department of Industry, Trade, and Tourism publishes the directory ***Fishing in Georgia Lakes;*** write P.O. Box 1776, Atlanta, GA 30301-1776, or call (404) 656-3590. Detailed boating and fishing maps are available from Wildlife Resources, the Army Corps of Engineers, and the Georgia Power Company. Frequently, Wildlife Resources stocks maps from all three of these sources. Among dozens of private publications on sportfishing in Georgia, the 152-page ***Georgia Fishing Digest*** lists professional fishing guides and other information. It's available from Pisces Press, Box 8-521, Athens, GA 30608, for $6.95 per directory, plus $1.50 for shipping (state residents add six percent sales tax). **Kingfisher's** laminated maps of 15 Georgia lakes note camps, markets, and access roads as well as topographical and navigational features; call (800) 326-0257 for a catalog and prices.

Even for nonanglers, a trip to an isolated fish camp can offer an authentic Southern cultural experience. Display at least a bamboo pole and line so they won't look at you funny, and what the hey—try your luck. Most camps offer low-rent campsites or cabins and small marinas or boat launches. Fish hatcheries across the state are also interesting local diversions.

Hunting

As with fishing, hunting in Georgia is a revered

tradition dating from frontier days (and the days of slim pickin's). Today, exclusive resorts in South Georgia are devoted to quail hunting, and you can see full-dress fox hunts near Augusta. More commonly, hunters stalk deer, feral hogs, wild turkeys, and small game such as opossum, raccoon, rabbit, and squirrel. For information on hunting seasons, restrictions, limits, licenses, and fees, and for maps of wildlife management areas, which can also be wonderful primitive places to hike and camp—when it's *not* hunting season—send for the annual ***Hunting Seasons and Regulations*** guide produced by the state's **Department of Natural Resources,** Wildlife Resources, 2123 U.S. Hwy. 278 SE, Social Circle, GA 30279, tel. (770) 918-6400, or see www.georgia.org/dnr/wild/.

Southerners display an impressive familiarity with the subtleties of animal behavior, bird migration and nesting patterns, minute distinctions in plantlife, and other intimate characteristics of the natural landscape. In the past, accumulating such knowledge was a simple matter of survival—hunters and anglers reading the signs to put dinner on the table—but now the tradition continues in the form of recreation and wildlife observation, as well as hunting and fishing.

SPECTATOR SPORTS

While Atlanta's professional sports franchises—the Atlanta **Braves** (baseball), **Falcons** (football), and **Hawks** (basketball)—are the state's greatest draw for spectator sports, the selection is expanding. Professional ice hockey franchises have sprung up around the state and are drawing crowds, perhaps unexpectedly for a subtropical region.

College football is also widely popular. When the University of Georgia **Bulldogs** play Georgia Tech's **Yellow Jackets,** you can't find a hotel room near town. Valdosta State University is also known for its football team.

As the home of Hank Aaron, Ty Cobb, and Fran Tarkenton, Georgia loves athletic competitions, particularly baseball. Throughout the state you can catch popular minor-league or hometown games with all the cultural attractions: muddy uniforms, cheering crowds, ballpark food, and plenty of hot sun.

All of these teams, sports, athletes, and traditions are celebrated in the new **Georgia Sports Hall of Fame,** opening in Macon in 1999. See www.gshf.com for updates.

ARTS AND ENTERTAINMENT

MUSIC AND NIGHTLIFE

Georgia's rich musical tradition ranges from the lyrical Elizabethan ballads of Appalachian mountaineers to the electrifying R&B of the likes of Ray Charles and James Brown—and you're never too far from Southern rock, country twang, urban rap, and arty punk. Feel the rhythm in smoky dives, waterfront saloons, country dance halls, plush box seats, and outdoor amphitheaters throughout the state.

Though not the style the region is most noted for, classical music is performed by symphonies in all the major cities (the **Atlanta Symphony** is most highly esteemed). Concerts held in the "jewel box" opera houses in Columbus and Macon are worth attending for the ambience alone; also watch for campus performances at the state's many colleges and universities. Traditional swing and cool piano-bar jazz still play on in Savannah, birthplace of songwriter and composer Johnny Mercer ("Jeepers Creepers," "That Old Black Magic").

Georgia's contribution to American music, particularly contemporary music, is celebrated in the new **Georgia Music Hall of Fame** in Macon, where more than 400 of the state's musicians and producers are honored with lively exhibits on jazz, swing, rock and roll, rhythm and blues, gospel music, and more; www.garocks.com.

Traditional Music

Appalachian **mountain music** evokes an Anglo-Saxon heritage preserved for hundreds of years in isolated mountain hollows ("hollers"). Homemade stringed instruments—dulcimers, banjos, and fiddles—accompany the old English songs that gave rise to such American ballads as "Tom Dooley" and "John Henry," now folk classics.

Today, **bluegrass** fiddlers, square dancers, and "cloggers" (a distinctively Appalachian form of foot-stompin' inherited from "African-American flat-footin'") whoop it up in plank-floored lodges and on festival stages throughout North Georgia. And the related sound of contemporary **country music** ("soul music for white people," according to *Late Show* bandleader Paul Shaffer) can be heard in dance halls throughout the state, with occasional hometown performances by such native recording artists as Trisha Yearwood and Alan Jackson.

Originating from similarly remote communities, **Sea Island music** weaves traditional African rhythms with musical traditions established in America during slavery—maintained uncommonly consistently down through the generations because of the natural isolation of Georgia's coastal islands. The Sea Island Festival at St. Simons Island each August highlights "Geechee" musical traditions and culture.

Throughout the state, **gospel music** carries evangelizing messages in churches, at festivals, and at all-night gospel "sings." Drawn from traditional African spirituals and mixed with the Afro-Christianity the slaves developed, gospel anthems became synonymous with resistance, particularly during the civil rights era ("We Shall Overcome," "This Little Light of Mine," etc.).

Contemporary Music

The roots of contemporary **blues** and **rhythm and blues** (R&B) reach back to the "slave songs" chanted for generations in cotton fields throughout the South. Local legends Curley Weaver, Emery Glen, and Ma Rainey established Georgia's blues tradition earlier this century. Today's greatest R&B musicians—Ray Charles, Otis Redding, and the "grandfather of soul," James Brown—all sprang from Georgia. Since Ray Charles transformed "Georgia on My Mind" into an American classic decades back, the state has served as musical inspiration for many, with such hits as "Midnight Train to Georgia" sung by Gladys Knight (also a Georgia native), and "Rainy Night in Georgia," and "Georgia Rhythm" by the Atlanta Rhythm Section.

An uncommon number of famous Georgia musicians came from Macon alone, not only Redding and Charles but also Little Richard, Randy Crawford, Lena Horne, and the Allman Brothers. Here the Allman Brothers Band spawned **Southern rock,** and established their Capricorn music studios right off Cherry Street. Filled with musical landmarks, Macon was a natural choice for the state's new **Georgia Music Hall of Fame.**

More recently, musical notoriety has shifted to Athens, a small college town where several art and punk bands rocketed to fame in the mid-1980s. Local legends such as Pylon and the Barbecue Killers were eclipsed by the national recognition gained by the B-52s (". . . I'm a Scorpio from Athens, GA") and R.E.M. *(Automatic for the People).* R.E.M. adds to its already considerable local reputation by touring infrequently and reluctantly (an anomaly on the nation's contemporary music bandwagon), preferring instead to hang around Athens and occasionally show up at the city's 40-Watt Club.

Atlanta's music scene has introduced Arrested Development (a group breaking ground for its spiritually correct "gospel rap"), TLC, and the Indigo Girls. Elton John has also been made an honorary native since he adopted Atlanta as a home.

Nightlife

Atlanta has the most exciting nightlife of any city in the state or region—folks start early and keep going till the bars close at 4 a.m.; a few all-night clubs draw in the more energetic. Plenty of clubs cater to specific styles or audiences, but the city's trademark mix keeps the categories and audiences so fluid that newcomers always feel welcome. Certain bands draw many Atlantans up to clubs in Athens on weekend nights. Savannah hosts a citywide block party on River Street nearly every weekend in good weather, and plenty of clubs and music festivals keep the city moving till the wee hours. Macon, the granddaddy of Georgia's contemporary music scene, continues to pound out Southern rock and various other styles in scattered nightclubs, but without the nighttime streetlife of Atlanta or Savannah. Columbus and Augusta are sleepier, conservative towns, yet each has a college population that frequents a limited number of local saloons and clubs.

Farther-flung across Georgia's backcountry you'll find roadhouses—usually windowless cinderblock joints with pickup trucks parked outside—that can range from lively honky-tonks with local entertainment to dens of iniquity: outlanders (particularly women) might want to proceed with caution.

PERFORMING AND VISUAL ARTS

Each major city has its own performing arts groups, some with a long history and fine reputation (such as the Atlanta Ballet). Georgia's elegant old opera houses, such as the **Springer Opera House** in Columbus (the official theater of Georgia) or the **Grand Opera House** in Macon, make any performance therein worthwhile. And a variety of contemporary venues are found in the cities, from intimate lofts to huge coliseums. Also look for local performances and exhibits at colleges and universities.

The visual arts are best viewed at Atlanta's **High Museum** and in smaller galleries throughout metro Atlanta, Savannah's **Telfair Museum** and the city's many contemporary art galleries, the **Georgia Museum of Art** in Athens, and the **Columbus Museum** in Columbus. Albany's **Museum of Art** is noted for its African art collection.

Folk Arts and Crafts

The finest of Georgia's many folk-art traditions comes from the Appalachian Mountains in the northern part of the state. For hundreds of years, local artisans and craftspeople have fashioned handiworks from native materials, handing down their skills from generation to generation. Among the best known Appalachian crafts are quilts and weavings, pottery made from local clay, basketry from local vines, whittling, hardwood furniture and cabinetry, and musical instruments. See the Blue Ridge Mountains chapter for more information.

Another rich folk tradition emanates from the Sea Islands, where descendants of the islands' slave plantations weave baskets from local vines, make fishing nets by hand, and carry on many other distinctive traditions.

Two folk artists in Georgia defy categorization, though they've been called "visionary environmental artists" (for lack of any other description). Howard Finster's **Paradise Gardens** in northwest Georgia presents a spiritual fantasia with angelic madonnas spouting Bible verses, abstract sculpture constructed from used bicycle parts, and such simple flourishes as twisted stalks of tinfoil dangling decoratively from trees.

KAP STANN

Folk art sculpture incorporates modern materials, but keeps its down home flavor and whimsy.

GEORGIA FESTIVALS, EVENTS, AND HOLIDAYS

Georgians love a "fest," so you'll find plenty of occasions to celebrate local history, ethnic heritage, folklore, regional cuisine, and recreation. Dramatic seasonal changes encourage festivals of every size in nearly every town. Some towns are notable for a single event only (in which case they are not listed again in the text). The state Department of Industry, Trade, and Tourism produces an annual calendar available from P.O. Box 1776, Atlanta, GA 30301-1776, which lists every catfish rodeo, flower show, and raft race along with major festivals and seasonal openings. Whichever event strikes your fancy, call first to confirm dates and times.

January

King Week, Atlanta, from January 15. A civic celebration of racial harmony and ethnic pride, honoring famed civil-rights leader and native son Martin Luther King, Jr.

February

Atlanta Storytelling Festival, Atlanta. One of the South's finest traditions, stories celebrating history, multicultural heritage, and life itself.

Founders Day, Savannah, first week of February. Reenactment of the founding of the colony on the First Saturday Heritage Day.

March

St. Patrick's Day Festival, Savannah, around March 17. The South's largest celebration of traditional Irish revelry, including a music weekend of jazz, blues, and rock, plus a parade, green beer flowing on River Street, Irish folk music and crafts, and merriment lasting a full week.

Cherry Blossom Festival, Macon, mid- to late March. The downtown historic district's wide avenues, lined with cherry trees, are closed to traffic for arts, crafts, music, and food in the city's landmark event.

Antebellum Jubilee, Stone Mountain, last weekend in March and first weekend in April. A living-history festival in a mid-1800s setting with authentic period buildings, costumes, and entertainment.

April

Dogwood Festival, Atlanta, mid-April. The local rite of spring, when thousands gather for entertainment, local arts and crafts, and such springtime entertainment as a canine Frisbee contest and hot-air balloon rides.

Masters Golf Tournament, Augusta, early April. One of the nation's premier golf events.

Riverfest, Columbus, mid-April. A weekend of barbecues, raft races, and children's carnival games and rides held on the newly swanked-up waterfront.

Springfests in many cities and state parks inaugurate the season with barbecue cookoffs, outdoor recreation, and concerts. North Georgia towns schedule ample festivals for the many visitors who come to observe spring wildflowers in the mountains.

May

Chehaw National Indian Festival, Albany, third weekend in May. Traditional dances, foods, and arts and crafts of 10 aboriginal nations, mythology and storytelling of the original Southeastern natives, pottery and basket-making workshops.

June

Bluegrass Festival, Dahlonega, late June. Fiddlers, cloggers, and overall-clad mountaineers fiddle away in the gold rush town.

Country-by-the-Sea, Jekyll Island, early June. Five-hour country-music festival on the beach features nationally known country stars such as Ronnie Milsap, Conway Twitty, and Georgia's own Trisha Yearwood.

July

Independence Day Celebration, July 4, Stone Mountain. Two days of music, food, and festivities culminate with a spectacular laser light show and fireworks display over Georgia's most famous natural landmark.

Peachtree Road Race, July 4, Atlanta. Up to 40,000 runners compete in this annual civic event, in which almost every Atlantan is either a runner or a spectator.

July Fourth Celebrations in every town bring out the South's patriotic fervor and fireworks; national military bases feature full-regalia showcases (such as paratrooper landings at Fort Benning, near Columbus).

Civil War Encampment, Atlanta, mid-July. The Atlanta History Center presents soldier-actors recreating history with period costumes, weapons, music and stories.

Appalachian Music Festival, Helen, second week. Traditional, folk, bluegrass, and old-time mountain music at Unicoi State Park.

August

Georgia Mountain Fair, Hiawassee, early August. Good old-fashioned county-fair-type rides, piglet races, gristmill and moonshine demonstrations, mountain crafts, bluegrass, and country music for nearly two full weeks.

Sea Island Festival, St. Simons Island, mid-August. Music, food, and crafts celebrating the African-rooted Geechee culture of the low country.

National Black Arts Festival, Atlanta, mid-August, even-numbered years only. The nation's largest celebration of African-American music, visual arts, dance, and theater in sites throughout the city.

September

Arts Festival, Atlanta, mid-September. The city's major outdoor exhibit of contemporary arts enlivens the city with bands, theater, food, and huge crowds to herald fall.

Jazz Festival, Savannah, end of September. Four days of legendary jazz and blues riverside.

October

Oktoberfest, Helen, late September through October. The complete German extravaganza—wursts, bier steins, and polkas—in Georgia's own little Bavarian village.

Big Pig Jig, Vienna, first week in October. Amateur and professional chefs compete in whole hog, sliced, and chopped pork divisions. Also a hog-calling contest, parade, and livestock show in the weeklong event.

Gold Rush Days, Dahlonega, third week in October. An old-time weekend of panning for gold and gemstones, and recalling the 1838 discovery of gold in Georgia.

Country Music and Bluegrass Festival, Hiawassee, mid-October. A yee-haw mountain-music celebration of Appalachian ballads, clogging contests, and fiddle playing; more than 100 bands perform.

Harvest Festivals of all kinds fill North Georgia as "leaf-lookers" flock to the hills to see scenic fall foliage. Also check for historic homes transformed into haunted houses for Halloween.

November

Mule Day, Calvary, first Saturday in November. Thousands from around the region pack this small South Georgia town to see the mule judging (in 10 classes) and show, mule parade, and such old-time folkways and diversions as cane grinding and a tobacco-spitting contest.

Christmas Tree Lighting, Atlanta, Thanksgiving. Kicking off the holiday season by lighting the Big Tree and singing Christmas carols at Underground Atlanta.

December

Old Fashioned Christmas, Atlanta, Savannah, Dahlonega, Jekyll Island, and Thomasville. Historical holiday celebrations evoke antebellum or turn-of-the-century times with period decorations, carolers, merriment, and food. A **Tour of Homes** takes visitors through historical houses, period-decorated for the holidays (in Madison, Macon, and Atlanta). Going back 2,000 years earlier for inspiration, Stone Mountain presents a **living nativity.**

HOLIDAYS

Holidays are celebrated with parades, festivals, and special events in most towns. On national holidays, federal and state offices and some businesses may close. State offices may close on holidays marked "State."

New Year's Day: January 1
Martin Luther King, Jr.'s Birthday: January 15; usually observed the third Monday in January
Robert E. Lee's Birthday (State): January 19
Presidents Day: third Monday in February
Easter Sunday: late March or early April
Confederate Memorial Day (State): April 26
National Memorial Day: last Monday in May (traditional start of summer holidays)
Jefferson Davis's Birthday (State): first Monday in June
American Independence Day: July 4
Labor Day: first Monday in September (traditional end of summer holidays)
Columbus Day: second Monday in October
Veterans Day: November 11
Thanksgiving Day: fourth Thursday in November
Christmas Day: December 25

And Eddie Owens Martin's out-of-this-world space station of bizarre humanoids and hallucinogenic patterns at **Pasaquan** in southwest Georgia must be seen to be believed.

LITERATURE

Southern writers in the early 20th century made tremendous contributions to America's literary history and defined a body of Southern literature that continues to enrich Southern and American culture. Georgia's esteemed artists joined ranks with William Faulkner, Tennessee Williams, Thomas Wolfe, and poets and writers in literary groups known as the Fugitives and the Agrarians in offering a distinctive vision rooted in the land, history, oral traditions, and culture of the South.

Flannery O'Connor *(Wise Blood,* A Good Man Is Hard to Find, *The Violent Bear It Away)* perfected the country surrealism so prevalent in Southern writing; a literary journal and a small library room at the local college near her hometown of Milledgeville are devoted to her work. The works of Georgia's **Carson McCullers** *(The Member of the Wedding, The Heart Is a Lonely Hunter)* and **Erskine Caldwell** *(Tobacco Road, God's Little Acre)* still captivate readers with powerful portraits of an earlier South.

Yet the work that eclipsed this literary revolution was **Margaret Mitchell's** classic Civil War romance *Gone with the Wind,* a thousand-page encyclopedia of Old South plantation mythology (one critic called it "America's favorite novel and no part of its literature"). The book sold more copies in its first few weeks than many major authors sold in their lifetimes. (See the special topic **The *Gone with the Wind* City Tour.**)

In the *Uncle Remus* stories, **Joel Chandler Harris** recorded African folk tales of the wily trickster Br'er Rabbit (entertainingly retold at Harris's Atlanta home to this day). **Conrad Aiken** and **Sidney Lanier** are much-celebrated Georgia poets.

Georgia continues this literary tradition with outstanding contemporary writers. **Alice Walker** relates the story of an African-American family set in a countryside similar to her hometown of Eatonton in *The Color Purple.* **James Dickey's** novel *Deliverance* presented a haunted vision of North Georgia, and his poetry and fiction are often set in evocative Southern scenes. For the flavor of the Georgia-South Carolina low country and Sea Islands, check out **Pat Conroy's** popular novels *Prince of Tides* and *The Water Is Wide* (titled *Conrack* in the film version). Macon-born **Reynolds Price** *(A Long And Happy Life)* also tells tales of the region.

A Georgia-born Manhattan transplant, **Roy Blount, Jr.,** produces commentaries that span both worlds. **Stanley Booth** is the state's preeminent music writer. **Bailey White's** South Georgia stories are broadcast nationwide on National Public Radio, and **Ludlow Porch** is a popular Georgian humorist.

A recent Gothic blockbuster written about Savannah was actually written by a (gasp) Yankee—

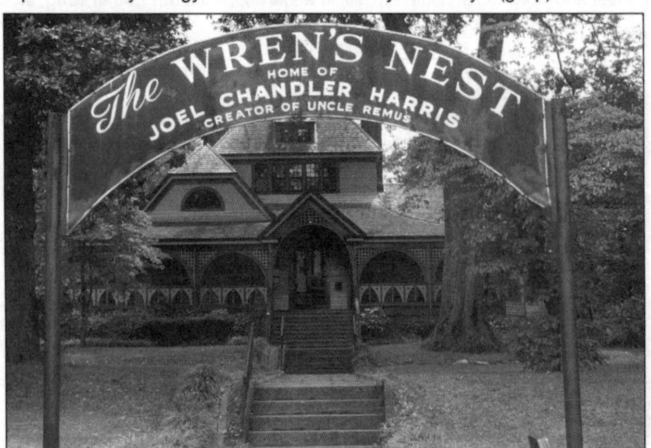

KAP STANN

The South's storytelling tradition carries on at the Wren's Nest in Atlanta.

John Berendt's nonfiction bestseller *Midnight in the Garden of Good and Evil* has been almost singly responsible for that city's skyrocketing tourist influx (see the special topic ***Midnight* Tours** in the Savannah chapter).

Many of the books mentioned above have been made into films that evoke Georgia and the Southeast in general. Other films introduce the region's African-American heritage, such as **Julie Dash's** portrayal of a Gullah community in *Daughters of the Dust,* and the story of the all-black Civil War regiment, the 54th Massachusetts, in *Glory.* Actors from Georgia include Joanne Woodward, Burt Reynolds, Julia Roberts, and Kim Basinger. Another hometown film note: Ted Turner owns all rights to MGM's *Gone with the Wind.*

Storytelling

Georgia's fine oral-history tradition has produced a culture that has raised storytelling to a high art. The **Wren's Nest,** the home of Joel Chandler Harris (reteller of the Uncle Remus stories), hosts storytelling programs and festivals bringing Br'er Rabbit to life. The **Atlanta History Center** sponsors an annual storytelling festival each spring, and a Christmas storytelling program is held evocatively at the Callanwolde mansion in Atlanta each January (at Old Christmas).

Elsewhere in the state, storytelling programs are found as part of local festivals, in state park programming, at historical sites and restorations—not to mention the stories to be told at the end of nearly every porch swing and park bench. (Immerse yourself in Southern literature and folktales to get an idea of what you're in for; see the **Booklist.)**

ARCHITECTURE

Some of Georgia's earliest buildings were constructed from a mixture of crushed oyster shells, lime, and sand—called "tabby." It was used first by native groups, then adapted by the Spanish into adobe-like missions and by the English into their colonial architecture.

Savannah has the richest collection of 18th- and 19th-century architectural styles in the state, beautifully preserved in a large but compact historic district. Georgian Colonial, Federal, Greek Revival, and Victorian styles with verandas, balconies, and high sweeping staircases are accentuated with a Creole flair for cast ironwork decoration. Throughout the state, historic public buildings, churches, homes, and house museums preserve antebellum architectural styles and interior decoration for the public to see (see **Historical Tours,** below).

Pioneer log cabins that once dominated the interior are also preserved; the unique dogtrot type once common to southwest Georgia connected rooms with a covered breezeway. Mountain communities still make much use of wooden cabin construction, and wood in general is one of the state's primary products and building materials. Red Georgia-clay bricks form the basis for more recent architecture, particularly of large public buildings. "Savannah gray" bricks are distinctively shaded by sandy coastal soils and are evident in the brick buildings there.

At the other end of the spectrum, arresting architecture strings out along country byways—shacks with swept lawns, country stores set behind ancient gas pumps, old road motels, and roadside stands—grassroots efforts that present eclectic personal visions and reveal distinctly Southern ways of defining shelter and using space.

TOURING AND SHOPPING

HISTORICAL TOURS

In Georgia, the land records a turbulent history. Contests between the Creek and Cherokee, the Spanish and English, redcoats and patriots, and Yankees and rebels were all fought here. Ancient tribes marked their civilizations with burial mounds and shell middens now thousands of years old, and arrowheads litter the ground. Civil War ruins—a standing chimney, an old fort, the crumbling walls of a paper mill that once produced Confederate dollars—stand as a daily reminder of the nation's defining struggle. And Georgians themselves, in their keen awareness and appreciation of their heritage, celebrate history in such a way that visitors are drawn in—to battlefields, cemeteries, and lookouts, to log cabins, earth lodges, and plantation homes—for story after story, legend after legend.

Aboriginal Historical Sites

Historians say three of the four most significant archaeological sites east of the Rockies are in Georgia: **Etowah Mounds,** north of Atlanta, an earthen mound center among the most significant sites in all of North America; **Ocmulgee Mounds** near Macon; and **Kolomoki Mounds** in southwest Georgia. A variation on these heaped-earth ceremonial mounds is the **Rock Eagle Effigy Mound** near Eatonton, where stones shape the image of a large bird. In North Georgia, you can see remnants of the impressive Cherokee Nation at its former capital of **New Echota.** The state tourist board publishes a driving map of aboriginal historical sites in North Georgia called the ***Chieftain's Trail;*** request one from P.O. Box 1776, Atlanta, GA 30301-1776 (enclose a business-size SASE for a prompt reply).

U.S. History

Georgia's restorations and historical sites offer glimpses of Southern life going back more than 260 years, from pioneer days to the turn of the century. At the **Atlanta History Center** and **Stone Mountain Park** in metro Atlanta, at the **Jarrell Plantation** in Central Georgia, at **Agrirama** and **Westville** in South Georgia, and at **Seabrook Village** on the coast, 19th-century farm communities have been re-created from original log cabins, mills, country stores, and craft shops. Cornfields, livestock, and period-costumed "living-history interpreters" set the stage for days gone by, and special events such as battle reenactments, Civil War encampments, and folklife festivals ("pioneer days," "sheep to shawl" demonstrations, and the like) bring it all to life. More than historical theme parks, these restorations and other smaller ones throughout the state, such as the **Jarrell Plantation** outside Macon, make a sincere and studied effort to carry on the region's heritage. In this way, they provide as much insight into contemporary Southern culture as they shed light on its past.

Adults and children alike can enjoy a visit to a period restoration. And if you're lucky enough to converse with one of the "old-timers" on staff (Georgia's "living treasures"), you'll likely be rewarded with memorable stories of the South's self-sufficient farming communities.

African-American heritage sites present stories not always told in Eurocentric history books. Georgia's major cities publish brochures on local African-American heritage sites. The most extensive of such sites is the **Martin Luther King, Jr., National Historic District** in Atlanta. In Savannah, the exceptional **Ralph Mark Gilbert Civil Rights Museum** and **Negro Heritage Trail Tour** incorporate much fascinating local history, and Macon maintains an African-American museum and gallery. Again, special events enliven this heritage; look for ethnic festivals such as Martin Luther King, Jr., Day on the third Monday in January, February's Black History Month events, and Juneteenth and Kwanzaa celebrations.

U.S. military history is also commemorated in several museums, including those at Fort Benning in Columbus, the Robins Air Force Base near Macon, and at Georgia Veterans State Park. The most powerful of all is the new **National P.O.W. Museum** in Andersonville, the most haunting museum outside of the Holocaust Memorial Museum in Washington, D.C.

Historic Homes and Districts

Popular guided tours of historic homes (called "**house museums**") show off the elegantly constructed and furnished mansions the South is famous for. Southerners take pride in and love to talk about fancy local homes, along with the history of the buildings and the people who lived in them. Among Georgia's most impressive are Savannah's **Davenport House** and **Owens-Thomas House** (among scores of others in that city's historic district), the Atlanta History Center's **Swan House,** Macon's **Hay House** and **Cannonball House,** and the millionaires' homes on **Jekyll Island.** Of many other historic homes open to the public throughout the state, several have been turned into inns; see **Accommodations and Food,** below.

You can find historic districts in major cities in the "old" downtown centers on the rivers (newer development follows highways). Savannah's is the oldest and most impressive—it's the largest urban historic district in the nation; Macon, Augusta, and Columbus have historic downtown areas of more recent vintage in various stages of renovation. In smaller country towns you'll find classic Southern town squares—typically a ring of storefronts set around a brick courthouse plaza—most notably picturesque in **Madison** and **Americus.** A state-supported "Main Street" program helps rebuild historic city centers throughout the state.

SPECIAL INTERESTS

Adventure Tours

Signing on to an organized tour in Georgia does not have to mean an amplified bus tour with a pack of tourists. It could be a canoe trip to deserted coastal islands, an expedition to remote swamp wilderness, or a hike to Appalachian backcountry. Some of the best, wildest land owned by the state, for example, is accessible only to occasional organized groups and not individuals. In other cases where the reservations or permit systems are complex or arcane—or the natural environment exceptionally challenging—linking up with seasoned pros is the only way to go. Contact local branches of the **Sierra Club** and the **Georgia Conservancy** in Atlanta or Savannah about trips at reasonable rates.

Keep handy these two indispensable numbers for ecotourist excursions: **SouthEast Adventure (SEA) Outfitters,** tel. (912) 638-6732, for paddling and camping adventures along the coast and in the swamp and in coastal rivers (also see links from www.gacoast.com), and **Appalachian Outfitters,** (706) 864-7117.

Work and Work-Exchange

Volunteering can mean a "working vacation" and a great cultural foray into local communities. One of the most worthwhile local endeavors is volunteering at the international headquarters of **Habitat for Humanity,** 121 Habitat St., Americus, GA 31709, tel. (912) 924-6935 or (800) HABITAT (800-422-4828), e-mail at info@habitat.org, or see www.habitat.org. Housing can be arranged for visiting volunteers.

The organization originated in a neighboring farming commune called **Koinonia** (from the Greek term for "fellowship"). Koinonia attracts volunteers to its ecumenical Christian community to plant, harvest, build, and repair, in exchange for room, board, and a small "living allowance." For more information, write to Koinonia Partners, 1324 Dawson Rd., Americus, GA 31709.

Campground hosts can stay free in state parks and Georgia's national forests in exchange for acting as a resource to other campers. Retired folks with well-equipped trailers typically fill these positions. For more information, contact the volunteer coordinator at Georgia's State Parks Division, tel. (404) 656-6539, or the state's U.S. Forest Service office, tel. (404) 536-0541. A directory of outdoor volunteer jobs nationwide occasionally lists positions in Georgia (most jobs include housing and a small stipend); call the American Hiking Society, tel. (703) 385-3252.

Job postings and bulletin boards at Georgia's many colleges and universities are good places to begin a search for local employment.

Children

The family-oriented, multigenerational Southern culture ensures that children's activities abound in Georgia. The Greatest Hits: **Six Flags Over Georgia** and **White Water** parks outside Atlanta, living-history and natural-science museums, as well as festivals, parades, and such regionally specific events as battle reenactments and storytelling marathons. North Georgia's diverse recreational opportunities are largely open to children; rafting excursions or strenuous group hikes may have minimum-age requirements (parental discretion, judgment, and responsibility are required), and gold-panning and exploring old mines are some mountain favorites.

State parks and many private campgrounds design special children's activities and entertainment during popular seasons; throughout the state, families don't need to look far to find amusements, arcades, water slides, batting cages, skating rinks, miniature golf, and swimming pools.

The author's daughter's hands-down favorite? Floating down the cool, calm Chattahoochee River in an inner tube on a hot summer day through the ersatz-Bavarian town of Helen.

Gays and Lesbians

Atlanta has one of the nation's largest gay populations, at its most visible in the Midtown district. Several bars and clubs downtown cater to gay men or lesbians, and a few free weekly newspapers *(Etcetera, Southern Voice,* and *G.A.)* carry news and events of particular interest to the gay community. Cosmopolitan Savannah is also a popular stop on the itinerary of gay travelers.

Yet Atlanta and Savannah can be very different from the rest of Georgia. While most places welcome all business, be aware that some conservative family operations may be less tolerant of alternative anything (which would include revealing dress, rowdiness, and drinking, as well as same-sex couples). Resorts and hotels throughout the state that cater mostly to city folk will be most welcoming to gay travelers.

Women

Georgia's cities are about the same as other American cities as far as a woman's safety is concerned; standard precautions apply (avoid walking alone late at night, no flashy jewelry, etc.). Traditional Southern chivalry has its charms, and can add to a woman's safety factor, but typically, this can also backfire if you're perceived as a "loose" outlander.

Women will find Atlanta's feminist bookstore **Charis Books and More** in Little Five Points to be a tremendous local resource for women's events (see **Bookstores** under Atlanta).

People with Disabilities

Atlanta prides itself on its ultramodern infrastructure and architecture, which means mostly barrier-free buildings and public transportation. Hartsfield International Airport is one of the most accessible in the country; several car-rental agencies offer lift-equipped vans; specially equipped tour companies offer guided city tours; and "all-access" nature trails are designed to accommodate wheelchairs and other mobility aids. For more information, contact the city's **Disability Coordinator** at (404) 330-6026.

One small historic town in southwest Georgia has evolved into a monument of sorts to the challenge of physical disability. It's Warm Springs, where natural mineral springs attracted polio-stricken President Franklin D. Roosevelt for soothing hydrotherapy. FDR's Georgia cabin, dubbed the "Little White House," is now a state historic site that emphasizes the man's triumph over disability. His specially adapted cars, wheelchairs, and cane collection are on display, and the site provides wheelchairs and guides to visitors by reservation. The nearby historic village, also fully accessible, is likewise extraordinarily sensitive to people with physical challenges. The Warm Springs hospital administers physical-therapy treatment, and restoration of the original mineral baths was completed in 1997.

Elsewhere around the state, special-needs travelers may find fragrance gardens, museums with tactile exhibits, and all-access fishing decks and trails.

SHOPPING

Atlanta is a shopping Mecca for Georgia's widest selection of nationally known brands, designer boutiques, and city style. **Lenox Square,** the largest mall in the Southeast, draws tourists and shoppers from around the region to more than 200 stores in its self-contained mini-metropolis. Dozens of shopping areas in town and in the suburbs (particularly the upscale northwestern perimeter) offer specialty shopping from haute couture to kitsch. Major cities—Savannah, Athens, Columbus, Augusta, Albany, and Valdosta—all have at least two malls (one spanking new, one older), so you're never too far from a **Gap** store. Of regional department stores found throughout the state, both **Parisian** and **Rich's** are more upscale; **Gayfer's** is more moderate. **Outlet malls** carry name-brand discounts; you'll find the most popular ones in Valdosta (off I-75 in South Georgia) and near Helen in the Blue Ridge.

Regional Specialties

Southern **folk arts and crafts** can be found throughout the state, but nowhere with a wider selection than in North Georgia. Appalachian quilts, basketry, "primitives," and all forms of woodwork can be found in handicrafts stores, artists' cooperatives, and antique stores, particularly in the eastern Blue Ridge Mountains. And nearly every small-town festival features handmade local crafts; you'll find treasure chests of old country wares—butter paddles, old wooden toys, manual coffee grinders, and suchlike.

Native American crafts, some locally made and others imported from Southeastern tribes banished to Oklahoma or Florida, can be found at many Native American historical sites: dolls in traditional Seminole costume, books of Southeastern nations' mythology and legends, beadwork jewelry, and ritual objects.

If you have room in your pickup, you might want to take home a symbol of Southern culture: a typical slat-back wooden **front porch rocker** (around $100). Look for them outside general goods stores near small-town squares. Rough-hewn furniture, crafted from unshaven or unusually shaped limbs, is another bulky one-of-a-kind souvenir that evokes the South.

ACCOMMODATIONS AND FOOD

In Georgia, you can stay in ultramodern deluxe mega-hotels, quaint country inns, historic landmark period rooms, tree lofts, a walk-in lodge, and Civilian Conservation Corps cabins, or camp in lush natural environments statewide.

HOTELS AND MOTELS

Budget

Georgia's interstate freeways and major exits are lined with the towering logos of hotel and motel chains. Among the lowest-cost chains of reliable quality are **Days Inn, Budgetel,** and **Super 8,** with prices that may vary from $35 in remote outposts at the off-season to twice that in metro Atlanta. You can find many independently-operated, super-cheap motels at a lower cost than these, some of which are authentically funky road motels; ask to see the room first to separate kitsch from sleaze.

Mid-Range

Many statewide national chains, such as **Holiday Inn, Best Western,** and **La Quinta,** offer standard rooms starting around $50 (again, prices vary dramatically by location and season). A few, such as **Courtyard by Marriott,** follow the trend of providing small kitchens—typically, a microwave, refrigerator, and coffee maker—and calling these suites. Although all-suite hotels are geared primarily toward business travelers, families find them comfortable as well. Author's pick: the well-maintained **Jameson Inn** chain has a particularly clean, crisp, classy style and friendly, efficient service; most locations have pools and small fitness centers, and offer continental breakfasts.

Deluxe

Most of Georgia's deluxe hotels are in metro Atlanta. Preeminent among a dozen or more of the city's "mega-hotels" are the regally classic **Ritz-Carlton** (with locations downtown and in the upscale Buckhead district), and deluxe versions of major hotel chains, such as the **Marriott Marquis** and **Hyatt Regency.** Standard rooms may start around $100 (in businesslike downtown Atlanta, only weekend rates would be this low) and skyrocket from there.

The **Cloister Hotel,** a four-star coastal resort on Sea Island (accessible by car from St. Simons Island), offers an exclusive retreat for the Old Money set.

Historic Hotels and Inns

Georgia's rich historic heritage makes it worth your while to seek out a historic inn for at least part of your stay. By and large, you'll pay no more for such unique lodgings than you would for a comparable-quality cookie-cutter chain hotel, making inns a great value for the one-of-a-kind experience they offer. Their style may vary considerably, from antique-furnished 19th-century restorations to modern hotels within a historic facade or building. Largely all concede to modern comfort with unhistoric central cooling or heating systems in addition to period ceiling fans and woodstoves. Many have at least a few barrier-free rooms (call to be sure), and some have an age minimum for children.

Savannah, with its beautiful historic district, offers the widest and most impressive selection. Dozens of grand-style inns have been artfully restored and furnished to reflect the district's 18th- and 19th-century character. Each holds its own charms, and is operated independently to offer a wide variety of "perks." Among the all-around favorites are **Magnolia Place Inn, River Street Inn,** (author's picks) and the **Gastonian.** Down the coast, the rambling Victorian **Jekyll Island Club Hotel,** once an exclusive millionaire's hideaway, now offers all vacationers a welcoming island resort. Remote island resorts, accessible only by boat, are in a class by themselves. Among the last bastions of the Southern oligarchy, the exclusive inns cost more than $200 a night (meals included) and often book up far in advance. Cumberland Island's **Greyfield Inn** (a rare private parcel on the island's national parkland) retains an aristocratic flair; picture formal summer dinners—men in jackets and women in heels—served on old china in a formal dining hall on a steamy subtropical island. The more rustic retreat on privately owned **Little Saint Simons Island** enables lodge and cabin guests to explore beaches, horse trails, and abandoned rice fields, among other island activities. It's described by the manager as "summer camp for adults."

In the Blue Ridge, the elegant **Glen-Ella Springs Inn** in Clarkesville reflects the town's origins as a century-old resort, and the **Lake Rabun Hotel,** nestled in the woods outside Tallulah Falls, offers a rustic wooden lodge across from the lake. In northwest Georgia, the 1847 **Gordon-Lee Mansion** served as army headquarters during the Civil War and is now an inn.

Elsewhere in the state, the newly restored **Windsor Hotel** in Americus, outside Plains, is a grand old brick hotel set among the feed stores and hardware shops of South Georgia. In Macon, you'll find the **1842 Inn** in the heart of the city's historic district (author's favorite historic hotel inland). The newly opened **Melhana Plantation** outside Thomasville aims to be among the South's most exclusive historic resorts.

Resorts

Georgia's popular modern resorts offer self-contained vacations—full-service hotels and impressive facilities provide lodging, dining, recreation, sightseeing, and usually an exhaustive opportunity for a wide range of activities. Families are particularly attracted to the all-inclusive convenience (kids' activities are plentiful, including day camps), as are people who love people—these aren't the places to get away from crowds. The popularity of resort-style vacations offers several other advantages as well—it "ups the ante" for standard amenities in hotels and state parks across the state (even campgrounds compete with bigger and better perks), and it leaves the wilderness to hearty adventurers.

Lake Lanier Islands sets two hotels, two golf courses, a water park, and a swimming beach on a string of small islands in a lake north of Atlanta (boat rentals, including sailboats and houseboats, are also available). **Jekyll Island,** practically a tropical-island theme park at the southern Atlantic coast, offers the beach, the marsh, fishing, boating, bicycling, three golf courses, and a tennis complex in a beautiful natural setting; guests can stay at the deluxe historic Jekyll Island Club Hotel or at one of many moderately priced motels.

BED AND BREAKFAST INNS

A wide range of bed and breakfast accommodations is available in Georgia, from restored plantation-style mansions that operate essentially as inns (with innkeepers in residence) to spare rooms in modest homes—a good route for travelers interested in personal touches and interaction with locals, often at moderate rates. The widest selection is in Savannah (and in October; when fall colors peak, nearly every house in the Blue Ridge becomes a B&B).

Outside major cities, however, be alert for situations that may not meet certain expectations,

KAP STANN

State park rental cottages offer lodging in beautiful locations for very reasonable prices.

such as, say, the necessity of sharing a single bathroom with the proprietor, hosts who are extremely talkative, or conservative folks who may frown on unconventional couples, drinking, or Sunday-morning recreation. If you're prepared to be deferential to your hosts, you may be rewarded with a very personal experience of local people and customs. Note also that not every guest room is automatically outfitted with double beds (some have twin beds), so be sure you know what you're getting. The B&Bs listed are the more-established inns, with owner-operators likely to be cosmopolitan enough to welcome a wide variety of travelers, with priority given to inns within walking distance of town centers.

One outstanding choice is **Ashford Manor Bed-and-Breakfast** in Watkinsville—a civilized country retreat an hour outside Atlanta. **Sixty Polk** in Marietta is another good choice.

Several agencies coordinate bed and breakfast lodging in Georgia. In Atlanta contact **Bed and Breakfast Atlanta** at (800) 967-3224. **RSVP Georgia and Savannah,** tel. (800) 729-7787, coordinates lodging statewide, specializing in Savannah and along the coast. The state tourism bureau produces the ***Georgia Bed and Breakfast Directory;*** write for a copy from the Georgia Department of Industry, Trade, and Tourism, P.O. Box 1776, Atlanta, GA 30301-1776, or call (404) 656-3590.

HOSTELS

Open to all ages, hostels offer low-cost dormitory lodging that holds a particular appeal for international travelers and students. In Atlanta and Savannah, **Hostelling International** hostels operate out of historic homes in centrally located residential districts. Reservations are advisable for the Atlanta location, and "not needed" in Savannah.

Prices range $12-14 per person per night for members of Hostelling International. A 12-month membership costs $25 for adults (ages 18-54), $15 for seniors 55 and over, or you can buy a temporary $3 membership good for a one-night stay. Discount rates are available for youths and families; call or write Hostelling International at P.O. Box 37613, Washington, D.C. 20013-7613, tel. (202) 783-6161, or contact the Georgia Council (located in the Atlanta hostel) at 233 Ponce de Leon Ave., Atlanta, GA 30308, tel. (404) 872-8844. HI-affiliated hostels might require you to do some light housework (sweeping, dishwashing, etc.) and to use your own sleepsack (available for purchase or rental at most locations). They may also close midday.

Georgia also has three independent hostels: in Decatur (metro Atlanta), in Watkinsville, and in Brunswick. Independent hostels generally operate under more casual policies than HI (accordingly, your experience may be less predictable, for good or bad). In addition, a couple of outfitters in North Georgia tend to put people up in dormitory situations to suit recreational excursions.

STATE PARK ACCOMMODATIONS

Georgia's state parks provide some of the nicest and best-value lodging in the state. They occupy prime locations throughout the state's several different bioregions, offering fully stocked cottages at most locations and modern hotel-type lodges at five. Accommodations in the most popular parks book up quickly—sometimes nearly a year in advance—so make sure to call ahead for reservations.

Of the many beautiful state parks (you can't go wrong making a state park your vacation destination), scenic Blue Ridge parks are the most sought after. But other parks around the state also hold great appeal. Tucked away in the state's remote northwest corner you'll find dramatic **Cloudland Canyon.** For the most exotic, **Stephen C. Foster** offers swampside cabins at the headwaters of the Suwannee River. Or seek out **FDR** for gracefully set 1930s CCC-built cabins surrounded by pines in an intriguing historical area.

Almost all parks have lakes and extensive water recreation, including boat launches and rentals, fishing, sandy swimming beaches, swimming pools, hiking trails, and other amusements (some golf and tennis, some historic museums) for no or low additional cost. For a map and general information, request a ***Great Georgia Getaways*** brochure along with fee information from Georgia State Parks, 1352 Floyd Tower East, 205 Butler St. SE, Atlanta, GA 30334 (enclose a business-size SASE for speedy reply). Also see www.gastateparks.org.

To reserve lodge rooms, cottages, or campsites, call the **toll-free reservation line** at (800) 864-PARK (800-864-7275). From metro Atlanta, call (770) 389-PARK (770-389-7275) for reservations. For general state park information, call (404) 656-3530, TDD (770) 389-7404.

Lodges

Five parks have lodges with guest rooms of mid-range hotel quality (or higher). The beautiful **Amicalola Falls Lodge,** overlooking a breathtaking Blue Ridge vista, has the feel of a remote Alpine resort. The new **Len Foot Hike Inn** here, designed to be low-impact, is up a 4.6-mile trail in Amicalola Falls State Park. **Unicoi Lodge** is more well-worn, with crowds of travelers drawn to the heart of Georgia's Blue Ridge. **Red Top Mountain Lodge,** set on a peninsula on Lake Allatoona, is only an hour and a half north of Atlanta. You'll find South Georgia lodges at **George T. Bagby** (alongside a quiet fishing lake) and at **Little Ocmulgee,** where a golf course is a big draw.

The lodges have 30-100 rooms each; guest rooms have one or two double beds, telephones, and televisions (barrier-free and nonsmoking rooms available). Rooms can be reserved up to 11 months in advance, and can be confirmed with an advance deposit or credit-card guarantee. Most lodges also feature a classically Southern restaurant, worth a stop in itself.

Guest room prices vary by size, location, season, and day of the week. Standard room rates start at $50 and vary by location and season. The biggest bargains are in winter at mountain parks, where rates drop from peak summer rates over $100 to about $40 a night for a room with a snowy view. Some off-season weekend specials and golf package deals are also usually available.

Cottages

Most of the parks offer cottages, from a handful to a dozen or more at each location. The cottages typically have one to three bedrooms (larger cottages are outfitted with double and twin beds), a large living room and dining table, a standard kitchen (stoves and refrigerators) and bathroom, air-conditioning and heating, and often an outside patio. Each is equipped with an ample set of dishes and cookware (bring your own garlic press), linens, pillows, and blankets. Some have fireplaces, barbecues, and even automatic coffeemakers; no phones, no TV. Several cabins share a central washhouse, which contains coin-operated washers and dryers, soda machines, and a public phone. At some parks, provisions and firewood are sold. To be safe, bring your own dishwashing soap, toiletries, eight-cup coffee filters, and food.

Though often described as "rustic," they're far from primitive (no army cots, no bare bulbs dangling from the ceiling); they're more like family vacation homes. And they provide a wonderfully relaxing atmosphere where families or friends can enjoy a vacation together in a natural setting—hiking, rafting, or just plain relaxing—without having to scrape two sticks together to get dinner started. (Note that the comfortable state park cottages are generally indicative of what you can expect from private cabin rentals as well.)

Cottage rates vary by size, season, location, and day of the week (weekends are higher than weekdays), generally starting at $50 for one-bedroom cottages, $65 for two or three bedrooms. Guests over 62 receive a 20% discount per night, and additional charges may apply for one-night stays (if allowed).

Call up to 11 months in advance for reservations. Reservations are taken for stays of two nights (minimum) to 14 days (maximum). A deposit of one night's lodging is due within five days of receipt of the reservation notice. During popular summer months, many parks require a one-week minimum rental (but you may fill "holes" in their schedules for fewer days as available). Less popular parks are more flexible about this one-week-minimum policy.

CAMPING

National Forest Campgrounds

To get as close as you can to the wilderness without backpacking, camp at one of the 21 Forest Service (FS) campgrounds, scenically located throughout Georgia's **Chattahoochee-Oconee National Forest.** Its Chattahoochee section encompasses most of North Georgia's Appalachian forest, while its Oconee parcel is in central Georgia's Piedmont forest. These camps are basic—just drinking water, tables, grills, vault toilets, and some cold showers at most sites. Prices can vary by campground or site, but are generally $5 a night. No reservations are accepted, and the length of stay is restricted to 14 days. Check with local ranger stations for where you might find vacant sites during the summer. The most popular campgrounds usually have volunteer "hosts" in residence during busy seasons who are knowledgeable about local regulations and recreation. Only three campgrounds stay open during the winter. Primitive camping is allowed anywhere in the national forest unless posted otherwise; no fee or permit is required.

State Parks

All but five of Georgia's state parks offer full-service family campgrounds set around Georgia's most attractive natural features. Most are exceptionally well-maintained, and provide water and electrical hookups, disposal stations, clean bathhouses with hot showers, coin-operated washers and dryers, and full access to park facilities (which often include swimming pools or lakes, amusements, and nature trails).

All campsites can be reserved through the toll-free reservation line: (800) 864-PARK (800-864-7275). Within metro Atlanta, you need to call (770) 389-PARK (770-389-7275) for reservations. Park gates lock at 10 p.m., and campers who miss this curfew are out of luck. (Gates close even earlier around the Okefenokee Swamp to discourage poachers.) Fees vary slightly depending on location and equipment—higher for hookups, lower for walk-in tent sites—but are generally around $14-16, with campers over 65 receiving a discount. Backpacking trails and primitive campsites (called "pioneer" camping in the park system lexicon) are also available. For park system brochures, write Georgia State Parks, 1352 Floyd Tower East, 205 Butler St. SE, Atlanta, GA 30334 (enclose a business-size SASE for speedy reply). See also www.gastateparks.org.

Utility and Private Campgrounds

Georgia Power Co. administers lakes created by damming rivers for hydroelectric power and operates several full-blown recreational areas that include camping (primitive camping also available). The most notable of these are recreation areas at **Lake Sinclair** and **Lake Oconee** in central Georgia.

Private resort campgrounds tend to mimic the high style of some state parks, and prices are generally comparable. More than a place to pitch a tent and eat, such camping resorts—many in North Georgia—feature swimming pools, trout ponds, river floats, and hayrides. For low-end camping, funky **fish camps** offer campsites often high in character but low in amenities near small marinas or boat launches. They're designed for anglers, so carry a pole and line to get in the spirit.

Throughout the state, you're never far from a place to camp, whether it's a deserted county park along a lone stretch of lazy river or a reliably paved **KOA** campground off the interstate. There's even an **all-Airstream** campground near Helen, full of the original silver bullet trailers (members only).

FOOD AND DRINK

Crispy skillet-fried chicken, hickory-smoked 'cue dripping with mustard-drenched sauce, honey-laced corn pone, buttery biscuits, catfish, succotash, and sweet potato pie—if it's Southern, there'll be mounds of it, and when your plate is clean you can go back for more.

Southern cooking draws generously from aboriginal and African influences. The region's three principal Native American crops—corn, beans, and squash—remain staples of Southern cooking today, and their main meal of "sofkee" survives as cracked hominy grits. African influences have carried over most notably in the low country, where okra was first brought to this country from Africa, and today's seaside cuisine is still stirred up by West African spices.

Throughout the state, you can choose from among many delicious regional specialties. In major cities, you'll also find ethnic cuisine. Atlanta has the widest array of international restaurants, representing Asian, Latin American, Middle Eastern, and European cuisines. Savannah, meanwhile, specializes in coastal shellfish and seafood.

Traditional Southern

Fried chicken is the hands-down regional favorite; you can buy it by the piece or by the barrel in nearly every restaurant. Other standard **country-cooking** entrees include country-fried steak (beef in a cream sauce called "sawmill" gravy, also popular over biscuits for breakfast), baked ham, and smoked trout or fried catfish. **Soul food** includes all the above, plus dishes such as chitterlings ("chittlin's," or fried tripe) and pigs' feet distinctive to the African-American tradition.

Of the dozens of fresh vegetables frequently served, you'll always find fried okra, corn, black-eyed peas (these "field peas" are always eaten on New Year's Day for luck), and greens served with hot pepper vinegar. But be on the lookout for fried green tomatoes, sweet potato soufflé, and gumbo—a casserole mixture of okra, tomatoes, and rice.

Add to your meal either a buttermilk biscuit or corn bread (called "hush puppies" in its round, fried form), and wash it all down with a "bottomless" glass of sweetened iced tea (free refills). This is what you get when you ask for "tea"; if you want the boiling variety you'd better specify "hot tea" and be prepared for strange looks. Finally, delectable dessert choices may include peach cobbler, banana pudding, and key lime or pecan pie.

Southerners like to eat a lot, both in variety and volume, so meals are frequently served at **buffets** (self-serve from a buffet table), in **cafeterias** (your selection is served to you), or **family-style** (presented in serving dishes for diners to dish out a portion and pass around). Typical lunches and dinners feature a choice of three entrees, four or five vegetables, and bread. Sunday spreads, served midday, are the most lavish. One fixed price means a tremendous value for hungry appetites; most restaurants also offer a reduced-price vegetables-only plate. Though some refined places make an elegant feast of Southern buffet, most often country cooking is served in a casual, inexpensive "down-home" style.

Regional chain restaurants offer a healthier alternative to fast food; cafeterias in particular are often just as cheap and quick (and you can see the food to pick out what looks good). Franchises offering a taste of the South include **Morrison's Cafeteria** and **Piccadilly Cafeteria.** For table service, there's the hick-themed **Po' Folks** and **Cracker Barrel** (the object of gay protests years back), and the more upscale newcomer **Black-eyed Pea.** Most **state farmers' markets** also house inexpensive cafeterias. Two local chains open around the clock are the ubiquitous **Waffle House** and **Huddle House.** On country roads, sample Georgia's agricultural bounty directly from **roadside produce stands,** seasonally offering muscadine grapes, Georgia peaches, pecans, roasted and boiled peanuts, sweet Vidalia onions, watermelons, and many other locally grown fruits and vegetables.

KAP STANN

Nita's of Savannah serves a mean plate of "low-country soul food" unique to the South.

Cultural notes: Southerners prefer food served less than piping hot, and that's how many restaurants serve it. Also, in family-style places, don't be surprised if the people next to you pause to say a blessing before eating; it would be considerate to stay quiet until they're done.

Barbecue

A local art form, Southern barbecue has subtleties that natives devote whole lives to deciphering, but visitors can pick up a few basics in a short trip. First, pork is the meat of choice, though chicken and beef are widely available. To many purists, "barbecued beef" is considered an oxymoron. Georgia humorist Ludlow Porch writes "If someone comes in and wants barbecue beef, the waitresses will all laugh and the cook will holler things about his mama till he leaves."

LUNCH MENU

All dishes served family-style to every table at Mrs. Wilkes Boarding House, Savannah

Fried chicken	Green beans
Beef stew	Potato salad
Rice and gravy	Tuna salad
Sweet potatoes	Corn bread
Collard greens	Biscuits
Squash	Iced tea
Butter beans	Strawberry shortcake
Chicken salad	

Chefs base sauces on tomatoes, vinegar, or mustard, or often a combination of all three. An entree is served with the standard slice of white bread and your choice of two side orders, usually cole slaw, baked beans, or the local gumbo-like beef and chicken mix called "Brunswick stew."

The best places to participate in this revered local tradition are roadside barbecue stands with sawdust on the floor and cords of hickory wood stacked up against the smokehouse. But barbecue restaurants may come in all shapes and sizes. A particularly festive, cheap, and delicious way to sample favorite recipes is at local festivals: follow all signs to a Barbecue Cookoff.

Low-Country Cuisine

Coastal Georgia and South Carolina comprise a distinct geocultural region called the low country. Cooking traditions here sprout from the Gullah or Geechee cultures and retain West African influences. Coastal fish and shellfish appear alongside fresh vegetables in peppery concoctions of okra soup—okra was introduced to this country by slaves—and she-crab soup. Pan-fried softshell crabs are another delicious low-country specialty.

Oysters, shrimp, crab, and other local seafoods can be inexpensively sampled at "raw bars" in restaurants or taverns and at streetside food stalls and many coastal festivals—or go down to the docks to buy fleet-fresh selections.

Liquor

Around the topic of liquor, two prominent Southern institutions collide—namely the Southern Baptist church with its tradition of abstinence, and a fine country moonshine tradition. Now that the days of homemade stills hidden from taxing "revenooers" have mostly passed, alcohol is served and sold in Georgia's cities without restriction except on Sundays. In some rural areas, however, counties may either prohibit the sale of alcohol entirely, restrict sales to beer and wine only, or approve the sale of liquor in bars but not in stores. Generally speaking, it's not in the culture to drink much alcohol, though a mint julep on the veranda or a cold six-er in the ice chest are fine Southern traditions. Nonalcoholic beverages are most often served with meals and offered to guests, though wine is widely available.

Wine, beer, and alcohol are sold in "package stores," the local euphemism for liquor stores; only select specialty shops in major cities stock California or imported wines. Relative to other costs, alcohol prices are high, but not prohibitively so.

Several local wineries within an hour or two of Atlanta offer tours and tasting in scenic settings. Braselton's **Chateau Elan,** the most elaborate, resembles a 16th-century French chateau with its own Parisian sidewalk cafe, guest lodge, and golf course. Nearby, try the tasting rooms at **Chestnut Mountain Winery** in Braselton and **Habersham Winery** in Baldwin. At any Georgia winery, be sure to sample the classic Southern muscadine wine among many other varietals.

TRANSPORTATION

GETTING THERE

By Air

Most people come to Georgia through Atlanta's Hartsfield International Airport, an airline hub so central it has inspired the joke, "Whether you go to heaven or hell, one thing's for certain: you'll need to change planes in Atlanta." Every year, 68 million passengers pass through the heavenly gates of the world's busiest airport. Hartsfield-based Delta Air Lines is among the 32 passenger airlines with domestic and direct international flights to and from Atlanta. From an airport terminal station, sleek modern light-rail trains whisk passengers downtown in 10 minutes. (See also **Transportation** in the Atlanta chapter.)

By Car

A web of interstate freeways connects Georgia with the Eastern seaboard (I-95) and Midwest (I-75), as well as with other parts of the South (I-20, I-85). **Georgia Welcome Centers,** run by the state tourist board, are situated at each interstate freeway entrance to Georgia, and there's one inland in Plains. Make a pit stop for information on local services and attractions, and pick up discount coupons for local lodging.

By Bus

Greyhound-Trailways operates a bus network linking major American cities with cities throughout Georgia. For information and fares call (800) 231-2222.

By Train

Amtrak operates two lines that pass through Georgia. The **Crescent** connects New York and Washington, D.C. with Atlanta, Birmingham, and New Orleans. It also stops in Gainesville, jumping-off point for the Appalachian Trail. The **Silver Meteor** runs the length of the Atlantic seaboard from Boston to Miami, stopping in Savannah—where Amtrak offers package deals (train fare and lodging)—and Jacksonville, Florida—closest city to Georgia's Okefenokee Swamp and Cumberland Island.

Though generally more expensive than regularly discounted air travel, riding the trains is a leisurely and civilized way to travel, and occasional special excursion fares make rates more competitive. For costs and schedule, call (800) USA-RAIL (800-872-7245).

By Boat

If you have a boat, a scenic way to come to Georgia is via the **Intracoastal Waterway,** a marsh-lined corridor largely sheltered between

KAP STANN

Georgia by bus

the mainland and barrier islands. The passage takes sailors past Georgia's port cities of Savannah and Brunswick. Marinas in Thunderbolt (outside Savannah) and at St. Simons Island make the most popular stops along Georgia's 100-mile coast.

GETTING AROUND

Driving

The most practical way to get around the state is by car, and it's the best way to get a flavor for the back-roads rural heritage of the South. You can rent a car at the airport or in any big city; all major car-rental agencies are well represented and most have toll-free 800 numbers to begin your inquiry. Daily rates are discounted for weekly or monthly rentals, and watch for special weekend rates. (See also **Transportation** in the Atlanta chapter.)

The maximum speed limit in Georgia is 65 miles per hour on interstates through rural stretches, 55 mph near urban areas. Georgia requires drivers to turn on their headlights whenever they use their windshield wipers—which makes common sense once you've seen a typically dark Georgian thundercloud advance on the horizon. You're permitted to turn right at a red light after coming to a complete stop, unless signs tell you otherwise.

Interstate freeways offer the quickest routes to and fro, but they can also be the least interesting. Before the interstates opened, state highways handled heavy vacationer traffic to and from Florida, giving rise to hundreds of road motels, roadside stands, and dinky small-town attractions designed to entice travelers en route. Since tourist business moved out to the interstates, many have fallen by the wayside into a sort of modern ruins, and those that have survived have aged deliciously into Route-66-like Americana classics. Georgia's old Atlantic Coast highway or the old Dixie Highway in North Georgia best illustrate this past heyday.

Through some curious loophole in constitutional law, Georgia sets up occasional drug checkpoints. Here highway police may wave select cars over and unleash a drug-sniffing dog to search out contraband. At the first sign of "Drug Check Ahead," you'll see drivers pull cars over to the shoulder and dart into the forest before continuing down to the checkpoint.

Trailers and RV owners are easily accommodated with wide passing lanes on country highways; plentiful campgrounds offer pull-though sites, hookups, disposal stations, and other services. Hitchhiking may well result in pleasurable encounters with hospitable locals who treat you to cheap colorful tours, but no one with any conscience could unreservedly recommend it, particularly for women.

Buses

Greyhound-Trailways runs regularly scheduled bus networks throughout the state; tel. (800)

231-2222. Charter bus companies also compete for passengers on the popular route from Atlanta to Savannah.

Trains

Considering how vital the railroads were to the development of the South, it's a shame you can't get around Georgia on a train more easily. Amtrak does stop in other Georgia towns besides Atlanta, Savannah, and the above-mentioned Gainesville, but not at times convenient for most tourist travel. An excursion train runs an hourlong trip in North Georgia.

Intrastate Flights

The busiest intrastate flight is the hourlong run between Atlanta and Savannah; call Hartsfield-based Delta Air Lines for a schedule. It is possible to take commuter flights between Georgia's cities, but considering that most major cities are concentrated on the Piedmont, surface shuttles are most often used instead.

Bicycling

Georgia's different topographic regions present increasingly easier terrain from north to south. North Georgia's mountainous country highways offer the greatest challenge, yet even at their most undulating, the shoulders are wide and the pavement smooth. The same excellent road conditions are maintained all through the state, across the rolling hills of the Piedmont and the long, flat expanses of the coastal plain. The scenery throughout—the outstanding natural environment, antebellum architecture, quaint town squares, orchards, and roadside produce stands —as well as the leisurely Southern pace, make bicycling a wonderful way to see Georgia.

As for specific routes, it would take an exceptional biker to tackle metro Atlanta's byways with their fast-paced traffic, winding narrow routes, and sprawling urban development—but it's been done. More rewarding long-distance routes would include the coastal highway, the stretch from Athens to Macon in central Georgia, and the areas around Plains, Thomasville, or along the Chattahoochee River in South Georgia. For a copy of state-designated bike routes throughout Georgia (emphasizing connections to the state parks), write the Georgia Department of Industry, Trade, and Tourism, P.O. Box 1776, Atlanta, GA 30301-1776; tel. (404) 656-3590. The Southern Bicycle League organizes long-distance trips; write P.O. Box 1360, Roswell, GA 30077 for more information.

INFORMATION AND SERVICES

HEALTH AND SAFETY

Tropical Precautions

One of the most pleasurable aspects of traveling in the Southeast is its generally mild and seasonal climate. During the summer, however, visitors unfamiliar with subtropical weather can find the extreme heat and humidity oppressive. Heed all cautions. Wear loose, light, long-limbed clothing and hats, sunglasses, and sunscreen (Photoplex or Shade UVAGUARD blocks both UVA and UVB rays). Drink and eat often, stay out of the sun, and avoid exertion during the midday heat. Travelers who presume their cool-climate stamina will remain unchanged may suffer heatstroke. It's no joke—heat exhaustion is the number one medical emergency in the summer. Scale down your ambitions.

Also in summer, insects are most active—again, by taking precautions you can reduce this bother to a minimum. Mosquitoes usually appear only around dusk, or around stagnant water. Use insect repellent—*Consumer Reports* rates a product called "Ultra Muskol" the highest, though locals use Avon's "Skin-So-Soft" hand lotion for everyday repelling—and carry an insect bite cream such as Benadryl. Wear long-limbed clothing and tuck pants into socks for the greatest protection against ticks, and perform a thorough tick check after a wilderness walk. Red rash-like patches are the sign of chiggers; get rid of them by covering the area with clear nail polish. Coastal residents complain of "no-see-ums" (gnats too small to see) and sand fleas most bothersome on windless afternoons; try to pick a breezy day for beach-going, or retreat indoors midday.

Hypothermia

Hypothermia—the inability to maintain sufficient body heat—presents another danger, and not just in cold weather. Overexertion coupled with coldness, wetness, and wind may bring on such symptoms as shivering and poor coordination even in mild temperatures. Avoid it by keeping clothing warm and dry, staying in motion, and, of course, seeking shelter. Always pack for emergencies: spare clothing, extra food and water, matches, a flashlight, a compass, and a stocked first-aid kit. Three toots on a whistle or three smoky fires set in a triangle signal distress. Wilderness adventurers should leave detailed itineraries with someone at home and at the appropriate ranger station.

Crime

Urban hazards are of a different nature, namely crime. As in most American cities, you must stay alert, aware of your surroundings, and exercise reasonable caution—for example, leave fancy jewelry home. Atlanta is no worse than comparably sized American cities, and security in tourist areas is high.

On the other side of the fence, you'll also want to avoid any needless encounters with local law enforcement, particularly in more rural regions. Obey speed limits to avoid speed traps common around small towns, and be aware that things "untidy"—such as a beat-up old foreign car, poor grooming, or sloppy or revealing dress—will often attract negative attention from backcountry police.

WHAT TO BRING

The perennial travel advice "the less the better" also holds for traveling to Georgia, particularly if you're flying into Atlanta and aim to take the train downtown. Pack clothes for seasonal change. In spring, dress in layers you could remove if it warms up; a light raincoat could come in handy. For spring or fall, a light jacket is all you need; pack a heavier one for winter (but not too heavy—this isn't Chicago). Fairly conservative day-to-day dress becomes even more formal in Atlanta's professional environment and at Sunday church services, Old Guard social dinners, and some fancy restaurants; even during hot and humid summer months men wear ties and jackets, and women wear stockings on these occasions. Though men and women wear shorts for casual wear, sleeveless shirts are considered too casual and may even be prohibited by the dress codes of some establishments. Old sneakers come in handy as "river shoes" for rafting or tubing. Water adventurists could also use dry bags, key pouches, and other waterproofing.

MONEY

Generally, prices in Georgia are lower than the U.S. average, making it an excellent travel bargain. Compared to other states, for example, gasoline (petrol) in Georgia is less expensive, and good food is cheap. Labor prices are dramatically lower than in other regions, and consequently travelers will find exceptional guides and staffed services to enhance their trip without tremendous additional costs. For example, for little more than it costs to rent canoe equipment in California, in Georgia you can not only rent the equipment, but also obtain the expert services of an experienced local guide.

As with the rest of the U.S., most establishments geared toward travelers accept major credit cards and traveler's checks. Banks are generally open from about 9 or 10 a.m. until about 3 or 4 p.m.; some have reduced hours on Saturday. Plentiful 24-hour automatic teller machines link up to interstate banking networks. Georgia sales tax is six percent; hotel tax varies depending on city, generally around 13%.

Discounts for admissions, tickets, restaurant meals, etc., are widely available to youths, people over 65, and members of the U.S. military (sometimes restricted to active military, or military in uniform). Student discounts are less widespread, but it can't hurt to ask. Some restaurants also offer discounts to clergy on Sundays.

Tipping: For taxi drivers, tip 10% plus $1 per bag; restaurant servers 15%; at buffets and counters, leave 10%, a little less for table clearers at cafeterias; hotel doormen services $1.

COMMUNICATIONS

Telephones and Emergency Numbers

Be forewarned: Georgia now has four different **area codes.** Folks had barely enough time to reprint stationery and adapt to the boundary shift of area codes in 1992, when another shift in late 1995 created a challenge for those trying to nail down a correct number.

As it stands, Atlanta now has two area codes: **404** is meant to apply closest to downtown and **770** to the wider metro region, but there is presently so much overlap that callers need to include the area code when making any local call in Atlanta—not, however, including the "1" you would generally need to dial before any area code.

In an interrupted region from north Georgia swinging around to Central Georgia, it's **706.** The boundaries of these regions continue to shift somewhat, so you may find literature that still lists an incorrect code. South and coastal Georgia's **912** area code remains unchanged.

Excluding local calls within metro Atlanta (see above), you must dial "1" before dialing a long distance number. For directory assistance within the same area code, dial 411. For a number outside the area code you're calling from, first dial 1, then the area code of the region you want to call, then 555-1212. Many businesses have toll-free (no charge) long distance numbers, which carry an 800 or 888 prefix in place of an area code. Some of these toll-free numbers only operate within the state.

In emergencies, dial 911. For traveler's aid, call (404) 527-7400. To receive tourist information, call (404) 656-3590, and for up-to-the-minute weather reports, call (404) 455-7141.

Business Hours

Business office hours are now fairly standardized to weekdays from 8 or 9 a.m. to 5 or 6 p.m. Most stores open later—about 10 a.m.—on weekdays and Saturdays, and stay open to early evening (often later in heavily trafficked urban areas and malls). Outside metro Atlanta, nearly all businesses shut down on Sundays (except for restaurants, many of which may serve a traditional midday dinner).

U.S. Postal Service hours generally run 8:30 a.m.-5:30 p.m. on weekdays; some open until noon on Saturdays. Private mailing companies (e.g., Mail Boxes Etc.) stay open longer hours and offer additional services such as wrapping, packaging, photocopying, and facsimile transmission.

Media

The Atlanta newspapers, the morning ***Atlanta Constitution*** and the afternoon ***Atlanta Journal*** (combined editions on Saturday and Sunday), carry the major news of the region. The Saturday edition carries a tabloid supplement titled ***Weekend,*** a comprehensive listing of entertainment and events in metro Atlanta and beyond. Atlanta's free alternative newsweekly ***Creative Loafing*** carries entertainment listings as well as news for the metro area; the coastal ***Creative Loafing*** covers Savannah. The other daily newspapers throughout the state are painfully unnotable, and it becomes harder than you'd expect to track down an Atlanta paper outside of the metro region. South Georgia hotels tend to distribute *USA Today* before either a local or Atlanta paper.

As for television, the **Cable News Network (CNN)** broadcasts out of Atlanta, so what's a worldwide update elsewhere is simply local news here. **Peach State Public Radio** syndicates an innovative slate of programs throughout the state—it's usually found at the low end of the FM band. Among its eclectic line-up are a Civil War music series and Click and Clack's car mechanics' talk show, sponsored by a local auto shop that "welcomes your car no matter what its make, model, or country of origin."

Internet

Public Internet access is readily available in metro Atlanta, but less so in other cities, and virtually unheard of in many rural regions. Besides hit-or-miss Internet cafes or cyberbars, one reliable source of Internet access is the copy shop **Kinko's** (tel. 800-2-KINKOS or 800-254-6567) which offers online computer access among its services. Many branches are open 24-hours. There are 20 Kinko's in Georgia (six of these in Atlanta); see www.kinkos.com for more information.

Maps and Information

Georgia's Department of Transportation sends out free state road maps by phone request to (404) 656-5336. An eager state Department of Industry, Trade, and Tourism produces many publications; its statewide directory includes a road map and list of state park services, and its semiannual events calendar covers standard Georgia travel. To request information, call or write the Georgia Department of Industry, Trade, and Tourism, P.O. Box 1776, Atlanta, GA, 30301-1776, tel. (404) 656-3590.

The *Georgia Atlas and Gazeteer* by DeLorme Publishers is a handy tabloid-sized atlas ideal for recreation and getting around rural regions. (See **Booklist** or www.delorme.com for ordering information.)

Seven state welcome centers off the interstate freeways at the Georgia border encourage pit-stoppers to walk in for information; frequently you'll find coupons good for discounts at local lodging. Many Georgia towns have local tourist offices or welcome centers; contact the convention and visitor bureaus listed in the text or the chambers of commerce. Nearly every town hands out a free driving map describing local historic buildings and sites.

INTERNATIONAL SERVICES

Language Assistance

Multilingual Visitor Services Representatives sponsored by the city and federal tourist boards meet all arriving international flights to Atlanta's Hartsfield International Airport to assist inbound and connecting passengers with translation and other needs. Also in the international terminal is an international "Calling Assistance Center," a computerized telephone system that displays information in six languages.

International Services Telephone Numbers

The area code for all of the following telephone numbers is **404.**

Austria 252-7920; Belgium 659-2150; Canada 577-6810; China 522-0182; Denmark 522-8811; Finland 446-1400; France 522-4843; Germany 659-4760; Greece 261-3313; Israel 875-7851; Italy 875-6177; Japan 892-2700; Korea 522-1611; Latin American countries 231-0940; Mexico 688-3258; Nigeria 577-4800; Switzerland 872-7874; United Kingdom 524-5856; Georgia Council for International Visitors 873-6170.

MISCELLANEOUS

Voltage

Power outlets in the U.S. run only on a 117-volt AC system, which means that only appliances of that approximate voltage will run as manufactured. You'll need a transformer to run a 200- or 220-volt appliance. Find transformers and adapter plugs to fit American appliances at department stores, electronics supply stores, specialty travel stores, or department stores.

Time Zone

Georgia follows eastern standard time (EST), five hours earlier than Greenwich mean time. From the first Sunday in April until the last Sunday in October, Georgia, like most of the U.S., goes on daylight saving time, which advances the clock one hour across all American time zones. Though Georgia's border with Alabama constitutes an official change in time zones, some border cities in Alabama maintain Georgia time (such as Phenix City, across the Chattahoochee River from Columbus).

ATLANTA

INTRODUCTION

Atlanta is a lively, sprawling city of 425,000 surrounded by rather ungainly suburban development, particularly to the north, which boosts the metro population to nearly 3.5 million. Much of that rise has been in the last few decades, as Atlanta has successfully positioned itself as a corporate center. Coca-Cola, CNN, Delta Air Lines, Holiday Inn, Ritz-Carlton, and UPS are a few of the corporate giants in town that have attracted a largely white-collar work force from all over the country. So while the influx means you can now find Internet cafes, haute cuisine, and world class art exhibits here, you'll also find gridlock, $3 caffe lattes, and more Northerners than any Southern town should be expected to absorb. The city can best be appreciated as a cosmopolitan oasis with an exciting nightlife and art and music scene, and as a convenient gateway to the rest of the state and to the South.

Since the Summer Olympic Games were held here in 1996, Atlanta has also established itself as a sports capital. The Atlanta Braves (1995 World Series winners) play at Turner Field—formerly Olympic Stadium, where Muhammad Ali ignited the Olympic Torch. The NBA Atlanta Hawks and a new hockey franchise, the Atlanta Thrashers, play in a new 20,000-seat arena downtown. And not only spectator sports—with more than 50,000 runners last year, the annual Peachtree Road Race is the largest 10K race in the world.

One of the reasons cited for Atlanta's successful Olympic bid was the city's reputation for progressive racial politics. Martin Luther King, Jr., was born here, preached here, and is now buried here; his tomb is a pilgrimage site for generations moved by his message of interracial equality and nonviolence. As the home of the nation's largest consortium of African-American colleges, Atlanta has also been called a mecca for African-American intelligentsia, from the likes of Andy Young to Spike Lee.

A racially diverse coalition headed up by African-American mayor Bill Campbell governs the city, which, despite its many business successes, is as beset by urban problems as any other American city. But this is the only one with a former President on the task: from the Carter Center east of downtown, President Jimmy Carter tackles vexing social justice issues through his Atlanta Project.

Atlanta's minority populations have seen recent increases in immigration, most notably in Latin and Southeast Asian communities. A vibrant gay and lesbian community, and pockets of Bohemian counterculture, also add to the city's dimension.

THE LAND

The wooded, rolling Piedmont Plateau surrounding Atlanta is broken only by one natural barrier, the Chattahoochee River, which snakes down from North Georgia to the Gulf of Mexico, passing along Atlanta's northwest perimeter. The clay-stained "'Hooch" remains wildly forested, with boulder-studded and marsh-lined shores, fast-water shoals, and stone ruins of old water-powered mills—all right at the city limits.

East of town, massive granite outcroppings pop inexplicably out of the landscape like gigantic helmets. Stone Mountain, the largest and most famous of these, measures seven miles in circumference and 825 feet high, the largest piece of exposed granite in the eastern United States. A huge carving in the face of the rock depicting three Confederate heroes on horseback—Jefferson Davis, Robert E. Lee, and (appropriately) Thomas J. "Stonewall" Jackson—is the centerpiece of this major recreational center for city folk. These geologically fascinating "monadnocks" harbor rare botanical communities and shed rock layers in exfoliated slabs like a peeled onion.

From the summit, visitors get a rare panoramic view of Atlanta. The city's thickly forested rolling hills, with no mountains or large body of water close at hand, make Atlanta hard to spot on a horizon. The few natural boundaries encourage sprawling low-rise development away from the city center, largely following original Indian trails or ridge routes. A good map is vital for getting around; narrow surface streets curve with a scenic disregard for typical urban grids, and many streets have similar-sounding names.

In town, the skyline of towering skyscrapers is framed by an abundance of trees, including dogwood, oak, hickory, pecan, poplar, willow, magnolia, crabapple, peach, cottonwood, and chinaberry. The trees bloom in spring, provide welcome shade in summer, and turn colors each fall. Of course, with this volume and variety of trees, you're never far from the sounds of birds and the rustle of squirrels, even in the central city. Wildlife in the woods and river areas also includes beavers, raccoons, opossums, and a great variety of fish and birds (such as herons, ducks, and an occasional osprey).

Climate

Mild weather most of the year and the scenic changes of the full four seasons make Atlanta pleasant to visit and ideal for outdoor recreation nearly year-round. In July and August, oppressive tropical heat and humidity are interrupted somewhat by afternoon thundershowers, but most residents become nocturnal in summer, venturing out of air-conditioned enclaves only at dusk. Fall is warm and dry; each winter a trace of snow appears; and in spring, temperatures may fluctuate from frosty or rainy one day to a sunny mid-80s (°F) day the next.

HISTORY

For hundreds of years before the Europeans came, the Creek and Cherokee nations settled the region around what is now Atlanta. A Creek settlement at the Chattahoochee River called Standing Peachtree and the land south of the river are said to have been won from the Cherokee in a ball-game competition played with land rights at stake. In 1814, Europeans built a small military outpost here (where the river meets Peachtree Creek) that developed into an active trading post.

Founding

But it was the railroads that put Atlanta on the map. In 1837, railroad interests decided to build a line that would connect Chattanooga, Tennessee, with rails already in place in Augusta, Georgia. They needed a midway point to link up the two, and the natural contours of the land led them to choose a site eight miles southeast of the Chattahoochee River. The white stone marker identifying the precise meeting point of the rail lines, the Zero Mile Post, can still be seen near Underground Atlanta today.

First named simply Terminus, then Marthasville (to honor the then-governor's daughter), the town that grew around the railroad depot was renamed Atlanta (for the Western & Atlantic Railroad) in 1845. It was ambitious from the start; as early as the 1850s, observers noted how Atlanta had "a bustle uncharacteristic of Southern cities."

Civil War

By the time Georgia seceded from the Union in 1861, Atlanta was already a major transportation hub with a population of 8,000. Its developed industry made the city critical for supplying the Confederacy. Union General William Tecumseh Sherman reckoned that crippling Atlanta would cripple the Confederacy, and with that aim he began his Atlanta campaign in May 1864.

"Atlanta was too important a place in the hands of the enemy to be left undisturbed," said Sherman, "with its magazines, stores, arsenals, workshops, foundries, and more especially its railroads, which converged there from the four great cardinal points."

Following the rail lines down from Chattanooga with 100,000 federal troops, Sherman engaged Confederate General Joseph Johnston's smaller army several times in North Georgia before arriving on the city's doorstep. After the Battle at Kennesaw Mountain northwest of Atlanta forced Johnston to withdraw on July 2, Confederate President Jefferson Davis replaced Johnston with General John Bell Hood.

The Battle for Atlanta

One of four engagements for possession of the city, the battle of Peachtree Creek began on July 22, 1864. Sherman's continued assaults on the perimeter and a 75-day siege crippled the city. Hood finally surrendered Atlanta on September 2, and the infamy known to history as Sherman's March to the Sea began. Although the terms of surrender were to leave citizens and property unscathed, Sherman ordered the city evacuated, then burnt it down, tore up the rail lines, and continued to burn a 60-mile-wide swath across Georgia out to the Atlantic Ocean. The rampage accomplished its objective and the South surrendered the following year. When Sherman left Atlanta, every business was leveled, as were most homes. Only 400 of the city's 4,500 buildings were left standing, inspiring a 1960s politician to call Sherman "Atlanta's first urban renewal director." Today, disgruntled locals display bumper stickers asking Where's Sherman When You Need Him?

Reconstruction and the "New South"

Rebuilding quickly regained for Atlanta its position as a regional center, and the city was named capital of Georgia in 1867, a decision spurred, it's said, by the refusal of hotel owners in the old capital of Milledgeville to rent rooms to black constitutional convention delegates. In the 1880s,

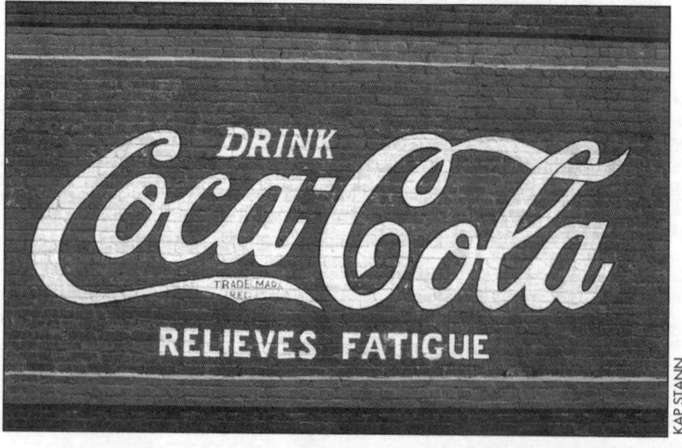

KAP STANN

In 1886, Coca-Cola sales totaled $50. Today, Coca-Cola Company products are consumed at the rate of more than one billion *drinks per day.*

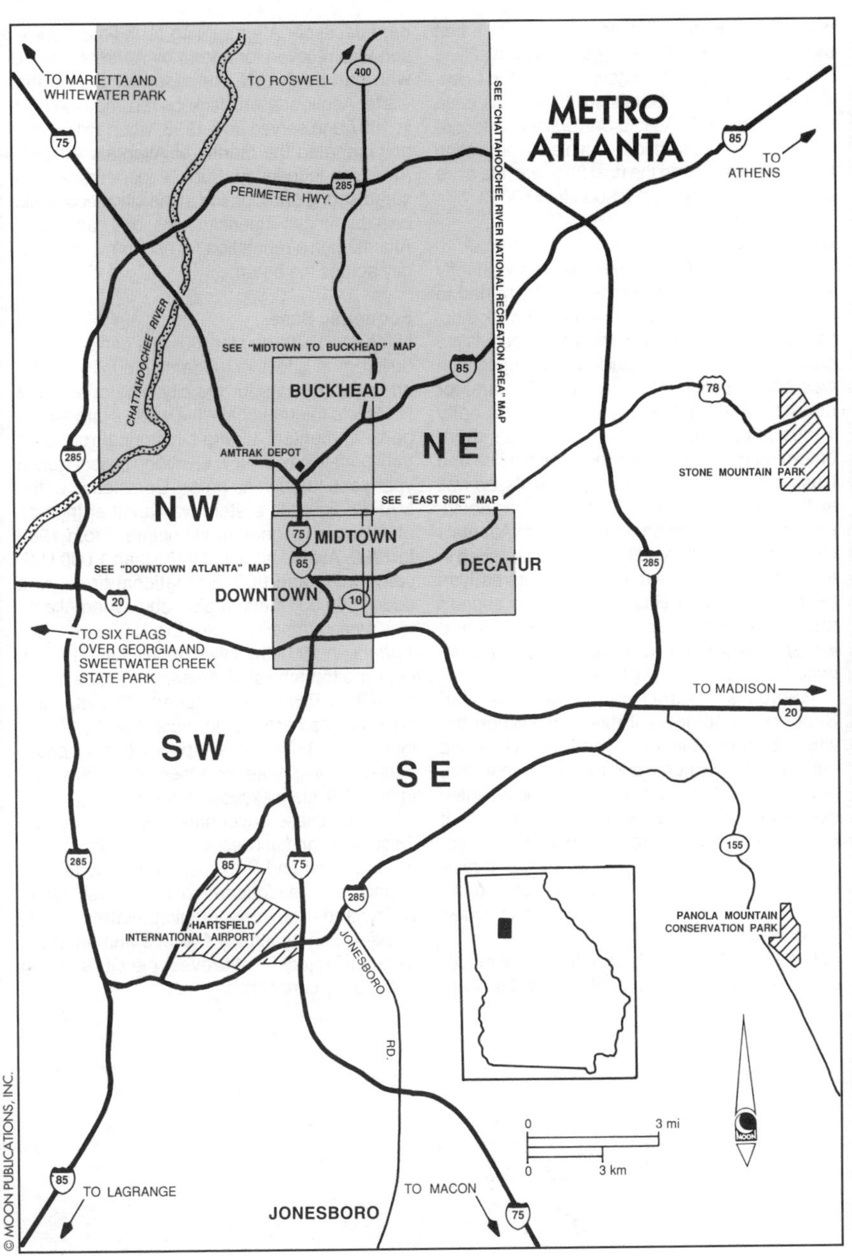
METRO ATLANTA
TO MARIETTA AND WHITEWATER PARK
TO ROSWELL
400
75
285
PERIMETER HWY.
SEE "CHATTAHOOCHEE RIVER NATIONAL RECREATION AREA" MAP
85
TO ATHENS
CHATTAHOOCHEE RIVER
SEE "MIDTOWN TO BUCKHEAD" MAP
BUCKHEAD
NE
AMTRAK DEPOT
78
STONE MOUNTAIN PARK
NW
SEE "EAST SIDE" MAP
MIDTOWN
DECATUR
SEE "DOWNTOWN ATLANTA" MAP
DOWNTOWN
10
20
TO SIX FLAGS OVER GEORGIA AND SWEETWATER CREEK STATE PARK
TO MADISON
SW
SE
155
HARTSFIELD INTERNATIONAL AIRPORT
JONESBORO RD.
PANOLA MOUNTAIN CONSERVATION PARK
0
3 mi
3 km
MOON
TO LAGRANGE
TO MACON
JONESBORO

when tiny Southern Bell opened the city's first switchboard, and a local drugstore began selling a new headache-and-hangover tonic called Coca-Cola, the start of Atlanta's solid business base took hold. In 1867, Atlanta University was founded as the first of six schools devoted to educating former slaves. During the next 30 years, the city's population swelled from 21,000 to 90,000.

Civil Rights

While originally Atlanta was so predominantly white that one citizen complained "men had to black their own shoes and dust their own clothes, as in the North," after the Civil War the population grew to 50-50 white and black. While segregation was official policy for more than 60 years, for the most part it gave way quietly in the early 1960s under the influence of Atlanta's then-emerging coalition of the progressive white and black elite, politicians, and industrialists, as well as the strong influence of Dr. King and his Southern Christian Leadership Conference. Atlanta's racially progressive reputation was established in the early days by such former mayors as Ivan Allen, Jr.—the only Southern mayor to support federal civil-rights legislation in 1963—and William Hartsfield, who in 1959 proclaimed Atlanta "the city too busy to hate."

Georgia's governor during this time, Carl Sanders, remembers it this way: "When the whole South was in turmoil and chaos over the questions of civil rights and matters of that kind, Atlanta took a responsible position and elevated itself above the demagoguery of the day. . . . It took a giant step forward. Because of that, people from other parts of the country were attracted to Atlanta, and today we have a cosmopolitan city with people from all parts of the world and all walks of life."

In 1973, Atlanta elected the first black mayor of a major Southern city, the formidable Maynard Jackson. After serving term limits, Jackson was relieved for a term by Andrew Young, who had been U.N. Ambassador during the Carter Administration. Jackson resumed the post in 1987 and served until 1993, when Bill Campbell inherited the mantle of Atlanta's African-American leadership. Such leadership has ensured strong participation in the city's economic base by African-American firms, and has helped Atlanta gain a reputation for economic opportunity across the board.

Economic Base

In the late 1970s and the '80s, the earlier work of building an effective leadership coalition paid off in boom years for the city. The opening of Hartsfield International—the world's largest airport—cemented Atlanta's historical role as a transportation hub. Now 68 million passengers a year pass through its gates. Completion of the MARTA light-rail system was another triumph of Atlanta's modern infrastructure. From 1980 to 1990, Atlanta attracted more than 1,000 U.S. companies and 300 international firms, and added 500,000 metro-region jobs. When Atlanta was named "America's Best City for Business" by *Fortune* in 1991 the city's population had shot near the top-ten list of America's largest cities. More than 75% of the Fortune 1000 companies have offices here, as do more than 1,400 foreign-based businesses representing 40 countries (including more Japanese companies than in any U.S. state except California).

The business environment is supported by 38 colleges and universities, the Centers for Disease Control and Prevention (the only federal agency with headquarters outside Washington, D.C.), and innovative public/private partnerships—such as Jimmy Carter's humanitarian "Atlanta Project"—that reveal the city's strong community connection.

DISTRICTS AND NEIGHBORHOODS

GETTING ORIENTED

To orient yourself to sprawling metropolitan Atlanta, it helps to visualize the city divided up by its north-south and east-west highways, bounded by the city's perimeter highway. With that scheme in mind, you'll find downtown at the center, the airport at the southern tip, and Buckhead at the northern tip (for areas beyond the perimeter, see **Vicinity of Atlanta,** later in this chapter). Yet a trip to Atlanta without exploring its cozier neighborhoods, particularly those nestled in the northeastern quadrant, would reveal little of the city's diverse character.

The following geographical guide characterizes the city's major districts, tells you how to get about, and introduces some of the outstanding sights, hotels, and restaurants to be found within. Major attractions are more fully described under **Sights,** below. Complete practical information on hotels and restaurants appears under **Accommodations and Food,** later in this chapter; also see **Transportation** at the end of this chapter for parking and transit information.

DOWNTOWN

Named for Standing Peachtree, the original Creek settlement at the banks of the Chattahoochee River, **Peachtree Street** runs for miles north from downtown—like Wall Street, Fifth Avenue, and Broadway laid end to end. Not to be confused with West Peachtree Street, Peachtree Center Avenue, Peachtree Road, or Peachtree Place, At-

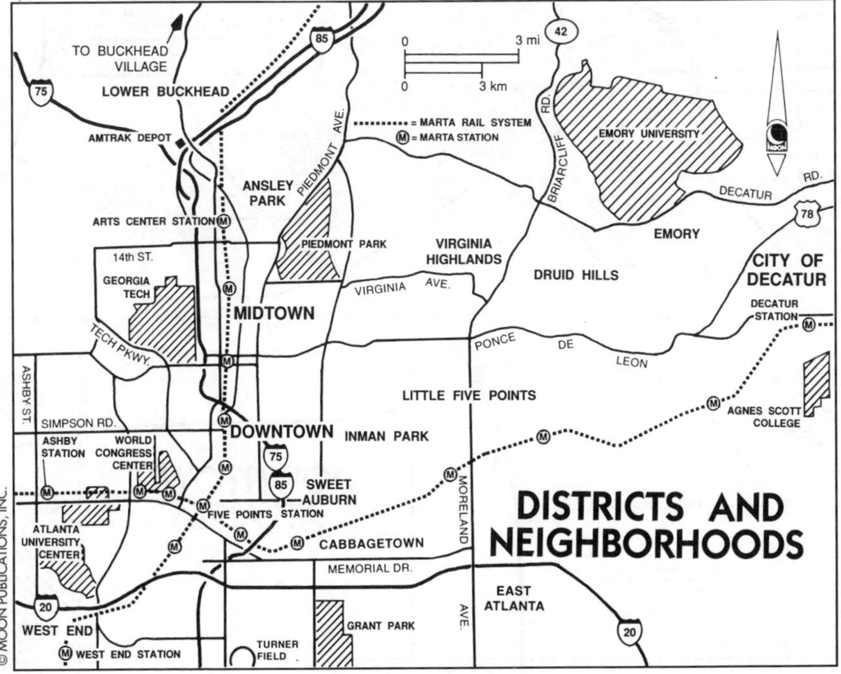

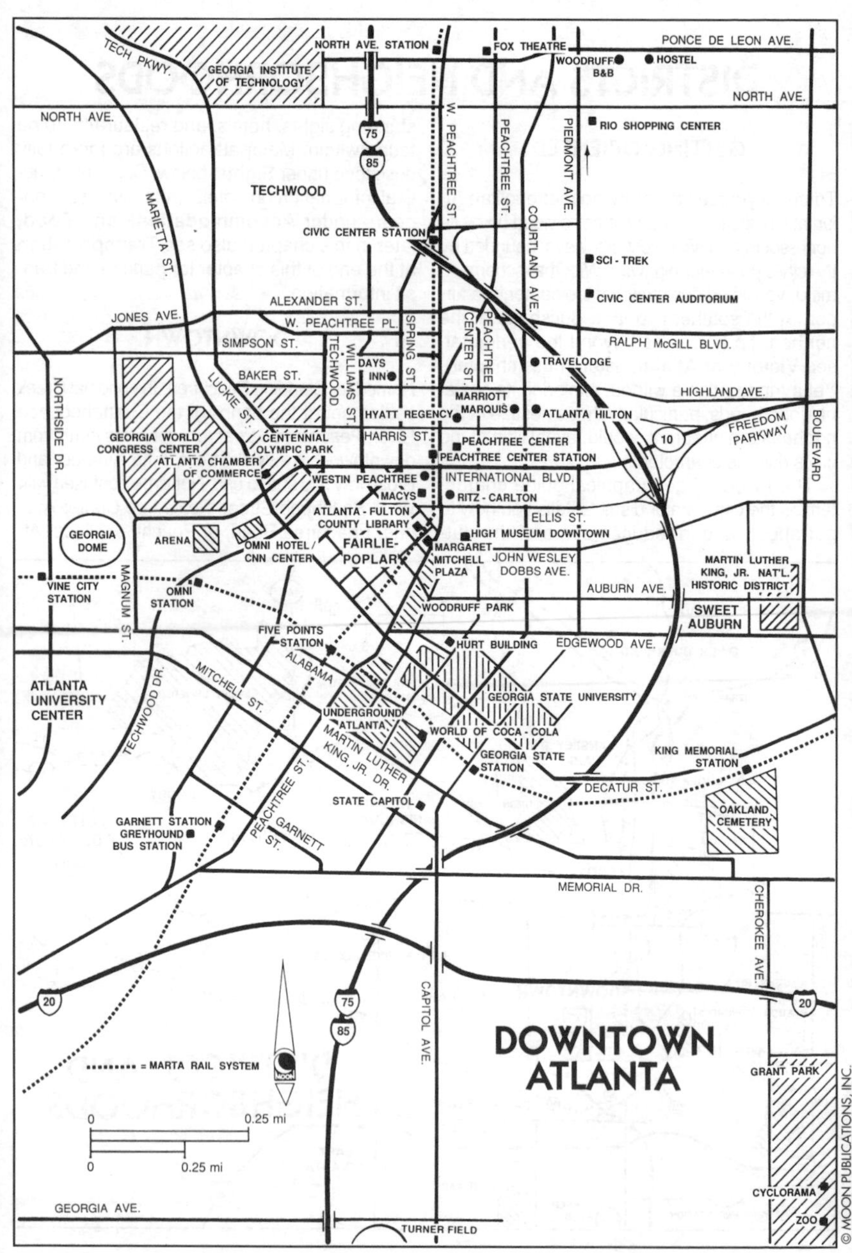
DOWNTOWN
ATLANTA
NORTH AVE. STATION
FOX THEATRE
PONCE DE LEON AVE.
WOODRUFF B&B
HOSTEL
NORTH AVE.
TECH PKWY.
GEORGIA INSTITUTE OF TECHNOLOGY
RIO SHOPPING CENTER
TECHWOOD
MARIETTA ST.
W. PEACHTREE ST.
PEACHTREE ST.
COURTLAND AVE.
PIEDMONT AVE.
CIVIC CENTER STATION
SCI - TREK
CIVIC CENTER AUDITORIUM
ALEXANDER ST.
JONES AVE.
W. PEACHTREE PL.
SIMPSON ST.
RALPH McGILL BLVD.
TRAVELODGE
BAKER ST.
DAYS INN
HIGHLAND AVE.
LUCKIE ST.
TECHWOOD
WILLIAMS ST.
SPRING ST.
CENTER ST.
PEACHTREE
MARRIOTT MARQUIS
ATLANTA HILTON
HYATT REGENCY
FREEDOM PARKWAY
BOULEVARD
NORTHSIDE DR.
GEORGIA WORLD CONGRESS CENTER
CENTENNIAL OLYMPIC PARK
HARRIS ST.
PEACHTREE CENTER
PEACHTREE CENTER STATION
ATLANTA CHAMBER OF COMMERCE
WESTIN PEACHTREE
INTERNATIONAL BLVD.
MACYS
RITZ - CARLTON
ATLANTA - FULTON COUNTY LIBRARY
ELLIS ST.
GEORGIA DOME
ARENA
OMNI HOTEL / CNN CENTER
FAIRLIE-POPLAR
HIGH MUSEUM DOWNTOWN
MARGARET MITCHELL PLAZA
JOHN WESLEY DOBBS AVE.
MARTIN LUTHER KING, JR. NAT'L. HISTORIC DISTRICT
VINE CITY STATION
MAGNUM ST.
OMNI STATION
AUBURN AVE.
WOODRUFF PARK
SWEET AUBURN
FIVE POINTS STATION
HURT BUILDING
EDGEWOOD AVE.
ALABAMA
ATLANTA UNIVERSITY CENTER
MITCHELL ST.
TECHWOOD DR.
GEORGIA STATE UNIVERSITY
UNDERGROUND ATLANTA
WORLD OF COCA - COLA
MARTIN LUTHER KING, JR. DR.
GEORGIA STATE STATION
KING MEMORIAL STATION
DECATUR ST.
PEACHTREE ST.
STATE CAPITOL
OAKLAND CEMETERY
GARNETT STATION
GREYHOUND BUS STATION
GARNETT ST.
MEMORIAL DR.
CHEROKEE AVE.
CAPITOL AVE.
20
75
85
10
= MARTA RAIL SYSTEM
MOON
0
0.25 mi
GRANT PARK
GEORGIA AVE.
CYCLORAMA
ZOO
TURNER FIELD
© MOON PUBLICATIONS, INC.

lanta's historic central artery is one of 32 streets with the word Peachtree in its name. Early prestige associated with having a Peachtree address prompted businesses to use the word liberally (also note that it's often written with the abbreviation "P'tree").

Five Points, the acknowledged epicenter of the city of Atlanta, gets its name from the star-shaped intersection linking Peachtree St. with Marietta St., Decatur St., and Edgewood Ave. The city's two MARTA lines also intersect here, providing the grand central station for the metro subway system.

Underground Atlanta

The **Zero Mile Post** at Underground Atlanta marks the spot designated in 1850 as the future intersection of the railroad lines that would put Atlanta on the map. When Atlanta's expanding rail yards congested downtown, the city built bridges over the rails. Over time the bridges evolved into streets, eventually fully enclosing the old storefronts and byways underground. After decades of disuse, the hidden ghost town was richly renovated in the late 1970s into a modern rendition of the original historic center.

Today Underground Atlanta, on Alabama St. between Peachtree and Central, tel. (404) 523-2311, is an appealing mix of old stone and terracotta facades—fading Coca-Cola advertisements remain on original brick walls—along with modern plate glass and track lighting. Cafe tables and hawkers' stalls lean slightly crookedly on the uneven cobblestone streets, now for pedestrians only. A particularly cool refuge in summer, the 12-acre complex supports 130 shops, restaurants, and clubs, inside and out.

Despite many mallish brand-name shops and personalized T-shirt souvenir stands, the historic ambience is evocative and worth seeing. Reasonably priced eateries (start at **Cafe du Monde** for coffee and beignets, or try **Mick's** for lunch or dinner), local wares, and ethnic crafts including many African-American specialties attract Atlanta's trademark mix of locals and visitors, professionals and shoppers, old and young of every shade. Find bars in the part that pours out onto a lower plaza, known as **Kenny's Alley.** Among the annual events at Underground, each December 31 revelers crowd around to watch the "giant peach" drop down to signal the New Year.

Above ground, a friendly **Visitor Center** distributes helpful free maps, event calendars, and city and state information (restrooms here too). A half-price ticket booth to performances at local venues is next door, along with a **Gray Line** ticket booth and a hall of free exhibits on the city's cultural and arts heritage.

The **World of Coca-Cola,** one of the city's most popular attractions, houses a Disneylike shrine to Atlanta's world-famous beverage in a striking modern building near Underground, in the plaza up from Kenny's Alley. A nice place to stay is the **Suite Hotel,** adjacent to Underground, which recreates turn-of-the-century elegance to blend into the historical setting. Underground Atlanta parking garages, while not cheap, are convenient to the freeway and avoid worse traffic farther north. Better yet, take MARTA.

Capitol Hill

Georgia's **State Capitol,** tel. (404) 656-2844, surveys the scene from atop the knoll of Capitol Hill. Topped with a gleaming dome of authentic Georgia gold, the white-columned 1889 building—home to the state legislature from January to June—displays flags-of-state, flora and fauna collections, historic artifacts, and a Hall of Fame honoring native sons and daughters. Visitors are welcome during business hours, no charge. Outside, statues and modern sculpture dot the landscaped lawns. Stately government buildings, many made with Georgia marble, surround the Capitol. One of these, the 17-story windowless **Georgia Archives** building, creates a dense, near one-dimensional silhouette on the skyline.

Georgia State University enrolls 32,000 students in six colleges at its sprawling urban campus downhill from the capitol. Among 25.5 acres of college facilities, the **Cinefest** theater in University Center offers cut-rate matinees of eclectic films you won't find screened elsewhere. Overlooking downtown in the eighth floor of South Library, a collection in the music library plays tribute to Georgia native Johnny Mercer, songwriter of such American classics as "Moon River," "Blues in the Night," and "That Old Black Magic." A jukebox plays Mercer classics. The twin "Sloppy towers," directly above the Georgia State MARTA station, are named for former politician James H. Floyd—affectionately nicknamed "Sloppy" (there's an inexpensive cafeteria on street level).

Capitol Avenue runs south from the state building across the freeway under a mile to **Turner Field.** Named for CNN mogul Ted Turner, the field is home to the Atlanta Braves baseball franchise and holds the Braves Museum.

South of the government center, Peachtree St. leads to an older, derelict corner of downtown. Artists are sparking a renaissance by inhabiting loft space in the Bowery-like district and in the adjacent warehouse district. Only the most intrepid pioneers would find themselves here, and there's nothing to see, but the site does occupy an appealing crest and it's an area to watch. Downhill, the Greyhound bus terminal is conveniently adjacent to the Garnett MARTA station.

North of Five Points

A block north of the Five Points MARTA station, **Woodruff Park** makes a shady retreat for brownbagging officeworkers, with its story-high fountain and occasional lunchtime concerts. (From the northeast corner, a walk along Auburn Ave. leads under a mile to the King memorial in the adjacent "Sweet Auburn" district; see the special topic **King's Legacy.**)

Margaret Mitchell Plaza, on Peachtree St. north of Five Points, was named for the author of Civil War Atlanta's saga *Gone with the Wind.* Here the central **Atlanta-Fulton County Library** contains a tribute to its native daughter with exhibits on the book. The library is always a nice place to duck in out of the weather and flip through local periodicals. Eat around the park at the inexpensive **Delectables** gourmet cafeteria or at the very trendy **Mumbo Jumbo.**

The **High Museum Folk Art and Photography Galleries** in the Georgia-Pacific Center offer a taste of the city art museum's collection. Exhibits and lectures are designed especially for the busy, walk-by downtown crowd, and admission is free.

Fairlie-Poplar District

Across Peachtree St. from Woodruff Park is the city's oldest commercial district, recently brought back to life after a long slumber. Buildings constructed between 1890 and 1920 trace the city's evolution from a pioneer railroad town to a modern city, with styles from Victorian to art deco. Highlights include early skyscrapers such as the 17-story 1906 Asa Candler Building, the triangular 1897 Flatiron Building, and the Corinthian-columned 1912 Hurt Building (with its acclaimed **City Grill** restaurant). In a city known for constantly remaking itself, preserved buildings such as these are rare examples of constructive re-use.

Three shady blocks of Broad St. offer a compact set of cafes and eateries between Peachtree and the MARTA station; for innovative cuisine head a few blocks north to the **Fairlie Poplar Cafe** and **Bona Petit** cafe. The neighborhood celebrates its revival at festivals and

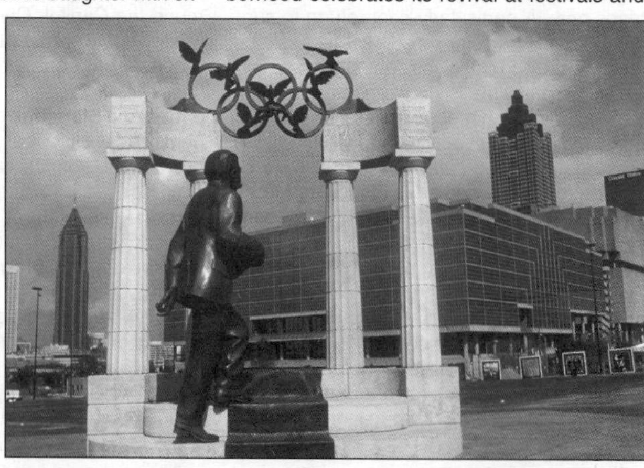

Centennial Olympic Park is home to many community events and festivals.

GEORGIA IT&T

street fairs unusually homey for downtown.

There are several good chain motel options in the neighborhood, including the Quality Inn and Comfort Inn.

Centennial Olympic Park

The 21-acre park constructed for the 1996 Olympics for $57 million is now Atlanta's downtown centerpiece, linking the convention center area to the west with the hotel district to the east. The attractive park is studded with fountains, shade trees, waterfalls, statues, and a memorial to the two people killed in the bombing here during the 1996 Summer Games. Maps are available at the visitor center (cafe inside, Atlanta Chamber of Commerce across the street).

The main attraction is the **Fountain of Rings,** where a sprinkler field in the shape of Olympic rings shoots up to music periodically—at any time it makes an playful place for children (and some adults!) to get totally soaked. An amphitheater and Great Lawn are the settings for many community events and concerts.

West of Centennial Olympic Park

Towering beside the park, the **Omni Hotel** occupies an atrium-centered building in the style of modern grand hotels. Surprisingly, the corporate headquarters of **Cable News Network (CNN)** shares this unlikely setting and leads tours of their international broadcasting studios within. A ground floor plaza of souvenir shops and food stalls includes a six-screen cinema, a good coffee bar, **Le Petit Bistro** for gourmet salads and roll-ups, and a British pub (that hosts a Great Loser's Party every July 4).

The **World Congress Center** here, built over what were once huge rail yards, is now the second-largest convention center in the U.S. (the largest is in Chicago). There is a city visitor center within (open during conventions only).

The new **arena** due to open in 1999 will house the Atlanta Hawks basketball team and a new ice hockey franchise. To the west is the huge **Georgia Dome** stadium for football and massive events of all kinds. All the above locations can be accessed via the Omni-Dome-WCC MARTA Station.

(The Vine City MARTA Station accesses the western side of the Dome. Also exit Vine City to reach Atlanta University Center across Northside Ave. from the Dome.)

Peachtree Center

As Peachtree St. rounds the bend at Ellis St., it lands in downtown's most elite hotel and shopping district: Peachtree Center. As the name describes not only the vicinity, but also the subway station, the underground mall, prestigious twin office towers, and the avenue behind Peachtree St., visitors should get specific directions if they have a destination in mind. All are part of a vast, interconnected pedestrian maze of sparkling skywalks, tunnels, steep escalators, elevators, and interior plazas.

From the MARTA subway station, it's tricky to find your way through the cool subterranean complex—as it's built underground and on a slope, "ground level" is relative and elusive. Yet the 13-acre high-tech, climate-controlled environment is an impressive marvel of modern engineering, architecture, and urban planning, with telltale elements of a futuristic theme park thrown in for fun. Within this human ant farm, visitors could survive indefinitely without confronting the elements—a particular advantage in the sweltering summer.

The city's major hotels lie within a radius of several blocks from here, in a compact and frenetic zone running from around Baker to Houston streets (north to south), and Piedmont Ave. to Spring St. (east to west). The **Hyatt Regency, Westin Peachtree, Ritz-Carlton, Marriott Marquis,** and **Atlanta Hilton** compete in the megahotel category, surrounded by more than a dozen smaller and less expensive hotels. Naturally, visitors can find all they need in the area, plus plenty of other bewildered visitors. **Macy's** heads up the shopping district (not a bad place to park either, if you're going shopping anyway—they validate parking).

If hotel restaurants in the area are too lavish, expensive, or won't stop revolving, and the food court won't do, try **Mick's,** at the corner of Peachtree Center Ave. and International; **Dailey's,** on International at Peachtree St., for more of a happy-hour crowd; or **Haveli's,** within the Gift Mart, for great Indian food.

Civic Center

Beyond the I-75/85 freeway overpass (look for the funky sculptures representing Georgia's best known folk artists as you speed by), the congestion of the hotel zone gives way to a quiet section of downtown, whose main attractions are **SciTrek,** the city's hands-on science museum, and

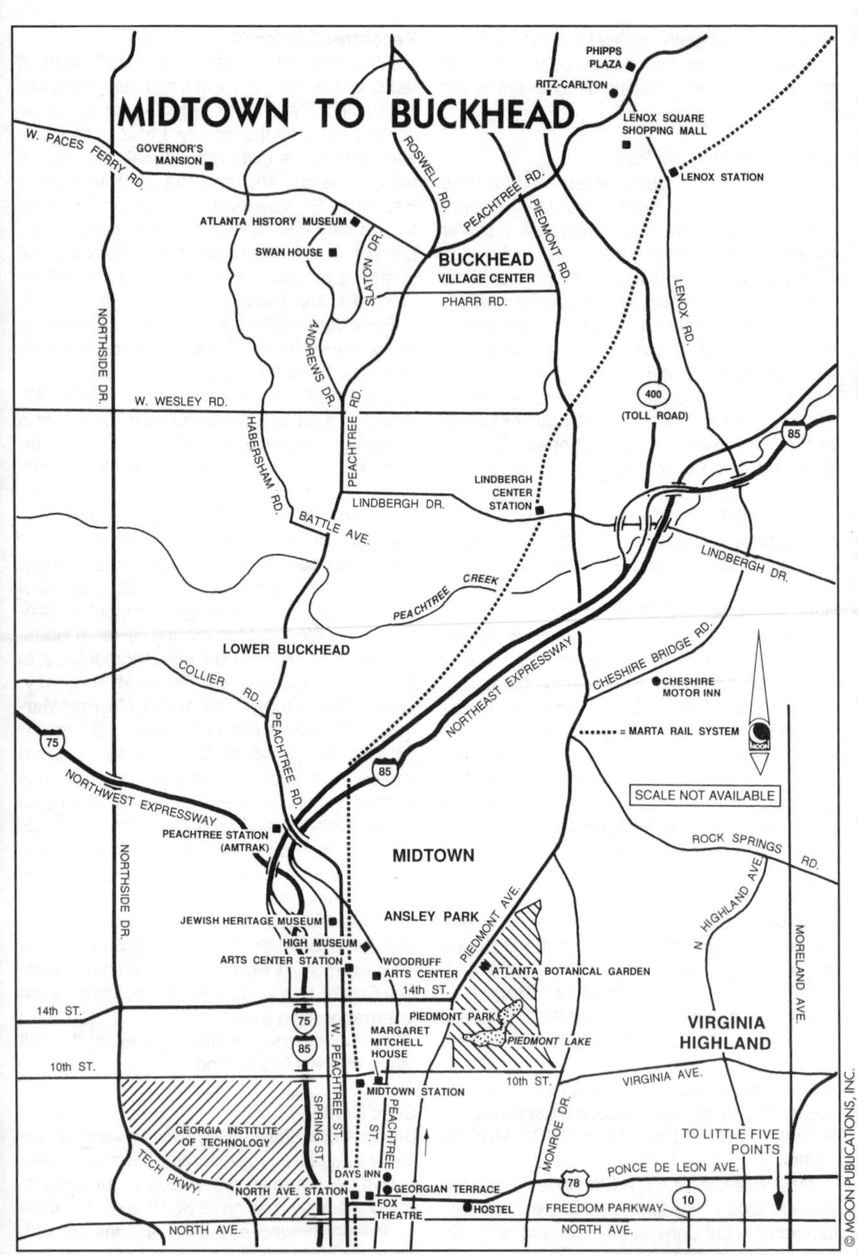

MIDTOWN TO BUCKHEAD
W. PACES FERRY RD.
GOVERNOR'S MANSION
ATLANTA HISTORY MUSEUM
SWAN HOUSE
ROSWELL RD.
SLATON DR.
PHIPPS PLAZA
RITZ-CARLTON
LENOX SQUARE SHOPPING MALL
LENOX STATION
PEACHTREE RD.
PIEDMONT RD.
BUCKHEAD VILLAGE CENTER
PHARR RD.
LENOX RD.
NORTHSIDE DR.
ANDREWS DR.
W. WESLEY RD.
HABERSHAM RD.
PEACHTREE RD.
400
(TOLL ROAD)
85
LINDBERGH CENTER STATION
LINDBERGH DR.
BATTLE AVE.
LINDBERGH DR.
PEACHTREE CREEK
LOWER BUCKHEAD
COLLIER RD.
NORTHEAST EXPRESSWAY
CHESHIRE BRIDGE RD.
CHESHIRE MOTOR INN
= MARTA RAIL SYSTEM
75
NORTHWEST EXPRESSWAY
85
SCALE NOT AVAILABLE
PEACHTREE STATION (AMTRAK)
MIDTOWN
ROCK SPRINGS RD.
N HIGHLAND AVE.
MORELAND AVE.
JEWISH HERITAGE MUSEUM
ANSLEY PARK
PIEDMONT AVE.
HIGH MUSEUM
ARTS CENTER STATION
WOODRUFF ARTS CENTER
ATLANTA BOTANICAL GARDEN
14th ST.
14th ST.
PIEDMONT PARK
PIEDMONT LAKE
75
85
MARGARET MITCHELL HOUSE
VIRGINIA HIGHLAND
10th ST.
10th ST.
VIRGINIA AVE.
W. PEACHTREE ST.
MIDTOWN STATION
SPRING ST.
PEACHTREE ST.
MONROE DR.
GEORGIA INSTITUTE OF TECHNOLOGY
TO LITTLE FIVE POINTS
TECH PKWY.
DAYS INN
PONCE DE LEON AVE.
78
NORTH AVE. STATION
GEORGIAN TERRACE
10
FOX THEATRE
HOSTEL
FREEDOM PARKWAY
NORTH AVE.
NORTH AVE.

Civic Center Auditorium, where concerts and performances are held, both off Piedmont Ave. Eat at the original **Mick's** at 557 Peachtree St., and use the Civic Center MARTA stop.

MIDTOWN

Midtown houses the city's premier arts center as well as an upscale business district and homey neighborhoods of Victorian cottages on shady lanes. Midtown holds a particular appeal for Atlanta's gay community. With several hotels and easy MARTA and freeway access, it's a convenient alternative for visitors wishing to avoid the hubbub of downtown.

North Ave.

North Ave. straddles the floating boundary between "downtown" and "midtown"—as a rule of thumb, if the joint's upscale, they call it midtown; if it hasn't yet been renovated, revitalized, or gentrified, it's downtown. By this quirky logic, the greasy spoon **Varsity drive-in** (on North Ave. at the interstate) is definitely downtown, while the avenue's attractive historic pocket a block away qualifies as "lower midtown."

The **Fox Theatre,** on the corner of Peachtree St. and Ponce de Leon Ave. (PONTS-de-LEEon) is a treasured local landmark. Rescued from Atlanta's rampant urban-renewal binge in the 1970s and '80s by a strong civic campaign, the Moorish/art deco fantasia was originally conceived as the Yaarab Temple Shrine Mosque. It bears the neo-Egyptian styling popular in the 1920s that was inspired by Howard Carter's discovery of King Tutankhamen's tomb. Seeing a performance here is the best way to view the theater; but the Atlanta Preservation Center also leads tours of the interior and surrounding neighborhood (see **Touring the City**).

This compact, walkable area offers a choice of lodging and several places to eat, making this a good base of operations for visitors looking to stay somewhere quieter than downtown by day, yet more populated after hours. The **Days Inn Midtown** is one nice choice. A few blocks east on Ponce de Leon Ave., the Victorian **Woodruff Bed and Breakfast Inn** offers lodging next door to **Hostelling International Atlanta.** For classic Southern plates, lunch at **Mary Mac's** across the street; for great Jamaican food, try **Bridgetown Grill** on Peachtree St.; for an artsy cafe, hunt down **Yin Yang** where 3rd dead ends at the interstate.

Use the North Avenue MARTA station to access this district. (Drivers note that Ponce de Leon Ave. leads east to Freedom Parkway access and to Virginia Highland and other east side neighborhoods.)

West of the interstate, **Georgia Institute of Technology,** site of the 1996 Olympic Village, is the state's well-ranked technology campus. Georgia Tech retains a dozen stately brick buildings dating from the 19th century on its original nine-acre campus.

Near campus, **Techwood** contains historic buildings of another kind. Built in 1935, it was the nation's first federal public housing project.

Around 10th St.

The Margaret Mitchell house on the corner of Peachtree and 10th Streets, where the author of

The Fox Theatre is an example of "neo-Egyptian," King Tut-inspired public architecture.

Gone with the Wind wrote her famous story, is one of the city's newest attractions. Mitchell met her death when she was struck by a taxi while she was crossing Peachtree St. three blocks farther north.

At **Piedmont Park,** Atlanta's Central Park, lush acres of woods give way to paved walkways, bike paths, and wide meadows—the scene of spring festivals and summer concerts (skate rentals available). At the park's northern tip are the grand conservatory and gardens of the **Atlanta Botanical Gardens.**

Lining the park between Piedmont Ave. and Peachtree St., are the wide winding lanes of **Ansley Park,** a historic residential district where 600 homes built between 1904 and 1930 remain beautifully preserved behind landscaped lawns and shade trees. The **Ansley Park Inn** here offers a graceful alternative to city hotels.

A cluster of eateries at 10th St. and Piedmont Ave. include a **Caribou Coffee** stop and **Blake's,** the neighborhood gay bar. **Einstein's** on Juniper and 10th, offers an eclectic menu and secluded patio seating. (Virginia Highland is a mile and a half due east via 10th St.; jog left to pick up Virginia Ave.)

Arts Center

The city's cultural arts nucleus, **Robert Woodruff Arts Center**—established to honor a hundred members of Atlanta's arts community killed in a plane crash en route to Paris in the 1960s—is home to the Atlanta Symphony Orchestra and the Alliance Theater. The **High Museum of Art** occupies a strikingly modern four-story building next door.

At Spring and 18th Streets, the **Center for Puppetry Arts** hosts performances and maintains a puppetry museum. The **William Breman Jewish Heritage Museum** across the street contains the most extensive Jewish heritage exhibits south of Washington, D.C. The studios of the **Atlanta Ballet,** the city's 60-year-old company, are on Spring St. nearby.

For a wonderful selection of places to eat, browse along **Restaurant Row,** on Crescent Ave. a block east of Peachtree. Here in a two block-stretch between 12th and 14th Streets there's the **Front Page News** (its Press Room bar is a local journalists' watering hole), casual **Vickery's,** upscale Italian at **Metropoli,** the swank **Martini Club,** and the more formal **South City Kitchen.**

Use the Arts Center MARTA Station for all sights.

BUCKHEAD

Three miles north of downtown, Buckhead is large and independent enough to be a city in itself—only four or five cities within the state are larger. The city's poshest district, Buckhead is home to Southern mansions on manicured lawns, swank mega-hotels, haute cuisine, and upmarket galleries, boutiques and shopping malls. But for all its exclusivity, Buckhead's many casual patio cafes, sports bars, beer gardens, and lively nightclubs also attract a young and varied crowd (anyone with lots of disposable income).

Lower Buckhead

Heading up Peachtree St. north of the Amtrak station, historical markers around Peachtree Creek recount day-by-day troop movements during the **Battle for Atlanta** fought here under command of Union General William Tecumseh Sherman and Confederate General John Bell Hood. The battle led to a 75-day siege that ended with the city's surrender, followed by the fire set by Sherman that destroyed all but 400 of the city's 4,000 buildings.

Every July Fourth, Peachtree St. through lower Buckhead closes to car traffic for the Peachtree Road Race, and tens of thousands of runners complete the 10K course despite summertime heat and humidity.

Miles of cafes and bistros along this route make this Atlanta's version of the Via Veneto—**R. Thomas** (open 24 hours), **Rocky's Pizza,** and **Cafe Intermezzo** are among the more notable.

Buckhead Village and Vicinity

Buckhead is centered where Peachtree St., Roswell Rd., and West Paces Ferry Rd. intersect. While nowhere near quaint, the compact modern "village" is full of shops, galleries, and cafes, and is easy to walk around provided you can find parking (pay lots available).

The city's premier historical homes and museums can be found a scenic drive down W. Paces Ferry Road. Among the wooded acres of the **Atlanta History Center** are the city's mammoth history museum and elegant **Swan House** (go south on Andrews Dr. for a beautiful exterior view), as well as a kid-friendly farmhouse that features farm animals and traditional crafts demonstrations. The Greek Revival **Governor's Mansion** at 391 W. Paces Ferry Rd. NW is also open to the public for limited hours.

The luxury hotel and shopping zone can be found on Peachtree St. north of the village. Here the **Ritz-Carlton Buckhead, Swissotel,** and **Grand Hyatt Hotel** provide Atlanta's most deluxe accommodations. More reasonably priced is the **Terrace Garden Hotel;** while the **Beverly Hills Inn** has the most historic character. The cheapest stay in Buckhead, and one of the best bargains in Atlanta, is the **Cheshire Motor Inn** next to the Colonnade Restaurant out Cheshire Bridge Rd. at the raggedy fringe of the exclusive district.

Buckhead is known for its many top-end restaurants. Among the most acclaimed are **Baccanalia, Cafe TuTu Tango, Pricci,** the **Dining Room** at the Ritz-Carlton; for haute diner cuisine try the **Buckhead Diner;** and for the most fun in a converted doughnut shop, **Fat Matt's Rib Shack** on Piedmont Avenue serves barbecue along with live jazz and blues.

The shopper's mecca is **Lenox Square,** largest mall in the Southeast, where Neiman-Marcus, Macy's, and Rich's department stores, Latitudes map store, a tourist bureau desk, an American Express office, cinemas, Mick's restaurant and California Pizza Kitchen are among hundreds of shops in the skylit complex. The elite **Phipps Plaza** shopping center includes Saks Fifth Avenue and Lord & Taylor.

Drivers should note that traffic is often snarled through the district, particularly along Peachtree St., Lenox Rd., and towards any freeway access. The Lenox Square MARTA Station is a convenient alternative for mall shoppers, and a new Buckhead MARTA station brings transit closer to the hotel zone, but by and large the district has been designed for drivers rather than pedestrians.

NEIGHBORHOODS

West End

Atlanta University Center (AUC) dominates the West End district. The campuses of Morehouse College, Spelman College, Morris Brown, and Clark-Atlanta University are surrounded by some comfortable residential neighborhoods that historically housed the city's African-American elite, and are still home to many local academicians. While the sprawling campuses hold attractive shady lawns and handsome buildings dating back to the school's founding in 1869, much of the district is in disrepair, particularly its commercial center around the West End MARTA station.

The campuses are linked by James P. Brawley Dr., the central collegiate drag of fraternities and a few isolated cafes and shops, including **Shrine of the Black Madonna,** with its "Black Holocaust" slavery exhibit.

Three house museums show the West End at its best. The **Herndon Home** displays upper-class urban life in the 1910 mansion of Alonzo Herndon, a former slave who rose to become a millionaire as founder of the Atlanta Life Insurance Company. The 1857 Victorian **Hammonds House** exhibits African-American artwork and also serves as a community center. **Wren's Nest,** the 1870 Victorian home of Joel Chandler Harris, holds a fanciful shrine to Br'er Rabbit, Br'er Fox, and all the other Uncle Remus characters recorded by the Atlanta journalist. Year-round storytelling programs bring the African folk tales to life.

The **Clark Atlanta University Art Gallery** can be found in the Trevor Arnett Bldg. on campus. The Atlanta Preservation Center leads tours of AUC campuses and the district (see **Touring the City**).

Now that the legendary **Paschal's** motel on Martin Luther King, Jr., Dr. SW—the site of civil rights negotiations during the movement's 1960s heyday—has been turned into an AUC conference center, there's no lodging available in the area. You can still enjoy a meal here, though, or follow your nose to **Aleck's Barbecue Heaven** across the street.

The Vine City MARTA Station is convenient to the Herndon Home; drivers may also want to park around here to avoid the narrow winding lanes of the district. The AUC campuses are a short walk away (cross the pedestrian bridge over Martin Luther King, Jr. Dr.).

Sweet Auburn and Vicinity

A thriving African-American commercial center from the 1890s, Sweet Auburn was known at the turn of the 20th century as "the richest Negro street in the world." While its heyday began to diminish in the 1940s, it was the center of civil rights movement leadership in the 1960s, as home to Ebenezer Baptist Church, the Southern Christian Leadership Coalition, and Martin Luther King, Jr. (see the special topic **King's Legacy**). After years of decline, the neighborhood has for the last decade been undergoing dramatic city- and federally funded preservation to restore Sweet Auburn to prominence as Atlanta's most historic African-American community. The street is the scene of the annual **Kingfest,** which brings arts, music, and performers to the neighborhood around Martin Luther King, Jr.'s birthday January 15.

Along a mile-long strip of Auburn Ave. east of Five Points to the King Center, visitors will find many community landmarks. From west to east, the Auburn Ave. Research Library maintains a special collection on African-American history and heritage, the APEX Museum holds art and heritage exhibits (see **Sights),** and the Southern Christian Leadership Conference continues to work for social change out of its offices in Prince Hall Masonic Building at 332 Auburn Ave. All sites are marked on a self-guided walking tour map of the district distributed at the National Park Service Visitor Center at 450 Auburn Ave. Both the NPS and the Atlanta Historical Preservation Society lead guided tours of the district (see **Touring the City**).

Beautiful Restaurant serves hearty Southern meat-and-three plates (diners choose one meat and three side plates from a buffet of options), or try **Thelma's** barbecue shack next to the interstate overpass. For local recreation, there's an indoor public pool across from the King Center.

The King Memorial MARTA Station is several blocks away from the King Center through a rundown residential neighborhood that's okay to walk through during the day, or pedestrians might prefer the more-traveled route down Auburn Ave. from downtown.

Oakland Cemetery, adjacent to MARTA, holds historic gravesites and monuments on several acres of rolling hills. Neighboring **Cabbagetown** is a so-so working-class residential district undergoing some gentrification (the **Cabbagetown Grill** is the most flavorful evidence), as is the neighborhood surrounding **Grant Park** to the south. Within Grant Park are two of the city's most popular attractions: **Zoo Atlanta** and the historic **Atlanta Cyclorama.** Across from the zoo, **Taco Mac's** is one of the few businesses in the largely residential area.

Virginia Highland

The sophisticated little village of Virginia Highland charms with a European flair—scones, cafes, chianti—mixed in with plenty of comfortable neighborhood pubs, arty boutiques, and used bookstores. The bouncy street life starts at dawn, when the first joggers hit the streets, and continues until the last joint closes its doors at 4 a.m.

The village is centered at the intersection of Virginia and N. Highland Avenues. Here a row of storefront cafes, taverns, and restaurants converge into one collective second-story patio out back, overlooking not much more than a parking lot, but with appealing back-alley style. Across the street, **Murphy's Deli** is another great stop, and **Moe & Joe's** bar serves as the unofficial neighborhood welcome center.

A short walk south on Highland from this central village is the nightlife strip anchored by **Blind Willie's** blues club and long-time saloon **Atkins Park;** the good restaurant **Dish** is nearby. Across Ponce de Leon Ave., **Manuel's Tavern** has the smoke-filled ambience of a local politico's hangout, which it is—a great place to watch election returns or bring up such subjects as the state flag or the 11th congressional district. For an all-hours greasy spoon, the **Majestic Diner** on Ponce de Leon Ave. will still be flipping hotcakes after the crowds have turned in.

Emory/Druid Hills

In the exclusive Druid Hills neighborhood, large homes such as those featured in the movie *Driving Miss Daisy* (filmed here) are set back on expansive landscaped lawns; among these, the

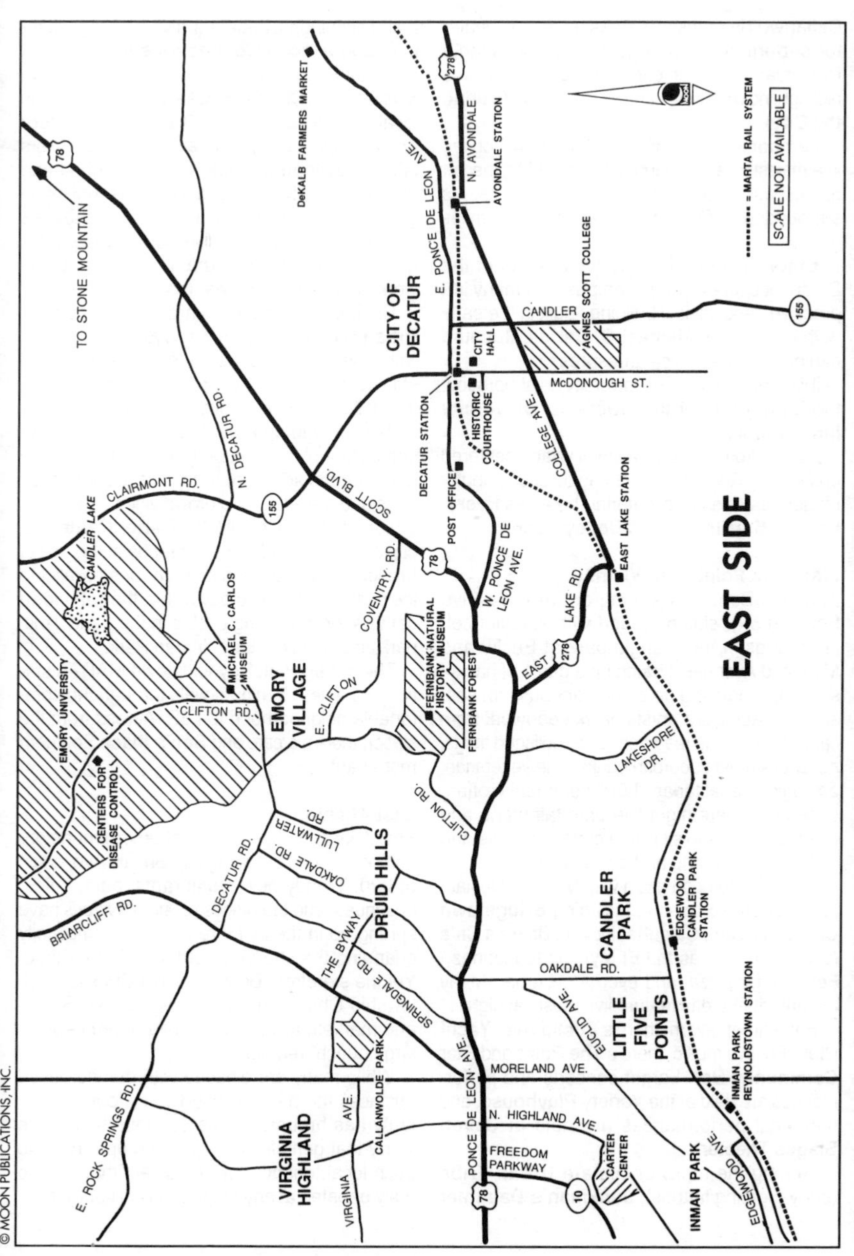
EAST SIDE
TO STONE MOUNTAIN
78
DeKALB FARMERS MARKET
278
N. AVONDALE
AVONDALE STATION
E. PONCE DE LEON AVE
CITY OF DECATUR
CANDLER
AGNES SCOTT COLLEGE
155
CITY HALL
McDONOUGH ST.
DECATUR STATION
HISTORIC COURTHOUSE
COLLEGE AVE.
POST OFFICE
W. PONCE DE LEON AVE.
EAST LAKE STATION
N. DECATUR RD.
CLAIRMONT RD.
SCOTT BLVD.
CANDLER LAKE
COVENTRY RD.
MICHAEL C. CARLOS MUSEUM
FERNBANK NATURAL HISTORY MUSEUM
FERNBANK FOREST
LAKE RD.
EAST
EMORY UNIVERSITY
CLIFTON RD.
EMORY VILLAGE
E. CLIFTON
CENTERS FOR DISEASE CONTROL
LAKESHORE DR.
CLIFTON RD.
LULLWATER RD.
OAKDALE RD.
DECATUR RD.
DRUID HILLS
BRIARCLIFF RD.
THE BYWAY
CANDLER PARK
EDGEWOOD CANDLER PARK STATION
OAKDALE RD.
SPRINGDALE RD.
EUCLID AVE.
LITTLE FIVE POINTS
CALLANWOLDE PARK
PONCE DE LEON AVE.
MORELAND AVE.
INMAN PARK REYNOLDSTOWN STATION
E. ROCK SPRINGS RD.
VIRGINIA HIGHLAND
VIRGINIA AVE.
N. HIGHLAND AVE.
FREEDOM PARKWAY
10
CARTER CENTER
INMAN PARK
EDGEWOOD AVE
= MARTA RAIL SYSTEM
SCALE NOT AVAILABLE
MOON

Callanwolde mansion serves as an arts center for performances and galleries. The Atlanta Preservation Center leads guided walking tours highlighting residential architecture (see **Touring the City**).

Fernbank Natural History Museum, housed in a majestic new building, offers an IMAX theater as well as three floors of science exhibits. It's surrounded by Fernbank Forest, with two miles of trails.

Emory University, the Ivy League of the South, occupies a huge campus with many impressive neoclassical buildings built in the early 20th century. Its **Michael C. Carlos Museum** exhibits archaeological treasures.

Two hotels serve the university neighborhood: the **Emory Inn,** or the lower-cost **University Inn at Emory.**

Across from campus, a small village centered on Decatur Rd. at Oxford St. holds such popular student eateries and watering holes as **Everybody's, Burrito Art,** and **Dolleys Bar.**

Little Five Points and Vicinity

Atlanta's Bohemians hang out at Little Five Points (L5P), sitting around with kerchief-collared dogs in the triangle park at Euclid and Moreland Avenues, kicking up a game of hackysack, or drumming up a spontaneous jam session. Dreadlocked artists hawk beadwork from carts, street poets read from self-published tracts, runaways meet suburban punks. The vegetarian, ecological, egalitarian "L5P" community offers cheap eats, late-night live entertainment, and plenty of places to sit with a coffee or bottle and watch the nose-ring and crystals crowd.

The neighborhood has a variety of good restaurants for ethnic cuisine, including **Bridgetown Grill** (Jamaican), **Calcutta** (Indian), **Baker's Cafe** (Cajun), as well as the **El Myr** "burrito lounge," **Fellini's** for pizza, and even a cyberbar. Many restaurants-by-day feature live music at night.

For a great tavern, there's **Euclid Ave. Yacht Club.** For live music, there's **The Point** and **Star Community Bar.** Larger concerts and performances are held at the **Variety Playhouse,** and theatrical performances are held at **Seven Stages Theater.**

Among the funky shops are **Urban Tribe** (body piercing/tattoos), **Junkman's Daughter** (used clothing), **Stefan's** (pristine vintage fashion), and **African Connections** for ethnic art and fashion. Find used books at **A Capella Books;** and **Charis Books and More** is the local feminist bookstore. **Outback Outfitters** rents camping equipment and sells and repairs bikes. **Sevananda Market,** the neighborhood grocery collective, has a deli case as well as organic produce and health foods (not cheap)—its community bulletin board lists such indispensable notices as used bongo drums for trade, bodywork, and roommates wanted.

Beside their shop of yard art and pottery, **Urban Nirvana** keeps a wild overgrown garden with lanes leading under archways and around statues past chicken coops and peacock pens. It's off DeKalb Ave. a mile west of Moreland.

Adjacent **Inman Park** down Euclid Ave. is Atlanta's first planned suburb. Here old Victorian and "Bungaloid" homes are set around large trees and gracefully overgrown vines and greenery. At the top of the hill, the **Carter Center** occupies a large landscaped campus at the end of Freedom Parkway (a bike path runs parallel to the parkway). On Saturday nights, the L5P crowd gathers for drumming circles in the Land Trust parkland in the center of Inman Park.

The Inman Park/Reynoldstown MARTA station is a quiet 15-minute walk through the comfortable neighborhood to L5P. Across from the station there's a cafe and **Son's Place** Southern restaurant.

East Atlanta

East Atlanta is the city's most emergent neighborhood, strung out along Flat Shoals Ave. south of I-20. Trendy new restaurants, bars, cafes, boutiques, and the offices of *Atlanta Press* have sprung up in the last three years, dramatically changing the character of the neighborhood. Yet the storefront Body of Christ Christian Fellowship Church, the Soul Zodiac Hair Salon, and markets advertising "Collards 99 cents—large bunch" remain.

While many are pleased with the increased business the neighborhood's newfound popularity has brought, some community leaders worry that gentrification will drive up rents and push local tenants out—a subject that can be hotly debated at any neighborhood counter.

Heaping Bowl and Brew, the **Flat Iron** restaurant, **Edible Art** Cafe, and **Burrito Art** serve some of the most unusual dishes in town (pierogies, lentil burgers, seafood balls, Asian meatloaf). For coffee, there's **Sacred Grounds.** The sleek Ayn Rand-inspired **Fountainhead** serves cocktails and a selection of California wines.

There's no practical mass transit and the neighborhood can be tricky for newcomers to find. It's a half mile south of the I-20 Moreland Ave. exit (NOT the Flat Shoals exit). Turn in at the "East Atlanta" sign on McPherson Ave. then turn right towards the library. Note that Flat Shoals Ave. is disjunctive; from surface streets you're better off approaching via Moreland Ave.

WITHIN THE BELTWAY

East side towns within the I-285 bypass are an easy reach for Atlanta visitors. For destinations outside the bypass—including Stone Mountain and northern suburbs—see **Vicinity of Atlanta.**

Decatur

Founded in 1823, Decatur let history pass it by when early town residents, fearing noise and pollution, refused to let the railroad stop there. So the railroad went on to Terminus instead, the depot town that evolved into Atlanta. Today Decatur is the home of **Agnes Scott College** and is a small-city alternative to bustling downtown Atlanta. Situated between Atlanta and Stone Mountain, Decatur is a quick 10 minutes from downtown by rail.

Decatur's compact downtown square is directly above the Decatur MARTA station. The 1889 **County Courthouse** has a small museum of local history and artifacts, including Union and Confederate memorabilia.

The **Holiday Inn Decatur** here is within walking distance of the square, as are several restaurants, including **Mick's. Eddie's Attic** above the square features largely acoustic music; a half-mile away is the **Freight Depot** for bluegrass music. Along the way, **Twains** is a great bar. The **DeKalb Farmer's Market** out E. Ponce de Leon Ave., offers much more than fresh produce—the hangar-size building attracts all sorts of people to its selection of ethnic and gourmet specialties (there's an inexpensive cafeteria too).

Chamblee and Doraville

North of Decatur, Chamblee (SHAM-blee) and Doraville have growing immigrant populations of primarily Asians and Latinos (they're derisively nicknamed "Cham-bodia" and "Doritoville"). Most of the action—including great ethnic markets and restaurants—can be found on a drive along the Buford Highway (see **Food and Drink**). Though both towns have MARTA stations, driving is really the only way to see these neighborhoods.

SIGHTS

FACTORY TOURS

Two of the world's most successful and visible businesses originated in Atlanta, and now operate two of the city's most popular attractions. Raising the factory tour to dazzling new heights are the Cable News Network (CNN) Studio Tour and the World of Coca-Cola.

CNN Studio Tour

On guided tours through CNN Studios, visitors are introduced to the history of Ted Turner's media empire—not only the Cable News Network (CNN), but also Turner Broadcasting Systems (TBS) and Turner Network Television (TNT). Turner also owns the rights to many classic films including the hometown saga *Gone with the Wind.* CNN's TalkBack program is filmed live in the central plaza weekdays at 3 p.m.; tickets are free.

A 45-minute guided **studio tour** culminates with a look at the kinetic central newsroom from a gallery overhead. Tours begin every half-hour 9 a.m.-6 p.m. daily. Adults pay $7, seniors $5, children 12 and under $4.50. Call (404) 827-2300 for reservations. Visitors must pass through a metal detector and bags are subject to search.

The 14-story **CNN Center** on Marietta St. at Techwood Dr. encloses offices and the **Omni Hotel** around a central atrium, all above a ground-level mall of restaurants, snack bars, shops, and a cinema (an unlikely place to find a worldwide broadcasting network). For souvenirs, the **Turner Store** sells videotapes of Desert Storm news coverage, CNN/TBS/TNT logo-emblazoned golf balls, and paraphernalia from the Turner-owned Atlanta Braves baseball team. CNN Center is above the Omni/WCC/CNN MARTA station.

The World of Coca-Cola

Designed "to entertain and enlighten soft-drink consumers from around the world," the World of Coca-Cola, tel. (404) 676-5151, pays tribute to the wildly successful marketing of Coke in 185 countries. The $15 million, three-story, carbonated, caffeinated fantasyland features continuously running Coke commercials, soda fountains from vintage to high-tech, and a store selling hundreds of products with the familiar red-and-white logo. Can't beat the feeling.

Across from Underground Atlanta at 55 Martin Luther King, Jr. Dr. SW, the Coke museum is open Mon.-Sat. 10 a.m.-5 p.m. and Sunday noon-6 p.m.(expanded summer hours). Adults pay $6, seniors and students $4, children $3 (under age five free); prices include all the Coke you can drink. The last entry is an hour before closing.

More Commercial Exhibits

The Federal Reserve Bank of Atlanta, 104 Marietta St. NW, tel. (404) 521-8764, maintains a **monetary museum** that explains the history of money, how money is made, and how the Federal Reserve system works. Gold coins minted in North Georgia and other rare coins are on display. It's across from Centennial Olympic Park and open 9 a.m.-4 p.m., weekdays only.

Southern Bell Center, 675 W. Peachtree St. NE, tel. (404) 223-2311, has a **telephone museum** of ancient telecommunications equipment at its plaza level.

ARTS AND SCIENCES

High Museum of Art

From 18th-century Oriental ceramics to soulful contemporary street expressions, the High Museum, 1280 Peachtree St. NE, tel. (404) 733-4437, houses four artful stories in a modern building so striking the *New York Times* called it "among the best any city has built in at least a generation" after it opened in 1989.

Inside, works of artists with Georgia roots (such as the visionary Rev. Howard Finster and self-taught painter Mattie Lou O'Kelley) are celebrated alongside an extensive sub-Saharan African art collection, 19th-century American paintings, and an inviting interactive children's gallery to boot. Wafting scents from the atrium coffee bar and a well-stocked museum store (regional-flavor art books and crafts, wearable art) enhance the welcoming come-as-you-are, see-art ambience.

Recent blockbuster traveling exhibitions have included the largest Impressionist exhibit in the Southeast and a colorful selection of Pop Art (special rates and extended hours may apply). Past film series have included a Latin American film festival, animation shorts, and a Johnny Depp retrospective; tickets are $4-5; call the film hotline at (404) 733-4570 for current screenings.

The museum is open Tues.-Sat. 10 a.m.-5 p.m., Sunday noon-5 p.m. (closed Monday). On Thursday it's free after 1 p.m.; all other times admission is $6 for adults, $4 for students and seniors, $2 for youths 6-17, under six free. The cafe within opens at 8:30 a.m. weekdays and 10 a.m. weekends. The museum is a block from the Arts Center MARTA station.

The satellite **High Museum of Folk Art and Photography** at Georgia-Pacific Center, 30 Wesley Dobbs Ave., tel. (404) 577-6940, brings exhibits within free-and-easy reach of the downtown crowd. It's open Mon.-Sat. 10 a.m.-5 p.m. (closed Sunday), no charge. Use Peachtree Center MARTA.

Michael C. Carlos Museum

Northeast of downtown in the historic quadrangle of the attractive Emory University campus, this art and archaeology museum, tel. (404) 727-4282, displays ancient artifacts from around the world and artwork from the Middle Ages to the 20th century. Exhibits include an Egyptian mummy, pre-Columbian pottery, and Greek statues. The museum is open Mon.-Sat. 10 a.m.-5 p.m., Sunday noon-5 p.m. A $3 donation is suggested. Adjacent to the museum is a bookstore and cafe.

Find the museum from the University's main entrance on Decatur Rd. at Oxford St. Bus #36 runs here from the Arts Center MARTA Station.

Other Galleries and Art Exhibits

Atlanta International Museum of Art and Design, in the Marriott Marquis Tower Two in Peachtree Center, tel. (404) 688-2467, brings exotic artwork from around the world within easy reach of the convention crowd.

Hammonds House, 503 Peeples St., tel. (404) 752-8730, displays Haitian art and work by Romare Bearden in a Victorian home in the West End district. Admission is $2 adults, $1 students (closed Monday).

On the AUC campus nearby, the **Clark Atlanta University Art Gallery,** James P. Brawley Dr., tel. (404) 880-6889, displays African art and contemporary African-American art in the Trevor Arnett Bldg. (closed Monday).

The **Atlanta College of Art** maintains a gallery of experimental student work at the Robert Woodruff Arts Center, 1280 Peachtree St. NE, tel. (404) 733-5050.

Center for Puppetry Arts, 1404 Spring St. NW at 18th St., tel. (404) 523-3141, maintains a small museum showcasing the sophisticated artistry of puppetry from around the world—a colorful and fun collection across from the Jewish Museum (on view weekdays and during performances).

For a brochure of dozens of galleries in town, call the Atlanta Gallery Association at (404) 390-0309 (also occasionally available in racks around town).

SciTrek

Ranked among the top 10 science centers in the nation, SciTrek, 395 Piedmont Ave., tel. (404) 522-5500, displays hands-on interactive exhibits that encourage visitors to make their own scientific discoveries about gravity, electricity, physics, sensory perception, and the like. Smaller children will love the playful bubble-filled kids' space, complete with soft cushions and face-paint vanities. It's open Mon.-Sat. 10 a.m.-5 p.m., Sunday noon-5 p.m. Adult admission is $7.50, youths and seniors $5, under three free. It's three decent blocks from the Civic Center MARTA Station.

Fernbank Natural History Museum

Fernbank's impressive museum, 767 Clifton Rd. NE, tel. (404) 370-0960, holds a popular IMAX theater (the only one in Georgia), fun "discovery room" play areas (one exclusively for preschoolers), and exhibits on plate tectonics, indigenous societies, and more bubble science. The state history exhibit traces the evolution of humans in Georgia's varied natural environments (including the Okefenokee Swamp as night falls and owls hoot, cicadas chirp, and alligators bellow). The nice cafe serves such daily specials as fried trout with roasted potatoes and vegetables for $4, also sandwiches and salads.

Admission to the museum only is $9 adults, $8 students and seniors, $7 children 12 and under. To see the IMAX movie only, knock $2 off those prices. Combination tickets for both museum admission and one IMAX movie cost $14 adults, $12 students and seniors, $10 children. The museum is open Mon.-Sat. 10 a.m.-5 p.m. (and Friday evenings for IMAX movies only), Sunday noon-5 p.m.

Fernbank's **Science Center** nearby holds more traditional exhibits on Georgia ecosystems, an Apollo spacecraft and astronomy exhibits; admission is free. Shows in its 70-foot-diameter **planetarium** (one of the world's largest) cost $2 adults, $1 students, seniors free; for a schedule call (404) 378-4311. Its **Observatory** houses a 36-inch reflecting telescope to view the celestial bodies and galaxies; it's open Thursday and Friday evenings from dark to 10:30 p.m. in clear weather only.

Nearly two miles of trails within the 65-acre **Fernbank Forest** lead hikers through undisturbed stands of large tulip trees, oak, beech, and hickory—a surprisingly wild pocket five minutes from downtown. Gates are open Sun.-Fri. 2-5 p.m. and Saturday 10 a.m.-5 p.m.; no fee. The **greenhouse** is open Sunday afternoons only, and visitors may be rewarded with a small plant as a souvenir.

Find the Fernbank complex and forest off Ponce de Leon Ave. in the Druid Hills district east of downtown. The #2 bus runs along Ponce de Leon from the North Ave. MARTA station.

Atlanta Botanical Garden

The lush displays in the strikingly modern and massive **Fuqua Conservatory** and the surrounding 15-acre hardwood forest make the Botanical Garden, tel. (404) 876-5859, a tranquil urban retreat. Tropical, desert, and endangered plants complement naturally profuse and flowering native varieties. The garden is adjacent to Piedmont Park, off Piedmont Ave., at the Prado; it's open Tues.-Sun. 9 a.m.-6 p.m. (till 7 p.m. during daylight saving time). Adult admission is $6; $5 for seniors, $3 for children 6 to 12 years, no charge on Thursday after 3 p.m. It's under a mile from the Arts Center MARTA Station.

Zoo Atlanta

Renowned for its primates, Zoo Atlanta, 800 Cherokee Ave. SE, in Grant Park, tel. (404) 624-5600, is best known locally as the residence of the city's unofficial mascot, Willie B. (also a proud father several times over—rare for gorillas in captivity.) They maintain natural habitat settings and representative species from Georgia's coastal and swamp regions, also an aviary and wildlife shows.

The ticket booth is open daily 9:30 a.m.-4:30 p.m.; the grounds stay open an hour longer. Admission is $9 adults, $6.50 seniors, $5.50 children ages 3 to 11 (under 3 free). Parking is free but the lot may fill on weekends. Bus #105 shuttles between the zoo and the West End MARTA station. There's fast food in the zoo; **Taco Mac's** is about the only restaurant nearby. See also www.zooatlanta.org.

HISTORY AND HERITAGE

Atlanta History Center

The Atlanta Historical Society manages the impressive collection of historical homes and interpretive centers that make up the Atlanta History Center, 130 W. Paces Ferry Rd. NW (at Andrews, a mile and some from Buckhead's central village), tel. (404) 814-4000. Set beautifully on 32 wooded acres in posh residential Buckhead, the Center opened its grand **Atlanta History Museum** in 1993. This vast $11 million facility, its architecture designed to evoke the city's railroad heritage, devotes 83,000 square feet to the city's historical and cultural milestones—"from Civil War to Civil Rights." Special mixed-media displays highlight Atlanta's early African-American elite society and regional folk arts; the most provocative exhibit critically examines whether commonly held perceptions of Southern history are "Fact or Myth." The '50s cafe serves lunch and snacks.

The Center's two historic home tours present contrasting views of mid-1800s rural Georgia and 1920s Atlanta high society. The **Tullie Smith Farm,** an 1840s plantation restoration, exemplifies the kind of simple two-story clapboard house Margaret Mitchell had in mind for Tara, not the white-columned vision of the filmmaker. The working farm with live animals includes demonstrations of sheep-shearing, weaving, open-hearth cooking, and other traditional skills and crafts. Visitors are free to explore the house and grounds; check at the Center's admission desk for a guided tour and demonstration schedules.

The majestic 1928 **Swan House** sits regally among acres of landscaped gardens (the exterior view is particularly impressive from Andrews Dr.). Period furnishings sculpted in exquisite detail—a swan motif appears throughout in furniture, stained glass, and even dishware—and the grand spiral staircase are most memorable.

KAP STANN

The Swan House at the Atlanta History Center reflects the lifestyle of prominent Atlantans in the 1930s.

Visitors are allowed through on guided tours only, offered every half hour.

A modern interpretive center houses additional exhibits, a casual museum cafe, gift shop, and archives. Give yourself at least half a day to explore all the offerings, and try to catch one of many special events.

An annual **storytelling festival** takes place in February, and lectures by nationally known historians and authors are held throughout the year. For a weekend each July, the Center hosts a **Civil War Encampment,** with costumed living-history interpreters acting out Civil War scenes.

The Center is open Mon.-Sat. 10 a.m.-5:30 p.m., Sunday noon-5:30. The admission price of $7 adults, $5 students and seniors, $4 youths ages 6-17 (under six free) includes most sites; for guided tours add $1-2. Special events may have a separate admission charge. From the Lenox MARTA station, take bus #23. See also www.atlhist.org.

(The Historical Society also operates **Atlanta Heritage Row,** a small history museum downtown—see **Underground Atlanta** below.)

Georgia State Capitol

Georgia's 1889 **Capitol,** 214 Capitol Ave., tel. (404) 656-2844, can be easily identified atop Capitol Hill with its gleaming dome of North Georgia gold. The stately white-columned building (home to the state legislature from January to June) displays flags-of-state, flora and fauna collections, historic artifacts, and a Hall of Fame honoring native sons and daughters. Statuary dots its landscaped lawns, including a metal sculpture honoring the 33 African-American legislators expelled during Reconstruction It's open weekdays during business hours. Use the Georgia State MARTA station.

Underground Atlanta

Underground Atlanta, on Alabama St. between Peachtree and Central, tel. (404) 523-2311, is more a contemporary mall than historic site. In 1986, Underground was reconstructed from the original ghost town that had been enclosed by overhead bridges in the early part of the 20th century. Today, shoppers promenade on original rail-inlaid cobblestone lanes, brick walls bear fading Coca-Cola ads, and historical facades of stone and terra-cotta evoke design. A particularly cool refuge in summer, the 12-acre complex supports more than a hundred shops, restaurants, and clubs.

The center connects directly with the Five Points MARTA station. Drivers may want to use Underground's easily accessible public parking lot to explore the downtown area.

Atlanta Cyclorama

The Cyclorama in Grant Park, tel. (404) 658-7625, tells the story of the 1864 Battle for Atlanta as the studio revolves around a massive painting and diorama completed in 1885. Despite the contemporary studio, the Cyclorama retains the slightly campy appeal of an attraction from another era, like an old talkie or giant camera obscura. Expect that overstimulated modern children might find it incredibly dull.

Admission is $5 adults, $4 seniors, $3 children ages 6-12 (under six free). It's open daily 9:20 a.m.-4:30 p.m. (5:30 p.m. in summers). Find the entrance at Georgia and Cherokee Avenues SE in Grant Park right next to the zoo.

Jimmy Carter Library and Museum

The National Archives operates the Carter Library and Museum, 441 Freedom Parkway, tel. (404) 331-0296. The museum displays artifacts from Carter's presidency, including a replica of the Oval Office, inaugural First Lady gowns, gifts from world leaders, and the notorious brown cardigan sweater Carter wore during his famous fireside chats. There's a 30-minute biographical film, and past scheduled events have included a reenactment of the Camp David accords. The gift shop sells all of Carter's books and fine china in the Carter White House pattern. The museum is open Mon.-Sat. 9 a.m.-4:45 p.m., Sunday noon-4:45 p.m. Museum admission is $5 adults, $4 seniors, under 17 free.

The **Carter Center** here houses private public-policy organizations devoted to global issues, conflict resolution, and human rights, which unfortunately are not included with the public exhibits. One highlight, the **Atlanta Project,** is devoted to the idea that "somewhere on earth, there is one place where poverty and the social ills associated with it can be overcome," according to President Carter.

The Center occupies a 35-acre hilltop landscaped with a rose garden, cherry orchard, wild-

KING'S LEGACY

I HAVE A DREAM . . .

. . . that one day on the red hills of Georgia, sons of former slaves and sons of former slave owners will be able to sit down together at the table of brotherhood. I have a dream that my four little children will one day live in a nation where they will not be judged by the color of their skin but by the content of their character. I have a dream!"

—Dr. Martin Luther King, Jr.,
1963, Washington, D.C.

Martin Luther King, Jr. (1929-1968)

Martin Luther King, Jr., was born in Sweet Auburn on January 15, 1929, a block away from Ebenezer Baptist Church, where, 39 years later, the city and the nation mourned the death of the man who founded the American civil rights movement. The tomb of the Nobel Peace Prize winner now rests next to the church where he, his father, and his grandfather had preached; its simple inscription reads "Free at last, free at last, thank God Almighty I'm free at last."

King's birth home, church, and gravesite—all national historic landmarks—make a stirring tribute to the American hero who moved the world with his passion for equal justice. But what truly memorializes Dr. King are the millions of visitors (around a half million each year) who pause before his grave, read his printed remarks, view his last effects, and explain to their children what the man and the time meant to them. How times have changed for minorities in America, how they haven't—it's the old people remembering, and the young people imagining, who create the most powerful memorial.

The King Center

The **crypt** of Dr. Martin Luther King, Jr. stands in the center of a long reflecting pool near an eternal flame at the King Center for Nonviolent Social Change, 449 Auburn Ave., tel. (404) 524-1956. Founded by King's widow Coretta Scott King and now administered by Dexter Scott King (King's younger son), the King Center continues Dr. King's work toward economic and social equality. Within their Freedom Hall offices, an exhibit hall houses a collection of King's personal effects and mementos, including exhibits on Mahatma Gandhi, who inspired King's dedication to nonviolence. Exhibits are on view daily 9 a.m.-5 p.m., no charge. The gravesite outside can be visited around the clock.

NPS Visitor Center

The National Park Service **Visitor Center,** 450 Auburn Ave., tel. (404) 331-3920, holds powerful exhibits on the history of American apartheid and the evolution of the civil rights movement. A well-done 30-minute film contains historical footage of civil rights marches and clashes. The visitor center is open daily 9 a.m.-5 p.m.

Birth Home

Martin Luther King, Jr. was born in an upstairs bedroom in a two-story Victorian house at 501 Auburn Ave. His father, Rev. Martin Luther King, Sr., and mother, the former Alberta Williams, had been married in the house three years earlier, and all three of their children were born here. The nine-room Queen Anne style house has been restored and furnished to reflect the time when "M.L." (as he was known) was growing up. Ranger-guided tours of the house begin at the NPS visitor center.

Ebenezer Baptist Church

Three generations of King family preachers presided over the historic sanctuary of Ebenezer Baptist Church, 407 Auburn Ave. In 1957, Martin Luther King, Jr., organized the Southern Christian Leadership Conference in the church's basement. In 1968, crowds of mourners paid last respects at Dr. King's funeral here after his assassination in Memphis. Another family tragedy occurred here in 1974, when Dr. King's mother was killed by an assassin's bullet while seated at the church organ.

The 750-person-capacity church became so popular as a civil rights shrine that an expanded sanctuary was built across the street for worship services, preserving the original 1922 church for tours and special services. The new church is due to open in 1999.

MLK, Jr. National Historic District

The King memorial sites are all part of a national historic preservation district within the surrounding **Sweet Auburn** neighborhood. The NPS oversees this district, and distributes maps to all historic sites from its visitor center.

The King Center is a mile from the Five Points MARTA station, a decent, usually well-traveled walk past many community landmarks; the #3 bus runs along this route. It's less than half that distance from the King Memorial MARTA station through a hard-luck residential district. Drivers will find ample signs pointing the way from major freeways to the parking lot behind the NPS Visitor Center.

flower meadow, ponds, and waterfalls within a formal Japanese garden. A dignified cafeteria serves inexpensive Southern lunches and snacks overlooking the gardens. There's no charge to wander the grounds, and diners can patronize the restaurant without paying admission.

APEX Museum

The **A**frican-American **P**anoramic **Ex**perience **APEX Museum,** 135 Auburn Ave., tel. (404) 521-2729, relates local African-American history through exhibits on the Sweet Auburn district (including a short video and a replica of a 19th-century pharmacy) and displays African art and contemporary artwork by local artists. It's open Tues.-Sat. 10 a.m.-5 p.m. (During February's Black History Month and in summer, it's also open Sunday 1-5 p.m.) Admission is $3 adults, $2 students and seniors, under four free.

William Breman Jewish Heritage Museum

Opened in 1996, the Jewish Heritage Museum, 1440 Spring St. NW, tel. (404) 873-1661, is the largest Jewish heritage museum south of Washington, D.C. Its Holocaust gallery chronicles the systematic murder of more than half of Europe's 11 million Jews by the Nazis and the failure of the world to react to the massacre—the exhibit winds up with a contemporary group photo of local survivors and their families. The heritage gallery tells the story of Atlanta's Jewish community from the first German immigrants in 1845.

Admission is $5 adults, $3 seniors and students (under age six free). It's open Mon.-Thurs. 10 a.m.-5 p.m., Friday 10 a.m.-3 p.m., and Sunday 1-5 p.m. (closed Saturday). It's next to the Center for Puppetry Arts.

Margaret Mitchell House

The Margaret Mitchell House, 990 Peachtree St. at 10th St., tel. (404) 249-7012, opens the home of the famous Atlanta native. Mitchell wrote *Gone with the Wind* here in a cramped basement apartment Mitchell called "the Dump"—not exactly Tara. The museum displays the typewriter on which the manuscript was written, Mitchell's Pulitzer Prize, and a great collection of movie posters. Hour-long guided tours of the house and apartment emphasize

"Peggy's" unconventional life and the pains of restoring the house, which nearly rival the author's drama.

The three-story Tudor Revival house had been carved up into apartments and was occupied until 1978, when it was abandoned and boarded up. It remained urban blight for nearly two decades. Early faltering restoration attempts went up in flames after arsonists struck in 1994. A German industrial group contributed $5 million for restoration, but 40 days before its scheduled opening in 1996 the house was again torched by arson. After repairs, the house opened to the public in May 1997.

Admission is $6 adults, seniors and students $5, under age six free. Purchase tickets at the visitor center, which displays photographs of the house fire and screens a 17-minute film on the author and the restoration. Tours are offered daily 9 a.m.-4 p.m. (closed on major holidays). It's next to the Midtown MARTA station.

Other Historic House Museums and Buildings
The **Wren's Nest,** 1050 Ralph D. Abernathy Blvd. SW, tel. (404) 753-7735, is the enchanting Victorian home of Georgia writer Joel Chandler Harris, chronicler of the Uncle Remus stories. The house is a fanciful shrine to Br'er Rabbit and all his br'erly shenanigans. Storytelling programs here bring the wonderful old African tales to life. Guided tours and plenty of memorabilia are also available. It's open Tues.-Sat. 10 a.m.-4 p.m., Sunday 1-4 p.m. Admission is $3 adults, $2 seniors and teens, $1 children (under age four free). It's a half-mile from the West End MARTA station through a run-down district.

THE *GONE WITH THE WIND* CITY TOUR

The Pulitzer prize-winning novel that's sold more copies than any book besides the Bible, *Gone with the Wind,* was written by native Margaret Mitchell in her Atlanta home in 1936. Selling more than one million copies in the first six months of its issue, the novel won the Pulitzer prize for its author in 1937 and has since been translated into 70 languages. In 1939, MGM released the film based on Mitchell's book—starring Clark Gable and then-unknown Vivien Leigh—which went on to become one of the most popular movies in film history.

Mitchell's compelling account of antebellum plantation life and the Civil War gained an international reputation for the author, and also for Atlanta, where the story was largely based.

Yet today, visitors coming to Atlanta expecting to find scenes out of the movie are bound for disappointment. Whatever antebellum homes and buildings Sherman didn't burn eventually succumbed to fast-moving Atlanta's urban renewal binges, now most of the "Capital of the New South" looks just about as classically Southern as Toronto. Nevertheless, those on a dedicated Margaret Mitchell tour of metropolitan Atlanta can hunt down traces of GWTW glory.

999 Peachtree St. The Margaret Mitchell House in midtown Atlanta, affectionately called "the Dump" by its most famous tenant, was where Mitchell composed the opus during a 10-year period. After being abandoned for years, boarded-up, and set ablaze twice, the three-story house has now been meticulously restored with special attention to the tiny Mitchell apartment downstairs. Daily tours start at the visitor center next door. (Mitchell's girlhood home at 1401 Peachtree St. was torn down at her request.)

Forsyth St. at Carnegie Way In the Atlanta Public Library "Peggy" consumed so many books her husband complained in frustration that he couldn't find any she hadn't read, so he bought her a typewriter and challenged her to write her own. Today the library maintains a small collection of mementos (mostly documents) at its central library downtown at (where else?) One Margaret Mitchell Square, first floor.

130 W. Paces Ferry Rd. The Atlanta History Center's **Tullie Smith House,** an 1840s farmhouse, was closer to what Mitchell had in mind for the fictional Tara than the opulent mansion pictured in the movie (which is more like the plantation houses found in Mississippi). Mitchell felt her story was a tale of survival, and disapproved of the way the movie romanticized the Old South. (Catch a behind-the-scenes view of the movie at the Center's exhibit of candid photographs taken on the GWTW set.)

The **Governor's Mansion,** 391 W. Paces Ferry Rd. NW, tel. (404) 261-1776, a Greek Revival house elegantly furnished with Federal-period antiques, opens to the public Tues.-Thurs. 10-11:30 a.m. only. Admission is free.

The **Herndon Home,** 587 University Place NW, tel. (404) 581-9813, showcases the 1910 mansion of Alonzo Herndon—a Georgian born into slavery who later established the first black-owned life insurance company. It's in West End near the Vine St. MARTA station. Hours are Tues.-Sat. 10 a.m.-4 p.m., no charge.

The **Fox Theatre,** 660 Peachtree St. NE, tel. (404) 881-2100, is the city's most potent symbol of historic preservation, as well as its quirkiest architectural landmark. Rescued from Atlanta's rampant urban-renewal binge in the 1970s and '80s by a strong civic campaign to "Save the Fox," the Moorish/art deco fantasia is now the most unusual venue in town. The Atlanta Preservation Center, tel. (404) 876-2041, organizes tours year-round on Monday, Thursday, and Saturday (adults $5, seniors and students $4; also inquire about walking tours around the surrounding neighborhood). Use the North Ave. MARTA station.

The city's most elegant house tour, of the 1920s **Swan House** mansion, is operated by the Atlanta Historical Society; for more information on this and an 1840s farmhouse and slave cabin also on site, see **Atlanta History Center,** above. For Martin Luther King, Jr.'s birth home, see the special topic **King's Legacy.**

Oakland Cemetery

Atlanta's most historic cemetery, on Oakland

659 Peachtree St. The glamorous Georgian Terrace Hotel here was where the movie's white cast members stayed for the film's premiere at Loews Theater. Segregation laws kept African-American cast members from attending the opening or staying at the hotel.

1296 Piedmont Ave. The Della Manta Apartments here (at the corner of S. Prado) was where Mitchell moved after leaving the Dump. (Exterior views only). A plaque at the door commemorates the author, who was named "Georgia's most famous person" by an act of the state legislature in 1985.

Peachtree and 12th Sts. At this intersection three blocks north of Mitchell's home in midtown Atlanta, a drunken off-duty taxi driver struck Margaret Mitchell on August 11, 1949 (the driver was charged with involuntary manslaughter). Mitchell died at Grady Memorial Hospital downtown five days later; her funeral service was held at Patterson's Funeral Home.

248 Oakland Ave. Oakland Cemetery is the eternal resting place of Margaret Mitchell and her husband John Marsh. Her grave is a pilgrimage site for die-hard fans, such as members of the ***Gone with the Wind* Fan Club,** based in South Carolina.

Margaret Mitchell House

Ave. at Memorial Dr., tel. (404) 688-2107, serves as the eternal home of some of the city's most famous residents, including Margaret Mitchell, Confederate Vice President Alexander Stephens, and golfer Bobby Jones, along with mayors and governors and the nameless Unknown Confederate Dead. Gravestones, statuary, and memorials clutter the scenic cemetery on its slight rise in Atlanta's Cabbagetown district, and the ambience is lively enough to attract lunchtime picnickers and joggers. A brochure available at the cemetery office identifies major sites. It's adjacent to the King Memorial MARTA station.

SCHOOLS AND LIBRARIES

Metropolitan Atlanta's 36 colleges and universities stimulate the city's intellectual community and enroll nearly 100,000 students. Many maintain galleries of interest to the public and host such public events as lectures, performances, concerts, and festivals. University Centers and cafeterias can be a networking resource for visiting students—check out bulletin boards and campus newspapers for notices and information. The following lists major campuses only.

Georgia State University

Second largest in the state university system, Georgia State, tel. (404) 651-2000, occupies a 25.5-acre urban campus in the heart of downtown (a block from Underground Atlanta and above the Georgia State MARTA station). GSU's six colleges enroll 32,000 students.

Visitors can find the Welcome Center in **Alumni Hall** and a tribute to native son Johnny Mercer in **Library South** (where a jukebox plays such Mercer classics as "Jeepers Creepers" and "Blues in the Night"). Its **Cinefest Theater** in University Center screens foreign and art films booked nowhere else (for program information, call 404-651-2463); performing arts take place in the restored **Rialto Theater** across Peachtree St.

Georgia Institute of Technology

Grown from its establishment in 1885 to the South's largest center for technological education and research, "Georgia Tech," 225 North Ave. NW, tel. (404) 894-2000, (part of the state university system) enrolls 12,000 students and ranks as one of the top tech schools in the nation. In 1996 it was the home of the Olympic Village, and its new bioengineering and bioscience building establishes the school as a major player in the biotechnology field. Tech's **Bobby Dodd Stadium** is the home of the beloved Georgia Tech Yellow Jackets football team.

Atlanta University Center

Atlanta University Center, tel. (404) 522-8980, is the largest African-American academic center in the country. Now a six-school consortium enrolling a total of 8,000 students, the institution has roots going back to the late 1860s, when a school for former slaves was founded here. The historic campuses of **Clark Atlanta University,** all-male **Morehouse College** and the **Morehouse School of Medicine,** all-female **Spelman College** (richly endowed early on by the Rockefellers, more recently by a $20 million gift from the Cosby family), **Morris Brown College,** and the **Interdenominational Theological Center** establish Atlanta as a hub for the African-American intelligentsia.

The schools host many public events, film showings (which may include the work of alumnus Spike Lee), and African-American art exhibits (see **Arts and Sciences**).

Emory University

Ranked by college presidents as one of the top 25 universities in the nation, Emory University, 1380 S. Oxford Rd., tel. (404) 727-6123, enrolls 9,400 students and occupies a large scenic campus in Druid Hills. Known for its extensive medical center and walloping $105 million Woodruff family (Coca-Cola) endowment, Emory also supports the **Michael C. Carlos Museum** (see **Arts and Sciences,** above). The **Centers for Disease Control and Prevention** occupy a federal enclave within the Emory Campus. The main gate is off N. Decatur Rd. at Oxford Rd.

Libraries

The Central Library of the **Atlanta-Fulton County Library** downtown at 1 Margaret Mitchell Square, tel. (404) 730-1700, maintains special collections on Georgia history, a small *Gone with the Wind* exhibit, and an inexpensive gourmet cafeteria, as well as plenty of local periodicals, community resource boards, and bulletin boards. The modern Auburn Ave. branch houses special African-American collections. There's also a cozy midtown branch, conveniently located along a busy stretch of Peachtree St. near the Arts Center and a branch near East Atlanta Village.

The **Georgia Department of Archives and History,** next to the Capitol, tel. (404) 521-8764, houses state records from 1733 to the present. The **Atlanta Historical Society's** archives are housed in its library at the Atlanta History Center. The **Jimmy Carter Library** at the Carter Center is open by appointment for students and scholars.

TOURING THE CITY

Guided Tours

Expert volunteer docents at the nonprofit **Atlanta Preservation Center,** 156 7th St., tel. (404) 876-2041, lead guided walking tours through 10 historic districts—including the Fox Theater area, downtown, Sweet Auburn, and West End—between March and November. The tours cost $5 adults, $4 seniors, and $3 students (under age four free); call for reservations or call their tour hotline for more information, tel. (404) 876-2040.

Gray Line, tel. (404) 767-0594 or (800) 965-6665, offers bus tours in town and out to Stone Mountain, including a Black Heritage Tour. Two-hour tours cost $20 adults, $18 children, and half-day tours cost $40 adults, $32 children. See their booth next to the visitor center at Underground Atlanta for more information.

For a list of other private tour companies, call the Atlanta Convention and Visitors Bureau at tel. (404) 521-6600.

Scenic Drives

To see classic Southern mansions, ride along **Habersham Road** (from Peachtree Rd. in lower Buckhead, turn west onto Battle Ave., then turn right onto Habersham Road), one of the nicest drives through scenic residential Buckhead. Several other city neighborhoods also make particularly pleasant drives or bike rides, among them midtown's **Ansley Park** (east of Peachtree St. at 15th, around the western perimeter of Piedmont Park) and **Druid Hills,** where the house featured in the locally shot film *Driving Miss Daisy* is typical (turn left off Ponce de Leon Ave. onto Springdale Road).

SPORTS AND RECREATION

SPECTATOR SPORTS

Tickets to major sporting events are available through **Ticketmaster,** tel. (404) 249-6400 or (800) 326-4000 outside Georgia; local Ticketmaster ticket centers include Blockbuster Music, Publix supermarkets, and Tower Records; also see www.ticketmaster.com.

Atlanta Braves Baseball

The Braves are as much of a local legend as Scarlett O'Hara. Owned by CNN's Ted Turner, who can often be seen enthusiastically delivering the "tomahawk chop" with his wife, Jane Fonda, at home games (the gesture has drawn protests from Native Americans), the Braves rose from obscurity to World Series champions in 1995. T-shirts proclaiming the banner headline "From Worst to First" are still proudly worn by loyal fans.

The Braves play at **Turner Field,** 755 Hank Aaron Dr., tel. (404) 522-7630, the state-of-the-art 1996 Olympic stadium with seating for 50,000. The stadium is off Capital Ave., three-quarters of a mile south of the Capitol. The **Ivan Allen Jr. Braves Museum** within, tel. (404) 614-2310, dedicates 4,000-square feet of the complex to a Hall of Fame and collection of baseball memorabilia, including Hank Aaron's 715th home run ball and bat. For schedules and tickets, call tel. (404) 249-6400, Ticketmaster (see above), or see the Braves Clubhouse store at CNN Center. Seats cost $1-25. See also www.atlantabraves.com.

Bus shuttles run between the Five Points MARTA station (Forsyth St. exit) and Turner Field for all stadium events, from 90 minutes before game time until the stadium is empty. It's free with a MARTA transfer or costs $1.50 each way.

Atlanta Falcons Football

Atlanta's professional football team plays in the **Georgia Dome,** tel. (404) 223-8687 (tours). The massive 71,500-seat stadium (future site of the 2000 Super Bowl) is as tall as a 27-story building and covers 8.6 acres. For Falcons ticket information, call (404) 223-8000.

Two MARTA rail stations, Omni and Vine City, serve both ends of the Georgia Dome (buy tokens in advance to avoid long lines). MARTA shuttles are available to outlying parking lots.

Other Professional Sports Franchises

A professional NBA basketball team, the **Atlanta Hawks,** tel. (404) 827-3800, will roost in new $213 million arena scheduled to open next to CNN Center in 1999. The **Atlanta Thrashers** will play ice hockey here.

Collegiate Athletics

For 75 years, the 46,000-seat **Bobby Dodd Stadium** at North Ave. and Techwood Dr., tel. (404) 894-5447, has been home to Georgia Tech's **Yellow Jackets** football team. Many football fans drive an hour east to Athens to watch the statewide mascots, the **Georgia Bulldogs,** play at the University of Georgia; see **Athens** under Central Georgia. The biggest competition in the state is when these two teams face off.

URBAN RECREATION

Favorite Parks

Centennial Olympic Park in the heart of downtown offers a romp through the sprinklers, climbable boulders, shady benches, a playground, and a cafe and visitor center within 21 acres. Many concerts and special events are held at its amphitheater and Great Lawn, as well as more impromptu street music in its plazas.

Midtown's **Piedmont Park,** with its dogwood-rimmed lake, rolling lawns, shady coves, and wooded walkways and paths, is a great place to run, bike, or skate; they also have a swimming pool, tennis courts, playgrounds, and ball fields. Rent skates or bikes (cruisers or 10-speeds) across from the main gate at **Skate Escape,** 1086 Piedmont Ave. NE, tel. (404) 892-1292. The shop is open Mon.-Sat. 10 a.m.-7 p.m., from 11 on Sunday.

The 60-acre **Atlanta Botanical Garden** adjacent to Piedmont Park (see **Sights,** above) offers 15 more acres of nature walks through lovely landscaped gardens and surrounding woods.

Grant Park holds two of Atlanta's most popular attractions, the **Cyclorama** (exhibited here since 1885) and **Zoo Atlanta,** as well as the old Confederate battery site of **Fort Walker.** The rest of the wooded, shaded acreage is devoted to lawns, recreation, and picnic areas.

See **Vicinity of Atlanta** for information on recreational parks beyond the beltway, including the major recreational center at **Stone Mountain Park,** 17 miles east of downtown, as well as less-developed areas in the Chattahoochee River Recreation Area north of downtown and at Sweetwater Creek State Park west of town.

Bicycling

A 15-mile city loop bicycle route east of downtown runs north from Irwin St. along Jackson St., through Piedmont Park and Virginia Highland. Midtown's Piedmont Park has miles of paved bike paths, and the wide streets of the adjacent Ansley Park neighborhood are ideal for bicycling. A bike path runs along the length of Freedom Parkway to eastside neighborhoods.

Request bike-route information from the **Southern Bicycle League** (P.O. Box 1360, Roswell, GA 30077, tel. 770-594-8350), the Georgia Dept. of Tourism (285 Peachtree Center Ave., Atlanta, GA 30303, tel. 404-656-3590), or ask at local bike shops (such as Skate Escape, 1086 Piedmont Ave. NE, tel. 404-892-1292).

Running and Walking

The monolithic **Peachtree Road Race**—considered "the Wimbledon of 10K"—inspires more than 50,000 runners to brave the summer heat every July 4 to run the course up Peachtree Street. It's sponsored by the Atlanta Track Club. If you'd rather just watch, cheering spectators congregate principally at the streetside patio restaurants of lower Buckhead, many of which set up elaborate "pit stops" for the athletes. The race ends up at Piedmont Park, where runners are cooled in huge sprays of water. Souvenir T-shirts for the runners are prized items. Plenty of other five km and 10 km races are held throughout the year; check local papers.

Joggers favor Piedmont Park, and, perhaps strangely, the cobblestone lanes of historic Oakland Cemetery off Memorial Drive. Another surprise to cool-climate folks may be "mall-walking": some Southerners seek out summer exercise in such climate-controlled environments as Lenox Square, either individually or in organized groups, usually when the doors open.

Hiking

For short in-city hikes, head to the 65-acre **Fernbank Forest,** adjacent to the Fernbank Science Centers near Druid Hills. Two miles of paved trails through thick tulip trees, oaks, beeches, and hickory are representative of the local terrain, flora, and fauna. Gates are open Sun.-Fri. 2-5 p.m., Saturday 10 a.m.-5 p.m. Midtown's 15-acre forest at the Atlanta Botanical Garden in Piedmont Park also makes for a nice stroll (see **Sights,** above). For more hiking right outside town, see **Vicinity of Atlanta,** below.

Swimming

The indoor **Martin Luther King Jr. Natatorium,** next to the King Center at 70 Boulevard, tel. (404) 658-7330, is open to the public year-round for $3 adults, $1 children. Seasonal outdoor pools are available at Piedmont Park, tel. (404) 892-0117, and Chastain Park, tel. (404) 255-0863. Most hotels and motels have pools (almost a necessity in summers), except for historic hotels, hostels, and bed and breakfasts. See **Centennial Olympic Park** for a quick way to cool off.

Golf

In Atlanta Memorial Park, the city's public **Bobby Jones Golf Course,** 384 Woodward Way, tel. (404) 355-1009, is named for the native Atlantan who rose to golf greatness. The 18-hole championship course occupies part of the site of the Battle of Peachtree Creek. You'll find many more deluxe courses in the northern suburbs, such as the **City Club** in Marietta, tel. (770) 425-0447, or out at **Stone Mountain Park** (see **Vicinity of Atlanta,** below). Free putting practice is offered downtown inside the Healey Building, 57 Forsyth St., tel. (404) 521-1451.

Recreational Resources

Outdoor-adventure groups, environmental-advocacy organizations, commercial outfitters, and outfitting stores are all great resources for finding out about area recreation. The **Sierra Club,** 1447 Peachtree St. NE, Ste. 305, Atlanta, GA 30309, tel. (404) 607-1262, sponsors a busy calendar of day and overnight adventures in addition to its legislative activism and environmental advocacy. Outings—often in North Georgia—include hiking, backpacking, rafting, fossil hunts, you name it. The preeminent statewide conservation organization, the **Georgia Conservancy,** 1776 Peachtree St. NW, Suite 400 South, Atlanta, GA 30309, tel. (404) 876-2900, produces detailed reference works on Georgia's natural areas and sponsors field trips.

The **REI** store at 1800 N.E. Expressway Access Rd. (I-85 exit 32 northeast of downtown), tel. (404) 633-6508, stocks the largest selection of outfitting gear in the city, rents camping equipment, and maintains a posting board of local events. **Geared to Go,** in lower Buckhead at 420 Armour Dr. off Piedmont Rd., tel. (404) 875-8828, rents backpacking and camping equipment and also organizes excursions; see also www.gearedtogo.com. In Little Five Points, **Outback Outfitters,** 1125 Euclid Ave. NE, tel. (404) 688-4878, sells and repairs bicycles and rents camping equipment.

For more recreation in the metro area, call **Go With the Flow** in Roswell, tel. (770) 992-3200, for canoe and kayak rentals, and **Atlanta Rocks** in Norcross, tel. (770) 242-7625 has indoor rock-climbing.

ENTERTAINMENT

Atlanta has a great range of entertainment to suit many tastes and styles. To find out what's going on, the daily *Atlanta Journal/Constitution* lists events, with a weekend roundup in Friday's edition and in Saturday edition's *Weekend* tabloid.

Creative Loafing, Atlanta's indispensable guide to nightlife, is a free weekly alternative newspaper found throughout town at vending machines. The alternative alternative, *Atlanta Press,* is less widely distributed.

Besides the box offices of the venues listed below, tickets to major events are available through **Ticketmaster,** tel. (404) 249-6400 or (800) 326-4000 outside Georgia. Local Ticketmaster ticket centers include Blockbuster Music, Publix supermarkets, and Tower Records; also see www.ticketmaster.com. **AtlanTix,** tel. (770) 772-5572, operates a half-price day-of-performance ticket booth next to the Visitor Center atop Underground Atlanta.

PERFORMING ARTS

Traditional

The **Woodruff Arts Center** in midtown Atlanta at 1280 Peachtree St., tel. (404) 733-5000, houses the city's premier performing arts organizations and hosts performances in its symphony hall, theaters, and auditoriums. The **Atlanta College of Art** is also located here, and the High Museum of Art is next door. The Center is connected directly to the Arts Center MARTA station via a covered walkway.

The **Atlanta Symphony Orchestra,** tel. (404) 733-4900, performs in Symphony Hall during its Master Season. It also holds a popular summertime concert series outdoors at Chastain Amphitheater. The **Alliance Theater Company,** tel. (404) 733-5000, presents classic and contemporary dramas at the Alliance Theater and also sponsors a children's theater.

The **Atlanta Opera,** tel. (404) 817-8700, performs at the historic **Fox Theatre,** 660 Peachtree St., tel. (404) 881-2100. Broadway shows are among the varied performances also held here, as well as at **Civic Center Auditorium,** 395 Piedmont Ave., tel. (404) 523-6275.

The 60-year-old **Atlanta Ballet,** tel. (404) 873-5811, the nation's oldest continuously performing regional ballet company, operates from studios on Spring St. near the Arts Center and performs at the Fox Theatre.

The **Center for Puppetry Arts,** 1404 Spring St. at 18th, tel. (404) 873-3391; entertains adults as well as children with its well-produced performances.

Experimental/Alternative Theater

Smaller scale, experimental, political, and original local theatrical productions can be found in midtown at the three-stage **Academy Theater,** 501 Means St., tel. (404) 525-4111, and in Little Five Points at **Seven Stages Theater,** 1105 Euclid Ave., tel. (404) 522-0911.

Among the most avant-garde venues, **Actors Express,** 887 W. Marietta St., tel. (404) 875-1606, is within the recycled King Plow Arts Center, and **Dad's Garage Theater Company,** 280 Elizabeth St., tel. (404) 523-3141, hosts an eclectic selection of comedy, bands, and underground performances; see www.dadsgarage.com.

NIGHTLIFE

Atlanta not only attracts national musical acts, it *creates* many of them; the city's musical reputation (and that of the outpost town of Athens) has grown along with the celebrity of such Georgia groups as Arrested Development, R.E.M., B-52s, Indigo Girls, and the late Tupac Shakur—not to mention the Georgia-grown classics: the Allman Brothers, James Brown, Ray Charles, Otis Redding, Little Richard, and Gladys Knight, to name a few.

Many of the city's nightspots host live music seven nights a week. A selective, highly subjective list follows. (Also see **Districts and Neighborhoods,** earlier in this chapter, for neighborhood bars, and **Accommodations and Food,** below, for late-night coffeehouses.)

Downtown and Vicinity

In Underground Atlanta, **Kenny's Alley** is what they call the back plaza where a handful of lively saloons feature live music, mostly rock and jazz for a fairly mainstream, after-work or convention crowd. Special events bring street parties.

The **Tabernacle,** 152 Luckie St., tel. (404) 659-9022, hosts such national acts as Big Bad Voodoo Daddy, Burning Spear, and RuPaul along with such musical happenings as an Ethiopian Music Festival or the Funk Jazz Kafe—all within a former Baptist church in the Fairlie-Poplar district. It's hard to catch—only open about once a week—but worth seeking out.

Out towards Grant Park, **Daddy D's,** 264 Memorial Dr., tel. (404) 222-0206, is an old barbecue joint where young white hipsters mingle with the local African-American crowd for live blues out on the patio on weekend nights. In the double-wide trailer a block farther east, **Dottie's,** Memorial Dr., tel. (404) 523-3444, is a rough redneck underground bar that's been adopted by a slumming salaried crowd with punk sensibilities. The entertainment takes it to the edge: films with graphic violence, the odd percussionist Typewriter Tim who performs with a children's typewriter. We wouldn't go twice if it weren't for the trash-talking women bartenders.

Midtown and Vicinity

Masquerade, 695 North Ave. NE, tel. (404) 577-2007, Atlanta's biggest dance club, hosts the likes of the Genitorturers, Girls Against Boys, the New Morty Show, and Liquid Soul in its three-story ("Heaven, Hell, and Purgatory") club. Special DJ'ed nights include '80s retro, techno, Sunday swing, and Dance-in-Foam Night ($2 off with scuba gear). The crowd varies with the band or event, but it's predominantly a young, white, hetero crowd. See also www.masq.com.

Backstreet Atlanta, 845 Peachtree St., tel. (404) 873-1986, is Atlanta's most popular gay dance club, with drag shows, disco music, and mixed crowds. **Blake's,** 227 10th St. NE, tel. (404) 892-5786, is a comfortable neighborhood tavern catering predominantly to gay men. **The Otherside,** 1924 Piedmont Rd., tel. (404) 875-5238, is the city's most notorious lesbian bar with DJ'ed dance music most nights and live music on weekends.

The **Yin Yang Cafe,** 64 3rd St., tel. (404) 607-0682, hosts acid jazz on Saturdays and Sundays in its back alley shack off Spring St. towards the freeway (reservations recommended). **Under-the-Couch** on the Georgia Tech campus attracts a young punk crowd for hardcore garage music and the like (there's always a loyal punk following at GA Tech).

Northside Tavern, 1058 Howell Mill Rd., tel. (404) 874-8745, is a classic blues dive in the middle of nowhere around a mile and a half west of Midtown along 10th, then right (north) on Howell Mill Rd. till you hear the lowdown blues. The **Somber Reptile,** 842 Marietta St., tel. (404) 881-9701, features cutting-edge rock in a graffiti-strewn industrial zone.

Buckhead

Visitors downtown might hear that Buckhead is the city's premier entertainment district. While it does have a tremendous number of bars and clubs, it is perhaps the most overrated district in town when you add up the crowds (traffic congestion), clientele (relatively conventional), and cost ($$$).

The **Roxy,** in the Village at 3110 Roswell Rd., tel. (404) 233-7699, is one of the largest venues and hosts a variety of larger-draw events; the CD release party of the local Cigar Store Indians was there on a recent visit. Nearby, **CJ's Landing,** 270 Buckhead Ave., tel. (404) 237-7657, offers a laid-back scene, with live music and a great balmy-night patio.

Fat Matt's Rib Shack, 1811 Piedmont Rd. NE, tel. (404) 607-1622, out in a far corner of the district, hosts no-frills blues, roots music, and finger-lickin' barbecue in a converted doughnut shop.

Virginia Highland

Blind Willie's, 848 N. Highland Ave., tel. (404) 873-BLUE (404-873-2583), Atlanta's most venerable blues club, serves as an excellent introduction to local nightlife. Even on weekday nights, a wonderfully mixed crowd—bikers, suits, students, suburbanites, barflies in dark sunglasses, couples, singles, groups—pack the tiny club to hear rocking Chicago-style blues.

A few doors down is **Atkins Park,** a great bar that draws a mostly young, white, hetero crowd.

Parking is tight on Highland but available on neighboring residential streets, and it's a short cab ride from downtown.

Little Five Points

L5P offers a great variety of live entertainment in a compact area, including theatrical performances at Seven Stages Theater (see **Performing Arts,** above). The **Variety Playhouse,** 1099 Euclid Ave., tel. (404) 521-1786 is the largest venue, and books such national acts as Southern Culture on the Skids and the David Grisman Quartet, along with jazz, rock, country, even Celtic music.

Find roots music at **Star Community Bar,** 437 Moreland Ave., tel. (404) 681-9018, which features such acts as Eugene Swank and the Atomic Honky Tonk, Drive-by Truckers, and Slim Chance and the Convicts in a casual downhome bar. Ask about the Elvis shrine, and watch for special tributes around the King's birthday in January and deathday in August. The small lounge downstairs is a cool stop for cocktails and swing hits on the jukebox.

The Point, 420 Moreland Ave., tel. (404) 659-3522, hosts many underground rock bands among its eclectic lineup, its beat clientele shoots pool out back, where there are also dark booths for conversation. Look for the League of Decency.

Decatur

The city of Decatur, east of Atlanta (10 minutes by train) has two great venues for live music. **Eddie's Attic,** 515 N. McDonough St. on the Square above the Decatur MARTA station, tel. (404) 377-4976, serves as metro Atlanta's acoustic central, and its spacious second-story club draws a laid-back crowd for all variations on folky music. The **Freight Room,** in a converted depot at the tracks around a half mile south on E. Trinity Pl. from the MARTA station, tel. (404) 378-5365, is the metro region's premier bluegrass music venue (look for Undergrass Blueground). Students from Agnes Scott College—an all-women school with a visible gay community—frequent both places, which attract a largely white, low-key suburban crowd. **Twains** is a nice bar and pool hall on E. Trinity Pl. near the Freight Room.

Outdoor Concerts

For outdoor performances, spectators pack elaborate picnics to accompany classical or popular music concerts at the 5,800-seat **Chastain Park** amphitheater, 135 W. Wieuca Rd. in Buckhead; bring candles to light at sundown.

Major concerts like the Lillith Fair are booked at the **Coca-Cola Lakewood Amphitheater,** off I-75/85 south of downtown, tel. (404) 627-9704. which seats 18,000 (additional spectators stake a claim on the lawn). Food and drink are sold inside; you can't take any in with you. Also here is a popular Sunday flea market.

Cinema

Georgia State University's **Cinefest Theater** in University Center downtown at 66 Courtland St., tel. (404) 651-2463, screens art films and old classics seen nowhere else. The film series at the **High Museum** (see **Sights**) shows more unusual selections, often scheduled to coincide with exhibits or lectures by directors and such.

Easily accessible multiscreen cinemas include the six-plexes at **CNN Center** (tel. 404-827-4000) and **Lenox Square** (tel. 404-233-0338. Discount theaters include **Buckhead Backlot Cinema & Cafe,** 3340 Peachtree Rd., tel. (404) 816-4262, and the **Plaza Theater,** 1049 Ponce de Leon Ave, tel. (404) 873-1939.

SHOPPING

Atlanta is the Hong Kong of the Southeastern U.S.—where people come to shop at exclusive department stores found nowhere else in the region. According to the local tourist bureau, Atlanta has more shopping center space per capita than any other city besides Chicago. But metro Atlanta's 53 malls are more than shopping emporiums: as clean, secure, climate-controlled environments, they have nearly replaced town centers, and nowadays people meet at the mall

ATLANTA FESTIVALS AND EVENTS

Some of the South's most entertaining spectacles can be experienced through local festivals, which are usually multifaceted affairs with plenty of local music, arts and crafts, parades, and local food and drink that bring out local character and community spirit. Spring and fall weekends are particularly packed with events. Note that as the city grows to use its new Centennial Olympic Park more fully, events that have been established elsewhere may move here.

January

King Week, the second week of the month, starts 10 days of cultural arts, entertainment, and action centering around the national holiday named for Martin Luther King, Jr.'s birthday on January 15. Speeches and interfaith services by Coretta Scott King and local religious leaders kick off the event; call the King Center at (404) 524-1956.

The Olde Christmas Storytelling Festival, scenically set at the Gothic Tudor-style Callanwolde mansion, brings the Southern Order of Storytellers out to celebrate the Christmas season, which traditionally began (not ended!) on Christmas Day. Dates depend on where the Twelve Days of Christmas fall; call (404) 872-5338.

February

The **Atlanta Storytelling Festival,** at the Atlanta History Center, brings folk tales, myths, and legends from around the world to life in this multicultural event, which also features jugglers, balladeers, and an evening concert.

The **Atlanta Flower Show,** a four-day event in February or March, previews the Southeast's spectacular spring blooming season through displayed gardens, landscapes, and an elegant opening gala benefiting the Atlanta Botanical Garden; call (404) 220-2209.

The **Hispanic Festival of Music and the Arts,** a new event reflecting Atlanta's growing Latin community, brings international guest musicians and cultural arts performances; call (404) 938-8611.

Mardi Gras merrymakers ramble through downtown in costumes, floats, and bands, ending up at Underground Atlanta; call (404) 392-1272.

March

The **Antebellum Jubilee** at Stone Mountain Park presents period costumes, arts and crafts, early folk music, open-hearth cooking, and a Civil War Camp for two weekends in March and April, call (770) 498-5702.

The **St. Patrick's Day Parade,** with century-old roots reaching back to early Irish Catholic settlers, marches thousands down Peachtree St. to festivities at Underground Atlanta with the usual revelry of bagpipes, politicians in convertibles, floats, and high school bands; spectators number 150,000. The party continues at Virginia Highland's Irish pub, **Limerick Junction,** and the **Fado's Irish Pub** in Buckhead.

April

The **Atlanta Dogwood Festival,** a major weeklong rite of spring for Atlanta, brings art and music to various city venues before culminating in weekend festivities at Piedmont Park. The mid-month event features art shows, favorite local bands, steaming-food booths, historic house tours, children's activities, hot-air balloons, and much more. Check the papers for full listings of events.

Easter Sunrise Services at Stone Mountain take place at its base or summit at dawn (the skylift starts running at 4:30 a.m., or climb the 1.3-mile trail to the top); later the park fills with family reunions celebrating the holiday at this traditional site.

Sweet Auburn Festival celebrates the revival of this African-American historical neighborhood with heritage tours, parades, ethnic foods, lively jazz, rhythm and blues, and gospel music; call the Sweet Auburn Merchants and Professional District Association at (404) 577-0625.

A Taste of Atlanta can be sampled at this annual cook-off by renowned local chefs. The three-day event attracts 50,000 hungry Atlantans to the award-winning cuisine, as well as side orders of entertainment, children's activities, and fireworks. It has been held at CNN Center; call the sponsoring Kidney Foundation at (404) 248-1315 for current venue.

The **Inman Park Festival** highlights Southern historical architecture and design with a tour of Victorian homes through this late-19th-century neighborhood. The streets are blocked off to cars and the pedestrian market fills with food, music, and craft stalls; call (404) 242-4895.

continues on next page

ATLANTA FESTIVALS AND EVENTS

continued

May

Kingfest, at the King Center all summer long, devotes performances every other Saturday to different musical genres (from gospel to zydeco), including special days for kids and international performances; call (404) 524-1956.

Springfest at Stone Mountain Park, where barbecue chefs compete in a massive "grill-off," celebrates the season in early May with live entertainment, arts and crafts, and plenty of barbecue; a rodeo follows in mid-May, call (404) 498-5702.

The Atlanta Film and Video Festival screens hundreds of entries from across the nation during a five-day period at the city's premier film and video center, Image; call (404) 352-4225.

The **Atlanta Jazz Festival,** reportedly the largest free jazz festival in the country, features eight days of free outdoor concerts around town, including a brown bag series in Woodruff Park.

June

The **Arts Festival of Atlanta,** one of the largest and oldest arts fests in the country, has for the last 40 years attracted huge crowds to view paintings, prints, ceramics, jewelry, and textile arts. Its location changed from Piedmont Park to Olympic Centennial Park for 1998; check for current location.

The three-day **Gay Pride Festival,** timed to coincide with the anniversary of the Stonewall riots, brought tens of thousands of participants to Piedmont Park each day for its 28th annual event in 1998; it culminates with a gay pride parade.

The **Georgia Shakespeare Festival** at Oglethorpe University stages three different Shakespearean classics under a giant open-air tent; spectators come early with picnics to enjoy the dulcimer-studded pre-performance entertainment.

July

On **July 4,** 50,000 runners race down Peachtree St. from Lennox Square to Piedmont Park in the annual 10K **Peachtree Road Race**—called the "Wimbeldon of 10K." An Independence Day **parade** courses through downtown Atlanta, reportedly the largest regularly scheduled Fourth of July parade in the country with 250,000 spectators. Nighttime fireworks explode over Stone Mountain and also above Lenox Square (largest fireworks display in the Southeast). The Symphony performs at Centennial Olympic Park.

The **Civil War Encampment** at the Atlanta History Center re-creates battlefield life with more than 100 Confederate and Union living history interpreters eager to share historical stories and anecdotes.

August

The **National Black Arts Festival,** the country's premier African-American cultural arts program, showcases dance, theater, various types of music (sacred steel drums, Mississippi blues, and gospel, to name a few), folklore, visual arts, and Afrocentric heritage programs in various venues for 10 days in even-numbered years.

September

The **Folklife Festival** at the Atlanta History Center re-creates daily life circa 1840 on the Tullie Smith farm by presenting traditional crafts (such as weaving, candlemaking, and soap making), costumed historians, and farm animals; call (404) 261-1837.

Around Labor Day, the **Montreaux Music Festival** brings eight days of free jazz, blues, gospel, pop, reggae, R&B, and more to outdoor stages

October

The **Scottish Games and Highland Gathering** at Stone Mountain brings kilted clans, pipe bands, folk dancing, and Scottish pageantry to this three-day event.

November

The **Veterans Day Parade** on November 11 or thereabouts runs south along the downtown strip of Peachtree, from West Peachtree to Woodruff Park.

Heaven Bound, a 60-year holiday tradition of Auburn Ave.'s Big Bethel AME Church is a religious musical pageant that presents medieval allegorical theater the first weekend of the month; call (404) 659-0248.

December

Country Christmas, sponsored by the Atlanta Botanical Garden on the first Sunday of the month, showcases natural decorations with wreath-making and popcorn-stringing activities, and features strolling mimes, carolers, bell ringers, and chestnuts roasting on an open fire (oh, a tree too); call (404) 876-5858.

Christmas at Callanwolde transforms the Gothic Tudor mansion to a yuletime fantasyland of interior design for the first two weeks of the month, accompanied by the sounds of choral groups and more bell ringers; call (404) 872-5338.

The **Candlelight Tour of Historic Homes** at the Atlanta History Center fashions period holiday celebrations at its 1920 Swan House mansion and a contrasting 19th-century country Christmas at the Tullie Smith farmhouse two evenings in early December; call (404) 261-1837.

The **Festival of Trees,** having expanded into the World Congress Center, has grown in popularity as visitors flock to the artfully decorated trees and holiday activities, a 10-day fundraising event for Emory University's Children's Hospital starting the first Saturday in December; call (404) 264-9348.

New Year's Eve at Underground Atlanta brings thousands of revelers out to watch the "Giant Peach" at midnight, while crowds dance in the streets.

to stroll (walking clubs meet in early mornings), eat (not just at food courts—malls have some great restaurants, too), and see films and performances, as well as shop.

What follows is a summary of the larger centers; see **Districts and Neighborhoods** earlier in this chapter for more specialty stores and funkier shopping districts.

Major Shopping Centers

Underground Atlanta, with its authentic historical setting, rates the highest marks for its unique design; it's full of local crafts (including Afrocentric wares) as well as national brand-names. It's where people might impulsively buy that book they've been wanting or a little something from Victoria's Secret—ambitious shoppers go elsewhere. Farther north up Peachtree St., the upscale **Macy's** department store anchors the central downtown shopping strip between Ellis and Harris.

Buckhead is the most exclusive shopping district, from unusual boutiques and galleries in its Village to huge malls at its perimeter. **Lenox Square,** anchored by Macy's and Neiman-Marcus, is the largest shopping mall in the Southeast (1.5 million square feet), with plenty of places to eat under its skylit atrium, cinemas, and even its own MARTA station. Across Peachtree St. from Lenox, the elite **Phipps Plaza** has the exclusive Lord & Taylor and Saks Fifth Avenue department stores.

(Another Lord & Taylor and the region's first Nordstrom are expected to open in 1999 in the **Mall of Georgia** currently under construction around 30 miles north of town at the I-85/I-985 split, which is due to surpass even Lenox Square in size. Freeway corridors in the northern suburbs are practically lined with retail.)

Bookstores

Two large national chain bookstores can be found in Buckhead: **Barnes & Noble,** 2900 Peachtree St., tel. (404) 261-7747, and **Borders Books and Music,** 3637 Peachtree Rd. NE, tel. (404) 237-0707. Each has a wide selection of periodicals and books (including local interest and Southern authors) and an adjacent cafe and author readings.

In Midtown, **Outwrite Bookstore,** 991 Piedmont Ave., tel. (404) 607-0082, declares itself Atlanta's "Gay and Lesbian Bookstore and Coffeehouse."

In Little Five Points, **A Capella Books,** 1133 Euclid Ave. NE, tel. (404) 681-5128, offers a great selection of inexpensive used books (particularly pertaining to counterculture), along with rare editions. **Charis Books and More,** 1189 Euclid Ave NE, tel. (404) 524-0304, is Atlanta's feminist bookstore that also serves as a local resource for women and lesbians; they have a thoughtful children's book selection too.

In West End, the **Shrine of the Black Madonna,** 946 Ralph D. Abernathy Dr., tel. (404) 752-6125 offers an Afrocentric collection of books, along with crafts and an "African Holocaust" exhibit.

ACCOMMODATIONS AND FOOD

The 449 hotels in the nine-county Atlanta area offer a combined total of 66,906 rooms. Downtown alone has more than 10,000 hotel rooms, most in the central hotel district around Peachtree Center—within walking distance of major convention and event facilities at the World Congress Center, Georgia Dome, and the new arena. Deluxe hotels are typically towering skyscrapers, and budget hotels are nearly all standard chains (most all have at least seasonal pools, exceptions noted). Every familiar hotel chain is represented at least once (many midrange chains have multiple locations and also offer deluxe and budget versions of themselves along with the original). Only a few select inns offer a historic ambience (see **Midtown** and **Buckhead),** and hostels serve low-budget travelers (see **Midtown** and **Decatur**).

The main hotel zone downtown, midtown hotels, and pricey Buckhead hotels are all easily accessible to MARTA light-rail, which connects directly to the airport. The subjective selections below emphasize centrally located properties near sights and services and within walking distance of MARTA stations. Major hotels offer shuttles to the airport or to the local MARTA station (or both).

DOWNTOWN LODGING

There are no strict budget accommodations in the downtown hotel zone. The lowest standard midweek rate starts at around $70, though prices fall may substantially on weekends (by as much as a third at higher-priced hotels). Inquire about special package rates and discounts for seniors, military, auto club members, or any other group or affiliation—prices are based on availability and it can't hurt to negotiate. Note that overnight parking downtown can easily add $15 a night to your hotel bill.

Moderate-to-Expensive

The **Quality Hotel,** 89 Luckie St., tel. (404) 524-7991 or (800) 228-5151, and **Comfort Inn,** 101 International Blvd., tel. (404) 524-5555 or (800) 535-0707, are both centrally located in the Fairlie-Poplar district, a more interesting place to walk around than the convention zone around Peachtree Center, particularly at night and on the weekends. They both start at $79 s.

TraveLodge, 311 Courtland St. NE, tel. (404) 659-4545 or (800) 578-7878, is a three-story road motel with a pool at a nondescript corner of the convention hotel district near the freeway (from $81 s with a continental breakfast and free parking).

The **Days Inn Downtown,** 300 Spring St.; tel. (404) 523-1144 or (800) 325-2525; maintains a nice 10-story building across from the Apparel Mart; it's a short walk to Peachtree Center or Fairlie-Poplar (from $89 s or d).

Premium-to-Luxury

The downtown hotel district specializes in "megahotels" catering to the business and convention trade—gleaming luxury skyscrapers towering over cavernous atrium-like lobbies with exotic foliage and glass elevators soaring to the top inside and out. Standard weekday rates start at more than $100. The 73-story **Westin Peachtree Plaza,** 210 Peachtree St. NW; tel. (404) 659-1400 or (800) 228-3000, is the tallest hotel in the Western Hemisphere (an outside elevator leads to a revolving restaurant with a panoramic view). With 1,671 rooms, the 47-story **Marriott Marquis,** 265 Peachtree Ctr. Ave., tel. (404) 521-0000 or (800) 228-9290, qualifies as the largest hotel in the Southeast; it's also among Atlanta's newest. Also in the Peachtree Center zone is the 29-story **Atlanta Hilton,** 255 Courtland St. NE, tel. (404) 659-2000 or (800) 445-8667. The granddaddy of this breed is the **Hyatt Regency,** 265 Peachtree St. NE, tel. (404) 577-1234 or (800) 233-1234, which was the first to introduce the atrium concept that revolutionized luxury hotel design (a tiny counter cafe here with Internet access is open around the clock).

The 15-story **Omni Hotel;** 100 CNN Ctr., tel. (404) 659-0000 or (800) 843-6664, is adjacent to CNN Center and across from Centennial Olympic Park, the World Congress Center, the new arena, and the Georgia Dome. With a small retail mall and restaurants at its base, a conventioneer's whole trip to Atlanta could be confined to a half-block radius (from $160).

The 27-story **Ritz-Carlton Atlanta;** 131 Peachtree St. NE, tel. (404) 659-0400 or (800) 241-3333, offers a refined luxury hotel with more classic style, including impeccable service and one of the city's most outstanding restaurants (from $185, no pool).

At the 16-story **Suite Hotel,** 54 Peachtree St. NE; tel. (404) 223-5555 or (800) 477-5549; a tasteful Old World design meshes nicely with its location in historical Underground Atlanta. Well-appointed modern suites cost from $135 weekdays, and can drop to $89 on weekends (no pool).

MIDTOWN

Budget

Hostelling International Atlanta hostel, 229 Ponce de Leon Ave., Atlanta, GA 30308, tel. (404) 875-9449, fax (404) 870-0042, occupies a sagging but comfortable three-story Victorian house with 75 dormitory beds and some private rooms. It is open only to travelers carrying a foreign passport or valid student I.D. It costs $13.40 a night for members, nonmembers an additional $3 to join; reservations are advisable. It's four blocks east of the North Ave. MARTA station; inquire about shuttles. The hostel closes noon-5 p.m. The office is in the back of the inn next door. E-mail them at rsvp@mindspring.com; see also www.hiayh.org.

Moderate

The **Days Inn Peachtree,** 683 Peachtree St. NE, tel. (404) 874-9200 or (800) 325-2525, has a wonderful location in the historic neighborhood (and even sports a historic facade). It's right near the Fox Theatre with several restaurants and MARTA within easy walking distance (from $63 with continental breakfast plus $6 parking, no pool).

The **Best Western Granada Suite Hotel,** 1302 W. Peachtree St. NW; tel. (404) 876-6100 or (800) 548-5631, a restored art deco court hotel of Spanish-style adobe with a red-tiled roof, has three floors of guest rooms facing an interior plaza and fountain. With easy freeway access it's centrally located for drivers. Even though the Arts Center and MARTA are only blocks away, the hotel is not really in a pedestrian area, so the hotel offers free shuttle service within a three-mile radius. Rates start at $79 including continental breakfast and free cocktail hour (add $8 for parking, no pool).

For bed and breakfast lodging from $89, **Woodruff Bed and Breakfast Inn,** 223 Ponce de Leon Ave., tel. (404) 875-9449, occupies a three-story 1915 Victorian at the edge of a walkable area near the Fox Theatre and several restaurants (the hostel is next door). All 10 guest rooms have private baths. In a better location, **Shellmont,** 821 Piedmont Ave. NE, tel. (404) 872-9290, occupies an 1891 house in a residential district a few blocks from the heart of Midtown's gay commercial district. Eight guest rooms with private baths are furnished with antiques.

Expensive

The **Ansley Inn,** 253 15th St.; tel. (404) 872-9000, luxuriously set in a Tudor mansion surrounded by landscaped lawns in a peaceful residential neighborhood, offers pristine and businesslike lodging with all the corporate amenities, but leisure travelers would be equally comfortable here. They have 22 rooms; rates start at $95. They also rent out a two-bedroom cottage down a gravel path.

BUCKHEAD

Inexpensive

Cheshire Motor Inn, 1865 Cheshire Bridge Rd. NE, tel. (404) 872-9628 or (800) 827-9628, is a great low-end option at the eastern fringe of what might be considered Buckhead. Convenient for drivers, it's 1.3 miles south of I-85 and right next to the Colonnade Restaurant, but the surrounding area is largely a neglected stretch of strip bars and thrift shops. Singles start at $40 in the older nine-unit building with tiny rooms, the more modern annexes run $58 s and $65 d (no pool).

Moderate-to-Expensive

Sheraton Four Points Atlanta Buckhead, 3387 Lenox Rd. NE, tel. (404) 261-5500 or (800) 241-0200, across from Lenox Square mall and a half block from MARTA, has taken over an older motel with 180 rooms (rates currently from $79; expect remodel and price hike).

The three-story 1920s **Beverly Hills Inn,** 65 Sheridan Dr. NE, tel. (404) 233-8520 or (800) 331-8520, a charming retreat, offers 18 rooms with period furnishings secluded in a quiet residential niche a few minutes' drive from the village and major Buckhead attractions (from $99, no pool).

Luxury

The 22-story metallic **Swissotel,** 3391 Peachtree Rd. NE, tel. (404) 365-0065, across from Lenox Square, brings modern European design and service to Atlanta (from $149).

The **Ritz-Carlton Buckhead,** 3434 Peachtree Rd. NE, tel. (404) 237-2700, the 22-story flagship hotel of the international luxury hotel chain headquartered here in Atlanta, offers gracious service, Old World interior design, and what's been called the finest restaurant in Atlanta. It's across from Lenox Square and Phipps Plaza shops (from $165).

The twin Georgian towers of the phenomenal **Grand Hyatt Atlanta,** 3300 Peachtree Rd., tel. (404) 365-8100 or (800) 233-1234, retains 25 stories of art and antiques, all corporate amenities, and a restaurant overlooking Japanese gardens, on 40 acres of manicured lawns (from $215).

OUTLYING AREAS

Airport

Budget choices from $30 in College Park (within striking distance of the MARTA airport terminus) include **Days Inn Airport West,** 4979 Old National Hwy., tel. (404) 669-8616 or (800) 342-3297, and **Red Roof Inn Airport,** 2471 Old National Hwy., tel. (404) 761-9701 or (800) 843-7663.

The luxurious **Renaissance Atlanta Hotel,** 1 Hartsfield Centre Pkwy., tel. (404) 209-9999 or (800) 468-3571, brings luxurious mega-hotel accommodations to a convenient location within the airport (from $165).

Decatur

The **Atlanta Dream Hostel,** 222 E. Howard Ave., tel. (404) 875-2882, offers a funky, casual stay in an adapted industrial building at the railroad tracks across from Agnes Scott College. A dorm bed, with access to kitchen and common areas, runs around $10 per night, no curfew. Inquire about transportation from the Decatur MARTA station.

The five-story **Holiday Inn Decatur,** 130 Clairmont Rd., tel. (770) 371-0204, is a nice option for Atlanta travelers who prefer a small town environment; it's within walking distance of MARTA and only a 10-minute train ride to downtown Atlanta (from $99).

Bargain Motels Elsewhere

Drivers have hundreds of low-priced modern motels to choose from at interstate exits away from downtown. To find the lowest of the low, cruise the pre-interstate highways within the perimeter—the northwestern Cobb Highway and the northeastern Buford Highway are lined with bottom-dollar road motels.

Camping

Atlanta proper offers no campgrounds, but several are scattered within the metro region. The closest is 10 miles west in Austell, next to the Six Flags Over Georgia amusement park—see **Vicinity of Atlanta** for more information on this and other campgrounds within a 20-mile radius, including campgrounds to the east at Stone Mountain, and to the northwest at Kennesaw Mountain.

FOOD AND DRINK

Atlanta has many wonderful restaurants offering a wide variety of cosmopolitan choices from exotic ethnic specialties to haute continental cuisine—the greatest variety in the state, and arguably the region—in settings from down-home to swank. Because of the number of vegetarians in town, many restaurants offer at least a couple of meatless entrees (and a "vegetable plate" remains a Southern standard).

The following selection emphasizes dependable local places travelers might be less likely to stumble upon independently (we're presuming you can find your way to revolving restaurants, Benihana, or dinner at the Ritz without our help), including several impressive new contenders on Atlanta's culinary scene.

KAP STANN

Cafes and restaurants merge into a collective patio cafe in the Virginia Highland neighborhood.

Southern

Particularly if your trip to the South is limited to Atlanta, be sure to sample Southern cooking at some of the city's most legendary institutions. Southern food comes plentiful, cheap, and accompanied by a bottomless glass of iced tea (some places serve no alcohol). On Sunday, many places serve a generous brunch buffet or midday dinner; meal times may change accordingly.

Downtown, **Thelma's Kitchen,** 768 Marietta St., tel. (404) 688-5855, dishes up full Southern breakfasts and plate lunch specials (such as fried chicken with mashed potatoes, okra cakes, and sweet peas) in a fairly bland storefront—their original cinderblock eatery was destroyed to make way for Centennial Olympic Park, and the new place doesn't quite have the old feel—but the food and clientele is as dependable as always (they say Ted Turner remains a loyal customer). It's open Mon.-Fri. 7:30 a.m.-4:30 p.m. and Saturday 7:30 a.m.-2:30 p.m. East towards Grant Park, **Daddy D's Bar-B-Que Joynt,** 264 Memorial Dr., tel. (404) 222-0206, serves "ba-a-d-to-the-bone" smoked spare ribs (half-slab $10), red beans and rice, and 'Que Wraps (like a deep-fried pork bun, $2.50 a half-dozen).

In Midtown, **Mary Mac's Tea Room,** 228 Ponce de Leon Ave. NE, tel. (404) 876-6604, cooks up such Southern classics as catfish, fried chicken, hush puppies, collard greens, apple brown betty, and banana pudding—a new menu every day. This Atlanta institution, set off in a clapboard storefront a shady stretch from Peachtree St., serves lunch and dinner to suited professionals, camera-swingin' tourists, white-gloved matrons, grunge hostelers, and anyone else with an appetite. It's open Mon.-Fri. 11 a.m.-4 p.m. and 5-8 p.m.

West of Midtown, **Silver Skillet,** 200 14th St. NW, tel. (404) 874-1388, is an old-fashioned coffee shop where the beehive hairdos are the same vintage as the formica counter, it's always packed for breakfast standards and lunch specials daily (Tuesday is pot roast day, $6). Between Midtown and Virginia Highland, **Silver Grill,** 900 Monroe Dr. NE, tel. (404) 876-8145, serves breakfast and meat-and-three plates with bread and tea for $6.75 from its small cottage near 10th St. (open weekdays only).

East of Buckhead, the **Colonnade,** 1879 Cheshire Bridge Rd. at Piedmont Rd., tel. (404) 874-5642, still dishes up such Southern classics as mountain trout, baked ham, and famous yeast rolls, as it has here since the 1940s. It's open for lunch and dinner Mon.-Wed. 11 a.m.-2:30 p.m. and 5-9 p.m., Thurs.-Sat. 11 a.m.-2:30 p.m. and 5-10 p.m., and for dinner Sunday 11 a.m.-9 p.m. (Find it 1.3 miles south of I-85.) On the same funky edge of town, **Fat Matt's Rib Shack,** 1811 Piedmont, tel. (404) 607-1622, barbecues pork ribs or chicken with traditional sides of slaw and beans, and roasts peanuts to snack on while blues bands heat the joint up at night. It's open Mon.-Thurs. 11:30 a.m.-11:30 p.m., Fri.-Sat. 11:30 a.m.-12:30 a.m., Sunday 2-11:30 p.m.

In West End, **Pashal's,** 830 Martin Luther King, Jr. Dr., tel. (404) 577-3150, a civil rights landmark, has fed its famous smothered chicken to generations of AUC students, city leaders, and loyal locals. Across the street, **Aleck's Barbecue Heaven,** 783 Martin Luther King, Jr. Dr., tel. (404) 525-2062, cooks up great ribs and a terrific side of Brunswick stew—a gumbo-like mix of chicken, meat, and vegetables—as it has since it opened in 1942 (they say Dr. King was a regular). It's open weekdays 10 a.m.-11 p.m., Fri.-Sat. until 2 a.m., Sunday noon-8 p.m.

In Sweet Auburn, **Beautiful Restaurant,** 397 Auburn Ave., tel. (404) 223-0080, serves hearty meat-and-three Southern plates for $4; banana pudding is the house specialty. It's open daily 7 a.m.-8:30 pm. **Thelma's Rib Shack,** 302 Auburn Ave., tel. (404) 523-0081, is a great barbecue dive next to the freeway a few blocks west of the King Center (follow your nose). It's open for lunch and dinner (closed Sunday and Monday).

On the east side in Inman Park, **Son's Place,** 1029 Edgewood Ave., tel. (404) 525-3415, (named for the son of Deacon Burton, who ran a legendary restaurant here until his death in 1993) serves a soulful selection of Southern specialties for breakfast and lunch Mon.-Fri. 4 a.m.-4 p.m. It's across from the Inman Park MARTA station.

In Little Five Points, **Baker's Cajun Cafe,** 1126 Euclid Ave., tel. (404) 223-5039, brings a taste of the Big Easy to the Big Peach with their muffalettas and frittatas.

American Standards

Buckhead has some of the best high-end American steakhouses in the country: **Bone's,** 3130 Piedmont Rd. at Peachtree, tel. (404) 237-2663, and **Chops,** 70 W. Paces Ferry Rd. at Peachtree Rd., tel. (404) 262-2675. They're "power-lunch" affairs, serving whole sides of meat to robust executives with silk ties slung over their shoulders. With all those expense accounts, naturally they're expensive (more than $50 for dinner and drinks for two).

The deluxe **Buckhead Diner,** tel. (404) 262-3336, may serve such familiar old standards as meatloaf and handmade potato chips, but the day's special is as likely to be calamari or fettucine—it's a diner with a wine list. Its blinding polished chrome and neon script faithfully recreate 1950s diner high style at 3073 Piedmont Road. Casual dress is okay, yet most local men wear jackets. Entrees are $10 and up.

Fish, pastas, and salads are among the daily chalkboard specials of contemporary American fare offered at the Peasant's reliable trio of bistro-style restaurants. All three offer good food, friendly service, and reasonable prices in comfortable settings. The original **Pleasant Peasant,** 555 Peachtree St., tel. (404) 874-3223, in Midtown near the Fox Theatre, set the pace and remains the traditional favorite. In Buckhead, find the **Peasant Uptown** in Phipps Plaza shopping center, tel. (404) 261-6341, or **The Peasant** at 3402 Piedmont Rd. in the village, tel. (404) 231-8740. Entrees are about $10-15. Operated by the same franchise, **Daileys,** tel. (404) 681-3303, offers huge portions of American classics, and a lively crowded bar downtown at 17 International Blvd. (at Peachtree St.).

Mick's is a glossy nouveau diner chain known for good burgers, dependable pasta specials, lively crowds, and friendly service—you can't go wrong. A hamburger with all the fixin's runs about $6.95. Its original (fairly composed) location is near Civic Center at 557 Peachtree St., tel. (404) 875-6425; splashier locations include Underground Atlanta, tel. (404) 525-2825, downtown at the corner of Peachtree Center Blvd. and International, tel. (404) 688-6425; lower Buckhead at 2110 Peachtree, tel. (404) 351-6425; and inside the Lenox Square mall, tel. (404) 262-6425.

In two locations, red-eyed skulls mark the entrances to **Vortex,** casual burger places with a great selection of beers. In Midtown one's at 878 Peachtree St., tel. (404) 875-1667, in Little Five Points at 438 Moreland Ave., tel. (404) 688-1828.

Anchoring Virginia Highland, **Murphy's,** 997 Virginia Ave., tel. (404) 872-0904, does deli, but with a bent. Traditional lox and bagels, morning oatmeal, and overstuffed sandwiches are served alongside vegetarian creations, pesto, and brie. Behind the bright deli counter, elegant cafe seating overlooks the triangular green at Virginia and Highland. Murphy's is open most mornings by 8 a.m. and closes at 10 p.m. weekdays, 12:30 a.m. weekends.

For low-end American, the **Varsity Drive-In,** 61 North Ave. in Midtown, tel. (404) 881-1706, is an Atlanta institution for cheap onion rings and hot dogs, sit-down or drive-through. It's above the I-75/85 North Ave. exit, down from the North Ave. MARTA station.

For **24-hour** low-end American, **Majestic Food,** 1031 Ponce de Leon Ave. NE at N. Highland., tel. (404) 875-0276, is the city's ultimate greasy spoon: red formica counter, original waitresses in those little white aprons, slick vinyl booths patched with duct tape. The action picks up around 4 a.m., when nearby Virginia Highland bars close and everybody's ordering the apple pie.

Radical American

For excellent, reasonably priced lunches downtown at Woodruff Park, **Delectables** cafeteria, 113-117 Peachtree St., tel. (404) 681-2909, offers such healthy gourmet specials as California chicken salad, Caesar salad with grilled salmon, and roasted eggplant on foccacia, along with familiar pimento cheese and ham-and-Swiss on rye.

West of Midtown in the warehouse district, **Food Studio,** 887 W. Marietta St., tel. (404) 815-6677, is a trendy dinner spot within the recycled King Plow Arts Center. A recent example of their "Bold American Cooking" was an elaborate acorn squash risotto served in its shell, among several other beautifully presented but complicated choices. It's two miles from CNN up Marietta St. (they'll try to throw you off at Howell Mill, so make the left turn to stay on Marietta).

In Midtown, **Einstein's,** 1077 Juniper St., tel. (404) 876-7925, offers an uncategorizable compendium of "quantum entrees" and "coefficients" (snacks). Try the pita pizza with grilled chicken, basil, and jack, or the generous vegetable stir. You can order at the bar inside, on the streetside patio, or on the sunken deck a block east of Peachtree St. It's open daily 11:30 a.m.-midnight, until 1 a.m. Friday and Saturday nights.

In East Atlanta Village, **Heaping Bowl and Brew,** 469 Flat Shoals Ave., tel. (404) 523-8030, specializes in innovative one-dish meals like their seafood bowl of swordfish, tuna, and calamari over linguini, or try the Italian sausage and sage-seared apples over pierogies. They also have a friendly bar. It's open for dinner 5-11 p.m. Mon.-Fri., for brunch, lunch, and dinner Saturday 10 a.m.-11 p.m., Sunday 10 a.m.-10 p.m.

A few doors down, **Edible Art,** 481A Flat Shoals Ave. SE, tel. (404) 587-0707, is an eight-table place with twisted takes on Southern themes—take the Hoppin' John stuffed pepper or Cajun grilled chicken-red bean-ravioli combo (entrees $9-16, soft drinks only). It's open Tues.-Fri. from 11 a.m.-2 p.m. and again from 5-9 p.m., Saturday till 10 p.m., and Sunday from 11 a.m.-2 p.m. and again from 4-8 p.m.

In Buckhead, **Bacchanalia,** 3125 Piedmont Rd. NE, tel. (404) 365-0410, serves inventive dishes that are a fusion of California and French cuisine (the chef studied with California cuisine guru Alice Waters). Their filet with dates and chunks of Parmesan is among the best meals in town. Look for the old house between Pharr Rd. and Peachtree Rd.

R. Thomas Deluxe Grill, 1812 Peachtree Rd., tel. (404) 872-2942, anchors Lower Buckhead's miles-long strip of patio restaurants. A converted Waffle House turned beautiful-people pit stop, the cafe serves artful healthy meals and snacks **24-hours** in a lush patio complete with birds and blooms. Go anytime for its juice bar, veggie tacos, or asparagus salad, but the freaks come out in the wee hours.

Italian

In Atlanta, Italian restaurants nearly outnumber burger joints, though Italian comes in wider varieties—from cheap and raucous pizzerias to high-class, high-tab *ristorantes*. But the best of the form comes in neighborhood bistros and cafes, perfect for lingering over a jelly glass of red wine while contemplating your cannoli.

Perhaps the best example is in Virginia Highland: **Capo's Cafe,** 922 Virginia Ave. at N. Highland, tel. (404) 876-5655, a decades-old tradition in Virginia Highland, dishes up hearty and inexpensive Italian standards in an intimate dark bistro setting. Open from 5:30 p.m. for dinner; closed Monday.

Across the way, the more casual **Everybody's,** 1040 N. Highland Ave., tel. (404) 873-4545, is where you find cheap and gooey pizza, decent pasta specials, a scenic patio, a lunch-counter bar, and tall wooden booths to linger in.

KAP STANN

You'll find ethnic eateries in Little Five Points, Atlanta's foremost bohemian neighborhood, as well as throughout the city.

Another, bigger Everybody's is across from Emory University at 1593 N. Decatur Rd., tel. (404) 377-7766. **Fellini's** is another popular local chain pizzeria that usually has big patio areas for hanging out.

A pizza refuge for New Yorkers, **Rocky's Brick Oven Pizza,** 1770 Peachtree St. in lower Buckhead (original location), tel. (404) 876-1111, is the hands-down local favorite. Try the Pizza Bianco (with white cheese) or calzone, all baked in wood-fired brick ovens. You can eat in Rocky's comfy booths or call for delivery. It's open Mon.-Thurs. 11 a.m.-10:30 p.m., Fri.-Sat. 5-11 p.m., Sunday 5-10:30 p.m.

For high-end Italian in Buckhead, **Pricci** (say Pree-CHEESE), 500 Pharr Rd., tel. (404) 237-2941, serves northern Italian classics such as homemade saffron pasta and polenta with veal sausage, along with legendary bread and Italian wines. The decor is cozy booths and tables in a sleek setting. It's open Mon.-Thurs. 11 a.m.-11 p.m., Fri.-Sat. 11 a.m. till midnight. On Sunday, dinners are served family-style 5-10 p.m. For an equally modern and expensive choice in midtown, there's **Veni Vidi Vici,** 41 14th St., tel. (404) 875-VICI (404-875-8424), which throws in alfresco seating and a bocce ball court to boot. From here you can also check out nearby "Restaurant Row" on a two-block stretch of Crescent Ave. south of 14th St. for several more options.

Mediterranean

The arty **Fairlie-Poplar Cafe & Grill,** 85 Poplar St. at Fairlie, tel. (404) 827-0040, is a wonderful new addition to this reinvigorated downtown neighborhood. Grilled vegetables or exotic meats (kabobs, lamb, pheasant) come glazed with pomegranate honey or wrapped in filo dough—also lots of feta and couscous. It's open weekdays for lunch ($10 buffet) 11:30 a.m.-3 p.m. and for dinner Mon.-Fri. 5:30-11 p.m. Entrees are $9-19.

Jamaican

Bridgetown Grill offers spicy island specialties in lively and colorful restaurants that attract a lively and colorful crowd for inexpensive entrees—try Jamaican jerk chicken served with black beans and rice—or just drinks and tapas. Two locations: in Midtown it's at 689 Peachtree Ave. NE, tel. (404) 873-5361, up from the Fox Theatre, or in Little Five Points at 1156 Euclid Ave., tel. (404) 653-0110.

Mexican and Dix-Mex

Nuevo Loredo, 1495 Chattahoochee Ave. NW, tel. (404) 352-9009, might well be the most authentic Mexican restaurant east of the Mississippi, right down to the bloody crosses, saints, and candlelit shrines. A bilingual menu is packed with *chorizo, flautas,* and *mole pollo* plates, including many vegetarian options. Try the Guadalajara-style barbecued shrimp ($13) with a chilled Bohemia. Lunch is served Mon.-Sat. 11:30 a.m.-3 p.m., dinner until 10 or 11 p.m. It's set off in a glen near nowhere five miles north of Centennial Olympic Park: take Marietta St. north of CNN and stay to the right as Marietta merges into Howell Mill Rd., then turn left (west) on Chattahoochee.

East of Midtown, **Tortillas,** 774 Ponce de Leon Ave., tel. (404) 892-3493, serves funky California-style Mexican fast food. As one local culinary pundit says, "it's cheaper than eating at home." It's open daily 11 a.m.-11 p.m.

In Little Five Points (L5P), **El Myr** ("rhymes with beer") **Burrito Lounge,** 1091 Euclid Ave., tel. (404) 588-0250, serves burritos, quesadillas and nachos—most selections under $5—at the bar, tables, or at comfortable couches in a cultivated dive setting.

Around L5P, **Gringo's,** 1238 DeKalb Ave. NE, tel. (404) 522-8666, has a great tropical patio for lingering over Mexican plates, but it's perhaps best known for exotic Margaritas made from a selection of 20 different tequilas (from $4).

With two locations on the east side, **Burrito Art** invents "Americanized" burritos, including a Southern BBQ chicken burrito, an Asian meatloaf burrito, and the veggie favorite, a grilled eggplant burrito with red pepper and roasted garlic (from $5). In Emory Village it's at 1451 Oxford Rd., tel. (404) 377-7786; in East Atlanta Village it's at 1259 Glenwood Ave., tel. (404) 627-4433. They're open daily, 11:30 a.m.-10 p.m. Mon.-Fri., from noon on Saturday and from 4 p.m. Sunday.

An isolated outpost off the tracks on the East Side, **Cabbagetown Grill,** 727 Wylie St. SE at the corner of Krog St., tel. (404) 525-8818, serves quesadillas and chimichangas along with daily specials all over the map (from bok choy to meatloaf). It's open 11 a.m.-11 p.m. Mon.-Fri., from 10 a.m. Sat.-Sun. for brunch till 3 p.m., then off the regular menu till 11 p.m. (From DeKalb Ave., it might be tricky to find the Krog St. underpass—particularly if you're working from a visitor center map which currently neglects to show where Krog goes through.)

Indian

Downtown, **Haveli,** 225 Spring St., tel. (404) 522-4545, North Indian lamb, goat, and vegetarian specialties in a finer dining setting in the Gift Mart. It's open for lunch Mon.-Fri. 11:30 a.m.-2:30 p.m. and Saturday noon-2:30 p.m., and serves dinner daily 5:30-10 p.m.

In Little Five Points, **Calcutta,** 1138 Euclid Ave., tel. (404) 681-1838, specializes in tandoori dishes.

Assorted Asian

The Buford Highway runs northeast of downtown up to Chamblee, where a large Asian community supports a Chinese mall and a Korean mall. The highway is lined with inexpensive ethnic eateries such as the **Queen of Thailand** at 3330 Buford Highway, **Bien Thuy** (Vietnamese) at 5095 Buford Highway, and **Pung Mie** (Chinese) at 5145 Buford Highway.

Taverns

Atlanta's taverns offer some of the best inexpensive spots in town to eat. The settings are often smoky, always lively, and seating is in comfortably worn booths or along crowded bars. Try some Sweet Georgia Brown Ale, Red Brick Ale, or Marthasville Pale Ale—three offerings from Atlanta's growing microbreweries. Of course, football fans like to get their hands around a Red Dog for that familiar bulldog logo.

Atkins Park, a well-established neighborhood eatery and saloon, anchors Virginia Highland at 794 N. Highland Ave., tel. (404) 876-7249. Also in Virginia Highland, **Manuel's Tavern,** tel. (404) 525-3447, the watering hole of local politicians and media types, offers alcohol-sopping chili dogs, wings, and other classic bar food at 602 N. Highland Ave. at North Avenue (the *New York Times* has called Manuel's one of its "10 favorite places in the world").

Coffeehouses

Atlanta's coffeehouses offer more than just coffee: they're places to come in out of the weather (or sit outside at patio tables and appreciate it), people-watch, rendezvous, read, write, or graze on baked goods or light meals. Many also offer gourmet coffee by the pound.

In Underground Atlanta downtown, **Cafe du Monde,** a branch of the famous New Orleans landmark, offers the same Crescent City beignets (square powdered doughnuts) and cafe au lait. At Five Points, **Starbucks,** 240 Peachtree St., tel. (404) 589-4522, overlooks Woodruff Park (upstairs, Kinko's offers Internet access). In Midtown, stop at **Caribou Coffee** on the corner of 10th St. and Piedmont Ave. a block east of Peachtree Street.

In Virginia Highland, **Cafe Diem,** 604 N. Highland Ave., tel. (404) 607-7008, quotes

Horace, Oscar Wilde, and Art Buchwald on its menu, while arty patrons fill the joint for cappuccino, combo sandwiches, *salades Niçoise,* and other goodies. It's open most days 11:30 a.m.-midnight (until 2 a.m. Friday and Saturday).

In Inman Park, **More Than Coffee,** 110 Hurt St., tel. (404) 577-7400, offers a quiet refuge with plenty of secondhand magazines across from the Inman Park MARTA station (open daily, weekdays till 6 p.m., weekends till 2 p.m.)

In East Atlanta Village, **Sacred Grounds,** 510 Flat Shoals Ave., tel. (404) 584-2253, offers morning treats, afternoon sweets (including Snickers cheesecake), and a range of coffee drinks along with a quiet place to sit and sip.

Farmers Markets

There's a lot more to Atlanta's farmers markets than groceries. You can experience a wide ethnic and cultural mix, eat at inexpensive cafeterias and bakeries, find exotic wines and cheeses—or just watch the eggs roll in. Decatur's **DeKalb Farmers Market,** 3000 E. Ponce de Leon Ave., tel. (404) 377-6400, operates an enormous food emporium out of a spiffy hangar-size building and has a helpful multicultural and multilingual staff. It's at open weekdays 10 a.m.-9 p.m., weekends 9 a.m.-9 p.m.

The **State Farmer's Market,** down by the airport at 16 Forest Pkwy., tel. (404) 366-6910, packs produce, poultry, pickles, plants, and more onto its 146 acres; a cafeteria serves fresh inexpensive food 24 hours.

TRANSPORTATION

GETTING THERE

By Air

Hartsfield International Airport, tel. (404) 530-6834, the largest passenger terminal complex in the world, serves 68 million passengers a year. Thirty-two passenger airlines—including Hartsfield-based Delta Air Lines—provide service to every major U.S. city and most major international cities.

Ten miles (16 km) south of downtown, near the junction of interstate freeways I-75, I-85, and perimeter highway I-285, the airport is a city in itself. At the main terminal, visitors pass through demanding security gates (allow extra time for close camera and computer inspection) and board tram trains to five outlying concourses, where gates are located according to airline. If you need help, go to the Traveler's Aid desk near baggage claim in the main terminal; here volunteers offer wide-ranging assistance from lodging information and language service to finding where you left your car. At baggage claim, you'll find courtesy phones to more than 30 hotels and motels that run shuttle van service to and from the airport.

From an in-terminal station near baggage claim, clean and efficient MARTA trains whisk passengers downtown in 10 minutes for $1.50. Taxi rates from the airport to the downtown hotel district are fixed at $15 for one passenger, $8 per person for two passengers, and $6 each for three or more. Single passenger rates to Buckhead's hotel district, north of downtown, run $25 for one.

By Car

Two major north-south interstate highways merge in northern Atlanta; the combined I-75/85 then splits again down by the airport. This combined interstate intersects with the major east-west route of I-20 at downtown Atlanta. All three interstates cross I-285, the perimeter route that encircles Atlanta, which can easily be the most confusing to newcomers. As directions in a circle are relative, "east" and "west" signs quickly turn to "north" or "south," and directional signs to Augusta or Birmingham don't help you find your way through town (Atlanta Braves pitcher Jose Peres once missed the beginning of a game because he was stuck in perpetual motion on the perimeter). To avoid this common pitfall, plan your approach carefully and avoid rush hours. Atlanta's prolonged rush hours run 6-10 a.m. and 3-7 p.m. Travel time then may be doubled or tripled, particularly along routes north.

By Train

Amtrak, tel. (800) USA-RAIL (800-872-7245), provides daily service from Atlanta to New York,

Washington, D.C., Philadelphia, and other northern cities, and to Mobile, Birmingham, New Orleans, and other points south. The Amtrak station at 1688 Peachtree Rd. (at I-85) is in a fairly isolated stretch of the Peachtree corridor, north of downtown and midtown (surprisingly forlorn, considering the city's origins as a railroad capital). Yet visitors can readily find taxi and bus service here, and a couple of restaurants are a short walk away.

By Bus

Greyhound-Trailways, tel. (800) 231-2222, provides bus service connecting Atlanta with the entire country. The downtown bus terminal south of Five Points at 232 Forsyth St. SW, tel. (404) 584-1731, is in a nowhere district but conveniently connected to the Garnett MARTA station for easy access to the airport and hotels and restaurants within reach of the MARTA line.

GETTING AROUND

Rental Cars

At Hartsfield Airport (near baggage claim) and also at branch locations throughout metro Atlanta, major car-rental agencies include **Dollar Rent-A-Car,** tel. (800) 800-4000; **Alamo,** tel. (800) 327-9633; **Budget,** tel. (800) 527-0700; **Hertz,** tel. (800) 654-3131; **Avis,** tel. (800) 331-1212; and **National,** tel. (800) CAR-RENT (800-227-7368). All offer weekly discounts, weekend packages, unlimited-mileage rates, and even such perks as cellular-phone rentals. Frequent-renter "clubs" offer additional advantages, including discounts and express service. In town, **Rent-A-Wreck,** tel. (404) 363-8720, offers lower rates; you get what you pay for. Summer travelers should select cars with air-conditioning and light-colored interiors.

Taxis

Taxis downtown charge a flat rate of $5 for a single passenger ($1 extra each for more than two passengers) traveling within the official downtown taxi zone. Bounded by Boulevard on the east, 14th St. (north of Georgia Tech) on the north, Northside Dr. on the west, and Turner Field on the south, "the zone" encompasses the major business district north to Midtown. Metered rates for all other destinations are $1.50 for the first one-sixth mile, 20 cents each additional sixth of a mile, and $1 per person for each additional passenger. Some special-event flat rates apply. For a cab, call **Atlanta Taxicab Association,** tel. (770) 269-7553, or **Checker Cab Company,** tel. (404) 351-1111. A 10% tip is customary, more for bags or special services.

MARTA Public Transit

The Metropolitan Area Rapid Transit Authority (MARTA), tel. (404) 848-4711, operates the buses and Atlanta's impressive light-rail system, a convenient alternative to driving around town. Clean, safe, and frequent MARTA trains run along two lines (east-west and north-south) that intersect downtown at the central Five Points subway station. Here passengers can pick up maps, schedules, discounted tokens (10 for $12), and weekly passes. Riders can buy tokens for $1.50 each for a trip of any length (includes a free transfer to bus lines) from self-service machines. While the machines accept bills up to $10, they dispense only tokens (no

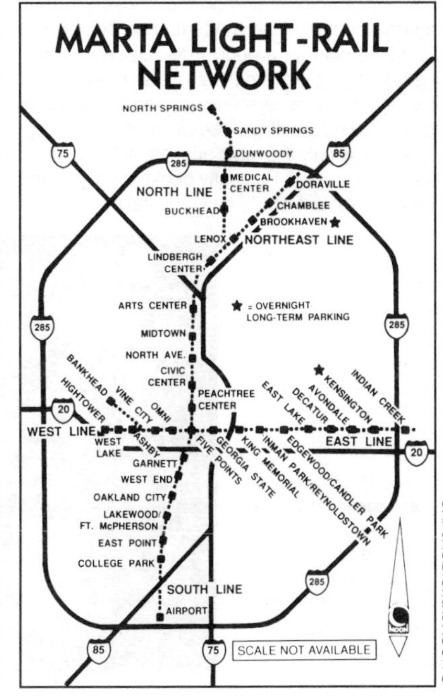

change), so it's smart to carry crisp one-, five-, or 10-dollar bills, small change, and a handful of tokens. Parking at some MARTA stations also requires exact change. Both locally and in this text, the term MARTA is used to refer to the light-rail system exclusively.

MARTA's bus lines traverse the city for $1.50 a ride. Less convenient to visitors than the trains (long rides and exposed bus stops without benches are pet peeves), the buses are most useful for short jaunts from train stations to city attractions.

For information on MARTA's handicapped services, call tel. (404) 848-5389.

Driving Maps and Tips

Though the MARTA line offers a relaxed alternative, most people get around Atlanta by car. This is straightforward enough in downtown areas, presuming you're familiar with urban driving patterns (one-way streets, traffic, and the like), but the wider metro region can be something else. With a city that sprawls like Los Angeles—yet without mountains on the horizon to help chart a course—metro Atlanta can be tricky to navigate without a good map. Get a comprehensive street map from auto clubs, gas stations, tourist outlets, or select newsstands. Hotels and tourist outlets distribute free city maps; these typically show only the main arteries, of limited help if you wander off. Specialty bookstores offer the widest selection of city and regional maps; you'll find **Latitudes** in the Lenox Square shopping mall (accessible from MARTA's Lenox station).

To park downtown and skirt the worst of the traffic, aim for Underground Atlanta's public parking lot off Martin Luther King, Jr. Drive. Around Peachtree Center, shoot for the public lot on Courtland Street at Harris. Or park at Macy's off Peachtree Street at Ellis; it validates parking with purchase. Private parking downtown is relatively expensive, more than $6 an hour.

INFORMATION AND SERVICES

Telephones

Two area codes serve the Atlanta area—404 is closer to downtown, 770 generally applies to the wider metro region, but because the two area codes may overlap *you must include the area code when placing any local call* within Atlanta, which can be quite a bother, particularly from pay phones or when using calling cards. Unlike all other calls requiring area codes, *do not dial 1 before the area code* for local Atlanta calls.

Important Telephone Numbers

Dial 911 for emergency assistance—police, ambulance, or fire. In nonemergency situations, call the police at (404) 658-6600, the fire department at (404) 659-2121, or ambulance service at (404) 521-4141. For local time and weath-

MARTA provides fast and comfortable public transit around town and to the airport with 240 cars on more than 40 miles of track.

KAP STANN

er, call (404) 455-7141. Traveler's Aid can be reached at tel. (404) 527-7400.

Tourist Offices

The **Atlanta Convention and Visitors Bureau,** tel. (404) 521-6600 or (800) ATLANTA, staffs information booths and distributes free information (including maps and events listings) at Underground Atlanta, the World Congress Center, Peachtree Center Mall, Lenox Square, and at the airport. Send inquiries by post to 233 Peachtree St., Ste. 100, Atlanta, GA 30303, by e-mail to acvb@atlanta.com, or see www.acvb.com.

The State of Georgia **Department of Industry, Trade, and Tourism,** tel. (404) 656-3590, at 285 Peachtree Center Ave., Atlanta, GA 30303, distributes statewide information including long-distance bike-route maps and local festival listings. The **Atlanta Chamber of Commerce,** 235 International Blvd. NW, tel. (404) 880-9000, is headquartered across from Centennial Olympic Park.

Publications

"Covering Dixie like the Dew" since 1868, the ***Atlanta Journal-Constitution,*** tel. (404) 526-5151, produces a daily morning and afternoon paper, and joint Saturday and Sunday editions. See Saturday's paper for the entertainment listings in the pull-out *Weekend* tabloid.

The free weekly alternative newspaper ***Creative Loafing*** is an indispensable guide to what's happening in the city—for the latest in local politics and activism as well as entertainment and humor. Find it at street corner bins all over town. The ***Atlanta Press*** has cropped up to compete for its share of the alternative press market, but it's less widely distributed.

For the upscale beat, find the four-color monthly ***Atlanta Magazine*** at newsstands. The ***Atlanta Daily World*** carries news of particular interest to the African-American population, as it has since 1928. ***Atlanta Asian News*** (in English), ***Georgia Magazine*** (in Japanese), and ***Mundo Hispánico*** (bilingual Spanish-English) are just a few of a dozen or more international publications produced in metro Atlanta that cater to Atlanta's diverse ethnic populations.

Online Access

Kinko's offers Internet access for $1 a minute at several locations: downtown at 100 Peachtree St. #101, tel. (404) 221-0000; in Midtown at 1371 Peachtree St., tel. (404) 262-9393; in Buckhead at 3637 Peachtree Rd. NE, tel. (404) 233-1329; and near Emory University at 1385 Oxford Rd. NE, tel. (404) 377-4639. In Little Five Points, **Cyberbar,** 1130 Euclid Ave., charges $6 an hour, $4 a half-hour. (The Hyatt Regency downtown currently has a online computer "free for guests" outside its 24-hour cafe.)

Security

Crime is a major concern in any American city, and Atlanta is no exception, though areas that attract visitors are among the best patrolled. An urban "ambassador" patrol instituted for the Olympics and still in place covers downtown Atlanta to help visitors find their way and to act as a deterrent to crime.

For added precaution, hide money and cards securely in a money belt or under clothing, and leave valuable jewelry home. Some seasoned urban travelers carry a spare money clip with a $10 or $20 bill wrapped around a wad of ones, so if ever accosted they can throw this mad money out and run in the opposite direction.

VICINITY OF ATLANTA

Sprawling metropolitan Atlanta encompasses 18 counties and 5,147 square miles. While the encircling perimeter highway (I-285) once encapsulated urban development, expanding suburbs now spread far beyond it, sparking calls for a second beltway farther out. Like Los Angeles, the car-dominated metro area consists of miles and miles of low-rise development, pockets of industry, and suburban-style strip malls. Yet unlike L.A., Atlanta's routes often roll and wind through thick deciduous woods under clear skies. Some of the metro area's best recreation and historical touring sites lie at its perimeter, just outside the I-285 beltway.

Clockwise from the west, **Six Flags Over Georgia** lies near a tranquil state park off I-20. West, the **Chattahoochee River National Recreation Area** sits at Atlanta's northwestern corner near the city's most established suburb of Marietta. Directly north is the city of Roswell, which manages to retain a small-town central core. To the east, **Stone Mountain** is a major recreational center for city dwellers. (Off I-20 east, the small towns of Middle Georgia are covered under Central Georgia.)

WEST OF ATLANTA

Six Flags Over Georgia

Six Flags, west of Atlanta off I-20, tel. (770) 948-9290, is one of a national chain of amusement parks; this one has a Southern theme. Names of rides such as the Georgia Cyclone, the Great American Scream Machine, and Mind Bender let you know that daring roller coasters are the specialty of the park, guaranteed to bring that cotton candy taste to the back of your throat. This gigantic amusement park features artificial whitewater rapids and live country music and performances.

Admission is $32, kids aged three to nine $22, two and under free. Hours change seasonally; summer hours run approximately Sun.-Thurs. 10 a.m.-10 p.m., Friday and Saturday till midnight. Call to confirm seasonal schedule and prices.

Sweetwater Creek State Conservation Park

A slice of wilderness only minutes outside metro Atlanta (I-20 exit 12), Sweetwater Creek State Park, tel. (770) 732-5871, features a placid creek, five miles of trails, fishing and boating on a reservoir (canoe and fishing-boat rentals and bait shop available), and Civil War-era textile mill ruins.

The **Factory Ruins Trail** follows Sweetwater Creek a half-mile through Piedmont hardwoods to the remnants of the New Manchester Manufacturing Company. Here cloth was made for Confederate troops, until Sherman ordered the factory burned on July 9, 1864. The blue-blazed trail continues a half-mile downstream to a platform overlooking waterfalls and the huge granite outcroppings at the water's edge. From here, you can retrace your steps back or follow an inland trail through moist coves and glens to the original trailhead. Pick up trail maps and interpretive guides at the park office. The conservation park is for day-use only; the fee to park is $3 per car. From I-20 exit 12, go south on Thorton Rd. a quarter-mile and turn right onto Blairs Bridge Rd., then turn left onto Mt. Vernon Rd. to the park.

Lodging and Camping

Several chain motels are clustered around I-20 exit 13; of these, **La Quinta Inn,** tel. (770) 944-2110, is among the lowest-priced (from $49).

The closest campground to downtown Atlanta, **Arrowhead Campground,** 7400 Six Flags Rd. at I-20 exit 13/13C in Austell, tel. (770) 732-1130 or (800) 631-8956, offers 160 RV sites for $27 and 150 tent sites for $18, a pool, and small store, all a five-minute walk from Six Flags and 10 miles from downtown (prices quoted are for two people, $3 each additional person over age three). A MARTA shuttle from the westernmost rail station to Six Flags brings many city sights within easy reach without driving.

CHATTAHOOCHEE RIVER NATIONAL RECREATION AREA

The Chattahoochee River National Recreation Area, tel. (770) 399-8070, a federally designated parkland along 48 miles of river corridor, offers the scenic natural beauty of the Piedmont region, recreational activities such as boating, fishing, and hiking, and ruins of old water-powered mills. Deciduous forests of oak, beech, and hickory line the river, along with huge rocks and cliffs that make for varied hiking challenges and scenic overlooks.

The river parkland stretches from Lake Lanier in the north to the outskirts of metropolitan Atlanta, not contiguous but cut up into distinct unconnected parcels called "units." The southernmost unit borders metropolitan Atlanta, 9.5 miles from downtown (see map). The day-use-only park system is great for hiking, jogging, biking, and rafting (no camping).

Park headquarters are on the Island Ford unit, a mile east of Hwy. 400 just south of Roswell. Request a brochure or trail maps from the superintendent's office, 1978 Island Ford Pkwy., Atlanta, GA 30350 (enclose a stamped, self-addressed business-size envelope); tel. (770) 399-8070.

"Shootin' the 'Hooch"

One of the most popular activities along the Chattahoochee is river rafting (locally called "Shootin' the 'Hooch"), a leisurely half-day-or daylong float down calm currents and across wide shoals (a Class I and II waterway). Enforcement by park officials against excessive rowdiness the last few years has enhanced the river's appeal to families and groups of all sizes, ages, and abilities, though it's still a tremendous hit with the sunbathing/beer chest crowd (alcohol okay, but glass containers of any kind are prohibited). This lazy, sunny float feels much farther away from the busyness of downtown than a mere 10 miles.

The **Chattahoochee Outdoor Center** tel. (770) 395-6851, a private raft-rental concessionaire, operates three outposts from the first weekend in May to the second weekend in September. You can rent rafts and canoes at the two upper outposts. The northernmost Johnson's Ferry Rd. outpost is open for rentals 9 a.m.-1:30 p.m. on weekends and 10 a.m.-1:30 p.m. on weekdays (take I-285 to Roswell Rd., then left on Johnson's Ferry Rd.). The central Powers Island outpost rents until 4:30 p.m. daily (from I-285 exit 15, backtrack along Interstate North Pkwy). The southernmost Paces Mill outpost at Hwy. 41 does not rent rafts, but it provides shuttles back upriver for rafters. (Alternatively, rafters could leave cars at the southernmost outpost and shuttle *up* to start their trip.) The only practical way to get to the river is by private automobile. Parking is free, but signs are scarce—carry a map or call for explicit directions to rafting outposts.

Rafting trips range from two to six hours, depending on where you put in and take out. Count on floating about one mile an hour. It's six miles from Johnson's Ferry to Paces Mill, four miles from Johnson's Ferry to Powers Island, and two miles from Powers Island to Paces Mill.

Four-person rafts rent for $42.50, six-person rafts for $62.50 and eight-person rafts for $82.50. Canoes rent for $35, or bring your own and put in at any one of these points or other launches along the river. A refundable $75 security deposit is required for each craft. Credit cards are accepted for deposit or rental. The shuttle bus costs $2.50 for adults, $1.50 for children. It runs to and from each outpost every 30 minutes daily 10 a.m.-8 p.m. weekdays, 9 a.m.-8 p.m. on weekends and holidays. Reservations are recommended for weekend trips.

Being prepared for a day on the river will make your experience more enjoyable. Bring a "dry sack" for your car key, shuttle tickets, and deposit receipt. Wear swimsuits and "river shoes" (old sneakers) or other wettable light clothing and footwear. Pack a picnic, a litter bag, and cool drinks (concessions sell some snacks and drinks). Two real dangers are heatstroke from hours in the direct sun—bring hats and sunblock—and hypothermia from the cold water (55° F year-round). Each craft is required to carry one lifevest for each passenger; they are provided free with rental.

(Spectators gather at **Ray's on the River,** 6700 Powers Ferry Rd., tel. (770) 955-1187, for an elegant Sunday brunch overlooking the streaming flotilla. The sunburned post-rafting crowd heads to patio cafes along lower Roswell Road.)

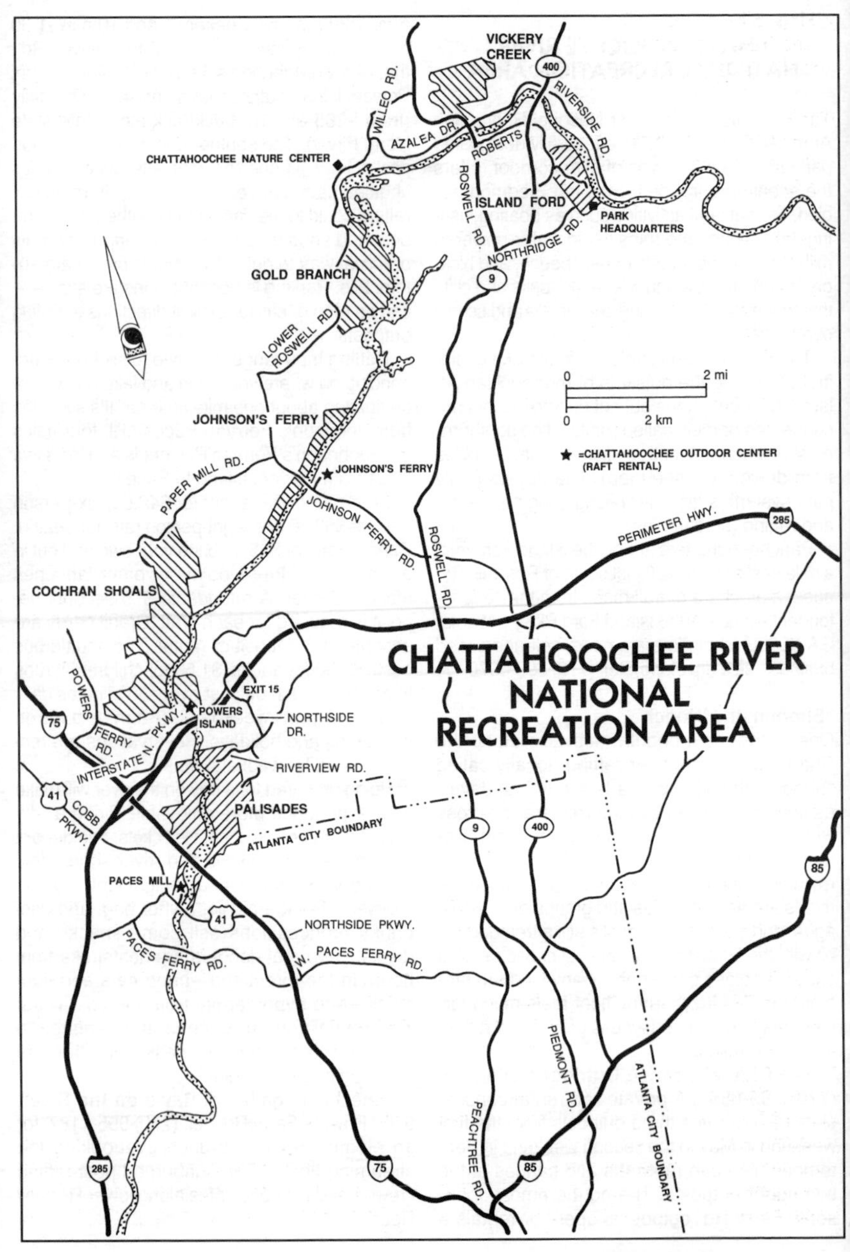

CHATTAHOOCHEE RIVER NATIONAL RECREATION AREA
VICKERY CREEK
400
RIVERSIDE RD.
WILLEO RD.
AZALEA DR.
ROBERTS
CHATTAHOOCHEE NATURE CENTER
ROSWELL RD.
ISLAND FORD
PARK HEADQUARTERS
NORTHRIDGE RD.
9
GOLD BRANCH
LOWER ROSWELL RD
MOON
0
2 mi
2 km
= CHATTAHOOCHEE OUTDOOR CENTER (RAFT RENTAL)
JOHNSON'S FERRY
PAPER MILL RD.
JOHNSON FERRY RD.
ROSWELL RD.
PERIMETER HWY.
285
COCHRAN SHOALS
POWERS FERRY RD.
EXIT 15
POWERS ISLAND
NORTHSIDE DR.
75
INTERSTATE N. PKWY.
RIVERVIEW RD.
41
COBB PKWY.
PALISADES
ATLANTA CITY BOUNDARY
PACES MILL
NORTHSIDE PKWY.
PACES FERRY RD.
W. PACES FERRY RD.
85
PIEDMONT RD.
PEACHTREE RD.

Hiking, Biking, and Fishing

Hiking trails wind along the river and through upland woods of the varied southern Piedmont, known for its beautiful seasonal colors in spring and fall, long-flowering trees and shrubs, and varied deciduous and coniferous trees. Giant rock outcroppings were once used by the native Creek and Cherokee for temporary shelter. Several still-standing stone foundations of old water-powered mills (grist, textile, or paper) have crumbled back into the natural landscape, as many such recent "ruins" in the South have done. Birdwatchers look for great blue herons, green herons, kingfishers, and ospreys. Look for tracks of raccoons, muskrats, mink, beavers, and otters along the river—look also for beaver dams, turtles, toads, and the river's 22 varieties of fish. From south to north, here are highlights of hiking trails, unit by unit. Contact park headquarters for trail maps and information.

Palisades Unit: Park at the rafting outpost parking lot off Cobb Pkwy. to reach the **West Palisades Trail.** After crossing under the freeway, the easy trail follows Rottenwood Creek up to the ruins of Akers Mill, a 19th-century gristmill about 1.5 miles from the start. Here a sandy beach and large boulders invite leisurely picnicking and sunbathing. East of the river, five miles of easy-to-difficult trails wind through wooded floodplains, ridges, and ravines, to a panoramic view of the river gorge at Devil's Race Shoals (so called because they were the "devil" to navigate, according to local legend). One of the park's largest rock shelters, once a Native American fish camp, can be reached a half mile north of Long Island Creek. You get to all eastern riverbank trails from the north: take I-285 to Northside Dr., drive southeast to parking lots and trailheads either at the foot of Indian Trail Rd. or Whitewater Rd. farther south.

Cochran Shoals Unit: The fully accessible three-mile **Cochran Fitness Trail**—open to cyclists as well as hikers—parallels a stretch of river wetlands, with stops at observation decks, picnic areas, and exercise stations. The moderately steep **Sope Creek Trail** leads to the ruins of the Marietta Paper Mill, where paper products—including Confederate currency—were produced from 1855 to 1902.

Rangers and volunteers operate free guided hikes of natural-history and cultural-history sites almost every weekend, and occasionally midweek; call (770) 399-8070 for a schedule.

Fishing is permitted in the Chattahoochee River. A valid Georgia fishing license is required, and a trout stamp is required to fish for trout; no live minnows are permitted as bait.

MARIETTA

Northeast of Atlanta along the historic railroad route demolished by Sherman's March, the 1824 town of Marietta has exploded into Atlanta's grandest suburb. This busy, affluent city mixes its historic town square with modern corporate towers; Civil War cemeteries border spanking-new housing developments. The aerospace industry drives the prosperous local economy; Lockheed builds fighter jets here, and the county receives more federal money than any other suburb outside of the D.C. area and the Kennedy Space Center.

Marietta is the county seat of the notoriously conservative Cobb County—the object of many progressively-led protests over the years from its comparatively liberal neighbor of Atlanta, from the civil rights era to most recently in 1996, when Olympic organizers considered rerouting the arrival of the Olympic torch to bypass Cobb. In 1993, Cobb County came to national attention as the first city in the U.S. to officially condemn homosexuality: the county commission declared homosexuality "incompatible with community standards" (one commissioner descriptively explained how "people are fed up with having the gay agenda crammed down their throats"). Cobb's reactionary stances can reach comic extremes: the city of Kennesaw responded to national gun-control trends by *requiring* each household to own a gun. Yet, as always, policymakers don't necessarily represent all residents. Many progressive folks from all over are drawn to the county's good jobs, good schools, and relief from urban congestion.

Visitors will also find many attractions in the area: historical touring downtown and at nearby Kennesaw Mountain battlefield, antebellum house tours, and the popular summertime White Water Park with its adjacent amusement park. The most notorious local landmark is the "Big

Chicken," a 56-foot-tall sheet-metal rooster that towers over the corner of Hwy. 41 and Roswell Road. It's so large that pilots use it for navigational purposes—so do locals; you'll hear directions such has "turn left at the big chicken."

Marietta Square

Even though Sherman's troops ravaged the town in 1864 en route to Atlanta, more than a hundred antebellum homes remain, and many more 19th-century structures are evidence of Marietta's quick recovery. The heart of the historic downtown is **Marietta Square.** In the center of the square, scenic **Glover Park** dates from 1852, and hosts summertime brown-bag concerts, art shows, and seasonal festivals. The lively square is lined with browseable antique shops, practical stores, cafes, restaurants, and the Theatre in the Square (see **Entertainment** below). Tour the square in style atop **horse-drawn carriages** that operate on weekends from the corner of North Park Square and Church, tel. (770) 499-9719.

The **welcome center,** 4 Depot St., tel. (770) 429-1115 or (800) 835-0445, in the 1898 railroad depot behind the square, distributes self-guided walking- and driving-tour maps, parking passes, and event calendars. Hours are Mon.-Fri. 9-5, Saturday 11 a.m.-4 p.m., Sunday 1-4 p.m. Also inquire about historic house tours. Across the street in the Kennesaw House, where Sherman shacked up while devising his Atlanta Campaign, the **Marietta Museum of History,** tel. (770) 528-0430, tells the town's illustrious history ($2 admission).

A block south of the square, the old 1909 post office has been converted into the **Marietta-Cobb Museum of Art,** 30 Atlanta St. at Anderson St., tel. (770) 528-1444. It's open Tues.-Sat. 11 a.m.-5 p.m. Admission is $2 for adults, $1 for students and seniors.

Northeast of the square, the 1866 **Marietta National Cemetery** off Washington Ave. contains 10,000 graves shaded by towering magnolias and oaks—24 acres speckled with monuments from many states honoring slain native sons. South of the square, the 1863 **Confederate Cemetery** holds the graves of 3,000 soldiers, a thousand marked "unknown"; take N. Marietta Pkwy. south.

White Water Theme Park

At White Water, 250 N. Marietta Pkwy., tel. (770) 424-9283, four million gallons of water create waves, pools, waterfalls, and plenty of daring slides in the shaded 35-acre water park north of Atlanta. It opens seasonally: weekends only in spring and daily from Memorial Day to Labor Day (opens 10 a.m.) An all-day pass to White Water for adults costs $20, for children three to four feet tall the cost is around $12. Once you dry off, an **amusement park** next door offers bumper cars, train rides, and an arcade. Take I-75 exit 113.

Accommodations

Sixty Polk Street, 60 Polk St., tel. (770) 419-1688 or (800) 845-7266, a bed and breakfast inn housed in a regal 1872 Victorian two blocks from the square, offers four guest rooms each with private bath ($85-150); in the morning your hosts Joe and Glenda Mertes serve a deluxe breakfast in the formal dining room.

National chain motels are clustered around I-75 exit 111, including the low-end **Motel 6,** tel. (770) 952-8161 (from $34), and **Howard Johnson,** tel. (770) 951-1144 (from $44).

Food and Drink

Le Cafe Crepe, 90 Marietta Station, tel. (770) 426-8003, serves delicate French lunches (*crêpe française* $4) on weekdays and fixed-price gourmet dinners (salmon with lobster sauce in puff pastry, $28) on Saturday nights by reservation. **Shillings on the Square,** 19 N. Park Sq., tel. (770) 428-9520, serves American and continental entrees from $15.

Java Blues, 10 Whitlock Ave., tel. (770) 419-0095, attracts a young suburban avant-garde set for pricey gourmet coffees ($1.61 for a cup of joe) and snacks during the day and smoky live blues, rock, and readings at night (see Atlanta papers for entertainment listings).

Entertainment

The award-winning **Theatre in the Square,** 11 Whitlock Ave., tel. (770) 422-8369, hosts six productions a year in its 170-seat theater; *Always Patsy Cline* was on the bill at last visit. The 1993 production here of a play with homosexual references sparked the controversy which led to the county's anti-gay measure; after a cut-off of county funds, supporters rallied to keep the arts group in production (backers included Georgia native Joanne Woodward and her husband Paul Newman). Check Atlanta entertainment pages or local papers for performance listings.

KENNESAW

Kennesaw Mountain Battlefield

Established in 1917, this national historic park north of Marietta commemorates the Battle of Kennesaw (KEN-a-saw) Mountain, in which the Confederates under General James Johnston forestalled the Union advance of Sherman's troops in defense of Atlanta. In June of 1864, Sherman's attack on Confederate entrenchments here (still visible today) was repelled by rifle fire, rocks rolled down the hillsides, and hand-to-hand combat. The mountains "couldn't have been more suited for defense than if they'd been designed for that purpose," a surviving Union soldier explained. Though Sherman returned to his previously successful flanking maneuvers to eventually capture Atlanta, Kennesaw Mountain was a proud Confederate victory. (And, as these things go, Confederate victory battlefields are often less well known and therefore more enlightening than their Union counterparts.)

The **visitor center** presents a slide show on the battle, and distributes maps detailing memorials, entrenchments, and trails. The quarter-mile **summit trail** is an easy walk. On weekdays you can drive to the top but on weekends you must park at the center and either walk or take a shuttle bus to the top. The center opens daily 8:30 a.m.-5 p.m. Take I-75 exit 116 and follow signs.

Whether or not you're drawn to see the battlefield, the scenic beauty of the valley is alone worth a visit, for a drive or a hike. Sixteen miles of **hiking trails** crisscross the 2,884-acre park, through Piedmont forests of oak and dogwood, and along hillsides overlooking fields, farmland, and stately homes.

Kennesaw Civil War Museum

The **Kennesaw Civil War Museum,** 2829 Cherokee St., tel. (770) 427-2117, is home of the famous locomotive named "General," stolen during the Civil War by Andrews' Raiders (a story told in the Disney movie *The Great Locomotive Chase*). Housed in an old cotton gin, the Civil War memorabilia museum is open Mon.-Sat. 9:30 a.m.- 5:30 p.m., Sunday noon-5:30 p.m. (reduced winter hours). Admission to the museum is $3 adults, $1.50 children (six and under free).

Camping

The **KOA North Atlanta** campground, 2000 Old U.S. Hwy. 41 via I-75 exit 116, tel. (770) 427-2406, offers 250 campsites near the Kennesaw Mountain Battlefield. The KOA has a pool and charges $18 for tents and from $26 for RVs.

ROSWELL

Directly north of Atlanta and east of Marietta, the growing suburb of Roswell retains at its core a small walkable village with a historic feel. Only 30 minutes out of town (if there's no traffic), it's popular with city visitors looking for a nice place to drive to where they can walk around and do a little shopping at a few quaint shops and antique stores.

The welcome center, 617 Atlanta St., tel. (770) 640-3253 or (800) 776-7935, directs visitors to historic walking tours, performing arts, and area lodging.

Historic House Museums

Bulloch Hall, 180 Bulloch Ave., tel. (770) 992-1731, opens the antebellum Greek Revival home of President Theodore Roosevelt's mother Mittie Bulloch. Exhibits relate family history and Civil War history, and period gardens are also on display. Hours are Mon.-Sat. 10 a.m.-3 p.m. and Sunday 1-4 p.m. Admission is $5 adults, $3 children.

The **Archibald Smith Plantation Home,** 935 Alpharetta St., tel. (770) 641-3978, offers tours through the 1845 home of the city's founder. Plantation outbuildings include an original slave cabin. Admission is $5 adults, $3 children. Tours are held Tues.-Fri. at 11 a.m. and 2 p.m., and Saturday at 11 a.m., 12 noon, and 1 p.m.

Chattahoochee Nature Center

Outside town, the **Chattahoochee Nature Center,** 9135 Willeo Rd., tel. (770) 992-2055, is a private, nonprofit environmental education and animal rehabilitation center that maintains a 128-acre riverside preserve, with walking trails out to the marshlands or up through the woodlands. Admission to the interpretive center (adults $3, children $2) includes guided walks at 1 p.m. and 3 p.m. weekends. Of the Center's many scheduled programs (most designed for children), most popular are two-hour canoe floats down the Chattahoochee River, Tuesday evenings from April to September. Access is from Azalea Rd. off Roswell Rd. (there are few signs; you might want to call for directions). Hours are Mon.-Sat. 9 a.m.-5 p.m., Sun. noon-5 p.m.

STONE MOUNTAIN

Stone Mountain Park

East of Atlanta, a huge granite bubble surfaces out of the rolling Piedmont landscape. The 825-foot-high natural landmark has been a meeting place since the time of the Creeks and early settlers. Now the unusual formation is the centerpiece of Stone Mountain Park, Hwy. 78, tel. (770) 498-5600, which attracts six million visitors annually. The 3,200-acre park ranks third in attendance nationally after both Disney parks, and it's Georgia's number-one attraction. Transformed into "Olympic Park" for the 1996 Summer Games, Stone Mountain Park and its 383-acre lake were the site of many Olympic competitions. (The park is overseen by state authorities but is not within the state park system.)

The geologically unusual rock "outcropping," is further distinguished by displaying the largest bas relief sculpture in the world. The landmark carving depicts three Confederate heroes on horseback: Confederate President Jefferson Davis, and Generals Robert E. Lee and Thomas ("Stonewall") Jackson. Originally begun in 1923 by Gutzon Borglum (who also carved Mount Rushmore), the three-acre design was not completed until 1970.

Park gates are open 6 a.m.-midnight, year-round. In summer, attractions are open 10 a.m.-9 p.m.; the rest of the year they close at 5:30 p.m. The entrance fee is $6 per car; the entrance fee to attractions is $4.25 for adults, $3.50 seniors, and $3.20 for children 3-11. Alcohol is prohibited in most public places except for designated picnic areas.

Natural History

A century ago, in its undeveloped state, Stone Mountain was crawling with naturalists and scientists observing and recording the dome's distinctive natural history. As the largest of only a dozen or so major granite outcroppings in the eastern U.S., Stone Mountain was highly valued for its unique geology, botany, and animal life.

Such "monadnocks" were formed during the volcanic collision of the African and North American continental plates half a billion years ago. The huge molten bubbles cooled, gradually rose toward the surface, and with erosion became exposed. Scientists theorize the rocks cooled in onionlike layers, and that's why the rock sloughs off in exfoliated slabs. Visible at the base of the mountain, some of these granite slabs are as big as houses.

Because the dense rock holds only thin soil, retains little water, generates heat, and exposes plants to much sun and wind, these outcroppings support plant life more commonly associated with the desert than with the lush Southeast. The rare botanical enclaves are made rarer still by the disjunctive occurrence of these outcroppings, scattered as they are through the Atlantic Coast Piedmont region. Because of this, you can be assured that any one you visit forms its own unique habitat.

Of the score of rare plants found here, the most celebrated is the Confederate yellow daisy *(Viguiera porteri)*. In early fall, bright yellow flowers spring from rock crevices and fill shallow soil pockets on the barren gray rock with vibrant color. The park's Yellow Daisy Festival marks the event. Eroded depressions in the rock form small freshwater pools that support tiny crustaceans.

Today heavy recreational use has blurred Stone Mountain's natural history, yet this granddaddy of granite domes remains a geological and botanical treasure. Smaller outcroppings in the region exhibit similar features, but are less developed, and hence more "natural." (See **Panola Mountain.**)

Sights

From the wide **Memorial Lawn,** site of the park's many festivals, you can look up at the massive rock and its defining sculpture. Or take a Swiss-made **skylift** to the summit for a bird's-eye view of the scene. From the top you'll see the panoramic view over the Piedmont, with city skyscrapers in the distance. The 1.3-mile **summit trail** leads from the mountain's base to the top along the rock slabs, where you can get a closer look at the mountain's rare botany.

The **Antebellum Plantation Village** displays 19 historical buildings, each restored and authentically furnished, including a plantation house, slave quarters, a country store, and craft shops, dating back as far as the 1790s. The **Memorial Hall Museum** contains an excellent collection of Civil War weapons, uniforms, flags, and other memorabilia. The **Stone Mountain Railroad,** featuring replicas of 19th-century locomotives, takes passengers on a five-mile loop around the mountain's base—from the reproduction of Atlanta's 1853 railway depot through surrounding forest and past old granite quarries. Or get the view from the three-deck **Paddlewheel Riverboat.**

On **wildlife trails** through natural woodlands, you may spot cougars, elk, bison, and other species once indigenous to Georgia; the petting zoo is home to domesticated species. The **Antique Auto and Music Museum** exhibits collectors' cars and nickelodeons.

Sports and Recreation

A lushly landscaped 27-hole **golf course** has golf cartways resembling a miniature autobahn; for tee-time reservations call (770) 498-5717. For **swimming and sunbathing,** the lake features an imported white-sand beach, lifeguard-staffed swimming area, and canoe, rowboat, pontoon boat, or pedalboat rentals. Other recreation includes an ice rink, tennis courts, batting cages, miniature golf, hiking, and fishing in the stocked lake "behind" the mountain (a valid Georgia license is required and sold, in season).

Accommodations, Camping, and Food

The classic white-columned **Stone Mountain Park Inn,** tel. (770) 469-3311 or (800) 277-0007, across from the central Memorial Lawn, is the traditional place to stay and eat—or just rest your feet in the front-porch rocking chairs. The inn's rates change seasonally, with highest summer rates starting around $80. Its **Dining Room** serves Southern buffets—it's an Easter-brunch, Mother's-Day-dinner kind of place.

The lavish 250-room **Evergreen Conference Center and Resort,** tel. (770) 879-9900, occupies a quieter corner of the park. Its modern hotel includes a dining room that features continental cuisine.

The park's nicely situated 441-site **campground,** tel. (770) 498-5600, has wooded and shady sites along the lakeshore, with a disposal station, grocery store, and full or partial hookups, 20 miles from downtown Atlanta.

Food service can also be found around the park. **Memorial Depot Chicken Restaurant** fries bird; the **Whistlestop Barbecue** at the base of the trail serves traditional barbecue and sides; and the **Memorial Plaza Deli** atop Memorial Lawn is mostly convenient. Picnic tables are sprinkled throughout. For restaurants outside the park, see **City of Stone Mountain.**

Special Events

The **Antebellum Jubilee** in late March-early April celebrates Southern heritage with folk music, storytelling, traditional arts-and-crafts demonstrations, and a Civil War encampment. A **Lasershow** on the natural one-million-square-foot "screen" of the mountain's face is put on nightly from early May to September 1 (then weekends only through October). The **Fourth of July** celebration brings major music acts along with all-American food and fireworks. Hear bagpipe music performed by kilted marchers at the **Scottish Festival and Highland Games** in October, and see the **Antebellum Plantation** traditionally decorated for Christmas starting in late November.

City of Stone Mountain

Adjacent to the park's south side sits the city of Stone Mountain, actually a quaint village of restored Victorian storefronts set across from an old-time railroad depot. A peanut stand, ice cream parlor, craft shops, and folk antiques complete the scene. It makes a small manageable stop—usually away from the crowds—for a meal, a short walk, or a quick bag of roasted goobers. Drivers with time on their hands may note that Memorial Drive runs a straight shot to downtown Atlanta from here—not a particularly scenic route, but a decent alternative to crowded freeways.

The **Basket Bakery,** 6655 Memorial Dr., tel. (770) 498-0329, serves attractive light meals accompanied by fresh-baked breads and treats. You can eat inside at cozy basket-laden tables or under umbrella tables on the wooden deck, or pick up a muffin and coffee to go at the bakery counter. It's open Mon.-Sat. 7 a.m.-7 p.m., Sunday 8 a.m.-5 p.m.

SOUTHEAST OF ATLANTA

Panola Mountain State Conservation Park

Panola Mountain, 18 miles southeast of Atlanta, is a huge granite outcropping resembling Stone Mountain. Yet unlike Atlanta's familiar landmark, Panola Mountain remains undeveloped, so that visitors here may better see the unique botanical and geological features of these mammoth rock mountains. A 617-acre state conservation park off Hwy. 155 (south of I-20 exit 36), tel. (770) 389-7801, preserves the natural day-use area. The parking fee is $2 per car, free on Wednesday.

Hikers enjoy six miles of trails. Access to the 3.5-mile **summit trail** to the top is restricted to protect the fragile habitat of the 940-foot dome. The trail is open for public use only on guided ranger walks on Saturday and Sunday. The one-and-a-quarter-mile **micro-watershed trail** and three-quarter-mile **rock outcrop trail** both start out behind the interpretive center and loop through the base hardwood forest; both trails are suitable for family outings. The park opens daily; the interpretive center is closed Monday except on major holidays.

JONESBORO AND VICINITY

From its start in southeast Atlanta, Jonesboro Road winds its way down through one of the city's most neglected districts into Clayton County, where it follows the railroad line into Jonesboro and becomes Main Street. In 1864, Yankees and Confederates fought along the route after Atlanta was burned. The Battle of Jonesboro is remembered in Jonesboro's **Confederate Cemetery** with the graves of nearly 1,000 unidentified Confederate soldiers—whose headstones are arranged to form the shape of the Confederate battle flag—at Johnson and McDonough Streets.

This Confederate history likely caught the imagination of young Margaret Mitchell, who traveled to Jonesboro often from her Atlanta home to visit relatives near Jonesboro. Mitchell wove scenes and stories from the battle into her famous novel, and today *Gone with the Wind* fans retrace her steps through the town's historic sites.

The **1898 Jonesboro courthouse** in the center of town was where Margaret Mitchell researched her novel. The 1867 depot now houses the local welcome center at 104 N. Main St., tel. (770) 478-4800 or (800) 662-7829, where they have driving-tour maps and audio cassette rentals, along with lodging and dining information. Also here is the **Road to Tara Museum** ("Road to Tara" was Mitchell's working title), tel. (770) 210-1017, which displays autographed first editions of GWTW, movie posters and costumes, and a hundred GWTW dolls among its exhibits. It's open Mon.-Sat. 10 a.m.-5 p.m. (closed Sunday). Admission is $3 adults, children under 12 free.

Visitors in search of the fictional Tara are directed to the 1839 Greek Revival **Stately Oaks Plantation,** 100 Carriage Lane, tel. (770) 473-0197, a 1839 Greek Revival mansion. Guides in period costume lead tours Mon.-Fri. 10:30 a.m.-3:30 p.m. for $5 adults and $2.50 children.

Fifteen miles south of town, **Fayetteville Academy,** built in 1855, was where the fictional Scarlett O'Hara went to school.

KATHY PETERSON

NORTHWEST GEORGIA

INTRODUCTION

Northwest Georgia's rugged outback—an arid Western-style landscape of singular mesa-topped mountains, long exposed ridges, and sheer-walled canyons—sharply contrasts with the moist coves and knobbly summits of the Blue Ridge Mountains in northeast Georgia. The region's ageless natural attractions draw hikers, spelunkers, hang gliders, and sightseers to the area, while historians come here to see remnants of Civil War battles and ancient aboriginal civilizations.

Outside Atlanta, the **Western Uplands** are a quiet corner of the state, sprinkled with moundworks, Civil War sites, and the hidden jewel of Cave Spring.

Three states meet in Georgia's **TAG Corner** —**T**ennesee, **A**labama, and **G**eorgia. Here on the Cumberland Plateau, the dramatic backcountry is so remote that until relatively recently it could be reached only from neighboring states—yet during the Civil War, the battles of Lookout Mountain and Chickamauga were waged in this impossible terrain. Besides its Civil War heritage, the area is known for hundreds of limestone caves—including two of the deepest in the country—and for its status as the premier hang gliding site on the East Coast.

East of TAG Corner, the high plateau gives way to a series of lesser ridges and valleys forming the high-basin watershed between the Cumberland Plateau and the Cohutta Mountains. Mountain folding along the long parallel ridges has disarranged ancient layers of strata, exposing a variety of rock at the forest floor. A unit of the Chattahoochee National Forest here offers trails, campgrounds, and recreation among woodlands, waterfalls, rock bluffs, and narrow ridges.

On its eastern flank, this region culminates in the long and broad "Great Valley," through which both the railroad and General Sherman entered Georgia. Today, I-75 runs through the valley, providing a modern conduit between Chattanooga and Atlanta. The hundred-mile neon-lit interstate corridor is never more than a few exits away from motorist services (the widest selections

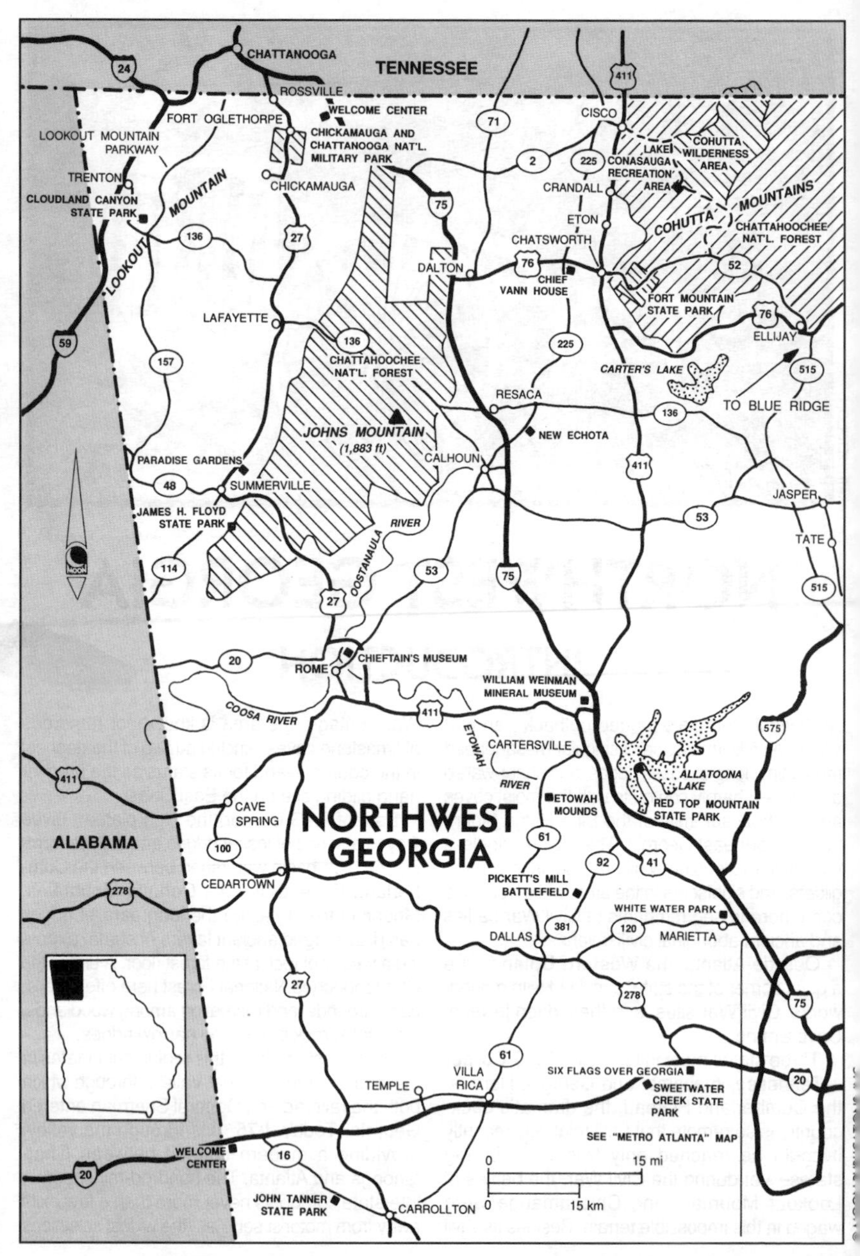

TENNESSEE
CHATTANOOGA
ROSSVILLE
WELCOME CENTER
FORT OGLETHORPE
CHICKAMAUGA AND CHATTANOOGA NAT'L. MILITARY PARK
LOOKOUT MOUNTAIN PARKWAY
TRENTON
CHICKAMAUGA
CLOUDLAND CANYON STATE PARK
LOOKOUT MOUNTAIN
CISCO
LAKE CONASAUGA RECREATION AREA
COHUTTA WILDERNESS AREA
CRANDALL
ETON
CHATSWORTH
COHUTTA MOUNTAINS
CHATTAHOOCHEE NAT'L. FOREST
DALTON
CHIEF VANN HOUSE
FORT MOUNTAIN STATE PARK
ELLIJAY
LAFAYETTE
CHATTAHOOCHEE NAT'L. FOREST
CARTER'S LAKE
TO BLUE RIDGE
RESACA
NEW ECHOTA
JOHNS MOUNTAIN (1,883 ft)
CALHOUN
PARADISE GARDENS
SUMMERVILLE
JAMES H. FLOYD STATE PARK
JASPER
TATE
OOSTANAULA RIVER
MOON
CHIEFTAIN'S MUSEUM
ROME
WILLIAM WEINMAN MINERAL MUSEUM
COOSA RIVER
ETOWAH RIVER
CARTERSVILLE
ALLATOONA LAKE
RED TOP MOUNTAIN STATE PARK
CAVE SPRING
ETOWAH MOUNDS
NORTHWEST GEORGIA
ALABAMA
CEDARTOWN
PICKETT'S MILL BATTLEFIELD
WHITE WATER PARK
DALLAS
MARIETTA
TEMPLE
VILLA RICA
SIX FLAGS OVER GEORGIA
SWEETWATER CREEK STATE PARK
SEE "METRO ATLANTA" MAP
WELCOME CENTER
JOHN TANNER STATE PARK
CARROLLTON
0
15 mi
0
15 km
24
411
71
2
225
75
76
52
136
27
59
157
225
515
136
411
48
53
114
53
75
515
27
20
411
575
61
100
92
41
278
381
120
27
278
75
61
20
16
20

of gas, accommodations, and food are clustered around Dalton and Calhoun), and many historical and natural wonders lie within easy reach of the highway. The area also marks the heart of Cherokee country. While the entire mountain and foothill region was once the province of the Cherokee, encroachment by settlers and countless broken treaties eventually distilled the Cherokee Nation into this Ridge-and-Valley region.

Farther east, the flat, industrialized valley ends abruptly at the western edge of the **Cohutta Mountains.** The Cohutta (co-HUT-a) range is a spur of the Smoky Mountains of Tennessee and North Carolina, and belongs to the easternmost Appalachian geological region, the Blue Ridge Province. In contrast to the secluded dens of the Blue Ridge farther east, the Cohuttas are drier and more wide open. Here the 34,100-acre Cohutta Wilderness challenges hikers and backpackers, and attracts fisherfolk to the finest trout streams in the state.

Climate and Travel Seasons

The mountains have warm summer days in the high 60s (°F), peaking in the mid- to high 70s in July and August. Nighttime temperatures hover in the low 60s, and afternoon cloudbursts are common. Fall continues warm, dry summer weather into October, when the crisp air turns cooler. By mid-month, daytime highs are down in the low 60s. Winter brings freezing temperatures, particularly in January and February, and snow falls every year, accumulating at higher elevations. Springs are cool and wet, with daytime highs in the low to mid-60s, nights in the 50s, and some periods of heavy rain.

Mountain scenery is always beautiful, but it's particularly dramatic when wildflowers bloom in spring and when leaves change color in fall. Summer's a popular time, because the mountains stay cool when the "flatlands" heat up. Winter brings the fewest visitors.

Tourist Information

The **Georgia Welcome Center** at Ringgold, tel. (706) 937-4211, inside the Georgia line off I-75 can orient visitors to the region. For further information on the area, write to the **Northwest Georgia Mountains** tourist bureau at P.O. Box 2497, Calhoun, GA 30703.

THE WESTERN UPLANDS

ALABAMA BORDERLANDS

John Tanner State Park

Ten miles from the Alabama line, John Tanner State Park, I-20 exit 3, tel. (770) 830-2222, offers the state's largest lakefront sand beach. The 136-acre park offers six motel-like efficiency units (from $50) and 78 campsites ($14 a night); call (800) 864-PARK (800-864-7275) for reservations. It also offers miniature golf, an exercise trail, a nature trail, bicycle rental, canoe and pedalboat rental, and a fall crafts show. The park is six miles west of Carrollton off Hwy. 16. Westbound drivers take I-20 exit 3 from Villa Rica and proceed 20 miles southwest via Highways 61, 166, and 16. The parking fee is $2 per car, free on Wednesday.

Cave Spring

Cave Spring is a charming little outpost at the Alabama border. The limestone cave for which the town is named is behind a miniature stone castle in **Rolater Park** in the heart of town, tel. (706) 777-8439. Here the castle matrons collect a dollar each from visitors (and place the bills in a cigar-box register) for tours of the cool (56° F) cavern. The cave is open daily in summer 11 a.m.-4 p.m., and on weekends in shoulder seasons, and also occasionally by request.

Outside, the zealous spring streams forth from the cave (at the rate of three to four million gallons a day) into the park's huge public **swimming pool,** whimsically constructed in the shape of the state of Georgia. Admission is $1.50. It's open summers only, from around June 1 through Labor Day 10 a.m.-5 p.m.

Beside the pool, an 1839 country schoolhouse is now open as the **Hearn Academy Bed and Breakfast,** tel. (706) 777-3382, which makes a nice small-town retreat. They charge $60 for rooms with shared bath, $70 with private bath. Also in the 29-acre park you'll find an old church and log cabin. The park is a short quarter-mile walk to the town square.

the entrance to Cave Spring, where it's a cool 56° F year-round

KAP STANN

The square surrounds a central garden park adorned with a gazebo. The row of shops around the square includes a nursery, cafes, antique shops, and gift shops behind historic storefront facades. The surrounding residential neighborhood holds many stately homes on the historic register. The town hosts arts festivals the second weekend in June and the fourth weekend in September.

On the square, **Gray Horse,** tel. (706) 777-8327, serves a lunch buffet of Southern meats and vegetables as well as menu selections; it's open for breakfast and lunch Mon.-Sat. 6 a.m.-5 p.m. and opens back up for dinner Fri.-Sat. **Todd's** off the square is known for its broasted chicken.

East of Cave Spring is **Chubbtown,** one of the few communities of free blacks in pre-Civil War Georgia. Descendants of the founding family still live here.

Atlanta drivers can reach Cave Spring by way of Rte. 278 to Cedartown, then Rte. 100 to Cave Spring.

CARTERSVILLE AND VICINITY

North to Cartersville

Off Hwy. 92 south of I-75 between Marietta and Cartersville, **Pickett's Mill Battlefield** on Hwy. 381, tel. (770) 443-7850, remains one of the best preserved Civil War battlefields in the nation. The state historic site recalls the 1864 battle, in which the Federal troops attempting an end run around the Confederate line were decisively repelled. In May, living-history programs demonstrate Civil War military drill, cooking, and weapons-firing by soldiers in period costumes. The battlefield is five miles northeast of Dallas.

Next door in **Dallas,** hungry visitors find the Hickory House at 531 W. Memorial Dr. (no phone). for cheap barbecue and Brunswick stew. From town, go west on Business Rte. 6 under a railroad bridge, and look for the small white cinderblock building on the right. Hours are Tues.-Sat. 11 a.m.-9 p.m., Sunday 11 a.m.-8 p.m.

Etowah Indian Mounds

Five miles southwest of Cartersville at Etowah Mounds on Hwy. 61, tel. (770) 387-3747, a well-preserved aboriginal earthwork center offers a glimpse of the ancient civilization that thrived here about 400 years ago. The hallowed mounds, up to 63 feet high, served as platforms and temples for the Priest-Chief and as burial sites for nobility.

Artifacts at the site date back much further, and provide evidence of an early continental trade network. The human statuettes and decorated mica sheets found at Etowah—the site's most acclaimed relics—clearly illustrate a style influenced by Mesoamerican designs (surmised to have been brought by traders).

The state-operated historic site is open Tues.-Sat. 9 a.m.-5 p.m., Sunday 2-5:30 p.m. (closed Monday except for legal holidays). Admission is $2-4.

Red Top Mountain State Park

At Allatoona Lake, a 1,950-acre peninsula holds this major state park, tel. (770) 975-4203, which features a 33-room lodge and restaurant overlooking the lake, a 125-site campground, 18 rental cottages, tennis courts, and a seven-mile nature trail.

Two-bedroom cottages at the park rent for $89-129; lodge rooms cost $69-109; camping costs $14-16. Call (800) 864-PARK (800-864-7275)for reservations. The lodge restaurant serves three meals a day. It costs $2 per car to park, free for restaurant patrons and on Wednesday. The park is two miles east of I-75 exit 123, less than an hour from the Atlanta perimeter.

NATIVE AMERICAN HISTORY SITES

Traces of the Southeast's illustrious Native American history remain visible throughout northwest Georgia. In fact, the region contains two of the most important historical sites in the Southeast, one of which, Etowah Mounds, is considered among the most significant archaeological sites in North America.

At **Etowah Mounds,** off I-75 outside Cartersville, a well-preserved aboriginal earthwork center offers a glimpse of the ancient civilization that thrived here about 400 years ago. The hallowed mounds, up to 63 feet high, served as platforms and temples for the Priest-Chief and as burial sites for nobility. The most acclaimed artifacts found at the site—human statuettes and decorated mica sheets—clearly illustrate a style influenced by Mesoamerican designs (archaeologists surmise the designs were brought by traders).

In the 18th century, when Europeans began to settle what is now Georgia, the Cherokee inhabited northwest Georgia. Unlike the Europeans, the Cherokee formed matrilineal societies, subscribed to a belief system of opposing forces (somewhat similar to the Chinese concept of yin and yang), divined the future with quartz crystals, and purified themselves at an annual Green Corn Ceremony. Other aspects of Cherokee culture, however, were far more familiar.

The natives grew corn, beans, and squash, ate hominy grits, cornbread, and succotash, woke up with a highly caffeinated black drink, smoked tobacco, fished, hunted, and played such a serious game of ball that the outcome was regarded a matter of life and death—all staples of Southern traditions to this day.

To head off threats to their land and independence, the Cherokee reorganized their society into a representative democracy, with a structure and constitution similar to the U.S. Government. In 1828, they named **New Echota** (off I-75 outside Calhoun) the capital of the new Cherokee Nation, and constructed buildings to house their Supreme Court, the *Cherokee Phoenix* (the bilingual English-Cherokee newspaper), and other state concerns. The courthouse and print shop are today among the restored buildings open during public tours at the site.

Several homes of Cherokee leaders remain standing. At the foot of the western Cohutta Mountains in north-central Georgia, the **Chief Vann House** in Chatsworth is the former residence of Cherokee Chief James Vann. The 1804 Federal-style brick mansion is furnished with period antiques and open to the public as a state historic site. In Rossville at the Tennessee line, the **Ross House** preserves the 1797 house of John Ross, principal chief of the Cherokees in 1828. On the banks of the Oostanaula River in Rome, the **Chieftains Museum** occupies the 1794 house of Major Ridge, a prominent Cherokee leader; the exhibits present a memorial to his life and the history of his people.

The Cherokee Nation was recognized as a sovereign power by the U.S. Supreme Court and accorded full diplomatic privileges until Andrew Jackson became president. President Jackson, notorious for his callousness toward native groups, sent federal troops to remove Southeastern natives, foremost the Cherokee, from their ancestral homelands. In 1838, soldiers rousted natives from their homes, imprisoned them in temporary removal forts (of 31 such forts throughout the Southeast, 13 were in Georgia), and exiled them on the Trail of Tears to Indian Territory (now Oklahoma, where the surviving Nation remains today).

The National Park Service plans to develop the Georgia-to-Oklahoma **Trail of Tears** into its historic trails network, which will incorporate many of the above sights. Meanwhile, a 150-mile driving tour called the **Chieftain's Trail** loops from Atlanta past the above sites and others in North Georgia. You can pick up a map of the town at listed heritage sights, the Georgia Visitor Center off I-75, or local welcome centers. Or write Chieftain's Trail, 300 S. Wall St., Calhoun, GA 30701, tel. (706) 625-3200; enclose a business-size SASE for the speediest reply.

Etowah pendant

William Weinman Mineral Center and Museum

Rock hounds will find gemstones, fossils, crystals, arrowheads, geodes, mastodon molars, petrified wood, and a simulated limestone cave in this mineral center, on the southwest side of the intersection of Hwy. 411 and I-75 exit 126, tel. (770) 386-0576. Hours are Tues.-Sat. 10 a.m.-4:30 p.m., Sunday 2-4:30 p.m. Admission is $2.

ROME AND VICINITY

Founded in the 1830s on the site of a former Cherokee Indian settlement at the head of the Coosa River Valley, the city sheltered an important cannon foundry for the Confederacy. Evading earlier threats by Union troops in 1863, Rome succumbed to the routing forces Sherman led through Georgia in 1864. But neither destruction of the town's industry at that time nor subsequent floods have kept Rome from keeping its status as northwest Georgia's industrial center.

Downtown Rome is centered along several busy blocks of Broad St. down from the river. The two most prominent landmarks downtown are the **1871 Old Town Clock** atop a long-empty 104-foot-tall water tower that houses a small museum at its base, and a **statue of Romulus and Remus** in front of City Hall, a gift from Benito Mussolini in 1929.

The **Rome Visitors Center,** 402 Civic Center Dr., tel. (706) 295-5576 or (800) 444-1834, is open daily in a turn-of-the-century train depot off Highways 20 and 27 for self-guided driving tour maps and other city information.

Chieftains Museum

The Chieftains Museum, 501 Riverside Pkwy., tel. (706) 291-9494, is housed in the white clapboard home of the man who signed the treaty that led to the removal of the Cherokee from the area. Chief Ridge went west with his fellow Cherokee, only to be executed there for selling off tribal lands.The small museum examines southeastern Indian history from the first to the 19th centuries. The museum is open Tues.-Sat. 10 a.m.-4 p.m. (closed on national holidays). Admission is $3 adults, $1.50 children.

Berry College and Berry Home

In 1902, Martha Berry founded the Berry School to educate Appalachian youths. The school evolved to Berry College, which today occupies 28,000 acres of handsome buildings set amid forests, fields, lakes, and streams north of Rome. The campus waterwheel makes a picturesque stop, and the Weaving Room displays handwoven items and other student crafts, all available for sale. Pick up a map at the main entrance off Hwy. 27.

Across the highway, **Oak Hill,** tel. (706) 291-1883, opens the Berry family's antebellum mansion and five acres of formal gardens. It's open Mon.-Sat. 10 a.m.-5 p.m., Sunday 1-5 p.m. Admission is $3 adults, students $1.50, children under six free.

"TAG" CORNER

The TAG corner—where Tennessee, Alabama, and Georgia meet—is the most intriguing region of northwest Georgia. Here a completely unexpected landscape of mesas, canyons, limestone caves, boulder fields, and weird rock formations rises up, covered with Appalachian forests. Cloudland Canyon is a hidden getaway for the few who seek it out.

The natural environment is enhanced by the region's rich history. The land is scarred with

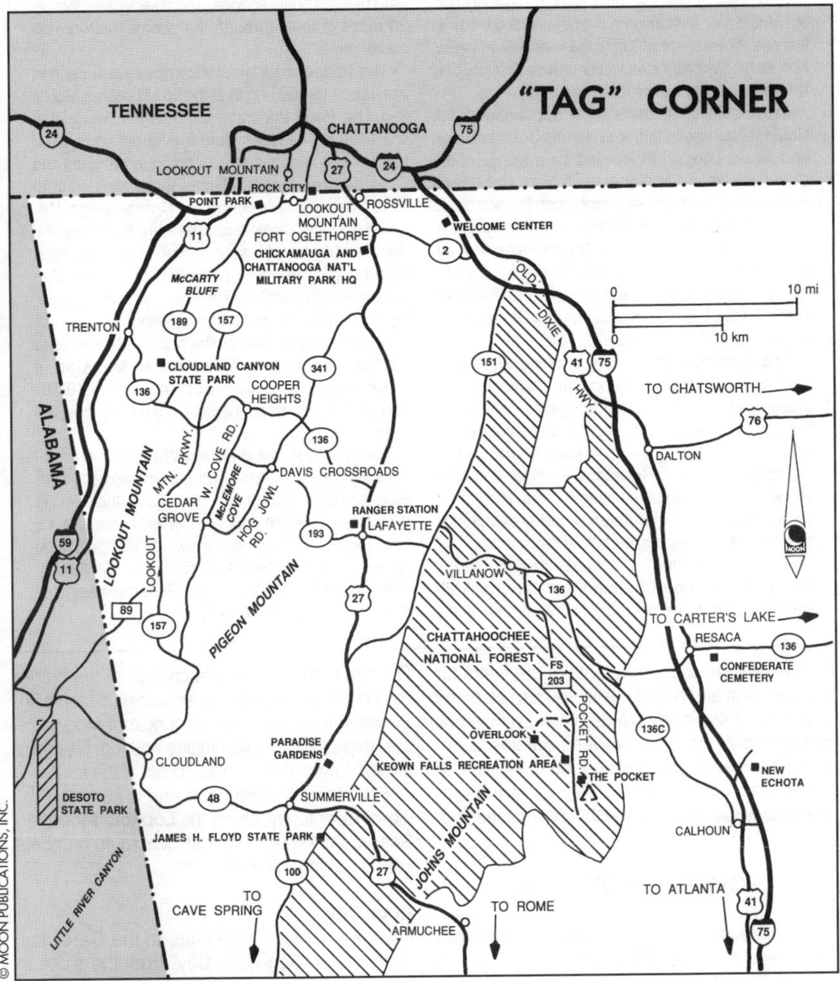

CIVIL WAR TOURING

The critical Civil War battles for Chattanooga and Atlanta were staged in the stark terrain of northwest Georgia. Here, a single glance at the unforgiving landscape delivers a finer appreciation for the hard-fought victories and defeats than a lifetime of imagining the scene.

Union infantry, heading south, came up against Lookout Mountain—a daunting hundred-mile linear barrier that rises like a sheer wall from the level valleys below. Narrow breaks channeled weary armies through, only to face equally formidable mesas beyond.

In the Chickamauga Valley in September 1863, Confederate troops led by Generals Braxton Bragg and James Longstreet repelled the advance of the Union armies under Generals William Rosecrans and George Thomas, yet at high cost. Remembered as the two bloodiest days of the Civil War, the Battle of Chickamauga Creek took 35,000 lives on both sides. In November, the "Battle Above the Clouds" atop Lookout Mountain and fighting on Missionary Ridge led to Union General Ulysses S. Grant's eventual control of Chattanooga.

The following spring, Union General William Tecumseh Sherman resumed the advance south into Georgia. With 100,000 troops he chewed up the path of the railroad, engaging the vastly outnumbered troops of Confederate General James Johnston in Dalton, Resaca, Cassville, and New Hope Church before assaulting Atlanta. His path is today strewn with monuments, old breastworks, cemeteries, old depots, and other landmarks.

Today, Civil War tours start naturally at the **Chickamauga and Chattanooga National Military Park,** the oldest and largest military park in the country. Established 25 years after the war on the urging of veterans from both sides, the historic park's headquarters are at the **Chickamauga Battlefield** site near Fort Oglethorpe, where Union and Confederate soldiers are buried side-by-side in the national cemetery. Frequent living-history programs here reenact battle scenes, and hikers can traverse 80 miles of trails through the scenic, history-rich countryside.

The military park also encompasses a second site, about 15 miles north at the tip of Lookout Mountain. This **Point Park** site, just over the Tennessee line, holds the **Cravens House,** a former home used as Civil War headquarters for both the Yankees and Confederates. Nearby, Rebel fans won't want to miss Chattanooga's **Battle for Chattanooga Museum** (formerly Confederama)—here 5,000 tiny soldiers glued to a 480-square-foot battle map illustrate troop movements with blinking red and blue Christmas lights while the whistling strains of "Dixie" loop continuously over loudspeakers.

A fitting way to explore the region's history is to stay overnight in the **Gordon Lee Mansion** in Chickamauga. This historic inn, built in the 1840s, served as Union headquarters and a troop hospital in 1863.

For a complete list of all Civil War sights in northwest Georgia, pick up a driving-tour map called the ***Blue and Gray Trail*** at the military park, the Georgia Welcome Center off I-75, or local visitor centers. Or write for a copy from the Northwest Georgia Travel Association, P.O. Box 184, Calhoun, GA 30703-0184, tel. (706) 629-3406; enclose a business-size SASE for the speediest reply.

Civil War battle sites, remnants of the fights for Chattanooga and Atlanta. And you can also find a couple of offbeat adventures: Howard Finster's otherworldly Paradise Gardens outside Summerville presents a hallucinogenic flip-side to the enchanted gnomes and fairies at the old-timey Rock City attraction at the Tennessee line.

LOOKOUT MOUNTAIN

Lookout Mountain stretches more than a hundred miles through all three TAG states. Its northern tip overlooks the city of Chattanooga at the Tennessee-Georgia border, and on each side of the border lies one of two towns named Lookout Mountain. So when folks direct you to "Lookout Mountain," they might mean the mountain's northern tip, one of the two towns, or the entire corner of the state.

For dramatic overlooks and a sense of regional topography, cruise the **Lookout Mountain Scenic Parkway** (note that local route numbers change along the way).

Rock City

From Knoxville, Tennessee, to the Carolinas, signs shout "See Rock City" from the sides of barns, birdhouses, and billboards. This old-time mountain institution, tel. (706) 820-2531, was designed in the late 1920s as a private walk-through garden. It displays the arresting rock formations of the Cumberland Plateau in entertaining ways that will enchant youngsters in particular.

Here visitors cross a swinging suspension footbridge over the rock canyons, walk through a narrow crevice called Fat Man's Squeeze, and see Balancing Rock and Lover's Leap. At the visitor center overlook (where the big-headed park mascot Rocky the Elf greets all comers), transparent sheets of colored paper cover the windows while captions explain, "This is what Chattanooga would look like if everything were orange," or red, or green, whatever. Throughout the park, small concrete gnomes peek from behind rocks and trees and Sugar Plum fairies (winged Barbie dolls) inhabit enchanted grottoes lined with glass crystals.

Admission is $5-9. Rock City is open every day except Christmas, 8:30 a.m. until sundown. Follow signs to Rock City from I-24; it's on Hwy. 157 off Hwy. 189.

FORT OGLETHORPE AND VICINITY

Chickamauga Battlefield

The oldest and largest military park in the country, **Chickamauga and Chattanooga National Military Park** has headquarters at Chickamauga Battlefield on Hwy. 27 south of Fort Oglethorpe. Established 25 years after the war on the urging of veterans from both sides, the park commemorates the 35,000 who died in two days of fighting—the two most costly days of the Civil War—over control of Chattanooga and Atlanta. The troop movements of Confederate Generals Braxton Bragg and James Longstreet, and Union Generals William Rosecrans and George Thomas (the "Rock of Chickamauga") are recounted with 1,500 historical markers and monuments, self-guided audiotape tours, summertime living-history reenactments, and ranger interpretive programs. Start at the **visitor center,** tel. (706) 866-9241, for a slide show that details the battle nearly hour-by-hour.

Because most visitors come to hear the human history and rarely stray from their cars, more than 80 miles of **hiking trails** through the Chickamauga Valley are generally quiet and untrampled. The rolling terrain is in a wide valley between two long ridges—a blend of thick forest, open meadows, and farm fields. Seven trails with interpretive signs explain the natural and human history of the region; a five-mile nature trail is the shortest and the 20-mile Perimeter Trail is the longest.

The visitor center distributes trail maps and guides. The center is open 8 a.m.-5:45 p.m. from Memorial Day to Labor Day; the rest of the year it closes at 4:45 p.m. From I-75, take exit 141 (Hwy. 2) west to Fort Oglethorpe, then turn south on Hwy. 27 to the park.

KAP STANN

breathtaking Cloudland Canyon

Gordon Lee Mansion

In the town of Chickamauga, the Gordon Lee Mansion, 217 Cove Rd., tel. (706) 375-4728 or (800) 487-4728, served as headquarters to General Rosecrans for a few fateful days in September 1863. Today it operates as a historic inn, and offers visitors guided day tours for a small fee May-Oct. (no tours on Monday). Nicely appointed bed and breakfast rooms have private baths (rates $75-125).

CLOUDLAND CANYON AND VICINITY

Tucked away in Georgia's northwest corner, Cloudland Canyon remained virtually unknown and inaccessible until roads were built into the area in the 1930s. Adventurers returned with tales of a breathtaking canyon with extraordinary scenery and waterfalls, and naturalists came to study the striped layers of exposed sandstone underlying Lookout Mountain. Now a state park at the rim lets drivers ride straight up to the panoramic vista to witness a topography you'd never expect from Georgia.

Cloudland Canyon State Park

Cloudland Canyon State Park, off Hwy. 136 between Trenton and LaFayette, tel. (706) 657-4050, remains an isolated retreat today. The park features a pool, tennis courts, cabins, and wonderful trails. The parking fee is $2 per car, free on Wednesdays.

Hikers can find magnificent views along two rim trails. The five-mile **West Rim Trail** crosses Daniel Creek and loops into a mixed hardwood forest (spectacular in autumn). **Falls trails** lead down hundreds of steps and switchbacks into the canyon to two dramatic waterfalls—the trip back up can be agonizing, but it's worth it. Backpackers must obtain permits to take the seven-mile **East Rim Trail** to two primitive campsites; rangers lead overnight backpacking trips each October.

Stay in one of 15 fully equipped and spacious cottages at the rim for $65-80 for a two-bedroom; three-bedroom cabins are also available at a slightly higher rate. Or camp at one of 75 sites near rim trails ($15 including water and electric hookups). Call (800) 864-PARK (800-864-7275) for reservations. Overnight visitors need to carry all necessary food to avoid a lengthy descent into Trenton for supplies.

THE LOWER PLATEAU

McLemore Cove

Between Cloudland Canyon and LaFayette, two mesas meet. Pigeon Mountain extends from Lookout Mountain in the shape of a thumb—the sheltered nook between them is McLemore Cove. You can overlook the pastoral valley from the Lookout Mountain Scenic Highway (Hwy. 157), or get a close-up look by descending into the cove on Hwy. 193 (about 15 miles east of Cloudland Canyon and eight miles west of LaFayette).

The isolated valley of dairy farms, croplands, farmhouses, and tall cedar stands, wedged between the sandstone cliffs, starts where Hwy. 193 meets Hog Jowl Rd. (Hwy. 341) and fans out to Hwy. 136. Bicyclists will find this a pleasant, quiet touring route, and can take loop trips of various lengths via either Highway 193 or 136.

Once in the cove, hikers can find the steep six-mile **Pocket Trail,** which climbs Pigeon Mountain for a view of the valley and an up-close look at the mountain's unusual rock formations. To reach the trailhead, take Hog Jowl Rd. 2.7 miles south from Davis Crossroads (the junction of Highway 193 and Hog Jowl Rd.) to the fork in the road, then veer left. Continue past the Baptist church to the top of the hill and turn left onto a paved road. The pavement ends after a half-mile, then turns rugged (four-wheel drive may be necessary after storms) and continues another 1.6 miles to a field where you can park. A wooden sign next to the stream marks the trailhead.

LaFayette

The town of LaFayette marks the western border of the Chattahoochee National Forest. Most of the forest's recreation areas are accessible via Hwy. 136 east. Travelers can pick up directions and trail guides at the Forest Service office, 806 E. Villanow St., tel. (706) 638-1085.

Summerville

About 18 miles south of LaFayette on Hwy. 27, the little town of Summerville has become known to folk art lovers worldwide as the home of Paradise Gardens, the folksy shrine of artist Howard Finster. Also here, a quiet state park draws locals for fishing and boating.

PARADISE GARDENS

Howard Finster, a visionary folk artist, has created his own eccentric personal wonderland outside of Summerville. Here at Paradise Gardens, twisted shards of aluminum foil dangle from tree branches, bicycle-part sculptures and folk Madonnas grace the grounds, and signs quote scripture and proclaim the mystery of Finster's folk philosophy.

Maintaining his gardens since the 1940s, Finster first came to national attention when his art was featured in *Esquire* in 1975. During the next 10 years, his work was exhibited around the country. His painting on the Talking Heads' "Little Creatures" album was selected best album cover in 1985 by *Rolling Stone.* Since then Finster's iconographic portraits and angels can be found among the folk collections of museums throughout the South and U.S.

The gardens are open Mon.-Sat. 10 a.m.-6 p.m. There's a $3 charge to visit the gardens (no charge on Tuesday, donations requested). The gallery and store are open to visitors for no charge. Also inquire about overnight stays in the folk art shrine.

You'll find Paradise Gardens three miles north of Summerville, about a hundred yards off Hwy. 27 (turn east on Rena St. between Jim's Auto Supply and Penn Auto Parts). It's open daily 9 a.m.-5 p.m.

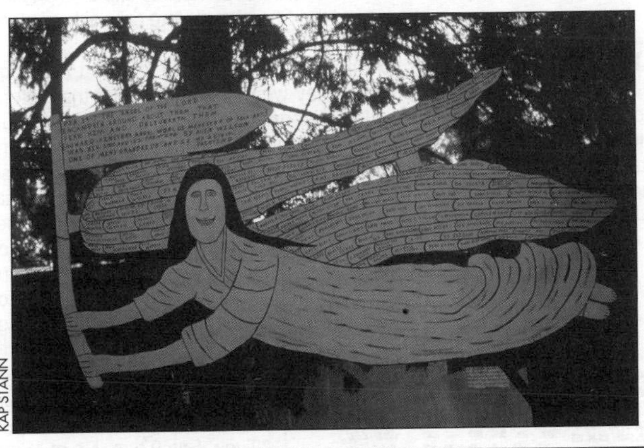

KAP STANN

a trademark Howard Finster icon

In town, Finster pilgrims, fishermen, and locals commune at **Armstrong's,,** 216 N. Commerce St., tel. (706) 857-9900, a breakfast and barbecue joint. It's open Wed.-Sat. 8 a.m.-9 p.m.

James H. "Sloppy" Floyd State Park
Named for a revered state legislator affectionately nicknamed "Sloppy," J.H. Floyd State Park, tel. (706) 857-0826, sits at the western edge of the national forest, off Hwy. 100 south of town. Its two lakes are popular for fishing and boating; boat rentals are available. A hilly, wooded 25-site campground charges $14 a night, including water and electric hookups; call (800) 864-PARK (800-864-7275) for reservations. The cost to park is $2 per car, free Wednesday.

DALTON

As "Carpet Capital of the World," Dalton (I-75 exit 136) presides over the region's economic mainstay—the carpet-producing mills of the central valley. More than 60% of the world's carpet is made here, and more than 100 carpet outlets—many along the interstate—offer discount carpet samples.

Twice a year, a major regional fair is held 10 miles north of the city. The **Prater's Mill County Fair,** in May and October (on Mother's Day and Columbus Day weekends), is staged at the site of a historic gristmill (off Hwy. 2 a mile east of Hwy. 71). The historic mill, built by slaves in 1855, is one of several historic structures to be seen at this celebration of rural folklife. The festival features mountain music, square dances, storytellers, and the original arts and crafts of 150 artisans—including the colonial art of hand-tufted bedspread-making that gave the town industry its start. The 1898 Prater's Store serves authentic Southern meals. Admission to the fairs is $4 for everyone 13 and older. The rest of the year, the historic grounds are open to the public dawn to dusk, no charge.

The **Dalton Welcome Center** in the northwest Georgia Trade and Convention Center off I-75 exit 136, tel. (706) 272-7676, organizes carpet mill tours and distributes downtown walking tour guides among other city information. It's open weekdays only: Mon.-Fri. 8:30 a.m.-5 p.m.

CALHOUN AND VICINITY

Beyond the Last Chance carpet outlets, Wal-Mart, budget motels, and other national chains found at its freeway exits, Calhoun hides a rich history. It was once the home of the 1828 Cherokee Nation, and the Atlanta Campaign's battle at Resaca occurred six miles outside town in 1864—the battle is reenacted annually in mid-May.

New Echota State Historic Site

The Cherokee Nation was organized in 1828, with a representative democracy and a constitution similar to that of the United States. **New Echota,** on Hwy. 225 one mile east of I-75, tel. (706) 629-8151, was named as its capital. Though the U.S. Supreme Court originally recognized the nation as a sovereign power, President Andrew Jackson sent federal troops to remove the Cherokee from their ancestral homelands. In 1838, troops forcibly expelled and imprisoned the Cherokee before exiling them along the Trail of Tears to Oklahoma.

A museum and several restored buildings here display what little remains of the historic capital. Visitors can tour the Supreme Court house, the printing shop that produced the bilingual ***Cherokee Phoenix*** (printed in both English and Cherokee), Vann's Tavern, and the original home of missionary Samuel Worcester, an advocate for Cherokee rights. Several annual events celebrate Cherokee heritage, including a living-history reenactment the fourth week in August and the **Cherokee Fall Festival** in October. The state-operated site is open Tues.-Sat. 9 a.m.-5 p.m., Sunday 2-5:30 p.m. (closed Monday except for legal holidays). Admission is $2 -4.

Johns Mountain

Six miles west of Calhoun, the Armuchee Ranger District of the **Chattahoochee National Forest** shelters the wooded ridges and valleys that stand between the central valley around Calhoun and the western Cumberland Plateau.

Johns Mountain overlooks Georgia's ridge-and-valley region. The 3.5-mile **Johns Mountain Trail** loops around

A as in FATHER
E as A in HATE OR SHORT as in PIT
I as I in PIQUE OR SHORT as in PIT
O as in LOW SHORT as in NOT
U as OO in FOOT SHORT as in PULL
V SHORT U NAZALIZED

THERE WAS NO SOUND OF P. B. J. R. CH or Z

The entire language could be spoken without closing the lips except for the sound of 'M'

CHEROKEE ALPHABET

Joseph Sequoyah, a visionary among the Cherokee, recognized that the written language of the European-Americans offered them a tremendous advantage over the Native-Americans, who at that time had no written language. So Sequoyah set to work developing a syllabary that expressed the sounds of the Cherokee language (essentially, an alphabet). Within a few years after the adoption of his 85-unit syllabary in 1819, thousands of Cherokee became literate. Considering how rarely in the course of human history language-writing systems have been developed, Sequoyah's written language stands as a remarkable Native American achievement.

the mesa-topped mountain with vistas of pastoral farms and fields not much changed since Sherman's troops marched through here in 1864. Find the trailhead from Hwy. 136, about 18 miles northwest of Calhoun and I-75. Turn left (south) onto FS Rd. 203 (Pocket Rd.) just before you reach Villanow; continue south on this route five miles to the two-mile rugged gravel road to the mountaintop.

About halfway around the Johns Mountain loop, hikers arrive at the top of Keown Falls. A spur trail descends to the base and connects with the 1.8-mile **Keown Falls Trail.** This trail runs from the wispy waterfalls, along a stream, to a scenic area near the 27-site FS **Pocket Campground** ($5 a night). The campground features another trail, a 2.5-mile loop through the surrounding wooded glen. To reach the campground and waterfalls trailhead, follow the directions to Johns Mountain above, and continue south on Pocket Rd. past the turnoff to the overlook trail.

THE COHUTTA MOUNTAINS

North Georgia's Cohutta Mountains are centered between the linear mesas of the Cumberland Plateau to the west and the knobbly Blue Ridge Mountains to the east. As part of the Blue Ridge geological province, the Cohuttas resemble the eastern Blue Ridge range with similarly rolling elevations laced with rivers and creeks. Yet with a less "enclosed" canopy and a drier climate, the Cohuttas feel more ruggedly Western than the moist and sheltered Blue Ridge.

The small towns surrounding the remote range can be characterized in much the same way. While more rugged and Western in style than the boutiquey towns farther east, the communities of north-central Georgia share the same Appalachian heritage; many of the traditions of the Blue Ridge Mountains can also be found here.

Highways run along three sides of the range—Hwy. 411 to the west, Hwy. 5/76 to the east, and Highways 52 and 76 to the south.

COHUTTA WILDERNESS

Some of the wildest and most rugged country left in the eastern U.S., the Cohutta Wilderness Area contains 35,000 acres of primitive backcountry bordered by a 95,000-acre wildlife management area. Fishermen claim the Cohuttas hold the best trout streams in the state—Jacks River and Conasauga River are favorites of anglers and hikers. The area was extensively logged in the 1920s, and now the old logging roads and beds of narrow-gauge railroads serve as hiking trails, with names such as Tearbritches Trail, Rough Ridge, and Penitentiary Branch. Bears, wild hogs, and white-tailed deer are a few of the larger species that lies here in isolated mountain coves and on forested ridgetops.

Forest Service roads skirt the perimeter of the wilderness; many have rough, narrow climbs not suitable for delicate cars, drivers, or passengers. From the west, adventurers can gain access from three entrances off Hwy. 411 north of Chatsworth—via the towns of Eton, Crandall, and Cisco. From the south, follow signs from Hwy. 52. From the east, take Hwy. 5 northwest of the town of Blue Ridge to Rte. 271.

Hiking and Backpacking

The 16.7-mile **Jacks River Trail** nearly crosses the wilderness from northwest to southeast. The trail runs largely along what was once the bed of a narrow-gauge railroad. It's a wet and demanding route with 30-some river crossings. Yet the rewards are great, with many scenic waterfalls and beautiful spots to camp (try around Horseshoe Bend). Bring a walking stick to help cross rivers, wear shoes that can get wet, and watch the weather to avoid raging waters after rains or flash floods during thunderstorms.

The 78-mile **Benton MacKaye Trail,** named for the founder of the Appalachian Trail, starts farther east at Springer Mountain. The trail winds its way west, skirting the eastern boundary of the Cohutta Wilderness up to the Tennessee line. Road crossings at Hwy. 60 and Hwy. 5/76 permit easy access. Contact the FS office on E. Main St. in Blue Ridge, tel. (706) 632-3031, for trail maps and Cohutta Wilderness maps.

For a 12-mile overnight backpacking loop within the Cohutta Wilderness, take the 3.4-mile **Tearbritches Trail** to the **Conasauga River Trail;** follow the river southeast for about five miles, then drop down south on the 1.8-mile **Chestnut Lead Trail.** The Tearbritches trailhead lies east of the Lake Conasauga recreation area; take FS Rd. 68 a half-mile north till the road forks, veer right and continue another half-mile east (still FS Rd. 68) to the trailhead on the north side of the road. The Chestnut Lead trail ends 1.5 miles down the road from the Tearbritches trailhead.

CHATSWORTH AND VICINITY

At the western foot of the Cohuttas, at the end of a long, dry drive from every direction, the remote town of Chatsworth vaguely resembles an old stage stop—isolated clapboard buildings are scattered off wide, dusty streets, stacked road

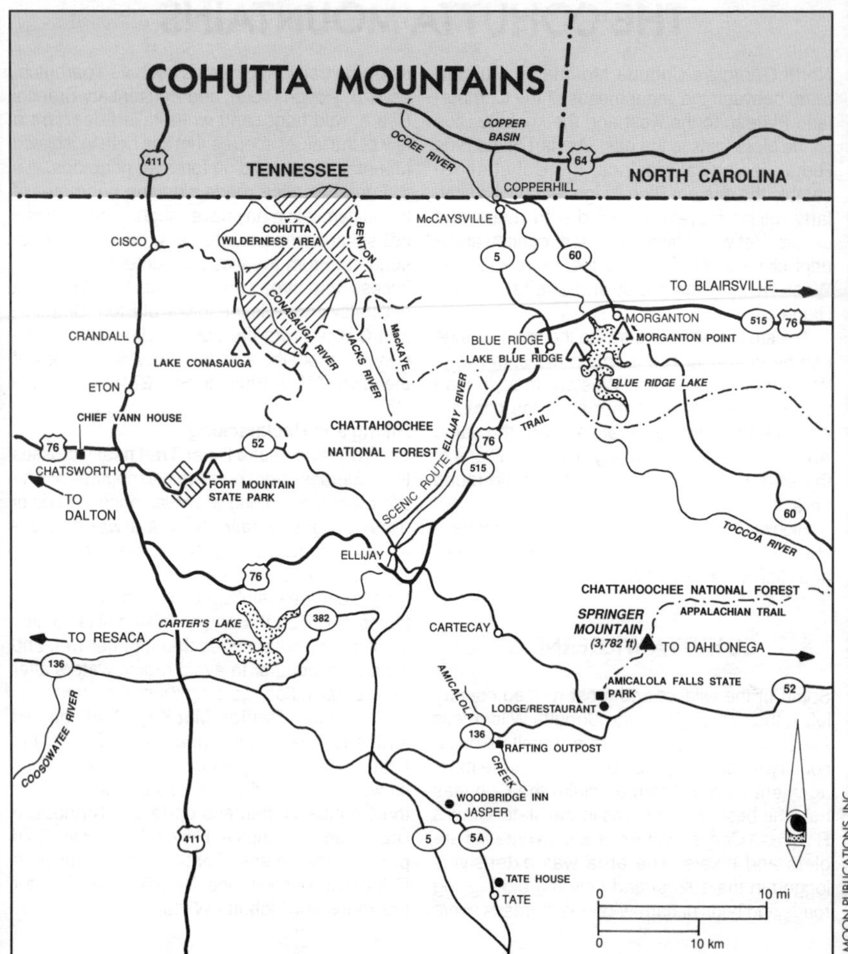

signs point to faraway destinations, and the mountains loom large in the background.

It's fitting that the town's major annual event is the **Appalachian Wagon Train** in July—up to 200 wagon trains and 2,000 horseback riders create a spectacular parade, and half-day wagon-train trips take passengers through local wilds.

In town, a **Forest Service office,** 401 Old Ellijay Rd., tel. (706) 695-6736, sells and distributes trail maps to the Cohutta Wilderness and other forest areas.

At lunchtime, find your way to **Edna's** on Hwy. 411, tel. (706) 695-4951 for inexpensive home-style Southern lunch and early dinner, topped off with peanut butter pie.

Chief Vann House

The town's main attraction is the Chief Vann House, at the junction of Highways 52A and 225, tel. (706) 695-2598. The two-story Federal-style brick mansion, built for Cherokee Chief James Vann in 1804, has been restored and furnished with period antiques. It's the only Native American mansion in America (a distinction best left to individual interpretation). The house is open Tues.-Sat. 9 a.m.-5 p.m., Sunday 2-5:30 p.m. Admission is $2-4.

Fort Mountain State Park

Fort Mountain State Park, on Hwy. 52 about five miles east of Chatsworth, tel. (706) 695-2621, occupies a mountain summit named for a mysterious stone wall. Because the 855-foot wall is aligned to the position of the sun at equinox, some speculate it was a religious center for the Woodland people who inhabited the area around A.D. 500. More romantic theorists assert instead that it was made by a nomadic Welsh prince who predated de Soto; the least romantic claim it to be the natural weathering of hard caprock.

Whatever the origin, the **Old Fort Trail** leads to the wall through an inviting forest of scarlet oak, gnarled white oak, and Virginia pine. The wall itself (about a quarter-mile out) is anticlimactic compared to the dramatic legends (how could it not be?); it resembles a typical New England property line. Beyond the wall, summit trails loop a mile or so to an observation tower and several overlook platforms. Backpackers hike the 8.2-mile **Gahuti Trail** across old logging roads, passing scenic vistas of the interior wilderness and three primitive campsites. Pick up maps to all trails at the park office.

Among the park's other outstanding features are a 17-acre lake—with a swimming beach, dock, and boat rentals—and a 400-foot waterfall. Three short nature trails (under a mile and a half) take hikers to a view of the falls and around the lakeshore. The park hosts a variety of interpretive programs, such as guided wildflower walks in early spring, traditional crafts demonstrations in summer, and overnight backpacking trips in early November.

Fifteen fully equipped cottages (two to three bedrooms each) rent for $65-80 a night. A 70-site campground at the lake's north shore charges

KAP STANN

It may not look like much now, but this stone wall at Fort Mountain State Park might once have been an ancient religious center.

$16 a night, including water and electric hookups. Call (800) 864-PARK (800-864-7275) for reservations. The cost to park is $2 per car, free on Wednesday.

Cohutta Lodge and Restaurant

Off Hwy. 52 about five miles east of Chatsworth, Quality Inn operates a low-key resort scenically perched on a panoramic hilltop. The Cohutta Lodge offers comfortable, moderately priced guest rooms and fine dining with a view in a modern wooden lodge. The amenities include a heated pool, miniature golf, tennis courts, and horseback riding; yet its most unusual diversion is a four-hour **pack-llama ride** through the mountains. For reservations and information, call (706) 695-9601 or (800) 325-6686 (out-of-state).

Lake Conasauga and Vicinity

At the end of backwoods drives south of the Cohutta Wilderness Area, the Forest Service **Lake Conasauga Recreation Area** lies along the shores of a 19-acre lake. Here folks can swim, sunbathe on a grassy ledge, launch boats, and fish for bass, rainbow trout, bream, and crappie. The two-mile **Songbird Trail** leads to a habitat of warblers, cuckoos, and chickadees; other trails lead around the lake and up to an old fire tower.

The 35-site campground ($5 per night) has tent pads, restrooms, and water. On summer weekends, it's often full, so there's an overflow camping area with portable toilets but no water. To reach the lake from Chatsworth, travel north on Hwy. 411 to Eton, turn right at the traffic light, and go east along this road until the pavement ends. Here it becomes FS Rd. 18; turn left on FS Rd. 68 and proceed northeast for 10 miles.

The five-mile **Windy Gap Cycle Trail** southwest of Lake Conasauga is designed for experienced mountain bikers. The trailhead is off Hwy. 411 north of Chatsworth. Turn right at the traffic light in Eton and go east around five miles. Turn left on FS Rd. 218 (Muskrat Rd.) and continue three miles to the trailhead. For other off-road-vehicle trails in the vicinity, contact the Forest Service office in Chatsworth (see above).

Carters Lake

The U.S. Army Corps of Engineers constructed 3,500-acre Carters Lake south of Chatsworth in 1977. It's now a self-contained recreational resort popular with anglers and families. You'll find maps of hiking trails, waterways, and general information at the **Resource Manager's visitor center,** tel. (706) 334-2248, open year-round, Mon.-Fri. 8 a.m.-4:30 p.m., weekends 10 a.m.-6 p.m.

Here, the **Blue Ridge Mountain Marina Resort** (a down-home, private concession) offers a public swimming beach, campgrounds, cabins (from $75), boat rentals (houseboats, fishing boats, and pontoon boats), guided fishing trips, and short hiking and nature trails. Modern, fully equipped rental cabins fit up to six people; houseboats fit eight.

TATE AND JASPER

Highway 5, which merges with Hwy. 76 north of Ellijay for a stretch, traces the valley that divides the Cohuttas to the west from the Blue Ridge Mountains to the east. In the foothills, only an hour and a half from Atlanta, two renowned country inns lie within five miles of one another in the marble-quarry region around Tate and Jasper.

In Tate, two miles east of Hwy. 5, the pink marble mansion of the **Tate House** on Hwy. 53, tel. (770) 735-3122, is a local landmark. Five luxury suites within are individually decorated with fine antiques, and each private bath is lined with locally quarried marble. Out back, nine log cabins each have a fireplace, sleeping loft, and hot tub. There's also a pool, tennis courts, and horse stables. Weekend rates run about $120 for two and include a country breakfast. The dining room is open to both guests and the public Saturday 6-9 p.m. for elaborate five-course dinners featuring prime rib, mountain trout, and other specialties (from $30 a person). A generous champagne brunch is served Sunday 11 a.m.-3 p.m.

Jasper, two miles east of Hwy. 5, hosts the **Georgia Marble Festival** each October. And here the **Woodbridge Inn,** 411 Chambers St., tel. (770) 692-6293, offers elegant dining in a rustic antebellum setting with a beautiful panoramic mountain view. The inn serves steak, fish, veal, and more, along with domestic and European wines. Dinner is served Tues.-Sat., and midday meals are served Wednesday and Sunday. Rooms in the modern lodge start at $60. From downtown Jasper, go north on Main St. and cross the small wooden bridge on the right to the inn.

ELLIJAY AND VICINITY

The "Apple Capital" town of Ellijay centers around a homey old square set on a wooded rise above a stream. Around the square, a streamside cafe and other dusty wooden storefronts selling country wares give the town a fine funky flavor, where kayakers and mountain bikers meet apple farmers over grits and coffee.

The town's trademark event, the **Apple Festival,** is held the second weekend in October, and features plenty of home-style apple treats, a pet parade, mountain music, and local crafts. A rodeo highlights local **Fourth of July** festivities; and you can check out the livestock at the **Gilmer County Fair** the second week in August.

Accommodations and Food

The **Elderberry Inn,** 75 Dalton St., tel. (706) 635-2218, offers bed and breakfast lodging in a welcoming Victorian house on a tree-covered slope above the main road, less than a half-mile from the square (about $60 double).

For home-cooking, the **Calico Cupboard Restaurant** on the square, tel. 635-7575, serves country breakfasts and lunch.

Coosawatee River Running

The Coosawatee River was once a long stretch of dramatic wilderness whitewater—some say it inspired novelist James Dickey's whitewater adventures in *Deliverance*—but its biggest rapids, highest cliffs, and scenic gorge were obscured by the dam that created Carters Lake (highest dam east of the Mississippi). Whitewater enthusiasts still enjoy the upper part of the wild river, which drops more than 500 feet in 22 miles. Yet these rapids do not exceed Class III, and their spacing allows paddlers time to enjoy spectacular scenery.

Gilmer County Park, south of the intersection of Highways 5 and 282, provides a put-in point; the take-out is at **Ridgeway Park** boat ramp administered by Carters Lake (see **Chatsworth and Vicinity,** above).

CITY OF BLUE RIDGE AND VICINITY

The city of Blue Ridge sits near the junction of three states and three mountain ranges. The long narrow valley from Ellijay to Blue Ridge (traced by Highway 76) divides the Blue Ridge Mountains on the east from the Cohutta Mountains on the west. North of Blue Ridge—where Georgia, Tennessee, and North Carolina come together—the Cohutta range becomes the Great Smoky Mountains. Across the border, Georgia's Toccoa River changes its name too, becoming the Ocoee River so familiar to whitewater rafters.

The city of Blue Ridge, the western gateway to the Blue Ridge Mountains, resembles more a town from the Old West than the hillside-hugging towns deeper in the mountains farther east. Downtown, flanks of brick storefronts surround a working depot with a steam train that offers scenic excursion rides, and folks can browse through antiques, folk art, and books while they wait. Mountain-music fans know Blue Ridge best for the bluegrass, country, and gospel music festivals and concerts held west of town, while serious recreationers find great hiking, fishing, and boating in and around Blue Ridge Lake and in the many natural areas in the vicinity.

The most modern development—in the form of supermarket shopping malls and familiar franchise outlets—lines Hwy. 76 on each side of the Hwy. 5 intersection. Find downtown tucked southeast of this intersection.

Sights and Events

Operating out of the old depot in the center of town, the **Blue Ridge Scenic Railway,** tel. (706) 632-9833 or (800) 934-1898, began offering excursion rides in 1997. Passengers board enclosed vintage passenger cars drawn by a massive, smoke-belching, whistle-blowing steam locomotive for a 13.5-mile trip to the Tennessee border. The trip takes an hour and a half, and there's about an hour layover in the humbly scenic riverside border towns of McCaysville and Copperhill (see **Copper Basin**). Excursions run weekends only, June-Oct., Saturday at 9 a.m. and 2 p.m., and Sunday 2 p.m. only. Tickets cost $20 adults, $10 children ages 4-12 (under four free).

The festive mountain-music concerts Blue Ridge is known for take place at the **Sugar Creek Music Park,** west of town off Hwy. 5 north. Regularly scheduled concerts include the two **Sugar Creek Bluegrass Festivals,** the second week in May and October (featuring cloggers, square dancers, fiddlers, and plenty of country cookin'), and July's **Bluegrass Weekend,** which includes free on-site camping with the price of admission. Country-western concerts usually follow bluegrass festivals by one week; and in December, the park hosts a Christmas Music Show. Downtown's city park hosts an **Appalachian crafts festival** the Saturday before Memorial Day, and the annual **Labor Day Barbecue.** October's **Harvest Festival** is celebrated at the **farmers market** on old Business Route 5.

Accommodations and Food

Several motels provide basic accommodations right off the highway. The **Fannin Inn Motel** on Hwy. 76 south, tel. (706) 632-2005, has a pool and rents rooms for about $45. Its home-style restaurant serves lunch, dinner, and a midday Sunday buffet. The newer **Days Inn** on Hwy. 76 north, tel. (706) 632-2100 or (800) 325-2525, charges $44 d. For camping, see **Blue Ridge Lake,** below.

Forge Mill Crossing, tel. (706) 374-5771, is on Forge Mill Rd. off Hwy. 5 six miles north of town. The mountain-view restaurant serves such hearty entrees as trout and steak along with lighter pasta salads. Lunch ranges $3.50-6; dinners about $7-13. It's open Tues.-Sun. 11 a.m.-2:30 p.m. and 5-9 p.m. (later on weekends). The Forge Mill complex also features shops selling crafts, gifts, and antiques.

Information and Services

The Blue Ridge Scenic Railway **depot** in the center of town serves as the local visitor center, or you can call the local chamber of commerce at (706) 632-5680 for more information or a schedule of events. The **Forest Service office,** Hwy. 515 E, tel. (706) 632-3031, provides guides and directories to trails and FS campgrounds nearby.

For groceries and supplies, two supermarket shopping centers are north of downtown: Ingles Market, visible from Hwy. 76 east, and the Piggly Wiggly on E. 1st Street.

Blue Ridge Lake

Blue Ridge Lake, a 3,290-acre impoundment of the Toccoa River maintained by the Tennessee Valley Authority (TVA), features 100 miles of shoreline with beaches, a full-service marina, public boat ramps, campgrounds, and of course, favorite fishing holes. Walleye, smallmouth bass, white bass, and bluegill are the most common catches. Water-skiing and motorboats are permitted on the lake.

At the north shore near the dam, the **Blue Ridge Lake Marina,** tel. (706) 632-2618, is the only commercial outlet on the lake for gas, food, and supplies. It also rents fishing boats. At **Morganton Point,** a FS recreation area offers swimming, boat launching, fishing, rock-hounding trails, and a 37-site campground ($5 a night). Take Hwy. 76 southeast from Blue Ridge for six miles, turn right at Morganton on paved County Rd. 616 and proceed for one mile to the campground.

At the south shore, the **Lake Blue Ridge** FS recreation area offers swimming, boating (launching ramps available), fishing, a short loop shoreline trail, and a 48-site campground ($5 a night). From Blue Ridge, go 1.5 miles down *old* Hwy. 76, turn right on Dry Branch Rd. and go three miles to the entrance.

The 8.8-mile **Rich Mountain Trail** leads from the south shore east of the FS campground up to the Rich Mountain Wilderness Area south of Blue Ridge Lake. The trail dead-ends near the middle of the 78-mile **Benton MacKaye Trail.** To find the lakeshore trailhead, take old Hwy. 76 to Aska Rd.; follow this road for three miles, then turn left on Campbell Camp Rd. and continue for two miles. For closer access to the MacKaye Trail, find the Hwy. 60 road crossing 15 miles south of Morganton.

Ocoee River

The Ocoee River, site of the 1996 Olympic whitewater rafting competition, races through Polk County, Tennessee, between two dams built by the Tennessee Valley Authority (TVA). The river ran dry for 63 years until a broken flume reflooded the riverbed and brought in whitewater enthusiasts. The monolithic TVA eventually agreed to let the waters run for recreation at certain times and divert it at other times for hydroelectric power.

The river's continuous series of Class III and IV rapids—with names such as "Broken Nose," "Diamond Splitter," "Tablesaw," and "Hell Hole"—makes it one of the Southeast's greatest whitewater runs. Because of its nonstop action, the overall rating is Class IV. Surrounded by the Cherokee National Forest, the Ocoee offers beautiful scenery as well as an outstanding whitewater challenge. Tennessee Hwy. 64 parallels the river, easing access for rafters and spectators.

From river outposts centered around Ocoee, Tennessee, a consortium of two dozen outfitters lead guided rafting expeditions downriver for half-day or full-day excursions ($45 and up). Some offer canoe and kayak rental, classes, overnight trips, wet-suit rentals, and package deals with overnight lodging. Try **Ocoee Rafting, Inc.,** tel. (800) 251-4800; **Southeastern Expeditions,** tel. (800) 868-7238; **Nantahala Outdoor Center,** tel. (800) 232-7238; or **Ocoee Outdoors,** tel. (800) 533-7767.

Copper Basin

The Copper Basin at the Georgia-Tennessee border, so named for the copper mines that created its stark desertlike environment, now stands out as an arresting scene of smooth red- and copper-hued hills against the surrounding lush green forested mountains. The mid-1800s mining industry generated enough copper sulfide fumes to devastate the area's vegetation (whatever was left over once the forest was cut to fuel the smelters). After the industry collapsed early this century, the Civilian Conservation Corps began a reclamation project to reseed the rolling hills.

By now the environmental nightmare has been transformed into a historic legacy, and today the principal industry is tourism from Ocoee River whitewater enthusiasts. Visitors can tour the old mines and visit historic districts in the neighboring border towns of **McCaysville, Georgia,** and **Copperhill, Tennessee.** Self-guided walking- and driving-tour maps available at the visitor center in downtown Copperhill, tel. (615) 496-1012, incorporate sites in both towns.

Within walking distance of the **Blue Ridge Scenic Railway** terminus you might be surprised to find a Japanese restaurant with decent sushi. Across from the platform, the casual **Michiko's,** tel. (706) 492-5093, serves sushi plates from $5 along with such other specialties as gyoza, yakitori, and udon (also $3 burgers for kids). Lunch and dinner is served Mon.-Fri. 11 a.m.-2 p.m. and 5-8 p.m.; it's open all day Saturday and closed Sunday. A short drive up Hwy. 5 in McCaysville, the local greasy spoon is **Pat's Country Kitchen** on Hwy. 5, tel. (706) 492-5477, where the conversation is likely to be better than the food—particularly if you're a smoker—but it's nearly always open (hours are Mon.-Thurs. 6 a.m.-9:30 p.m., Fri.-Sat. 6 a.m.-10 p.m., Sunday 7 a.m.-10 p.m.).

LOUISE FOOTE

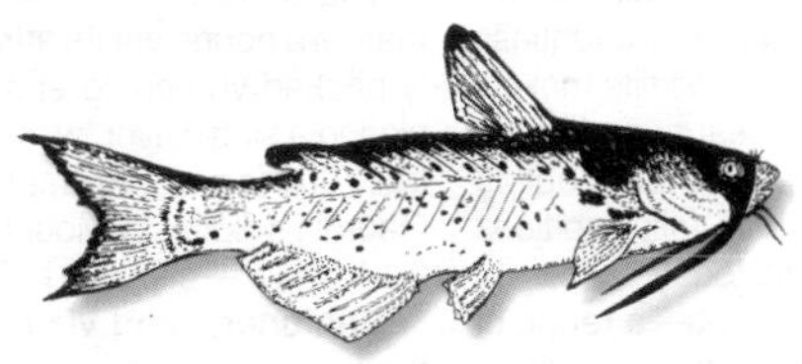

channel catfish

KATHY PETERSON

BLUE RIDGE MOUNTAINS

INTRODUCTION

Two hours north of Atlanta, the Appalachian Mountains rise up into a spectacular landscape of thickly forested ridges, soft hidden "coves," and rushing waters. But the terrain isn't all that changes. The Southern Appalachians also give rise to the mountaineer culture that has captured the American imagination since the days of English rule.

Early visitors called it an Eden. Its 1,500 blooming plant types, 130 tree varieties (compared with only 85 in all of Europe), countless streaming waterfalls, and rustling wildlife make it easy to see why. The natural beauty and bounty attracted America's first pioneers, peopling the wilderness with Appalachian folk traditions still practiced in North Georgia today.

Here the Blue Ridge Mountains—a range of legendary beauty and history—get their start. Yet for all the Blue Ridge's renown, few people outside the South realize that Georgia has mountains at all, much less such a celebrated range.

Most of Georgia's Blue Ridge lies within the 727,000-acre Chattahoochee National Forest. Wild and rugged, yet inviting and accessible, these mountains are made to explore—a single cove, one sunlit spider web, one stairstep waterfall at a time. Built to a human scale, the Appalachians can best be described as the subtle, intimate difference between the terms *forest* and *woods.*

You could cross this fabled landscape in less than two hours, yet its attractions are so densely packed you could easily spend a week exploring a single river, wood, or trail. One of these trails, the famous **Appalachian Trail,** begins at Georgia's Springer Mountain and extends north 2,144 miles—clear up to Maine.

Dahlonega and vicinity is a great place to begin your exploration of Georgia's Blue Ridge. The historic town boomed during the nation's first gold rush in 1828. The gold-country valley below it extends south and west over to Amicalola Falls State Park. To delve deeper into

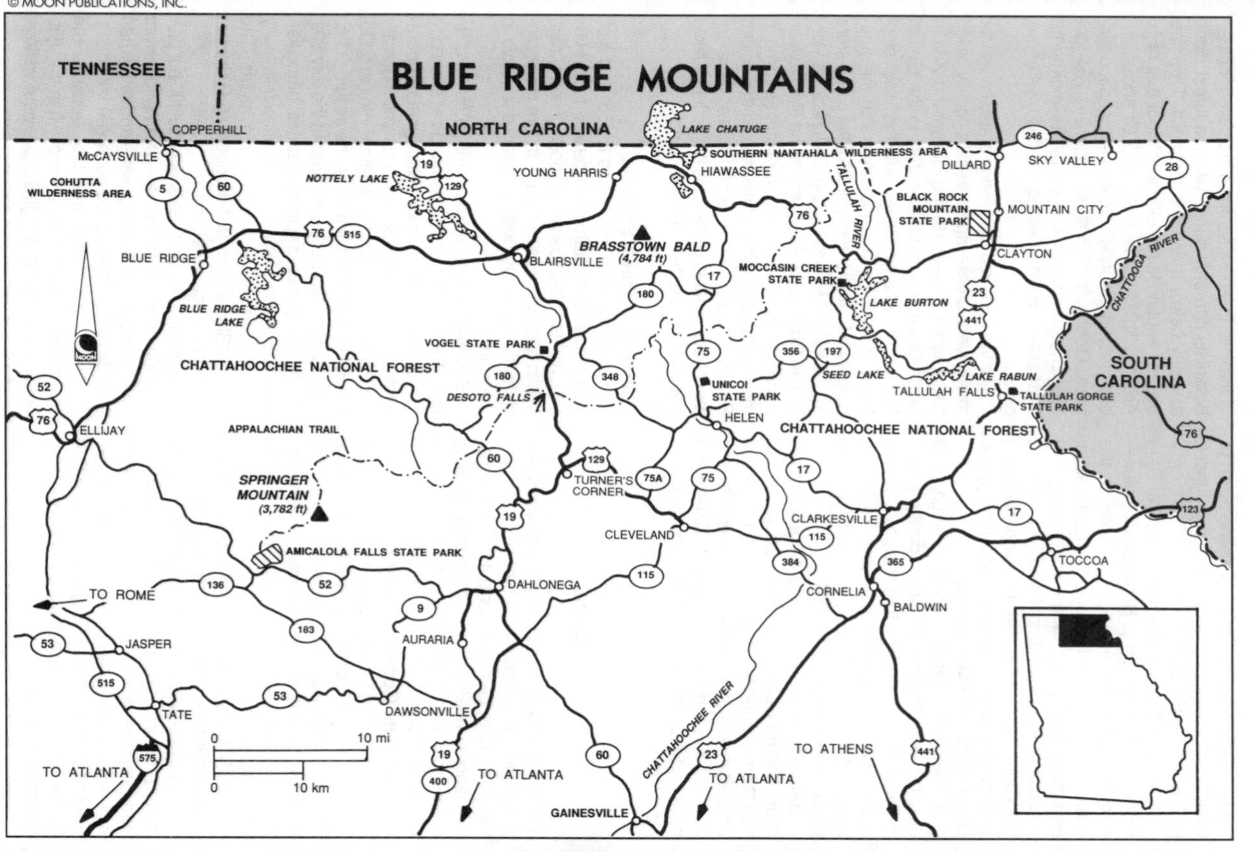
© MOON PUBLICATIONS, INC.
BLUE RIDGE MOUNTAINS
TENNESSEE
NORTH CAROLINA
SOUTH CAROLINA
COPPERHILL
McCAYSVILLE
COHUTTA WILDERNESS AREA
BLUE RIDGE
BLUE RIDGE LAKE
NOTTELY LAKE
BLAIRSVILLE
YOUNG HARRIS
LAKE CHATUGE
HIAWASSEE
SOUTHERN NANTAHALA WILDERNESS AREA
TALLULAH RIVER
DILLARD
SKY VALLEY
BLACK ROCK MOUNTAIN STATE PARK
MOUNTAIN CITY
CLAYTON
CHATTOOGA RIVER
BRASSTOWN BALD (4,784 ft)
MOCCASIN CREEK STATE PARK
LAKE BURTON
SEED LAKE
LAKE RABUN
TALLULAH FALLS
TALLULAH GORGE STATE PARK
VOGEL STATE PARK
CHATTAHOOCHEE NATIONAL FOREST
DESOTO FALLS
UNICOI STATE PARK
HELEN
ELLIJAY
APPALACHIAN TRAIL
SPRINGER MOUNTAIN (3,782 ft)
AMICALOLA FALLS STATE PARK
TURNER'S CORNER
CLEVELAND
CLARKESVILLE
TOCCOA
DAHLONEGA
CORNELIA
BALDWIN
TO ROME
JASPER
AURARIA
TATE
DAWSONVILLE
CHATTAHOOCHEE RIVER
TO ATLANTA
TO ATHENS
GAINESVILLE
0
10 mi
10 km
MOON
5
60
19
129
76
515
52
180
17
348
75
356
197
23
441
246
28
129
75A
123
136
53
183
9
115
384
365
575
400

the Blue Ridge, head over the ridgeline **north to Blairsville,** a hardy mountain town surrounded by forest and lake adventures.

The route through Georgia's central Blue Ridge runs from **Helen to Hiawassee.** Helen—a re-created Alpine village, right down to the edelweiss—is the most unusual town in the state, and bounded by the compelling beauty and serenity of the Chattahoochee River valley to the south. North of Helen, the highway leads through Unicoi Gap to Hiawassee, the popular site of many mountain festivals.

Heading to the easternmost Blue Ridge, you'll pass through **Clarkesville and vicinity,** a turn-of-the-century resort area that retains its historic sophistication. Between here and Toccoa, a branch of the national forest offers natural areas within easy reach of urban folk.

Set apart in the northeastern corner of the state, **Rabun County** attracts hotdog river runners from around the country to the Chattooga River's whitewater wilderness (the river's Section Four is for daredevils; run Section Three if you have dependents). City weekenders flock to its placid high-country lakes.

THE LAND

The **Blue Ridge Province,** the eastern Appalachian geological region that occupies two-thirds of North Georgia, consists of two separate ranges: the Blue Ridge Mountain front range to the east, and the Cohutta Mountains to the west. (The Cohutta Mountains are covered in the **Northwest Georgia** chapter.)

From Georgia through eight states to Pennsylvania, the lush landscape of the Blue Ridge Mountains has inspired a lexicon all its own to describe its unique topographical features: visitors enter a land of "coves, balds, gaps, knobs, licks, and cataracts."

Thickly forested low rises ("knobs") spread throughout the mountains create small fertile valleys in between called "coves." These secreted niches supported most agriculture of early settlers, while hunting revolved around naturally occurring salt deposits ("licks") that attracted wild animals. "Gaps" may be either "water gaps" in river valleys or "wind gaps" in mountain passes.

Inexplicably bare summits are called "balds." Botanists can only guess why the forest stops abruptly below these grassy knolls. Tree line doesn't explain it; the elevation's not that high. Are they lightning-set fire scars? Or ancient Indian sacred grounds? No one explanation suffices. Georgia's highest elevation—4,784-foot Mt. Enotah, better known by its nickname **Brasstown Bald**—belongs to this mysterious group.

The well-watered Blue Ridge is also known for many rivers, creeks, and waterfalls (locally called "cataracts"). The eastern continental divide in North Georgia separates waters to the Gulf of Mexico, the Atlantic Ocean, and the Mississippi River. In a rainstorm, you can watch this phenomenon from the front porch of the camp store at Black Rock Mountain State Park near Clayton.

The Chattooga River, where the film *Deliverance* was made, is known to rafters as some of the most challenging whitewater in the United States. Rivers impounded for power development have created contiguous high-country lakes popular with boaters and paddlers.

Climate and Travel Seasons

Early spring in the mountains is cool and wet, with midday temperatures in the low- to mid-60s (°F), nights in the 50s, and periods of heavy rain. In mid-May, the weather starts to turn more consistently summery, with warmer, drier days in the high 60s.

Summer temperatures climb to the mid- to high 70s in July and August; tropical afternoon cloudbursts are common. Nighttime temperatures slip to the low 60s. Indian summers typically stretch warm dry summer weather into early October. When fall finally arrives, the air turns crisp and daytime temperatures drop to the low 60s. Winter brings freezing temperatures, particularly in January and February, and snow falls every year, accumulating at higher elevations. The famed "Blizzard of '93" dropped 16 inches of snow in a single weekend.

Mountain scenery is always beautiful, but particularly dramatic in spring—when wildflowers bloom and rivers run highest—and fall, when crowds of "leaflookers" come to see fall colors. Summer's a popular time too, because the mountains remain relatively cool when the "flatlands" heat up. Winter gets the fewest visitors;

some businesses shut their doors until spring. Because many flatlanders are wary about winter driving, drivers unafraid to encounter the possibility of snow and ice can have the scenic winter mountains to themselves.

Budget travelers may want to take seasonal demand into account when making plans. Prime October lodging may cost up to twice as much as the same room come winter, and you may want to consider camping. Whichever way, book early for October; popular state park cabins may book up 11 months in advance!

FLORA AND FAUNA

The Appalachian Forest

In the Blue Ridge, you'll find a lush, storybook wood with a surprise discovery at every step. Overhead, the leafy forest ceiling shades the 130 tree species, 1,500 blooming species, 350 mosses and related plants, and 2,000 types of fungi below.

Besides its compelling beauty, the variety of the Appalachian forest sustained its inhabitants and defined mountain culture. Trees vital to the mountain economy were revered with near-animist regard. The mighty **chestnut,** for example, provided the Appalachian people with a strong and durable wood, and nuts for eating and attracting game. Earlier this century, a devastating chestnut blight wiped out most of these giants, and mountain communities mourned their passing with a heartfelt grief beyond economic loss. The **red cedar** was sacred to the Cherokee; they carved religious objects from it and forbade its use as firewood. Even today, old-time mountaineers know the properties of trees intimately, like a hunter knows the habits of wild animals.

When white settlers arrived, most of the forest was already second growth—natives typically cleared lands for firewood and to attract game. Later, logging and farming further reduced the original Great Appalachian Forest to a few patches, where giant stands of old-growth **hemlocks** and **yellow poplars** remain (see Cooper Creek near **Blairsville,** and Ellicott's Rock Wilderness in **Rabun County**).

Dominating the Southern Appalachian forests are **oaks, hickories, poplars, sweet gum,** and **pines,** accompanied by the blooming varieties of **magnolia, dogwood, yellowwood, silverbell,** and **tulip poplar.** You'll hear the term "hardwoods" used to describe the deciduous trees (those that lose their leaves every autumn), while the term "softwoods" refers to evergreens (coniferous varieties with needles).

Below the towering canopy, 30-foot-high **rhododendron** and **mountain laurel** thickets create a flowering substory so dense that mountaineers call them rhododendron "hells." Look closely to distinguish the two: rhododendron *(Rhododendron maximus)* has leaves a foot long and two to three inches wide; mountain laurel *(Kalmia latifolia)* leaves never exceed four inches in length. The peak flowering season for both runs from April to June.

Understory Plants

In spring, **trilliums, violets, lilies, hydrangeas,** and pink and yellow **lady's slippers** (the Cherokee call them "partridge moccasins") bloom among many other varieties. But perhaps the **sunflower** is the one that makes the most lasting impression—whole fields of flowers tall as posts turn their broad faces to follow the arc of the sun from dawn till dusk.

A green fern bed lines the forest; the **cinnamon fern** turns its spicy color in fall, while

'SANG HUNTIN'

Ginseng *(Panax quinquefolium),* an understory plant that produces a root highly valued for its medicinal properties, grows wild in the Southern Appalachians. As early as the 18th century, Blue Ridge settlers harvested it for sale to China. Believing that plant shape influences its value, the Chinese hold the human-shaped ginseng root in high regard as an all-around stimulating tonic. Appalachian families likewise incorporated the herbal tonic into their own folk medicine. (The word "panacea" is believed by some to come from ginseng's Latin name.)

Raised ginseng didn't match the quality of the wild plant, so farmers went "'sang huntin'," searching hillsides and coves for the thin-leafed plant. The conservative "sanger" dug roots only in the fall and reseeded a harvested area by taking only a portion of the root, yet extensive collecting has made the once-prolific ginseng a rare find.

Throughout the Blue Ridge whole fields of sunflowers follow the sun, marking the passage of summer.

stocking-shaped blades distinguish the **Christmas fern. Galax,** another Christmas favorite, turns red in December; its leaves are harvested for decorations in spite of a skunklike odor. Edible wild plants grace mountain tables with fresh fruits and berries, including the exotic pawpaw fruit and "coon" grapes, as well as wild greens and herbs used for seasonings and medicines.

Mammals

The **white-tailed deer,** hunted down to small numbers by the native Cherokee, now verges on overpopulation. **Razorback hogs** (domestic pigs gone wild) and the larger and fiercer **European wild boar** (introduced for sport) fostered the country ham tradition carried on in the mountains today. Other mammals occasionally encountered by visitors include **black bears, wild mink,** and **beavers.** Small game animals abound: look for **rabbits, squirrels, raccoons,** and **possums.**

Two centuries ago, the Appalachians sheltered the timber wolf, bison, and puma, each now practically exterminated (the elusive **puma** may be an exception).

Reptiles

The mountains' venomous snakes—**timber rattlers** and **copperheads**—usually stay clear of people, yet a hiker venturing beyond worn trails would be wise to keep an ear and eye out for their distinctive sounds or markings.

Birds

The forests of North Georgia are home to a variety of bird species more commonly associated with points north, such as the **Canadian warbler.** The mild climate and location along the winter migration flyway bring hundreds more species to its treetops.

Game species include **quail** and **ruffed grouse** (often called partridge, locally pronounced "pah-tridge"). Florid historical accounts describe once-huge herds of **wild turkey** (still found in smaller numbers), and flocks of pigeons so large they "darkened the sky" as they flew overhead.

HISTORY

While previously only the coast was known to support ancient societies, excavations of the Nacoochee Mound near Helen earlier this century revealed skeletons and relics that may date back 10,000 years. Nearby petroglyph carvings date back 3,500 years, and in the north-central mountains, a stone wall of mysterious origins at Fort Mountain is ascribed to aboriginal tribes.

Inheritors of this ancient past, the Cherokee inhabited North Georgia when the first Europeans arrived. In 1539, the Spanish explorer Hernando de Soto led a 600-man expedition from Florida to North Georgia in search of gold. His journey and those of other European explorers decimated the Cherokee by introducing diseases against which the natives had no natural immunity.

British pioneers from coastal Charleston, and Scotch, Irish, and German emigrants from Pennsylvania began settling on the Appalachian frontier in the mid-1700s. In their wilderness isolation, many pioneers maintained independent ways; they remained loyal to the Crown during the American Revolution, and later refused to fight for the Confederacy during the Civil War.

White settlers fought with the Cherokee over territory, yet surprisingly, the two radically different groups managed to coexist peacefully much of the time, learning from one another's culture. From the Cherokee, the pioneers learned how to make the best use of natural resources, and in turn, the Cherokee adopted many European ways. They established the Cherokee Nation, with a representative system of government based on that of the United States. Yet their sovereignty and homeland nonetheless fell victim to U.S. expansionism (see the **Northwest Georgia** chapter), triggered by the discovery of gold on Cherokee territory.

Gold Rush

In 1828, a hunter named Benjamin Parks kicked up what resembled "the yellow of an egg," and what turned out to be a large gold nugget propelled the first major gold rush in American history (predating California's "'49ers"). Centered in the boomtown of Dahlonega (Cherokee for "yellow"), the rush brought thousands of miners to the area. The federal government founded a branch of the U.S. mint in Dahlonega that produced more than $6 million in gold coins before it closed at the onset of the Civil War. The town's Gold Museum recounts gold-rush days.

1865-1930s

After the Civil War, the economic and environmental destruction wrought by overfarming, hydraulic mining, overlogging, the chestnut blight, and the boll weevil added up to decades of hard times for mountain communities. Forced to rely more than ever on what could be drawn from the land, the mountaineers heightened their reliance on folkways—customs and crafts now regarded as some of America's most creative pioneer expressions. Their extreme isolation began to diminish with the first rural postal delivery, highway construction, and later with radio and television, yet many mountaineers continued to practice traditional folkways in earnest for several more decades. The aging population of "oldtimers" in the mountains today represents the last of a hardy breed.

Chattahoochee National Forest

In the 1920s and '30s, the federal government bought most of North Georgia's land to establish the national forest. Land "reclamation" projects, designed to restore flora in areas of environmental devastation, were accomplished by the Depression-era Civilian Conservation Corps. Several CCC-built state parks, stone cabins, and lodges remain in active use today. The Wilderness Act of 1964 set aside the Cohutta and Ellicott Rock wilderness areas, and in December 1991, 56,000 more acres were designated as wilderness.

PEOPLE

Traditional Appalachian Culture

The southern Appalachians are united not only geologically, botanically, and historically, but also culturally. In many ways, North Georgians hold more in common with mountain folk three states removed than with flatlanders in their own state.

The forest provided the means to their self-sufficiency. From log cabins to the smallest peg, virtually everything on an Appalachian farm was made from wood. Nut trees provided an important source of protein and attracted small game animals easily hunted. Wild fruits ripe for the pickin' grew profusely, including red mulberries, wild plums, wild cherries, black haws, persimmons, crabapples, wild strawberries, and pawpaws (described as "somewheres between a banana and a persimmon"). Plenty of "pick-your-own" fields still dot the region today. Wild onions ("ramps") and wild garlic seasoned cultivated crops.

Like the Cherokee, the mountaineers crafted many useful items from the bottle gourd plant, including dippers, water jugs, cups and bowls, and even banjos. But today, you'll most commonly see the gourds used as birdhouses to attract the purple martins that keep the local insect population down.

Folk Beliefs

Traditional Appalachian farmers subscribed to a strong belief in astrology. The signs of the zodiac and phases of the moon determined auspicious times to plant and harvest, and even influenced when to get a haircut, paint a house, or wean a child. Each sign was identified with a different part of the body, so, by example, folk logic would hold that the best time to plant beans was with the moon in Gemini ("the arms"). Root crops were best gathered with the moon in Capricorn or Aquarius (the knees or ankles), and all crops that yield below the ground were best planted in a waning moon—those that yield above were best planted in a waxing phase.

With few trained health-care practitioners, farm families relied on folk medicine. This ranged from sound herbal remedies (whose physiological properties have been long ignored by modern science) to superstition. Common ailments were treated with herbal teas and poultices, kerosene oil, and healthy doses of homemade whiskey. More ingenious treatments included: carrying buckeye seeds to combat rheumatism, turning shoes upside down overnight to relieve cramped feet, and burying hair under a rock to cure headaches (it's said old-timers would never allow their cut hair to be thrown away because it was too valuable). Faith healing also carried weight; to test faith, some Primitive Baptists handled venomous snakes and drank poison.

Arts and Crafts

Appalachian baskets, pottery, quilts, weavings, and all manner of woodworking are prized Appalachian crafts. Skilled artists demonstrate these crafts today at mountain fairs and festivals, and sell their wares at local craft shops. Look for baskets woven from honeysuckle vines and oak splits; clay pottery shaped into "face jugs" (believed to derive from African traditions and English Toby mugs); and whittled carvings, wooden toys, and hardwood furniture (either rustic or refined). Natural expressions of folk art decorate gravestones, road signs, and side yards throughout the mountains; similar "primitives" are sold in craft and antique shops.

Music, Dance, and Entertainment

Bluegrass music emanates from the mountains, where it's performed at all local festivals and on front porches throughout the region. Folk and traditional music, accompanied by homemade dulcimers, fiddles, and banjos, date back generations to Old English ballads. Today's "mountain music" also includes gospel and country-western.

"Clogging" is a distinctively Appalachian dance form, which originated from the "flat-footin'" African-American style introduced earlier this century. Most festivals feature clogging performances. Square dancing is also a popular mountain pastime.

Storytelling reaches a pinnacle in the mountains. A strong oral-history tradition, a flair for

Bottle gourds attract nesting purple martins, which help keep the local insect population down.

KAP STANN

grandiose hyperbole, and mountaineer idiom and accent combine to make mountain storytelling an entertaining art form. Tales of local "haints" (haunts) are particularly popular, especially around mountain campfires.

GETTING THERE

By Car

Wide, smooth, well-maintained highways throughout the mountains offer spectacular scenery and gentle slopes with few steep climbs. Wherever a new highway bypass has been constructed, visitors with time to spare will naturally find the "old" highways more scenic.

Forest Service (FS) roads through the Chattahoochee National Forest present a far greater challenge. Unpaved—and likely steep, narrow, and pocked—FS roads are not recommended for delicate vehicles, drivers, or passengers (four-wheel drives are ideal). Speeds slow considerably, so leave plenty of time to reach your destination before dark. Navigating can be tricky even in daylight—signs are small, few, and often hidden by foliage. So carry a good map, a compass, and emergency supplies including a flashlight, whistle, and first-aid kit, and extra food, water, and clothes. Also be aware that during summer's thundershower season, flash floods may block roads.

By Bicycle

Bicycle touring is a scenic and adventurous form of transportation in the mountains. Wide, smooth highways of changing elevations provide spectacular scenery and a range of challenges, and there are plenty of camps or country inns at which to stay along the way. One of the many statewide routes mapped by the state tourist bureau, the "Mountain Crossing" route traverses North Georgia east to west. To request a free biking guide from the bureau, call (404) 656-3590.

Several organizations and excursion companies arrange or list bicycle tours in the mountain region; write the **Southern Bicycle League** at P.O. Box 1360, Roswell, GA 30077 for more information. Forest Service roads are great for mountain biking.

By Train

Amtrak runs service through Gainesville and Toccoa, with direct service from Atlanta and many Eastern Seaboard and Southern cities. Call (800) 872-7245 for schedules and fares. The Gainesville stop, a well-worn path for Appalachian Trail hikers, is serviced by taxi (about $38 plus tip to the lower Blue Ridge; call **Gainesville Taxi** at 706-287-3221).

By Bus

Regular bus service runs between Atlanta and Gainesville (50 miles north). Buses leave daily from Atlanta's downtown terminal; call (404) 522-6300 for routes and fares.

On Foot!

Among the region's hundreds of miles of hiking trails, several long-distance trails enable hikers to cross the region on foot. The **Appalachian Trail** from Georgia to Maine is best known. Its initial 78-mile segment traverses Georgia's Blue Ridge. Two other trails also offer long-distance hiking. The 50-mile **Benton MacKaye Trail** runs from Tennessee through north-central Georgia and into the Blue Ridge, where it joins the Appalachian Trail. The 37-mile **Bartram Trail** (which follows the route of naturalist William Bartram's 1791 travels) traverses Georgia's northeastern tip on its route through the Carolinas.

PRACTICALITIES

Camping

The **Chattahoochee National Forest** offers the best escape from civilization. The Forest Service maintains 19 developed campgrounds with water, toilets, and, at some sites, cold showers. They range in cost $3-10 per night (most typically $5), depending on facilities. Sites are available first-come, first-served for a maximum stay of 14 days, from late spring to early fall. A couple of them are open year-round. No hookups are available, and the maximum trailer length is 22 feet. Primitive camping is allowed anywhere in the national forest unless posted otherwise; no fee or permit is required.

State park campgrounds offer water and electrical hookups, bathhouses with hot showers and flush toilets, and often other conveniences such as groceries, supplies, coin laundry, and phones. Rates range $8-16 per night—higher for hookups, lower for "walk-in" camps, reduced rates for seniors—and an additional $2 per vehicle parking fee is charged except on Wednesdays.

Private campgrounds, while occasionally simple and primitive, are most often developed attractions with such family diversions as pools, playgrounds, hayrides, and hoedowns. Rates are roughly comparable to state parks, higher for deluxe camps.

Accommodations

Rustic to luxurious country inns, cabins, lodges, and motels offer a wide range of prices and "perks." Scenically set **state park cottages and lodges** offer some of the best values and set a standard for private cabin facilities as well.

Lodging rates vary widely according to season and degree of luxury—popular parks, suites and view rooms cost more. Rooms in the highly desirable month of October may cost twice as much as the same room come winter. Weekend nights (Fri.-Sat.) cost more than weekday nights. Prices quoted in the text are average for spring and summer weekends.

Business Hours and What to Bring

Most tourist-oriented businesses such as restaurants are open long weekend hours and close midweek (Tues.-Wed.), other businesses typically close on Monday. Also note that Sunday dinners are traditionally served midday. Gas stations may be open late on weekends but aren't open 24 hours. Gas up when you can; mountain climbs consume gas quickly. A few old-time businesses still hang out a Gone Fishin' sign on Wednesday afternoons.

Supermarkets in larger towns stock ample supplies, but bring what you need if you're headed to remote areas. Depending on season and elevation, temperatures and weather can change quickly; dress in layers, and pack a hat and something waterproof. Bring an extra pair of old sneakers to use as "river shoes."

BLUE RIDGE MOUNTAIN STATE PARKS

One of the best places to start exploring North Georgia's Blue Ridge is a state park. Some of the best land, views, and trails, and the best hideaway cabins and lodges (at excellent values) lie within the six mountain region state parks. Many offer recreation such as swimming (pools or beaches), fishing, boat rentals, hiking, and backpacking. Festivals, mountain music concerts, guided backpacking trips, Appalachian and Cherokee crafts demonstrations, and guided nature walks and workshops for low or no cost add to the attractions. All vehicles must purchase a $2 park pass, except on Wednesdays when entrance is free.

Lodging rates for cottages vary by location, by weekday or weekend, and by size (one- to three-bedroom) anywhere from $55 to $135. Lodge rooms range $69-119. For all reservations, call toll-free (800) 864-PARK (800-864-7257).

Amicalola Falls; Star Rte., Dawsonville, GA 30534; tel. (706) 265-2885; campground, cottages, lodge and restaurant, new Len Foote Hike Inn, Appalachian Trail terminus.

Black Rock Mountain; Mountain City, GA 30562; tel. (706) 746-2141; remote, campground, cottages, near "wild and scenic" Chattooga River.

Moccasin Creek; Rte. 1, Lake Burton, GA 30523; tel. (706) 947-3194; modest fish camp on beautiful Lake Burton.

Tallulah Gorge; Hwy. 441, Tallulah Gorge, GA 30573; tel. (706) 754-8257; panoramic views of dramatic gorge and waterfalls, rock-climbing, mountain biking, campground.

Unicoi; P.O. Box 849, Helen, GA 30545; tel. (706) 878-3366; Granddaddy of Blue Ridge Parks, campground, cottages, lodge and restaurant, rental boats, central location.

Vogel; Rte. 1 Box 1230, Blairsville, GA 30512; tel. (706) 745-2628; campground, cottages, rental boats, beach, hiking trail network

FOR MORE INFORMATION

The **Northeast Georgia Mountains Travel Association** distributes free publications to the region; write P.O. Box 464, Gainesville, GA 30503.

Chattahoochee National Forest

The 749,444-acre Chattahoochee National Forest, encompassing most of North Georgia, offers hundreds of miles of trails, three wilderness areas, 455 developed and primitive campsites, and many scenic recreation areas. Contact the Chattahoochee National Forest headquarters in Gainesville (508 Oak St. NW, Gainesville, GA 30501, tel. 770-536-0541) for a trail guide and recreation directory. Enclose a business-size SASE for the quickest reply. Or stop by one of the Forest Service district offices in the Blue Ridge Mountains.

SCOTT TEEPLE

Maps and Directories

Local welcome centers distribute free maps of major routes in the mountain region, particularly for the popular Blue Ridge region. For off-road travel in any region, you'll need a more detailed map from either the Forest Service or from private sources. (In the Blue Ridge, you'll find local maps at the Hometown Bookstore in Dahlonega.)

The Georgia Conservancy's ***North Georgia Mountains*** guide contains an exhaustive listing of the region's natural areas (see bookstores or call 404-876-2900). ***Northern Georgia Canoeing*** by Don Otey is the prime paddler's reference. Check with the Georgia Department of Natural Resources for local fishing and hunting regulations.

opossum

APPALACHIAN TRAIL

Every spring, thousands of eager and overpacked hikers flock to North Georgia to undertake the demanding 2,144-mile Appalachian Trail in hopes of reaching trail's end in Maine before winter. Beginning at Springer Mountain northeast of Dahlonega, the trail follows the front ridge of the Appalachian range through 14 states and seven national parks. Oldest continuously marked footpath in the world (according to the Appalachian Trail Conference), the Appalachian Trail is known to trekkers as simply the "A.T."

Georgia's 78-mile stretch of the A.T. crosses terrain more rugged than in neighboring states, allowing hikers to test their mettle. Clearly marked and well-maintained, the trail passes through thick deciduous woods, scales panoramic overlooks, and skirts the many beautiful waterfalls for which Georgia's Blue Ridge is famous. March through May is the season for "thru-hikers" (trekkers attempting the journey to Maine), but anyone can enjoy the trail anytime from one of several access points and road crossings.

History and Development

The A.T. is largely a product of the vision of one man, Benton MacKaye (rhymes with "pie"), who originally conceived of the idea of a continuous trail along the backbone of the Appalachians in 1921. The idea developed into a crusade, and the following year the first section opened to the public in New York. By 1937 the original 1,200-mile route was completed. Since then, urban growth has pushed the route farther into the mountain wilderness, adding 800 miles to its length.

The Appalachian Trail Conference (ATC), a private nonprofit entity that works in cooperation with the National Park Service, administers the trail. Scores of small volunteer organizations—such as Georgia's local A.T. club—raise shelters and repair and maintain the trail. The National Park Service holds overall responsibility for the A.T., so you could call it the narrowest park in the nation.

Georgia's A.T.

The A.T.'s 78-mile starting stretch (for hikers who started in Maine, it's the final heat) lies entirely within the Chattahoochee National Forest. Although rising to elevations over 4,400 feet, the ridgeline trail hovers for the most part around elevations of about 3,000 feet. Occasional steep ascents are rewarded by scenic vistas.

White "blazes" (eye-level tree cuts painted white) mark the length of the A.T.; blue blazes

Springer Mountain is the trailhead for the Appalachian Trail; only 150 hikers annually complete the entire 2,144-mile trek to Mt. Katahdin, Maine, in one season.

KAP STANN

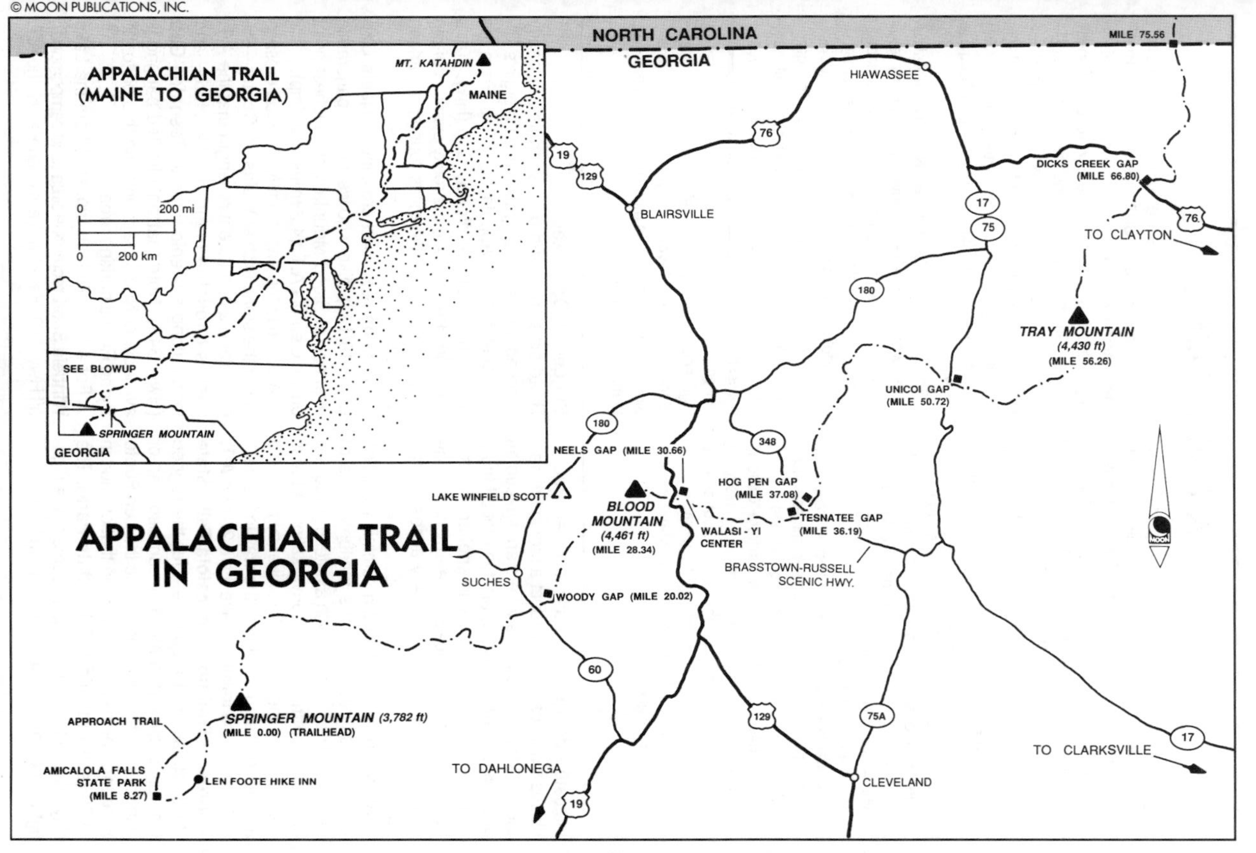
© MOON PUBLICATIONS, INC.
APPALACHIAN TRAIL (MAINE TO GEORGIA)
MT. KATAHDIN
MAINE
0 200 mi
0 200 km
SEE BLOWUP
SPRINGER MOUNTAIN
GEORGIA
NORTH CAROLINA
GEORGIA
MILE 75.56
HIAWASSEE
76
19
129
BLAIRSVILLE
DICKS CREEK GAP (MILE 66.80)
17
75
76
TO CLAYTON
180
TRAY MOUNTAIN (4,430 ft) (MILE 56.26)
UNICOI GAP (MILE 50.72)
180
348
NEELS GAP (MILE 30.66)
HOG PEN GAP (MILE 37.08)
LAKE WINFIELD SCOTT
BLOOD MOUNTAIN (4,461 ft) (MILE 28.34)
WALASI - YI CENTER
TESNATEE GAP (MILE 36.19)
BRASSTOWN-RUSSELL SCENIC HWY.
APPALACHIAN TRAIL IN GEORGIA
SUCHES
WOODY GAP (MILE 20.02)
60
SPRINGER MOUNTAIN (3,782 ft) (MILE 0.00) (TRAILHEAD)
APPROACH TRAIL
AMICALOLA FALLS STATE PARK (MILE 8.27)
LEN FOOTE HIKE INN
TO DAHLONEGA
19
129
75A
CLEVELAND
17
TO CLARKSVILLE

A.T. MYSTIQUE

Why hike on a path as traveled as the Appalachian Trail when other trails offer more seclusion? The first answer is factual: the well-marked, well-maintained A.T. crosses some of the most spectacular country in North America, a narrow ribbon of wilderness from Maine to Georgia that passes through as many eons of natural history as it does miles.

But the second answer is less tangible. There's something about the A.T. that *draws* people. Much more than a hike, the A.T. has come to mean a quest by thousands of dedicated "thru-hikers" who "went the distance," and by the thousands more who arrive in North Georgia every spring with high hopes and a heavy pack.

Aspirants anticipating the 2,144-mile walk create an infectious optimism and energy—comments alongside hikers' names and pack weights at the A.T. register at Amicalola Falls State Park run from "Go for it!" and "Just DO it!" to "I've promised myself this for 20 years." The average backpack weighs out at about 50 pounds, though the frequently scrawled "Too Much" is the most common measure (and perhaps also the most accurate).

By the first road crossing 20 miles north, reality hits. The postmaster at Suches stays busy mailing back home every extraneous ounce weary neophytes are eager to shed. The next road crossing at Neels Gap boosts the confidence and morale of hikers when the encouraging proprietors snap Polaroids to add to a thick album of A.T. hopefuls. (By this point, hikers have usually adopted "trail names," the Native-American likes of "Lightfoot" or "Eagle Feather.")

Thru-hikers are a hardy breed. Not simply a walk in the woods, thru-hikes require painstaking research, planning, and preparedness; hikers clear their calendars for six months or more for the journey, and supplies and expenses can add up to $4,000-5,000. Of the thousands who start out at Springer Mountain each year, only about 150 make it all the way to Mount Katahdin in Maine. Those tenacious souls share a lifetime solidarity, retelling "war stories" of Pennsylvania's boulder fields, soaked river crossings, and blistered feet, as well as tales of generous fellow hikers and favorite all-you-can-eat buffets along the way. The A.T. is much more than a trail—to many, it is a *path.*

indicate side trails and trails to water. Double blazes signal caution—expect a turn in the trail. Eleven three-sided trail shelters are spaced an approximate day's hike apart. On Blood Mountain, a CCC-built stone cabin shelters hikers. Four road crossings lead to nearby communities and allow day hikers easy access to the trail.

At the **Springer Mountain** summit, you'll find a whimsically incongruous mailbox—one of many that line the trail—with a notebook register of hikers' comments and conversation. A brass plaque bears the classic A.T. hiker symbol, and a huge road sign proclaims the way to Maine.

To reach the trailhead, take the 8.27-mile **A.T. Approach Trail** from **Amicalola Falls State Park,** considered a good test for the rugged Georgia section to come. You can also start or end your trip by detouring over to the **Len Foote Hike Inn,** the new walk-in lodge that opened in 1998 (see **Amicalola Falls State Park**). The day hikes listed below include some of the highlights of Georgia's Appalachian Trail.

Suggested Day Hikes

Road crossings and access trails are easily reached from several spots along Georgia's 78-mile stretch of the Appalachian Trail. From the first road crossing at **Woody Gap** (Hwy. 60), a hike north takes you to the rocky overlook of Big Cedar Mountain—two miles roundtrip, parking available.

From the next road crossing at **Neels Gap** (Hwy. 19/129), hikers go west to the panoramic overlook at Blood Mountain, the highest point on the Georgia A.T. (4.2 miles roundtrip).

A 5.5-mile trip east from Neels Gap crosses under the stone arch at **Walasi-Yi Center**—the only place along its entire length that the A.T. passes through a manmade structure—and leads along a scenic ridge to **Tesnatee Gap** (Hwy. 348). Note that only limited parking is available at Neels Gap; drive north a bit to the Byron Reese parking area.

For a 5.3-mile loop trip, start from the **Lake Winfield Scott** recreation area (and campground), off Hwy. 180. Here two trails connect with the A.T.

to create a triangular loop. Starting from the lake, hike south to **Jarrard Gap,** then north on the A.T. to **Slaughter Gap,** then back west to the lake. Or detour one mile north on the A.T. at Slaughter Gap for the view from Blood Mountain before descending back down to the lake.

At **Unicoi Gap** (Hwy. 17/75), a 10.4-mile roundtrip hike leads north to views from Tray Mountain's rocky summit. The summit can also be reached by a one-mile roundtrip north on the A.T. from FS Rd. 79.

Fifty-Mile Backpacking Loop

Three long-distance trails converge in a triangle in North Georgia's remote Blue Ridge wilds, enabling backpackers to sample all three on a localized backpacking adventure. Depending on individual pace, the trip might take a week or two; you could also tack on an overnight at the Amicalola Falls State Park trailhead. Starting at **Springer Mountain,** the A.T. heads north and connects with the **Duncan Ridge Trail,** which leads west to the **Benton MacKaye Trail,** which heads back south to Springer Mountain. Consult topo maps, Chattahoochee National Forest trail maps, or park rangers to plan the details.

Precautions

A.T. elevations invite colder and rainier weather than in mountain towns; hikers who start out early in the spring should prepare for freezing temperatures and rain. Water is available right off the trail, but it should be treated or boiled. Watch for snakes sunning themselves on rock ledges. November and December are deer-hunting months in North Georgia, and cautious hikers wear orange vests and pack covers.

Transportation and Parking

To reach Amicalola Falls State Park from Atlanta, take Hwy. 400 north to Hwy. 53 west past Dawsonville, then take Hwy. 183 north to Hwy. 52 east. From Dahlonega, take Hwy. 52 west. Free long-term parking is easily arranged at the visitor center—$2 per vehicle is charged to enter the park except on Wednesday. Forest Service roads could take you closer to the trailhead, but they aren't recommended for drivers unfamiliar with the area.

Public transportation from Atlanta reaches only as far north as Gainesville; from there hikers can take a taxi or meet a prearranged shuttle. **Appalachian Outfitters,** tel. (706) 864-7117, can help arrange shuttles from the Gainesville station to Amicalola Falls State Park (about $45 for up to three hikers, deposit required).

Long-term parking within the gates of Amicalola Falls State Park is easily arranged with the visitor center (no charge over and above the $2 entrance fee per car). Short-term parking is available at road crossings, but cars may be vulnerable if left overnight.

Resources and Information

Walasi-Yi Center (wal-a-SEE-a), the CCC-built stone lodge at Neels Gap (where the A.T. crosses Hwy. 19) houses the **Mountain Crossings** outfitting store, tel. (706) 745-6095, a well-rounded resource for maps, freeze-dried foods, and other supplies. From March to May—"thru-hiker season"—supportive proprietors and experienced A.T. hikers Jeff and Dorothy Hansen operate a casual hostel out of the basement of their home, and throughout the year they may be able to help arrange point-to-point shuttles.

Write the **Appalachian Trail Conference** at P.O. Box 807, Harpers Ferry, WV 25425-0807 (tel. 304-535-6331) for a brochure and list of publications. You can buy the ATC *Guide to the Appalachian Trail in North Carolina and Georgia* at local outdoor stores (or order it from the ATC, above, item #110, $15.95). Contact the all-volunteer **Georgia Appalachian Trail Club** at P.O. Box 654, Atlanta, GA 30301. (If requesting information, enclose a business-size SASE and a small donation to defray costs.)

For more information about Amicalola Falls State Park, see **Dahlonega and Vicinity,** below, or contact the park at Star Rte. Box 213, Dawsonville, GA 30534, tel. (706) 265-2885.

TRAIL ETHICS

Built and maintained by volunteers, the Appalachian Trail demands that hikers share responsibility for keeping the trail in good shape. Don't shortcut switchbacks (correcting erosion damage is the most difficult part of trail maintenance), carry out all trash, avoid camping in heavy-use areas (camp beyond sight of the trail when possible), and carry a small cooking stove to avoid campfires, or use only downed wood in an established fire ring to minimize the impact on the environment. Respect the flora and fauna, and keep water sources clean (always wash away from water sources, especially if you're using soap). Where no privy is available, dig a "cat hole" at least six inches deep, at least 75 feet from water sources, and bury all waste and paper.

Of course, this no-trace ethic applies to all outdoor areas, not just the A.T.

DAHLONEGA AND VICINITY

In 1828, the discovery of gold near Dahlonega propelled thousands of fortune-seekers to descend on the region, heralding the nation's first major gold rush and producing more than $6 million coined at a local branch of the U.S. Mint. Gold mines, panning operations, and hydraulic mining changed the face of the hills and added a new element to traditionally conservative Appalachian communities, a discernibly freer spirit still felt today.

Gold-country pleasures are centered in Dahlonega (dah-LON-ah-ga), a bustling country town that makes the most of its unique heritage. In the surrounding woods and rivers of the Chattahoochee National Forest, visitors can hike, run rivers, ride horses, and try their hand at goldpanning. Amicalola Falls State Park west of Dahlonega, named for its dramatic 729-foot waterfall, offers lots more recreation, along with a campground, lodge, and new walk-in lodge. The park is the traditional starting point for Appalachian Trail thru-hikers.

Less than an hour and a half from Atlanta, Dahlonega can be reached by taking Hwy. 400 north to Hwy. 60/19 north. To reach the state park from Dahlonega, take Hwy. 52 west (a 40-minute drive from town). To go directly to the state park from Atlanta, you can bypass Dahlonega by taking Hwy. 136 west off Hwy. 400 just past Dawsonville, to Hwy. 183 west to Hwy. 52 east.

History

Named from the Cherokee term *talonega,* meaning "yellow," Dahlonega was chosen as county seat of the new gold-rush region in 1835, displacing Auraria (which faded into the ghost town still visible today south of Dahlonega). In 1838, the federal government built a branch of the U.S. Mint in Dahlonega, stamping the town's name on $6 million worth of gold coins before the operation was shut down at the onset of the Civil War. Today Price Memorial Hall of Dahlonega's North Georgia College stands on the site, with a gleaming crown crafted of local gold.

When California's 1849 gold rush threatened to lure miners away, miners were implored to stay in Dahlonega with the now-famous call "there's gold in them thar hills!" Gold mining and panning operations continued in earnest until the early 1920s, when legislation fixing the price of gold at $35 an ounce was enacted and mining suddenly became unprofitable.

Though panners still try their luck in nearby streams, the region is now richest in its gilded history, attracting visitors to its historic gold museum, spelunky gold-mine tours, and festivals that celebrate Appalachian mining traditions. Dahlonega's mother lode today is tourism, bringing in $20 million annually.

SIGHTS

Set against a backdrop of the pristine Appalachian forests, Dahlonega's historic **town square** makes the most inviting sight of all. Revolving around the 1838 Greek Revival courthouse that now houses the gold museum, the busy square is lined on all sides with colorful two-story Victorian storefronts. The windows of the square's antique stores, bookshops, jewelers, and general store display the town's heritage—you can find antique scales used for weighing gold, audiocassettes of mountain music, and even pans and glass vials to help you try your luck. Strollers saunter down brick walkways lined with flower barrels, past monuments, park benches, and the old town well. At night the old-fashioned streetlights let off a hazy glow.

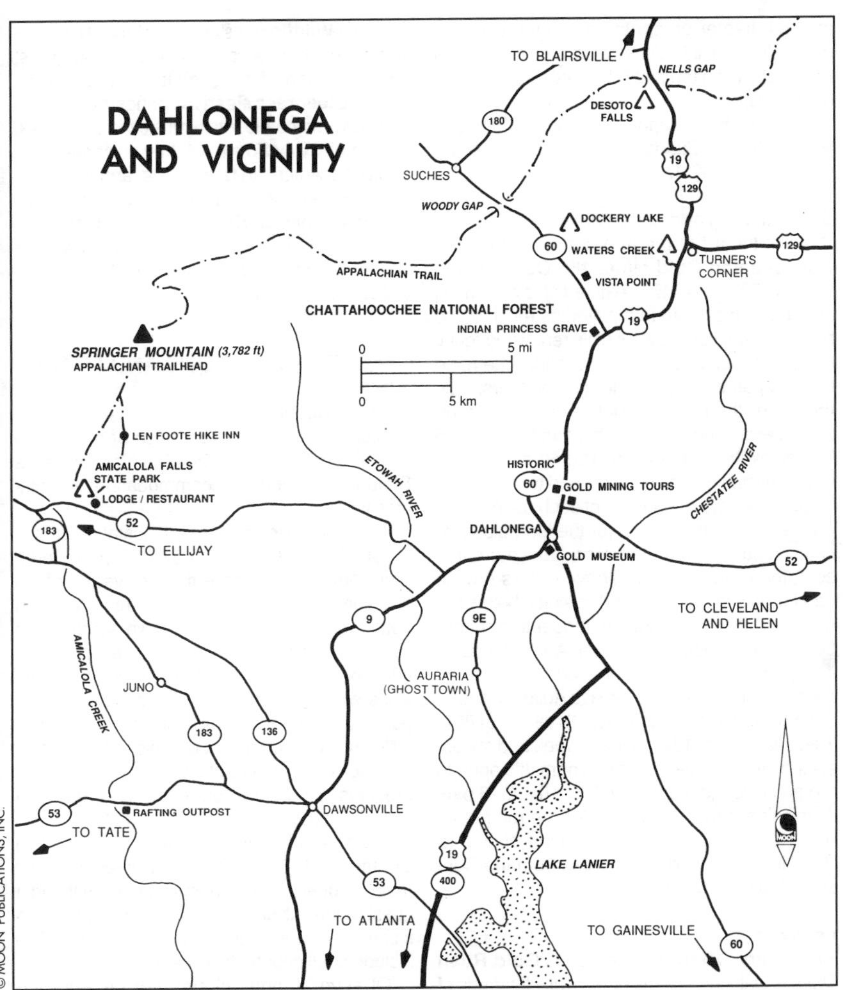

A few minutes from town, the ghost town of **Auraria** had a population of 10,000 in its heyday in the booming 1830s. The town declined once Dahlonega was named county seat, and today Auraria contains only a handful of residents and a historical marker to attest to its bustling past (from Dahlonega, take Hwy. 52 to Auraria Rd., drive south two to three miles, and pass the Gold Dust Lodge).

Gold Museum

The Dahlonega Gold Museum, tel. (706) 864-2257, occupies the oldest building in North Georgia, in the center of the Dahlonega town square. The former courthouse was constructed in 1838 with locally cast bricks; look carefully and you may see gold flecks. The state-operated gold museum exhibits gold nuggets, coins, and tools of the mining trade on the ground floor. Upstairs, a small theater presents an enlightening 20-minute film that introduces gold-rush history and Appalachian culture through interviews with local old-timers.

The museum is open year-round Mon.-Sat. 10 a.m.-5 p.m., Sunday 10 a.m.-5 p.m. The admission fee is $2-4.

Gold Panning and Mine Tours

State-of-the-art at the turn of the century, the **Consolidated Gold Mine,** 185 Consolidated Rd., tel. (706) 864-8473, featured electrical wiring and a railcar system that pulled as much as 50 pounds of gold per day out of its renowned "glory hole." After extensive re-excavation, the mine is now open to the public for guided tours. Visitors enter the mine through a dramatic stone passageway and descend stairs and cuts to 125 feet below the water table. The 40-minute tour covers mining history, geology, and technique, including displays of equipment such as the "widowmaker"—a drill named for the lung-disease-causing dust it generated. Back above-ground, costumed "prospectors" show visitors how to pan for gold in rows of wooden sluice boxes behind the gift shop. Tours run frequently throughout the day 10 a.m.-4 p.m. daily. Adult admission is $10, $5 children 6-12 (five and under free). It's north of town off the bypass (follow signs).

Crisson Gold Mine, Hwy. 19, tel. (706) 864-7998, dates from 1847, and is owned and still operated by fourth-generation miners. It's open to the public for gold panning daily 10 a.m.-6 p.m. Admission is free, but prices for ore run from a dollar a pan to $8 for a five-gallon bucket (a "find" is guaranteed). It's across from the Consolidated Gold Mine.

Festivals

Held every October since 1954, **Gold Rush Days** is Dahlonega's major festival. Hundreds of thousands of visitors descend on the tiny town (resident population: 3,000) to witness and enjoy such rural pastimes as a greased pig chase, tobacco-spitting and hog-calling contests, Wild West shoot-outs, clogging dances, gold panning, and plenty of local foods and crafts. In recent years, the event has drawn more than 250,000 visitors, so if you *don't* plan to attend, steer wide—approach roads get snarled.

May's **Wildflower Festival of the Arts** highlights traditional Appalachian arts and crafts, such as wood carving, quilting, and pottery. June's **Bluegrass Festival** brings out fiddlers and down-home mountain music the third week. The **Family Day Fourth of July** celebrates with traditional American fare, music, and fireworks. Each December, the town dresses up for an **Old Fashioned Christmas,** stringing miniature white lights and decorations—a picturesque scene accompanied by mountain holiday festivities and caroling.

ACCOMMODATIONS AND FOOD

Accommodations

Dahlonega makes a great base of operations for a visit to the Blue Ridge. See also Amicalola State Park for lodge accommodations 40 minutes west.

The **Smith House,** 84 S. Chestatee St., tel. (706) 864-2348 or (800) 852-9577, a revered Blue Ridge inn for more than 70 years, offers overnight lodging in a turn-of-the-century Victorian house a half block from the town square. The sunny yellow three-story farmhouse, reportedly built above a gold mine, blooms with flowering vines wound around its porches, trellises, and pool. Sixteen guest rooms upstairs and a modern suite annex are comfortably furnished in keeping with the country inn spirit—practical, nothing too precious. Standard room rates start at $55; a typical summer weekend rate runs $88 d.

The 1845 **Worley Homestead,** 410 W. Main St., tel. (706) 864-7002, is a well-established resident-operated bed and breakfast with eight guest rooms (all private baths), in a nice location a short walk west of the square. Rates from $60 include a full country breakfast.

Of several motel chains not far from the square, **Econolodge** Hwy. 19 N, tel. (706) 864-6191 or (800) 55-ECONO (800-553-2666), is among the oldest and least expensive (moderate rates from $45, pool), yet still decent and conveniently located a short half-mile walk north of the square. Newer chains are clustered on Hwy. 60 at the bypass (less practical for pedestrians), including **Days Inn,** tel. (706) 864-2338, and **Howard Johnson,** tel. (706) 864-4343, with prices mostly in the moderate range.

Outside town, **Mountain Top Lodge,** Old Ellijay Rd., tel. (706) 864-5257 or (800) 526-9754, offers 13 secluded guest rooms in a two-story barnlike lodge set on 40 forested acres. The inn features great views, a spa, and fireplaces in some rooms. Rates range $60-125 d, including breakfast.

The least expensive lodging outside town is available at the hostel operated by the **Amicalola River Rafting Outpost,** Hwy. 53 five miles west of Dawsonville, tel. (706) 265-6892, dormitory rates are around $10 per bunk.

Camping

Three basic Forest Service campgrounds with water and vault toilets only are within a half hour's drive north of Dahlonega: **Waters Creek** sits beside a beautiful mountain stream 12 miles north of town on Hwy. 19, then left on paved FS Rd. 34 for one mile; **Dockery Lake** has sites near a popular three-acre trout lake off a gravel road from Hwy. 60; and the campground at **De-Soto Falls,** (easily approached from Hwy. 60) is near the namesake waterfalls. Most sites are $5 per night.

See **Amicalola Falls State Park** for additonal camping 40 minutes west.

Food and Drink

Renee's Cafe and Wine Bar, 135 N. Chestatee St., tel. (706) 864-6829, is the best place to eat (and drink—there's a wine bar upstairs). In its busy bistro-like setting two blocks up from the square, a friendly staff serves such entrees as Greek shrimp over saffron rice, exotic mushroom pasta, grilled salmon, and gourmet pizza (entrees $11-17). Dinner is served Tues.-Sat. from 5 p.m. (Couples might opt for the romantic tables on the screened porch.)

Folks come from all over to go to the **Smith House,** 84 S. Chestatee St., tel. (706) 864-2348, for all-you-can-eat family-style Southern meals (up to 2,000 meals are served on popular Sundays), but lately the prices have gotten so out of reach it's hard to recommend it as still a good value (particularly for families) unless money is no object or y'all have enormous appetites. Fixed price Sunday dinners are $15 adults, $10 ages 10-12, $7.50 ages 4-9 (under four free), paid in advance. They're closed Monday, except on major holidays and during October.

Other choices around the square include the casual Italian fare at the friendly **Caruso's** and the **Front Porch** for light lunches on the deck overlooking the square. Locals eat out at the **Wagon Wheel** on Hwy. 19 one mile north of the square, tel. (706) 864-6677, for Southern plates (fried chicken and "all-u-can-eat" catfish nights on Fri.-Sat.) served cafeteria style.

See also **Amicalola Falls State Park** for its lodge restaurant listing.

OTHER PRACTICALITIES

Shopping

Downtown's 19th-century courthouse square offers some scenic shopping. Antiques, mining memorabilia, old-time penny candy, locally mined and made gold jewelry, and mountain crafts and music are among the distinctive souvenirs to be found. The biggest bargain is a five-cent cup of coffee at the **General Store** which you can sip while you browse through the store's tinny treasures.

At the **Hometown Bookstore** off the square, tel. (706) 864-7225, Deborah and Bill Kinsland sell regional guides, books, mountain-music cassettes, and topographical maps. They also serve as an unofficial visitor information center, gathering comprehensive information on climate, autumn colors, and the like, and distributing it free of charge.

Appalachian Outfitters on the square, tel. (706) 867-6677, sells outdoor gear, supplies, and clothes, and also organizes paddling excursions from its river outpost (tel. 706-864-7117).

Chestatee Crossing, tel. (706) 864-9099 or (800) 326-9613, specializes in Native American arts, including headdresses, drums, mandalas, fetishes, jewelry, and baskets.

Information and Services

The **Dahlonega Welcome Center** on the square, 13 Park St. South, Dahlonega, GA 30533, tel. (706) 864-3711 or (800) 231-5543, opens daily 9 a.m.-5:30 p.m. to distribute local maps and information (free restrooms here too).

There's a little gold panning station right next door ($3).

A **Forest Service visitor center,** 1015 Tipton Dr., tel. (706) 745-6928, distributes information on local recreation in the Chattahoochee National Forest. It's open Mon.-Sat. 8 a.m.-4:30 p.m., Sunday 11:15 a.m.-5:15 p.m.

For medical emergencies, contact **St. Joseph's Hospital,** two miles south of town on Hwy. 60, tel. (706) 864-6136.

RECREATION

Water Sports

The Chestatee River, popular with paddlers for canoeing or kayaking, crosses highways 60 and 52 south and east of Dahlonega. First-timers and families usually choose its Class I lower section; experienced paddlers may prefer its more challenging Class II-III upper section.

KAP STANN

Amicalola Creek features the "Edge of the World" Class IV rapids.

Appalachian Outfitters, tel. (706) 864-7117, rents canoes and organizes guided paddling excursions from its river outpost on Hwy. 60 at the river (southeast of town). They also help arrange shuttles for paddlers and hikers (around $1 a mile).

The Amicalola Creek southwest of Dahlonega on Hwy. 53 offers a chance to swim, canoe, kayak, raft, tube, or hike in the protected corridor of this scenic Appalachian river. Under the Hwy. 53 bridge six miles west of Dawsonville, you'll find a put-in point with a river marker and a trail down the eastern bank. This trail leads south to the swimming hole, with natural slides for inner tube riders and a refreshing cold-water "natural jacuzzi."

Amicalola River Rafting Outpost, Hwy. 53, tel. (706) 265-6892, rents rafts, canoes, and tubes, and organizes guided river trips and Native American programs. Inquire about dormitory lodging in their stone-and-wood mountain cabin a mile east of the river.

AMICALOLA FALLS STATE PARK

At Amicalola Falls State Park, 18 miles west of Dahlonega via Hwy. 52, visitors enjoy scenic overlooks of the centerpiece waterfalls and wooded trails through the park's 1,210 acres. The most famous of these hikes is the 2,144-mile **Appalachian Trail,** which draws thousands of ambitious backpackers to the park each spring to begin the long trek north. Like many mountain state parks, the park has so much to offer that a solace-seeker could stay weeks without venturing off the mountain except to hike.

Pick up a park guide, trail maps, and interpretive information at the visitor center near the base of the falls. Contact Amicalola Falls State Park at Star Rte., Box 215, Dawsonville, GA 30534, tel. (706) 265-8888. For lodging and camping reservations, call (800) 864-7275. The park is open year-round. A $2 per vehicle fee is charged, except on Wednesday.

Sights and Trails

Amicalola Falls' dramatic 729-foot cascade—three times taller than Niagara, though a fraction as wide—can be seen from scenic overlooks a short walk from parking lots at the lower Reflection Pool or at the summit (where you'll find the classic Blue Ridge panorama so often photographed). Or you can hike to scenic overlooks off 3.5 miles of falls trails.

The **Appalachian Trail** (A.T.) officially begins at Springer Mountain, out in the Blue Ridge wilds just beyond the park boundary. The classic route to get there is the **A.T. Approach Trail,** which starts behind the park's visitor center near the base of the falls (or you can pick up the trail near the summit lodge). Considered a good test for thru-hiker hopefuls, the approach trail offers a taste of the rugged backcountry to come along Georgia's 78-mile A.T.

A moderate 4.6-mile trail leads to the new **Len Foote Hike Inn;** it's another 2.5 miles from here to Springer Mountain.

A challenging **mountain bike trail** runs over 20 miles on an old gravel road; pick up a map from the visitors center.

Accommodations and Camping

The modern four-story **Amicalola Falls Lodge,** tel. (706) 265-8888, sits majestically atop a steep summit. The three-story glass lobby, restaurant, and all 57 guest rooms have a panoramic view of the surrounding Blue Ridge wilderness—a beautiful scene anytime, and most dramatic in the fall. Many of the modern, tastefully appointed rooms have porches and lofts, and several are especially equipped for handicapped guests. Standard rooms start at $79 d.

Fourteen fully equipped cottages, some with fireplaces, are nestled in the woods a short drive from the lodge (except for #1-5, which are more exposed near the base of the falls). Rates start at $105-135, depending on size (one to three bedrooms).

A moderate 4.6-mile trail leads to the new **Len Foote Hike Inn,** where hikers can find rustic overnight shelter and meal service in a low-impact lodge operated by a nonprofit affiliate of the Georgia Appalachian Trail Club and managed by the unsinkable thru-hiker Sonie Green. The cost is $75 single or $55 double occupancy in two-bunk cabins with shared bathrooms and communal dining. Families and kids are encouraged; there's even a handicapped-accessible room (reserve transportation in advance).

Each of the park's 17 wooded **campsites** hooks up to water and 110-volt power; nearby bathhouses have hot showers, flush toilets, coin laundry facilities, and soda machines. Because of the entrance road's 25% grade, trailers must be under 16 feet. Sites cost $17 per night, $19 in October.

Lodge Restaurant

The glass-walled 200-seat Maple Restaurant at the lodge serves generous buffets, enough to make your mouth water at the thought after a long strenuous hike. Roast turkey, baked ham, or fried catfish may be among the dinner entrees; the rest of the spread includes four types of vegetables, soup, salad, and desserts. The hot breakfast buffet includes eggs, grits, hotcakes, sausage, ham, bacon, and biscuits and gravy. Three meals are served Mon.-Sat.; on Sunday only breakfast and midday dinner are served (until 2 p.m.). Prices are reasonable; note that no alcohol is served.

Services, Facilities, and Programs

The **visitor center** at the park entrance displays natural history exhibits, distributes trail maps, and sells books, gifts, and firewood (more maps, guides, and scenery books can be found at the lodge gift shop). Inquire about a full slate of interpretive programs and special events, including backpacking expeditions. Seasonal trout fishing within the state park, as elsewhere in Georgia, requires a Georgia fishing license and trout stamp.

Outside the park, **Burt's Pumpkin Farm** a short way west of the entrance on Hwy. 52, sponsors hayrides, Saturday night hoedowns, and other farmy family diversions.

Vicinity

In sleepy Dawsonville, the 1858 Greek Revival Dawson County Courthouse adorns the central square. Off the square, the **Dawsonville Pool Room,** 101 E. First St., tel. (706) 265-2792, has short-order meals—burgers, steak sandwiches, and the like—and tributes to native son and racing champion Bill Elliott. The **Bill Elliot Showroom and Racing Facilities** racetrack is nearby.

NORTH TO BLAIRSVILLE

North of Dahlonega, the country highway climbs through wind gaps and water gaps up to the ridgeline traced by the Appalachian Trail. The primary route through Georgia's central Blue Ridge is through Neels Gap (Hwy. 19/129), largely carved by the Nottely River. To every side, trailheads lead into Blue Ridge wilds—here hikers find the tallest peaks, the panoramic ridge, towering stands of cathedral pines, and sparkling waterfalls framed by flowering thickets of mountain laurel and rhododendron. Its human history is retained by ancient petroglyphs, the grave of a Cherokee princess, and local legends of Spanish explorers and arklike canoes of mythological proportions.

Over the ridge, the no-nonsense mountain town of Blairsville leaves the trim latticework and lace curtains of valley towns far behind. Cafes open before sunrise to fry eggs and fling hotcakes for farmers wearing well-worn overalls, and most shopping to be done is at the local feed-and-grain. But visitors find all they need to outfit themselves for weeks backpacking in the wilderness, fishing and boating at high-country lakes, or relaxing in cozy pondside cabins tucked into Blue Ridge coves.

Follow Hwy. 60/19 north from Dahlonega nine miles to its split. From here, Hwy. 60 leads northwest to Woody Gap and Forest Service camps and creeks; Hwy. 19 continues north, merging with Hwy. 129 five miles up and heading to Blairsville through Neels Gap—the route de Soto marched through in the mid-1500s in search of gold.

HIGHWAY 60 WEST

The 35-mile stretch of highway between the Hwy. 19 split and Morganton bisects the thick of the national forest. To either side of Hwy. 60, rugged Forest Service (FS) roads wind up the mountains to remote camps, cool creeks, and prime fishing holes. The split is marked by a shoulder-high rock pile in the center of the road. This is said to be the grave of Cherokee Princess Trahlyta—the native custom was to heap stones

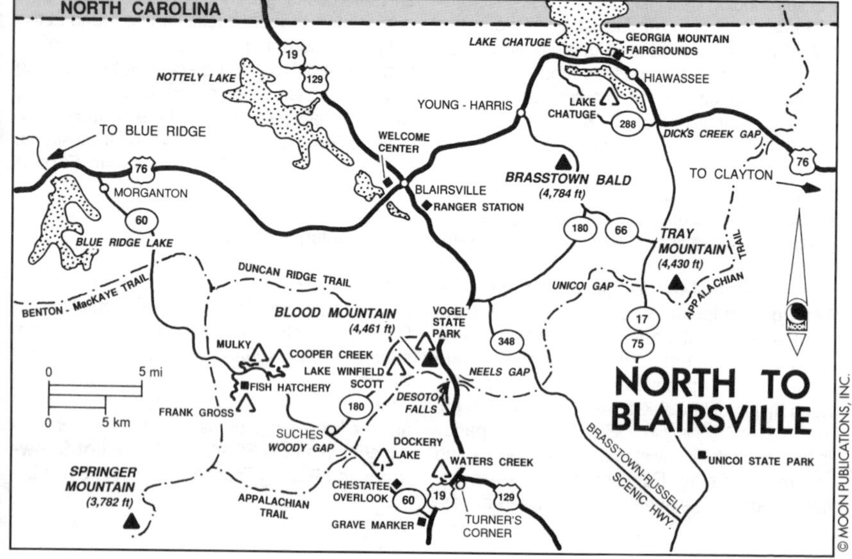

on a grave to show you've been there to pay your respects.

Five miles northwest of the grave marker, a mile-long gravelly turnoff east leads to **Dockery Lake,** where an 11-site FS campground ($5 per night), trailhead parking lot, and popular three-acre trout lake are set in a large cove accented in May by white dogwood blossoms and purple rhododendron. A half-mile barrier-free trail leads around the lake, and a 3.4-mile trail north provides access to the Appalachian Trail. The **Chestatee Overlook,** on Hwy. 60 just north of this turnoff, provides a scenic roadside vista of Blood Mountain cove.

A mile farther north, the road meets the A.T. at **Woody Gap.** Park here for easy access to the 2,144-mile trail; a two-mile roundtrip hike north takes you to the rocky overlook of Big Cedar Mountain. Picnic tables at the turn-out provide a nice view too.

The beautiful little town of **Suches** (on Hwy. 60 a mile north of Woody Gap) is set in a picturesque valley of pasturelands, red barns, and sparkling lakes. Its post office is a landmark for hikers—when overloaded thru-hikers hit this first road crossing after 20 rugged miles on the A.T., they detour to the Suches post office to mail home every extraneous ounce.

Hwy. 180 leads northeast from here to **Lake Winfield Scott,** another bucolic little find nestled away in the high country. The **Winfield Scott Grocery and Motel** here on Hwy. 180, tel. (706) 747-2061, offers the least expensive rooms around ($35 s or d). It's 22 miles from Blairsville, 18 miles from Dahlonega, and accessible from the A.T. via either Henry Gap or Jarrard Gap.

About 10 miles northwest of Suches on Hwy. 60, FS roads lead off to remote recreation areas and campgrounds north and south of the highway. Drivers should note that FS roads, though scenic, may be narrow, steep, and offer few places to turn around—not recommended for delicate cars, drivers, or passengers. The cautious driver planning on extensive back-road travel would carry emergency supplies. FS roads make great trail-biking routes; just watch out for those trailers coming around the bend.

Beyond the FS areas described below, Hwy. 60 continues northwest 14 miles to Morganton and sights around Blue Ridge Lake.

Forest Service Areas North

About 10 miles northwest of Suches, FS Rd. 4 leads from Hwy. 60 six miles east through rugged backcountry to the 1,240-acre **Cooper Creek Scenic Area.** Besides a few faint traces of human habitation or fire, the area represents largely untouched original forest. In stands of large hemlock and white pine (just about the southern geographic limit of both varieties), many trees measure three to four feet in diameter. To see these giants, follow the southern riverbank from the bridge over trout-stocked Cooper Creek (about a half-mile south of FS Rd. 4 on Cavender Creek Rd., also labeled FS Rd. 236). From here a rough fisherman's path passes through a white pine grove, rhododendron thickets, and hemlock stands a quarter-mile in.

The 20-site **Cooper Creek** campground, adjacent to the scenic area (at the FS Rd. 4 junction with FS Rd. 236), and the 10-site **Mulky Creek** campground (slightly west off FS Rd. 4), both provide drinking water, picnic tables, grills, and vault toilets. Most sites are $5; premium creekside sites may be more, and farther-flung primitive sites are free.

Forest Service Areas South

Slightly west of the Cooper Creek turnoff, the FS **Deep Hole** campground on the south side of Hwy. 60 provides eight sites along the trout-stocked Toccoa River. Take the next turnoff south (FS Rd. 69) to reach the trout-rearing "raceways" (outdoor tanks) of the **Chattahoochee National Fish Hatchery** (open daily 7:30 a.m.-4 p.m.) and the 11-site **Frank Gross** FS campground and picnic area, five miles south of Hwy. 60 along Rock Creek. (See notes on FS campground prices above.)

HIGHWAY 19 TO NEELS GAP

From a round wooden table in the cafe at **Turner's Corner,** you can look out to the crossroads of two country highways. Coming in from the direction of the cash register is Hwy. 19. Highway 129 up from Cleveland is out behind the swinging saloon door that leads to the kitchen. As the last low-level stop before committing to crossing the mountain, a meal at Turner's Corner almost invariably marks the brink of an adventure.

Step outside to where the ancient gas pump totems stand, and you'll see the bridge over Waters Creek. If you follow the creek up a half-mile or so (paved FS Rd. 34 leads around from Hwy. 19), you come upon the prettiest little (eight sites) campground right off the side of the road. It's set right against a bend in the creek, and there's not a spot where you can sit and not hear the rushing waters.

Seven miles farther up the narrowing Hwy. 19 you'll find **Blood Mountain Falls,** where a mountain stream flows about 20 feet through a rock cut, creating a churning sluice of water. A trail on the right leads 0.8 miles from the road to the falls.

DeSoto Falls Scenic Area

The highlights of the 650-acre DeSoto Falls Scenic Area (west of Hwy. 19/129) are the spectacular waterfalls. Legend has it that a piece of armor found near these falls belonged to the 1540s expedition of Hernando de Soto, thus the name. A 24-site campground ($5 per night), near clear streams for fishing and wading, provides water, grills, flush toilets, and cold showers.

Drivers can pull over to view the falls from the highway, but for a closer look, hike the three-mile **DeSoto Falls Trail.** The trail leads easily to the lower falls, which cascade 20 feet, then continues more steeply up to the most scenic 80-foot middle falls, and finally to the upper falls, which surge 200 feet down a granite rock incline.

Neels Gap

At Neels Gap, the ridgeline A.T. meets the historic route now carved by Hwy. 19/129 (eight miles north of the junction of those two highways; 10 miles south of Blairsville). This is the hiking epicenter of Georgia's Blue Ridge Mountain range. Within several miles of here, many of the most adventurous Blue Ridge trails converge into a vast trail network—the wilderness equivalent of a major freeway cloverleaf.

The gap is marked by the **Walasi-Yi Center** (wal-a-SEE-a), a sturdy stone lodge with a terraced overlook constructed by the Civilian Conservation Corps in 1934. Approximately 1,000 thru-hiker hopefuls annually pass through its breezeway—the only place on the 2,144-mile route that the A.T. cuts through a manmade structure. The state-owned historic lodge now houses the **Mountain Crossings** outfitting store, tel. (706) 745-6095. Supportive proprietors Jeff and Dorothy Hansen photograph ambitious A.T. hikers on their way to Maine, and sell backpacks, Patagonia-wear, freeze-dried foods, "mountain art," and trail maps.

Day hikers can head west for the scenic views from atop 4,458-foot **Blood Mountain,** the highest point on Georgia's A.T. (4.2 miles roundtrip). A 5.5-mile A.T. trip east leads along the scenic ridge to **Tesnatee Gap** (Hwy. 348). Note that only limited parking is available at Neels Gap and hiker parking displaces shoppers and short-term sightseers; drive north a bit to the Byron Reese parking area and take the short A.T. access trail up the hill.

VOGEL STATE PARK

Vogel State Park, off Hwy. 19/129 south of Blairsville, tel. (706) 745-2628, is among the oldest and prettiest of Georgia's state parks, nestled around a shaded lake in a large cove. This full-service park offers water sports, lodging, camping, prime hiking and backpacking trails, and a full slate of entertaining and interpretive programs and events.

Lake Trahlyta, named for a Cherokee princess, is stocked with trout and ringed by a swimming beach, boathouse with boat rentals, and lakeside trail. At the park office you can find a small well-stocked camp store, trail maps, and a coin laundry; outside you can play miniature golf and volleyball, or join the kids on the playgrounds. The compact facilities and dramatic scenery make it one of the most desirable mountain parks for camping and cottage rental.

This jewel of a resort park is so popular, however, that it's nearly loved to death by its admirers. "Yard for yard, we see as many people as Yosemite," says one ranger. In high seasons (summer and October) the park comes to resemble an outdoor metropolis, with crowds of spatula-wielding barbecue chefs, kids riding Big Wheels, and "camp potatoes" watching TV inside massive trailers, running the generator to keep the air-con at full blast. It's a scene. If you're looking for rustic, seek out the walk-in campsites, get out on the rugged backpacking trail, or come back in the off-season.

Many special events and interpretive programs—including such kid-friendly diversions as a foot-powered wheel race, wiffleball tournaments, and a ranger-supervised planetarium field trip—are listed on a weekly schedule available at the office. The annual highlight is rousing **Old Timers Day** in August, a celebration of mountain music performed by old-time Appalachian fiddlers, accompanied by handicrafts booths and traditional foods. You can write the park at Rte. 1 Box 1230, Blairsville, GA 30512. The parking fee is $2 per car, free on Wednesday.

Hiking and Backpacking

Besides the park's own 19 miles of trails, Vogel connects with a wider trail network, offering impressive opportunities for many different hiking adventures. Backpackers can arrange overnight secured parking at the park office. Short walks include a mile-long trail that loops around the lake and spurs off to a rushing waterfall (also visible from the highway), and a half-mile-loop nature trail that features interpretive signs.

The orange-blazed **Bear Hair Trail** is a moderate-to-strenuous four-mile loop over rocks and logs, across a footbridge, through a hardwood forest, and up a steep rhododendron thicket. It's best to hike the loop in a counterclockwise direction (though you can hike it either way). About a third of the way in, a green-blazed spur trail climbs to the 3,260-foot summit overlook (a mile roundtrip). Beyond the midpoint, the trail merges with the backpacking trail (see below); a sign at the junction marks the way south to the A.T. or north back to the park, both about two miles one-way.

The demanding 12.7-mile-loop **Coosa Backcountry Trail,** also best hiked counterclockwise, is recommended for experienced hikers only. Obtain the required permit and a trail map for no charge at the park office. The yellow-blazed trail climbs one rounded summit after another, fords streams, crosses Hwy. 180 twice, and merges with the Duncan Ridge Trail for two miles. At Slaughter Gap, the backcountry trail's southernmost point, hikers can either continue to follow yellow blazes back to the park or take a short spur trail over to the A.T.—from here you can hike a mile one-way south to the beautiful views of 4,461-foot Blood Mountain, the highest point on Georgia's A.T. Hardy day-hikers wishing to see Blood Mountain can follow the Coosa trail clockwise from the trailhead (turn left—south—at the end of the access trail) to the A.T. and continue south on the A.T. to the summit (3.6 miles one-way).

Cottages and Camping

The park's 36 fully equipped cottages range in size from compact studios to spacious three-bedroom cabins; all have fireplaces. The nicest ones are the CCC-built stone-and-wood cottages by the lake (#31-36) and the cabins nestled up the hill (#21-30); the remaining central cabins are exposed near roads in the thick of the action and traffic—not the place to get away from

SASSAFRAS

With three differently shaped leaves on the same tree, sassafras *(Sassafras albidum)* inspired a Cherokee folktale. As legend has it, a young brave enters the forest alone on a vision quest. Facing the bracing cold, the resourceful young brave is warmed with a hat made from the oval-shaped leaves of the sassafras tree, mittens made from its mitten-shaped leaves, and socks from its three-lobed foot-shaped leaves.

The tree bark was also used by the Cherokee and Appalachian mountaineers; a tea infusion served as an all-around tonic.

crowds and activity. Prices range $50-90, depending on size.

The 110-site campground charges $16 a night, including water and electric hookups at most sites. Ten walk-in sites are secluded from the glare of the trailer encampments. The campground is packed in high seasons, but if you like activity you'd be lucky to get a site here.

For cottage or camping reservations, call (800) 864-7275.

Vicinity

A rugged FS road off Hwy. 19/129 south of the park leads to **Helton Creek Falls,** a set of three majestic waterfalls that drop a total of 100 feet. A short trail leads to both ends of the lower falls, but be careful—rocks are deceptively slippery. From the park, go south on Hwy. 19/129 one mile; turn left onto an unpaved road that leads east (Helton Creek Rd./FS Rd. 118). Take this narrow rocky route 2.1 miles, and watch for the orange paint on a pine tree to your right; park at the wide spot in the road and follow the 300-yard trail to the falls. You can turn your car around three-tenths of a mile farther down the road. The route is not recommended for cars with low suspension; four-wheel drive or mountain bikes would be best.

Several scenic recreational sights lie west off Hwy. 180, within seven miles of its junction with Hwy. 19/129 a mile north of the park. The **Sosebee Cove Scenic Area** shelters 175 acres of prize hardwood timber, a forest floor lined with ferns and wildflowers, a boulder field, and babbling creeks. A half-mile trail encircles the area, starting from the trailhead in the parking pullout. At **Lake Winfield Scott,** a FS recreation area provides a 32-site campground ($5 a night), picnic areas, trails, boating, fishing, and swimming around the 18-acre lake. From here, two trails lead to the A.T., enabling hikers to take a triangular 5.3-mile loop trip.

Two miles north of the park, Hwy. 180 leads northeast to Brasstown Bald; after a mile the Brasstown-Russell Scenic Hwy. (Hwy. 348) shoots off this route southeast towards Helen (see **North of Helen,** below).

BLAIRSVILLE

Tucked in the national forest, the mountain town of Blairsville is centered around its 1898 courthouse. The town offers a nice respite from hearty hiking with all-you-can-eat restaurants, motels, supplies, and plenty of fraternizing with friendly folks.

Recreation and Events

North of town, **Lake Nottely,** a 4,180-acre TVA impoundment of the Nottely River off Hwy. 19/129, attracts fisherfolk to its high-country shores in pursuit of largemouth bass, crappie, and striped bass. South of town, the **Nottely River Campground** on Hwy. 19, tel. (706) 745-6711, rents inner tubes for leisurely floats downriver, and will shuttle you back up.

The town's largest annual event, the **Sorghum Festival,** takes place the second through fourth weekends in October. Watch sorghum-crushing demonstrations, and try the cooked syrup served sticky on biscuits in the festival's "Biskit Eatin' and Syrup Soppin'" contest. Competitions—including greased-pig catching, log-sawing, and tobacco-spitting—and square dances round out the event.

Accommodations and Camping

The 26-room **Seasons Inn** at the square, tel. (706) 745-1631 has clean rooms at inexpensive-to-moderate prices (no pool). The **Best Western** a block off the square has a pool and moderate prices.

In a small cove off Hwy. 19/129 a quarter-mile north of Vogel State Park, **Goose Creek,** tel. (706) 745-5111, rents rustic wooden cabins (no phone, no TV, no a/c) by a lake. Rates range $35-65, depending on size and season. You don't need a license to fish at the private stocked lake; the owners provide a bamboo pole and line, and charge by the pound for your catch. Seasonal creekside camping, with water and electric hookups, is also available. (A.T. hikers should inquire about shuttles to nearby Neels Gap and hiker discounts.)

Food and Drink

The **North Georgia Restaurant,** on the square, tel. (706) 745-5888, serves down-home biscuit-drippin' country breakfasts daily starting at 5 a.m., and lunches until 2:30 p.m. The comfortable booths at the cozy corner cafe are full of friendly locals—a warm welcome sight on a crisp mountain morning. You can pick up the Atlanta paper in a vending machine outside.

For all you can eat, chow down at the **Blairsville Restaurant,** a block behind the square to the west, tel. (706) 745-6921. Three meals a day (except Sunday) are all served buffet-style here, allowing diners to help themselves; hours are Mon.-Sat. 5 a.m.-2:30 p.m. and 5-9 p.m.

Millie's at the overpass, is the most presentable and has all-around good food, good prices, and a comfortable atmosphere. You can find a boiled-peanut stand nearby.

Blair House, on Hwy. 19 five miles north of town, tel. (706) 745-3399, serves moderately priced seafood and sit-down nautical fare in a shell-and-net-laden cabin at the eastern shore of Nottely Lake. (It also rents two cabins, from $55.)

Information and Services

The **visitors center,** on the rise above Hwy. 76 west of town, distributes maps and lists of local lodging with prices. Or contact the local **chamber of commerce** for information: P.O. Box 727, Blairsville, GA 30512, tel. (706) 745-5789. The **Forest Service office** on Hwy. 19/129 south of town, tel. (706) 745-6928, distributes and sells maps and directories to national forest recreation areas, campgrounds, and hiking and ORV trails.

For medical emergencies, call **Union General Hospital,** at 714 Hospital Dr. a mile north of the town square, tel. (706) 745-2111. Call the police at (706) 745-2005.

East to Hiawassee

Highway 76, the major east-west route through the upper Blue Ridge, cuts a smooth path through the high valleys and rolling knobs to each side. To the east, between Blairsville and Young-Harris, a turn south on Trackrock Rd. takes you 2.2 miles to the **Trackrock Archaeological Area,** where ancient petroglyphs are etched in sandstone boulders above the road. The 3,500-year-old petroglyphs, depicting images of animal tracks, are today protected of necessity by unfortunate metal frames. Park at the turnout south of the historical marker and backtrack up the short trail. The 5.5 mile Arkaquah Trail ascends to the Brasstown Bald Summit from the petroglyphs. Nearby, a private camping resort, **Trackrock Campground,** off Trackrock Rd. south of the petroglyphs, tel. (706) 745-5252, offers guided horseback trips through the quiet valley in the shadow of Brasstown Bald. The resort also has campsites with hookups, cabins, and a swimming lake.

In Young-Harris, nine miles east of Blairsville, the campus of **Young Harris College,** tel. (706) 379-3111, holds a planetarium (open to the public for occasional programs) and presents a living nativity in December. On campus, a trail leads from behind the women's dormitory to Brasstown Bald, Georgia's highest peak (see **Highway 75 to Helen and Hiawassee,** below).

Brasstown Valley Resort, 6321 Hwy. 76, tel. (706) 379-9900 or (800) 201-3205, offers deluxe accommodations (lodge rooms from $99, cottages from $109) along with golf, tennis, horseback riding, hiking, and other recreation on 503 acres.

HIGHWAY 75 TO HELEN AND HIAWASSEE

The Bavarian-style town of Helen, Georgia's most popular Blue Ridge destination, flanks the Chattahoochee River at the head of a large pastoral valley studded with gristmills and country inns. Behind it to the north, the mountains rise up dramatically, cresting at Brasstown Bald—highest point in the state. Highway 75 winds its way north over these mountains and down to Hiawassee on the other side, passing one of Georgia's most beautiful state parks along the way.

The central location of the region around Helen makes it a convenient base of operations for visitors, if you're up for the scene. It's less than an hour away from any Blue Ridge destination in Georgia—except during festivals, when it takes nearly that long to clear downtown Helen; choose other routes at busy times if you don't plan to attend.

Cleveland

Cleveland is the largest foothill town between the tourist centers of Helen to the north and Dahlonega to the west. Situated on Hwy. 129, Cleveland is also a gateway to the deeper Blue Ridge around Neels Gap.

All roads lead to the town square, where a few country antique shops and cafes make Cleveland a welcoming stop. In the center of the square, the **Old White County Courthouse,** constructed around 1857 by slaves and paid for in Confederate dollars, stands as a small-scale imitation of Philadelphia's Independence Hall. The **White County Chamber of Commerce,** housed in a renovated jail built in 1901, provides information about local attractions and businesses. It's on Hwy. 129, tel. (706) 865-5356.

Once prominent as a gold-mining town, Cleveland is now best known as the birthplace of the Cabbage Patch doll craze that swept the country years back. **Babyland General Hospital** on 19 Underwood St., tel. (706) 865-5164, has produced more than 100,000 Cabbage Patch Kids since 1978. In the "hospital," actually housed in a 1919 clinic building, the yarn-haired babies sprout from fantasyland cabbage fields strung with twinkling lights—a sight bound to astound (and confuse) curious children. Uniformed nurses deliver the babies to consumers after completing the adoption papers. The doll hospital is open Mon.-Sat. 9 a.m.-6 p.m., Sunday 1-6 p.m.; admission is free.

East of town, you'll find one of the Blue Ridge's most unusual craft shops off Hwy. 17. **Gourdcraft Originals,** Duncan Bridge Rd. (Hwy. 384), tel. (706) 865-4048, creates household items and whimsical decorations from hollow bottle gourds (an ancient Native American practice handed down to Appalachian settlers) and displays gourdcraft from around the world.

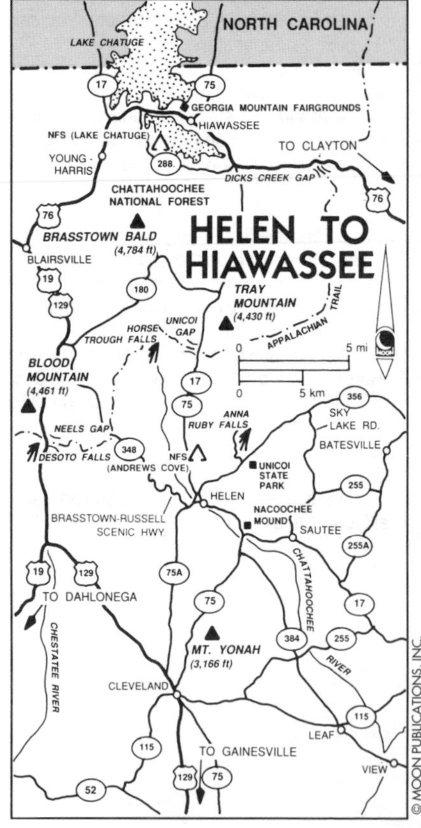

West Family Restaurant, on Hwy. 75 north of town, offers excellent value buffets in a convenient location.

Sautee-Nacoochee Valley

The gazebo-crowned **Nacoochee Mound,** whose excavated artifacts date back 10,000 years, marks your arrival to the magical intersections of Tyrol and Appalachia in Georgia's central Blue Ridge. From here, follow Hwy. 75 north to Helen or Hwy. 17 east to Sautee. With its sight-studded, smooth country highways made for slow-paced rambling, the Sautee-Nacoochee valley is ideal for leisurely drives or bicycle touring, if it's not too congested.

At the crossroads in Sautee, the **Old Sautee Store** hasn't changed much since it opened for business 115 years ago; farmers still find the basics here. Next door, the **Sautee Inn,** tel. (706) 878-2940, serves a country buffet at lunch and dinner, daily except Tuesday from May to mid-December.

A mile or so north on Hwy. 255, **Stovall House,** tel. (706) 878-3355, provides guest rooms in a Victorian farmhouse (rates from $70 d). Dinner is served Tues.-Sun. 5:30-8:30 p.m., or come for the midday Sunday brunch.

Farther north off Hwy. 255, see the smallest **covered bridge** in Georgia (36.8 feet long), and order a soda at the old-fashioned counter of the **Skylake Country Store** on Skylake Rd., tel. (706) 878-2940.

HELEN

Helen started out in 1913 as just another lumber town. Named for a local official's daughter, Helen floundered after the logging bust until several native sons put their heads together to drum up a scheme that could save the town. With fond memories of his travels to Germany, one entrepreneur suggested redesigning the town to resemble a Bavarian village, and in 1969, the tiny town of 300 was transformed into "Alpine Helen." Never ones to quibble about geography, the locals' concept is elastic enough to include things Belgian, Dutch, Scandinavian, and Danish, as well as strictly Swiss or German.

The townspeople work with admirable cohesiveness to present their play to the public, and by casual observation, they enjoy it. By coincidence, a trace of German ancestry exists in Southern Appalachia (from 18th-century Pennsylvania emigrants), though Anglo-Saxon stock predominates by far (so why not a Scottish Highland wonderland with bagpipes and plaid?). Yet success like this—three million vacationers annually, 300,000 for Oktoberfest alone—is bound to turn plain folks into *volks.*

Coming into Helen on the Hwy. 75 corridor, you're introduced to the local Tyrolean flavor by the gabled roofs of modern motels, billboards written in Renaissance script, and an unusually high number of German bakeries per capita for a

GREG KNOBLOCH

Wilkommen *to Helen, where Bavaria meets Appalachia.*

rural Georgia town. But what is perhaps more surprising in this Appalachia-meets-Bavaria village, is that through all its styling, downtown Helen can actually manage to charm.

At the entrance to the village, a particularly scenic bend of the **Chattahoochee River** crosses under the narrow bridge of Main Street. Shade trees, patio cafes, hotel balconies, and the FestHalle line the river. Cobblestone byways skirt a small plaza adorned with park benches, flower boxes, and fountains. Inviting plazas and tiny shops line the main street. Browsing among the dozens of shops you'll see products found nowhere else in Georgia—giant handpainted cowbells, decorated beer steins, cuckoo clocks, Hummel figurines, and pipes worthy of Heidi's grandfather.

Throughout the town, shopkeepers parade in felt caps, and horse-drawn carriages carry sightseers to the next strudel-laden meal or pint of beer. Sure it's kitsch, yet no matter how you feel about accordion music or grown men wearing *lederhosen,* to find *Wiener schnitzel, schwartzwaldtorte,* and draft Heineken in rural Georgia is a welcome rarity.

Sights

In the castle on Main Street (you can't miss it), the **Museum of the Hills,** tel. (706) 878-3140, illustrates Helen's transformation from pioneer days to fairyland kingdom with historic photographs and other exhibits. Main Street's **Doll and Toy Museum,** tel. (706) 878-3493, displays a collection of more than 2,000 antique dolls.

Back down on Hwy. 75 south of Helen, the **Nora Mill Granary** features an old gristmill powered by the Chattahoochee River; the granary still produces and sells stone-ground grains. At the **Gold Mines of Helen** off Hwy. 75 around the bend, tel. (706) 878-3052, a self-guided tour leads visitors down 325 feet into an old mine. Admission is $3-5. It's open 10 a.m.-6 p.m.

Oktoberfest

The biggest annual event in the region, Oktoberfest draws 300,000 revelers to two months' worth of fall festivities. The German holiday of Oktoberfest originated in 1810, when King Leopold declared his son's rousing engagement bash to thereafter be an annual holiday. For years, Helen has likewise celebrated the holiday, with Bavarian dances and costumes, oom-pah-pah sing-alongs, polkas, waltzes, and plenty of German food and beer.

While the whole town works itself into a celebratory frenzy, the main event takes place in the **FestHalle,** an open-air pavilion set out over a bend in the river two blocks east of the Main Street bridge. The fest begins the Thursday after Labor Day and runs through the last weekend in October—Thurs.-Sat. in September, then Mon.-Sat. in October. On Saturday the event begins at noon, the rest of the week at 6 p.m. Admission to the FestHalle costs $6-8.

Other Seasonal Events

In winter, the Old-World **Altstadt Christmas Market** brings out citywide decorations in December. Outdoor booths under red-and-white striped tents sell crafts and plenty of hand-warming beverages and holiday treats. The town's official tree-lighting ceremony takes place in the central Marketplatz the Friday after Thanksgiving; a 60-foot tree is illuminated and Santa arrives in a horse-drawn carriage. In January or February, **Fashing Karnival** re-creates a costumed German Mardi Gras for four merrymaking weekends (Friday and Saturday nights).

In spring, a Bavarian **Volksmarch** has *volks* heading through the forest on 3K, 10K, and 20K hikes the third weekend in April. On the first weekend in May, the **MayFest** celebrates a mini-Oktoberfest in the Festhalle.

In summer, the annual **Hot Air Balloon Race** to the Atlantic takes off the first Thursday in June; later in the month there's the **Square Dance Festival** in the FestHalle. The **Fourth of July** sends tubing parades down the Chattahoochee River and brings out all-American fare and fireworks.

Nearby Unicoi State Park hosts many additional festivals, most of which celebrate traditional Appalachian arts and music.

Recreation

The calm, shallow stretch of the **Chattahoochee River** around Helen is fun for summertime tubing, swimming, or basking; several riverfront companies rent tubes or small rafts and offer shuttle service to return swimmers back upstream (about $7 for adults). Downriver, an outpost at the Hwy. 117 road crossing arranges canoe and raft trips down the Class II and III waterway. For canoe rentals and guided river trips, call **Appalachian Outfitters,** tel. (706) 864-7117. For mountain bike rentals, find **Woody's,** tel. (706) 878-3715, next to Fred's Famous Peanuts on the way to Unicoi. At the **Alpine Amusement Park** on Hwy. 75 south near the outlet mall, kids enjoy a 40-foot Ferris wheel, miniature golf, and of course, the *autobahn.* A steep 18-hole golf course and tennis club at the **Innsbruck** resort up off Hwy. 75 south, tel. (706) 878-2400, are part of a complex with condo rentals and a restaurant. An 18-hole public course, **Skitt Mountain Golf Course,** tel. (706) 865-2277, is in nearby Cleveland.

Accommodations and Camping

Because of its popular attractions, the Helen area's 1,233 guest rooms cost more than comparable accommodations elsewhere in the mountains. Standard price fluctuations apply: higher in October and during festivals and holidays, lower for weekdays and winter. Naturally, hotels along the Chattahoochee are most scenic, and premiums may be charged for riverfront rooms. (Unfortunately, some local proprietors put more stock in the exterior appearance of their property than they do the interior: check out the room before you accept it.)

Festival-goers note: A hotel beyond your walking distance from town means competing with day-trippers for overflowing $2 parking spots—unless the hotel provides shuttles, as many do.

Unicoi State Park, four miles north of Helen, offers lodge rooms ($69-109 d) and lakeside cottages ($95-135 for a one-bedroom).

Five properties are scenically set on the river right downtown. This list runs from north to south: the busy, lively **Chattahoochee Riverfront Motel,** 8949 N. Main St./Hwy. 76, tel. (706) 878-2184 or (800) 830-3977, with a pool, restaurant, river floats, and rates from $40 up, up, and up, depending on season; new freestanding cabins on stilts at the quiet **River Bend Chalets,** 152 Dye St., tel. (706) 878-3000 or (800) 247-7761; a brand new **Hampton Inn,** tel. (800) 426-7866, in a quiet residential area; cute motel exterior/somewhat shabby interiors at **Chalet Kristy,** 134 River St., tel. (706) 878-2155; and the **Helendorf River Inn,** tel. (706) 878-2271 or (800) 445-2271, in the thick of all the action at the Hwy. 75 bridge.

The new modern chain motels are clustered in a flat, less interesting area south of the Main St. bridge. These include Holiday Inn Express, Ramada Inn, Comfort Inn, Econo Lodge, Best Western, and Super 8. You'd pretty much have to drive downtown (it's not far, but not designed for pedestrians).

For campers, **Unicoi State Park,** four miles north of town, offers a 99-site campground with many amenities (see below). Campsites nestled alongside a mountain stream in **Andrews Cove,** a Forest Service recreation area five miles north of Helen off Hwy. 75/17, are available for $5 a night. An Appalachian Trail access route leaves from the campground.

Food and Drink

Not many rural Georgia towns serve the variety of Swiss-German-Dutch-Scandinavian cuisine you can find in Helen. The area's 35 restaurants may not be Munich, but it's a change of pace from fried chicken (there's that too). Helen is also one of the few places in the conservative mountains where you can get a mixed drink.

Budget travelers have their pick of *wurst* (knockwurst, bratwurst, and Polish sausage are common choices) in a bun, heaped with sauerkraut (as it happens, pickled sauerkraut is an authentic Appalachian tradition), and served with a side of German potato salad and a cold draft beer—available at low cost from many cafes and stands. Plenty of gingerbread cottage bakeries present a beautiful assortment of morning Danish, as well as strudel, cookies, and *torten* (including Black Forest cake). Belgian waffles are a local breakfast specialty, and you can even find strong European-style coffee—all right, maybe not *that* strong, but richer than usual.

In places like the **Hofbrauhaus Inn** on Main St., tel. (706) 878-2248, you might just want to lift a stein at the beer garden deck while strolling minstrels play Rhineland favorites, unless you want the full-scale stroganoff, fondue, and schnitzel with noodles.

At **Paul's** on Main St., tel. (706) 878-2468, the oldest restaurant in town, prime rib accompanied by country-western music and riverside views are the specialties of the house (closed Sunday). **Mountain Valley Kitchen** on Chattahoochee St., tel. (706) 878-2508, serves country cooking, including stone-ground grains from nearby Nora Mill.

AUTUMN COLORS

People familiar with the deciduous forests of eastern North America are sometimes surprised to realize how rare such forests are around the world. The familiar annual cycle of broadleaf trees turning spectacular colors and shedding their leaves in fall, and renewing their growth each spring, happens elsewhere in Europe, central China, and a few other places 30 to 60 degrees of latitude from the equator, but that's it. The best and most extensive of these forests is in North America, on the slopes of the Appalachians.

The Cherokee tell a legend of how the trees came to lose their leaves: the Great One told all the plants and animals to stay awake for seven days, yet as the nights wore on all but a few succumbed to sleep. The ones who remained awake—the cedar, pine, spruce, holly, and laurel—were rewarded by remaining evergreen, while the rest must lose their leaves each fall.

The following list of autumnal shades may help to identify a few dominant tree types in the fall forest:

American beech—yellow and orange
Black cherry—yellowish orange
Dogwood—scarlet
Hickory—yellow and orange
Red maple—from yellow to red to orange
Sassafras—orange
Scarlet oak—scarlet
Sourwood—dark red
Sugar maple—reddish yellow
Sumac—brilliant red
Sweet gum—scarlet, purple, and gold (sometimes all three shades on the same tree)
Yellow poplar—brilliant yellow

The timing and brilliance of the fall display depend on several factors, such as temperature and seasonal rainfall, but you'll most likely see colors from mid-September to mid-November, peaking the third week in October. Plan early for popular October accommodations.

For farm-fresh produce, barbecue meats, a deli, penny candy, and other provisions artfully arranged in a nouveau old country store, go to **Betty's Country Store** on Hwy. 75 north of town, tel. 878-2943. Toward Unicoi State Park three or so miles north of Helen, **Fred's Peanuts** sells boiled peanuts—a mountain specialty—along with other local food items. One of the best-value buffets in the region is served at the lodge in **Unicoi State Park.**

Information and Services

The **Alpine Helen-White County Convention and Visitors Bureau,** P.O. Box 730, Helen, GA 30545, tel. (706) 878-2181 or (800) 858-8027, fax (706) 878-4032, operates the welcome center at 726 Bracken Strasse at Edelweiss St., south of the Main St. bridge in the chain motel gulch. Discount coupon booklets are available upon request from the welcome center. They're open Mon.-Sat. 9 a.m.-5 p.m.

Parking lots behind Main St. charge $2 (lots may fill on busy weekends). Park south of town by the river to avoid the fee and the bridge bottleneck that slows all north-south traffic through town.

UNICOI STATE PARK

Unicoi State Park, five miles northeast of Helen, is the granddaddy of Georgia's mountain parks. With a jewel-like lake for boating, access trails to cascading Anna Ruby Falls, beautifully set lodging in cabins or lodge rooms, and an impressive schedule of festivals, Unicoi is a popular mountain destination. There's a $2 parking fee per vehicle, free on Wednesday. Contact the park at P.O. Box 849, Helen, GA 30545, tel. (706) 878-2201. For lodging and camping reservations call (800) 864-7275.

Anna Ruby Falls

Though technically within the national forest, access to Anna Ruby Falls is through Unicoi State Park, so it is most appropriately treated here. Follow the winding road off Hwy. 356 to the interpretive center parking lot (no $2 parking fee for falls hikers). From here, a paved path of just less than half a mile climbs moderately through a lush glen to two observation decks overlooking the spectacular waterfalls. Anna Ruby's unique double waterfall, the most popular stop on the Blue Ridge "cataract" itinerary, is formed from

KAREN McKINLEY

two separate creeks originating from underground springs at Tray Mountain to the north.

Recreation and Facilities

At **Lake Unicoi,** the 53-acre park centerpiece, you can swim, boat, or fish. The boathouse rents canoes and paddleboats. Four lighted **tennis courts** are also available. A 2.5-mile hiking trail leads around the lake, and another trail follows Smith Creek five miles up to Anna Ruby Falls. The four-mile moderate-difficulty **Helen Trail** leads into town—a rustic approach to the town's enchantments—also accessible to mountain bikes. Find trail maps at the lodge, the camp store, and the information center at the lake.

Accommodations and Camping

Unicoi Lodge houses a restaurant, meeting rooms, shops, and the lodge desk in the central building; outlying two-story lodge buildings contain guest rooms with interior corridors. Guest rooms may show a little wear (and were undergoing renovation at last visit) but are nevertheless an excellent value in a prime location (rates run $69-119).

Thirty fully equipped **cottages** are sprinkled at lakeshore and farther up Smith Creek. One-bedroom cabins rent for $95-135.

The 99-site **campground** creates a camp city in the woods, with a playground, amphitheater, nightly summertime campfire programs, and "trading post" camp store. Secluded wooded sites are available, including 33 walk-in tent sites and "squirrel's nest" platform shelters. Sites cost $16-18.

Lodge Restaurant

The Unicoi Lodge restaurant serves delicious reasonably priced buffets in a beautiful setting. The dining hall occupies a spacious room with a cathedral ceiling and massive stone fireplace; its glass-walled patio overlooks the woods. Georgia mountain trout is the house specialty, but catfish, barbecued chicken, and glazed ham are also often served. The dining room serves a generous breakfast buffet 7-10 a.m. (until 10:30 a.m. on weekends); lunch is served noon-2 p.m. daily (though on Sunday that means the all-out midday dinner, and higher prices); dinner is served daily from 5 p.m. Restaurant patrons aren't required to buy the $2 parking pass.

Programs and Events

Highlighting the park's full schedule of special events are its Appalachian arts festivals, such as the **Spring Bluegrass Concert and Dance** the third week in March, April's **Whittle Inn** (woodcarvers display their skills and sell their wares), June's **Mountain Living** festival (blacksmithing, weaving, and quilting demonstrations), and the **Appalachian Music Festival** in July (an old tradition that brings fiddlers from all over for folk and traditional music as well as bluegrass). In busy seasons, a daily list of activities for children and adults may include guided hikes, crafts programs, volleyball games, movies, and wildlife talks.

NORTH OF HELEN

Ravens Cliff and Vicinity

The Brasstown-Russell Scenic Hwy. (Hwy. 348) traverses a high leisurely route from Helen to Vogel State Park. (From downtown Helen, take Hwy. 75 north to Hwy. 75A and turn left. Hwy. 348 is a short distance down on the right.) On a clear day, drivers can overlook a Blue Ridge skyline of Slaughter Mountain, Turkey Pen Flats, Lordamercy Cove, Saddle Gap, Stoney Knob, and the Blue Ridge escarpment. As it forms the northern boundary of the Ravens Cliff Wilderness Area, the route provides easy roadside access to pristine waterfalls and adventurous trails—including the Appalachian Trail.

At 2.3 miles in from Hwy. 75A, a mile-long trail leads to **Dukes Creek Falls,** which drop 150 feet down a sheer granite canyon. An observation deck at the parking lot overlooks the falls. At 2.8 miles in, you'll find the trail to **Raven Cliff Falls** on the southern roadbank. Follow a 2.5-mile blue-blazed trail to these unusual falls, which emanate from a split in the face of a solid rock outcropping and drop 100 feet to Dodd Creek.

Unicoi Gap

Highway 75 leads from Helen through Unicoi Gap and the Hiawassee River valley to the town of Hiawassee at the North Carolina line. At **Andrews Cove,** off Hwy. 75 five miles north of Helen, a secluded 11-site FS campground lies along a beautiful mountain stream. From here, an old logging road heads two miles north up the ridge to connect with the Appalachian Trail (A.T). Farther north up Hwy. 75, the A.T. crosses Unicoi Gap. Park here to take a 10.4-mile roundtrip hike north to Tray Mountain. The rocky summit overlook, with remarkable panoramic views and a challenging boulder field on its north face, can also be reached by a one-mile roundtrip hike north on the A.T. from FS Rd. 79.

You'll find the road to **Horse Trough Falls** on Hwy. 75 eight miles north of Helen; turn left on FS Rd. 44 (Wilkes Creek Rd.) and continue 5.4 miles to an open camping area. Take the dirt road on the right for two-tenths of a mile to an iron gate and park; then, on foot, take the left fork of the old road and follow the winding blue-blazed trail through a serene forest to these 70-foot falls.

High Shoals Falls grace a 170-acre scenic area off Hwy. 75. Eleven miles north of Helen, turn right (east) onto the rugged dirt-and-gravel Indian Grave Gap Rd. (FS Rd. 283); ford a small stream and continue up the hill. A parking area is about 1.3 miles in from the highway. From here a moderately steep 1.2-mile trail winds its way to the succession of five falls (total vertical drop of 500 feet) framed by rhododendron and mountain laurel. An abandoned access road parallels the falls for inspiring views from two observation platforms.

Brasstown Bald

In the Cherokee version of Noah's Ark, the canoe that holds the surviving People comes to rest here, on the top of Brasstown Bald. As with other bald summits throughout the southern Appalachians, the exact cause for the missing forest is unknown.

The 360-degree view from Georgia's highest mountain encompasses four states: South Carolina, North Carolina, Tennessee, and Georgia. The steep half-mile paved **Brasstown Bald Trail** leads to the 4,784-foot summit (officially dubbed Mt. Enotah); shuttles are available for a small fee. At the top, the visitor center presents a short film on the region's cultural and geological heritage, and observation-deck placards identify sights in the distance. At the parking lot trailhead, a small concession sells local products and some refreshments.

Three trails connect at the approach to the summit (off-road parking available). **Arkaquah Trail** descends 5.5 miles along ridgeline to the petroglyphs at Trackrock. **Jacks Knob Trail** runs 4.5 miles south until it intersects with the Appalachian Trail. The original double-rutted **Wagon Train Trail** spurs off the paved summit trail and heads northwest six miles through the surrounding Brasstown Wilderness, ending behind the women's dormitory at the Young-Harris College campus (unmarked at both its beginning and end).

HIAWASSEE

Straddling the North Carolina border on the southern shore of Lake Chatuge, Hiawassee is best known for the popular mega-events staged at its 2,000-seat lakeside pavilion and fairgrounds. Plenty of local recreation areas, motels, restaurants, and bait-and-tackle shops cater to concertgoers and fisherfolk.

Entertainment and Events

In August, the **Georgia Mountain Fair** brings two weeks of mountain merrymaking to North Georgia. Ferris wheels, arcade games, pig races, and other amusements fill the fairgrounds, while the music hall hosts one lively mountain music act after another. Old-timers hold forth from wooden shacks, demonstrating the revered Appalachian arts of pot-throwing, whittlin', and moonshine-making. Admission is $5 (fair-goers in overalls are admitted free on "pioneer day"), and you may want to go back several times for different musical acts such as bluegrass, country-western, gospel, and traditional.

The play ***The Reach of Song*** tells the story of Appalachian history and heritage with a traditional music score. Fiddle pickin', two-steppin', and storytelling—it's all here (call 800-262-SONG or 800-262-7664 for more information). More homegrown mountain music can be heard at **Music Festivals** in mid-May and mid-October, and at a **Fiddlers Convention** in late October.

Recreation

The Forest Service's Lake Chatuge recreation area, on Hwy. 288 a mile south of Hwy. 76 west, provides access to the 7,050-acre **Lake Chatuge,** an angler's favorite for spotted and largemouth bass. Here a 32-site FS campground ($5 a night) is set on a pine-covered peninsula jutting into the reservoir. The nearby **chamber of commerce** on Hwy. 288 right off Hwy. 76, tel. (706) 896-4966, can direct you to commercial marinas, launches, and other services around the lake and throughout Hiawassee.

Eleven miles east of town, Hwy. 76 meets the Appalachian Trail, the fourth and final road crossing in Georgia from the Springer Mountain trailhead. The A.T. heads north from here five miles or so into the **Southern Nantahala Wilderness Area** before crossing over into North Carolina.

Accommodations and Food

The **Fieldstone Inn and Restaurant** on Hwy. 76 at the western shore of Lake Chatuge, tel. (706) 896-2262 or (800) 545-3408, offers a full-service hotel complex. A sleek stone-and-glass lobby leads to 66 modern guest rooms, all with balconies overlooking the lake (rates from $79). Boat rentals are available at the hotel's boathouse, and a swimming pool, tennis court, and restaurant are also on the premises. At the low end, **Mull's Motel,** 213 N. Main St., tel. (706) 896-4195, offers basic rooms for about $55 and can arrange shuttles to the A.T.

The **Georgia Mountain Restaurant** on Hwy. 76, tel. (706) 896-3430, serves popular country cooking for three meals in the thick of the action. It's open daily 6 a.m.-9 p.m.

At the **Deer Lodge** on Hwy. 75 south, tel. (706) 896-2726, crowds gather before the doors open—scratch your name on the notepad tacked outside, take your ticket, and wait for your number to be called. It's worth the wait for its meaty steaks, delicious mountain trout, and other hearty entrees served in cozy wood-paneled rooms. Dinners are served Tues.-Sun. 5-10 p.m., and the lodge also rents cabins up the hill.

Highway 76

From Hwy. 76, you can easily travel west to Blairsville or east to Rabun County.

CLARKESVILLE AND VICINITY

The oldest resort in North Georgia, Clarkesville sits at the lower slope of the river valley that stretches southeast from Helen. The surrounding countryside is perfect for a leisurely drive or bike tour past an old mill here, a covered bridge there, and renowned Glen-Ella Springs, an elegant country resort. North of Clarkesville, Highway 441 leads to high-country lakes and the deeper wilds of Rabun County.

To the east, between Clarkesville and the foothill city of Toccoa, the southernmost branch of the national forest offers natural areas within easy access to urban travelers. At the intersection of the Blue Ridge and Piedmont provinces, the forest here exhibits species from both physiographic areas. Most of the region's recreation areas are easily reached from Cornelia.

CORNELIA AND VICINITY

Cornelia, the southernmost Blue Ridge town, borders the most readily accessible branch of the national forest. Besides that, the town is known for its Giant Apple Monument, a tribute to the local industry, on Route 23 downtown. Visitors to town and forest areas east follow Hwy. 441 business; a modern bypass skirts the town for through-travelers.

About 20 minutes south of Cornelia, the **Habersham Winery** off Hwy. 365 in Baldwin, tel. (706) 778-WINE (706-778-9463), allows visitors to sample its local favorite white muscadine wine, as well as other varieties. A gift shop sells Georgia food items along with the winery's products. It's open Mon.-Sat. 10 a.m.-6 p.m., Sunday 1-6 p.m.

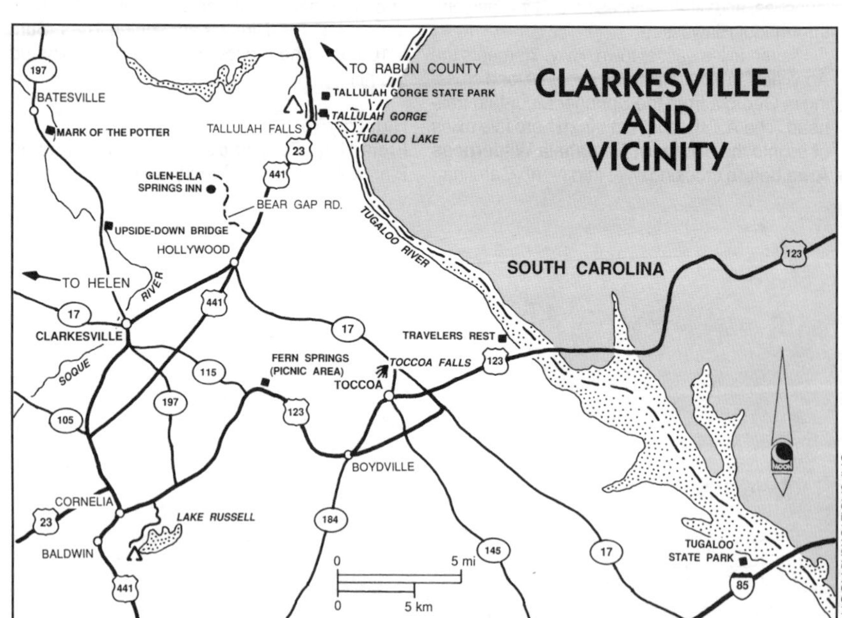

Trails and Recreation

At **Lake Russell,** 3.5 miles southeast of Cornelia, the Forest Service (FS) operates a recreation area for swimming, fishing, boating, camping, and hiking. The recreation area is set around a 100-acre lake with a grassy beach. From Cornelia, take Hwy. 123 toward Toccoa 1.5 miles, turn right on FS Rd. 59 (Lake Russell Rd.) and go two miles to the recreation area. The beach parking lot charges $2 per vehicle during its season from Memorial Day to Labor Day.

The 4.6-mile **Lake Russell Trail** follows the southern shore of the lake from dam to dam; the entrance road along the northern shore provides an alternate loop trip back. The other two trails start in the group camp area around Nancytown Lake. The 6.2-mile **Ladyslipper Trail,** a horse and foot trail, leads one mile up to a loop around Red Root Mountain with its panoramic views and a few steep climbs. The 2.7-mile loop **Sourwood Trail,** ideal for families and less ambitious hikers, reaches Nancytown Falls a mile in, passes a beaver pond, and follows a creek through the woods back along Red Root Rd. to the trailhead.

The 42-site Lake Russell campground is one of the few FS camps open year-round. It also has a trailer dump station (one of only two; the other is at Rabun Beach, north in Rabun County) and cold showers, as well as water, tables, grills, and toilets. Sites are $5 per night.

Fern Springs, a nice wooded picnic area set around a mountain spring, lies off Hwy. 123 six miles north of Cornelia.

CLARKESVILLE

More than 150 years ago, coastal families seeking refuge from the oppressive summer heat at the shore established Clarkesville as a cool summer home resort. Today this little mountain town tucks urbane delights into its rustic country setting.

Several major country crossroads come together in Clarkesville. Visitors from the south likely arrive via Hwy. 441, which continues northeast to Rabun County. Highway 17 leads west through the Sautee-Nacoochee Valley to Helen. Highway 197 follows the scenic Soque River—across a ford in a stream affectionately called "the upside-down bridge"—north to Batesville and Lake Burton.

Take this last route to the **Mark of the Potter,** an old mill perched at the waterfalls of the Soque River. Here at this Blue Ridge landmark you can feed the pet trout from the second-story balcony, view the millwork underpinnings, and browse around the handcrafted pottery on display. Toward Batesville, other scattered shops and studios specialize in handcrafted furniture, stained glass, and wooden duck decoys.

Where Highways 197 and 255 meet, the **Batesville General Store,** tel. (706) 947-3434, sells all manner of groceries, gas, and bait, and a cafe out back specializes in cinnamon rolls, biscuits, and burgers. It's open daily.

Sights and Events

Downtown Clarkesville's three-block row of wooden storefronts is centered around a shaded plaza where many town festivals take place. Colorful quilts in centuries-old Appalachian patterns flutter outside corner flea markets and antique boutiques, and a small art gallery exhibits more contemporary "collectibles." A bank, drugstore, book cellar, bakery, and sandwich shop round out the stores. Forty buildings around town, mostly former summer homes, are listed on the National Historic Registry.

Each May, the town continues a 30-some-year tradition with the **Mountain Laurel Festival,** a weeklong arts celebration on the square featuring a parade, street dance, and exhibited artwork, crafts, and antiques. The **Chattahoochee Mountain Fair** comes to town the third week in September with livestock shows, arts and crafts, exhibits, and rides and games. The downtown **fall festival** features homemade musical instruments—Appalachian fiddles, banjos, and dulcimers—and wraps up with a hoedown.

Accommodations and Food

Hundred-year-old **Glen-Ella Springs Inn,** on Bear Gap Rd. off Hwy. 441 north, tel. (706) 754-7295 or (800) 552-3479, is North Georgia's premier country inn. Set on 17 lush acres tucked away down miles and miles of country roads, the historic two-story lodge holds 16 guest rooms (from $75 d), each of which opens to a porch with rocking chairs. The landscaped grounds feature a pool and wide sundeck and manicured lawns leading to woods and nature trails along Panther Creek. From the inn, you can conveniently reach all eastern Blue Ridge destinations—that is, if you can roust yourself from the pool or rockers. The **dining room** serves an elegant dinner Tues.-Sat. from June to December, and a buffet Sunday brunch that is open to nonguests by reservation.

The town square bistro, **Taylor's Trolley,** tel. (706) 754-5566, set in a 1907 storefront with authentic turn-of-the-century decor, serves such daily chalkboard specials as mountain trout and prime rib. Or slide up to the green marble-topped counter for a quick ice-cream soda or coffee-and-cobbler. It's open for lunch and dinner (closed Sunday).

In a long wooden cabin south of town, **Adam's Rib** on Hwy. 441, tel. (706) 754-4568, serves a hearty breakfast of homemade biscuits and gravy, country ham, steak and eggs, and hotcakes. At lunch there's a barbecue buffet.

Information and Services

For more information, call the chamber of commerce at (706) 778-4654, or write the Clarkesville Business and Community Association, P.O. Box 711, Clarkesville, GA 30523. A **Forest Service office** on Burton Rd. (Hwy. 197), tel. (706) 754-6221, sells and distributes maps and guides to local FS trails and recreation areas.

RABUN COUNTY

Bordering both Carolinas in Georgia's northeast tip, Rabun County packs natural wonders, outdoor adventures, and down-home Appalachian spirit into one small isolated corner made famous by *Foxfire* and infamous by *Deliverance.* Chattooga River whitewater (rated among the top 10 river runs in the U.S.) is the biggest draw, and sightseers take in the spectacular 600-foot drop of sheer-walled Tallulah Gorge.

Christmas-tree farms, dairies, and car graveyards dot the old-time mountain towns, and country dogs run free. Rooted residents in homey cabins and old trailers grow corn in sideyards, hang hollow bottle gourds for nesting purple martins, and advertise "Mountain Honey for Sale" on handpainted wooden signs.

Such rugged communities contrast sharply with the posh picture-postcard resorts bordering the county's high-country lakes. Generations of Atlanta's elite have summered in stately "cottages" around Lake Rabun, whose boathouses alone are more elaborate than most county residences.

Towns are laid out linearly through the valley along Hwy. 441. Modern stretches of the "new" highway bypass the more serendipitous "old" highway.

TALLULAH FALLS

Tallulah Falls, balanced precariously over the precipitous gorge and thundering cascades of the Tallulah River, has an illustrious history—the dramatic sheer-walled gorge has both haunted and attracted people for centuries. The wary Cherokee heeded legends that warriors who ventured in never returned, and many a curious settler had a waterfall or pool named in his honor—posthumously, after an untimely slip. Yet word of the natural wonder spread, and crowds were drawn to the breathtaking sight.

By the turn of the century, Tallulah Falls was a fashionable resort, with several elite hotels and boardinghouses catering to lowland sightseers. A railroad transported visitors to the rim. But fortunes changed once the power company set sights on harnessing water power for hydroelectricity. Over public objections, the completed dam slowed the water—and the crowds—to a trickle. Despite the impressive sight of the dry gorge, the once-famous resort of Tallulah Falls likewise faded, and reverted to an earthy Blue Ridge mountain community.

Cyclists find many rewards along the state's quiet country roads.

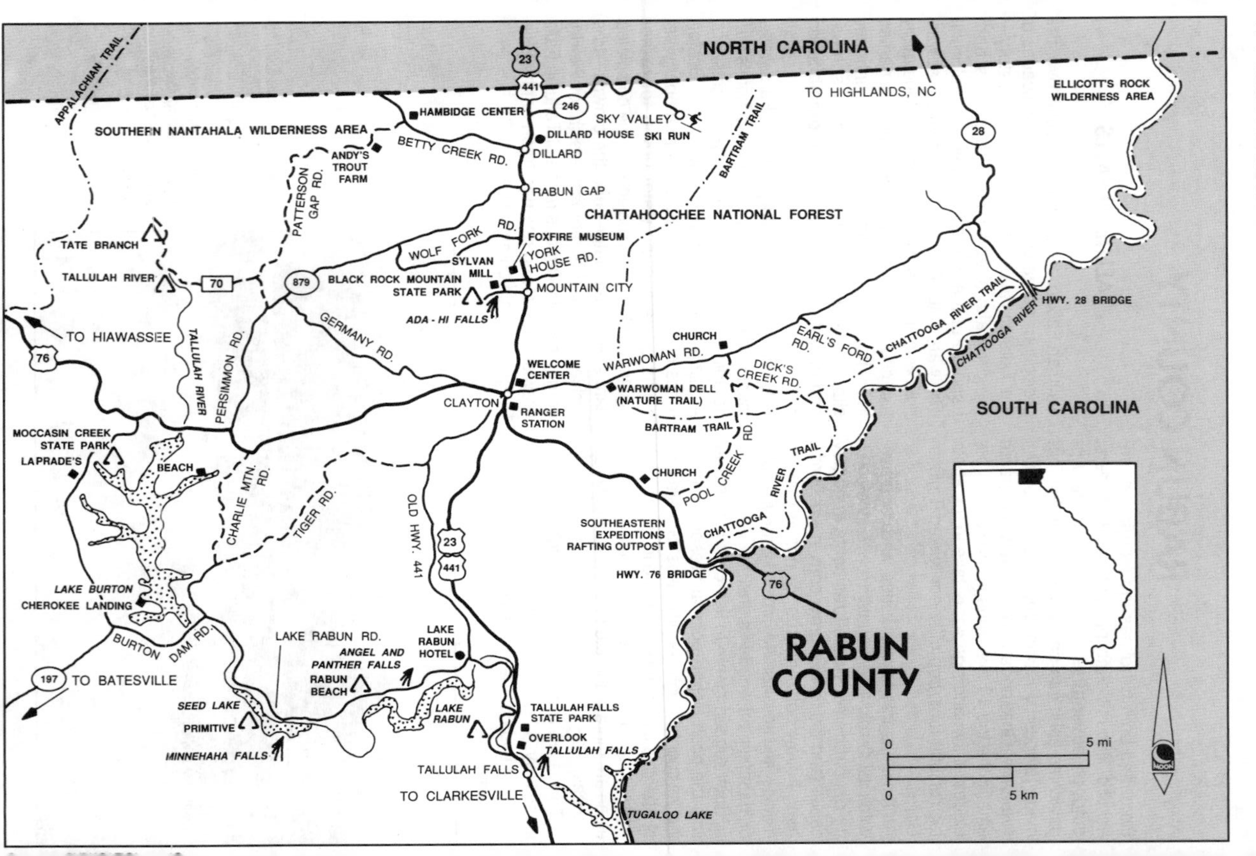
NORTH CAROLINA
APPALACHIAN TRAIL
23
441
246
TO HIGHLANDS, NC
ELLICOTT'S ROCK WILDERNESS AREA
HAMBIDGE CENTER
SOUTHERN NANTAHALA WILDERNESS AREA
SKY VALLEY
DILLARD HOUSE
SKI RUN
BARTRAM TRAIL
28
BETTY CREEK RD.
DILLARD
ANDY'S TROUT FARM
PATTERSON GAP RD.
RABUN GAP
CHATTAHOOCHEE NATIONAL FOREST
WOLF FORK RD.
FOXFIRE MUSEUM
TATE BRANCH
YORK HOUSE RD.
SYLVAN MILL
TALLULAH RIVER
70
879
BLACK ROCK MOUNTAIN STATE PARK
MOUNTAIN CITY
ADA - HI FALLS
CHATTOOGA RIVER TRAIL
HWY. 28 BRIDGE
TO HIAWASSEE
GERMANY RD.
CHURCH
EARL'S FORD RD.
CHATTOOGA RIVER
76
PERSIMMON RD.
WARWOMAN RD.
WELCOME CENTER
DICK'S CREEK RD.
WARWOMAN DELL (NATURE TRAIL)
CLAYTON
RANGER STATION
SOUTH CAROLINA
BARTRAM TRAIL
MOCCASIN CREEK STATE PARK
LAPRADE'S
BEACH
CHARLIE MTN. RD.
CHURCH
POOL CREEK RD.
CHATTOOGA RIVER TRAIL
TIGER RD.
OLD HWY. 441
SOUTHEASTERN EXPEDITIONS RAFTING OUTPOST
HWY. 76 BRIDGE
LAKE BURTON
CHEROKEE LANDING
BURTON DAM RD.
LAKE RABUN RD.
LAKE RABUN HOTEL
RABUN COUNTY
ANGEL AND PANTHER FALLS
197
TO BATESVILLE
RABUN BEACH
SEED LAKE
LAKE RABUN
TALLULAH FALLS STATE PARK
PRIMITIVE
OVERLOOK
TALLULAH FALLS
MINNEHAHA FALLS
TALLULAH FALLS
TO CLARKESVILLE
TUGALOO LAKE
0
5 mi
0
5 km
MOON

After decades of talk about restoring the gorge's former glory, in 1993 the power company agreed to test the waters and send the Tallulah River spilling through the gorge once again.

Tallulah Gorge

When you take in the beautiful sight of Tallulah Gorge, imagine walking a tightrope suspended across its breadth, 1,200 feet above the gorge floor. In 1886, such a feat was accomplished by Professor Leon (despite a stumble). In 1970, the flying Karl Wallenda replicated the historic feat. Drivers can pull over from Hwy. 441 to see the sight, or park and take one of several trails along the rim. At the privately owned **Overlook** concession stand, the outside view is free. The **North Rim Trail** reaches an overlook about a quarter-mile from Tallulah Gorge State Park.

Hang gliders enjoy the dramatic float over the gorge; gliders congregate at the **Hang Glider Heaven** cabins around the southeast rim, tel. (706) 782-6218.

Tallulah Gorge State Park

Established in 1993,Tallulah Gorge State Park, located off Hwy. 441,tel. (706) 754-7970, features an impressive interpretive center set out on the north rim of the gorge. Inside a dramatic film tells the story of the gorge and town; outside, rim trails lead to scenic overlooks. A six-mile mountain biking trail leads to Tugaloo Lake; the trailhead is near the gatehouse.

At Tallulah Lake, the 63-acre impoundment of the Tallulah River, there's a small swimming beach. A 50-site campground (call 706-754-7979 for reservations) is nicely set among woods; a short spur trail leads to the top of the gorge.

WEEKENDER LAKES

In the 1920s, Georgia Power constructed several more dams to impound the once-raging Tallulah River. The resulting placid lakes—Rabun, Seed, and Burton—now offer beautiful mountain scenery and recreation easily glimpsed from a smooth, slow-moving drive or an ideal bicycle tour. For a scenic flatwater canoeing adventure, cross the three lakes west-to-east, with short portages past two dams. Contact **Appalachian Outfitters** at (706) 864-7177 for canoe rentals and shuttle information.

To reach the lakes from Hwy. 441, drive two miles north of Tallulah Falls, crossing the gorge bridge, a second bridge, and turning left immediately before the third bridge. Continue 2.5 miles (crossing yet another bridge), and turn left onto Lake Rabun Road.

Lake Rabun

Lake Rabun, a clubby colony of 400 lakeshore homes for Atlanta's elite, also shelters one of the best Forest Service recreation areas in the Blue Ridge. All sights are accessible from Lake Rabun Road.

The **Lake Rabun Hotel,** tel. (706) 782-4946, has offered guests a high-style rustic retreat since 1922. The stone mountain lodge resembles a classic hunting lodge, with dark wood paneling, thick beams, and bowl-sized white porcelain sinks in the rooms (from $60 for a double with breakfast). There's an appealing pub downstairs for grub and beers. Innkeepers tell the story of one guest named Rabun (after the lake); his parents say he was conceived at the hotel on their honeymoon, and he grew up to reserve the same room for his own honeymoon.

At **Hall's Marina,** you can find a boat launch and fishing and boating supplies. The adjacent Boat House, an open-air pavilion over the lake, is treasured as the scene of rousing weekend concerts and parties in its past heyday. Today the only gatherings religiously held are the Sunday morning services called forth to a floating congregation. But you might get lucky—check at the marina for any bluegrass concerts or other events that might be taking place during your stay.

At the Forest Service **Rabun Beach** recreation area, a small strip of sandy beach brings sunbathers and families to the lifeguard-supervised swimming area. A boat launch is available, and a trail to waterfalls begins across the road (see the special topic **Waterfalls.**) The attractive 50-site FS campground across the way offers many secluded sites on a gently sloping hillside—it's one of the nicest places to camp in the region ($5 a night, first-come, first-served).

WATERFALLS

Something about a waterfall is compelling—the beauty, the roar, the spray—and the Blue Ridge is full of these graceful primal attractions. Nearly every stream has one, at some point, and each scene is guaranteed to be framed by thick lush growth and blooms, or sparkling with winter ice. You'll find the grand, well-known Amicalola Falls and Anna Ruby Falls, along with many other scenic waterfalls, farther west, and Toccoa Falls farther south, yet Rabun County's many waterfalls have a distinctive quality—tranquil and removed, yet easily accessible to the casual hiker.

Mountaineers use such terms as "misty," "cascading," or "thundering" to describe their favorite local "cataracts" (from Middle English for floodgate). Waters may spill down in "double falls," "stairstep falls," "free falls," or "shoals."

Rangers warn against climbing near any falls. The prime local hazard is slipping off slick rocks, and getting stuck endangers rescuers. "Blazes" are eye level rectangular gashes in trees, painted to indicate a trail.

Becky Branch Falls

A steep walk through the dense Warwoman Dell leads to the tranquil waterfalls of Becky Branch ("branch" is an Appalachian synonym for "stream"). The Bartram Trail—named for 18th-century Quaker naturalist William Bartram—begins a hundred feet below the falls. Nearby, old stone steps lead to an abandoned railroad bed.

From Clayton, drive east on Warwoman Rd. (County Rd. 5) to the junction with Pool Creek Road. Go 2.8 miles and park on the left. Walk 200 yards up the steep trail at the right side of the falls to the bridge.

Dick's Creek

Here water spills 60 feet into the federally designated "Wild and Scenic" Chattooga River, and an observation platform overlooks the sheer drop.

Take Warwoman Rd. east six miles out of Clayton to Pool Creek Road. Follow for 0.6 miles and turn right on Dick's Creek Rd. (also called Sandy Ford Rd.). Follow this road 3.5 miles past the second ford to where it crosses the Bartram Trail. Park and walk north along the trail for 600 yards.

Martin Creek Falls

Naturalist William Bartram wrote admiringly of these falls—then called Falling Branch Falls—in *Travels,* the 1791 account of his Southeastern expeditions. To get to this series of three falls on Martin Creek, follow Warwoman Rd. east from Clayton 2.5 miles. Drive up Martin Creek Rd. a half-mile and park, then hike up the west side of the creek.

Holcomb and Ammons Creek Falls

These picturesque waterfalls on the Holcomb Creek Trail drop and shoal for 150 feet, first at Holcomb Creek, then at Ammons Creek a third of a mile up.

Take Warwoman Rd. east of Clayton 10 miles. At Hale Ridge Rd., turn left and go nine miles; the 1.5-mile trail starts at the intersection of Overflow Road.

Mud Creek Falls

The falls cascade for 350 feet with a spouting flume down the middle.

Take Hwy. 441 north from Clayton, then north on Hwy. 246 to Sky Valley. Go through the main gate down Sky Valley Way, turn right on Tahoe Rd., pro-

Lake Seed

On Lake Seed, the power company maintains primitive campsites without water; follow signs off Lake Burton Road. The same turnoff leads to Minnehaha Falls.

Lake Burton

Lake Burton, the biggest and most remote of the three, is the fisherman's favorite. A mile or so west of the dam at the lake's southern end, signs off Hwy. 197 lead drivers down dirt roads to **Cherokee Landing.** Here you'll find a marina, boat launch, bait store, burger joint, and a scattered collection of cabins.

The lake's public swimming area, **Timpson Cove Beach,** lies at the northeastern shore, off Hwy. 76 west of Clayton. A cluster of activity at the western shore holds all other lakeside services.

The old-time fishing resort of **LaPrade's** off Hwy. 197, tel. (706) 947-3312, dates back to the town of Burton, which has been submerged under its namesake lake since 1925. Around the lodge, small tin-roof cabins with screen porches are scattered up the hillside. Rates of $38 per person include three meals a day. In the lodge, hearty mountain meals—chicken and dumplings, fried chicken, country ham, and your ceed three-quarters of a mile to the "three forks" intersection and park. Walk 500 yards down on left (grills and picnic tables available).

Angel and Panther Falls
Along the trail you'll first find 50-foot Angel Falls; half a mile upstream along the climbing trail lies Panther Falls.

Head south from Clayton on Old Hwy. 441 to Lake Rabun Rd., then turn in to the Rabun Beach recreation area, which is divided into two sections. Look for trail signs in Area Two.

Minnehaha Falls
One hundred feet high, this beautiful waterfall drops and shoals from the top of a secluded path that gently climbs through rhododendron and mountain-laurel thickets.

Go south from Clayton on Old Hwy. 441 and follow Lake Rabun Rd. to the west, which takes you around the north side of the lake. One mile past the Rabun Beach recreation area, you'll see the dam. Cross the bridge, bear left onto Bear Gap Rd., and continue straight after the full stop for 1.6 miles. Trail markers disappear mysteriously; watch for the bend with a widened left shoulder to park, and follow the narrow footpath across the way to the half-mile trail.

Tallulah Falls
Recently released after being bottled up for half a century, the magnificent falls at Tallulah Gorge again roar through the dramatic 1,000-foot gorge—now the centerpiece of a new state park; overlook trails have a panoramic view.

Follow signs off Hwy. 441 north of the gorge bridge.

MARSHALL BURGAMY

a short walk, a light lunch, and water on the rocks . . .

choice of biscuit or cornbread—are served family-style with a view of the lake. Breakfast is served Wed.-Sun. 8-9 a.m., lunch and Sunday dinner are served 12:30-2 p.m., dinners are served Wed.-Sat. 7-8 p.m. Call to confirm times open and make reservations weekends.

Across the road, LaPrade's marina features a boat launch and rentals.

Moccasin Creek State Park

This postage-stamp-sized park—Georgia's smallest state park—is nestled invitingly on the shores of Lake Burton off Hwy. 197, tel. (706) 947-3194. The 54 campground sites are close parking spots with only a few trees to shade you from your neighbor, but it nevertheless makes a good base of operations if you don't covet your privacy. Naturally, it attracts mostly trailer-camper fishing families. Campers can fry their daily catch or take all their meals at the nearby LaPrade's. The park sponsors a homemade music hoedown the first week in October, among other programs and events. From a trailhead at the trout hatchery intake across the road, the 6.2-mile **Moccasin Creek Trail** follows a scenic trout stream to high falls about an hour's hike away. It costs $12-18 to camp, including hookups; call (800) 864-PARK (800-864-7275) for

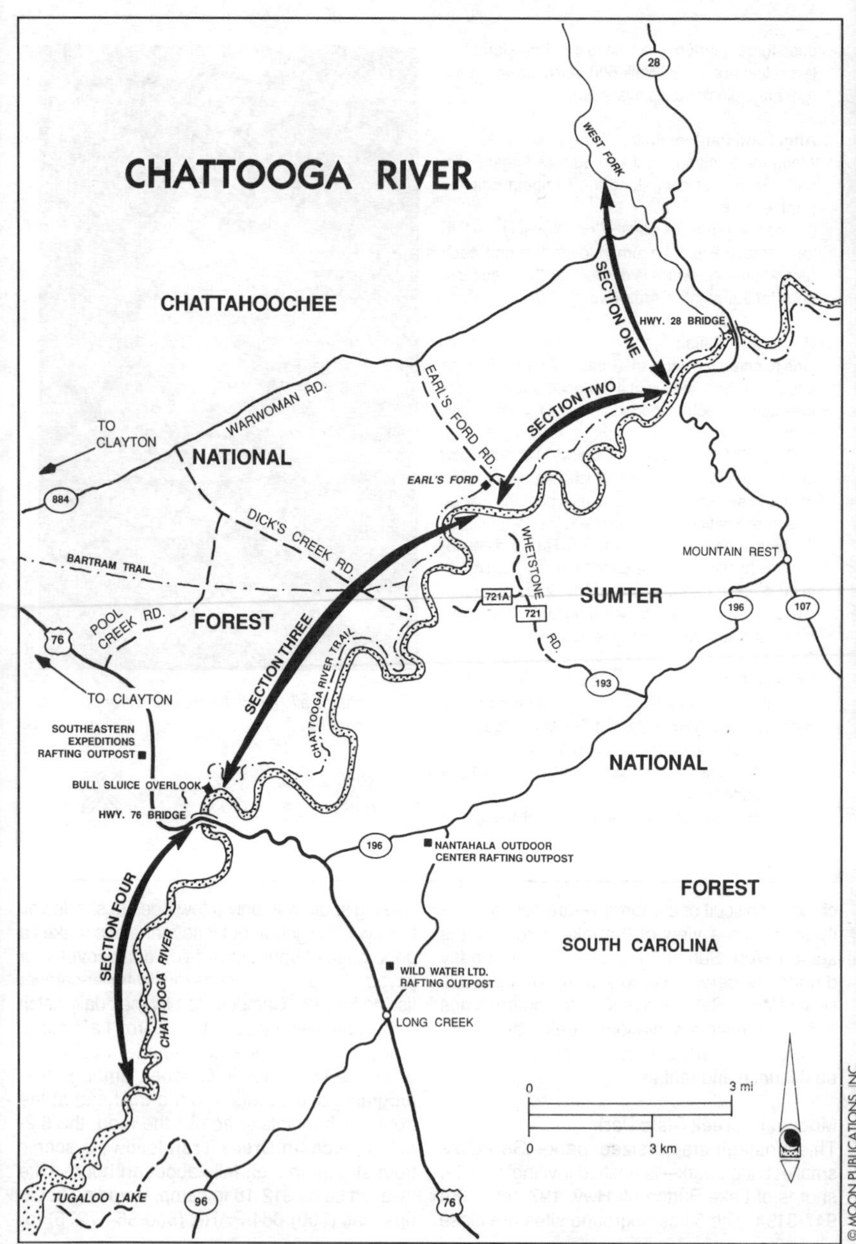
CHATTOOGA RIVER
CHATTAHOOCHEE
NATIONAL
FOREST
SUMTER
NATIONAL
FOREST
SOUTH CAROLINA
WEST FORK
SECTION ONE
HWY. 28 BRIDGE
SECTION TWO
SECTION THREE
SECTION FOUR
WARWOMAN RD.
EARL'S FORD RD.
EARL'S FORD
DICK'S CREEK RD.
BARTRAM TRAIL
POOL CREEK RD.
WHETSTONE RD.
721A
721
MOUNTAIN REST
196
107
193
28
884
76
96
TO CLAYTON
TO CLAYTON
SOUTHEASTERN EXPEDITIONS RAFTING OUTPOST
BULL SLUICE OVERLOOK
HWY. 76 BRIDGE
CHATTOOGA RIVER TRAIL
CHATTOOGA RIVER
NANTAHALA OUTDOOR CENTER RAFTING OUTPOST
WILD WATER LTD. RAFTING OUTPOST
LONG CREEK
TUGALOO LAKE
0
3 mi
0
3 km
MOON

reservations. The parking fee is $2 per car, free on Wednesday.

THE CHATTOOGA RIVER

Slicing through the Appalachian wilderness at the junction of three states, the "Wild and Scenic" Chattooga River rates among the nation's top 10 whitewater river adventures. The "world-class" river attracts 100,000 visitors a year to Rabun County for rafting, canoeing, kayaking, tubing, swimming, fishing, and bankside hiking, but you wouldn't know it from the desolate feel of the wilderness.

Rated Class IV overall, the river is divided into four sections of increasing difficulty. **Section One,** mainly the west fork above the Hwy. 28 bridge, is a shallow preserve of fly fishermen and frolicking inner tubers. **Section Two** picks up the pace; families and beginners enjoy light paddling with some rough-water rapids. **Section Three** is where the action starts—a dozen miles of fast water with as many Class III and IV rapids, plus the kicker, Class V Bull Sluice ("Decapitation Rock" gives you an idea of this rapid's thrills). **Section Four** follows with hardcore whitewater such as the "Screaming Left Turn," "Deliverance Rock," and an eye-of-the-needle run through "Crack in the Rock." Some of these rapids rate up to Class VI and are more hazardous in higher water. *There are no atheists on Section Four.*

While professionally guided rafting excursions have reliable safety records, independent paddlers be forewarned: the river is extremely dangerous and only experienced paddlers should attempt it. The movie *Deliverance,* based on the book by Georgia novelist James Dickey, was filmed on the river. Ever since the movie was released, authorities have been pulling bodies out of the river—not toothless mountaineers but overconfident river runners who underestimate the whitewater's power.

Rafting Excursions

To minimize traffic and wear-and-tear on the river, only three companies are licensed to operate on the Chattooga: **Southeastern Expeditions,** tel. (800) 868-7238; **Nantahala Outdoor Center,** tel. (800) 232-7238; and **Wild Water Ltd.,** tel. (800) 451-9972. All three run daily trips March-October; most trips take about six hours and cost roughly $60-80 (weekday rates are lower, Section Four is higher). All offer overnight or weeklong excursion trips—some combined with biking, hiking, or horseback riding—and package deals combine rafting prices with overnight accommodations at local lodges.

All outfitters provide lifevests, helmets, rafts, paddles, food, shuttle service from outposts, and car-key containers. Stow your valuables safely out of sight in your car or hotel. You need to bring a towel and change of clothes to leave in the car. In summer, wear shorts or a bathing suit, and old sneakers or river shoes. In cold weather, wear wool socks and a wool cap or the modern equivalent.

Hiking and Backpacking

The 20-mile **Chattooga River Trail** follows the river upstream from the Hwy. 76 bridge, crossing Hwy. 28 and continuing north another 15 miles into South Carolina. The route is blazed with both a metal diamond marker and yellow paint to indicate that the river trail and **Bartram Trail** merge here. With notably scenic exceptions, the trail passes through the thick mixed-hardwood forest largely out of sight of the river, though you can hear the roaring rapids. The Forest Service office in Clayton sells detailed river maps.

CLAYTON AND VICINITY

The down-home mountain town of Clayton, largest city in Rabun County, is a good base of operations for excursions into the wild forest and river areas to the east. Main Street, a three-block length of wooden storefronts on a sunny rise, still looks like a place you might hitch a horse outside to do your trading and salooning. Most of today's deals, however, involve bait-and-tackle, and heavy drinking means bottomless mugs of coffee at the local cafe.

Recreation

The 57-mile **Bartram Trail,** named for the naturalist William Bartram, who mapped this route in 1777, stretches from the North Carolina line through Georgia's tip downhill to South Carolina. Hikers can pick up the trail midway by parking at **Warwoman Dell,** a Forest Service area east of Clayton off Warwoman Road. A half-mile **na-**

ture walk here identifies native plants. From this point, the Bartram Trail heads east to the river and merges with the Chattooga River Trail.

Accommodations and Food

Out Hwy. 76 a half-mile east of town, **A Small Motel,** tel. (706) 782-6488 or (800) 786-0624, caters to river runners with a neat and friendly set of rooms ($38 and up), seven miles from the Chattooga River. The **Old Clayton Inn** on Main St., tel. (706) 782-7722, is a nice spot right downtown popular with rafters (rates from $50-60). The **Beechwood Inn,** 220 Beechwood Dr., tel. (706) 782-5485, is a quiet bed and breakfast operating from a two-story wooden lodge in the woods (rates from $85).

The **Clayton Cafe** on Main St. downtown slings down-home breakfasts, burgers, and other basic diner fare from a syrup-stained menu (open 6:30 a.m.-2:30 p.m., closed Sunday).

Green Shutters on S. Main St., tel. (706) 782-3342, serves three family-style meals a day, accompanied by cinnamon rolls, sweet potato bread, buttermilk biscuits, and corn muffins. It's open Wed.-Mon. 8-10 a.m., 11 a.m.-2 p.m., and 5-9 p.m. (also ask about overnight lodging).

From a small rise above Warwoman Rd. just east of the highway, the **Stockton House,** tel. (706) 782-6175, overlooks a forest-framed view of Screamer Mountain. It serves steaks, seafood, and pasta plates alongside Southern standards at buffet lunches (about $5), and dinners and elaborate midday Sunday suppers (about $10). City folk appreciate the rare wine list. It's open 11 a.m.-2 p.m. and 5-9 p.m.

Information and Services

The enthusiastic folks at the Rabun County Chamber of Commerce run the resourceful **welcome center** on Hwy. 441 north of Warwoman Rd., tel. (706) 782-5113. The **Forest Service office** on Hwy. 441, tel. (706) 782-3320, sells comprehensive Chattooga River maps and distributes guides to recreation areas in the surrounding national forest.

For provisions, look for the supermarket shopping centers off Hwy. 441. The laundromat on Hwy. 76 one block east of Main Street offers drop-off laundry service.

For medical emergencies, call **Rabun County Hospital,** tel. (706) 782-4233.

MOUNTAIN CITY

Coming into Mountain City from the south at the end of the day, drivers watch the monolith of Black Rock Mountain impose an early twilight on the broad valley to its east. Behind scruffy roadside cabins with their lean-to signs, the granite mountain's shadow slowly reaches past grazing black-and-white cows and tractors parked between haystacks. Turn left, and a winding route climbs to the summit where it's still bright with daylight.

Continue north another mile on the highway to S. Wolf Fork Road. If you turn in toward the mountain, you'll pass an old garage overtaken with flowering vines and a red storybook barn before coming to **Sylvan Mill,** sitting next to a waterfall pouring over gleaming granite. A red waterwheel standing two stories high churns through the silver water, still grinding hominy into speckled grits. The miller now operates the mill as a bed and breakfast.

On York House Rd. east of the highway, beyond the cows and hay and over the gully bridge, the trim white **York House,** tel. (706) 746-2068, banks up against the forest wall. This historic inn has been open for business since 1896, and not much has changed since then, except the addition of indoor plumbing in every room. The antiques weren't antique then, just furniture, and the fireplaces still work. The second-story veranda catches the last stretch of valley sun before the light goes out. Guests pay from $69 for a comfortable historic room with a continental breakfast.

Foxfire Museum

Inside the Foxfire Museum on Hwy. 441, tel. (706) 746-5318, a crowded collection of Appalachian handicrafts symbolizes a radical cultural and educational movement begun in the 1960s. At that time, local schoolteacher Eliot Wigginton, frustrated in attempts to motivate his uninspired high-school students, assigned them the task of interviewing their elders about how things were in the old days. It lit a spark. The students, jazzed with the newly discovered richness of their Appalachian heritage, assembled the written interviews into a magazine, which they named *Foxfire* (after a luminescent local fungus). The magazine expanded to a series of

KAP STANN

Mountain honey and Appalachian crafts are among the pleasures of country roadside stands.

books by the same name that exhaustively documented fading Appalachian folkways. The program's twofold success—educational innovation and folklife preservation—further broadened as the then-emerging back-to-the-land movement seized upon the books as vital how-to manuals for subsistence farming, animal husbandry, and crafts-making from found materials.

High schoolers built the traditional Appalachian log cabin that houses the museum. Inside, you can quietly peruse through the wooden toys, dolls, tools, smithwork, quilt patterns, and other farm equipment and housewares. A small bookshop here sells the *Foxfire* books and cassette tapes of the Foxfire Boys—now accomplished fiddlers who started playing when they were students in the program (you can hear them around town every now and again). The doors are open Mon.-Sat. 9 a.m.-4:30 p.m. See also www.foxfire.org.

Docents lead guided tours of a Foxfire village of handmade cabins constructed with period authenticity—every bean tells a story—with a five-adult minimum, weekdays only ($7.50 adults, $1-3 students).

BLACK ROCK MOUNTAIN

The temperature drops as you climb 2,700 feet up the steep grade to the top of Black Rock Mountain. At the wind-worn 3,640-foot summit, a visitor center and flagstone terrace look out over a grand south-facing Blue Ridge panorama. If there's no fog, you can see clear to the South Carolina Piedmont 80 miles away. The rocky crest also marks the eastern continental divide—from here waters part to follow a path to either the Atlantic Ocean or the Gulf of Mexico.

A local legend tells the story of a Cherokee chief's son who asked a neighboring Catawba chief for his daughter's hand in marriage. The girl's reluctant father told the prospective bridegroom he would grant consent only if the boy found "where the waters part"—likely a native version of "when hell freezes over." Well, it happened that the boy stumbled upon this mountaintop divide, and though he reported back to the chief with joy that his hopes would be fulfilled, the Catawba still refused him. So the young lovers ran off together to Hiawassee.

The highest state park in Georgia now occupies the legendary mountain. At **Black Rock Mountain State Park,** tel. (706) 746-2141, you'll see contrasting views from several observation platforms. The north-facing campground overlook spans a view across the Blue Ridge to the southern Nantahalas and the Great Smoky Mountains. At sunset, look for the Tennessee Rock overlook, just beyond the visitor center and a short jaunt up from the sign on the right. The 1,803-acre park also features 10 miles of trails, hideaway cabins, and a 17-acre lake stocked with trout. In winter, at least a light dusting of snow covers the higher elevations, and rangers can show you photos of the blizzard that dropped a foot of snow at the year-round park several winters back.

Hiking and Backpacking

Though the trail to **Ada-Hi Falls** is only a fifth

of a mile, in that length it drops 220 feet. Naturally, the trip up feels a whole lot longer. The sloping trail and steps dead-end at a wooden platform that overlooks the small (but worth the climb) waterfall. The two-mile yellow-blazed **Tennessee Rock Trail** largely follows the contour of the eastern continental divide, climbing 440 feet across the forested ridge crest. The 7.2-mile orange-blazed **James E. Edmonds Backcountry Trail** covers similar territory, but drops lower, climbs higher, crosses two creeks, and passes under stands of white pine, a hemlock forest, and thickets of fragrant mountain laurel. Midway in, the trail spurs off to a primitive campsite and vista point on 3,162-foot **Lookoff Mountain.** Ask for trail maps and interpretive nature trail guides at the visitor center. The park sponsors a guided overnight **backpacking trip** led by staff naturalists the last weekend in October; call for reservations and information.

Cottages and Camping

Ten spacious cottages are set off in a ring at the top of the mountain. The lucky campers in cottages 1-6 get the panoramic view, but all cabins are exquisitely removed from lowland civilization—no phones, no TVs, just fireplaces and porch rockers. The cottages sleep up to 10 people, and are rented year-round—a nice snowy winter retreat. The cost is $60-80 for a two-bedroom. Call (800) 864-PARK (800-864-7252) for cottage or camping reservations.

A 64-site wooded **campground** sits high atop the eastern continental divide. Eleven walk-in tent sites offer additional seclusion. All sites are $16. The red wooden Trading Post at the entrance to the campground sells a bare-bones assortment of batteries, charcoal, ice, and firewood. Sometimes when it rains, rangers open up the camp store's dusty attic for video shows to entertain the kids; if you sit on the porch, you can watch the waters part on the pavement out front.

DILLARD AND VICINITY

The Dillard name dates from the 1700s in these parts. For generations, the Dillard family has run a local hospitality empire. In addition to the rambling landmark inn, the family oligarchy operates a row of roadside businesses off Hwy. 441, selling "collectibles," "keepsakes," and even supplies.

Dillard House

A sprawling set of bungalows, lodges, and halls all go by the name Dillard House, off Hwy. 441, tel. (706) 746-5348. Heading them up is the restaurant, famous for its all-you-can-eat country cooking. From its glass-walled patio, diners can look out over the broad green valley to see horses in the pasture. Brisk waiters deliver plates of classic country ham, fried chicken, pan-fried trout, vegetables, cornbread, and assorted relishes and desserts. Grown to meet the mushrooming demands of flocks of tourists, the legendary institution may today impress you as more institution than legend—nevertheless, you never leave hungry. Guest rooms are around back—in low-slung lodges scattered near a swimming pool and tennis courts—and nearby at the original inn. Prices run from about $59 d.

At the **Dillard House Stables,** guests and visitors alike can inquire about hour-long, half-day, and overnight horseback-riding trips—an adventurous way to see the mountains' wild side.

Betty's Creek Road

From Dillard, a left turn onto Betty Creek Rd. leads west through one of North Georgia's most beautiful valleys. The gently rolling, winding route is perfect for bicycle touring.

At **Andy's Trout Farm,** five miles up, tel. (706) 746-2550, you don't need a license to fish for rainbow trout, and Andy's lends you a pole and line. They also rent wooden cabins around the ponds for $48 and up—that way you can stay over for the nightly square dances.

The **Hambidge Center,** six miles west of Dillard, tel. (706) 746-5718, was founded by Mary Hambidge—a cultural artist, iconoclast, and environmentalist—to preserve traditional Appalachian crafts. The Center houses a gallery, studio, cabins, and administrative buildings on 600 picturesque acres. It sponsors an on-site artists-in-residence program and hosts occasional programs devoted to Appalachian heritage. An old gristmill on the premises is still in operation; on Fridays and Saturdays neighbors bring in grain to be stone-ground. Visitors are welcome to roam about the grounds, providing that they first check in at the office. The center is open Mon.-Sat. 10 a.m.-4 p.m.

Sky Valley

Sky Valley, tel. (706) 746-5302 or (800) 437-2416, east of Dillard via Hwy. 246, is home to the southernmost ski resort in the eastern United States. Here, in an isolated niche within Georgia's northeasternmost wilderness, an exclusive year-round resort occupies a small valley at the base of the 3,320-foot runs. The length of the winter-sports season varies with the weather, though the resort "blows snow" if it's cold enough. Besides the winter sports, the deluxe resort is open year-round for guests to enjoy the remote setting, an 18-hole golf course and pro shop, swimming pool, tennis courts, restaurant, and bar. Chalet and condominium rentals start at $135 a night for a place that sleeps six. Ask at the office about nearby trails.

Quilt makers traditionally include a deliberate error in their patterns so as not to mimic the perfection of God.

KATHY PETERSON

CENTRAL GEORGIA

INTRODUCTION

The Piedmont region between the mountains of North Georgia and the southern coastal plain constitutes Central Georgia. This plateau holds most of the state's population and its major cities, including Atlanta. Unlike the bustling capital however, Georgia's other heartland cities retain a slow Southern pace of life. Residents greet one another with a generational familiarity, as their granddaddy and great-granddaddy done. The strong Southern sense of history and nostalgia for time-honored rural traditions continues to hold sway.

Fifty miles from Atlanta, **Lake Lanier** is a popular playground for city folk seeking a quick getaway. At the fringe of the metro region's suburban sprawl, the Army Corps of Engineers reservoir is easily accessible via Hwy. 400 or the I-985 spur. At its shores, Gainesville is also the gateway to the northern mountains. Several wineries and other detours in the region aim to divert weekenders off the highways.

Athens, home of the University of Georgia, is the seat of the state's intellectual and literary community. In recent years the low-key town has earned a national reputation for its hip music scene. Several nightclubs, Georgia Bulldog games, and state museums draw audiences from Atlanta, 60 miles away. Watkinsville, six miles from Athens, offers an arty rural retreat nearby.

At the remote South Carolina border 150 miles east of Atlanta, **Augusta,** colonial Georgia's second city, rests on its historical laurels. The sleepy city comes alive each April for Masters Week, the Olympics of golf.

Southeast of Atlanta, the lively towns of **Middle Georgia** share a common geography and history. Here in the thick hardwood forests laced with rivers and lakes, the destruction of Sherman's March was most devastating; the remaining antebellum architecture, monuments, and ghost towns are markers of regional pride. Highway 441 makes a particularly nice route for leisurely driving or bike touring through the area.

Smack in the center of the state, **Macon** is a friendly city that's a convenient stop for heavy

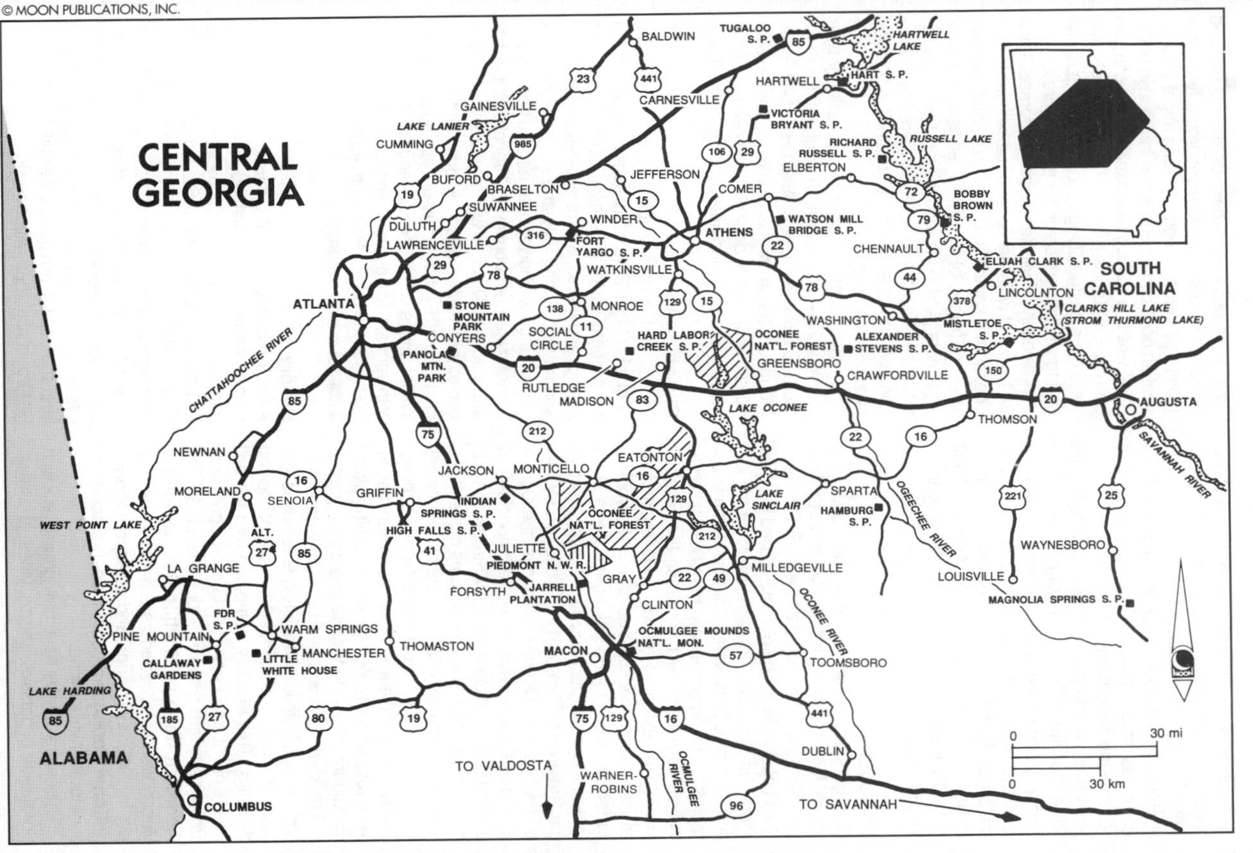

© MOON PUBLICATIONS, INC.
CENTRAL GEORGIA
SOUTH CAROLINA
ALABAMA
BALDWIN
TUGALOO S.P.
HARTWELL LAKE
HARTWELL
HART S.P.
CARNESVILLE
VICTORIA BRYANT S.P.
RICHARD RUSSELL S.P.
RUSSELL LAKE
ELBERTON
GAINESVILLE
LAKE LANIER
CUMMING
BUFORD
BRASELTON
JEFFERSON
COMER
BOBBY BROWN S.P.
SUWANNEE
WINDER
ATHENS
WATSON MILL BRIDGE S.P.
DULUTH
LAWRENCEVILLE
FORT YARGO S.P.
CHENNAULT
ELIJAH CLARK S.P.
WATKINSVILLE
LINCOLNTON
ATLANTA
STONE MOUNTAIN PARK
MONROE
WASHINGTON
MISTLETOE S.P.
CLARKS HILL LAKE (STROM THURMOND LAKE)
CONYERS
SOCIAL CIRCLE
HARD LABOR CREEK S.P.
OCONEE NAT'L FOREST
ALEXANDER STEVENS S.P.
PANOLA MTN. PARK
GREENSBORO
CRAWFORDVILLE
RUTLEDGE
MADISON
CHATTAHOOCHEE RIVER
LAKE OCONEE
AUGUSTA
THOMSON
SAVANNAH RIVER
NEWNAN
EATONTON
JACKSON
MONTICELLO
MORELAND
SENOIA
GRIFFIN
SPARTA
INDIAN SPRINGS S.P.
OCONEE NAT'L FOREST
LAKE SINCLAIR
HAMBURG S.P.
WEST POINT LAKE
HIGH FALLS S.P.
OGEECHEE RIVER
ALT.
WAYNESBORO
JULIETTE
LA GRANGE
PIEDMONT N.W.R.
GRAY
MILLEDGEVILLE
LOUISVILLE
FORSYTH
JARRELL PLANTATION
CLINTON
MAGNOLIA SPRINGS S.P.
FDR S.P.
PINE MOUNTAIN
WARM SPRINGS
OCMULGEE MOUNDS NAT'L. MON.
CALLAWAY GARDENS
LITTLE WHITE HOUSE
MANCHESTER
THOMASTON
MACON
OCONEE RIVER
TOOMSBORO
LAKE HARDING
DUBLIN
TO VALDOSTA
WARNER-ROBINS
OCMULGEE RIVER
COLUMBUS
TO SAVANNAH
0 30 mi
0 30 km

through-traffic on I-75 and I-16. Its renowned musical history makes this a logical site for the new Georgia Music Hall of Fame.

Southwest of Atlanta, a lonesome stretch of I-85 heads off to Alabama. Drop down Hwy. 27 to reach **Pine Mountain,** an old-fashioned resort town that's home to Callaway Gardens and the Pine Mountain Trail, and neighboring Warm Springs, a charming town that evokes its most famous resident, Franklin Delano Roosevelt. At the base of the I-185 spur, **Columbus** is another isolated riverfront outpost like Augusta. (Gulf-bound vacationers pass by on the way to Alabama Hwy. 431.)

The Land

Georgia's urban belt sits on the high plateau of thickly forested rolling hills between North Georgia's Appalachian mountains and South Georgia's coastal plain. The plateau—called the Piedmont—is separated from the plain by the "fall line," the drop in elevation that creates a line of rapids on inland waterways from Georgia on up the eastern seaboard. Because these rapids marked the extent of inland navigation, and because water power could be harnessed from the waterfalls, cities formed along the rivers at the fall line. For example, Augusta was established on the Savannah River in 1735, followed by Milledgeville on the Oconee, Macon on the Ocmulgee, and Columbus on the Chattahoochee; all at the fall line. Interestingly, urban growth has never developed along the lengths of the rivers, leaving surprisingly wild corridors of clay-stained rivers above and below these historical ports. Today, many of the rivers have been dammed for reservoirs or hydroelectric power, adding placid backcountry lakes to the Piedmont topography.

The early towns thrived primarily on cotton and lumber, both land-depleting enterprises that cleared forests and eroded the soil of the red clay hills. This erosion, combined with the boll weevil blight and finally the Great Depression, drove many farmers to abandon their lands. The **Piedmont National Wildlife Refuge** north of Macon was established as a reclamation project in 1939; the refuge and adjacent **Oconee National Forest** represent model restorations of natural environments.

The central forests have now grown back with a profusion of grasses, shrubs, vines, and trees, including pines and hardwoods such as oak and hickory. A walk through a Piedmont forest exhibits this verdant regrowth, and might also reveal an occasional abandoned farmhouse under thick vines, a rusting moonshine still, or an old barbed-wire fence running through forests that were once pasture. Dogwood, redbud trees, and spring wildflowers color the mature forest.

A diversity of wildlife inhabits the forests. Look for tracks of white-tailed deer, rabbits, raccoons, opossums, squirrels, foxes, quail, and wild turkeys, or traces of the more reclusive bobcats and bears. And in the remaining old-growth hardwood patches, listen for endangered red-cockaded woodpeckers with their distinctive "Woody Woodpecker" cries.

Unusual ecosystems thrive on solid granite outcroppings that appear throughout the Piedmont. Smaller versions of Atlanta's famed Stone Mountain, these "monadnocks" support isolated communities of desert plant species able to survive thin soils and harsh rocky conditions.

Climate

Temperatures in early spring may fluctuate from cool rainy 50s (°F) to warm sunny 70s, with more consistently warm days in late spring. Summers are hot and humid, with temperatures in the 90s and beyond during July and August; typical afternoon thundershowers interrupt the heat. Warm summer weather continues through September and into mid-October with dry skies, and then cooler fall weather sets in. Midday temperatures in the 60s (°F) drop to near freezing overnight. Winter brings some freezing temperatures, mostly in January or February, and occasional snowfall higher up on the Piedmont (only rarely does it collect on the ground).

History

After the coast, central Georgia was the next part of the state to be settled by European immigrants. The Georgia colony spread from the first coastal settlement of Savannah upriver to Augusta in 1736. The growing importance of inland agricultural products (cotton, tobacco, and lumber) soon overshadowed coastal production, and consequently, political power moved inland as well. Augusta became capital in 1784; later the capital moved to other fall-line cities—first Louisville, then Milledgeville.

KAP STANN

Central Georgia's lush vegetation envelops a cemetery near Athens.

But Europeans weren't the first to discover the value of this land. Native groups had long recognized the value of establishing communities along the fall line. Ocmulgee (now Macon), for example, was the seat of the Creek Confederacy. Logically, frontier trading posts were built at these sites, and the communities that grew up around them were incorporated into cities once the natives were pushed out to lands farther west.

The Revolutionary War brought fighting to the area and created a rift in the populace. Loyalist sympathies were strong in parts of the region; Augusta in particular was a Tory stronghold. The state was consumed by Revolutionary War fighting, and mass confusion and property confiscation followed once the British occupation ended. Yet even at that, the Revolutionary War toll doesn't hold a candle to what central Georgia endured during the Civil War. On Sherman's March to the Sea in 1864, his 50,000 troops swept through the region burning homes and towns. While this meant long-awaited liberation for slaves, to landowning families it stood out as an unprecedented attack on an unarmed civilian population—largely women and children, as most men had left to fight the war. Ruins from this time are still evident; spared towns or isolated structures provide a glimpse of antebellum architecture.

The advent of hydroelectric power brought renewed development to fall-line cities, and modern water power ran the textile mills that were established at the waterfalls. Old mills and mill towns—company-built rows of identical small cottages—still dot riverbanks.

The expansion of manufacturing industries broadened the economic base of Piedmont cities, as did the U.S. military. The major fall-line cities became home to significant military bases (Fort Gordon outside Augusta, Warner Robins outside Macon, and Fort Benning outside Columbus), vastly accelerating their growth and population.

Today a renewed push to revitalize downtown areas—long abandoned in favor of generic urban sprawl around freeway corridors—has resulted in the restoration of many historic buildings, breathing new life and character into the original commercial districts.

LAKE LANIER

The closest Atlanta has to a coastal resort, Lake Sidney Lanier (named for a Georgia poet from Macon) is casually considered Atlanta's beach. An hour north, the lake draws party crowds of boaters, water-skiers, swimmers and anglers to cabins, camps, and hotels around its shores. On some summer weekends the water gets so wild with speedboats and jet skis that local patrols began a crackdown to reduce the number of accidents attributable to drivers who were underage or "BUI"—boating under the influence of alcohol.

The 38,000-acre lake was created in 1957 when the Army Corps of Engineers (COE) built Buford Dam to impound the Chattahoochee River. To the engineers' surprise, when the new lake filled up, a string of hilltops at its southern end remained above water. Turning miscalculation into opportunity, the islands were turned into resort parklands, today managed by a consortium of federal, state, and private authorities. Close proximity to the 3.5 million population of metro Atlanta makes Lake Lanier the most visited COE reservoir in the United States.

Along 540 miles of shoreline you'll find 20 public swimming beaches, 10 marinas, 54 boat launches, and 10 COE campgrounds. For a map of all public facilities, stop by the **Resource Manager's Office** off Buford Dam Road, tel. (770) 945-9531, between Buford and Cumming, where there's also a boat launch. The impressive 192-foot dam is worth a look itself. A mile or so east of the dam, **Thrill Sports,** tel. (770) 614-1602, rents boats from $40 an hour along with ski equipment; see www.thrillsports.net.

Below the dam, paddlers and floaters navigate the protected shoals of the 'Hooch through the Bowmans Island Unit of the **Chattahoochee River National Recreation Area.** For recorded river conditions call tel. (770) 945-1466; for general park information call (770) 952-4419. Paddlers from the metro region can rent canoes and kayaks for $35 a day from **Go With the Flow** in Roswell; call (770) 992-3200 for reservations and directions.

To get to the dam from I-85, take I-985 exit 1 to Hwy. 20 and continue 6.8 miles to Suwanee Dam Rd. and turn right; after 2.2 miles this dead-ends into Buford Dam Rd.; turn right and you're a mile from the dam. From Hwy. 400 exit 14, take Hwy. 20 6.2 miles to Suwanee Dam Rd.; turn left then proceed as above.

The closest COE campground to the dam is **Shoal Creek,** 6300 Shadburn Ferry Rd., tel. (770) 945-9541, open seasonally from April to September. As with all COE camps, rates are $10-18 and hookups are available.

Lake Lanier Islands

This island resort complex on the southeastern shore, tel. (770) 932-7200 or (800) 840-5253, features sandy beaches, swimming pools and a water park, deluxe golf courses, and lodging in hotels, campgrounds, and houseboats. The facilities are open to overnight guests and daytrippers alike. The **Welcome Center** at the entrance gate distributes maps, full schedules of activities and events, and pamphlets listing current fees. Drivers pay $6 per car to park. It's accessible from I-985 exit 2 north of Buford.

For one admission price, access to the **swimming area** includes the beach, a dozen water slides and rides, pools, and deck cafes. Paddleboats and canoe rentals are also available. Admission is $19.95 for guests over 42 inches in height, $12.95 for children under 42 inches; children under two years are free. Swimming areas are open daily June through Labor Day, and weekends in May; hours are 10 a.m.-6 p.m. weekdays, until 7 p.m. weekends and holidays.

Two deluxe 18-hole golf courses occupy a scenic peninsula near the resort's two hotels. **Emerald Pointe Golf Club,** tel. (770) 945-8787, is part of the Hilton Resort, and **PineIsle Golf Course,** tel. (770) 945-8921, is affiliated with the Renaissance Pine Isle Resort. Greens fees are about the same, from $60 weekdays.

Special events at the resort include the **Beach Music Blast** kicking off the high season on Memorial Day weekend, a concert and fireworks display on July Fourth. On summer Fridays, they host free concerts from beach music to blues.

See also www.lakelanierislands.com.

Resort Accommodations

Two hotels within the Lake Lanier Islands resort offer a choice of luxurious accommodations. Each has its own golf course, tennis courts, pool, hot tub, restaurants, and other upscale amenities. The **Lake Lanier Islands Hilton Resort,** tel. (770) 945-8787 or (800) 768-5253, offers 216 rooms from $159; the **Renaissance PineIsle Resort,** tel. (770) 945-8921 or (800) 535-4028, has 250 rooms from $166. Note that rates may vary by season and are highest on summer weekends and holidays.

Thirty new **cabins,** tel. (770) 831-9400, rent from $200 for a one-bedroom that sleeps four, from $225 for a two-bedroom that sleeps six. **Camping** at 300 sites costs from $15.50 for tents and from $25 for hookups; they charge a premium for lakeside sites and offer weekly discounts. Call (770) 932-7270 for camping reservations. **Houseboat rentals** run about $349 a night in summer for boats that sleep 10; call (770) 932-7255 for houseboat reservations and weekly rates.

Around the Lake

Among the more unusual getaway offerings in the region, **Hidden Valley** off Hwy. 136 north of the lake, tel. (706) 265-6110, offers a family naturist ("nude but not lewd") resort on 110 acres with swimming, tennis, dances, and a restaurant. Day rates run from $20 singles; they also offer motel lodging from $45 as well as camping. It's 1.7 miles east of Hwy. 400 then a rugged mile down Cothran Rd.

In Cumming, **Lanierland Country Music Park** on Jot 'Em Down Rd., tel. (770) 887-7464, hosts such renowned country music performers as Merle Haggard, Loretta Lynn, and the Oak Ridge Boys. Concerts are held from April to November; tickets start at $22 (see Atlanta's entertainment listings for schedule).

Outside **Suwanee,** the NFL Atlanta Falcons practice at their 140-acre camp off I-85 and Suwanee Road; some summer practices are open to the public for avid fans. The Best Western **Falcon Inn** motel here, tel. (770) 945-6751, also houses the broadcasting studio of Ludlow Porch, one of the South's most popular radio personalities.

GAINESVILLE

Poultry Capital of the World, Gainesville sits at the eastern shore of Lake Lanier and was the site of the 1996 Olympic rowing and canoe/kayak competitions. Incorporated in 1821, the town retains an active downtown square on Main St. a block past the courthouse and an attractive residential district of 19th-century Victorian and neoclassical homes most readily seen along a mile-long stretch of Green St. north of downtown.

As a gateway to Georgia's Blue Ridge Mountains, Gainesville's local **Convention and Visitors Bureau,** 830 Green St. NE, tel. (770) 536-5209, distributes mountain region maps and brochures as well as city information. Forest Service headquarters at 1755 Cleveland Hwy. (Hwy. 129), tel. (770) 536-0541, distributes recreation directories to national forest areas (weekdays only).

Sights

The **Georgia Mountains Museum,** 311 Green St, tel. (770) 536-0889, relates city history including exhibits on its Appalachian heritage for $2 admission. Appalachian arts and crafts are on display daily at **Quinlin Art Center,** 514 Green St., tel. (770) 536-2575. The Big Chicken statue in **Poultry Park** a block west of the downtown square celebrates the local industry. Concerts and performances are held at the modern **Georgia Mountains Center** near the courthouse, tel. (770) 534-8420, and the newly restored **Arts Council Depot,** at the head of Spring St., tel. (770) 534-2787, which also has a sculpture garden.

The **Elachee Nature Science Center,** Old Atlanta Hwy., tel. (770) 535-1976, is a woodland museum devoted to local wildlife and ecology within a 1,200-acre nature preserve.

In Rabbitown at Gainesville's northern fringe, folk artist R.A. Miller (famous in primitive art circles for his "Blow, Oscar" tin paintings imploring a neighbor to honk) can often be found working outside his cottage under a mile east of I-985 exit 7; if you see the whirligigs atop the hillside south of the road, then you've just passed the small dirt drive that leads to Miller's cottage.

Accommodations and Food

In a restored 1910 house in the historic district, **Dunlap House,** 635 Green St., tel. (770) 536-0200 or (800) 276-2935, offers sophisticated bed and breakfast lodging with all the modern conveniences to make either business or leisure travelers comfortable. Ten guest rooms furnished with period reproductions and private baths start at $85 and include a full breakfast served in the lobby. It's on a shady stretch of the main Hwy. 129 drag near galleries and across from the city's premier restaurant.

Rudolph's, 700 Green St., tel. (770) 534-2226, in the English Tudor mansion across from Dunlap House, serves prime rib and fresh Georgia trout among other continental menu selections in an upscale setting.

On the Main St. square, **Penny University,** tel. (770) 287-3664, opens early for muffins and gourmet coffee, and stays open late to host such local bands as the Tone Deaf Pig Dogs in their back room on weekend nights (closed Sunday). There are a few officeworker lunch places on the square, but the franchise **Schlotsky's Deli** on Jesse Jewel Parkway (Hwy. 129) two blocks east near the courthouse has longer hours and is always a good bet.

Getting There

Gainesville offers the closest Amtrak station to North Georgia's mountains, as such it's the first stop for many Appalachian Trail hikers; call (800) USA RAIL (800-872-7245) for fares and schedules. The station is at the foot of Main St. a mile south of the downtown square in a so-so warehouse district a couple of businesses (including a new cafe) are struggling to gentrify. **Appalachian Outfitters** of Dahlonega, tel. (706) 864-7117, can help arrange shuttles to trailheads by advance reservation.

The Greyhound bus depot and Western Union desk is off Hwy. 129 on Myrtle St. around a half-mile from the train station. Call tel. (800) 231-2222 for fares and schedules.

Drivers may exit off I-985 at Hwy. 129, along which several sights and main services are found. Local signs identify Hwy. 129 as E.E. Butler Parkway until just past downtown, when the name changes to Green St. for a ways before it becomes the Cleveland Hwy. The I-985 spur ends a couple miles north of town, but Hwy. 23 picks up the seamless route north to Tallulah Falls.

OFF I-85 EAST

Braselton

What resembles an 18th-century French chateau above the interstate in Braselton is the **Chateau Elan** winery and resort, I-85 exit 48, tel. (800) 233-9463. Guests sample local wines and wander through grand interior plazas adorned with murals of French landscapes past shops, restaurants, cafes, even an Irish pub with live Irish music. Five stories of deluxe hotel accommodations start around $169 single or double in winter, $215 peak season. Four golf courses, an equestrian center, a health spa, pools, and tennis courts are among the amenities on the 2,400-acre grounds (open daily).

Chestnut Mountain Winery, I-85 exit 48, tel. (770) 867-6914, offers free tastings and a wine-cellar tour on its 30 acres of wooded grounds (closed Monday).

For the juvenile version of the winery tours, take the kids through the **Mayfield Dairy,** I-85 exit 48, tel. (706) 654-9180, where a friendly heifer leads tours of the milk-processing plant. Free tours are offered Mon.-Sat. 9 a.m.-4 p.m.; there are no tours on Sunday, but the ice cream parlor is open.

Victoria Bryant State Park and Vicinity

Two miles north of Franklin Springs on Hwy. 327, this 406-acre park tel. (706) 245-6270, offers a nine-hole golf course, a swimming pool, a fully stocked fishpond, and five miles of hiking trails. A 25-site campground charges $14 a night tent or RV; call (800) 864-PARK (800-864-7275) for reservations. The park hosts a bluegrass festival on July Fourth weekend. The parking fee is $2 per car, free Wednesdays.

In Royston east of the park, the **Ty Cobb Museum,** 461 Cook St., housed in the medical center endowed by Cobb, honors the baseball great nicknamed "the Georgia Peach." In Carnesville west of the park, the 132-foot **Cromer's Mill Covered Bridge** dates from 1906. It's off Hwy. 106 six miles west via Hwy. 51.

Tugaloo State Park

Five miles north of I-85 on a rugged peninsula jutting out into 56,000-acre Hartwell Lake, this 393-acre park, tel. (706) 356-4362, offers fishing, boating, a swimming beach, hiking, tennis, miniature golf, and lakeside cottages and campsites; also inquire about mountain-music programs.

Twenty fully equipped two-bedroom cottages rent for $55-75 a night; 120 tent and trailer sites cost $14 a night, including hookups; call (800) 864-PARK (800-864-7275) for reservations. The parking fee is $2 per car, Wednesday free. Take I-85 exit 58 to Hwy. 17 and follow park signs to the right.

Hart State Park
Two miles east of Hartwell via Hwy. 29 (take I-85 exit 59), this 147-acre state park, tel. (706) 376-8756, also sits alongside Hartwell Lake. A swimming beach and boat ramp are the primary draws. Admission to the lifeguard-staffed swimming area costs $2-3 per day. Anglers cast for largemouth bass, black crappie, bream, rainbow trout, and walleyed pike. Inquire about Memorial Day and Labor Day festivals.

Two-bedroom cottages rent for $55-75; a 65-site campground charges from $12 per site a night, including hookups; call (800) 864-PARK (800-864-7275) for reservations. The parking fee is $2 per car, free on Wednesday.

ATHENS AND VICINITY

The University of Georgia (UGA), home of the Georgia Bulldogs and Georgia's intelligentsia, dominates the stately town of Athens and nearly doubles the town's residential population with a student enrollment of 30,000. As the home of the University of Georgia Press and the well-respected *Georgia Review,* Athens is also the seat of the state's literary community.

But music lovers across the country know Athens best for its reputation as an incubator for cutting-edge bands, starting with R.E.M. and the B-52s in the 1980s and more recently the Black Crowes and Widespread Panic. This alternative scene is the one that dominates the club life and cafe society downtown.

The center of the action is the compact, walkable downtown across from the UGA campus. Within 12 square blocks or so of early 20th-century buildings from the intersection of Broad St. and College Ave. you'll find bookstores, restaurants, cafes, bars and clubs, a cinema, theater, and stores selling vintage clothes, beads, crystals, and locally made art glass, mosaics and textiles.

For hanging out, wandering through gardens or museums, for a ball game, and particularly for entertainment, the lively college town makes a great destination within easy access of metro Atlanta.

SIGHTS

University of Georgia
The University of Georgia, America's oldest chartered state university, was founded near an old Cherokee trail crossing and frontier settlement at the banks of the Oconee River in 1785. Today the esteemed University has grown to 13 colleges and professional schools with a total enrollment of around 30,000, and serves as headquarters for the statewide university system.

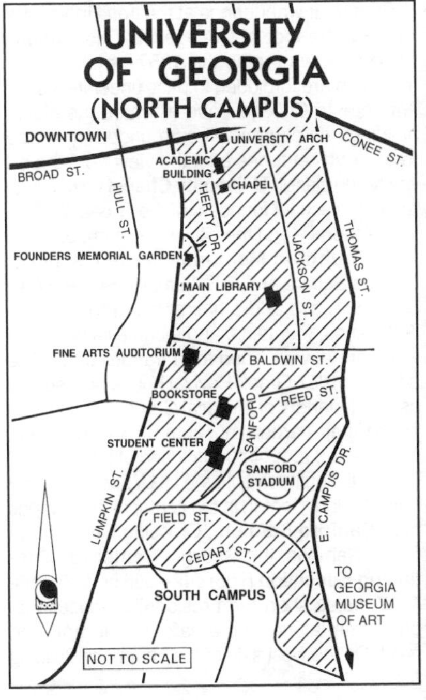

The University of Georgia embodies the Golden Age of Athens, Greece, in its many classical structures constructed before 1850.

KAP STANN

The UGA campus, tel. (706) 542-3000, occupies 40,000 acres in the heart of downtown Athens. The following highlights begin with North Campus, the historic head of campus adjacent to downtown, and proceed southward across Cedar St. to the newer adjacent South Campus.

Start your wanderings at the iron **University Arch** at the foot of College St. This campus trademark was raised in 1857—by tradition, freshmen are forbidden to pass under it—as the entrance to College Square, where the oldest buildings on campus sit surrounded by shade trees. Two centuries ago, the view from the hill where the classic **University Chapel** now stands reminded school founders of the Greek Acropolis in Athens—and the city was renamed.

At **Founders Memorial Garden,** south of College Square at 325 S. Lumpkin St., tel. (706) 542-3631, two-and-a-half acres of formal garden rooms, fountains, and a camellia walk and arbor are always open for a tranquil stroll. The adjacent 1857 Greek Revival house now serves as headquarters of the local Garden Club, which opens their garden museum for $1 admission weekdays 9 a.m.-4 p.m. (closed at lunch).

A walk south leads to the UGA bookstore and Tate Student Center, in the center of the campus near **Sanford Stadium.** Crossing Cedar St. to South Campus, the **Georgia Center for Continuing Education** (706) 542-2056 or (800) 488-7827, holds short-term residential educational programs, along with a cafe, restaurant, and hotel. On the west side of the Pharmacy Building is the test garden of the Department of Agriculture; to the east of the Pharmacy Building is the modernist Warnell Memorial Garden adjacent to the Forestry Building (an office of the U.S. Forest Service is in a nearby building).

Stegeman Coliseum holds basketball games and gymnastics events. The **Butts-Mehre Heritage Hall Sports Museum** on Pinecrest Drive houses UGA athletic memorabilia, including Herschel Walker's Heisman trophy. The **Tennis Hall of Fame** adjacent to the tennis stadium is usually open during tournaments.

On a hilltop to the east, the **Georgia Museum of Art** and **UGA Performing Arts Center** are the university's most impressive new additions, along with the $40 million **Ramsey Center for Student Activities** sports complex nearby. The visitor center on College Station Rd. at River Rd., tel. (706) 542-0842 conducts campus tours (open daily except on University holidays). See separate listings for the museum, theater, stadium, coliseum, and lodging on campus; also see www.uga.edu.

Georgia Museum of Art

In the modern home of the Georgia Museum of Art on UGA's South Campus at 90 Carlton St., tel. (706) 542-4602, elegant intimate galleries display the state's collection of 7,000 paintings, drawings, and sculptures of 19th- and 20th-century American artists and others. Recent shows have included photography and textile exhibits, interpreted with artist lectures and family activities. A Wednesday night film series screens art films and highlights of national film and video festivals (admission $3). The gift shop carries locally made arts, and the cafe has a nice view of the museum's hilltop perch. Gallery hours are Tues.-Sat. 10 a.m.-5 p.m. and Sunday 1-5 p.m. (closed Monday and most state and federal holidays). It's well worth a visit—and admission is free.

State Botanical Garden
This peaceful 313-acre enclave at 2450 S. Milledge Ave., tel. (706) 542-1244, alongside the Middle Oconee River, is full of sculpted gardens inside and out. An impressive three-story-high tropical **Conservatory** overlooking the International Garden serves as the visitor center, and also holds galleries, a gift shop, and cafe. Outside, five miles of **nature trails** lead through

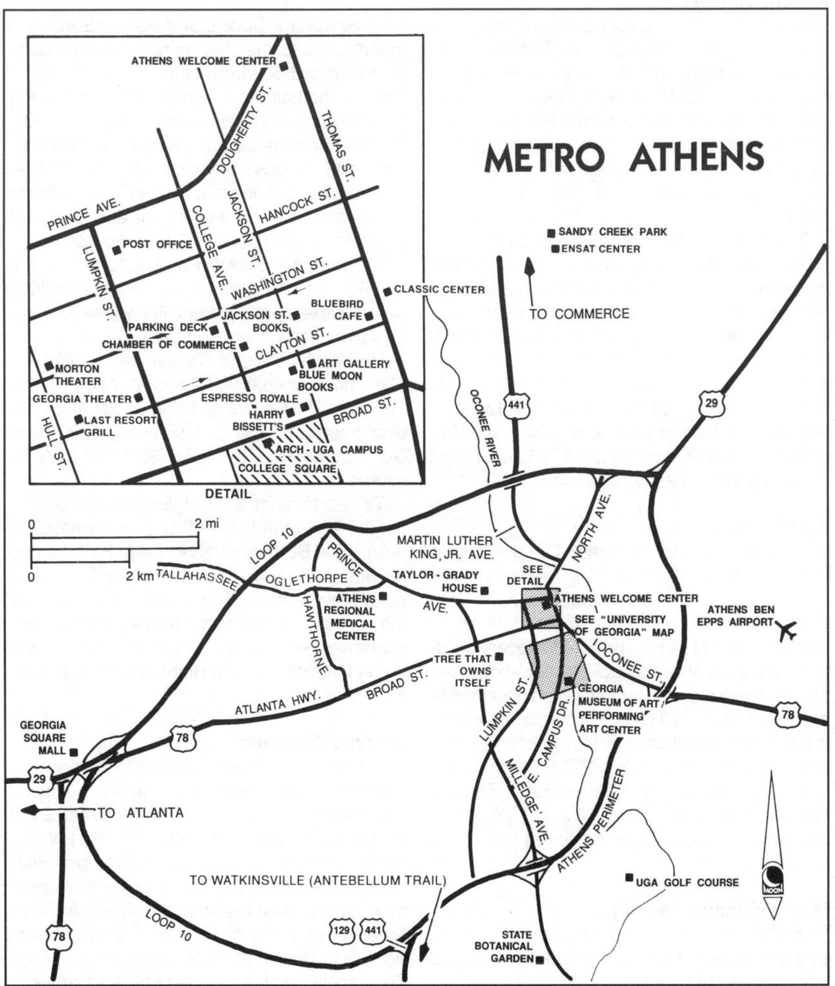

rhododendron dells, rose gardens, and shady woodland coves populated by deer, raccoons, squirrels, and many different bird species. The Conservatory is open Mon.-Sat. 9 a.m.-4:30 p.m. and Sunday 11:30 a.m.-4:30 p.m.; the Garden Room Cafe here serves lunch daily. The grounds are open daily 8 a.m.-sunset. A beautiful spot—and all admission is free.

Historic Houses

Athens has many beautiful old homes, several of which are open to the public as historic house museums, including the Welcome Center housed in the 1820 Brumby House. Inquire here about the 1825 Wray-Nicholson House and the 1903 Arnocroft House currently under restoration as house museums, about self-guided tour maps, and about seasonal house-and-garden tours.

Taylor-Grady House at 634 Prince Ave., tel. (706) 549-8688, the mid-1840s Greek Revival mansion home of *Atlanta Constitution* editor and "New South" spokesperson Henry Grady, occupies an entire city block and is furnished with period antiques. It's open Mon.-Fri. 10 a.m.-5 p.m. (closed for lunch); admission is $3 adults.

The city's newest restoration, the **Lyndon House Arts Center** at 293 Hoyt St., tel. (706) 613-3623, opens the original 1856 house and modern annex as a municipal arts center.

ENSAT Center

The **ENSAT Center** at Sandy Creek Park on Hwy. 441, tel. (706) 613-3615, opened in 1998 as a revolutionary facility dedicated to Environment, Natural Science, and Appropriate Technology (thus "ENSAT"). The 11,400-square building is a model of sustainable "green" construction, built with recycled materials and designed to maximize energy efficiency. Ecological exhibits inside highlight wetlands, woodlands, and urban environments, and include a 2,000-gallon aquarium and crawl-through beaver lodge. The exhibits are open Tues.-Sat. 8:30 a.m.-5:30 p.m. A boardwalk trail outside is designed to be fully accessible.

More Ecological Wonders

One of the city's most unusual landmarks is the **tree that owns itself.** The white oak sits in a small square at Dearing and Finley Streets—it was deeded its small plot of land by its owner, a former UGA professor who enjoyed its shade for many years. The original tree was destroyed in a 1942 storm but was sentimentally replaced by a seedling from one of its own acorns, which has now grown into a quite respectable tree.

SPORTS AND RECREATION

UGA Spectator Sports and Recreation

In the center of the University of Georgia campus, **Sanford Stadium** is the home of UGA's Bulldog football team (whose English bulldog mascot's image can be seen on T-shirts, caps, and license plates around the state). The fifth-largest on-campus college stadium fills with over 86,000 fans cheering "Go Dawgs!" during home games each fall. The stadium was also the site of Olympic soccer in the 1996 Summer Games.

Stegeman Coliseum on Carlton St. is the 11,000-seat arena where the Georgia Bulldog basketball team and the nationally ranked women's gymnastics team compete.

University Tennis Center, tel. (706) 542-4584, hosts annual NCAA tennis championship matches, and visitors can sign up to use the indoor courts. The 18-hole **University of Georgia Golf Course,** tel. (706) 369-5739, offers a par-72 course.

Tickets to most UGA athletic events can be purchased at the ticket office (open weekdays only) in the **Butts-Mehre Heritage Hall** (named for famed Georgia coaches Wally Butts and Harry Mehre—if only they'd switched the order of the names it wouldn't sound like the campus joke it has regrettably become) on South Campus at Pinecrest Dr. and Rutherford St., tel. (706) 542-9036.

Outdoor Recreation

For swimming at a lakeside beach, fishing, canoeing (rentals available), hiking and camping, head north up Hwy. 441 to **Sandy Creek Park and Nature Center,** tel. (706) 613-3631. While the beach is open only from April through September, the rest of the well-maintained, scenic park remains open year-round. The Sandy Creek Nature Center is open Tues.-Sun. 7 a.m.-9 p.m., April-Oct., closing at 6 p.m. the rest of the year. The park is also home to the ENSAT Center.

Broad River Outpost, tel. (706) 795-3243, runs paddling adventures down the Broad River north of Athens; see www.broadriver.com.

ENTERTAINMENT

Athens has a tremendously varied arts and entertainment scene for a city its size, thanks to UGA, the rarefied population, and Athens' proximity to metro Atlanta—a dynamic combination which lends the city exceptional performers and supportive audeinces. Find entertainment listings in Atlanta papers. Visitors may note that many local schedules coincide with the traditional academic calendar, and the town is quiet during school breaks and over the summer.

UGA's Performing Arts Center

This impressive modern venue in South Campus on River Rd., tel. (706) 542-4400, showcases world-class performances primarily in music and dance. Recent seasons have featured the Stuttgart Philharmonic Orchestra, the San Francisco Western Opera Theater performance of *Carmen,* Jean-Pierre Rampal, the Atlanta Ballet and the Atlanta Symphony (followers say the acoustics here are better even than the Symphony's home in Atlanta). See www.uga.edu/pac.

Classic Center

The new Classic Center downtown, behind the Athena statue at 300 N. Thomas St., box office tel. (706) 357-4444, a modern complex built around and to match the restored 1912 brick fire house that now holds the Athens Convention and Visitors Bureau, has featured an impressive slate of performances since its opening in 1995. Broadway shows, Holiday on Ice, Celtic dance, Marvin Hamlisch, and children's theater were featured in a recent season from October to April.

Morton Theater

The 1993 restoration of the 1910 Morton Theater, 195 W. Washington St., tel. (706) 613-3770, revives a historic African-American vaudeville theater as a 544-seat community performing arts venue (featured in an R.E.M. music video).

Georgia Theater

A sometimes-cinema, sometimes-concert hall, the always-groovy Georgia Theater on the corner of Lumpkin and Clayton Streets downtown, tel. (706) 549-9918, is a casual and cheap place to watch Michael Moore documentaries or hear local bands (it also has a kitchen and full bar).

Nightclubs

The musical acts that rocketed Athens to underground fame—Pylon, Love Tractor, or the better known B-52s and R.E.M.—created overnight acclaim for the Athens sound one critic describes as "chime-filled janglerock, earthy hippie music, and/or quirky, campy retro dancerock." WUOG 90.5 FM broadcasts who's playing where. The free weekly *Flagpole* tabloid distributed across town contains entertainment listings and distributes its own guide to Athens music from its office at 112 S. Foundry St. downtown. Atlanta's *Creative Loafing* also lists Athens events.

The **40 Watt Club,** 285 W. Washington St., tel. (706) (706) 549-7871, is the granddaddy of the alternative music nightclubs that fade in and out on the Athens scene, and attracts national acts and an underground audience just as wide; see www.40Watt.com.

The **High Hat,** 321 E. Clayton St., tel. (706) 549-5508, is an intimate blues dive/supper club-by venue that hosts live music and a songwriters' showcase Tuesday nights.

Boneshakers, 433 E. Hancock Ave., tel. (706) 543-1555, is pretty much the only dance club in town. It started out as a gay club, but now draws a mixed audience for DJed music and occasional cabaret drag shows. The **Uptown Lounge** on Washington St. west of College St. has a swing night on Mondays.

Local groups rumored to be among the favorites of R.E.M.'s Michael ("we like being backwater") Snipes are the Elephant 6 Collective, Jucifer, Vic Chestnutt, Jack Logan, the Star Room Boys, and Man or Astroman?

ACCOMMODATIONS AND FOOD

Accommodations and Camping

The decent **Bulldog Inn,** Hwy. 441 north, tel. (706) 543-3611, a mile north of downtown, has the lowest rates (from $35) and ample truck parking.

The **TraveLodge,** 898 W. Broad St., tel. (706) 549-5400 or (800) 578-7878, runs $40 s/$48 d and it's right downtown a half mile from campus. The **Econo Lodge,** 2715 Atlanta Hwy., tel. (706) 549-1530 or (800) 553-2666 runs $38 for one bed and $42 for two beds, but it's an older property three miles west of downtown in a drab area. The **Downtowner Motor Inn,** 1198 S. Milledge Ave. (Hwy. 15), tel. (706) 549-2626, offers comparably priced accommodations in the fledgling Five Points neighborhood near South Campus, with a couple of cafes nearby.

UGA's **Georgia Center for Continuing Education** on campus at 1197 S. Lumpkin St., tel. (706) 542-2056 or (800) 488-7827, is a residential conference center with a cafe, restaurant, and 200 rooms from $52 for people visiting the campus.

Best Western Colonial Inn, 170 N. Milledge Ave., tel. (706) 546-7959 or (800) 528-1234, charges $59 for a single or double; it's in town a half mile from campus. More mid-range motel chains can be found along the Atlanta Hwy. west of downtown. Among these are the lavish new **Hampton Inn,** tel. (706) 548-9600 or (800) 426-7866, two miles west near the State Farmer's Market (rates from $60); and farther out, **Comfort Inn,** tel. (706) 227-9700 or (800) 228-5150, with rates around $72 weekends, and **Perimeter Inn,** tel. (706) 548-3000, with rates from $48, both five miles west near Georgia Square Mall.

Holiday Inn, 197 E. Broad St., tel. 706) 549-4433 or (800) 465-4329, is the premier property in town and closest to campus; rates run from $84. They also have an indoor pool and complimentary airport transportation from Atlanta.

Magnolia Terrace, 277 Hill St., tel. (706) 548-3860, offers bed and breakfast accommodations in a 1912 house in a historic residential district in town a short walk from The Grit restaurant.

Except for UGA's Georgia Center and Magnolia Terrace, all the hotels listed above have pools. Expect prices to rise—as much as double—on fall football weekends.

Year-round primitive camping is available at secluded wooded sites in Athens' **Sandy Creek Park,** tel. (706) 613-3631, with access to the park's lake and varied amenities. More campgrounds are available at Fort Yargo State Park (cottage rentals too) and at Watson Mill Bridge State Park (both within 20 miles of Athens).

Food and Drink

You'll find a wide selection of cheap eats downtown at sidewalk cafes, food stalls, smoothie stands, and mobile espresso bars across from College Square—everything from veggie pizza to burritos, gyros to grits.

Start with coffee and pastry at the faux marble **Expresso Royale** at 297 E. Broad St. and wind up with Pop-Tarts at a 1960s dinette table at **Jittery Joe's,** 243 W. Washington St.—both excellent places to linger, read, or converse. **Hard Drive Cafe,** 175 N. Lumpkin, tel. (706) 227-0477, offers Internet access; it's open daily.

For inexpensive American diner fare, **The Grill,** 171 College Ave., tel. (706) 543-4770, serves neon-lit burgers, squiggly fries, and milkshakes around-the-clock. Breakfasts range from traditional ham-and-cheese omelets to granola or lox and bagels. Besides classic burgers, it serves veggie burgers under $5. **Varsity Drive-In** on the Atlanta Hwy. a half-mile west of campus, serves reliably smothered hot dogs and fries.

Wilson's Soul Food Inc., 350 N. Hull St., tel. (706) 353-7288, serves no-frills, downhome plates of chittlins and greens (breakfast and lunch served Mon.-Sat.). **Weaver D's Fine Foods,** 247 E. Washington St., tel. (706) 353-7797, also serves soul food and is a musical landmark: its automated cafeteria service motto "Automatic for the People" inspired R.E.M.'s 1992 album title (lunch served Mon.-Sat.).

For healthy alternatives to standard Southern cuisine, the casual **Bluebird Cafe,** 493 E. Clayton St., tel. (706) 549-3663 serves such hearty breakfasts as Bulldog tofu scramble 8 a.m.-3 p.m. daily. On weekdays, they also serve lunch specials 11 a.m.-3 p.m. (shrimp stir-fry for $7.50 was one recent chalkboard favorite) and they serve dinner Friday and Saturday nights only 5-10 p.m.

Marrakech Express, on Washington St. near the 40 Watt, tel. (706) 548-9175, has good falafels and other inexpensive Mediterranean specialties. **Khun Al,** 149 N. Lumpkin St., tel. (706) 548-9222 is a decent Thai restaurant downtown with vegetarian specials (though some locals prefer **Thai of Athens** out the Atlanta Hwy. west of town).

The **Last Resort Grill,** 174 W. Clayton St., tel. (706) 549-0810, takes its name from a legendary local nightclub and offers inventive California cuisine in an arty, airy storefront that opens onto the street. Exotic quesadillas from $5.50 (veggie, shrimp, or salmon-and-black-bean), roasted eggplant or fried green tomato sandwiches ($4) and pasta topped with grilled shiitake mushrooms, herbs, and feta ($6 lunch, $9 dinner) are some of the house specialties. They have a full bar and espresso drinks too. It's open daily: lunch is served 11 a.m.-3 p.m. (on Sunday it's brunch); dinner is served from 5 p.m.

Athens Sushi Bar Utage, 440 E. Clayton St., tel. (706) 227-9339, offers a crisp setting for good sushi by-the-piece (including such local favorites as "oyster po' boy roll" and spicy Bulldog roll) from $6 an order; they also have $6.50 rice bowls at lunch. Lunch is served Tues.-Fri. 11:30 am-2 p.m.; dinner is served daily from 5 p.m.

Harry Bissett's, 279 E. Broad St., tel. (706) 353-7065, remains about the fanciest spot downtown, offering Cajun specialties New Orleans style—or just pay by the shell at the oyster bar.

A half-mile from downtown, **The Grit,** on Prince Ave. near the fire station at Barber St., is a casual vegetarian restaurant started up by R.E.M. musician Michael Stipes (his residence is behind the big gates a few blocks away on Grady Ave.).

Three miles west of downtown, **Caliente** is a family-run Mexican restaurant that serves excellent tamales, Cuban sandwiches, and mango shakes out of a little trailer just north off the Hwy. 10 bypass Tallahassee Rd. exit.

A few miles south of town, **Charlie William's Pinecrest Lodge** off Whitehall Rd., tel. (706) 354-7900 serves mammoth dinner buffets of fried catfish, boiled shrimp, barbecue ribs, vegetables, and all the fixin's for $14 adults, children 7-12 half-price, six and under eat free. It serves these feasts only on Friday and Saturday 5-10 p.m. and Sunday noon-9 p.m. Find it near the UGA golf course about a mile southwest of College Station Rd.

Bars

The three coordinates of Athens' "Bar-muda Triangle" are the **Globe,** at 199 N. Lumpkin St., a comfortable two-story English pub-like place that hosts occasional readings in the smoke-free upstairs, along with the more rugged **Georgia Bar** at 159 W. Clayton St., and the **Roadhouse** at 149 N. Lumpkin Street.

For the best jukebox in town, look for the **No Where Bar,** 240 N. Lumpkin St., where the volume is kept low enough that you can actually carry on a conversation. **Hole In The Wall,** 263 W. Washington by the 40 Watt, is smokefree except Monday.

A brewpub atmosphere is found at **Athens Brewing Company** 312 E. Washington St.; they also serve food. Also wholesome is **The Winery,** 495 E. Clayton, for $2 house wines and live jazz.

Special Events

Among the more unusual special events in Athens are **Athfest,** a summer music festival that brought crowds of 20,000 to hear 150 bands performing in 25 venues in 1998, and the four-day **Kudzu Film Festival** in mid-October. For a full calendar of special events, contact the visitor center, tel. (800) 653-0603.

OTHER PRACTICALITIES

Getting There

Athens is 60 miles northeast of Atlanta; from Atlanta take I-85 north to Hwy. 316 east; exit onto Hwy. 78 east. Hwy. 78 west of Athens is called "the Atlanta Highway" west of Athens, once you're in town it's Broad St.

From Athens south to Macon, a scenic hundred-mile stretch of Hwy. 441 is known as the "Antebellum Trail." The route passes many natural, historical, and recreational high points, including several in Watkinsville, eight miles south of Athens, and in Madison, 30 miles south. Leisurely Atlanta drivers may want to loop to or from Athens via I-20 through Madison.

Getting Around

Downtown streets are identified as either East or West of College Ave. The most convenient parking lot downtown near the University is at the corner of College Avenue and Washington St. On-campus visitor parking is available at the Visitors Center on College Station Rd. at River Rd. and in three other areas: behind the UGA bookstore, next to the Tate Student Center, and in the parking deck next to the Georgia Center for Continuing Education.

Shopping

Among practical shops and fun boutiques downtown are **Wolf's Camera** on College Ave.; **Junkman's Daughter,** 458 E. Clayton, for vintage clothes; and **Musician's Warehouse,** 447 E. Clayton St., tel. (706) 548-7233, for Athens music.

The **Georgia Square Mall** on the Atlanta Hwy. just outside the Perimeter Hwy. sells all the necessities. Here you'll also find a **Morrison's Cafeteria.**

For a cultural adventure and all the trailer trash you can carry, the **J & J Flea Market** is held weekends four miles north of town on Jefferson Hwy.

Information and Services

The **Welcome Center** at 280 E. Dougherty St., tel. (706) 546-1805, is a good place to pick up city and campus maps. The Center occupies one of the city's oldest houses, and they're happy to show you around. It's open daily; Mon.-Sat. 9 a.m.-5 p.m., Sunday 2-5 p.m. Also inquire here about daily guided city tours for $10 per adult.

For more city information, contact the **Athens Convention and Visitors Bureau,** 300 N. Thomas St., Athens, GA 30601, tel. (706) 357-4430 or (800) 653-0603, www.visitathensga.com.

For UGA campus information, call the Information Line at (706) 542-0842 or see www.uga.com. For short-term educational programs, contact UGA's **Georgia Center for Continuing Education,** tel. (706) 542-2056 or (800) 488-7827.

A 24-hour **Kinko's,** 2235 W. Broad St., tel. (706) 353-8755, 2.3 miles east of downtown on the Atlanta Hwy., offers round-the-clock Internet access. A 24-hour supermarket is next door.

For police (nonemergencies), call (706) 613-3345. In an emergency, dial 911. For medical attention, call the **Athens Regional Medical Center,** 1199 Prince Ave., tel. (706) 549-9977.

VICINITY OF ATHENS

Fort Yargo State Park

Fort Yargo State Park is west of Athens in Winder off Hwy. 81, tel. (706) 867-3489. The park features one of four blockhouses built by settlers in 1792 to protect themselves against local Creek and Cherokees. Besides the well-preserved historical relic, the highlight of the 1,850-acre park is its 260-acre lake, where folks swim at a sandy beach, fish, and go boating—the park rents canoes, pedalboats, and skiffs. Four tennis courts, miniature golf, and hiking trails are among its other facilities.

Three fully equipped two-bedroom cottages rent for about $50-65 a night ($40 handicapped). A 47-site campground charges $12-14 per night; call (800) 864-PARK (800-864-7275) for camping or cottage reservations. The parking fee is $2 per car, free on Wednesdays.

The park's **Will-A-Way Recreation Area,** designed for visitors with disabilities, was the first of its kind in any state park nationwide when it opened in 1971. All facilities are barrier-free, including a fishing bridge. A half-mile paved trail leads around the marshy lake edge, crosses a flat bridge, and loops around a gazebo set in a tranquil hardwood cove.

Watson Mill Bridge State Park

East of Athens and three miles south of Comer off Hwy. 22, this is one of Georgia's most picturesque parks, named for the longest original-site covered bridge in the state. The 144-acre park, tel. (706) 783-5349, also offers a five-acre mill pond for boating and fishing. Camp in one of 21 campsites for $12-14; call (800) 864-PARK (800-864-7275) for reservations. There's a $2 parking fee per car, free on Wednesdays. From Athens, take Hwy. 72 northeast to Hwy. 22 and go south three miles.

Watkinsville

Eight miles south of Athens, Watkinsville—with its arty community, sophisticated bed and breakfast, and quality shops—is a nice small town that's a tranquil refuge for city dwellers who like their country *very* civilized.

The historic **Eagle Tavern** on Main St., tel. (706) 769-5197, has been restored from an 1801 stagecoach stop to a local welcome center and crafts shop. They distribute studio guides, downtown walking tour maps, road maps, and information on sights along Hwy. 441's "Antebellum Trail." It's open Mon.-Sat. 10 a.m.-5 p.m. and Sunday 2-5 p.m.

Five miles south of town, the **Elder Mill Covered Bridge** across Rose Creek has remained a picturesque sight for two centuries, and now a little garden at the entrance adds to its appeal. Find it off Hwy. 15 South; turn right onto Elder Mill Rd.

Get away overnight downtown at **Ashford Manor Bed-and-Breakfast Inn,** 5 Harden Hill Rd., tel. (706) 769-2633. Proprietors Jim and David Shearon and Mario Castro are Chicago transplants who bring big-city style and service to their rural four-acre retreat. ("We knew we were here to stay when we decided to trade in our classic Thunderbird for a King Cab pickup," says Dave.) They offer seven "costumed" rooms (including one dog-friendly nook) in a lovely two-story Victorian for $95 d with private bath and full hot breakfast; cocktails are served poolside on the landscaped terrace overlooking the woods beyond. Find them behind the stone wall on Main St. next to the Methodist Church.

The bargain option is **Hawks Nest Hostel,** five miles east of town at 1760 McRee Mill Rd., tel. (706) 769-0563. A local family offers a tiny loft cabin beside their house in the woods for $10 a night. The cozy bed-wide cabin has running water and a tub but for full plumbing guests need to use the bathroom in the family's house.

Eat downtown at **Gautreau's Cajun Cafe,** 24 Greensboro Hwy., tel. (706) 769-9330, where a Louisiana couple re-creates such bayou specialties as crawfish étouffee, fried oysters, and barbecue shrimp here on the Georgia prairie. They're open Tues.-Fri. 11 a.m.-2:30 p.m. and again 6-10 p.m., also Saturday 1-10 p.m. (closed Sunday). Lunch entrees start at $6, dinners from $9; BYOB.

For morning treats and afternoon sweets, **Main St. Coffee Cake,** 21 N. Main St., tel. (706) 769-1003 makes an easy stop. They also serve soups and sandwiches; hours are Mon.-Sat. 7:30 a.m.-4 p.m. (closed Sunday).

Wander along the antique shops and art galleries for finds from estate jewelry and ironwork bedposts to art glass and funky folk sculptures. To see local artists at work, the **Oconee Cultural Arts Foundation** on School St., tel. (706) 769-4565, can guide you to individual studios, or pick up an artist directory at the Eagle Tavern (also inquire about arts festivals in May and October).

A consortium of artists operate out of **Happy Valley Pottery** on Carson Graves Rd., tel. (706) 769-5922, nine miles south of Watkinsville via Colham Ferry Rd. Here potters, glass blowers, and sculptors ply their crafts; their 24-hour open-door shop operates on the honor system.

Piccadilly Farms on Whippoorwill Rd., tel. (706) 769-6516, showcases their specialty nursery display garden of perennials and woodsy plants (also watch for local farms selling u-pick-'em strawberries, blueberries, and pumpkins in season).

Out in the country out Hwy. 15 South towards Greensboro, you can see a massive 2,000-lb. iron horse that was put out to pasture here after the sculpture was rejected by the University of Georgia.

Greensboro and Vicinity

From Watkinsville, Hwy. 15 bisects a parcel of the Piedmont's **Oconee National Forest** and runs through Greensboro on its way to I-20. Twelve miles north of Greensboro, off Hwy. 15 at the Oconee River, the Forest Service-maintained **Oconee River Recreation Area** provides river access and a six-site campground ($5 a night).

The ghost-town ruins of **Skull Shoals,** a 1784 trading post and frontier settlement, lie an easy one-mile trail upstream from the boat launch near the campground. In 1811, Georgia's first paper mill operated here, and the town's industry grew to include a gristmill, cotton gin, and sawmill. At its peak in 1850, the town had 500 residents. Erosion from unsound farming practices, a severe flood in 1887, and the decline of farming eventually caused the town's demise. The largely abandoned area was incorporated into the national forest in 1959. Today, the charred ruins of a brick boardinghouse still stand. From here, hikers can cross over unpaved roads a half-mile to the trailhead that leads to a set of aboriginal mounds—take the road a quarter-mile to the first junction; turn left and continue a quarter-mile.

In Greensboro, the **Gaol** is a Bastille-like jail built in 1807; open by appointment, tel. (706) 453-7592. The **Towne House Restaurant** at the corner of Main St. and Broad St. (Hwy. 15), serves a down-home plate lunch for $4; try the sweet potato fries and homemade pies. The **Chile Pepper** a few doors down E. Broad St. offers pepper poppers and sangria on its tropical patio. A supermarket and pharmacy provide most necessities.

Crawfordville

Downtown Crawfordville paints a poignant portrait of a Southern gothic landscape—dusty storefronts appear largely abandoned, a lone pickup is parked at the curb, and you could practically imagine a hound dog sleeping in the middle of the street.

Alexander H. Stephens State Historic Park downtown, tel. (706) 456-2602, memorializes the vice president of the Confederacy, who, after the Civil War, returned to Washington, D.C. as a U.S. senator. Stephens' residence, the two-story Liberty Hall, was built in 1875. Guided gaslight house tours are held year-round. The adjacent museum houses a large collection of Confederate artifacts. Admission is $2 adults. Tours are offered Tues.-Sat. 9 a.m.-5 p.m. and Sunday 2-5 p.m.

In the woods beyond the tranquil home, the 1,189-acre park offers a fishing lake with boat rentals, trails, a pool, and a 36-site campground ($14 including hookups, call 800-864-PARK or 800-864-7275 for reservations). You'll find the park off I-20 exit 55; follow signs north on Hwy. 22 for two miles.

Southern Magnolia on Main St., tel. (706) 456-3333, serves a lunch buffet ($7) and dinner entrees from $9—Thursday is all-you-can-eat crab legs, Friday it's catfish. It's open daily, Mon.-Sat. 11 am-9ish, Sunday 11 a.m.-4 p.m. **Heavy's B-B-Q** is on Hwy. 22 south of town (open weekends only) and there's a truck stop cafe at I-20.

Washington

Washington, Georgia, was the first city chartered to honor the first president, and George Washington acknowledged the tribute on his trip through the town in 1791. Its tree-shaded courthouse square, red-brick storefronts, and landscaped antebellum homes make Washington a nicely preserved Southern town, and quiet county seat.

The region was settled two centuries ago—here references to past battles usually refer to the American Revolution—though the region's role in the Civil War is the source of more avid speculation. Washington was the last city to harbor the legendary Confederate treasury, a long-sought half-million dollars in gold, moved here from Richmond in April 1865 and never seen again.

Robert Toombs Ave. (Hwy. 78) leads directly to the courthouse square in the center of town. Inquire about self-guided tour maps and house tours at the Chamber of Commerce, in a Greek Revival house at 104 E. Liberty St., tel. (706) 678-2013.

The **Washington Historical Museum,** 308 E. Robert Toombs Ave., tel. (706) 678-7760, tells city history with Native American artifacts, antebellum furnishings, Civil War relics, and other memorabilia. Hours are Tues.-Sat. 10 a.m.-5 p.m., Sunday 2-5 p.m.; admission is $1-2. The stately red-brick 1888 **Mary Willis Library,** 204 E. Liberty St., is ornamented with stained-glass windows designed by Louis Comfort Tiffany.

A couple of blocks from the square, the **Robert Toombs House,** 216 E. Robert Toombs Ave., tel. (706) 678-2226, opens to the public the historic home of the senator who led Georgia to secession. A successful planter and lawyer, Toombs served in the U.S. Congress and Senate before his alliances shifted to the Confederate States of America. Though he aspired to the presidency of the Confederacy, he served instead as its Secretary of State. After the Civil War, Toombs steadfastly refused to take the oath of allegiance to the United States and died an unreconstructed rebel. The state-operated historic site is open Tues.-Sat. 9 a.m.-5 p.m., Sunday 2-5:30 p.m. Admission is $2 adults.

Eight miles south on Hwy. 44, the cemetery at **Kettle Creek Battleground,** marks an important patriot victory during the Revolutionary War. Here in 1779, acclaimed local son Elijah Clark led fellow countrymen in battle against the Tories. The patriot victory broke the hold of the British and saved Georgia from total capitulation to British occupation.

Callaway Plantation, five miles west on Hwy. 78, tel. (706) 678-7060, holds a city-sponsored history center featuring historic farm buildings and traditional skill demonstrations (closed Monday, admission is $1-4).

On the square, **Another Thyme,** tel. (706) 678-1672, serves light lunches (croissant sandwiches, salads) Mon.-Sat. 11 a.m.-2 p.m., and dinner (pastas, grilled meats, catfish, and oysters) Tues.-Sat. 6-9 p.m. If you're looking for an overnight, the nice **Jameson Inn** motel chain, 115 Ann Derard Dr., tel. (706) 678-7925, offers rooms from $39. The Chamber of Commerce, tel. (706) 678-2013, can direct you to several local bed and breakfast inns.

AUGUSTA

Around Augusta, a forgotten world of full-dress fox hunts, cutting-horses, and choral performances in gilt cathedrals lives on—a tranquil life steeped in history, tradition, and stability, where people are identified by congregation and their grandmother's maiden name. Then comes Masters Week, and the place fills with spectators come to see one of the world's premier golf tournaments, played on the Augusta National Golf Course.

Colonial Georgia's second city, Augusta was founded in 1736 on the banks of the Savannah River at an old native river crossing. Establishing itself as the capital of cotton production, Augusta soon became the state capital as well. Remaining untouched during the Civil War, Augusta was able to supply munitions to Confederate armies. Nature wrought a greater damage; the overflowing banks of the Savannah River flooded the town half a dozen times during the last 250 years. Today, dams and canals block the free-flowing Savannah into a series of placid lakes and gently streaming currents. (Every year, the community sends thousands of yellow duckies downstream for the annual Rubber Duck Race.)

The Medical College of Georgia (the health sciences campus of the state university system), Augusta State University, and Paine College are here, and students invent a bit of activity. But for the most part, the city reposes in its august history. The boyhood home of Woodrow Wilson and James Brown, quiet Augusta is today more Wilson than Brown.

SIGHTS

Riverwalk Attractions

Augusta's Riverwalk compact promenade, the city's central attraction, creates an inviting plaza

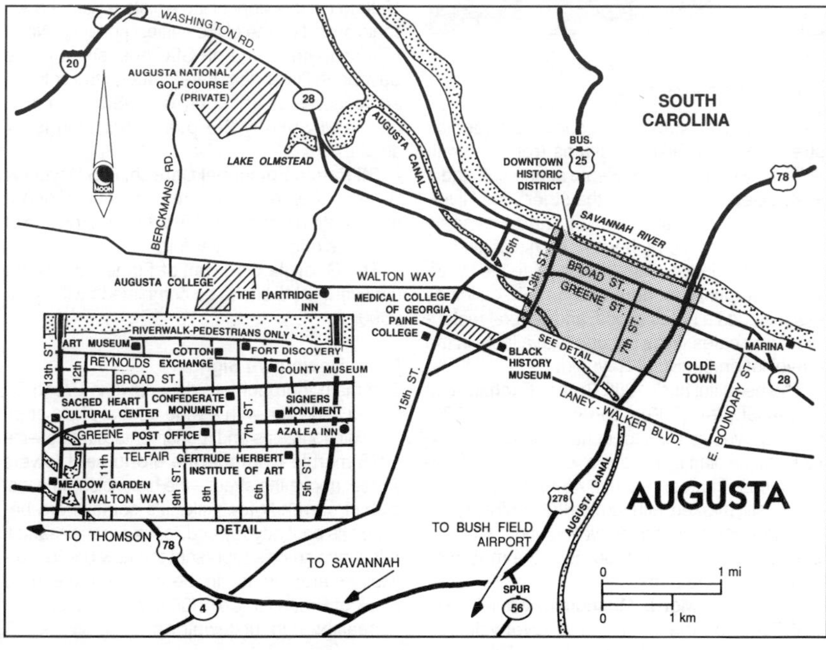

KAP STANN

The deconsecrated Sacred Heart Cathedral now serves as a cultural center.

along the river atop the high levee. It's a nice stretch by foot, bike, or skates (rentals available) between the art museum at one end and a lively science museum at the other. The Riverwalk entrance plaza is at 8th and Reynolds Streets (notice the high-water marks of past floods in the levee tunnel). Alongside the Riverwalk is a mix of modern and historic buildings that includes a hotel, shops, and several restaurants and cafes. Free parking is available in the gravel lot on 6th St. at Reynolds.

The beautiful brick 1886 **Cotton Exchange** at 32 8th St., tel. (706) 823-6600 or (800) 726-0243, serves as a visitor center and houses exhibits explaining its historic role as arbiter of cotton prices. The centerpiece 45-foot-long chalkboard, still marked with turn-of-the-century rates, was uncovered during renovation under layers of sheetrock. Hours are Mon.-Sat. 9 a.m.-5 p.m. and Sunday 1-5 p.m.

The modern **Morris Museum of Art,** tel. (706) 724-7501, on the west end of Riverwalk at 1 10th St. maintains an extensive collection of traditional oil paintings by Southern artists grouped by such themes as antebellum portraiture, Civil War art, and Southern landscapes, though one small gallery is devoted to lively and colorful contemporary folk art. The museum is open Tues.-Sat. 10 a.m.-5:30 p.m. and 12:30-5:30 p.m. on Sunday. It's free on Sunday, otherwise $3 adults, $2 students and seniors.

The spacious **National Science Center's Fort Discovery,** on the east end of the Riverwalk at 1 7th St., tel. (706) 821-0200 or (800) 325-5445, offers 128,000 square feet of high-tech playground, with highwire bike rides, an Air Chair, robotics, virtual sky-diving, Internet access, Lego sculptures, and water fountains that shoot up when you hit the target with lasers. Admission is $8 adults, $6 seniors and children ages 4-16, three and under free; sensory theater admission is an additional $3. Fort Discovery is open Mon.-Sat. 10 a.m.-6 p.m. and Sunday noon-6 p.m. There's fast food inside and pay parking below.

The **Augusta-Richmond County Museum,** 560 Reynolds St., tel. (706) 722-8454, opened in 1996 to tell the story of local history from the Archaic period (some of the earliest pottery in North America was found on Stallings Island in the Savannah River near here) through the colonial and cotton eras. It's open Tues.-Sat. 10 a.m.-5 p.m. and Sunday 2-5 p.m. Admission is $4 adults.

St. Paul's Episcopal Church, 605 Reynolds St. at the Riverwalk, the "mother church" of Augusta dating back to 1750, is built on the site of the city's original frontier fort.

The **Georgia Golf Hall of Fame** planned for the riverfront is due to be completed by the year 2000.

Other Downtown Sights

The main thoroughfare downtown is Broad St. Grand in design with a wide central plaza studded with fountains and monumental statues—the 1878 marble **Confederate Monument** towers 72 feet above the street—the historic commercial district currently feels like it's somewhere between its past heyday and its future renaissance. A few businesses represent the new breed, particularly arty studios in the middle of the 1000 block of Broad St. Colorful murals add a kidlike appeal throughout downtown.

One of the most venerable landmarks is **Signers Monument,** in the 500 block of Green St. Raised in 1848, the 50-foot obelisk marks the graves of two of Georgia's three signers of the Declaration of Independence.

The **Gertrude Herbert Institute of Art,** 506 Telfair St., tel. (706) 722-5495, holds classes and galleries inside the distinctive Federal-style mansion, which by itself is an impressive display. The 1818 mansion features an elliptical interior spiral staircase among its extravagant architectural details. It's open for tours Tues.-Sat. 10 a.m.-5 p.m.; adult admission is $2.

Meadow Garden, 1320 Independence Dr., tel. (706) 724-4174, is the oldest documented house in the city. The 1794 cottage of George Walton, one of the state's signers of the Declaration of Independence and a two-time Georgia governor, is open for tours weekdays only 10 a.m.-4 p.m. Adult admission is $3. Inquire at the visitors center about other historic homes open to the public.

Laney-Walker Sights

The Laney-Walker Historic District bounded roughly by Laney-Walker Blvd., Walton Way, Twiggs St., and Dent Blvd., honors educator Lucy Laney. Born into slavery, Laney became an influential community leader after founding a school in 1883 that became the pride of Augusta's African-American community. The school is now named **Lucy Laney High School,** at 1339 Laney-Walker Blvd. Laney, who died in 1933, is buried on school grounds. Laney's restored home nearby, now the **Lucy Craft Laney Museum of Black History,** 1116 Phillip St., tel. (706) 724-3576, holds heritage exhibits but operates largely as a conference center; it's open weekend mornings by appointment.

The most soulful approach from downtown is down 9th St., which becomes **James Brown Boulevard** as it nears the neighborhood. The Godfather of Soul owns WAAW 94.7 FM, a local radio station that features his granddaughter Tonya Brown on the air from studios downtown at the corner of 9th and Broad Streets. A mural depicting Brown appears on 10th St. between Jones and Reynolds.

For other sites, request an *African American Heritage* brochure from the visitor center.

RECREATION AND ENTERTAINMENT

Savannah Lock and Dam

Outdoor recreation can be found northwest of town around the **Savannah Rapids Pavilion,** 3300 Evans-To-Lock Rd. in Martinez, tel. (706) 868-3349, which provides a scenic overlook of river rapids and the historic Augusta Canal built in 1845. A nine-mile hiking and biking **trail** follows the towpath worn by mules to tow barges up the canal from downtown to the dam. Paddlers can put-in for a leisurely float down the canal or a wilder ride downriver.

The local outfitter **American Wilderness Outfitters Ltd.** (its motto: "Go AWOL") rents canoes and kayaks, runs shuttles, and can organize paddling trips, 2328 Washington Rd., tel. (706) 738-8500. **Clyde Dunaway Bicycles,** 215 12th St., tel. (706) 722-4208, rents bikes by the Riverwalk.

More water recreation can be found at the **Riverwalk Marina** at 5th St., tel. (706) 722-1388, including boat rentals.

Golf

The national shrine of golf is here in Augusta: **Augusta National Golf Course** at 2604 Washington Rd., tel. (706) 667-6000, is where the Masters Golf Tournament is held each April. Unfortunately the private course is open to members only. Visitors might try one of the city's two 18-hole public golf courses, **Augusta Golf Course,** 2023 Highland Ave., tel. (706) 796-5058, and **Forest Hills Golf Club,** 1500 Comfort Rd., tel. (706) 733-0001, or one of a dozen other semiprivate golf courses around Augusta. The **River Golf Club** across the river in North Augusta, South Carolina, tel. (706) 860-8872, is the region's newest. Contact the visitor center for a full list of courses, practice ranges, equipment and supplies.

Music and Performing Arts

Refined cultural-arts groups perform in venues about the city. Call the **Greater Augusta Arts Council** at (706) 826-4702 for schedules of the Augusta Ballet, Augusta Players, Augusta Symphony, and Augusta Opera.

Home to several arts organizations, **Sacred Heart Cultural Center,** at the corner of 13th and Greene Streets, tel. (706) 826-4700, also holds performances in an impressive 1891 Romanesque Revival building that was once a Catholic cathedral (now deconsecrated). Major acts are often booked at the **Civic Center Auditorium;** which is also where the Augusta Lynx play ice hockey from October to March.

Riverwalk nightspots such as the **Cotton Patch,** 816 Cotton Lane around 8th St., tel. (706) 724-4511, feature live entertainment; the **Soul Bar** at 984 Broad St. is a laid-back local hangout downtown that attracts young professionals and medical students. Pick up the free **Spirit** weekly tabloid for entertainment listings.

Special Events

"Like Mardi Gras without the costumes or floats" is how one bartender describes the city's *raison d'être* event, the **Masters Golf Tournament,** held the first full week in April. Hundreds of thousands of visitors descend on the sleepy city, packing roadways, restaurants, hotels, and houses (many residents leave), and pumping an estimated $94 million into the local economy annually. Held at the Augusta National Golf Course on Washington Rd., the event draws world-renowned champions to the Olympics of golf. Though the tournament is not open to the public, visitors can call (706) 667-6000 to get an application for tickets to a practice round. The tickets are awarded by lottery.

At the riverfront, there's a **St. Patrick's Day** celebration; the **Spring Festival** is held mid-May; and a laser light show and fireworks on the **Fourth of July.** September's **Arts in the Heart of Augusta,** one of the city's premier annual events, brings local cultural-arts performances to many venues around the city. In October, a rubber duck race and Oktoberfest are held, and the city decorates for a **Christmas festival and parade** in December.

ACCOMMODATIONS AND FOOD

Accommodations

Downtown, the cheapest accommodations are available at the **Augusta Budget Inn,** 441 Broad St., tel. (706) 722-0212. Across the street, the **Days Inn Downtown,** 444 Broad St., tel. (706) 724-8100, offers accommodations in a newer motel with a pool. The preeminent hotel in town is the 10-story **Radisson Riverfront Hotel,** 2 10th St., tel. (706) 722-8900, which offers several restaurants, a lounge, a pool, and 237 rooms, some with river views (rates from $100). **Azalea Inn,** 312-316 Greene St., tel. (706) 724-3454, offers 16 bed and breakfast rooms in two houses in a nice Victorian residential district adjacent to downtown (rates from $79).

West of downtown, the historic **Partridge Inn,** 2110 Walton Way, tel. (706) 737-8888 or (800) 476-6888, heads up the city's affluent Summerville district, a residential neighborhood of historic homes known locally as "The Hill." The original 1890 inn has been subsequently expanded and now has 155 rooms and a pool. It's a nice comfortable place, particularly the inviting wide veranda outside its bar-and-grill, but for rates of $100 and up you might expect something more historic than the modernly furnished rooms.

Modern chain motels are concentrated at I-20 exit 65, on Washington Rd. four miles west of downtown. Here an Econo Lodge (no pool), Hampton Inn, La Quinta Inn, Masters Economy Inn, Shoney's Inn, Homewood Suites, another Days Inn, Courtyard by Marriott, and Amerisuites compete for weary interstate drivers. A cheaper independent with rooms from $30 is **West Bank Inn,** 2904 Washington Rd., tel. (706) 733-1724, no pool.

Note that during Masters Week, room rates will likely double or even triple, and some establishments will take reservations only for a four- or seven-night minimum.

Food and Drink

At the Riverwalk, the **King George Pub** at 2 8th St., tel. (706) 724-4755, offers some English specialties along with classic American fare for lunch and dinner; they say James Brown is a regular on Sunday nights. Downtown, the most venerable place is old-time **Luigi's,** 590 Broad St., tel. (706) 722-4056, a traditional Italian restaurant operated by the same family for four generations (great jukebox). For more modern fare, **Word of Mouth Cafe,** 724 Broad St., tel. (706) 722-3477, serves upscale dinners of pasta, seafood and steak, often accompanied by live jazz, in a beveled-glass interior (closed Monday). Trendier still is **White Elephant,** 1135 Broad St., tel. (706) 722-8614, for fresh ethnic dishes and a good wine selection. A quicker stop, and open late, is the **Pizza Joint** at 1032 Broad. For coffee stops, there's the **Boll Weevil Cafe** on 9th off the Riverwalk at 9th, or **Java Hut** down on Reynolds, operated by a couple from Seattle.

South of town, another Augusta institution is **Sconyer's Barbecue,** on Sconyers Way via I-520 exit 6, tel. (706) 790-5411, was rated among the nation's top 10 barbecue restaurants by *People* magazine. Hickory-smoked ribs and sandwiches drenched with tangy sauce in a family restaurant setting. Take I-520 exit 6 to Peach orchard; turn left on Sconyers Way.

Among the many generic chain restaurants in the interstate gulch at I-20 exit 65 is a rare local find: lively **Rhinehart's Oyster Bar,** 3051 Washington Rd. west of I-20, tel. (706) 860-2337 serves you-shuck-'em oysters, rock shrimp, crawfish, and chowder on big picnic tables inside or out. Most everything is under $7. A totem pole, darts, margaritas, students, sports fans, and four TVs complete the scene.

Across the river in North Augusta, **Sno-Cap** offers an original 1950s-style drive-in, where teenage servers bring 95-cent burgers and banana milkshakes out to your car. From downtown Augusta, cross the 13th St. bridge and go uphill, then turn left on Jackson.

OTHER PRACTICALITIES

Getting There and Around

To reach Augusta from Atlanta (139 miles), take I-20 east to exit 65 and follow Washington Rd. east four or five miles into town. For a large city on an interstate corridor, downtown Augusta is surprisingly off the beaten path.

Augusta's **Bush Field Airport** is served by Delta and USAir. Taxis and limousine services are available at the airport, and major car-rental companies are well-represented among them.

For schedules of buses serving the downtown terminal on Greene St., tel. (706) 722-6411, call Greyhound at tel. (800) 231-2222.

Shopping

The **Augusta Mall** off I-520 on Wrightsboro Rd. has a Macy's, Sears, and Morrison's Cafeteria. The high-end retail **Surrey Center** across from Augusta National has a Talbot's, PJ's gourmet coffee, and the popular French Market Grille for Americanized Cajun food (go a mile east of I-20 exit 65, then two miles south on Berckman's Rd.).

Information and Services

The helpful **visitors center** at the Cotton Exchange near the Riverwalk, tel. (706) 724-4067, can start you off with maps and a sense of cotton's history in the region. A Georgia Visitor Center off I-20 at the South Carolina border provides statewide as well as local information. Or write the **Augusta Metropolitan Convention and Visitors Bureau,** P.O. Box 1331, Augusta, GA 30903-1331, tel. (706) 823-6600 or (800) 726-0243; or see www.augustaga.org.

Kinko's, 3435 Wrightsboro Rd., tel. (706) 733-1002, offers 24-hour Internet access.

In emergencies, dial 911; the police business phone is (706) 821-1000. The **Medical College of Georgia Hospital and Clinics** is at 1120 15th St., tel. (706) 721-0211.

NORTH OF AUGUSTA: THE BIG LAKES

On the eastern Piedmont north of Augusta, "Big Lake" parks line the border with South Carolina. Created by impounding the Savannah River, Clarks Hill and Russell Lakes offer remote campsites popular with anglers and boaters. The widest range of lakeside services are at scenic shoreline state parks. For maps detailing all access points, marinas, boat launches, and camps at the Army Corps of Engineers-managed lakes, inquire at the Resource Manager's Office, tel. (706) 722-3770, on Hwy. 221 at the Clarks Hill Lake dam (on the South Carolina side of the river northeast of Pollard's Corner, Georgia). The Georgia Visitor Center at I-20 inside the border also distributes lake maps.

Clarks Hill Lake

Georgia shares this lake with South Carolina, though they're unwilling to share a common name for it—on the South Carolina side, the 70,000-acre reservoir was officially renamed Strom Thurmond Lake, yet Georgians haven't taken to the change. Georgia maps doggedly continue to label it Clarks Hill, even if it means crossing out the new name on federal literature and writing in the sentimental favorite. Fisherfolk will find friendly reciprocity; you can carry either a Georgia or South Carolina license to fish border lakes.

Mistletoe State Park

At the southern branch of the lake, closest to Augusta, Mistletoe State Park, tel. (706) 541-0321, lies off Hwy. 150, 12 miles north of I-20's exit 60. Earlier this century, the area was a popular holiday gathering place nicknamed Mistletoe Junction. Today a swimming beach and five miles of hiking trails are highlights of the 1,920-acre shoreline park.

The white-blazed 1.3-mile **Cliatt Creek Trail** and the yellow-blazed 1.2-mile **Turkey Trot Trail** both loop through clearings and new growth on abandoned cropland that was farmed as recently as the 1950s; both trails start and end at the park entrance. A two-mile trail links the campground and the beach. Pick up trail maps at the park office.

The cottage area and a 107-site campground are set out on peninsulas. Ten fully equipped two-bedroom cottages rent from $55; campsites cost $14 including hookups. Call (800) 864-PARK (800-864-7275) for reservations. The parking fee is $2 per car, free on Wednesday.

Elijah Clark Memorial State Park

At the middle of Clarks Hill Lake, on Hwy. 378 six miles northeast of Lincolnton, is Elijah Clark Memorial State Park, tel. (706) 359-3458. Named for a Georgia Revolutionary War hero, the park also holds his gravesite. A pioneer museum displays 18th-century artifacts, and reconstructed log cabins are open to weekend tours. Boating, water-skiing, swimming, and fishing are popular activities at the 447-acre park, which features a white-sand beach and bathhouse among its facilities. An annual bluegrass festival is held here the first week in May.

Twenty fully equipped two-bedroom lakefront cottages rent for $55-75 a night; $14 to camp at one of 165 campsites; call (800) 864-PARK (800-864-7275) for reservations. The parking fee is $2 per car, free on Wednesday.

Bobby Brown State Park

At the juncture of the Broad and Savannah Rivers at the remote northern end of Clarks Hill Lake, Bobby Brown State Park, tel. (706) 213-2046, occupies the site of the old town of Petersburg, which thrived here in the 1790s. The 665-acre park, south of Hwy. 72, between Middleton and Chennault, features a pool, boat ramp and dock, and a 1.9-mile trail leading to a lake overlook. A 61-site campground charges $14, including hookups; call (800) 864-PARK (800-864-7275) for reservations. The parking fee is $2 per car, free on Wednesday.

Richard B. Russell State Park and Vicinity

On 26,500-acre **Russell Lake** adjacent to Clarks Hill Lake, this state park, tel. (706) 213-2045, is nine miles northeast of Elberton, on Ruckerville Rd. via Hwy. 77. The 2,700-acre park is open for day-use fishing, boating (rentals available), and swimming on an imported sand beach. As one of the state's newest parks, Richard Russell State Park is also one of the most thoroughly wheelchair-accessible. The parking fee is $2 per car, free on Wednesday. The park lies near an excavated site used by Paleo-Indians more than 10,000 years ago, now underwater.

Other mysterious phenomena are the **Georgia Guidestones** up Hwy. 77, a set of modern granite monoliths inscribed by an unknown hand with "a message for future generations" translated into 12 languages.

OFF I-20 WEST

Thomson

Thirty-five miles west of Augusta off I-20, downtown Thomson centers around its 1870s courthouse square. The old train depot off Main St. now houses the local tourist bureau, tel. (706) 595-5584, stands behind a monument dedicated to women who loyally supported the Confederate cause (depot open weekdays only). Inquire here about "Upcountry Plantation Tours" of historic houses, including the Rock House, among the oldest dwellings still standing in Georgia. The fieldstone building dating from about 1785 was built by an ancestor of President Jimmy Carter.

Thomson hosts the **Belle Meade Fox Hunt** every Wednesday and Saturday from November through March. Spectators can join the scene and watch a traditional fox hunt from the seat of a "tally-ho" wagon. The hunting season opens with a blessing of the hounds the first Saturday in November.

Hamburg State Park

About 30 miles south of I-20, this 750-acre state park, tel. (912) 552-2393, features a 1921 water-powered gristmill that continues to grind corn into hominy and meal (sold at the country store). A pioneer museum displays old-time artifacts of rural country living. Rent boats at a 225-acre stocked lake, or camp at one of 30 sites ($12-14, including hookups). The parking fee is $2 per car, free on Wednesday. Park rangers lead **canoe trips** down the neighboring Ogeechee River in March and April.

SOUTH OF AUGUSTA

As a fall-line city, Augusta sits at the junction of the Piedmont Plateau and the coastal plain. South of Augusta, the plain flattens into a wide expanse of piney woods and sandy soils. Georgia's largest export product, kaolin, is manufactured here. This earthy substance is used in the manufacture of fine china (and China is the only other country to produce this raw material, essential to make such luxurious brands as Limoges and Wedgwood). In this remote region of quarries, small towns, and quiet wooded rivers, drivers pass through the Kaolin Capital of the World, the Bird-Dog Capital of the World, yet another Old State Capital, and some hideaway state parks. As for famous sons, Elijah Muhammad, leader of the Nation of Islam and once Malcolm X's mentor, hailed from Washington County.

Louisville

Louisville (LOO-is-ville), one of colonial Georgia's first inland settlements, was named after King Louis XVI. Strategically situated on the banks of the Ogeechee River, the town grew into an important port and even served as the state capital from 1795 to 1805. Most historic structures were destroyed by Sherman's troops on their way to Savannah. Today the town's political might is limited to being the seat of Jefferson County. The county courthouse, built in 1904, sits on the site of the old capitol in downtown Louisville. The current population of 3,500 is nearly half what it was when it was the state capital.

At the center of Broad St. downtown, the **Market House** remains standing from its construction about 1758. Here, in addition to the auctioning of cotton, land tracts, and household goods, slaves were once sold in antebellum days. Inside the market house hangs a bell cast in France in 1771. On Hwy. 24 east of town, a small cemetery contains graves from the colonial era.

Find **Pansy's** downtown for such Southern buffet specialties as baked and fried chicken (closed Saturday).

Magnolia Springs State Park

Among Georgia's prettiest state parks, Magnolia Springs, on Hwy. 25 five miles north of Millen, tel. (912) 982-1660, takes its name from the park's clear natural springs—nine million gallons a day are estimated to flow from the source. During the Civil War, this ample fresh-water source led to the site's selection as a Confederate P.O.W. camp—Camp Lawton once imprisoned 10,000 Union soldiers, and its ruins are still visible. Today the springs attract an abundant variety of wildlife—ducks, herons, egrets, deer, tortoises, and alligators appear on its shores. Hike a half-mile loop nature trail (pick up an interpretive brochure and trail map at the office) or the three-mile **Upper Loop Trail,** which follows the eastern shore of the lake and crosses over a wooded swamp of cypress, tupelo, and maple.

The lushly wooded 948-acre park also offers a swimming pool and canoe or fishing boat rentals. Their special events include a biannual Confederate encampment, a canoe trip down the Ogeechee in spring and fall, and a clogging and square-dancing weekend in November.

Five fully equipped two-bedroom cottages rent from $50-65, and the 26-site campground charges $14, including hookups. Call (800) 864-PARK (800-864-7275) for reservations. The parking fee is $2 per car, free on Wednesday.

Waynesboro

The Bird-Dog Capital of the World, Waynesboro displays its hunting heritage at the **Burke County Museum,** 536 Liberty St., tel. (706) 554-4889, along with historical artifacts from colonial and cotton days (open daily). The **Boll Weevil Plantation** on Thompson Bridge Rd., tel. (706) 554-6954, which opens to the public, is one of many hunting plantations in the region.

Mobley's Restaurant at 222 E. 6th St., tel. (706) 554-4477, for home-cooked Southern specialties. It's open daily, Mon.-Fri. 6 a.m.-9 p.m., Sat.-Sun. 9 a.m.-3 p.m.

MIDDLE GEORGIA

"Middle Georgia" is the name for an egg-shaped region that encompasses the mid-central Piedmont from Atlanta on past Macon, widening farther south and dipping into the coastal plain. This fertile region, fed by the Ocmulgee and Oconee Rivers, was soundly trounced by Sherman on his march from Atlanta to Savannah. As a result, Middle Georgia shares a common history and culture distinct from other regions. (The southernmost reach of Middle Georgia, south of Macon, is covered in the **South Georgia** chapter.)

For travelers, the area within the triangle created by Atlanta, Macon, and Athens is among the state's most interesting rural regions, easily accessible from all three cities. Picturesque small towns cherish their remaining antebellum homes, and courthouse squares remain lively community centers. The paths are strewn with monuments, historical markers, and tributes to the citizenry that fought to defend the land from outsiders. That allied camaraderie, pride, and shared grief has been passed down for generations. Here in Middle Georgia, "the war" refers strictly to the one between the states.

Off I-20 east of Atlanta, sprawling suburbs have subsumed many of the region's northernmost towns, but a Middle Georgia heritage—boardinghouse restaurants, cowboy bars, and tranquil retreats in remote woods—still lies beyond the freeway's neon corridor. Picturesque Madison, with its many antebellum homes spared from Sherman's torch, is particularly scenic and accessible—within an hour from downtown Atlanta. It also offers a variety of historic bed and breakfast houses that make a great base of operations for exploring the region.

From Madison to Milledgeville along Hwy. 441, an intriguing set of historical attractions varies from a prophetic effigy mound and rivers named in native tongues to the white columns of the state's antebellum capital and the mischievous antics of trickster Br'er Rabbit. Side trips allow for traditional Southern respites on boats or beaches along interior lakes. The leisurely pace of the country highways and the close proximity of stops for sightseeing, refreshments, and recreation make the 40-mile route ideal for bicycle touring. Stretch out the route to Athens up north or Macon down south for a hundred miles of urban and rural appeal. (Drivers need to detour off Hwy. 441 bypasses to see historic areas.)

The I-75 route between Atlanta and Macon allows easy access to more Middle Georgia pleasures—you'll find a working plantation, historic mill ruins, and a wildlife refuge within the welcoming woods of the Oconee National Forest. Eat at saucy barbecue joints or order fried green tomatoes at the original Whistle Stop Cafe. Around Macon you'll enter peach country—orchards in bloom in spring, and stocked roadside fruit stands in summertime.

ATLANTA TO MADISON VIA I-20

Conyers

Since 1990, over a million visitors have visited the **Nancy Fowler Farm** at 2324 White Rd., tel. (770) 922-8885, to hear religious messages channeled through Mrs. Fowler. According to the local tourist bureau, "Jesus continues to appear every day to Mrs. Fowler and the Virgin Mary appears on occasion." It's open daily 11 a.m.-5 p.m.

A more venerable religious landmark, the **Monastery of Our Lady of Holy Spirit,** on Hwy. 212 eight miles southwest of town, tel. (770) 483-8705, was founded in 1944 by monks who practice self-sufficiency. Visitors may tour the church and grounds—a scenic duck pond and bonsai greenhouse offer a tranquil urban refuge. Mass is offered daily, including 11 a.m. Sunday; visitors are welcome. At the gift shop, the monks sell books, religious ornaments, and fresh breads baked on the premises. Overnight religious retreats are available for men only.

Conyers is also a noted equestrian center; its **Georgia International Horse Park,** on Centennial Olympic Parkway, tel. (770) 860-4190, hosted the 1996 Olympic equestrian events.

Social Circle

According to a plaque at the town well in the center of this attractive little community, Social Circle was named for the friendliness of its residents. More than 50 19th-century homes and buildings decorate its historic district downtown, four miles north of I-20. The Victorian storefront drugstore still sells penny candy.

But its most widely known landmark is the grand Greek Revival mansion that now houses the **Blue Willow Inn,** 294 N. Cherokee Rd., tel. (770) 464-2131. The Inn raises Southern buffet to aristocratic heights and is open daily for lunch and dinner. Friday and Saturday nights feature a special seafood buffet. Hours are Mon.-Fri. 11 a.m.-2:30 p.m. and 5-9 p.m., Saturday 11 a.m.-3:30 p.m. and 4:30-9:30 p.m., Sunday dinner served 11 a.m.-9 p.m. Prices range from $10-16, including drinks and dessert.

The trout-inclined can find a **fish hatchery** on Hwy. 278, southeast of town (take I-20 exit 48). The state **Wildlife Management** office next door at 2123 Hwy. 278, distributes information on statewide hunting and fishing, and maintains an interpretive trout habitat along Little Amicalola Creek.

Rutledge

Downtown Rutledge is a charming little crossroads dating from 1871 that gets enough sideroads traffic from Madison and the nearby state park to support several businesses appealing to visitors and a nice restaurant open daily.

Among the historic storefronts downtown you'll find a 75-year-old hardware store that sells such interesting garden accessories as ceramic bird feeders and yard art, and a bicycle shop that's a popular stop for local bicycle tours (currently no rentals). The red caboose sells homemade fudge and serves as an unofficial welcome center.

Housed in a 19th-century drugstore, the **Yesterday Cafe,** 120 Fairplay St., tel. (706) 557-9337, is plastered with local historical photographs, farm tools, and other rural tchotchkes. Its nouveau Southern menu delivers such comfortable staples as biscuits and gravy, buttermilk pancakes with sugarcane syrup, and pan-fried catfish alongside fresh vegetables, soups, salads, and pasta. Breakfast and lunch are served Mon.-Fri. 7 a.m.-2 p.m., Sat.-Sun. 8 a.m.-3 p.m. Supper is served Thurs.-Sat. 5:30-9:30 p.m. (entrees $10-15, beer and wine available).

A giant bouquet of colorful metal flowers downtown is sculpted by local folk artist Blue Chilton, best known for his whimsical animal sculptures made with old car parts. See his creatures inhabiting the lane to his studio a couple miles from downtown. From the bouquet at the corner of Hwy. 278 and Newborn Rd., take Newborn Rd. to Walter Shepard Rd. to Chilton Wood Rd. and look for the dragon.

A few miles west of downtown, just inside the Morgan County line, **Cowboy's Feed Lot,** 7201 Hwy. 278, tel. (706) 557-9552, serves "steaks and stuff" and features country-western bands and dancing on the huge dance hall's sawdust-sprinkled floors. Beef-lovers order the house specialty—a 22 oz. T-bone named "the Stud"—baby-back ribs, or the euphemistically named "calf fries" (testicles). It's open Wed.-Sat. nights; country dance lessons take place Thursday. If you left your 10-gallon hat at home, pick one up at the adjacent western-wear store—also chaps, bolo ties, boots, and other cowboy gear. A Saturday flea market runs year-round here. It's 2.25 miles east of I-20 exit 48.

Hard Labor Creek State Park

The busiest state park in Georgia, this full-service 5,805-acre park two miles north of Rutledge, tel. (706) 557-3001, draws plenty of city folk to its 5,805 acres packed with recreational facilities. The area is particularly nice for bike touring—it's 14 miles roundtrip to Madison—and rentals are available at the park.

Golfers know it best for its popular creekside 18-hole course ($24 for 18 holes on weekends), which offers cart rentals, a pro shop, and a cafe. Two shaded lakes provide swimming, fishing, and boating (rentals available); trails accommodate hikers, cyclists, and horses (bring your own).

Twenty fully equipped two-bedroom cottages rent for $65-80. A 49-site campground charges $16, including hookups. For reservations, call (800) 864-PARK (800-864-7275). The parking fee is $2 per car; golfers are exempt and Wednesdays are free.

MADISON AND VICINITY

Established in 1807, early Madison prospered on the cotton economy. Wealthy planters built the town's many elegant houses in ornate period styles between 1830 and 1860; today the remaining 19th-century structures lend the town its charm. Many homes are still owned by descendants of the original residents.

The tidy town of Madison was spared from the destruction of Sherman's 1864 March to the Sea.

KAP STANN

The town was lucky to be spared the wrath of Sherman, who brought 50,000 troops within blazing range of town on his 1864 March to the Sea. The story goes that Madison resident Senator Joshua Hill rode out to ask Sherman that no harm come to Madison—and as Hill was a staunch Unionist who resigned his congressional seat rather than agree to secession, Sherman spared the town. A fire in 1869 was not so merciful, however. The construction wave that followed endowed the town center with its late-19th-century flavor.

Today, Madison's classic Southern town square remains as vibrant as many such downtowns were half a century ago, before modern malls and suburban sprawl robbed them of their vitality. The 1905 Beaux Arts courthouse, with its cupola towering above massive oaks and magnolias, continues to dominate the square (city auctions are still held on its steps). Brick sidewalks line the square, dotted with colorful flowerboxes and park benches. Inviting shops in Victorian storefronts are pleasant to browse through for antiques, local arts and crafts, along with more practical sundries. Attractive residential neighborhoods surround the square, with dozens of historic homes and tidy gardens.

Tourism is now Madison's second-largest industry, after agriculture. Under an hour from downtown Atlanta, the tourist-friendly town draws crowds of frustrated Atlanta visitors who find little that resembles their notion of the antebellum South in the state capital. A good place to start is the welcome center on the square.

Sights

A range of historic house tours highlight architectural details while shedding light on antebellum caste society. At **Heritage Hall,** 277 S. Main St., tel. (706) 342-9627, guides describe high-class life in a glamorously restored 1833 doctor's residence a block from the square. Admission is $5 adults; hours are Mon.-Sat. 10 a.m.-4:30 p.m. and Sunday 1:30-4:30 p.m. Two restorations beside the courthouse, tel. (706) 342-4454, are the 1810 **Rogers House,** an example of where an antebellum middle-class white family might have lived, and the 1891 **Rose Cottage** across the gravel garden path, built by a former slave to house an African-American family. Tours include both houses; admission is $2.50 adults. Hours are Mon.-Sat. 10 am-4:30 p.m. and Sunday 1:30-4:30 p.m.

The 1895 Romanesque Revival **Madison-Morgan Cultural Center,** 434 S. Main St., tel. (706) 342-4743, has been transformed from a schoolhouse into an impressive multipurpose regional arts center. Downstairs, several rooms of exhibits tell the town's story, highlighting 19th-century decorative arts and interior design, and an evocative 395-seat theater hosts seasonal performances. Upstairs, one classroom has been restored to its Victorian origins, and another serves as an art gallery (winners of a regional competition were recently on view). The museum and gallery are open Tues.-Sat. 10 a.m.-4:30 p.m. and Sunday 2-5 p.m.; admission is $3 adults.

At the **Morgan County African-American Museum,** 156 Academy St., tel. (706) 342-9197, former schoolteacher Rev. Thelma Lee leads visitors through three rooms of a small Victorian cottage describing the life of its former residents. As she shows the museum's African art collection she mentions the visit of African athletes training nearby for the 1996 Summer Games—despite not speaking any English, the athletes shared a natural affinity with the community through the common heritage of art and musical instruments on display, according to Rev. Lee. The house is generally open Tues.-Fri. 10 a.m.-4 p.m. and Saturday noon-4 p.m., but hours may vary. Admission is $3 adults.

Accommodations and Camping

Madison has four bed and breakfast inns with rates from around $85 a night for two people including breakfast. The two inns right in town can keep you out of your car for the length of your visit—a highly recommended way to experience Madison. **Burnett Place,** 317 Old Post Rd., tel. (706) 342-4034, is operated by a hearty couple in their 80s, who offer spacious guest rooms in their two-story Federal home built about 1830. **Brady Inn,** 250 N. 2nd St., tel. (706) 342-4400, offers six rooms with private baths in an 1800s Victorian cottage.

Outside town around the dairy farms and horse pastures surrounding Madison, a young family renovating several farm buildings operates **The Farmhouse Inn,** tel. (706) 342-7933, with a row of country-decor guest rooms across from their house. Most unusual is a dude ranch called **Southern Cross,** tel. (706) 342-8027, operated by a bilingual German family catering to guests who want to ride.

Modern chain motels are clustered along Hwy. 441 around I-20 exit 51, including Ramada Inn, Super 8 (no pools), Comfort Inn, Days Inn (adjacent chain cafeteria), Holiday Express, and Hampton Inn (priciest, best breakfast buffet). The independent **Budget Inn** here goes as low as $25.88.

Camping is available at the 30-acre **Talisman Campark,** on Hwy. 441 1.7 miles south of I-20, tel. (706) 342-1799, which offers 67 sites in a nicely wooded area on the southern fringe of town with nature trails and a pool. Rates for two people are $12 for tents, $16-19 for RVs. (Also see **Hard Labor Creek State Park** for more camping options.)

Food and Drink

Ye Olde Colonial Restaurant, 108 W. Washington St., tel. (706) 342-2211, is a landmark for hungry visitors. The cafeteria-style restaurant is housed in an old bank building—sit in the vault if you like—and serves such classic Southern buffet choices as fried chicken, country-fried steak, sweet potatoes, butterbeans, corn bread, and cobbler, with bottomless iced tea. It's open Mon.-Sat. 6:30 a.m.-8:30 p.m. More modern fare is served around the square inside or out at **Amici's** Italian restaurant for lunch and dinner (and occasional live music) and the **Snapdragon Cafe,** for morning muffins and light lunches. Just off the square on S. Main St., **Same Old Place** is the local hangout for homestyle Southern food (fried pork chops are their specialty); it's open for breakfast and lunch from 5 a.m.-2 p.m.

Near the interstate, **Crowe's,** on Hwy. 441 1.4 miles north of I-20, tel. (706) 342-7002, serves good hickory-smoked 'cue for lunch only.

Entertainment and Events

The Madison-Morgan Cultural Center, tel. (706) 342-4743, holds its acclaimed summer theater festival in August, and hosts other theatrical productions and concerts throughout the year. Bobby McFerrin, the National Theatre of the Deaf, and the Vienna Boys Choir are among the artists who have performed here.

Spring house tours held in April and May take visitors through homes not generally open to the public. Seasonal tours include haunted house tours at Halloween and candlelit Christmas tours the first weekend in December.

Recreation

Sixteen miles east of Madison, on the northernmost reaches of Lake Oconee, the **Parks Ferry Recreation Area,** a few miles south of the freeway off Parks Ferry Rd., tel. (706) 485-8704, offers a swimming beach along with fishing and boating. See **Hard Labor Creek State Park** above for more local recreation west of Madison and **Greensboro and Vicinity** for national forest areas to the east.

Getting There and Away

Madison, 50 miles east of Atlanta, is easily accessible north of I-20 exit 51 to Hwy. 441 north three miles to downtown. This Hwy. 441 corridor

TALES FROM THE HEARTLAND

"The writer operates at a peculiar crossroads where time and place and eternity somehow meet. His problem is to find that location."

—*Flannery O'Connor,*
The Regional Writer

Three great fiction writers somehow found that elusive meeting place in this small rural patch of Georgia heartland.

Joel Chandler Harris, born in Eatonton in 1848, began chronicling the African-American folktales of a fictional character named Uncle Remus in his *Atlanta Constitution* column in 1879. The tales, transformed with Southern details when brought to America, featured a wily trickster named Br'er Rabbit and his antagonist Br'er Fox ("Br'er" is short for "Brother"). *Br'er Rabbit and the Tar Baby* was the most famous of these Uncle Remus stories. Harris recorded the tales in his version of black folk dialect of the period—barely intelligible for many contemporary readers (and possibly objectionable, with such patronizing terms as "Uncle" which were then in common use). Yet Harris's sincere admiration for the imaginative tales is undisputable. Disney's animated feature film *Song of the South* re-created Harris's folktales, and easy-reading modern versions of the stories are now widely available.

Eatonton's **Uncle Remus Museum** on Hwy. 441 contains memorabilia from the life and times of Harris and his Remus and Rabbit characters. Housed in two authentic slave cabins, the museum is open Mon.-Sat. 10 a.m.-5 p.m. (closed for lunch), Sunday 2-5 p.m. (closed Tuesday Sept.-May).

The contemporary writer **Alice Walker** also hails from Eatonton. Her Pulitzer-prize winning novel *The Color Purple* (which Steven Spielberg made into a film) was set in this rural Georgia countryside in the 1930s. Now a California resident, Walker established the Color Purple Foundation in Eatonton, which sponsors local educational enrichment programs. The Eatonton-Putnam County Chamber of Commerce, tel. (706) 485-7701, has an Alice Walker Driving Tour guide which maps the author's birthplace and former residences.

Flannery O'Connor, born in Savannah in 1925 (her home there is open for tours), wrote her famous novels, *Wise Blood* and *The Violent Bear It Away,* and such short stories as "A Good Man is Hard to Find," on the 1820 Milledgeville ranch called Andalusia (311 W. Greene St. off Hwy. 441 north of the bypass, west side). She attended the local college—now Georgia College—which maintains a collection of her manuscripts and memorabilia in the **Flannery O'Connor Room** (upstairs in the main library). College scholars produce the journal *The Peacock's Feet* devoted to O'Connor's work. The title refers to O'Connor's observation that a peacock's pride in his stunning plumage is humbled by his awkward feet. The O'Connor Room is open weekdays 8 a.m.-5 p.m. when the college is in session, and librarians can make available maps of other O'Connor landmarks in town. Her gravestone is in Memory Hill cemetery.

KAP STANN

is part of the "Antebellum Trail" from Athens to Macon—known through these parts as "the Eatonton Highway." There's no taxi or bike rental in town; bike rentals are available at **Hard Labor Creek State Park,** above.

Eastbound I-20 through-travelers should note that the freeway between Madison and Augusta has relatively few services; you might want to stock up and gas up around Madison.

Information and Services

The **Madison/Morgan County Chamber of Commerce** housed in the Welcome Center downtown at 115 E. Jefferson St., tel. (706) 342-4454 or (800) 709-7406, distributes walking-tour maps, audio tours, calendars of events, and brochures in French, German, and Spanish, and is happy to let you use their restrooms. They organize guided walking tours emphasizing local architectural highlights; also inquire about seasonal horse-drawn carriage tours. It's open daily: Mon.-Fri. 8:30 a.m.-5 p.m., Saturday 10 am-5 p.m., and Sunday 1-4 p.m.

EATONTON AND VICINITY

The small country town of Eatonton is surrounded by the dairy farms that constitute the mainstay of the local economy—the town's **Dairy Festival** in June highlights the industry. But tourists here will be most drawn to two quintessentially Southern sights.

The home of literary legends Alice Walker and Joel Chandler Harris Eatonton attracts visitors to its folksy **Uncle Remus Museum,** set in a small park on Hwy. 441 downtown (see the special topic **Tales from the Heartland**). A statue of the famous trickster Br'er Rabbit adorns the courthouse square. North of town, an aboriginal mound presents a moving memorial to ancient tribes.

The newest addition to the culturally rich mix in town is the Nuwaubian Nation of Moors, who have peppered their 476-acre compound off Shady Dale Rd. with pyramids, obelisks, colorful flags and a sphinx. The group has drawn crowds of 6,000 for its five-day Savior's Week celebration in June. The sect is led by Malachi York, who, according to local papers, "claims he is an incarnated being from another galaxy." The group hopes to build a family theme park in the future, but have been encountering opposition from city zoning officials.

(Antebellum Trail followers note they need to detour off the Hwy. 441 bypass to stay on the Trail to downtown Eatonton.)

Rock Eagle Effigy Mound

As you look down from the observation tower, the thousand-year-old aboriginal Rock Eagle effigy mound (on Hwy. 441 five miles north of Eatonton) resembles a bird of prey standing upright with outstretched wings. The effigy, believed to be an eagle because of the eagle's high place in native mythology, measures 102 feet from wingtip to wingtip. The eagle takes its shape from thousands of rocks, laboriously transported here and heaped into a huge mound. Rock Eagle is the only effigy site in Georgia, and it remains eerily pristine. Though now guarded by a tall wire fence, it looks as if no stone has been touched for centuries. Perhaps its earliest visitors heeded the parting words of a Creek chief, now inscribed on a marker at the site:

Tread Softly Here White Man
For Long Ere You Came
Strange Races Lived, Fought, and Loved

The site lies within a 1,452-acre 4-H center, tel. (706) 485-2831, that specializes in environmental education. On Memorial Day weekend, the center hosts a Southern **Folk Festival,** featuring regional handicrafts and bluegrass music as well as workshops on native culture.

Recreation

Lake Oconee and Lake Sinclair, two power-company impoundments of the Oconee River, are Middle Georgia's playground for boating, fishing, and swimming. The reservoirs meet at the Hwy. 16 dam, 15 miles east of Eatonton, where Georgia Power's **Land Department Field Office,** tel. (706) 485-8704, distributes maps to all public facilities and campgrounds around the lakes.

The Oconee National Forest abuts the lakes. The **District Ranger Office** on Hwy. 441 six miles

KAP STANN

LINK GRAVE MARKERS

Tucked away in Milledgeville's Memory Hill Cemetery, "slavery-time" graves are marked by small chains. Those with one link mark the grave of a person born into slavery; two links means the deceased was born and lived in slavery; and a three-link chain memorializes a person who was born, lived, and died a slave. The cemetery lies two blocks down the hill from the Governor's Mansion as you head away from town. Famous native daughter Flannery O'Connor is also buried at Memory Hill.

north of Eatonton, tel. (706) 465-7110, provides recreation directories and trail maps.

Within the national forest, the seasonal **Lake Sinclair Recreation Area,** offers a staffed swimming beach and campground ($7 a night, first-come first-served, hookups available). It's open from Memorial Day in late May to Labor Day in early September. Parking costs $2. There's also a family-friendly hiking trail that winds two miles (one-way) through a canebrake then follows the lakeshore (accessible year-round). To get there from Eatonton, go 10 miles south on Hwy. 129, then three miles east on Hwy. 212 to FS Rd. 1062; turn left and follow signs for two miles.

The busy center of lake activity at the Hwy. 441 crossing between Eatonton and Milledgeville features a marina, a swimming beach, campground, and **Choby's Landing** seafood restaurant, tel. (706) 453-9744, all in the shadow of a monolithic coal-fired power plant on the far shore. (The Sierra Club and other environmental advocacy groups have complained for years that heated discharges from the plant endanger local fish populations.)

For Oconee River excursions, call Gabe Gaddis at tel. (912) 453-0351.

MILLEDGEVILLE

Founded at the fall line on the Oconee River in 1803, Milledgeville served as state capital for more than 60 years, until Atlanta was named capital during Reconstruction in 1868. Union General William Sherman bivouacked here on his March to the Sea. Union officers staged a mock session of the Georgia legislature in the state capitol, and troops tossed government documents out the windows and fueled fires with Confederate money. Into the midst of this frivolity straggled a couple of emaciated Union soldiers who had escaped from the notorious Andersonville prisoner of war camp farther south. After Sherman heard their tales of conditions there, he continued his routing march with an increased vengeance.

Today the small city (population 14,000) is the home of three major state institutions: Georgia College and State University, Georgia State Military College, and Central State Hospital.

Downtown is wrapped around the Georgia College campus. Neither the circa 1950s commercial district nor the jam-packed campus is particularly scenic, but the city is nevertheless appealing with a certain hard-working, no-nonsense citizenry that loyally supports independent businesses and keeps the town from being overrun with chains. Attractive residential neighborhoods of old homes and tidy gardens line the south side of campus and downtown.

Old State Capitol

Set on the original Statehouse Square, the Old Capitol is now part of the **Georgia Military College** campus, 201 E. Greene St., tel. (912) 445-2700. The turreted Gothic three-story structure, built in 1807, is currently under renovation to house a community museum. The imposing entrance gates were constructed in the 1860s of bricks from the arsenal destroyed by Sherman's troops.

Georgia College and State University

The public liberal arts university of Georgia, Georgia College, 231 W. Hancock St., tel. (912) 445-5004, holds a few sights of interest to visitors.

The 1838 **Governor's Mansion,** 120 S. Clark St., tel. (912) 453-4545, an elegant peach-colored building that over the years was home to 10 Georgia governors, now houses the school's administration building. The mansion is open to the public for guided tours Tues.-Sat. 10 a.m.-4 p.m., Sunday 2-4 p.m.; $5 adult admission.

In historic houses opposite the mansion, the 1900 **Museum and Archives of Georgia Education,** 131 S. Clark St., tel. (912) 453-4391, displays exhibits on the development of education in Georgia, and 1910 **Blackbridge Hall** houses the art department (visitors welcome).

Tucked away in the Ina Russell Library at Georgia College, the **Flannery O'Connor Room** honors the Milledgeville native with a collection of manuscripts and memorabilia (see the special topic **Tales from the Heartland**).

For more information, see www.gscu.edu.

Lockerly Arboretum

Off Hwy. 441 south, this horticultural laboratory, tel. (912) 452-2112, showcases flora native to the Piedmont region on 45 acres of a former plantation. It's open Mon.-Fri. 8:30 a.m.-4:30 p.m. and Saturday 10 a.m.-2 p.m. for no charge.

Central State Hospital

Founded in 1842 as the Georgia Lunatic Asylum, Central State Hospital, tel. (912) 453-4371, has now grown into a major psychiatric hospital that serves 1,800 patients and employs 4,000 workers on its 1,000-acre campus off Hwy. 441. Its Victorian depot on Broad St. relates the asylum's history Wednesday 1-5 p.m. or by appointment.

Accommodations

Chain motels are strung out along Hwy. 441 around three-to-four miles north of town; including the usual Holiday Inn, Days Inn, and Comfort Inn, as well as the Jameson Inn. The **Jameson Inn,** 2251 N. Columbia St., tel. (912) 453-8471 or (800) 541-3268, is a tidy favorite, up off the road with rates from $39.

For bed and breakfast style, **Mara's Tara,** 200 W. Hancock St., tel. (912) 452-4687, offers four rooms with private baths in an 1825 Federal-style mansion within a quiet residential district not far from downtown; rates start at $65.

Food and Drink

Sit at the bar or in well-worn wooden booths at **The Brick,** 136 W. Hancock St., tel. (912) 452-0089, for pizza (the "environmentally correct" one is topped with spinach, mushrooms, onions, feta, and provolone), calzone, sandwiches, and salads. **Brewer's,** 138 W. Hancock, tel. (912) 452-5966, is also a nice place to drop in for a light lunch or coffee in a casual bistro-like setting.

Milledgeville Natural Foods, 111 W. Hancock, tel. (912) 452-6877, is a rare holistic find for fresh plates. For old-time country cooking, **Cafe South,** 132 Hardwick St., tel. (912) 452-3164, serves all the Southern staples.

Entertainment and Special Events

Even city folk from Macon drive up to **Cowboy Bill's** on Hwy. 441 north of town, tel. (912) 453-9902, to stomp to country rock bands in their huge warehouse-like dance hall. See listings in local or Macon papers.

The city's **Allied Arts, Inc.,** 201 N. Wayne St., tel. (912) 452-3950, hosts performances, including a Town-and-Gown series with Georgia College. More performances are held on campus.

The third weekend in October, the **Browns Crossing Craftsmen's Fair** presents a major regional exhibition of handmade arts and crafts along with bluegrass, blues, and folk music. It's held nine miles outside town at 400 Browns Crossing Rd. NW, on the site of an extinct cotton-ginning town.

Getting There and Around

As is true all along Hwy. 441, you will need to detour off the bypass to see the historic downtown; the route through town is along Columbia St. Southbound from Milledgeville you can blast to Macon on Hwy. 49 or detour through Gray (Hwy. 22 to Hwy. 129) to see the small town of Clinton.

Information and Services

The Milledgeville Convention and Visitors Bureau, 200 W. Hancock St., tel. (912) 452-4687 or (800) 653-1804, operates the visitor center downtown. Inquire here about trolley tours, interpreters, and guided "ghost walk."

The handy mall at 2400 N. Columbia St. has a market, a discount store, photo supplies, and a bank machine, as well as a six-plex cinema.

Clinton

Georgia's fourth largest city in 1820, Clinton was devastated by Sherman's March and never recovered. Civil War battle reenactments each April replay 1864 scenes and are best watched from the vantage point of a covered-wagon ride. What's left of the town retains a New England appearance, with many early 19th-century structures still standing.

The **Old Clinton Barbecue,** on Hwy. 129 10 miles north of Macon, tel. (912) 986-3225, serves a mean barbecued pork daily in a classic no-frills setting: concrete block building, picnic tables, sawdust on the floor. Hours are Sun.-Thurs. 10 a.m.-7 p.m. and Fri.-Sat. 10 a.m.-8 p.m.

ATLANTA TO MACON VIA I-75

The 80-mile freeway corridor between Atlanta and Macon cuts through thick Piedmont forests and offers ample services clustered at freeway exits. Beyond the freeway lie the lively parks, squares, and countryside of Middle Georgia bounded by the swells of the Ocmulgee River to the east and the Flint River to the west. Drivers considering parallel alternatives to the freeway might consider the largely four-lane Hwy. 19/41, which travels through several busy small towns, or the secluded Hwy. 23, a two-lane road through the Piedmont forest past several parks.

Jackson

Jackson is a lively, friendly town centered around its historic 1898 courthouse square. The visitor center, 206 E. 3rd St., tel. (770) 775-4839 is a block east of the square.

Fresh-Air Barbecue on Hwy. 23 a mile and a half south of town, tel. (706) 775-3182, originally opened in the 1940s. Little has changed since then. Pad through the sawdust and slide up to the long family-style tables in the wooden cabin; it's open Mon.-Thurs. 8:30 a.m.-7:30 p.m. (later Fri.-Sun.). For a backcountry adventure, seek out **Mathis Brothers Barbecue** on Barnett Bridge Rd., tel. (770) 775-6562, for barbecue turkey, chicken filet, and fish-and-chips, in addition to the down-home pork, beef, and chicken barbecue standards. It's open Thurs.-Sat. only, 11 a.m.-8 p.m. (later on weekend nights). From Hwy. 16 E, take Hwy. 36 north eight miles to Barnett Bridge Rd.; turn right at the BP station, it's a couple of miles in.

Indian Springs State Park

Indian Springs State Park, off Hwy. 42 (10 miles east of I-75 exit 67), tel. (770) 504-2277, offers a rich history, historic mansion, native-history museum, and clear springs surrounded by lush woods. The park's impressive stone masonry and craftsman carpentry are the hallmark of the Civilian Conservation Corps; annual CCC reunions are held here. The 523-acre park also features a 105-acre lake, with a swimming beach and boat rentals. Ten fully equipped two-bedroom cottages rent for $60-70. A 90-site campground charges $12-14, including water and electric hookups. For cottage or camping reservations, call (800) 864-PARK (800-864-7275). The parking fee is $2 per car, free on Wednesdays.

Indian Springs draws its name from the Creeks, who believed the spring had special healing powers. They brought their sick and dying to drink of its waters—a practice adopted by some early Europeans. Here a Creek chief built a beautiful mansion, which variously was the scene of a notorious treaty signing (1825), a Yankee Civil War encampment (1864), an exclusive spa resort (late 1800s), and finally a state park (1927).

The historic **Indian Spring Hotel** was built in 1823 by Chief William McIntosh, leader of the lower Creek Nation. Today the inn is the only Creek building that remains standing in the Southeast. Here McIntosh, despite threat of death by fellow Creeks, signed over 4.7 million acres of Creek territory to whites in the Treaty of 1825. For his betrayal, the upper Creeks executed McIntosh, scalped him, and publicly displayed the scalp on a pole. Though the treaty was soon declared illegal by the federal government, state authorities disagreed and pressed for the eventual removal of all the Creek from their ancestral homelands. Today, the county historical society charged with restoring the building opens it for special events and on weekends from April-November.

High Falls State Park

High Falls, 1.8 miles east of I-75 exit 65 at High Falls Rd., tel. (912) 993-3053, occupies the site of an early 19th-century town on the banks of the Towaliga River. The 995-acre park has a lake, swimming pool, and miniature golf. The park's 142 wooded campsites offer water and electric hookups for $14 a night; for reservations call (800) 864-PARK (800-864-7275). The parking fee is $2 per car, free on Wednesday.

The half-mile **Historic Ruins Trail** begins below the dam and leads past ruins of the once-prosperous town. An observation platform overlooks the 100-foot Towaliga River falls. The half-mile **Nature Trail** leads to the riverbank and extends into a loop through the pine-and-hardwood forest. The yellow-blazed **Non-game Trail** begins on the west side of Campground 2 and loops 2.2 miles through a more mature forest and past a lush "Fern Gully" of Christmas ferns (the fronds take the shape of stockings). Rangers lead **canoe trips** in early spring; call the park for reservations and information.

Forsyth

Downtown Forsyth revolves around an 1896 courthouse square, where old brick row-shops, cotton warehouses, an 1889 pharmacy, and an 1873 hardware store still stand. The old train depot houses a small museum operated by the local historical society, tel. (912) 994-5070; hours are Tues.-Fri. 10 a.m.-5 p.m., Saturday 10 a.m.-1 p.m. and Sunday 1-5 p.m. Its gift shop sells antiques, crafts, and souvenirs. Pick up a walking-tour map to all historic sights at the chamber of commerce, 102 E. Johnston St., tel. (912) 994-9239.

Forsyth's location at I-75 makes it a frequent pit-stop for passersby; gas stations, mini-marts, and other services are situated around the overpass. The Forsyth turnoff is also the exit for the remote region around Juliette.

Juliette

The revived town of Juliette, 18 miles east of Forsyth on Juliette Rd., was established on the banks of the Ocmulgee River at the early part of this century. Today it is best known as the home of the Whistle Stop Cafe, the movie set for the film version of Fannie Flagg's novel *Fried Green Tomatoes at the Whistle Stop Cafe.* Flagg's story is emblematic of hundreds of rural Southern towns—including Juliette—whose thriving tight-knit communities of the early 1900s fell ruin to modern times and urban flight.

After the turn of the century, Juliette supported the world's largest water-powered gristmill, five stores, schools, churches, a courthouse, post office, an active railroad depot, and surrounding farms—a life punctuated by train whistles, the hiss of steam locomotives, the clanking of Model Ts on the wooden toll bridge, and the roar of the water over the dam. The industries began to decline in the 1950s, until in 1957 the cotton mill finally closed—leaving the six-story mill in ruins and turning Juliette into a ghost town until its modest revival this past decade.

Sample fried green tomatoes at the **Whistle Stop Cafe,** at the tracks. The cafe serves Southern specialties at breakfast and lunch daily, year-round, Mon.-Sat. 8 a.m.-2 p.m., Sunday noon-7 p.m. A few shops recognizable in scenes from the movie operate around the cafe, tempting visitors with fudge, sweets, antiques, and a wine-tasting cellar.

Jarrell Plantation

Southeast of Juliette, the Jarrell Plantation, tel. (912) 986-5172, exhibits an intact working farm from the 1850s with 20 historic buildings. At the

Order fried green tomatoes at Juliette's Whistle Stop Cafe.

end of a long country drive through Middle Georgia, the living-history center makes a peaceful side trip at any time, yet it is best seen during special events, when many traditional skill and craft demonstrations bring the place to life. Jarrell hosts traditional Labor Day and July Fourth celebrations, "sheep to shawl" days, monthly quilting bees, cane-grinding and syrup-making demonstrations, and candlelit Christmas tours. It's open Tues.-Sat. 9 a.m.-5 p.m., Sunday 2-5:30 p.m. Admission is $2-4. From Atlanta, take I-75 exit 60 in Forsyth east to Juliette, cross the river, and follow signs south. From Macon, take I-75 exit 55B north to Hwy. 18 east across the river and follow signs north.

Piedmont National Wildlife Refuge

The Piedmont National Wildlife Refuge, 25 miles northeast of Macon, is restoring 35,000 acres of former cropland exhausted from 100 years of cotton farming. The second-growth preserve is still sprinkled with human history—a wisteria-laced stone chimney here, rockpiles from cleared fields there, and old fences found deep within the pine-and-hardwood forest. The refuge shelters deer, opossums, raccoons, bobcats, and 200 species of birds.

The **visitor center,** tel. (912) 986-5441, off Juliette Rd. 18 miles east of Forsyth, distributes bird lists, interpretive trail maps, tick precaution pamphlets, and hunting and fishing regulations, as well as information about the adjacent 109,000-acre Oconee National Forest. Also at the visitor center, a six-mile **nature drive** winds through the woodlands; the little-used gravel road is also suitable for hiking or mountain biking.

Two short hiking trails begin at the parking lot beyond the visitor center. The one-mile **Allison Lake Trail** loops out to a small scenic lake populated with wood ducks. The 2.5-mile loop **Woodpecker Trail** leads to a colony of red-cockaded woodpeckers a mile in. These endangered birds nest in mature loblolly pines, carving a cavity out of the heart of the tree about 15 feet above the ground. Pause at a bench in front of the white-ringed nesting trees for the chance to see the black-and-white birds with the red caps (recognizable also by their famed "Woody Woodpecker" cries).

Lake Recreation

Georgia Power operates two reservoirs in the vicinity for fishing, boating, and hunting. East of Jackson, 4,750-acre **Lake Jackson** has a 135-mile shoreline around which fishermen troll for bream, catfish, crappie, and largemouth bass. West of Juliette, 3,600-acre **Lake Juliette** cools the coal-fired power plant on-site. Fishing is allowed, and the remote lake is adjacent to the Rum Creek Wildlife Management Area for seasonal hunting.

LOUISE FOOTE

snowy egret

MACON

From ancient Mississippian chiefdoms to contemporary American rock icons, a revered history bolsters the working city of Macon. Quintessentially Southern and Georgian (you almost cannot hear the name "Macon" without hearing "Macon, Georgia"), the established city of Macon once competed with upstart Atlanta for the title of Georgia's number one metropolis. But that competition was settled more than a century ago when Atlanta was named capital and soon eclipsed its former rival with its growing national stature. Macon (population 107,000), settling

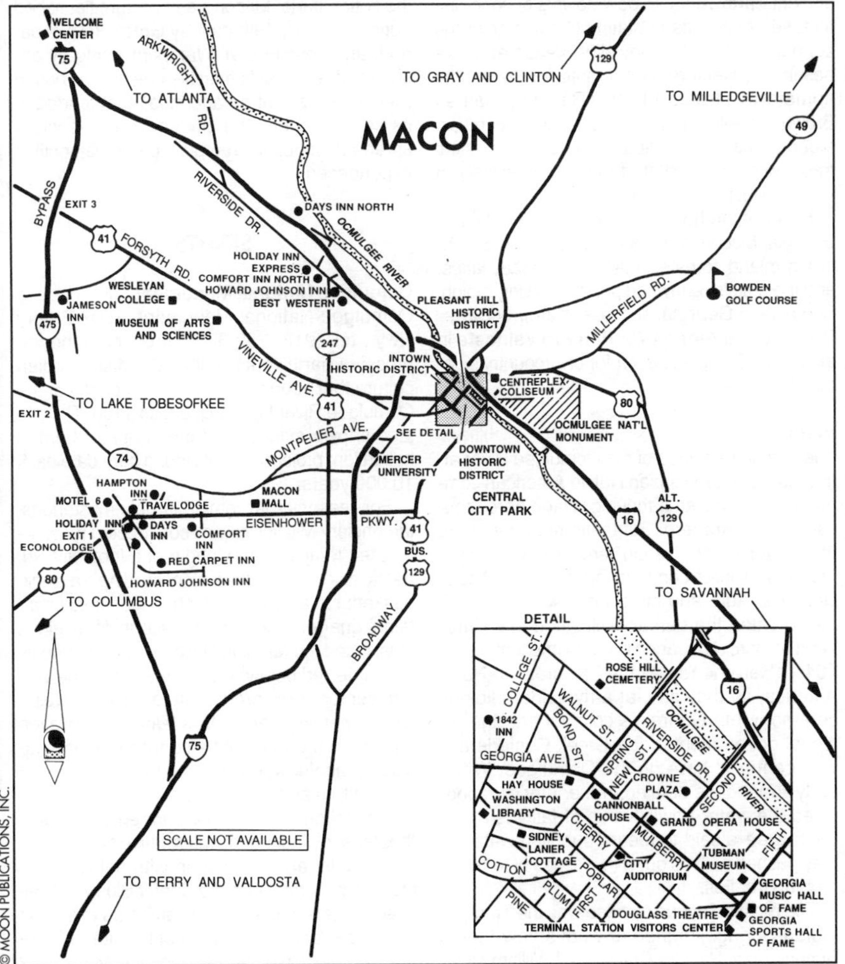

comfortably into its role as the heartland favorite, plays up its past like Atlanta plays the future.

The city is best seen in March during the Cherry Blossom Festival, when the blossoming of 200,000 cherry trees signals not only the start of spring but a weeklong celebration of local arts and community spirit. No matter when you come through, visit Ocmulgee National Monument; climb its Temple Mound, sit in the earth lodge, and linger to sense the power of magnificent ancient earthworks. In downtown's historic district, see hundreds of stately Grecian columns supporting the city's enviably preserved antebellum architecture. Get a taste for the soulful hometown streets of Otis Redding, James Brown, the Allman Brothers, and the other music legends Macon has spawned—a rich musical tradition commemorated most impressively in its new Music Hall of Fame.

Heart of the homespun region called Middle Georgia, Macon is surrounded by classic Southern farmland, forests, small towns, shady lakes, and the state's renowned peach-growing region. See **Middle Georgia,** above, and **Jimmy Carter Country** and **Along I-75: Perry to Valdosta** in the South Georgia chapter for backcountry sidetrips from Macon.

History

The rich bottomlands of the Ocmulgee River attracted the Mississippian Native American community to establish a thriving village here thousands of years ago. Fantastic monuments to their complex civilization remain at Ocmulgee Mounds. A later combination of faded Mississippian culture and indigenous woodland culture created the Lamar civilization that European explorer Hernando de Soto encountered in 1540. (Here he raised the first cross in North America, so they say, at a riverside religious ceremony.) In Georgia's colonial era, the regional government of the Creek Confederacy was centered here on the Ocmulgee. When early Americans settling in the interior recognized the water-power value of fall-line areas (*ocmulgee* is said to mean "bubbling waters"), they pushed natives out with a series of territory-robbing treaties.

The most notorious of these was the Treaty of Indian Springs, signed at what's now Indian Springs State Park by Creek Chief William McIntosh. When the Creeks discovered that McIntosh had signed their land over to the white man, they sentenced him to death and executed him before they were all exiled to Alabama. The frontier **Fort Hawkins** on the Ocmulgee, built in 1806, was Macon's first European-American settlement.

The city of Macon was established in 1823—laid out in a stately grid of broad avenues still preserved in the historic district—and thrived on the cotton trade. Macon's architecture flourished during the early 19th-century Greek Revival period, and despite Civil War skirmishing by offshoots of Sherman's march—one historic house marks the path of a cannonball that landed in its central foyer—the city escaped the widespread destruction Georgia's other major cities experienced.

SIGHTS

Ocmulgee National Monument

Ocmulgee National Monument, 1207 Emery Hwy., tel. (912) 752-8257, preserves the impressive earthworks of the late Mississippian culture that flourished here on the banks of the Ocmulgee River from A.D. 900 to 1100. The site also shows evidence of much earlier human habitation; projectile points found here date back 10,000 years.

For reasons that remain largely mysterious, the ancient Mississippians constructed massive earthen temples—the length of a football field, nearly as high as a three-story building—a single basketful at a time. The high mesas held chieftains' quarters, or were the scene of religious rituals, and the remains of high-status individuals were interred below. A short walk from the visitors center, a restored earth lodge recreates a typical meeting place. Trails lead not only to the top of the mounds, but also through the spacious graceful woodlands and along the riverside bottomland.

The visitors center houses ancient artworks, a theater showing a good interpretive film, hands-on exhibits, and a gift shop with native-made crafts. Concurrent with the Cherry Blossom Festival, rangers leads lantern-light tours to the top of Temple Mound, with tales of the site's history that will give you an appreciation for the complex

effigy figure from Ocmulgee Mounds

civilization buried underneath. At other times, the park sponsors storytelling programs (Indian ghost stories are most popular), nature walks, and basketmaking workshops. The park is open daily 9 a.m.-5 p.m. except on Christmas and New Year's Day (no admission fee).

Also administered by the Park Service, the nearby **Lamar Mound** site features a rare conical mound with a spiral mount, preserved in its natural setting. Though the property is not improved for public access, curious visitors can make arrangements with rangers to see the remote site—inquire at the visitor center. A long-debated fall-line freeway proposal threatens the sanctity of these ancient earthworks; direct objections to the State Legislature, Capitol Building, Atlanta, GA 30303.

Across Emery Hwy. stands the 1806 frontier fort blockhouse replica of **Fort Hawkins,** marking modern Macon's birthplace. After the 1805 treaty with the Creeks, the Ocmulgee River was also the Southwestern boundary of the United States, and the fort was most active in organizing resistance to Indian uprisings. The replica, constructed in 1938 by the Works Progress Administration, is maintained by the city and occasionally open to the public; call (912) 743-3401 for more information.

Historic Districts

Downtown Macon, like many such cities, suffered near abandonment as development followed the interstate highways, but recent efforts to revitalize the city's **historic commercial district** has brought new attractions, entertainment venues, cafes, restaurants, and new life downtown. The revived commercial district along Cherry St. features a broad park-like promenade of cherry trees, benches, and statues in its central median. While the diagonal route of historic Cotton Ave. was cut to expedite the town's chief export to port, today the city's financial district centers along Mulberry St.

In a compact cluster off Martin Luther King, Jr. Blvd. between the Otis Redding Memorial Bridge and the **Macon-Bibb County Convention and Visitors Bureau** in the massive Terminal Station at the foot of Cherry St. are the city's splashiest new attractions: the Georgia Music Hall of Fame, Georgia Sports Hall of Fame, and the renovated Douglass Theater.

The city's **Historic Intown** residential district centers along Georgia Ave., where the city's most impressive historic house museum—the Hay House—is located, on College St., where one of the best historic inns in Georgia is located, and around Bond St. to the crest of the hill overlooking Macon and the Ocmulgee River. City tours take visitors by the architectural highlights of this neighborhood, which can also be seen to good effect at night when many of the elegant antebellum mansions and the old shade trees surrounding them are dramatically lit.

North of downtown, the **Pleasant Hill Historic District,** bordered by College, Vineville, Rogers, and Neal Streets is the heart of Macon's historic African-American neighborhood, dating from the 1870s. Among the clapboard Victorian homes in the community is the birth home of "Little Richard" Penniman; also of note is the Otis Redding Memorial Library inside the Booker T. Washington Community Center at 391 Monroe St., and Linwood Cemetery, the final resting place of the city's most influential African-American leaders.

Georgia Music Hall of Fame

The Georgia Music Hall of Fame, 200 Martin Luther King, Jr. Blvd., tel. (912) 750-8555 or (888) 427-0257, opened in 1996 to commemorate the

THE BROTHERS AND SISTERS TOUR

The Allman Brothers Band (ABB), a trailblazing group that hit the music scene in the 1960s and came to define the era and its fans as the Southern equivalent of the West Coast's Grateful Dead, sprang to fame here at Capricorn Records in downtown Macon. Macon remains a pilgrimage site for fans ("brothers and sisters") rocked by such phenomenal ABB hits as "Whipping Post" and "In Memory of Elizabeth Reed."

The **Georgia Music Hall of Fame** (see **Sights**) screens ABB music videos and tells the story of Macon native Phil Walden, a white boy ostracized by schoolmates during segregation for his attraction to "race music," who later established Capricorn and launched the careers of the Marshall Tucker Band and Elvin Bishop in addition to the famed ABB. The former **Capricorn Records** studio at 536 Broadway now houses Phoenix studios, which uses the original Capricorn mixing board and sound booth. Nearby, the **H & H Restaurant** at 807 Forsyth St. served as a regular ABB hangout, and displays ABB photographs and memorabilia.

ABB archivist Kirk West and his wife Kirsten today maintain a small museum and store devoted to ABB paraphanalia at the "Big House"—ABB's home from 1970-72—at 2321 Vineville Ave., tel. (912) 742-5005.

Duane Allman died in a motorcycle accident October 29, 1971, at Hillcrest and Bartlett Streets, and band member Berry Oakley was killed in a motorcycle accident November 11, 1972, at Napier and Inverness Streets. The two are buried in **Rose Hill Cemetery** in side-by-side graves marked with the outline of electric guitars. ABB fans have made the site into an impromptu rock 'n' roll shrine, making pilgrimages, holding candlelight vigils, and leaving mementos, despite protests by some family members. Rose Hill gravestones served as inspiration for ABB's songs "Little Martha" and "In Memory of Elizabeth Reed," and the cemetery's Overlook Monument was pictured among other Macon scenes on the band's first album cover. (The cemetery office off Riverside Dr. distributes maps to all sites.)

The Georgia Allman Brothers Band Association (GABBA), P.O. Box 6354, Macon, GA 31208, hosts a GABBA festival as part of the city's Peach Music Festival in September. The Allman Brothers Band tour information hotline is tel. (912) 742-2888. The official ABB home page can be found at www.netspace.org/allmans.

state's rich musical heritage with a series of "audio landscapes" in the exhibition hall of a new 43,000-square-foot complex (which also houses musical archives). From Johnny Mercer, Ma Rainey, and Otis Redding to James Brown, R.E.M., the Indigo Girls, and Arrested Development, Georgia's musical stars are celebrated in a lively (but nevertheless scholarly) "Tune Town" recreating swing-era jazz streetlife, an R&B club, a country music cafe, a vintage vinyl rock-and-roll record store, a 1950s soda fountain (complimentary soft drinks), and a gospel chapel. Outrageous costumes from the 1960s and '70s, the now somewhat anachronistic genre of album cover art, and biographies of key players in Georgia music history are on display. Mini-theaters screen rare film footage, video interviews with artists and producers, and lots of foot-stomping, heart-pounding music (the 18-minute gospel film is particularly moving). The Wall of Fame showcases the achievements of 450 inductees in genres from Christian to urban, with plenty of jazz, blues, folk, and rock in between. Short of annexing a smoky roadhouse serving iced bottles of Bud from a Coleman ice chest, the museum is the best introduction to the state's contribution to contemporary music. (Director of Visitor Services, tour guide, and ardent music scholar Marty Willet can be counted among the state's natural musical resources himself.)

Live performances are occasionally held at the museum. The gift shop has an excellent and uncommon selection of recordings by 115 Georgia artists (including rare vinyl) along with books and periodicals devoted to a variety of music styles. No admission is required to visit the store. At the foot of Mulberry St. (take I-16 exit 4 south), the museum is open Mon.-Sat. 9 a.m.-5 p.m., Sunday and holidays 1-5 p.m. Admission is $7.50 adults, $5.50 students and seniors, $3.50 ages 6-16 (under six free). See also www.gamusichall.com.

Georgia Sports Hall of Fame

The state's splashy new Sports Hall of Fame, 301 Cherry St., tel. (912) 752-1585, opened in 1999 in a spacious $8.3 million building with a strikingly modern design of red brick and wrought iron intended to evoke the look of a classic old ballpark. A 14,000-square-foot exhibition hall highlights renowned Georgia college teams from UGA, Georgia Tech, Georgia State, and Valdosta as well as professional, amateur, and international sports, with impressive interactive exhibits including wheelchair basketball, video golf, and a NASCAR simulator. The Hall of Fame honors 281 inductees, including Heisman trophy winners, Olympians, and sportswriters, along with such Georgia greats as Bobby Jones, Ty Cobb, and Hank Aaron. For admission prices and hours, see www.gshf.org.

Museum of Arts and Sciences

Meet "Ziggy," a 40-million-year-old whale fossil, at the entrance to the splashy new Discovery House at the city's renowned Museum of Arts and Sciences, 4182 Forsyth Rd., tel. (912) 477-3232. Ziggy is part of an archaeological "dig" that is one of the many interactive exhibits emphasizing creativity in the arts and sciences. An artist's studio features a weaving loom, and an inventor's laboratory offers hands-on computers. The wonderland includes plenty of sheer whimsy—such as a Velcro wall, a musical staircase, and a darkened sound-filled "dream room." Walk across to the Tree House, an elevated wooden deck overlooking roaming animals. Live animal shows, science theater, and daily planetarium shows are all part of the package. The art galleries go beyond merely the visual into the realms of the aural, tactile, and fragrant.

The museum is open daily: Mon.-Thurs. and Sat. 9 a.m.-5 p.m., Friday 9 a.m.-9 p.m., Sunday 1-5 p.m. Admission is free all day Monday, and also Friday evenings after 5. All other times it's $5 adults, $2 children.

The museum also oversees Brown's Mount and Bond Swamp, an archaeologically and ecologically rich wilderness downriver, and occasionally sponsors field trips there to examine the riverine ecosystem and unusual spiral mound (where, they say, the first cross was placed in North America, by de Soto in 1540).

Tubman African American Museum

The Tubman Museum, 340 Walnut St., tel. (912) 743-8544, houses a collection of African art and colorful contemporary local arts and crafts, African-American inventions (ask about "the real McKoy"), a "Soul on Rice" exhibit on African contributions to American cuisine, a mural of African-American history and leaders (highlighting Macon's own), and exhibits that bring that history to light. (One told the remarkable story of the feisty light-skinned slave woman Ellen Craft, who made her escape to freedom disguised as a white *male* slaveholder while her husband pretended to be her slave.)

The museum is open Mon.-Sat. 9 a.m.-5 p.m., Sunday 2-5 p.m. Admission is $3 adults. The gift shop has an unusual selection of Afrocentric art, jewelry, crafts, and books.

Historic House Museums

The Italian Renaissance **Hay House,** 934 Georgia Ave., tel. (912) 742-8155, is the city's premier historic house museum, and among the finest in the region and the state. Built between 1855 and 1859, the ornate 24-room mansion show-

KAP STANN

The Hay House in downtown Macon is one of Georgia's finest house museums.

cases a ballroom, stained glass, an elevator, marble trompe l'oeil walls, and hidden passages (though docents discount the popular legend that the treasures of the Confederacy were once stored here). Restored and maintained by the Georgia Trust for Historic Preservation headquartered here, the Hay House is open Mon.-Sat. 10 a.m.-4:30 p.m., Sunday 1-4:30 p.m. (closed on major holidays). Adult admission is $6, seniors $5, students $1-2, children under six free.

The **Cannonball House,** 856 Mulberry St. (a few doors down from the Hay House), tel. (912) 745-5982, earned its nickname during the Civil War, when struck by a cannonball during the 1864 federal attack. The ball itself is among the antique furnishings displayed at the 1853 home. A small **Confederate museum** out back holds more Civil War memorabilia. The Cannonball House is open Tues.-Fri. 10 a.m.-1 p.m. and 2-4 p.m., Sat.-Sun. 1:30-4:30 p.m. Admission is $4 adults, $1 students, and 50 cents for children under 12 (under six free).

The **Sidney Lanier Cottage,** 935 High St., tel. (912) 743-3851, is the delicate, sparsely furnished home of the celebrated poet, whose two famous poems set in Georgia—*The Marshes of Glynn* and *Song of the Chattahoochee*—are memorized by the state's schoolchildren. It's open Mon.-Fri. 9 a.m.-1 p.m. and 2-4 p.m., and Saturday 9:30 a.m.-12:30 p.m. Admission is $3 adults.

Colleges and Universities

Chartered in 1836 as the first college in the world for women, private liberal-arts **Wesleyan College,** 4760 Forsyth Rd., tel. (912) 477-1110, offers degrees in 28 subjects to undergraduates. Here in 1840, Catherine Brewer Benson became the first woman in the nation to receive a college degree. The College's Midsummer Macon program hosts performances and instruction in the arts, and its fine-arts department sponsors events throughout the academic year.

The Baptist-affiliated **Mercer University,** 1400 Coleman Ave., tel. (912) 752-2650, founded in 1833, offers undergraduate and graduate programs in seven schools, including liberal arts, law, medicine, engineering, and business. Its music department holds six annual public performances.

Macon's **Georgia State Academy for the Blind,** 2895 Vineville Ave., tel. (912) 751-6083, has sensitized the community to special interests of the visually impaired; city festivals and museums frequently include touch and scent exhibits.

Macon State College, College Station Dr., tel. (912) 471-2700, is the newest college in the university system. Also within the state educational system, **Macon Technical Institute,** 3300 Macon Tech Dr., tel. (912) 757-3504, offers more than 105 programs in predominantly technical fields.

RECREATION

Spectator Sports

The minor league hometown baseball club the **Macon Braves**—farm team for the Atlanta Braves—compete in the 1929 Luther Williams Stadium in Central City Park during their April-to-August season (and some weekends in March and September). For ticket information call (912) 745-8943. General admission is $5.50, children $3.50. The field is one mile from the junction of I-75 and I-16 via the I-16 Coliseum exit 4.

The **Macon Whoopee** professional ice hockey team (Central Hockey League) compete in the Macon Coliseum from mid-October to mid-April. For ticket information call (912) 741-1000.

Municipal Parks and Recreation Facilities

The 250-acre **Central City Park** southeast of downtown, is one of the city's original parks, dating from the 1820s. It consolidates much of the city's urban recreation, including sports fields and shaded picnic spots, around a pond. Its attractive 1871 bandstand is the scene of many city festivals and performances—in the summer, you'll find concerts here most every weekend.

The public 18-hole **Bowden Golf Course,** 3111 Millerfield Rd., tel. (912) 742-1610, features a driving range, pro shop, and snack bar (greens fees about $10). Two staffed city tennis centers maintain 36 lighted tennis courts at N. Ingle Place and in Tattnall Square Park (Oglethorpe and College streets); call (912) 741-9196.

Around a 1,750-acre lake three miles west of I-475, the county-maintained **Tobesofkee Recreation Area,** 6600 Mosley Dixon Rd., tel.

(912) 474-8770, offers fishing, swimming, camping, and boating with a full-service marina. The entrance fee is $3, children under age six are free. North shore parks are accesssible from I-475 exit 2 (Hwy. 74 W).

ENTERTAINMENT

Performing Arts

Of more than a dozen performance venues around town, the **Macon Centreplex Coliseum,** 200 Coliseum Dr., tel. (912) 751-9152, packs in the largest crowds for concerts, circuses, and big-time shows. Its design mimics the shape of the nearby aboriginal mounds.

The **Grand Opera House,** 651 Mulberry St., tel. (912) 752-5460, offers Old South elegance in the beautifully restored 1884 theater from the plush-and-gilt era. Broadway shows and local events are held during its season; tours are also available by appointment.

The 1921 **Douglass Theatre,** 355 Martin Luther King, Jr. Blvd., tel. (912) 742-2000, hosted such black entertainers as Bessie Smith, Count Basie, and Dizzy Gillespie in its "Chittlin' Circuit" heyday, and launched the careers of James Brown, Little Richard, and Otis Redding in the 1960s before it was left abandoned for more than two decades. Today the 312-seat theater (newly restored in 1997) presents live performances, community events, and film series (including IMAX-format and a great laser preview featuring a soulful rendition of "Georgia on My Mind" by Ray Charles). Tours are also available Tues.-Sat. for $2 adults.

Nightlife

In a block-long strip of Cherry St. around 3rd St., several clubs present a variety of live entertainment. **The Rookery,** 543 Cherry St., tel. (912) 746-8658, features live Southern rock, jazz and blues in a comfortable tavern that draws a nicely mixed crowd from college kids to folks their parents' ages, of many shades, to seats at the friendly bar or intimate loft booths. Cover charges vary; $2 is typical.

Elizabeth Reed Music Hall, 557 Cherry St., tel. (912) 741-9792 (also called "Liz Reed's"), draws a young crowd for pool besides their bar downstairs and disco music in their upstairs dance hall. (Inquire about a new club the owner was planning to open for grown-ups in 1999). The cover charge is $3 for 21 and over, $10 for ages 18-21.

Coffee Connection, 517 Cherry St., tel. (912) 745-0070, is a tiny cafe that hosts "road warrior musicians" and poetry readings at night. A folk trio was playing political songs there on a recent visit. They're open from 2 p.m. to around midnight or later, and also offer Internet access ($3 an hour).

Judging by the motorcycles lined up out front every night, a new blues club downtown holds promise: **Riverfront Bluez,** 550 Riverside Dr., tel. (912) 741-9970, is run by the ex-wife of the Atlanta Rhythm Section's lead singer, who "really pulls in the talent" according to one local fan.

More diverse entertainment can be found outside town. Country music fans head 40 miles north to Cowboy Bill's in Milledgeville (see **Middle Georgia,** above). For traditional country, gospel, and bluegrass, **Swampland Opera House** 30 miles east in Toomsboro on Hwy. 57 at Hwy. 112, tel. (912) 628-5314 or (912) 933-5713, hosts live performances Saturdays 4-11 p.m. Fourteen miles south in Warner Robins, nightclubs at the outskirts of the air force base specialize in bikini contests and Bare-As-You-Dare nights.

Friday's *Macon Telegraph* newspaper features an "Out & About" tabloid with entertainment listings.

Festivals

The city's largest annual event, the **Cherry Blossom Festival** in late March, brings 10 days of activities that range from refined to wacky—bed races, hog-calling contests, storytelling, floats, parades, hot-air balloons, and many cultural arts performances—a major Southern-style block party that fills downtown. Rated (by those who rate festivals) as among the top 10 regional festivals in the Southeast, the Cherry Blossom fest is also one of the most scenic, as 200,000 cherry trees bloom with the light pink blossoms that herald spring.

July's **Midsummer Macon** brings three weeks of arts performances and workshops to town.

In September, the new **Peach State Music Festival** is destined to become an annual celebration of American music—the first one celebrated jazz, blues, and Latin jazz.

In October, the **Georgia State Fair,** since 1851 bringing traditional carnival games, livestock shows, and arts and crafts to Middle Georgia, is held the third week at the fairgrounds east of the city.

Each December, **White Columns and Holly, Christmas in Macon** dresses up historic homes (including ones not regularly open to the public) with period decorations and costumed docents. On New Year's Eve, **First Night Macon** is designed as a family event with performances and fireworks downtown.

ACCOMMODATIONS

Downtown

Arguably the most classic historic inn in Georgia, the **1842 Inn,** 353 College St., tel. (912) 741-1842 or (800) 336-1842, is housed in a stately Greek Revival mansion dating from (of course) 1842. It's set down a manicured lawn within a block from the Hay House and other antebellum restorations in the residential fringe of the downtown historic district. White columns, beveled glass, crystal chandeliers, oriental carpets, ceiling fans, and antique furnishings fill the two-story house; rooms in the inn's adjacent Victorian cottage across the garden courtyard are similarly period-furnished. All 22 guest rooms have private baths and such modern amenities as TVs, phones, central heating and air-conditioning. Service is impeccable but gratefully not stiff. Rates from $95 d include breakfast. Locals use the salon as a gathering spot for cocktails.

The major 16-story hotel downtown is now the **Crowne Plaza,** 108 First St., tel. (912) 746-1461, having undergone three ownership changes in less than 10 years (rates from $89). Locals mention the hotel's nightclub as a hot spot, but we must have caught it at an off night.

Off Interstate Exits

Most of the city's 4,000 hotel rooms are in chain motels clustered at interstate exits along Riverside Drive off I-75 or along Eisenhower Parkway off I-475.

Along Riverside Drive via I-75 exit 54, the older 123-room **Best Western Riverside Inn,** 2400 Riverside Dr., tel. (912) 743-6311 or (888) 454-4565, has a pool, a home-style Southern restaurant, and rates from $59 s or d. Also here is a Howard Johnson Inn, Days Inn North, Comfort Inn North, and Holiday Inn Express, with comparable rates.

Off I-475, TraveLodge, Comfort Inn, Motel 6, Econolodge, Red Carpet Inn, Super 8 ,and Hampton Inn compete for road-weary travelers along Eisenhower Parkway exit 1 near Macon Mall. Off I-475 exit 3, the Jameson Inn, tel. (912) 474-8004, is among the nicest chains, in a quieter zone with a pool and rates of $55 d including breakfast.

Camping

The county maintains two campgrounds with 120 first-come, first-served sites around a 1,750-acre lake at the **Tobesofkee Recreation Area,** three miles west of I-475, tel. (912) 474-8770. The north shore's Claystone Park campground can be reached via Hwy. 74 (I-475 exit 2), and the south shore's Arrowhead campground can be reached via Hwy. 80 (I-475 exit 1). Rates start at $10, hookups available.

FOOD AND DRINK

Downtown

A wonderful selection of Italian gourmet sandwiches, soups, and salads are served at **Cherry Corner,** 502 Cherry St. at 3rd St., tel. (912) 741-0086, along with such Italian bakery treats as exotic breads (pesto, sourdough, raisin walnut) and tempting desserts (cannoli, Napoleons, tortes). The asparagus/artichoke heart/braised fennel salad, a sandwich of wild mushrooms and provolone on ciabatta, gelati, and a selection of Italian wines are among the rare finds. It's open Mon.-Fri. 8 a.m.-8 p.m., Saturday 8 a.m.-5 p.m. (closed Sunday). They're gearing up a cybercafe adjacent (also inquire about the new Italian restaurant the owner plans to open a few blocks away).

The traditional Southern favorite is **Len Berg's** tucked away in Old Post Office Alley (follow the locals), tel. (912) 742-9255. A Macon institution since 1908, Len Berg's seats diners in well-worn wooden booths in small dark anterooms for daily specials, such as fried chicken, baked turkey with dressing, pimento-cheese sandwiches, and salmon croquettes (also sample the cream-topped macaroon pie). Hours are Mon.-Sat. 11 a.m.-2:30 p.m.

Soul food is on Mama Louise Hudson's menu at the **H & H Restaurant** at 807 Forsyth St., tel. (912) 742-9810, for full Southern breakfasts and meat-and-two plates for $5.30. A landmark haunt of the Allman Brothers, H & H has ABB photographs and memorabilia on the walls. It's open Mon.-Sat. 7 a.m.-7 p.m.

Through-travelers may want to detour to **Good to Go,** at the corner of Spring and Walnut, tel. (912) 743-4663, a great takeout eatery for generous daily specials (Friday is fried chicken, served with two vegetables for $5.25, vegetables alone for $2.99). It's five blocks across the river from I-16 exit 2.

Off Interstate Exits

Macon's favorite barbecue joints, readily accessible off interstate exits, make decent local alternatives to the standard fast food choices. Off I-75, **Fincher's,** 3947 Houston Ave., tel. (912) 788-1900, claims distinction as the only barbecue ever shot into space—astronaut Sonny Carter (who trained at Robins AFB south of town) took some Fincher's barbecue with him aboard the space shuttle. Fincher's is open Mon.-Sat. 9 a.m.-11 p.m. and Sunday 10 a.m.-10 p.m. From I-75 exit 49B, go east, take a left at the first traffic light to Fincher's on the left. Also off I-75, the sentimental favorite is **Fresh-Air,** 3076 Riverside Dr., tel. (912) 477-7229 (though loyalists drive an hour north to its original Jackson location; see **Middle Georgia,** above). Right off I-16 exit 4, you can't beat the barbecue at **Satterfield's** for convenience.

Off I-475 exit 1, find a food court and Morrison's Cafeteria at Macon Mall on Eisenhower Parkway. The **State Farmers Market** is a few blocks east of the mall.

GETTING THERE AND AROUND

By Air

Macon's **Lewis B. Wilson Airport** is 10 miles south of town at 1000 Terminal Dr., tel. (912) 788-3760. From here, **Atlantic Southeast Airlines,** tel. (912) 788-6310 or (800) 282-3424, connects with Delta and flies daily to Atlanta, yet most Macon-bound air travelers simply fly into Atlanta's Hartsfield Airport and take **Groome Transportation,** tel. (912) 471-1616, for the hour-and-a-quarter drive to Macon.

By Bus

Greyhound bus service connects with major cities from its station at 65 Spring St., tel. (912) 743-5411 (where Macon native "Little Richard" Penniman wrote "Tutti Frutti" while washing dishes before he took the bus out to stardom). In temperate weather, you could walk the five long blocks to the Music Hall of Fame and other downtown sights from here.

Local bus service is provided by the **Macon-Bibb County Transit Authority,** tel. (912) 746-1318.

By Car

Three interstate freeways provide easy access to Macon: I-75 runs north-to-south through town, I-475 skirts it to the west, and I-16 shoots off east to Savannah. To get downtown, take I-16's Coliseum Dr. exit 4, south across the Otis Redding Bridge over the Ocmulgee River to reach the Music Hall of Fame, Terminal Station visitors center, and other downtown sights. Parking is rarely a problem.

INFORMATION AND SERVICES

Information and Tours

The **Macon-Bibb County Convention and Visitors Bureau (CVB),** can be reached by post, phone, fax, e-mail, or via the Internet. Contact the CVB at 200 Cherry St., Macon, GA 31201, tel. (912) 743-3401 or (800) 768-3401, fax (912) 745-2022, maconcvb@maconga.org; also see www.maconga.org.

Two welcome centers distribute city maps and information. The **I-75 Welcome Center** is within the rest area just above the northern split of I-75 and I-475 (open daily 9 a.m.-5:30 p.m.). The downtown **Terminal Station** welcome center is at the foot of Cherry St. off 5th St. Here within the historic railway terminal, the center shows a short video on the city's history and highlights, and distributes city maps and information, including self-guided walking-tour and driving-tour maps and an African-American heritage brochure. It's open Mon.-Sat. 9 a.m.-5:30 p.m.

They also sponsor **Sidney's Tours** (named for native Georgian poet Sidney Lanier), two-hour guided bus tours of historic districts that also take in the city's three house museums. Tours depart Mon.-Sat. at 10 a.m. and 2 p.m. from Terminal Station. Contact the CVB at the numbers above for reservations.

Shopping

Among the most distinctive shops downtown, the **Karsten-Denson Co.** on 3rd St. at Poplar, restores an evocative old hardware store and now stocks outfitting gear (from hiking boots to canoes) and garden ornaments (from purple plastic gourd birdhouses for $5.50 to red porch rockers for $119) in addition to seed-by-the-scoop sold out of galvanized tin buckets. It's open Mon.-Fri. 8:30 a.m.-5:30 p.m., Sat. 8:30 a.m.-1 p.m. Photographers from across the country send equipment to **Coke's Camera Center,** 735 Cherry St., tel. (912) 746-3286 for repair.

Karla's Shoe Boutique on the corner of Cherry and 2nd Streets is operated by Zelma and Karla Redding, the widow and daughter, respectively, of famed musical legend Otis Redding.

Macon Mall, 3661 Eisenhower Pkwy. (a mile east of I-475 exit 1) features more than 200 shops, including the anchor department stores Rich's and Sears, along with a nine-screen cinema, food court, and Morrison's Cafeteria.

Bookstores

Downtown, **Golden Bough,** 371 Cotton Ave. at Cherry St., tel. (912) 744-2446, is a wonderful bookstore with used and rare books, Middle Georgia titles and authors, and meditative and New Age music in its reading room (open Tues.-Sat. 10 a.m.-6 p.m.). Off I-75 exit 55A, **Barnes & Noble Booksellers,** tel. (912) 757-2216, is in the North Park Shopping Center on Tom Hill Sr. Blvd. off Northside Dr. **Books-A-Million,** 3760 Eisenhower Pkwy, tel. (912) 785-1070, is near Macon Mall.

Emergencies

In an emergency, dial 911. For medical attention, call the **Medical Center of Central Georgia,** 777 Hemlock St., at (912) 633-1000.

VICINITY OF MACON

Warner-Robins

Fourteen miles south of Macon on the Robins Air Force Base, the **Museum of Aviation** off I-75 exit 45, tel. (912) 926-6870, displays scores of historic aircraft dating from WW I. It also exhibits military memorabilia and presents audiovisual programs on the history of air power. It's open 10 a.m.-5 p.m. daily except major holidays, no charge.

PINE MOUNTAIN AND VICINITY

Pine Mountain is the southernmost rise on the Piedmont Plateau, and a welcome landmark to altitude-seeking flatlanders. Northbound travelers will see Pine Mountain's wide ridge looming on the horizon like a huge temple mound.

Franklin Delano Roosevelt was the area's most famous part-time resident, drawn to the therapeutic mineral waters on Pine Mountain's eastern slope. His Little White House and the charming town of Warm Springs still evoke his memory. The city of Pine Mountain, at the western end of the ridge, and Callaway Gardens similarly recall this earlier time—the days before air-conditioning—when walking in a landscaped Southern garden or fishing in a quiet pond was all you could want out of a vacation. Despite modern conveniences and novel attractions, the beauty of Pine Mountain today remains in that simplicity. Hikers and backpackers find the 23-mile Pine Mountain Trail the greatest highland hike this side of North Georgia, and a ridgetop state park squirrels away CCC-era cabins around a wooded lake.

ALONG STATE HIGHWAY 85

State Highway 85—not to be confused with I-85—meanders through a scenic stretch of the eastern Piedmont from Atlanta to Warm Springs, past pasturelands and cornfields, gristmills and pit barbecues. Outside Atlanta, the route is largely a seven-lane expanse of urban sprawl, but it thins to a two-lane country highway once you hit the old downtown in Fayetteville.

In the tiny town of **Senoia,** tucked a mile west of Hwy. 85, the **Culpepper House Bed and Breakfast,** 35 Broad St., tel. (770) 599-8182, offers a romantic getaway less than an hour from Atlanta. The beautifully restored two-story yellow clapboard house features a wide veranda custom made for porch-rocking. Or try the **Veranda,** 252 Seavy St., tel. (770) 599-3905, a historic hotel that also features a restaurant (no alcohol). Room rates at both places start around $80 per couple including breakfast.

If you can give up a long read on the porch, you can walk or bike to the local feed-and-tack or to a couple of antique shops in downtown Senoia. There's also a **Buggy Shop Museum** on Main St., tel. (770) 599-1222 (open weekends only 9 a.m.-6 p.m.), and you can pick up a self-guided driving-tour map of historic local homes and sites at City Hall or the local library.

The aptly named **Cross Road Restaurant,** where Hwy. 85 and Hwy. 6 meet in Senoia, tel. (770) 599-3003, serves Southern breakfasts from 6 a.m., a reasonable midday lunch buffet, and daily specials until 8 p.m.

KAP STANN

Rockin' away the days of summer at Culpepper House, Senoia.

Down Hwy. 85 South a lick, the town of **Gay** hosts a Cotton-Pickin' County Fair at an old cotton-ginning complex the first weekend each May and October.

In **Woodbury,** Hwy. 85S splits into Highway 85E to Manchester and Highway 85W to Warm Springs. Pine Mountain-bound travelers veer to the right toward Warm Springs, past sheep farms, tidy ranch houses, and handmade signs advertising Rabbits for Sale.

ALONG I-85

The interstate route from Atlanta to Columbus is largely a monotonous corridor of four-lane blacktop and kudzu-lined forest straddling a region between the Flint and Chattahoochee Rivers.

A stop for barbecue at a local culinary landmark can break up a trip to Pine Mountain or Columbus. In operation since 1926, **Sprayberry's Restaurant** is well-known for its hickory-smoked barbecue pork or beef slathered with a vinegar-based sauce ("Double Aristocratic" plates run around $8). There are two locations: the newer one on Hwy. 34 right off I-85 exit 9, tel. (770) 253-5080, open Mon.-Sat. 7 a.m.-9 p.m. The original location is north of town at 229 Jackson St. (where Hwy. 70 and Hwy. 29 meet), tel. (770) 253-4421, open Mon.-Sat. 10:30 a.m.-9 p.m. The drive through town passes the attractive historic residential and commercial districts of downtown Newnan, and you may be drawn in by several inviting antique shops and flea markets along the way.

If you're headed to Pine Mountain, you can drop down Hwy. 27A at **Moreland,** the birthplace of two of Georgia's most celebrated writers. Readers captivated by such works as *God's Little Acre* and *Tobacco Road* may pay homage at the birthplace of author Erskine Caldwell (1903-1987), whose graphic tales of rural life scandalized the South in their time (they're *still* pretty racy!). His restored birth home, called **The Little Manse,** in the Moreland town square, tel. (770) 251-4438, serves as a small museum, open Sat.-Sun. 1-4 p.m. or by appointment. There's an old mill next door open on weekends. Another native son, Lewis Grizzard, was a beloved and local humorist who gained national notoriety with his collections of essays, such as *Aim Low Boys, They're Riding Shetland Ponies.* (Unfortunately, his romantic career was less successful—inspiring the local bumper sticker "Honk If You've Been Married to Lewis Grizzard!") A small museum at 27 Main St., tel. (770) 304-1490, commemorates his work; it's open Saturday 10 a.m.-4:30 p.m. and Sunday 1-4:30 p.m.

La Grange

At the Alabama frontier, the county seat of La Grange is an isolated outpost of perhaps surprising sophistication. The town of 26,000 has two art museums and retains a well-preserved historic courthouse square downtown set around a statue of Lafayette, for whose home in France the town was named (*La Grange* means "The Barn" in French). Surrounding the square, attractive residential districts of 19th-century homes are set along shady lanes of towering magnolias.

At La Grange College, 601 Broad St., tel. (706) 882-2911, a private Methodist school dating back to 1831, the **Lamar Dodd Art Center,** tel. (706) 882-2911, exhibits paintings in its modern gallery by the Georgia artist for whom the center is named.

The **Chattahoochee Valley Art Museum,** 112 Hines St., tel. (706) 882-3267, houses an impressive permanent collection of more than 400 works and intriguing traveling exhibits within a renovated county jail from the Victorian era. Its hours are Mon.-Fri. 9 a.m.-5 p.m., Saturday 9 a.m.-1 p.m. (and open Tuesday evenings till 8 p.m.). The annual La Grange Arts Festival in spring further promotes the visual arts and local artist community.

The local historic house museum is named **Bellevue,** 204 Ben Hill St., tel. (706) 884-1832, a stately 1850s Greek Revival mansion adorned with Ionic columns, porticos, and balconies (open Tues.-Sat. from 10 a.m.-noon and 2-5 p.m.). Admission is $4 adults.

The local chamber of commerce, 111 Bull St., tel. (706) 884-8671, distributes information about the town and nearby West Point Lake.

West Point Lake

Five miles north of La Grange, this 25,900-acre impoundment of the Chattahoochee River at the Georgia-Alabama border is maintained by the

U.S. Army Corps of Engineers (COE). The COE **Visitor Center** near the stateline dam off US 29, tel. (706) 645-2937, distributes maps to 33 developed areas for swimming, fishing, boating, and camping ($12-16, hookups available).

The COE **Earl Cook Recreational Area** offers a day-use beach with bathhouse and nature trails; $1 per person or $3 per carload. Take Hwy. 29 south of La Grange about five miles and go north on Lower Glass Bridge Rd. to the water.

The **Highland Marina** resort, 1000 Seminole Rd. off Hwy. 109, tel. (706) 882-3437, offers boat, water-ski, and inner tube rentals, along with a full-service marina, waterfront restaurant, campground, and cabin rental. All 33 modest, fully equipped cabins are on the water (rates from $55, depending on size).

CITY OF PINE MOUNTAIN

The welcoming little town of Pine Mountain, nestled at the eastern slope of its namesake rise, centers around the old City Hall downtown. The **Welcome Center** here at 101 Broad St., tel. (706) 663-4000 or (800) 441-3502, distributes local maps and directories to local dining, lodging, and recreation (open daily). A quaint collection of shops, galleries, and cafes (with thankfully few chains) make it a nice town to explore. Its most popular attractions are nearby Callaway Gardens and FDR State Park (see more on both below).

Pine Mountain is an hour and a half south of Atlanta. Take I-85 and drop down to two-lane Hwy. 27A at Newnan, to GA 18.

Wild Animal Park

At the Wild Animal Park, 1300 Oak Grove Rd., tel. (706) 663-8744 or (800) 367-2751, a four-mile safari ride may reveal exotic animals from six continents, including zebras, ostriches, and rhinos. Visitors drive through the 500-acre park themselves or take a guided tour bus. An alligator pit, serpentorium, petting zoo, concession stand, and hayride are part of the package. Tickets are $12 for adults, $9 for children ages three to nine. It opens daily at 10 a.m.; find it off Hwy. 27 three miles north of town.

Accommodations and Camping

There are three modest, well-kept motels in town. The 13-room **White Columns Inn,** 19727 Hwy. 27, tel. (706) 663-2312, is invitingly tucked away in quiet woods, but still within a walk from some shops (from $35 winter). The tidy old-fashioned **Pine Mountain Motel,** Hwy. 27, tel. (706) 663-2306, is right downtown, closer to all the action (from $40). The **Fireside Inn,** tel. (706) 663-4141, is the least attractive of the three, standing between an auto parts store and a gas station, but it's decent, has a pool, and is also downtown (from $40). Rates climb in summer. More area lodging is available at the Callaway Gardens resort; cottage rental and camping is found at **FDR State Park,** below.

Pine Mountain Campground, Hwy. 27, tel. (706) 663-4329, is little more than a lot in a pasture right along the highway but is nevertheless convenient and welcoming and has a pool. For scenery, camp at the state park.

Food and Drink

McGuire's, Hwy. 27, tel. (706) 663-2640, offers down-home Southern breakfasts (all day) and buffets at lunch and dinner (as well as a la carte items) in a casual country cabin right downtown. Buffets cost from $7 lunch, more on all-you-can eat barbecue rib and seafood buffet nights (presently Thursday and Friday, respectively), and come with quart-sized glasses of bottomless sweet tea (no alcohol). It's open daily 6 a.m.-9 p.m.

The comfortably elegant **Bon Cuisine,** 113 Broad St., tel. (706) 663-2019, is a wonderful little restaurant squirreled away downtown. They serve fresh and healthy entrees of grilled chicken, pasta plates, steaks, and seafood. Lunch is served Tues.-Fri. 11 a.m.-2 p.m. (all around $6), dinner Tues.-Sat. from 5:30 p.m. (from $17, reservations recommended, bring your own bottle.)

Moe's and Joe's Sportsman's Grill, Hwy. 27 at Hwy. 354, tel. (706) 663-8064, is a friendly pub for burgers, sandwiches, and other American standards, patio tables too.

Gourmet coffee and treats are served in the back of **Gallery 111,** 155 Main St., tel. (706) 663-2782, which also displays a great collection of whimsical and colorful folk arts and crafts (closed Monday).

CALLAWAY GARDENS

Callaway Gardens, Hwy. 27, tel. (706) 663-2281 or (800) 225-5292, is a private resort like no other. Callaway encompasses 2,500 acres of blooming woodlands and natural attractions that make the most of the beauty of lush Southern landscapes. Outdoor recreation is particularly compelling in this setting, and many visitors come for the day to hike or bike along flower-rimmed trails, golf at four manicured courses, play tennis, water-ski, and sunbathe and swim at the mile-long lakefront beach. Guests may also stay overnight at several resort lodges (see below). Interestingly, the crowd is more racially mixed than one might expect of such a traditional Southern upmarket resort, but pretty homogeneous class-wise. The standard day-use gate admission is $10 per adult and $5 per child (ages 6-12); most sights are free with this gate fee, additional recreational and special event fees may apply.

Sights

Callaway's most outstanding and unusual attraction is the **Cecil B. Day Butterfly Center,** a 7,000-square-foot towering glass atrium filled with lush tropical plants and a thousand free-flying butterflies. Fifty colorful varieties from around the world, some as big as small birds, swoop overhead and frequently alight on visitors (the experience will likely dazzle, but may overwhelm small children). Surrounding outside gardens are designed to attract native butterflies.

The horticulturally inclined will want to walk through the 20,000-square-foot **John A. Sibley Horticultural Center** for an introduction to native plants, or around the vegetable garden and Victory Garden (scene of the PBS television show by the same name). Kids enjoy the whimsical topiary garden—here such recognizable Wonderland characters as the Mad Hatter and the White Rabbit take perfect shape in ivy. The streamside **Memorial Chapel,** patterned after 16th-century wayside chapels, is an ideal spot for quiet meditation.

Daily programs include guided tours and walks, storytelling, and concerts. Major seasonal programs include a spring festival in March or April to coincide with the blooming peak, an acrobatic circus in summer, an autumn festival in October, and a "Fantasy in Lights" Christmas show in December. The map guides visitors to plants in bloom month-by-month.

Recreation

The 65-acre Robin Lake is the center of much recreation. Here a mile-long lifeguard-staffed **beach** ("largest inland man-made white sand beach in the world," so they say) attracts swimmers and sunbathers. Pedalboats and a frequent steamboat tour are free with gate admission; fishing, canoe rental, and water-skiing are also available for additional fees.

A 7.5-mile **bike trail** winds through the beautiful woodlands. A ferry near the midpoint of the trail transports riders across Mountain Creek Lake. The bike barn rents cruisers, mountain bikes, and tandems, for fees starting at $5 an hour (helmets also available). Miles of paved **hiking trails** weave through the gardens.

Four manicured golf courses carry green fees ranging from $32 (walking) at the Sky View course to $100 (including cart) at the Mountain View course. Tennis and racquetball fees start at $5 per person (doubles).

Lodging and Dining

Callaway provides lodging in its modern 349-room **Callaway Gardens Inn,** on Hwy. 27, tel. (800) 225-5292, in nearby townhouses, or in detached cottages tucked away in the woods. Rates start around $96 a night, but there are many combination recreation and weekend package rates available.

Within the Inn (no gate fee required), the **Georgia Room** offers the most deluxe and formal setting (dinner only, dress code, entrees from $18). The **Plantation Room** here serves generous, bottomless Southern buffet (breakfast $9, lunch $10, dinner $17, seafood Friday $20, Sunday brunch $16, kids 6-12 pay half price, no charge under six). Beachgoers watching their budgets and diet can bring a picnic to avoid fairly high-priced fast food at the beach pavilion.

Most accessible and casual is Callaway's mountaintop **Country Kitchen,** on Hwy. 27 at Hwy. 190, which serves Southern breakfasts (all day, from $4), classic country meat-and-two platters for lunch and dinner (from $7), and a kid's menu, all with a panoramic view. Given the menu variety and long hours, it's always a good sure thing: it's open daily 7 a.m.-9 p.m. year-round. The country store within sells a wonderful selection of foodstuffs (speckled grits, muscadine jams, pickled okra, relishes), distinctive garden ornaments, crafts, and jewelry, and great toys emphasizing outdoor activities (kites, bug boxes, ribbon wands).

WARM SPRINGS AND VICINITY

The 1930s set the tone for Warm Springs and Pine Mountain—thanks to the area's famous former part-time resident, Franklin Delano Roosevelt. The thermal waters of Warm Springs drew the polio-stricken FDR for their therapeutic value (as they had drawn the Creeks for centuries), and his love for the area led him to establish a presidential hideaway in these woods. The "Little White House" now stands as a memorial as enchanting and powerful as the man himself. Today, to stay in a Civilian Conservation Corps (CCC)-built log cabin at FDR State Park, cruise Warm Springs' two-square-block downtown and nearby pools, tour FDR's cottage, and stroll among the

CHRIS PARMENTER

Franklin Delano Roosevelt (1882-1945), 32nd President

traditional flowering gardens at neighboring Callaway Gardens, is to be transported back to prewar days of fedoras, rumble seats, the wireless, and an era of simple pleasures.

Today the Roosevelt Warm Springs Institute for Rehabilitation continues the therapeutic treatments that began with the outdoor mineral baths FDR frequented from 1924 until his death in 1945 (the baths on Hwy. 27A have now been restored and were rededicated with much fanfare by President Clinton among many other dignitaries in 1995).

The old clapboard depot in the center of town where FDR would arrive now serves as a **welcome center,** tel. (706) 655-3322 or (800) 337-1927. A vintage passenger rail car is now a gift shop. Along Main St., dozens of tiny shops and cafes invite visitors to poke around—particularly in the appealing alleyway courtyard that's hidden behind the storefronts (find restrooms here too).

Little White House

This state historic site, on Hwy. 85W a quarter mile from the depot, tel. (706) 655-5870, stands as a powerful memorial to Franklin Delano Roosevelt, who as governor of New York and frequent visitor to the therapeutic waters of Warm Springs, had the house built in 1932. After FDR was elected president, the house was inaugurated as the "Little White House." The site serves as an intimate tribute to the complex man who led the U.S. through a rocky stretch of its history and to his courageous triumph over disability.

The simple six-room house itself can be appreciated for its clean symmetry and spare craftsmen design. FDR died of a cerebral hemorrhage here in 1945—the portrait he was posing for remains incomplete, propped on its easel. The garage houses his specially adapted 1938 roadsters, one with the license plate "FDR 1."

A path lined with stones from all 50 states leads uphill to the museum, where a short biographical film features plenty of old newsreel footage. Exhibits on FDR's life and legacy include buttons and banners bearing National Recovery Administration (NRA), CCC, and Works Progress Administration (WPA), and other "alphabet soup" insignia, along with such artifacts as FDR vintage antiques, and a collection of gift canes from around the world.

The train depot where FDR used to arrive is now the Warm Springs Welcome Center.

KAP STANN

Special commemorative events are held on FDR's birthday (January 30), Franklin and Eleanor's wedding anniversary (March 17), on Fala Day in November (Fala was FDR's cherished lap dog), and around Thanksgiving (which FDR had made into a community tradition). Understandably, the park is extraordinarily accommodating to the needs of visitors with disabilities—wheelchairs and electric carts are available on request for no charge. The visitor center sells an unusual collection of New Deal-era memorabilia.

Admission is $4 adults, $2 for children ages 6-18. Hours are daily 9 a.m.-5 p.m.; the last tour is at 4 p.m.

Accommodations and Food

In the center of town, the four-story 1907 **Hotel Warm Springs,** 17 Broad St., tel. (706) 655-2114 or (800) 366-7616, captures the FDR era perfectly with handsome but modest rooms outfitted with cast-iron beds, chenille coverlets, ceiling fans, and tiny porcelain sinks in the corner of the room (rates from $50). There's also a new motel presently under construction outside town.

Feast on generous Southern buffets at the **Bulloch House,** Hwy. 27A, tel. (706) 655-9068, as well as such entrees as ribeye steak and catfish. They serve lunch daily, and dinner on Friday and Saturday nights. The **Victorian Tea Room** on Broad St., tel. (706) 655-2319, also serves lunch buffets (open daily). In the trailer around the corner from the main drag, **Mac's Barbecue,** Hwy. 27A, tel. (706) 655-2472, serves good quick barbecue plates and snacks daily 11 a.m.-8 p.m.

Recreation

Some of the nicest stretches of the Flint River are east of Warm Springs, accessible off Hwy. 36 between Woodland and Thomaston. Here you'll find the **Flint River Outdoor Center,** tel. (706) 647-2633, an outpost that organizes canoeing, rafting, and tubing adventures on the river's Class I-III rapids. Shuttle service, rentals, camping, and customized excursions are available.

To romp in the shoals and soak in a cool "natural jacuzzi," follow signs from Hwy. 36 to **Big Lazer Creek** (LIZA Creek) and head for the falls. For more information about fishing in the wildlife preserve lake there, call (912) 995-4486.

FRANKLIN D. ROOSEVELT STATE PARK

The 10,000-acre FDR State Park, tel. (706) 663-4858, sits atop Pine Mountain, offering fine views of the surrounding countryside. A stone CCC-built **visitor center and overlook** sits atop the scenic ridge route that connects with downtown Pine Mountain to the west and Warm Springs to the east (Hwy. 190). The parking fee is $2 per car, free on Wednesdays.

Hiking and Backpacking

The 23-mile **Pine Mountain Trail** starts at the Callaway Gardens Country Store at the intersection of Hwy. 27 and Hwy. 190 and weaves east up and over the wooded ridge to trail's end at a radio tower parking area on Hwy. 85W.

The trail gets better the farther east you go; buy trail maps at the FDR State Park visitor center.

Off the backpacking trail, the beautiful six-mile **Wolfden Loop** from the eastern terminus passes through a fern-lined forest of mountain laurel and provides views of scenic waterfalls and beaver dams along Wolfden Branch. The 4.3-mile **Dowdell's Knob Loop** takes hikers to FDR's favorite picnic spot and overlook—park at the Dowdell's Knob spur road off Hwy. 190 and follow the white-blazed trail.

Other Recreation

Roosevelt Riding Stables, on King's Gap Rd. off Hwy. 354, tel. (706) 628-4533, a private concession within the park, takes riders out for short trips, longer cookout rides, or overnight adventures.

Other park facilities include a **swimming pool** (free for overnighters, $2-3 for day use) and two small lakes for fishing and pedalboating.

Accommodations and Camping

Twenty-one fully equipped cottages, in scenic locations on lakeview hills or on the panoramic ridge, make great hideaways. Many are the original log cabins with stone chimneys constructed by FDR's New Deal CCC. The cottages rent from $50 for a one-bedroom weeknights to $80 for a three-bedroom on weekends. Spacious wooded sites at a 140-site **campground** go for $14 a night, including water and electric hookups. For reservations, call (800) 864-PARK (800-864-7275).

COLUMBUS

The second-largest city in the state (population 300,000), Columbus sits at the banks of the Chattahoochee River on Georgia's "West Coast" border with Alabama. Here the Chattahoochee drops 125 feet within two and a half miles, which has sculpted the region's history as an ancient native settlement, final city in the 13 original colonies, Civil War target, and Southern mill town. Columbus today makes the most of this riverine heritage with a renovated historic district behind an attractive new Riverwalk.

Columbus is home to Columbus State University and the largest infantry training center in the world at Fort Benning (and its notorious School of the Americas). It's also the birthplace of several Southern legends—Coca-Cola entrepreneur Robert F. Woodruff, the "Mother of the Blues" Ma Rainey, and author Carson McCullers, whose novels *The Heart Is a Lonely Hunter* and *Member of the Wedding* provide moving personal vignettes of small-town Southern life in towns much like Columbus once was.

Columbus lies at the end of I-185, which deadends at Fort Benning. Several historical, cultural, and natural attractions can be found a short day trip from Columbus (see **Pine Mountain and Vicinity,** above, and **Jimmy Carter Country,** under South Georgia).

History

Southeastern natives had a long history along the navigable lengths of the Chattahoochee—excavations in the river valley have uncovered Archaic period habitation from 5000 B.C. The Creek dominated several native groups in the area around "Bull Creek" when the first Europeans appeared on the scene. From a trading post the town developed into the farthest west frontier of colonial America, though the city wasn't chartered until 1828. Here industry flourished on fall-line water power, and when the Civil War broke out, the factories converted to weapons production.

Untouched by the war until 1865, Columbus was finally attacked by Union General James H. Wilson's troops (remembered locally as "Wilson's raiders") in the last land battle of the Civil War on April 16, 1865. Wilson had not yet heard of Lee's surrender at Appomattox a week earlier, and he left the city in ruins after setting fire to almost all its industry (a blessing in disguise, as the modernized rebuilt mills propelled economic recovery). Textile mills flourished, and traditional water power was later converted into hydroelectricity.

SIGHTS

Riverwalk

The 12-mile Riverwalk offers a scenic waterfront promenade along the clay-stained Chattahoochee from the historic district south to Fort Benning's National Infantry Museum at the trail's

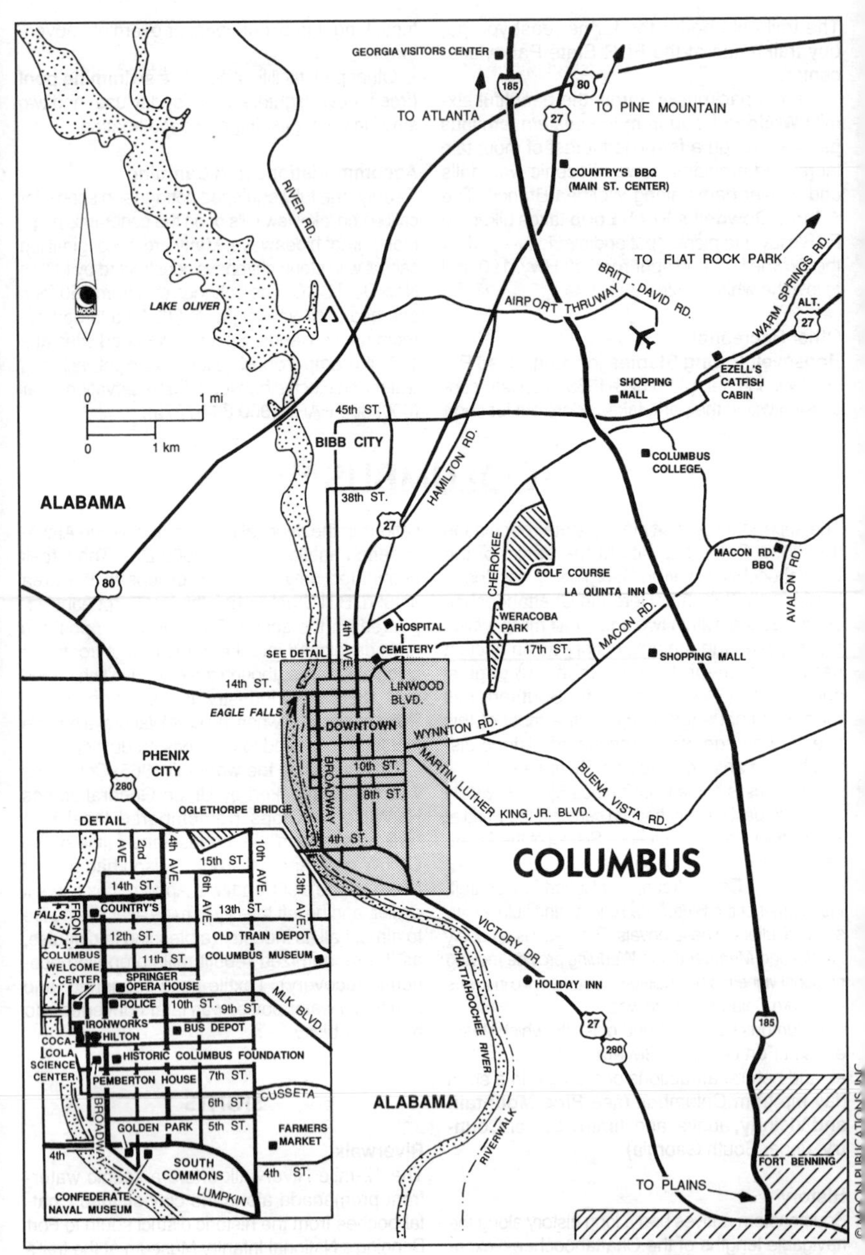
GEORGIA VISITORS CENTER
185
80
TO ATLANTA
TO PINE MOUNTAIN
27
COUNTRY'S BBQ
(MAIN ST. CENTER)
RIVER RD.
TO FLAT ROCK PARK
WARM SPRINGS RD.
BRITT - DAVID RD.
AIRPORT THRUWAY
ALT.
27
LAKE OLIVER
MOON
EZELL'S
CATFISH
CABIN
SHOPPING
MALL
0
1 mi
1 km
45th ST.
BIBB CITY
HAMILTON RD.
COLUMBUS
COLLEGE
ALABAMA
38th ST.
27
CHEROKEE
MACON RD.
BBQ
AVALON RD.
80
GOLF COURSE
LA QUINTA INN
WERACOBA
PARK
4th
AVE.
HOSPITAL
MACON RD.
SEE DETAIL
CEMETERY
17th ST.
SHOPPING MALL
14th ST.
LINWOOD
BLVD.
EAGLE FALLS
DOWNTOWN
WYNNTON RD.
PHENIX
CITY
10th ST.
BROADWAY
MARTIN LUTHER KING, JR. BLVD.
BUENA VISTA RD.
280
8th ST.
OGLETHORPE BRIDGE
DETAIL
4th ST.
COLUMBUS
2nd
AVE.
4th
AVE.
10th
AVE.
15th ST.
6th
AVE.
13th
AVE.
14th ST.
13th ST.
FALLS
FRONT
COUNTRY'S
12th ST.
OLD TRAIN DEPOT
VICTORY DR.
COLUMBUS
WELCOME
CENTER
11th ST.
COLUMBUS MUSEUM
SPRINGER
OPERA HOUSE
CHATTAHOOCHEE RIVER
HOLIDAY INN
POLICE
10th ST.
9th ST.
MLK BLVD.
IRONWORKS
HILTON
BUS DEPOT
27
185
COCA-
COLA
SCIENCE
CENTER
HISTORIC COLUMBUS FOUNDATION
280
PEMBERTON HOUSE
7th ST.
CUSSETA
6th ST.
ALABAMA
BROADWAY
GOLDEN PARK
5th ST.
FARMERS
MARKET
RIVERWALK
4th
SOUTH
COMMONS
4th ST.
FORT BENNING
LUMPKIN
CONFEDERATE
NAVAL MUSEUM
TO PLAINS
© MOON PUBLICATIONS, INC.

end (see below). Studded with fountains and monuments and with nice views of the falls, old brick mills, Ironworks, and arched bridges, the downtown Riverwalk makes a scenic place to stroll, bike, or in-line skate. Future plans call for extending the path northward towards Lake Oliver.

An 1880s riverboat takes visitors on river cruises (call 706-324-4499). Bike rentals are set up at a small kiosk near the dock (call 706-322-2802 for schedule). The city's convention and visitors bureau is across from the Riverwalk at 1000 Bay Ave.

Historic Districts

On a bluff at the water's edge, the city's 30-block historic commercial district features several newly renovated blocks of Broad St. on both sides of a nicely landscaped central strip. New businesses are gaining a foothold after years of flight and drawing more people downtown after hours to restaurants and clubs. The compact district is easily toured on foot or bike.

The elegant 1871 **Springer Opera House,** 103 10th St., tel. (706) 327-3688, is the centerpiece of the historic district. Officially designated the "State Theater of Georgia," the intimate theater continues to hold performances and contains a small museum highlighting luminaries who have graced the Springer's stage, including Oscar Wilde, Ethel Barrymore, and John Philip Sousa. Guided tours are available by appointment.

Many old buildings have been admiringly recycled to suit modern uses. Among the most notable are the **Columbus Hilton Hotel** at 800 Front Ave., carved out of a former mill, and the old **Ironworks** across the street, now a convention center and performance venue.

Adjacent to this commercial center is the city's Uptown historic residential district of tidy Victorian homes along several cobblestone blocks of lower Broadway. At the river, the Chattahoochee Promenade is an attractive riverside park with a Liberty Bell replica, a Civil War cannon, and a Carson McCullers memorial.

Here the **Historic Columbus Foundation,** 700 Broadway, tel. (706) 322-0756, housed in an immaculate 1870 Italianate villa, offers guided walking tours of its historic headquarters and nearby landmark homes. The tour includes a trader's log cabin, a farmhouse, and the 1855 Pemberton House, residence of the inventor of Coca-Cola. Tours are held Mon.-Fri. at 11 a.m. and 3 p.m., and Sat.-Sun. at 2 p.m. ($4 adults). The foundation distributes walking-tour maps describing the architectural history of more than two dozen historic buildings in the area.

At the southern foot of the historic district, **Bladau's Goetchius House** at 405 Broadway offers fine dining in a Victorian mansion overlooking the river. **Minnie's Uptown Restaurant** at 100 8th St. is the neighborhood's down-home cafeteria.

Across busy 4th St. surrounded by the South Commons Olympic ball stadiums, salvaged re-

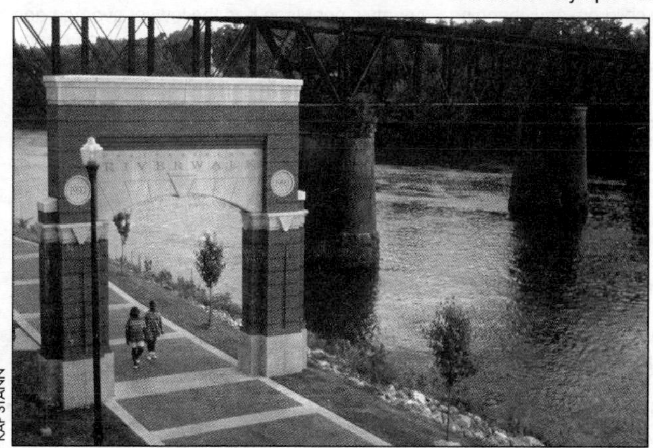

KAP STANN

The 12-mile Chattahoochee Riverwalk in Columbus is a delightful stroll.

SCHOOL OF THE AMERICAS

The School of the Americas (SOA) has graduated some 60,000 soldiers from Central and South America since its founding in Panama in 1946 (it moved to Fort Benning in 1984). SOA has come under increasing international criticism for its human rights record since the assassination of six Jesuit priests and two women colleagues in San Salvador in 1989. A UN Truth Commission investigation revealed that 19 of 26 Salvadoran Army officers involved in the massacre were trained by SOA. The report prompted Maryknoll Father Roy Bourgeois to found **SOA Watch,** which serves as an watchdog agency alerting the public and U.S. government to charges of wrongdoing by the school and its alumni.

SOA Watch has been instrumental in bringing to light some notorious allegations against SOA, including the exposure of a manual with instructions for torture methods, execution, false imprisonment, and extortion, according to the *Catholic Voice.* Despite Rep. Joseph Kennedy's (D-MA) efforts to introduce legislation to cut SOA funding, Congress continues to fund the SOA with nearly $20 million a year.

Since 1990 SOA Watch has sponsored annual vigils at Fort Benning, attracting 7,000 protesters from around the country to the base in 1998. Though in the past acts of civil disobedience led to arrests, no arrests were made in 1998—a reaction organizers attributed to mounting crowds and publicity (including support by such celebrities as Martin Sheen and Susan Sarandon). Protesters may note that some local hotels have been known to offer discounted room rates for those attending the vigil.

For more information about SOA Watch, call tel. (202) 234-3440 or see www.soaw.org.

mains of two Confederate gunboats sunk in the Chattahoochee are on display at the **Woodruff Museum of Civil War Naval History,** 202 4th St., tel. (706) 327-9798, displays ship models, blockade-running mementos, and more. It's free, and open Tues.-Fri. 10 a.m.-5 p.m., Sat.-Sun. 1-5 p.m.

Coca-Cola Space Science Center

Opened in 1996, this new science center, 701 Front Ave., tel. (706) 649-1470, features an "Omnisphere" theater (next generation planetarium) for laser light shows, science fiction movies, films designed for young children, and changing space shows (admission $3-6), along with an observatory (call for show and observation schedule). Lobby exhibits (no charge) include the snout of a space shuttle and an Apollo capsule, and the gift shop sells great glow-in-the-dark space stuff and freeze-dried astronaut food.

Columbus Museum

The pristine and spacious Columbus Museum, 1251 Wynnton Rd., tel. (706) 649-0713, is the major arts center for the region, housing historical, cultural, and visual-arts exhibits. Catch the impressive film *Chattahoochee Legacy,* shown throughout the day, and the historical exhibit surrounding the theater (particularly the southeastern natives exhibit). Its permanent collection is enhanced by traveling shows and special programs, including films, lectures, workshops, and guided tours. A hands-on children's room downstairs features a block area, tactile exhibits, and doable art. The museum is open Tues.-Sat. 10 a.m.-5 p.m., Sunday 1-5 p.m. Admission is free.

Fort Benning

Established on an old plantation site south of Columbus in 1918, the Army's Fort Benning has since grown to become the largest infantry training center in the world. As the fort occupies most of Chattahoochee County, it's no surprise that the county's populace has the lowest average age and the largest number of single men of any county in the United States. In town, large numbers of soldiers in combat boots and camouflage uniforms make Columbus seem like a city under friendly siege.

The embattled **School of the Americas** here is the constant source of protests by opponents charging the school trains graduates who go on to prop up military dictatorships in Central and South America (see **School of the Americas**).

On base, visitors can tour the three-story **National Infantry Museum,** tel. (706) 545-2958, which traces American infantry history from the French and Indian War to the Persian Gulf. It's open Tues.-Fri. 8 a.m.-4:30 p.m., Sat.-Sun. 12:30-4:30 p.m. Admission is free; a dress code forbids too-casual wear, such as sleeveless shirts.

RECREATION

Spectator Sports

The **Columbus Redstixx,** farm team for the Cleveland Indians, plays ball April-August at the 4,000-seat Golden Park, 100 4th St. on the Columbus South Commons, an attractive site of several ball fields where the 1996 Olympic women's fastpitch softball competition was held. Call (706) 571-8866 for schedules and ticket information (tickets around $5). **Georgia Pride,** a women's softball league, also plays at South Commons.

The **Columbus Cottonmouths** of the professional Central Hockey League play ice hockey at the Civic Center. Call (706) 571-0086 for schedules and ticket information (tickets from $8).

Outdoor Recreation

In town, **Weracoba** ("Lake Bottom") **Park** at Cherokee Ave. and 17th St. draws neighbors to ball fields, tennis courts, playground, and creek in an attractive residential section north of downtown.

Out by the airport, a natural rock slide at **Flat Rock Park** on Flat Rock Rd. offers a slippery down-home swimming hole.

Fishing folk and boat owners are drawn to large placid lakes formed by Chattahoochee River impoundments directly north (Lake Oliver, Goat Rock Lake, and Lake Harding, the largest one with the most services), and south (Walter F. George Reservoir); the small marina at scenic Lake Oliver north of town is the closest launch site.

ENTERTAINMENT

Performing Arts

The beautiful **Springer Opera House,** 103 10th St., tel. (706) 324-5714, an intimate red plush-and-gilt jewel box of a theater, hosts musicals, dramatic performances, and children's shows (*Driving Miss Daisy* and the bluegrass gospel musical *Smoke on the Mountain* were on a recent bill). Springer's second stage **Cafe Theater** also features live performances and frequent jazz concerts. The **Columbus Symphony Orchestra,** tel. (706) 323-5059, is awaiting a new home downtown.

The **Columbus Georgia Convention and Trade Center** on Front St., tel. (706) 327-4522, strikingly recycled from the old 19th-century Ironworks, is the scene of such large events as the city's annual Riverfest in April, which draws up to 100,000 participants over three days. Rooms spill out onto a shaded riverfront plaza beside the Riverwalk and railroad bridge.

Nightlife

Downtown, **The Loft** on Broad St., tel. (706) 563-0542, features live jazz in a small, low-key cafe setting. **Pillow Talk** on 4th St. offers an alternative scene with live music and occasional drag shows. North of downtown, stomp to C&W at the **Chickasaw Club,** 3472 Macon Rd., tel. (706) 561-3000. South of downtown, sleazy topless nightclubs and lingerie modeling storefronts line Victory Dr. near the army base to cater to the largest infantry training center in the world.

See Friday's *Columbus Ledger-Enquirer* for complete entertainment listings.

Cinema

Hollywood Connection, 1683 Whittlesey Rd. off Hwy. 80, tel. (706) 571-3456, offers a mind-boggling set of family entertainment including 10 movie theaters (four with stadium seating), roller-skating to contemporary Christian music, a carousel, an arcade, laser tag, and a restaurant in its 125,000-square-foot center north of town.

In the cinema complex west of I-185's airport exit, the **Screening Room** shows international films.

Festivals

The city's largest annual event is held the last weekend in April: the **Riverfest Weekend** city fair features a barbecue "Pig Jig," a children's carnival, outdoor arts and crafts, and plenty of folk food, music, and traditions on the riverbank. Fort Benning's **Fourth of July** celebration presents an amazing military pageant of skydiving paratroopers, gleaming bands, single-step parades in full BDU ("battle dress uniform"), and fireworks from the folks who know how.

ACCOMMODATIONS AND FOOD

Lodging and Camping

The **Columbus Hilton,** 800 Front Ave., tel. (706) 324-1800 or (800) 524-4020, offers not only lodging but a tourist hub and a gathering place for locals. Set attractively in the shell of a century-old gristmill at the boundary between the historic commercial district and historic residential district, the city's "Big House" provides airport transportation, a Delta Air Lines desk, summer sunset pool parties, a rendezvous lounge, and the only coffee shop in town with muesli-topped yogurt on the breakfast menu. Room rates start at $75.

In the Uptown historic district, the **Woodruff House Bed-and-Breakfast,** 1414 2nd Ave., tel. (706) 320-9300 or (800) 320-9309, offers bed and breakfast lodging in 13 suites (from $85) in the birthplace of Coca-Cola entrepreneur Robert Woodruff.

The least expensive motel lodging downtown is found along Victory Drive near the army base. Not far from South Commons, the **Days Inn,** 3170 Victory Dr., tel. (706) 689-6181 (from $39), and **Motel 6,** 3050 Victory Dr., tel. (706) 687-7214 (from $39). From here the strip quickly descends to more questionable choices.

Many modern motel chains are represented out at interstate exits, including La Quinta Inn, Sheraton, Holiday Inn, Budgetel, and another Days Inn.

The closest camping is on nice shaded hillside sites overlooking **Lake Oliver,** a first-come, first-served intimate campground with a small marina store, off Hwy. 80 north of town (at the river).

Food and Drink

Barbecue is revered in these parts—the local preference is for hot and spicy mustard sauce—and Columbus splits loyalties three ways when it comes to picking a favorite. The hard-core **Macon Road Barbecue** on Avalon Rd. at Macon Rd., tel. (706) 563-0542, is traditionally set in a cabin in the woods a mile or so east of I-185's Macon Rd. exit; hours are Mon.-Sat. 10 a.m.-8 p.m. Another local haunt is **Hamilton Road Barbecue,** 3930 Manchester Expressway, west of I-185, tel. (706) 323-8676, which serves good and cheap biscuit sandwich breakfasts—the Southern precursor to the Egg McMuffin—in addition to its saucy barbecue. It's open Mon.-Sat. 6 a.m.-10 p.m.

Perhaps the best place for a visitor to sample barbecue, along with a full range of other menu options, is downtown at **Country's on Broad,** 1329 Broadway, tel. (706) 596-8910. Set in an actual 1930s bus depot spiffed with retro chrome, it's a nice all-around lively restaurant equally comfortable for singles (slide up to the gleaming counter), families, or packs of teenagers. Country's also has two other locations in northside shopping malls.

Minnie's Uptown Restaurant, 100 8th St. at 1st Ave., tel. (706) 322-2766, offers cafeteria service for hearty meat-and-three plates for $5.25 in the Uptown neighborhood (call 706-322-1466 for a recording of daily specials). It's open for lunch weekdays only: Mon.-Fri. 10:45 a.m.-2:45 p.m.

More down-home Southern favorites can be found at **Ezell's Catfish Cabin,** 4001 Warm Springs Rd., tel. (706) 568-1149, a comfortable family restaurant that fries up all-you-can-eat catfish, "popcorn" shrimp, and other seafood plates (it's a mile or so east of I-185). Hours are Mon.-Thurs. 4:30-9:30 p.m., Fri.-Sun. 11:30 a.m.-10 p.m.

The lunch counter at the **Dinglewood Pharmacy** on Wynnton Rd. concocts the local specialty "scrambled dog"—a hot dog buried under chili, onions, and oyster crackers (an acquired taste). The counter is open 10:30 a.m.-6:45 p.m.

For dress up, go Uptown to **Bladau's Goetchius House** (GET-chez) at 405 Broadway, tel. (706) 324-4863, for frog legs bourguignonne, chateaubriand, swordfish, or lobster in the 1839 mansion's formally appointed dining room, or just meet for a drink and oysters in the speakeasy downstairs; then surface to the riverview patio for espresso. It's open 5-10 p.m., until 11 p.m. Fri.-Sat., closed Sunday.

The **Columbus State Farmers Market,** 318 10th Ave., tel. (706) 649-7448, sells farm-fresh produce off 4th St./Victory Dr. near South Commons.

OTHER PRACTICALITIES

Getting There and Around

By car from Atlanta, take I-85 to I-185 south—keep to the speed limit along I-185 (a notorious speed trap).

At the **Columbus Airport,** tel. (706) 324-2449, 10 minutes north of downtown, a handful of commercial carriers operate shuttle service to Atlanta and other destinations, but Atlanta travelers may find ground transportation more affordable and practical. **Groome Transportation,** tel. (706) 324-3939 or (800) 584-6734, runs shuttle van service between Atlanta's Hartsfield Airport and Fort Benning.

Greyhound, 818 4th Ave. (at 9th St.), tel. (706) 323-5417, also serves the Atlanta-to-Columbus route from its downtown terminal.

Shopping

Two shopping **malls** directly off I-185 (one off the Macon Rd. exit, the other off the Manchester Expressway exit) supply all necessities, including restaurants and movie theaters. Major department stores here are Sears, JCPenney, and the regional Parisian. **Wickham's Outdoor World,** tel. (706) 563-2113, sells and rents outfitting gear in the Cross Country Shopping Center just west of I-185 off Macon Road. It's the prime local reference for outdoor recreation. You can find similar gear in chocolate-chip camouflage patterns in **army surplus stores** on Victory Dr. off the interstate (one advertises "Conquer the Outdoors!"). Pick up fresh produce at the **farmers market** around Tenth and Victory Drive.

Information and Services

The **Georgia Visitors Center,** I-185 exit 8, tel. (706) 649-7455, provides statewide information, discount coupons for lodging, and help finding lodging, daily 8:30 a.m.-5:30 p.m.

Downtown, the **Columbus Convention and Visitors Bureau,** 1000 Bay Ave., Columbus, GA 31901, tel. (706) 322-1613 or (800) 999-1613 (24-hour recorded hotline 706-322-3181), across from the Riverwalk, is open Mon.-Fri. 8:30 a.m.-5 p.m., Saturday 10 a.m.-4 p.m., and Sunday 1-4 p.m. Tune in **1610 AM** for more visitor information. E-mail ccvb@msn.com and also see www.columbusga.com/ccvb.

The ***Columbus Ledger-Enquirer*** publishes daily, and the ***Columbus Times,*** devoted to African-American news and events, publishes weekly. You can find a selection of local and out-of-town papers in machines around the downtown courthouse.

In an emergency, dial 911. The non-emergency police number is (706) 596-7000. For medical attention, call the **Medical Center Hospital,** 710 Center St., at (706) 571-4262.

CHRIS PARMENTER

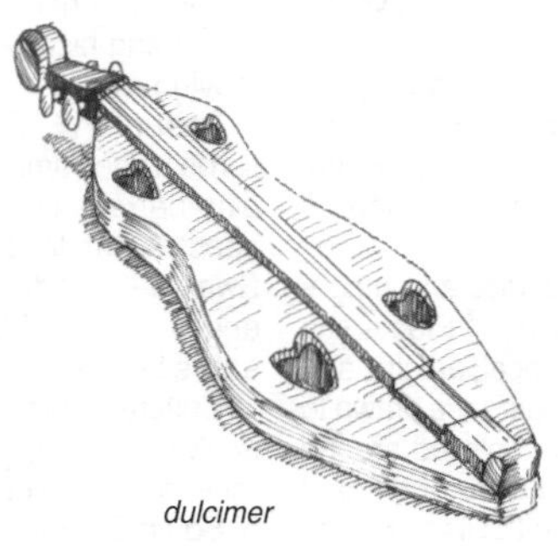

dulcimer

KATHY PETERSON

SOUTH GEORGIA

INTRODUCTION

The state's prime agricultural region, South Georgia remains overwhelmingly rural today. Only two cities of any size—Albany and Valdosta—bring urban development to the coastal plain region that occupies half of Georgia's land. Within this broad expanse of peanut fields, peach orchards, and piney woods—where tractors, pickups, and logging trucks outnumber cars—visitors discover the remnants of native, antebellum, and folk traditions, and the most primordial wilderness in the nation.

The southwestern plain is particularly intriguing. Jimmy Carter's hometown of Plains sits around an unusual set of historical, artistic, and natural attractions. And vacationers are drawn to the "Plantation Trace" region centered around Thomasville—a pine-scented area of elegant old homes and resorts that attest to its history as a cotton-producing area before the Civil War and an elite retreat at the turn of the century.

Farther east, I-75 cuts through the heart of wiregrass country. As part of the main route from the Midwest to the vacation mecca of Florida, this stretch of freeway is one of the nation's busiest. Under the corridor's iconographic spires advertising every franchise known to man lie several pre-neon pleasures, including Agrirama's living-history village and two favorite slow-moving rivers.

East of I-75, South Georgia's prime attraction is hidden among hundreds of square miles of pine barrens in the southeastern interior. The spectacular landscapes of the Okefenokee Swamp—moody cypresses, "trembling earth," and watery prairies—offer one of the Southeast's best wilderness adventures.

Culturally, the southernmost third of the state is divided at an imaginary boundary called the "gnat line"; subtleties separate the folk traditions of South Georgia's wiregrass region from those of the more urbanized Piedmont directly north. This folk heritage can best be seen at the region's many homespun festivals, such as Gnat Days and mule parades, sugarcane-grinding

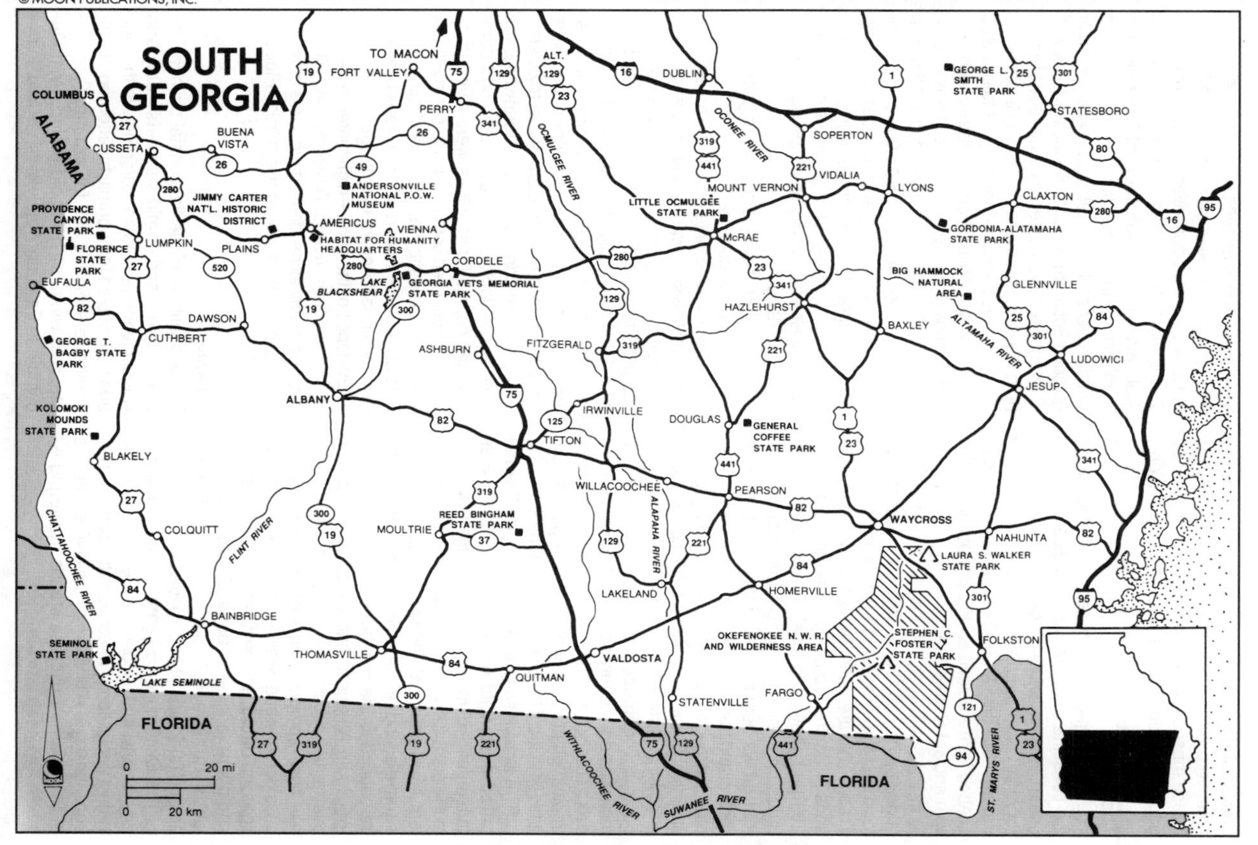

SOUTH GEORGIA
ALABAMA
FLORIDA
FLORIDA
TO MACON
COLUMBUS
CUSSETA
BUENA VISTA
LUMPKIN
PLAINS
AMERICUS
FORT VALLEY
PERRY
CORDELE
VIENNA
ASHBURN
ALBANY
DAWSON
CUTHBERT
EUFAULA
BLAKELY
COLQUITT
BAINBRIDGE
THOMASVILLE
MOULTRIE
QUITMAN
VALDOSTA
TIFTON
FITZGERALD
IRWINVILLE
WILLACOOCHEE
LAKELAND
STATENVILLE
HOMERVILLE
FARGO
DOUGLAS
PEARSON
WAYCROSS
NAHUNTA
FOLKSTON
HAZLEHURST
McRAE
MOUNT VERNON
DUBLIN
SOPERTON
VIDALIA
LYONS
BAXLEY
JESUP
LUDOWICI
GLENNVILLE
CLAXTON
STATESBORO
PROVIDENCE CANYON STATE PARK
FLORENCE STATE PARK
GEORGE T. BAGBY STATE PARK
KOLOMOKI MOUNDS STATE PARK
JIMMY CARTER NAT'L. HISTORIC DISTRICT
HABITAT FOR HUMANITY HEADQUARTERS
ANDERSONVILLE NATIONAL P.O.W. MUSEUM
GEORGIA VETS MEMORIAL STATE PARK
LAKE BLACKSHEAR
REED BINGHAM STATE PARK
SEMINOLE STATE PARK
LAKE SEMINOLE
LITTLE OCMULGEE STATE PARK
GENERAL COFFEE STATE PARK
BIG HAMMOCK NATURAL AREA
GORDONIA-ALATAMAHA STATE PARK
GEORGE L. SMITH STATE PARK
LAURA S. WALKER STATE PARK
STEPHEN C. FOSTER STATE PARK
OKEFENOKEE N. W. R. AND WILDERNESS AREA
CHATTAHOOCHEE RIVER
FLINT RIVER
OCMULGEE RIVER
OCONEE RIVER
ALTAMAHA RIVER
ALAPAHA RIVER
WITHLACOOCHEE RIVER
SUWANEE RIVER
ST. MARYS RIVER
0 20 mi
0 20 km

parties and turkey-calling contests. But at any time, you can visit roadside stands, antebellum house museums, tobacco auctions, or peanut-packing factories to get a flavor for the region.

The Land

The **coastal plain** region, between the fall line—the coastline of an earlier geological era—and ocean, retains evidence of its underwater history. Several "sandhill" ridges—former sand dunes—on the 35,000-square-mile former seabed form a unique ecological habitat studded with ancient sharks' teeth.

In the southwest, the sandy soils are overlaid with the rich "black belt" soils responsible for the cotton-producing heritage of Plantation Trace. This area also holds the highest elevations in South Georgia, peaking at a whopping 283 feet above sea level. The wiregrass midlands take their name from the coarse grass that grows beneath the pines. The **pine barrens** inland from the coast, originally virgin yellow pine, came to be dominated by fast-growing strains of planted loblolly and slash pine in stick-straight rows (courtesy of the local logging industry). Throughout the region, swampy bottomlands draw **cypress, gum, tupelo,** and **live oak.** The hot and humid climate invites such tropical plants as **sugarcane** and **palms,** and a favorite local fruit called the **mayhaw.**

The forests support a varied wildlife. **White-tailed deer, wild turkeys, quail,** and **doves** (the primary game species that attracts hunters to the area) can be found along with such prevalent small mammals as **raccoons, possums, squirrels,** and **rabbits.** The unusual **armadillo,** introduced to the Southeast when a couple of the South American natives escaped from an overturned circus truck in Florida about 1900, has now reproduced in such numbers that it's considered "weed wildlife." The rivers shelter **alligators, otters,** and **beavers,** as well as **catfish** and many varieties of **bass.** Coastal plain wetlands attract songbirds, herons, and storks among hundreds of bird species.

The Okefenokee Swamp has a natural history, botany, and resident wildlife all its own—the largest population of alligators in the state, turtles, frogs, bears, and birds enjoy the distinct habitats of the swamp's cypress stands, quivering islands, and open prairies.

The Great Flood of 1994

The region's clay-stained rivers course through fertile and swampy bottomlands in the flat terrain. To the west, the Chattahoochee River borders Alabama and joins with the Flint River at Lake Seminole. In the midsection, the Alapaha and Withlacoochee Rivers attract paddlers to their graceful Southern currents. To the east, the wild Okefenokee Swamp serves as headwaters to both the Suwannee and St. Marys Rivers.

In July 1994, record-breaking rainfall caused the worst flooding in Georgia's history, and several of these rivers overflowed their banks, causing 31 deaths, damaging more than $112 million in infrastructure, and leaving 15,000 people temporarily homeless. Fifty-two counties were declared federal disaster areas, primarily those bordering the Flint, Ocmulgee, and Chattahoochee Rivers. The city of Macon went without water for 19 days.

Scenes from the flood zone were grim: towns submerged, coffins unearthed, residents evacuated from treetops into boats. The smaller stories were no less powerful: of snakes and critters collecting on high ground, the mosquito onslaught, the foul stench, the lost crops and lost pets. Environmental pollutants from flood-zone factories, hazardous-waste dumps, landfills, junkyards, and sewage-treatment plants were unleashed downriver, to blend into a toxic stew with unknown consequences. Meanwhile, the Rev. Jesse Jackson surveyed the flood damage and charged that waters were diverted toward impoverished communities to spare affluent areas—proclaiming that "God didn't rain on one side of town; He rained on both sides of town!" County officials denied the charge.

Evidence of the flood—high-water marks visible on buildings, riverbank erosion—is still visible, and nearly all residents have a tale or two of their own to share about the "Great Flood of 1994."

Climate

The low latitude of the flat coastal plain invites tropically hot and humid summers—July and August temperatures are commonly in the high 90s (°F), cooled temporarily by afternoon thundershowers. Spring and fall are most temperate, and winter's short cold period, from December to February, rarely reaches freezing.

Seasonal change brings variety to the area, with the wildflowers and blooming orchards of spring giving way to full-fruited early summers, then fall colors sprinkled among the evergreens. Winters attract migratory birds to the region's many wetlands.

History

Georgia's oldest aboriginal mound center, Kolomoki Mounds, is evidence of a culture that thrived on the banks of the Chattahoochee 700 years ago. This ancient civilization spawned the modern-era Creek nation, named for its riverine culture. Later, some Creek left the tribe, becoming known as Seminoles (which means "runaway" in Creek). All indigenous groups were exiled by the U.S. government in the Indian Removal of 1836. Most headed on the Trail of Tears to Oklahoma; the Seminoles managed to retreat farther south into the swamps of Florida. Representatives of these and other native nations return to the area each May for the Chehaw National Indian Festival, a celebration of their traditional heritage on ancestral homelands.

Hernando de Soto was the first European to explore the area. He marched 6,000 troops through the area around the Flint River in 1540 on his search for gold throughout the Southeast. Yet South Georgia remained the last region of the state to be settled by Europeans; the Chattahoochee remained wild frontier until the mid-1800s. Then it developed with a flourish, particularly as planters recognized that cotton grew well in the rich dark soils. Many plantations were built in the southwest, while the pine barrens of the southeastern interior were logged.

Settlements first developed at rivers, to facilitate shipping out the agricultural products grown in the interior, yet the earliest communities were made up mostly of subsistence farmers. The war destroyed the cotton plantations in the southwest, but that scenic region readily recovered as an elite retreat for wealthy Northerners. As one local resident put it, "We soon discovered a Yankee was worth two bales of cotton, and was twice as easy to pick."

When the railroads arrived in the late 19th century, a traditional, nearly medieval way of life came to an abrupt end, bringing newcomers, modernization, and industry to isolated rural communities. Entrepreneurs saw a fortune in the virgin yellow-pine forests, which were clear-cut for lumber and replaced by cropland. Farmers turned to raising cotton for cash instead of growing subsistence crops, and the resulting oversupply of cotton depressed prices and depleted lands, even before the boll weevil blight took its toll. But as agriculture faltered, industry boomed; towns developed around railroads and manufacturing centers, with the logging industry leading the way.

Logging remains a major industry today—for paper and pulpwood production as well as lumber—but other crops grew in importance. Now South Georgia is the center of production for the state's number one cash crop—peanuts—as well as for pecans, peaches, and many other agricultural products. Tourism became a contributing factor to the southwestern region's economy as early as the 1870s. And since the opening of I-75—one of the busiest stretches of freeway in the nation—tourism has had an impact on the south-central region as well.

JIMMY CARTER COUNTRY

Below the fall line between the Chattahoochee and Flint Rivers, where the scent of peanut fields overwhelms even the magnolias, a typical South Georgia landscape appears. Farmhouses with militarily trim lawns adjoin shacks with swept yards, mailboxes are crafted from plowshares, tractors slow traffic on country highways, and drivers lift a few fingers off the wheel to greet every passing car. At night, electric bug zappers glow iridescent blue and interrupt the nocturnal drone of the cicadas.

Within this ordinary backcountry, visitors see traces of an extraordinary heritage. Here a peanut farmer rose to international leadership, an idealistic commune gave birth to a worldwide movement to improve substandard housing, and an eccentric folk artist constructed his otherworldly vision. Here too, Civil War ghosts haunt a notorious P.O.W. camp and a village recreates 1850s Georgia in a remote setting eerily convincing.

Beyond its pitchforks and pines, the region also shelters Providence Canyon—"the Little Grand Canyon"—which drops vistas reminiscent of the American Southwest into this remote corner of the Southeast. And wild stretches along the wide Chattahoochee hide ancient moundworks and fishing camps among the broken levees of abandoned plantations.

MONTEZUMA AND VICINITY

The sister cities of Montezuma and Oglethorpe were founded in the mid-1800s at facing banks of the Flint River. When the Flint overflowed its banks in 1994, downtown Montezuma was almost entirely under water. The local chamber of commerce on 316 S. Dooley St. (slightly north of the railroad tracks) distributes driving-tour maps of the many distinguished old homes in the area, particularly on the route north to Marshallville.

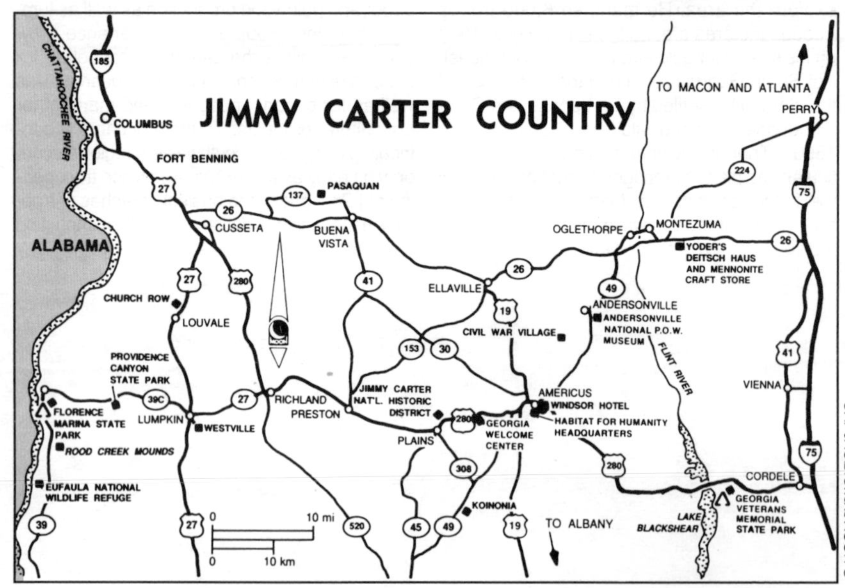

Several miles east of the river in Montezuma, mailboxes display distinctly German names, the likes of a Hershberger or Schwartzimmer, all Samuels or Nathans. Here 100 Mennonite families operate dairy farms and carry on a traditional way of life, as they have since 1954 when 11 families transplanted themselves here from Virginia (expanding military bases there propelled them to leave). Like the Amish, followers of the faith wear plain clothes—bonnets and long skirts for the women, men in beards, caps, and suspenders. Yet unlike the Amish, Mennonites do not forsake modern machinery.

At **Yoder's Deitsch Haus,** tel. (912) 472-2024, members of the community serve a wonderfully fresh cafeteria-style buffet in a large restaurant open to the public. Choose entrees such as roast beef, fried chicken, or Texas hash, served with two vegetables, rice, and iced tea; pick up goodies and fresh bread from the bakery around back. Three miles east of Montezuma on Hwy. 26, the restaurant is open Tues.-Sat. 11:30 a.m.-2 p.m. for lunch, and daily (except Wednesday) 5-8:30 p.m. for dinner.

A gift shop next door sells some of the best handmade country crafts this side of North Georgia: furniture that's either fine or rough-hewn, whirligigs, birdhouses, dolls in Mennonite garb, quilts, and homemade foods and candies.

(Visitors would show respect to dress conservatively here and in other rural areas; over-exposed limbs and feet draw unwelcome attention, so keep a stash of cover-ups handy.)

ANDERSONVILLE

History

During the 19th century, Andersonville was a small Georgia village near the end of the Southwestern Railroad. In early 1864, Camp Sumter was established here to house Union prisoners moved south away from the front lines in Richmond, Virginia. The P.O.W. camp grew to become the largest and most notorious of all Confederate military prisons. During the 14 months it existed, more than 45,000 Union soldiers were imprisoned here—of these, almost 13,000 died from disease, poor sanitation, malnutrition, overcrowding, or exposure to the elements. Once its conditions became public knowledge after the war, public outrage was so great that the camp's commandant was hanged in Washington, D.C., in 1865—the only person to be convicted and executed for war crimes during the Civil War.

Also in 1865, the **Andersonville National Cemetery** was built here adjacent to the old camp site to inter P.O.W.s and Civil War soldiers known and unknown. States from around the Union sent monuments to commemorate the loss of life. The veterans cemetery remains in operation today.

National Prisoner of War Museum

Opened in 1998, the new National Prisoner of War Museum, on Hwy. 49 10 miles north of Americus, tel. (912) 924-0343, is a hauntingly powerful memorial to American prisoners of war. Outside of the Holocaust museum in Washington, D.C., it might well be the most moving museum we've seen. (In fact, the quality of this P.O.W. museum resembles world-class museums in the nation's capital.) Yet as strongly as anyone would recommend visiting, parents should be aware that it is designed to disturb; exercise caution with young children.

Some of its most raw exhibits are from the Vietnam War era, where bamboo "tiger cages" invite visitors to consider what life was like for prisoners trapped within. Next door a tiny dark cell has cast-iron leg shackles cemented in place. On the back wall, a bank of video monitors loops interviews with P.O.W. families to suggest the agony endured by those who remained at home.

The museum leads visitors out from the exhibits to the former P.O.W. camp site, where a reconstructed camp stockade leads the visitor to imagine tens of thousands of soldiers confined within its small frame.

In addition to the well-crafted exhibits, the museum maintains a P.O.W. database and research library (available by appointment), along with a book shop that has an excellent, unsentimental selection of titles on military history. The museum is open 8:30 a.m.-5 p.m. daily, closed on Christmas and New Year's Day (no charge for admission).

On the site of a notorious Civil War P.O.W. camp, this powerful museum memorializes all American P.O.W.'s.

KAP STANN

Andersonville Village and Vicinity
Off Hwy. 49 south of the cemetery, the Civil War village of Andersonville was where 45,000 captured federal soldiers arrived by rail in 1864. Now restored, the five-acre park sets shops and picnic areas around the historic depot, which now serves as a visitor center, tel. (912) 924-2558. It's open daily 9 a.m.-5 p.m. The reconstructed village hosts a fair and battle reenactment the first weekend in October.

AMERICUS

Founded in 1831, Americus (population 18,000), first gained statewide recognition as the home of the grand Windsor Hotel, built in 1892. With Jimmy Carter's campaign for president in 1976 from neighboring Plains, the county seat of Americus was brought to national attention. Today the town is perhaps best known as the global headquarters of Habitat for Humanity. An attractive town with interesting people, and good places to stay and eat, Americus makes a great base of operations to explore all the region has to offer.

Downtown, the central square is dominated by the landmark Windsor Hotel, which also serves as a local gathering place and is home to a gallery within. Surrounding the hotel is an intriguing set of shops, cafes, and a great bookstore; the town's historic residential neighborhood can be found behind the square around Lee, Taylor, and College Streets. The reopening of the renovated Rylander Theater on W. Lamar St. planned for 1999 will add to the town's attractions.

The local chamber of commerce **visitor center,** 400 W. Lamar Street, tel. (912) 924-2646 or (888) 278-6837, fax (912) 924-8784, directs visitors to the county's attractions and distributes county maps along with lodging and dining guides. There's a branch visitor center off the Windsor Hotel's lobby.

Habitat for Humanity
Americus is the international headquarters of Habitat for Humanity, 121 Habitat St., Americus, GA 31709, tel. (912) 924-6935 or (800) HABITAT (800-422-4828), e-mail at info@habitat.org, or see www.habitat.org.

A nonprofit housing ministry, Habitat for Humanity developed out of the personal vision of Millard and Linda Fuller. Millard Fuller had been a successful Alabama lawyer and entrepreneur before he and his wife decided to reevaluate their priorities—they sold everything they owned, donated most of the proceeds to charity, and joined the Koinonia farming commune, which inspired them to start their housing ministry.

Since the Fullers founded Habitat for Humanity in 1976, the organization has overseen the construction of more than 20,000 houses in the U.S. and around the world. The organization depends on the work of thousands of volunteers who work alongside new owners to raise affordable housing.

Habitat for Humanity sponsors **guided tours** of its local operations weekdays: Mon.-Fri. at 8 and 10 a.m. and 1 and 3 p.m. (or at other times by appointment), no charge. Guides take visitors around Habitat's first urban development and to one of its most recent subdivisions. The highlight of the tour is the International Village, where samples of houses constructed in Zaire, Kenya, Papua New Guinea, India, and Guatemala provide an enlightening comparison of differences in culture, climate, and building materials. A **self-guided tour brochure** is also available at Habitat headquarters to guide you to these sites on your own.

Koinonia

Fifty years ago, the racially integrated farming commune of Koinonia (koy-no-NEE-ah, a Greek term for "fellowship") represented a radical departure from local cultural norms, and was fiercely condemned by local segregationists. The ecumenical Christian community nevertheless managed to sustain itself with a mail-order candy-making operation. After the Fullers joined the community and founded **Habitat for Humanity,** the first Habitat development was constructed at Koinonia, on Dawson Rd. (Hwy. 49) south of Americus, tel. (912) 924-0391.

Today, the small community continues to farm, make candy, and live by its utopian ideals. Stop

HABITAT FOR HUMANITY

"I've learned more about the needy than I ever did as a governor or president. The sacrifice I thought I would be making turned out to be one of the greatest blessings of my life. I don't know of anything I've ever seen that more vividly demonstrates love in action than Habitat for Humanity."

—Jimmy Carter

Habitat for Humanity, based in Americus, is a nonprofit housing ministry that has overseen the construction of 20,000 new homes around the world since its founding in 1976. Habitat depends on volunteers, who work alongside future homeowners to construct not only houses, but communities. Among its most supportive volunteers have been Jimmy and Rosalynn Carter, neighbors from Plains, who continue their hands-on work with Habitat today.

For information about volunteering at the international headquarters or on international Habitat projects, contact the organization at 121 Habitat St., Americus, GA 31709, tel. (912) 924-6935 or (800) HABITAT, e-mail at info@habitat.org, or see www.habitat.org.

RAY SCIOSCIA/HABITAT FOR HUMANITY

Jimmy and Rosalynn Carter put their hands where their hearts are, at work on a Habitat for Humanity housing project.

by for a tin of bittersweet pecan bark or other organic goodies, and if it's not too busy someone will show you around. If you're interested in a longer stay, inquire about the volunteer program, which provides room-and-board and a small stipend to selected folks over 18 willing to help out around the farm for summers or longer. The office is open weekdays 8-11:45 a.m. and 12:45-5 p.m.

Accommodations

The grand **Windsor Hotel,** 125 W. Lamar St., tel. (912) 924-1555 or (800) 252-7466, occupies an entire city block in the center of town. An elegant 53-room brick hotel built in 1892, the sprawling Victorian hotel features an attractive three-story central atrium, with the original sloping wood floors, crystal chandeliers, and carved oak paneling. Rooms are furnished with light wood period reproductions and ceiling fans along with all modern conveniences including elevators, remote-control color TVs, and central heat and air. The fourth-floor honeymoon suite in the hotel's rounded tower is lavishly furnished with a tasseled canopy bed. Standard rooms start around $75.

Chain motels along highways outside downtown include **Days Inn,** Hwy. 19 S, tel. (912) 924-3613; **Holiday Inn Express,** Hwy. 280 E, tel. (912) 928-5400; **Ramada Inn,** US 19 S, tel. (912) 924-4431; and Jameson Inn, Hwy. 280 E, tel. (912) 924-2726. (Habitat for Humanity maintains a simple RV park in town with hookups, for volunteers only.)

Food and Drink

The Windsor **Dining Room** is the place for the most proper meal with such entrees as roasted pork loin and Dijon lack of lamb (dinner entrees from $15). They serve breakfast daily 7-10 a.m., a luncheon buffet Sun.-Fri. 11 a.m.-2 p.m., and dinner Mon.-Sat. 6:30-9:30 p.m. With a second-floor veranda overlooking the main street, the hotel's **Floyd's Pub,** offers more casual meals and snacks, such as a nice chicken Caesar salad, chicken wings, or jalapeno poppers (all around $5).

Lee's Bakery Deli, 200 Windsor Ave., tel. (912) 924-9887, offers a wonderful gourmet selection of deli sandwiches made with fresh vegetables and herbs on fresh bakery breads—great muffins and cookies too. Their roasted vegetable sandwich made with tomatoes, peppers, goat cheese, olives, and red leaf lettuce is under $5.

The **Talking Bean,** 142 S. Lee St., tel. (912) 924-2299, a funky cafe a couple of blocks from the Windsor, serves gourmet coffees, croissant sandwiches, salads, Dix-Mex burritos and quesadillas, desserts, and smoothies—all under $5. They occasionally host live music or readings. **Pat's Place,** 1526 S. Lee St., tel. (912) 924-0033, serves pub food and hosts live music; weekday happy hour beers are 94 cents from 4-8 p.m.

PLAINS

Founded in 1940 as the Plains of Dura, Plains is a small town even by South Georgia standards—not much more than a strip of shops surrounded by peanut fields and country roads. Now it's known worldwide as the birthplace of the 39th president of the United States; the town was thrust into the national limelight when then-governor Jimmy Carter launched his presidential campaign from the old Plains depot.

Plains Country Days, the town's major festival the third weekend in May, features a parade, street dance, and hayrides, accompanied by lots of country cooking, homespun music, and crafts.

A former Carter family home, the **Plains Bed and Breakfast Inn,** 100 W. Church St., tel. (912) 824-7252, now offers B&B lodging in the gracious pink-and-ivory two-story Victorian on Hwy. 280 across from the depot (rooms from $60).

The inviting **Georgia Visitor Information Center,** east of town on Hwy. 280, tel. (912) 824-7477, operates a room reservation service and distributes statewide information from a lakeside cabin. It's open daily 8:30 a.m.-5:30 p.m.

Jimmy Carter National Historic Site

The Jimmy Carter Museum, 300 N. Bond St., tel. (912) 824-3413, is housed in the old Plains High School where Carter went to school (his prescient principal, Julia Coleman, often told the students "someday one of you will grow up to be president of the United States"). There are several classrooms restored to the Carter boyhood era, and personal exhibits on the Carter family and on Carter's political career. A biographical film screens in the auditorium, and there's also a touching video of the Carters walking people through their home in Plains pointing out the furniture Jimmy made and the treasured presents from family and world leaders.

They offer a select collection of books by and about Carter, and such souvenirs as Carter-Mondale campaign buttons. Hours are 9 a.m.-5 p.m. daily.

Jimmy Carter National Historic District

Self-guided driving-tour maps (with accompanying audiocassette rental) available at the historic site visitor center on Bond St. direct visitors to the quaint **Plains Depot,** from which Carter ran his presidential campaign (across from a small park at the tracks), Carter's **Boyhood Farm,** the private **Carter Family Compound** (off-limits), and the **Maranatha Baptist Church,** where Jimmy Carter delivers Sunday School lessons to this day.

The best photo opportunity is at the Giant Goober up from the high school.

LUMPKIN AND VICINITY

Lumpkin's major attraction, Westville, re-creates an 1850s village, and anachronistic Lumpkin itself appears frozen in time. Once a stop on the old stagecoach route, **Bedingfield Inn,** at the corner of Broad and Cotton Streets on the square, now operates as a visitor center, tel. (912) 838-6419 (open Tues.-Sun. 1-5 p.m.). Pick up guides to more than two dozen historic buildings in town; among these the **Singer Co.** on Main St. bills itself as "the oldest hardware store in Georgia."

Follow Main St. one block east to an impressively folksy collection of **whirligigs** in front of the home of Mr. John Byrd. You'll likely see Mr. Byrd himself, clad in overalls, repairing his handiwork or tending his flowers outside.

Eat at **Michelle's,** tel. (912) 838-9991, 109 Main St., where they serve a generous buffet of catfish, ribeye steak, fried chicken, assorted vegetables, cornbread, and breakfast all day in a homey little place (open 5:30 a.m.-9 p.m. daily).

Westville

One of the state's top three living-history centers, Westville is an authentically re-created 19th-century village on 57 acres outside Lumpkin (a mile and a half from the square, follow signs). Its 32 structures include a plantation house, schoolhouse, smithy, and bootery. Descendants of the original cast wear period dress, perform traditional crafts, and answer questions in character; just walking along the double-rutted red-clay roads recalls a bygone era.

The place comes to life during special folkways demonstrations in early April, early May, on July Fourth, and in mid- to late December. But the biggest festival runs from mid-October to mid-November—the 17-day **Fair of 1850** brings homemade music, open-hearth cooking, sugarcane-grinding, syrupmaking, basketmaking, weaving, woodworking, and demonstrations of the only animal-powered cotton gin in Georgia.

A private, nonprofit educational museum, Westville, tel. (912) 838-6310 or (888) 733-1850, is open Tues.-Sat. 10 a.m.-5 p.m., Sunday 1-5 p.m. Adult admission is $8, $7 seniors, $4 grades K-12.

Providence Canyon

The two-lane blacktop of Hwy. 39C cuts through miles and miles of solid stick-straight pinewoods, which makes all the more unexpected the first glimpse of Providence Canyon. Called Georgia's "Little Grand Canyon," its pastel-shaded canyon walls bring Southwestern contours smack dab into South Georgia's forested plain. As such a stark departure from the surrounding environment, the erosion-worn canyon (actually 16 of them, some as deep as 150 feet) shelters a rare botanical community, notably the rare plumleaf azalea, which blooms from July to September.

The canyon is protected as a 1,108-acre conservation area within the state park system. An **interpretive center,** tel. (912) 838-6202, explains the unusual geology and can also arrange guided canyon tours. Park gates stay open 7 a.m.-9 p.m. April 15-Sept. 14, till 6 p.m. the rest of the year. The entrance fee is $2 per car, free on Wednesday.

You'll see dramatic views at several overlooks close to parking. The three-mile **rim trail** loops largely around the perimeter, then dips down by wide switchbacks into the canyon at the interpretive center. Here hikers go from the dry, well-drained ridge to the moist and shaded canyon floor (slightly muddy during wet weather). A seven-mile **backcountry trail** invites backpackers to explore further. The red-blazed trail spurs off the loop trail deep down in the canyon and climbs back up to the ridge, where the trail continues through forested backcountry to five campsites along the next ridge. Then the trail drops down to a footbridge across the creek that flows from the canyons and loops back to the rim trail. Pick up free maps and permits at the interpretive center before backpacking.

Florence

What they now call Florence is largely **Florence Marina State Park,** tel. (912) 838-6870, built on the site of an abandoned 19th-century town. This small quiet refuge draws local anglers and boaters to the 150-acre park, which features a 66-slip marina with rental slips, a lighted fishing pier, a swimming pool, two tennis courts, and a "clubhouse" used for wedding receptions and other local get-togethers. Ten fully equipped cottages rent year-round for $40-50 for a one-bedroom, $70-80 for a two-bedroom. A 44-site campground provides full water-electric-sewage hookups for $16. Call (800) 864-PARK (800-864-7275) for cottage or camping reservations. The parking fee is $2 per car, free on Wednesdays.

The park's **Kirbo Interpretive Center,** tel. (912) 838-4706, displays exhibits related to the submerged town, native flora and fauna, and the nearby **Rood Creek** archaeological site. At the site, eight ceremonial mounds date from A.D. 900-1540, when a village of 3,500 inhabited the area. The site is only accessible on a tour; guided tours meet at the interpretive center Saturday at 10 a.m. (or call to arrange an appointment).

Eufaula National Wildlife Refuge

Abandoned farmland along the Chattahoochee River (off Hwy. 39 south of the state park) is now protected as a wildlife preserve. Here, the ruins of silos house bats and owls, armadillos frolic under strewn rusting tractors, alligator trails cross from pond to pond, and overhead you'll see anhingas, herons, and glossy ibis. The old roadbed and levees serve as trails; park at the sign where the road's blocked off.

Louvale

A favorite gathering place for fishermen and hunters, the tiny town of Louvale is the only action on a long forested stretch of Hwy. 27 between Lumpkin and Cussetta, unless you count bait shops. Louvale consists of an old-fashioned post office, a local barbecue, gas station, market, and above town, an unexpected collection of historic churches on display in an overgrown field. You'll find a free Army Corps of Engineers

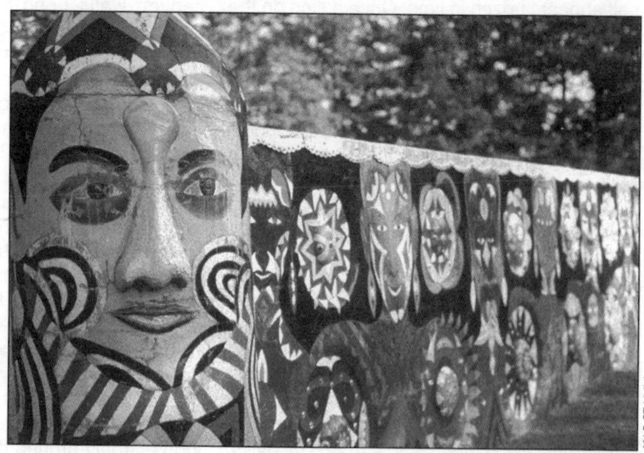

Once St. EOM got started painting and creating, he just couldn't stop. Pasaquan is the result of decades of work.

KAP STANN

campground with water and pit toilets down Riverbend Rd. on Walter F. George Lake.

BUENA VISTA

Buena Vista (BEWna VISta) has been placed on the map by a local eccentric who built his visionary art environment at the outskirts of town. Since the death of its creator, its discovery and exposure have brought art students and supporters of primitive expression to town. Fortunately, the town also has a bed and breakfast with its own restaurant, so that visitors could make Buena Vista and its environs into an interesting extended outing in the rural Georgia outback.

Ray and Donna Armer operate the **Sign of the Dove,** Church St. at 4th Ave., tel. (912) 649-3663 or (888) 690-3663, in a 1909 Georgia cottage with a wraparound porch in downtown Buena Vista. Rooms with private bath are $75 single or double, which includes a continental breakfast. Their restaurant features a Southern buffet, served Thurs.-Sun. 11 a.m.-2 p.m. They put out a seafood dinner buffet Fri.-Sat. 5:30-8:30 p.m. (reservations required for large groups).

Pasaquan

Four acres of an old South Georgia farmhouse and grounds have been transformed into a extraordinary folk-art environment by the late Eddie Owens Martin (1908-1986). Martin called himself "Saint EOM" (a derivative of his chant-like initials), and was a free spirit, fortune-teller, and bane of the local community for years until his death in 1986. He liked to consider himself the "Bodacious Mystic Badass of Buena Vista," and his biographer Tom Patterson *(St. EOM in the Land of Pasaquan)* called him "a cross between Walt Whitman, Sun Ra, Montezuma, Lord Buckley, and Boy George."

Over the years Martin designed and constructed walls and outbuildings from wood and poured concrete, which he molded, sculpted, and painted in hallucinogenic patterns and shades. He called the place Pasaquan—a term that appeared to him in a dream—which he explained as a combination of the Spanish word for pass and *"quoyan,"* purportedly an Asian term for integrating the past and present. He considered the place temple grounds, and his art reflects the influence of Asian, African, and Native American mythologies. Other beliefs were his alone—such as the unusual cone-like hairdos on his painted figures, designed to draw energy upward.

Now operated by the county historical society (and maintained by volunteers—grab a brush at a painting party), Pasaquan is open weekends only, Saturday 10 a.m.-6 p.m., Sunday 1-5 p.m., or by appointment. Admission is $5 adults, $3 seniors, free to children under 12, tel. (912) 649-9444.

Buena Vista is 35 miles southeast of Columbus. Take Hwy. 280 south from Columbus to Hwy. 26; go east on Hwy. 26 2.7 miles to where it splits. Take the left fork (Hwy. 137, the sign says Camp Darby) and continue five miles or so. Watch for a small white sign in the woods, and turn up a small paved road on the left. Drive up to the fence and a short toot will alert the caretaker to your visit.

SOUTHWEST GEORGIA

Among the live oaks draped with Spanish moss, Southern magnolias, poplar arcades, and orchards in the state's southwestern corner, visitors stumble upon sleepy courthouse squares, peanut-processing plants, sugarcane fields, aboriginal mounds, New Deal murals, frontier forts, and Native American totems. Country signs advertise "Goats for Sale—Barbecue Size," and pecan pie's the local specialty.

The Chattahoochee River flows along the region's western edge, forming the border with Alabama. Native American monuments sprinkled

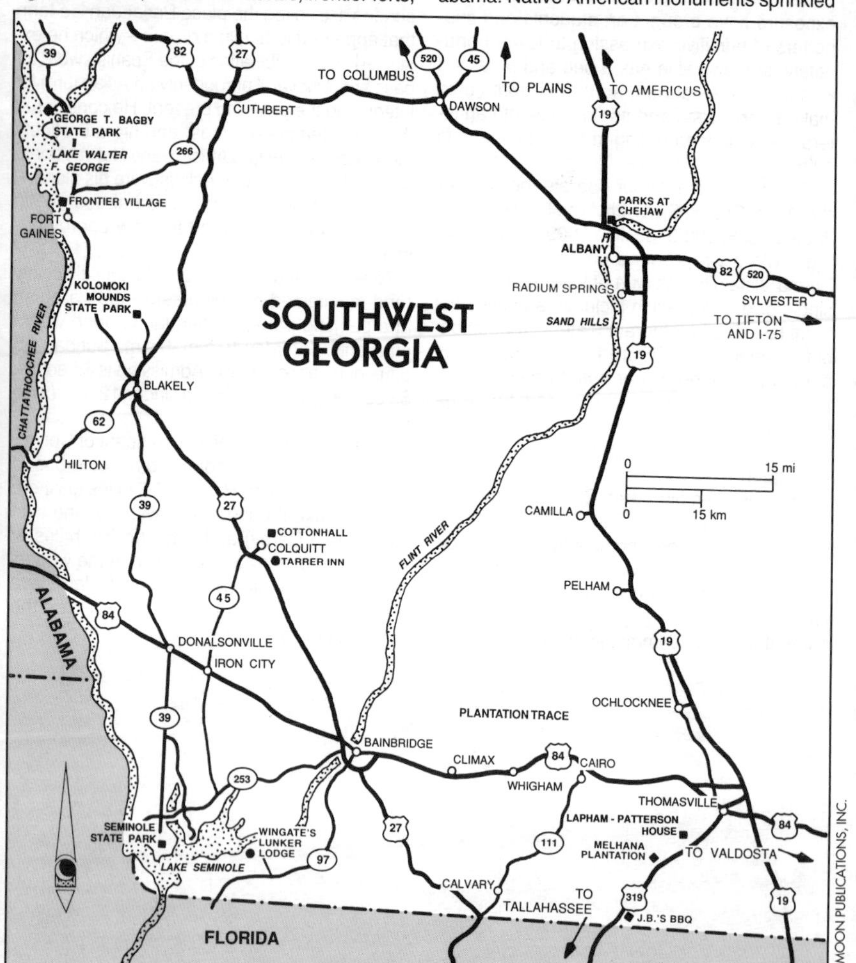

through the area attest to early human habitation along the river. But the wild and remote character of the lands here made for a sparsely settled frontier during colonial days. Much of the area remains wild today, although several dams along the Chattahoochee have tamed the river, creating placid lakes that draw anglers to their shores. The Flint River bisects the region, and evidence remains of the devastation caused when it overflowed its banks in the Great Flood of 1994.

The stately Plantation Trace region renowned as an elite resort at the turn of the century, and noted for its aristocratic hunting resorts to this day, is centered in Thomasville.

FORT GAINES AND VICINITY

In 1814, Fort Gaines was established on the Chattahoochee River boundary of the American frontier. In 1836, the resident Creek who had occupied this region for hundreds of years were forcibly removed, first through the fort, then along the Trail of Tears to Oklahoma. During the Civil War, the fort flew the Confederate flag, and today a replica of the fort draws visitors to the historical river bluff.

Even without the history, the site makes a nice change of scene; it's unusual in this flat coastal plain region to have any kind of contour. Besides the fort replica (off Hwy. 39 south of town), the small **Frontier Village,** tel. (912) 768-2984, features scattered log cabins, a Confederate cannon, and grist and cane mills. An 18-foot-tall oak statue memorializes the area's exiled Creeks. It's open daily 9 a.m.-5 p.m.

Downtown Fort Gaines presents an anachronistic glimpse of small town life as yet untouched by modernization. Tidy homes fly flags above well-tended flowerboxes, the hardware store is the local gathering place, and an old mural advertises "Drink Coca-Cola—Relieves Fatigue." A self-guided historical driving tour map available at either the local library or the state park lodge desk (see below) describes historic buildings and sites.

Just north of town lies Lake Walter F. George, a 48,000-acre impoundment of the Chattahoochee River administered by the Army Corps of Engineers (COE). The Alabama side is more developed (there the reservoir is known as Lake Eufaula), while the Georgia side remains remote and less developed, with the exception of a modern full-service state park. The COE **Resource Manager's Office,** tel. (912) 768-2516, a mile or so north of town on Hwy. 39, serves as an interpretive center. The office distributes maps that show all public facilities around 640 miles of shoreline, including COE campgrounds (some free), swimming areas, picnic spots, boat launches, and marinas. The office is open Mon.-Fri. year-round, and weekends March-October.

George T. Bagby State Park

Three miles north of Fort Gaines off Hwy. 39, a shoreline state park overlooks Lake Walter F. George. The 300-acre park, tel. (912) 768-2660, offers a full-service marina, lodge, boat rentals, swimming pool, tennis courts, and a sandy swimming beach.

A series of interconnected loop trails up to three miles long leads hikers past gopher-tortoise holes, armadillo diggings, and even an old whiskey still. The hand-packed sand trails, a boardwalk over a pond (a favorite alligator-spotting site), and a scenic gazebo with a ramp are all inviting to wheelchairs; pick up trail maps at the interpretive center or lodge.

At the modern lakeside lodge, diners can help themselves at the restaurant's buffet table and stay overnight in one of 30 comfortable lodge rooms for $42 and up. Fully equipped two-bedroom cottages rent for $65-85. For lodging reservations, call (800) 864-PARK (800-864-7275). The parking fee is $2 per car (no charge for restaurant customers or on Wednesdays).

East of Fort Gaines

At the intersection of Highways 27 and 82, the town of **Cuthbert** is most famous for its annual turkey-calling contest, which pits gobblers from around the state in heated competition each March. The town's antebellum historic district revolves around its 1885 courthouse square and includes several attractive private homes and the 1854 Andrews College building. Two other notable local landmarks are the home of jazz great Fletcher H. Henderson, Jr., on Andrews St., and the New Deal mural in the post office (corner of W. Pine and Court Sts.) titled "Last Indian Troubles in Randolph County." The town's historic architecture is further described on a driving-tour map available from the chamber of commerce at the square, tel. (912) 732-2683.

BLAKELY AND VICINITY

Blakely's courthouse square, the crossroads of Highways 27, 39, and 62, contains two potent cultural symbols. The first is a Confederate flag pole, the only one left standing in the state, and the other is a concrete monument to the peanut. In the local post office at Liberty and S. Main Streets, you'll see a classic New Deal mural titled "This Land is Bought from the Indians."

Yet Blakely's most significant landmark predates the town by several thousand years—the Kolomoki Mounds site is considered one of the most significant archaeological sites east of the Mississippi.

A short drive southwest of Blakely, nine miles down Hwy. 62 to Hilton, you'll find the 96-foot **Coheelee Creek Covered Bridge** on Old River Road. Built in 1891, it's the only covered bridge remaining south of Macon in Georgia.

Kolomoki Mounds

Six miles north of Blakely off Hwy. 27, seven pre-Columbian mounds preserve religious centers built by Swift Creek and Weeden Island natives in the 12th and 13th centuries. Georgia's oldest temple mound rises here, along with two burial mounds and four ceremonial mounds. Here in the state's remote southwestern corner, visitors can view these ancient mounds with only a few interpretive signs to distract from their silent majesty, unlike the more heavily visited mounds on the Piedmont.

The mounds were painstakingly constructed basketful-by-basketful. For the largest mound—56 feet high and 325 feet by 200 feet at its base—that translates to an estimated *two million* basketfuls. The mounds formed the center of village life for an estimated population of 1,500-2,000.

An **interpretive museum,** tel. (912) 723-5296, built directly into a partially excavated mound retains skeletons and artifacts exactly as left by archaeologists. An audiovisual show and other exhibits further describe Kolomoki culture, and maps and guides to the site's **nature trails** identify the local plantlife that sustained the native population through the centuries. The mound museum is open Tues.-Sat. 9 a.m.-5 p.m., Sunday 2-5:30 p.m. Admission is $2-4.

The mounds are just one part of 1,293-acre **Kolomoki Mounds State Park,** a major recreational center. Facilities include two small lakes for fishing and boating (rentals available), two swimming pools, miniature golf, and a calendar of special programs—such as October's Indian Artifact Day. Visitors can stay overnight for an after-dark look at the mysterious mounds; a 42-site campground provides water and electric hookups for $14; call (800) 864-PARK (800-864-7275) for reservations.

one of several pre-Columbian mounds centered at Kolomoki

KAP STANN

Colquitt

On Hwy. 27 between Blakely and Bainbridge, **Colquitt** is the undisputed "Mayhaw Capital of the World." This South Georgia fruit, which tastes faintly like guava, is hand-picked in the swamps and ponds of South Georgia for a relatively short harvest season each spring, an event marked by the town's **Mayhaw Festival,** held the third weekend in May.

The town celebrates its folk life heritage with its acclaimed *Swamp Gravy* theater production held several times a year in Cotton Hall, tel. (912) 758-5450, a 60-year-old warehouse. Joy Jinks operates **Tarrer Inn,** on the square downtown, tel. (912) 758-2888, an 1861 boarding house now restored as a lavish historic inn in this remote corner of Georgia.

BAINBRIDGE AND VICINITY

A 1903 brick courthouse clocktower presides over the square in downtown Bainbridge, a city of 27,000 on the banks of the Flint River. The one-time port hosts many events and concerts in the shady park green. The city's trademark festival, the **Riverside Artsfest,** puts a fresh spin on small town festivals—the first weekend each May, Bainbridge celebrates the cultures, arts, foods, and traditions of a state in the United States—a different one each year. The chamber of commerce, tel. (912) 246-4774, operates a welcome center in an antebellum house just off Basin Rd. in the riverside **Earl May Park.**

Many sporty travelers know Bainbridge best as the gateway to Lake Seminole, an impoundment of the Chattahoochee and Flint Rivers that covers 58 square miles. Get to the southern shore via Hwy. 97, or the northern shore via Hwy. 253. No bridge or ferry crosses the lake.

Lake Seminole

Ranking fifth among the best bass-fishing spots in the U.S., Lake Seminole draws fisherfolk to 12,000 acres of stump-filled waters, 5,000 acres of grassy beds, a couple of thousand acres of lily pads, 250 islands, and natural lime sink ponds. Lake waters average only 15 feet deep, shallow for a lake of this size. Besides largemouth and white bass, you can also net stripers, bream, crappie—in fact, more fish varieties than in any other lake in the state.

Wingate's Lunker Lodge, tel. (912) 246-0658, is the local fish camp mecca. Fishing sage and raconteur Jack Wingate presides over the south shore operation, which includes a marina, supply store, lodge, campground, and an 18-bed men's dormitory called the "Stag Hangout." And there's never any shortage of fishing or hunting advice. Sixteen lodge rooms have heat or air-conditioning, and color TV; the antler-adorned lodge restaurant serves seafood and catfish plates. Take Hwy. 97 south from Bainbridge to State Rd. 310 and turn right; it dead-ends at the lodge.

Farther down Hwy. 97 near the state line, see the Army Corps of Engineers **Resource Manager's Office** for detailed maps listing every COE campground, swimming area, boat launch, and picnic site, as well as boating and fishing services around the lake.

Seminole State Park

Seminole State Park, tel. (912) 861-3137, occupies a remote peninsula jutting out into Lake Seminole at the northern shore. The 343-acre park squirrels away a swimming beach, motorboat rental facilities, and a miniature golf course. The 2.2-mile Gopher Tortoise Nature Trail interprets the local wiregrass habitat.

Ten hideaway two-bedroom cottages rent for $60-75. A 50-site campground provides water and electric hookups; sites cost $14-16. For reservations, call (800) 864-PARK (800-864-7275). The park is accessible from the north, via Hwy. 39 (drive 16 miles south from Donalsonville), or from the east, via Hwy. 253 (drive 23 miles west from Bainbridge). The parking fee is $2 per car, free on Wednesdays.

ALBANY

At the head of navigation of the Flint River, Albany was founded in 1836 by Henry Harding Tift (for whom Tifton is named). He named the town after New York's capital, though here it's pronounced al-BENNY. Largest city in South Georgia (population 120,000), Albany is the center of the state's pecan- and peanut-producing area.

The **visitor center,** 225 W. Broad Ave., tel. (912) 434-8700, distributes lodging and dining information.

Albany Museum of Art

The Albany Museum of Art, 311 Meadowlark Dr., tel. (912) 439-8400, is best known for its African art collection, begun by former African ambassador and Albany resident Stella Davis. The museum also displays 19th- and 20th-century American art. It's open Tues.-Sat. 10 a.m.-5 p.m., no admission charge.

The Parks at Chehaw

The city's major attraction, multifaceted Chehaw Park, tel. (912) 430-5275, offers trails, a boat dock, picnic areas, camping, historical exhibits, and a wildlife preserve, on 700 forested acres on the Flint River. The park is open daily 9 a.m.-7 p.m. in summer, until 5 p.m. in winter (closed Christmas Day). Enter from Philema Rd. (Hwy. 91), off Hwy. 82/19 north of town (follow signs). Gate admission is $2 per vehicle.

The **Chehaw Wild Animal Park** is home to elephants, bison, zebras, llamas, wallabies, ostriches, emu, elk, and many other species. The animals roam in a 293-acre natural setting; the park also features a petting zoo, concession stand, and a miniature train that operates on weekends. The Wild Animal Park is open daily 9:30 a.m.-5 p.m.; admission is $2, ages 6-11 $1, under six free.

Mt. Zion Albany Civil Rights Movement Museum

Housed in the old Mt. Zion Church, where Martin Luther King, Jr. preached in 1961, this new museum, 326 Whitney Ave., tel. (912) 432-1698, commemorates the role Albany played in the civil rights movement. The museum is open Wed.-Sat. 10 a.m.-4 p.m., Sunday 2-5 p.m.; admission is $3 adults; $2 ages 6-17, 65 and over, and children under six free.

THOMASVILLE

In its heyday at the turn of the past century, ten thousand Northerners descended on Thomasville each winter to unwind in the heart of Georgia's graceful Plantation Trace region. Dozens of posh hotels and guesthouses catered to the aristocratic likes of the Goodriches and Rockefellers, and many of the country's elite built elegant estates in town and throughout the countryside.

They say it all started when a doctor published an article in 1870 asserting the therapeutic qualities of the region's pine-soaked air—and it sure is true, no one could help but feel healthier after inhaling the sultry scent. But even decades before that, Thomasville found itself an unlikely set of promoters—the Union prisoners who were temporarily moved down here from the P.O.W. camp at Andersonville returned north with tales of the region's "balsam breeze, long-blooming roses, and bobtail quails behind every hedgerow."

Today, Thomasville retains the old-timey appeal of a bygone resort, grateful the crowds are gone but eager to host the curious few who make their way here. The **Welcome Center** on the square, tel. (912) 226-9600, is always happy to give out information, including driving-tour maps of the area, and it also sponsors tours of local plantations. It's open daily except Sunday.

For a fine introduction to the area, read Bailey White *(Mama Makes Up Her Mind, Sleeping at the Starlight Motel)*, a former schoolteacher who chronicles South Georgia life regularly on National Public Radio from her Thomasville home.

Sights

The many varieties of roses in beautiful bloom around town has led to Thomasville's nickname, the "City of the Roses," and you can see its cozy new **Rose Test Gardens,** laid out around a latticework gazebo, east on Hwy. 84 (restrooms and a small lake are nearby). The natural landmark downtown is a 300-year-old **Big Oak** at E. Monroe and E. Crawford St., towering 75 feet high with a limb-spread of 162 feet. **Paradise Park,** centrally located in town on S. Broad St., retains the look of wild woods—18 acres of pine, dogwood, and crape myrtle.

Two impressive historic house museums recall the town's hotel era. The Victorian **Lapham-Patterson House,** 626 N. Dawson St., tel. (912) 225-4004, offered state-of-the-art conveniences when it was built in 1884—gas lighting, hot and cold running water, and indoor plumbing—and today it's beautifully restored to period splendor. The house is specially decorated for tours during the Rose Festival in April and at Christmastime; year-round it's open Tues.-Sat. 9 a.m.-5 p.m. and Sunday 2-5:30 p.m. (open Monday on major holidays only). The charge is $2 for adults.

The **Pebble Hill Plantation,** tel. (912) 226-2344, off Hwy. 319 five miles south of town, opens to the public an exquisite estate typical of winter hunting resorts built earlier this century. Guided tours take guests through the high-style mansion, from its dramatic black-and-white foyer with the French curved staircase through period-furnished rooms filled with artwork (much horse-and-hound imagery attests to the local leisure pursuit). One room is devoted to native artifacts from the region, and you can also see antique automobiles and carriages on display. You can wander through the grounds and gardens for $3 adults and $1.50 children. Guided tours of the house are offered for $7 (age 12 and older) Tues.-Sat. 10 a.m.-5 p.m., Sunday 1-5 p.m.; closed in September as well as major holidays.

At the **Thomas County Historical Museum,** 725 N. Dawson St., tel. (912) 226-7664, the local historical society displays a set of interesting exhibits, old hotel artifacts, and antique costumes recalling its past heyday. Outside there's a Victorian era bowling alley, farm house, and vintage cars. Tours are offered Mon.-Sat. 10:30 a.m.-3:30 p.m., Sunday 2-5 p.m., for $4 adults, $1 students 6-18.

Events and Entertainment

Thomasville's weeklong **Rose Festival** in mid-April is the city's answer to Pasadena's New Year's display. September brings the **Deep South Fair,** and about mid-December, the town decorates for a **Victorian Christmas Celebration** featuring a living nativity along with traditional music, games, and entertainment; historic homes are likewise dressed up for the season.

Local performing-arts productions are held at the **Thomasville Cultural Center,** 600 E. Washington St., tel. (912) 226-0588, a remodeled 1915 schoolhouse that also houses a library and a gallery with a permanent collection of antiques and fine arts. It's open Tues.-Sat. 1-5 p.m.

Accommodations

Four bed and breakfasts provide quiet retreats in grand Victorian houses with sweeping verandas and manicured lawns, all within walking distance of the historic downtown. Room rates start about $70 a night for antique-filled rooms and an ample breakfast.

At the **1884 Paxton House,** 445 Remington Ave., tel. (912) 226-5197 or (800) 278-0138, Susie Sherrod offers rooms in her gothic Victorian home or in a garden cottage. Anne Dodge operates the **Grand Victoria Inn,** 817 S. Hansell St., tel. (912) 226-7460. Kathy and Ed Middleton of **Serendipity Cottage,** 339 E. Jefferson St., tel. (912) 226-8111 or (800) 383-7377, let out rooms in their 1906 "Foursquare" home. Or try **Evans House,** 725 S. Hansell St., tel. (912) 226-1343 or (800) 344-4717.

South of town, the **Melhana Plantation** on Hwy. 319, tel. (888) 920-3030, opened in 1997 with an aim to take a place among the most select luxurious historic inns in the South. The gracious 40-acre estate—with beautiful horse pastures, sunken gardens, a pool house, and even its own Showboat Theater—holds guest rooms in a meticulously restored antebellum house, a carriage house, cottage, barns, and stable—rates start at $200 and include breakfast.

Food and Drink

The **Billiard Academy** on Broad St. downtown sells hundreds of chili dogs daily (85 cents each) through a streetside window, as it has since 1949 (when a dog cost a dime). **Fallin's Barbecue,** 2250 E. Pinetree Blvd., tel. (912) 228-1071, is a comfortable family restaurant serving lunches from 11 a.m. and dinners such as all-you-can-eat ribs for $8.99.

True barbecue aficionados drive the 12 miles south of town to **J.B.'s Bar-B-Que & Grill** on Hwy. 319 S, tel. (912) 377-9344, where J.B. cooks up meaty pork ribs ($8.75) along with barbecue chicken, mullet, and shrimp with all the traditional sides in a family-style restaurant. Neighbor Jimmy Buffett is among the biggest fans of J.B.'s 'cue. It's open daily except Monday from noonish to ten-ish.

You'll find acres of farm-fresh produce at the **state farmers market** on Smith Ave. at Hansell St., tel. (912) 225-4072 (closed Sunday).

VICINITY OF THOMASVILLE

Outside Thomasville, rolling hills densely covered with pinewoods harbor a lush fern understory. The scenic countryside is washed over by that trademark balsam breeze. Stately riverside towns hold tidy bandstand parks, while dustier outback communities have a more down-home flavor. Courthouse squares, roadside produce stands, and eccentric local festivals offer plentiful excuses for detours.

West of Town

Out Hwy. 84 west, **Cairo** (KAY-ro) is the home of Roddenbery's *Cane Patch Syrup.* The family-owned, 101-year-old firm distills syrup from South Georgia's native sugarcane. You'll find local agriculture celebrated in the New Deal mural "Products of Grady County," which graces the post office at 203 N. Broad Street. The town hosts an **Antique Car Rally** the second weekend in May that features a gaslight parade, street dance, and car displays.

Big-draw festivals at tiny towns can swell the local three-figure population to up over 50,000. In **Whigham** (on Hwy. 84 west of Cairo), a **Rattlesnake Roundup** held the last Saturday in January captivates onlookers with daring snake demonstrations and other entertainment. South of Whigham in **Calvary** (on Hwy. 11 near the Florida border), **Mule Day** is held the first Saturday in November (rainout date: the second Saturday). The festival features traditional country activities (cane grinding, syrup making), contests (tobacco spittin', greased pig catchin'), 600 booths hawking crafts and country wares, and the crowning event: the hundreds-strong mule parade (prizes awarded for ugliest and most ornery). Barbecue, fish fry, gospel, bands, clogging, and a square dance round out the event.

Out Hwy. 84 west of Whigham, the town of **Climax** hosts **Swine Time** the Saturday after Thanksgiving. Locals celebrate the indispensable stock animal of subsistence farmers, source of meat, lard, soap, and leather—pigs parade in costume, and are served in every dish imaginable, accompanied by country music, bluegrass, and gospel. For more information call (912) 246-0910 (SoooEEE!).

North of Town

Three towns north of Thomasville off Hwy. 19 also make good detours at festival time. **Ochlocknee** presents **Old South Days** the second Saturday in November, paying tribute to lost antebellum glory with traditional arts, crafts, entertainment and food, a country fair, cane syrup making, races and games; tel. (912) 574-5151. In **Pelham,** November's **Wildfest** highlights the sporting pastimes the region is famous for. In **Camilla,** the second and third weeks in June bring **Gnat Days,** featuring boat cruises, a professional tennis tournament, juried arts and crafts shows, the Gnat Market and regional foods; tel. (912) 336-5255.

Hunting

The thick woods of southwest Georgia draw hunters after deer, grouse, dove, wild turkey, and quail. Exclusive hunting plantations provide all necessary equipment, up to the customary horses and hounds. Operations are often seasonal and sporadic, so contact local chambers of commerce for area resorts, or call **Quail Unlimited** (Albany chapter tel. 912-432-2058).

Locals hunt in the region's many Wildlife Management Areas; see **Department of Natural Resources** for state regulations information.

ALONG I-75: PERRY TO VALDOSTA

From the I-75 corridor, which slices through the middle of wiregrass country, South Georgia looks like one great fluorescent strip of 24-hour gas stations, fast-food chains, and budget motels. Yet visitors looking beyond that find notable remnants of pre-neon history, such as Victorian mansions, gristmills, canoe trails down sandy Southern rivers, and boardwalks through moist coastal plain woodlands.

The central towns of Perry, Cordele, Tifton, and Valdosta—spread evenly along the 150-mile route from Macon to Florida—make logical pit stops for through-travelers on I-75. In fact, long stretches of empty highway in between the towns make them virtually *necessary* stops.

PERRY AND VICINITY

Once an old stagecoach stop, Perry continues to treat travelers with its small historic district and landmark New Perry Hotel. The small and scenic downtown, lined with antique and craft shops, lies two miles east of I-75 off the I-75 business loop.

The Georgia Agricenter south of town at I-75 houses such major events as the nine-day **Georgia National Fair** in early October. Another famed local event is the **Mossy Creek Barnyard Arts and Crafts Fest** held the third weekend in both April and October just outside town—festivities include storytelling, traditional music, mule rides, and such old-time crafts as handmade horse-drawn buggies and corn husk dolls. Stop by the **Perry Welcome Center** off I-75 exit 42 for a schedule of local events.

New Perry Hotel and Restaurant

The New Perry Hotel, 800 Main St., tel. (912) 987-1000, is a light, airy, and spacious old-time hotel built in 1925 to replace the "Old" Perry Hotel built in 1870. The hotel retains its original thick Venetian blinds, white chenille bedspreads, and potted geraniums, but also seems modern in its own retro-'40s way. The grandmotherly staff greets guests with such endearments as "sweetie" and "sugar."

The 39 rooms are split between the two-story 1925 building or an attractive motel of more recent vintage out back. An inviting patio between the two buildings surrounds a small pool. Room rates start at $27 for singles.

Three classically Southern meals a day are served on white tablecloths in the dining room at reasonable rates. The mimeographed menu changes daily, and may feature such entrees as ham with corn relish, grilled catfish, and fried chicken. Choose from among a half-dozen side dishes, such as squash Lorraine, fried eggplant, or congealed fruit salad. Of course, there's nearly always pecan and peach pie for dessert. Breakfast is served 7-10 a.m., lunch 11:30 a.m.-2:30 p.m., and dinner 5:30-9 p.m.

West of Perry

Eleven miles northwest via Hwy. 341, **Fort Valley** is the Peach Capital of the World. Georgia's prime peach-growing region encompasses much of the area between Fort Valley and Perry. See the orchards in full flower in early April, and find fresh fruit at roadside stands—or pick your own at do-it-yourself orchards—from late May through July.

West of Perry off Hwy. 341 (take I-75 exit 42), the American Camellia Society opens to the public the colorful **Massee Lane Gardens,** 1 Massee Ln., tel. (912) 967-2358. The camellias bloom from November to March, and in springtime visitors can see the flowering azaleas, dogwoods, irises, and many annuals and other perennials. The nine-acre site also shelters an art gallery, gift shop, and a tranquil Japanese garden, complete with koi pond. From November to March, hours are Mon.-Sat. 9 a.m.-5 p.m. and Sunday 1-5 p.m. Off-season hours are Mon.-Fri. 9 a.m.-4 p.m. Admission is $2, children under 12 free.

South of Perry

Ten miles north of Cordele and a mile west of I-75, **Vienna** (VI-enna) is famous for its finger-lickin' **Big Pig Jig**—Georgia's official barbecue cooking competition—held the second weekend in October. Downtown's stately turretted brick courthouse presides over a small historic district laced with gingerbread detailing, widow's walks, stained glass, columns, and other Victorian flourishes. The local chamber of commerce at 204 W. Union St., tel. (912) 268-4554, distributes city guides.

CORDELE AND VICINITY

With its miles-long strip of franchise restaurants, budget motels, and discount shopping centers along Hwy. 280, Cordele makes a handy pit stop for I-75 through-travelers. Others follow Hwy. 280 out nine miles to a major state park or another 20 miles or so to the intriguing area around Americus (see **Jimmy Carter Country,** above).

Lake Blackshear

Cordele's greatest recreational attraction is 8,700-acre Lake Blackshear, a Georgia Power impoundment of the Flint River. Around its 77-mile shoreline are municipal and utility beaches, campgrounds, and boat launches. You'll find marinas at the Hwy. 280 bridge and off Hwy. 300 at the south side near the dam. Pick up maps at the **Resource Manager's Office** by the dam, tel. (912) 273-3811.

Nine miles west of I-75 exit 33, **Georgia Veterans Memorial State Park,** tel. (912) 276-2371, is a major recreational resource on the lake. The 1,322-acre park offers boating (rentals available), fishing, a swimming beach, a pool, and a lakeside 18-hole golf course. The most distinguishing feature of this memorial park is its **military museum,** which displays weaponry, uniforms, and other artifacts inside, and planes, cannons, and tanks outside. Museum hours are daily 8 a.m.-4:30 p.m., no charge. Accommodations at the park include 10 two-bedroom cottages overlooking the lake ($60-75). An 85-site campground charges $14-17 per site, including water and electric hookups. Call (800) 864-PARK (800-864-7275) for reservations. The parking fee is $2 per car, free on Wednesday.

At the **Catfish Festival** held here each May, the bottomfeeder is cooked up and judged in three categories—fried, stewed, and extraordinaire. **Memorial Day** and **Veterans Day** celebrations are also very big here, for obvious reasons.

South to Tifton

Outside of Ashburn, at the shoulder of southbound I-75, the **World's Largest Peanut** stands perched atop a 15-foot-tall brick pedestal. The 10-foot-tall goober rests in a golden crown, which boasts "Georgia: 1st in Peanuts."

TIFTON AND VICINITY

Originally Creek territory and under Spanish rule until 1763, the area was settled by marine engineer Henry Harding Tift in 1872, who set up a lumbering operation that grew into the city of Tifton. Today you'll see Tifton in the dateline of breaking agricultural news; its Agricultural Experiment Station is foremost in the field of agricultural research nationwide. Also here is Agrirama, one of South Georgia's premier attractions.

The original downtown, a mix of restored and dusty storefronts dating from the 1940s, is along Main St. between 4th and 9th Avenues. Here you'll find an art deco movie theater, old shops anchored by a classic western-wear store, a homey art gallery at the tracks, and a **welcome center** in the old depot (at 100 Central Ave., tel. 912-382-6200, open weekdays only). Stretch your legs or picnic in one of several shady parks —Fulwood Park at Tift and 8th features a unique "musical playground." Take I-75 exit 19 to go downtown; follow 2nd Ave. east to Main (note that the numerical street order gets jumbled; 2nd Ave. is at one point between 4th and 9th Avenues).

Agrirama

Despite its hee-haw name, Agrirama, I-75 exit 20, tel. (912) 386-3344, presents an impressive "living-history" village that takes visitors back in time to the late 19th century. More than 40 restored structures on 95 acres replicate South Georgia farm and village life, including a distinctive South Georgia "dogtrot" cabin, a gristmill, lumber mill, print shop, Masonic lodge, cotton gin, and two-story Victorian house. Agrirama is largely staffed by old-timers wearing period costumes, who speak from their personal experience as they shell peas, grind corn, distill syrup, and spin yarns—catch these Southern "living treasures" while you can. A logging train ride, barnyard animals, and an operating antique drugstore soda fountain add to the experience.

The annual highlight of Agrirama's special events is the Folklife Festival in April, which features traditional crafts, games, and foods. Other festivals here include the Spring Frolic in March, Independence Day and Labor Day celebrations, and mid-December's Victorian Christmas gala. At the Opry stage next door, Agrirama hosts a **Wiregrass Opry** on Saturday nights April-Oct., featuring country, bluegrass, and gospel music (separate admission).

Admission is $8 for adults, $6 for seniors over 55, $4 for children ages 4-16 (no charge for children under four). Agrirama is open Tues.-Sat. 9 a.m.-5 p.m., then is closed either Sunday or Monday depending on the season (call for current schedule). Even without touring the grounds, you can pull over for a restroom/picnic stop and visit the country store (no charge).

Vicinity

In **Irwinville,** 15 minutes northeast of Tifton via Hwy. 125, a park marks the site where Jefferson Davis, president of the Confederate States of America, was captured in 1865. A small museum on Hwy. 32 displays Civil War artifacts, including part of the tree under which Davis was found (open Tues.-Sat. 9 a.m.-5 p.m., Sunday 1-5 p.m., adult admission $1).

Reed Bingham State Park, tel. (912) 896-3551, is conveniently located six miles west of I-75 exit 10 between Tifton and Valdosta (on Hwy. 37 between Adel and Moultrie), but this 1,620-acre park remains remote and unspoiled. Its 375-acre lake allows for fishing, boating, and swimming at a small sandy beach. Special gardens are designed to attract butterflies and hummingbirds. A 3.5-mile boardwalk **nature trail** traverses the wooded coastal plain lowlands, the highlight of four loop trails that cross through a variety of habitats—bay swamps, river swamps, flat woods, southern mixed hardwoods, and old fields. Camp at one of 46 sites ($14-16, hookups available); call (800) 864-PARK (800-864-7275) for reservations. The parking fee is $2 per car, free on Wednesday.

The **Catfish House** right outside the park entrance opens for dinner Thurs.-Saturday.

VALDOSTA AND VICINITY

Valdosta (population 48,000) is home to Valdosta State University (enrollment 7,500) and Moody Air Force Base, and is surrounded and supported by its agricultural industries—pine, peaches, pecans, and tobacco. In fact, tobacco is such a big player in the local economy that schools may delay opening if the harvest is behind schedule.

Downtown Valdosta's historic district centers around the 1905 courthouse square on E. Central Ave. (off Hwy. 84, about a mile east of I-75 exit 4), which is surrounded by attractive residential streets with many old homes. Around this agricultural county, you can attend tobacco auctions and tour pecan-processing plants, or visit pick-your-own cotton fields, peach orchards, and farms. The **Valdosta-Lowndes County Convention and Visitors Bureau,** 1703 Norman Dr., tel. (912) 245-0513, arranges agricultural tours and distributes self-guided driving tour maps emphasizing architectural highlights.

Accommodations and Food

At I-75 exits 2-6, nearly 3,000 motel rooms give travelers the choice of many national motel chains a stone's throw from the freeway. Budget travelers will find the four-story **Jolly Inn Motel** at exit 5 (a quarter-mile east of I-75), tel. (912) 244-9500. It has a pool and doubles run $28-36.

Beyond the standard interstate franchises, a local seafood shack overlooks a cypress swamp landscape. The family-operated **Fish Net** on Sportsmans Cove Rd., tel. (912) 559-5410, serves fresh fish dinners, including all-you-can-eat catfish and trout for $6.95. Or for the absolute freshest fish, catch one yourself at the adjacent public fishing ponds and the chef will prepare it for you. Hours are 5 p.m. until at least 9:30 p.m. Wed.-Sat. only. Take I-75 exit 2 west along Hwy. 376 a half mile, turn right onto Loch Laurel Rd. and go two miles to Sportsmans Cove Rd. (follow signs).

Morrison's Cafeteria in the Valdosta Mall off I-75 exit 5 serves traditional Southern plates.

Shopping and Diversions

At I-75 exit 2, you'll find **factory outlet shopping malls** offering a hundred stores in all, including Acme boots, Levi-Strauss, and London Fog, as well as restaurants and motels. For nonshopping traveling companions, the **Francis Lake Golf Course,** 340 Golf Dr. S, tel. (912) 559-7961 (east behind the malls), invites short-timers. You'll find department stores, boutiques, a food court, and a six-plex cinema at the **Valdosta Mall** off I-75 exit 5.

Information and Services

Stop at the **Georgia State Visitors Center** off I-75 between exits 1 and 2 for a helpful staff, a computerized resource to local lodging and camping, and discount coupons to accommodations or shopping. It also has a picnic area and free clean restrooms. The center is open daily 8 a.m.-5:30 p.m.

River and Lake Recreation

The **Alapaha River,** one of the South's most beautiful swamp rivers, flows through central wiregrass country east of I-75. Meandering through timberlands of pine, live oak, and tupelo—at times narrow enough for trees to form an overhead canopy—the Class I river is lined with snow-white sand banks where you'll likely see beaver, otter, wild turkey, and deer. A designated **paddling trail** begins outside Willacoochee (28 miles east of Tifton, where Hwy. 135 crosses the river), and runs south 83 miles to the Hwy. 94 crossing outside Statenville, six miles north of the Florida border. Road crossings divide the length into four convenient day-long stretches, and four primitive campsites are stationed along the way. Experienced paddlers can easily run the river's rapids (strongest at periods of low water), and beginners can easily portage around.

For guided canoe trips or rental equipment, call **Suwannee Canoe Outpost,** an outfitter on Hwy. 129 at the Suwannee across the border near Live Oak, Florida, tel. (904) 364-4991 or (800) 428-4147. The Outpost also runs the Withlacoochee River west of Valdosta—Class III rapids here attract experienced paddlers at certain times in the year—and the Suwannee from Okefenokee Swamp headwaters.

Fish for bluegill and redbreast (Jan.-June is best) on the Alapaha or Withlacoochee rivers, or head to **Banks Lake** National Wildlife Refuge 22 miles northeast of Valdosta (off Hwy. 122 outside Lakeland). The 3,900-acre lake teems with exceptionally large bluegill and largemouth bass, and dramatic cypress-swamp landscapes also attract naturalists and birders. Banks Lake is operated by Okefenokee Swamp authorities, tel. (912) 496-3331.

raccoon

SOUTHEASTERN INTERIOR

Countless even rows of stick-straight Georgia pine line southeastern highways, interrupted by rust-red logging roads used to transport the state's signature product to mills. Deeper into the interior the forests break into open farmland; roadside stands sell peaches, peanuts, pecans, and the regional agricultural oddity—the sweet Vidalia onion. While quiet country towns make diverting detours, most folks know this region best as the agonizing stretch of blacktop that's the necessary means to a beach vacation. The coast's distinct culture can be better understood and appreciated after crossing what seems even today like a daunting barrier.

Statesboro, the Big City in these parts, is home to 10,000 Georgia Southern University students. Smaller towns hold other prized distinctions: Vidalia is the namesake of the sweet onion, McRae proudly displays a 32-foot wooden replica of the Statue of Liberty, Glennville boasts of having the world's largest cricket farm, and Claxton calls itself the Fruitcake Capital of the World. As is true throughout South Georgia, secreted parks—often at the shores of a lazy Southern river or fishing lake—display the coastal plain habitat at its best.

Whether you're lollygagging or blasting through, the best advice is to be prepared to avoid getting stranded in areas with few services. Summer travelers should note that this region has the most unrelentingly hot and humid climate of the whole state, which can turn seemingly minor car trouble or unrequited thirst and exposure into a serious event.

The major route through the region is I-16 between Macon and Savannah (I-75 from Macon through Valdosta is covered in the previous section). This 150-mile stretch of freeway holds few services for those uninterested in straying far from the highway, though you can find intermittent food stops and gas stations. It's best to get gas and stock up around Macon.

Freeway highlights are limited to passing the precise geological center of Georgia around exit 7 (no services), and a local favorite barbecue restaurant only a quarter-mile south of the freeway off exit 5 (in Soperton, see **Dublin and Vicinity,** below). Most services cluster around I-16 exits for Dublin (45 miles outside Macon) and exit 23 around Statesboro (60 miles west of Savannah).

DUBLIN AND VICINITY

In 1812, Irish townsfolk named their community Dublin, and today the city continues to celebrate its Irish heritage. On St. Patrick's Day, two weeks of festivities aim to rival Savannah's grand holiday events. Although the town center is four miles north of I-16, most of the modern development naturally occurs at the freeway exits.

Drive along Bellevue Ave. to the town center to glimpse its earlier design. If you can catch it open, the 1904 **Dublin-Lauren County Museum** at Bellevue and Academy streets, tel. (912) 272-9242, displays native artifacts, vintage clothing, and local history exhibits, and also distributes walking-tour maps to 19th-century buildings around town. Hours are Tues.-Fri. 1-4:30 p.m. Near the downtown courthouse, eat at **Ma Hawkins Cafe,** 124 W. Jackson St., tel. 272-0941. The family cafe, in operation since 1931, serves such Southern specialties as fried chicken, greens, grits, and corn bread. It's open for three meals a day (closed Sun.).

Outside of town, head east to see evidence of a civilization that inhabited the area 3,000 years ago. Along Rte. 19 at the Oconee River is **Fish Trap Cut,** a 100-yard slice into the bank believed to be an aboriginal fishing hole that dates from 1000 B.C.; two ceremonial mounds are also on-site. Dublin's riverside park is nearby.

On Rte. 441 13 miles north of Dublin, the 1811 **Chappell's Mill,** tel. (912) 272-5128, still grinds corn by the old dry-mill process. You can watch the operation (call first for operating hours) and pick up a bag (two pounds for 60 cents); you can also find the stone-ground grains at local markets.

Soperton

To the east, Soperton (I-16 exit 17, then southeast on Rte. 29) is home to **Sweat's Surf N**

Turf, a misnamed concrete block restaurant known for the barbecue sauce that has drawn crowds here for inexpensive barbecue-soaked meats and sides since 1966. The parking lot holds a hearty mix of 18-wheelers, pickups, and beach-bound Mercedes sedans. Hours are Mon.-Sat. 11 a.m.-9 p.m., closed Sunday, tel. (912) 529-3637.

There's a tiny **visitor center,** tel. (912) 529-6263, housed in an 1845 pioneer cabin at the off-ramp, which presents local history exhibits and antique furnishings as well as tourist information (open daily 9 a.m.-5 p.m.).

McRAE AND VICINITY

South of Dublin at the intersection of five country highways, McRae displays its own all-American **Liberty Square.** Here a wooden replica of the Statue of Liberty towers to 32 feet (half actual size!), a turn-of-the-century fire bell has been rechristened Liberty Bell, and copies of the Declaration of Independence and Constitution are on exhibit. But the main event for this tiny crossroads is a major state park north of town.

Little Ocmulgee State Park

Little Ocmulgee State Park, tel. (912) 868-2832, two miles north of McRae on Hwy. 441, is a popular stopping point for drivers bound for Golden Isles resorts. The 1,397-acre lakeside park holds lodging, extensive recreational facilities, and a lake, all in a representative coastal plain environment.

Boating and fishing are popular activities at the park's 265-acre lake, and boat rentals are available. An 18-hole golf course is also a major draw, and package rates combining lodging and greens fees are a good value for avid golfers. A swimming pool and tennis courts provide additional diversion. Of special recreational and naturalist programs held throughout the year, the highlight is a regional crafts festival the first weekend in April. Check at the lakeside **visitor center** by the fishing pier for a schedule and trail maps.

The three-mile **Oak Ridge Loop** trail allows hikers to experience a great variety of habitats. Start from the lodge parking lot and first you will cross a boardwalk over a swampy lowland filled with tupelo, cypress, sweet gum, and live oaks—all lined with a green bed of ferns. The trail continues along the lake to an observation platform—an ideal spot to watch wood ducks, herons, egrets, anhingas, and other native and migratory birds. Then the trail gently climbs to a sand ridge, evidence of the area's geological history as an ancient seabed. Watch for gopher tortoise burrows, marked by small mounds of white sand at the entrance, and note how the scrubby oaks are dwarfed because of the nutrient-starved soil. The trail loops back and backtracks to the lodge. The 1.7-mile **Magnolia Loop** trail cuts off the larger loop, skipping the platform and sand ridge.

The park's **Pete Phillips Lodge,** tel. (912) 868-7474, offers 30 guest rooms, many of which overlook the landscaped golf course for $50-75 d. The lodge restaurant overlooks the sixth tee and serves generous Southern buffets and menu selections, all at reasonable prices. It's open for breakfast daily 7-10 a.m.; for lunch Mon.-Sat. 11:30 a.m.-2 p.m.; and for dinner Mon.-Sat. 5-9 p.m., Sunday 11:30 a.m.-2 p.m. Ten fully equipped rental **cottages** are set against the lake ($55-70 for a one-bedroom). A 58-site campground set among the pines charges $14 per night, including water and electric hookups. For lodge, cottage, or camping reservations, call (800) 864-PARK (800-864-7275). The parking fee is $2 per car; no charge for golfers and restaurant patrons, or on Wednesday.

VIDALIA AND VICINITY

Fifteen miles south of I-16, Vidalia is known nationwide by gourmands for its delectable brand of onions. In 1931, a Toombs County farmer named Mose Coleman discovered that the onion crop he had planted produced onions so sweet they could be eaten raw, like apples—an oddity attributed to a fortuitous combination of seeds and soil. Today gourmet Vidalia onions support a $30 million local industry; one crop represents an entire year's income.

In late April and early May, you'll have no trouble following your nose to the **Vidalia Onion Festival**—10 days of festivities scheduled to coincide with the brief harvest. You can taste onion-laden concoctions and witness the crowning of a Miss Vidalia beauty queen.

The astrally connected may have heard of Vidalia for its numerous UFO sightings over the years (local Holiness preacher Rickey Monroe claims to have witnessed 13 alien sightings alone).

The **Vidalia Welcome Center,** 2805 E. First St., tel. (912) 538-8687 (open Mon.-Fri. 8:30 a.m-5 p.m.) arranges tours of local onion farms and processing plants in the spring; cotton and tobacco tours are available in the fall.

The **Altama Museum of Art and History** at the corner of Jackson and 6th Streets, tel. (912) 537-1911, displays a collection of antique porcelein and other interior design arts in the restored 1911 Brazell House. It's open Monday, Tuesday, Thursday, and Friday 10 a.m.-4 p.m.

Sweat's, 215 N.W. Main St., tel. (912) 537-3934, is a local branch of the famous Soperton barbecue restaurant.

Lyons

Five miles east of Vidalia in downtown Lyons, the local pharmacy doubles as a Christian bookstore and the hardware store has a bridal registry. Also here in a restored turn-of-the-century commercial complex called Robert Toombs Square is the **Robert Toombs Inn,** 101 S. State St., tel. (912) 526-4489, which lets 14 period-furnished guest rooms and five suites. Room rates are inexpensive and include a continental breakfast (or just stop in for a drink or meal).

Gordonia-Altamaha State Park

In Reidsville, 25 miles south of I-16 (16 miles southeast of Lyons), this 280-acre state park, tel. (912) 557-6444, presents typical coastal plain terrain around a 12-acre lake. A nine-hole golf course, miniature golf, and a pool are available. A 23-site campground costs $14 per night, including water and electric hookups; for reservations, call (800) 864-PARK (800-864-7275). The park is off Hwy. 280; take I-16 exit 23 south. The parking fee is $2 per car; no charge for golfers or on Wednesday.

(By the way, Reidsville's the home of the Georgia State Prison—say you're "going to Reidsville" and folks will figure it's involuntary.)

STATESBORO

Statesboro, 60 miles west of Savannah, is home to Georgia Southern University (GSU), whose 10,000 students dominate the city's population of 16,000. The original town was ravaged by Sherman in his march through in 1864. Downtown's "new" Bulloch County Courthouse was built in 1894.

Along downtown's Main Street, a 1921 bungalow serves as the town's **welcome center,** 204 S. Main St., tel. (912) 489-1869. Folks here distribute walking-tour maps of the 19th-century buildings and sell a small selection of gifts and crafts.

Georgia Southern University

Georgia Southern is a four-year school, part of the state university system. On campus, the **Georgia Southern Museum,** tel. (912) 681-5444, displays a 26-foot Mosasaur skeleton—a meat-eating sea serpent once native to the prehistoric seas that covered South Georgia during the Mesozoic era—as well as exhibits ranging from arts and folklife to coastal crustaceans and antique autos. During the academic session (excepting holidays), the museum is open Mon.-Fri. 9 a.m.-5 p.m. and Sunday 2-5 p.m. (and it's occasionally open Tuesday evenings for lectures by GSU faculty). Summer hours are Mon.-Fri. 10 a.m.-5 p.m. Ask at the museum for an interpretive guide to the trail that runs through the adjacent **Herty Nature Preserve,** and also look for the 10-acre **Magnolia Garden** on campus.

Accommodations and Food

The **Statesboro Inn & Restaurant,** 106 S. Main St., tel. (912) 489-8628, set in a two-story 1904 Victorian house with a wraparound porch, offers 15 guest rooms from $75 d; the restaurant serves dinner only. The **Trellis Garden Inn** across the street at 107 S. Main St., tel. (912) 489-8781 charges from $44. Both are within walking distance of the university, downtown shops, and restaurants.

Eat at the **Beaver House Restaurant,** 121 S. Main St., tel. (912) 764-2821 (Hwy. 301 downtown). Set in a large white-columned mansion built in 1911, the restaurant serves classic Southern meals boarding house style—for one price, you're served everything on the menu, and you bring your plate to the kitchen when you're done. A typical spread includes fried chicken, rice and gravy, pole beans, fried okra, creamed corn, stewed tomatoes, black-eyed peas, macaroni and cheese, scratch biscuits, and cobbler (all for $5.49). Lunch is served daily 11 a.m.-2:30 p.m., dinner Mon.-Sat. 5:30 -9 p.m.

Vandy's Barbecue, 22 W. Vine St., tel. (912) 764-2444, barbecues delicious pork, beef, and chicken—a whole picnic-size fryer is $5.50 to go. It's a block behind the main street; hours are Mon.-Sat. 7 a.m.-6 p.m. (a second location is at the local mall).

VICINITY OF STATESBORO

George L. Smith State Park

About 24 miles west of Statesboro and 10 miles east of Swainsboro, George L. Smith State Park, tel. (912) 763-2759, encompasses 1,355 acres of natural coastal plain environment around a 412-acre lake. Fishing and boating are popular activities, or rent canoes to course through three miles of cypress-lined trails. A historic gristmill on the premises offers tours, and an 1880s covered bridge makes a scenic backdrop for a picnic. The park charges $14 a night to stay in its 21-site campground, including water and electric hookups; call (800) 864-PARK (800-864-7275) for reservations. The park is about 10 miles north of I-16 exit 23. The parking fee is $2 per car, free on Wednesdays.

South of Statesboro

The north-south Hwy. 301 thoroughfare that passes through Statesboro brought crowds of northern travelers to Florida before the interstates were built. At roadside produce stands along this route in summertime, expect to find blueberries, cantaloupes, corn, grapes (muscadine or scuppernong), raspberries, snap beans, strawberries, watermelons, and of course, peaches, peanuts, and pecans.

On Hwy. 301 south of I-16 you'll find **Claxton,** the Fruitcake Capital of the World (what—you thought that was in California?). If it's the second weekend in March, detour for its Rattlesnake Roundup. Snakes are judged in several categories (longest, fattest, etc.), and the event also features snake milking, parades, and home-cooking. In fruitcake season (Sept.-mid-Dec.), you'll find the Claxton Bakery open Mon.-Sat. 8 a.m.-6 p.m. at 203 W. Main St., tel. (912) 739-3441, for free samples of the six million pounds of fruitcake they produce per year. **Glennville,** meanwhile, boasts of the World's Largest Cricket Farm. You'll find Armstrong's cricket farm at Gordon and Russian streets, tel. (912) 654-3408, about 15 miles south of Claxton via Hwy. 301.

ALTAMAHA RIVER BASIN

The southeastern interior surrounding the Altamaha, a river formed by the conjunction of the Ocmulgee and Oconee Rivers near Lumber City, remains nearly as wild now as when it served as a critical source of food, trade, and transport for native groups many centuries back. In colonial

KAP STANN

The lumber industry, along with paper and pulpwood production, is a mainstay of the state's economy.

days, the river formed the frontier between land claimed by the British to the north and the Spanish to the south. In early Georgia statehood, European settlement spread out upriver to the navigational limits at Milledgeville and Macon, and the southeastern forests were cleared by simply floating logs downriver to the port at Darien.

Today the wide river basin is one of the most remote stretches in the state. Public boat launches at nearly every major road crossing draw fisherfolk and boaters to its shores, and the state opens wildlife management areas seasonally to hunters. Most river areas are accessible off Hwy. 341, also a popular route for city travelers headed for Golden Isles resorts.

Big Hammock Natural Area

Big Hammock Natural Area, on the northeast bank of the Altamaha River at the Hwy. 121/144/169 crossing (18 miles east of Baxley), presents the most expansive example of the strange sand ridges found in South Georgia's coastal plain. The sand dunes of the ancient sea that covered the plain a million years back, the hundred-foot-high ridges now form the only contour in the otherwise flat terrain. Trails traverse the ridge, providing a close-up look at the distinct wildlife habitat the sand hills support.

To find the trailhead, go two miles north of the bridge to the first paved road on the right, and take this road 1.3 miles to the stone monument identifying the preserve. Park here and follow short fiberglass trail markers. The longest loop trail is six miles, and it traverses two parallel sand ridges. For a 1.5-mile loop hike, return on the cutoff between the ridges. Several short spur trails lead out to a cypress head, a lake, and the swamp and swamp forest around the sand hills.

The ridges present an abrupt contrast to the surrounding base. Only a select group of hearty plant species tolerates the dry conditions, and even these appear stunted and wiry. Prickly pear cactus, Georgia plume, sand spikemoss, and twisted oaks and pine appear. Find mole trails, armadillo diggings, and the burrows of the gopher tortoise—oval holes marked by piles of white sand at the entrance. This is also the home of the eastern diamondback rattlesnack and the endangered indigo snake, both nocturnal species rarely seen.

Highway 341 Towns

Jesup, 40 miles inland, sits at the intersection of highways 301 and 341. The town offers tours of its principal industry, the "largest chemical cellulose-producing pulp mill in the world." Five public boat launches are on the Altamaha River north of town; one, the Jaycee Landing on Hwy. 301 has a general store for food and bait, and cheap camping with hookups, tel. (912) 427-7987. If you're downtown in time for lunch, try **Jones Kitchen** on Main St., tel. (912) 427-4100; for all-you-can-eat daily lunch buffets 11 a.m.-2 p.m.

Twelve miles north of **Baxley** on Hwy. 1, the visitors center at the **Hatch nuclear power plant,** tel. (912) 367-3668, attempts to explain the benefits of nuclear energy, and encourages visitors to picnic with a view of the cooling towers. Hours are Mon.-Fri. 8:30 a.m.-5 p.m., Sunday 1-5 p.m.

In McRae, **Little Ocmulgee State Park** is the area's major recreational resource, and also has lodging and a restaurant on the premises—stop here for a buffet meal, a quick round of golf, or to fish in Little Ocmulgee Lake, see **Dublin and Vicinity,** above, for more information.

EAST OF I-75

Fitzgerald

Founded in 1895, Fitzgerald was named for an Indianapolis journalist who, together with a Georgia governor, conceived of resettling veterans of the Union army here. Townspeople say they had to build a hotel to accommodate all the people who wanted to come see a Yankee. The town's west-side streets are named for Confederate generals: Union generals on the east. Other streets are named for Northern and Southern trees and flowers.

The **Blue and Gray Museum** in the old depot building in the center of town, tel. (912) 423-5375, houses Civil War memorabilia from both sides and other local history exhibits. It's open April 1-Oct. 1, Mon.-Fri. 2-5 p.m., free admission.

General Coffee State Park

Six miles east of Douglas on Hwy. 32, General Coffee State Park, tel. (912) 384-7082, is a 1,490-acre preserve around the Seventeen-Mile

River. The river pauses at a cypress swamp, where it creates four small lakes. The relatively common gopher tortoise and the endangered indigo snake are among the many species attracted to the rich wetland habitat. A swimming pool, short hiking trails, and a frontier village replica are among the recreational and historical attractions. In June, the park hosts a Pioneer Skills Day. A 250-site campground charges $14, including water and electric hookups; call (800) 864-PARK (800-864-7275) for reservations. The parking fee is $2 per car, free on Wednesday. From General Coffee State Park, it's about 35 miles southeast to Waycross, the doorway to the brooding, primordial Okefenokee Swamp.

OKEFENOKEE SWAMP

The Okefenokee Swamp is a place of mystery, but not the haunted foreboding kind most people associate with swamps. This pristine 680-square-mile wilderness is an ecological wonder, spiced with bizarre landscapes, exotic wildlife, and pioneer-spirited swamp folk.

As if passing through a looking glass, visitors step from the slatted South Georgia pine forest into a different environment altogether, where 80-foot cypresses rise out of black water, ground that appears stable gives way, and swampers who know the alligators by name pole shallow-draft skiffs through fern-lined channels. Even the climate changes: cooler, crisper, with a trace of echo under the canopy. Breezes stir draped Spanish moss, owls hoot in the middle of the day, and you know you're not in Waycross anymore.

The swamp's peculiar ecology of floating peat, which barely supports a person's weight, led the Seminoles to refer to the place as *ecunnau finocau*—"earth trembling"—and Okefenokee it became. From ancient mound-builders to turn-of-the-century canal-diggers, humans have left their mark on the swamp, but most traces of civilization have long since been reclaimed by nature.

As headwaters for two rivers, the swamp sends spring-fed Okefenokee black water to either the Atlantic or the Gulf of Mexico. St. Marys River, notorious as one of the crookedest rivers in the world, divides Georgia from Florida as it flows 175 miles from the swamp to the ocean—a distance of only 65 miles as the crow flies. The gulf-bound Suwannee earned its fame from the misspelled refrain in Stephen C. Foster's classic American folk song "The Old Folks at Home":

Way down upon the Suwanee River
Far, far away,
There's where my heart is turning ever
There's where the old folks stay . . .

Rivaling a tropical rainforest for the diversity of life within, the Okefenokee's delicate wetlands provide a critical habitat for abundant resident wildlife and migratory birds. Today a protected national wildlife refuge, the primitively beautiful Okefenokee Swamp remains a true great American wilderness.

THE LAND

Technically, the Okefenokee is not a swamp but a vast peat bog. Rising to 130 feet above sea level, it's higher than some surrounding towns. Its waters are neither brackish, stagnant, nor muddy—but pure, drifting, and set on sand.

A million years ago, the Atlantic Ocean covered this part of Georgia. Over the eons, a sandbar took shape offshore, and when the ocean eventually receded, this rising ridge trapped the sea water inside. Salt gave way to fresh water, a clear lake gave way to plants, and vegetation decayed into peat. The oldest peat in the Okefenokee dates back only 8,000 years. So as primordial as the brooding vistas appear, on a geological scale the Okefenokee Swamp is practically newborn.

Okefenokee "black water," as dark as oversteeped tea, enhances dramatic swamp scenery with its silvery reflection. The color comes from tannin produced by decaying vegetation. (Tannin is actually red, although the water appears black at depth.) Tannic acid acts as a natural preser-

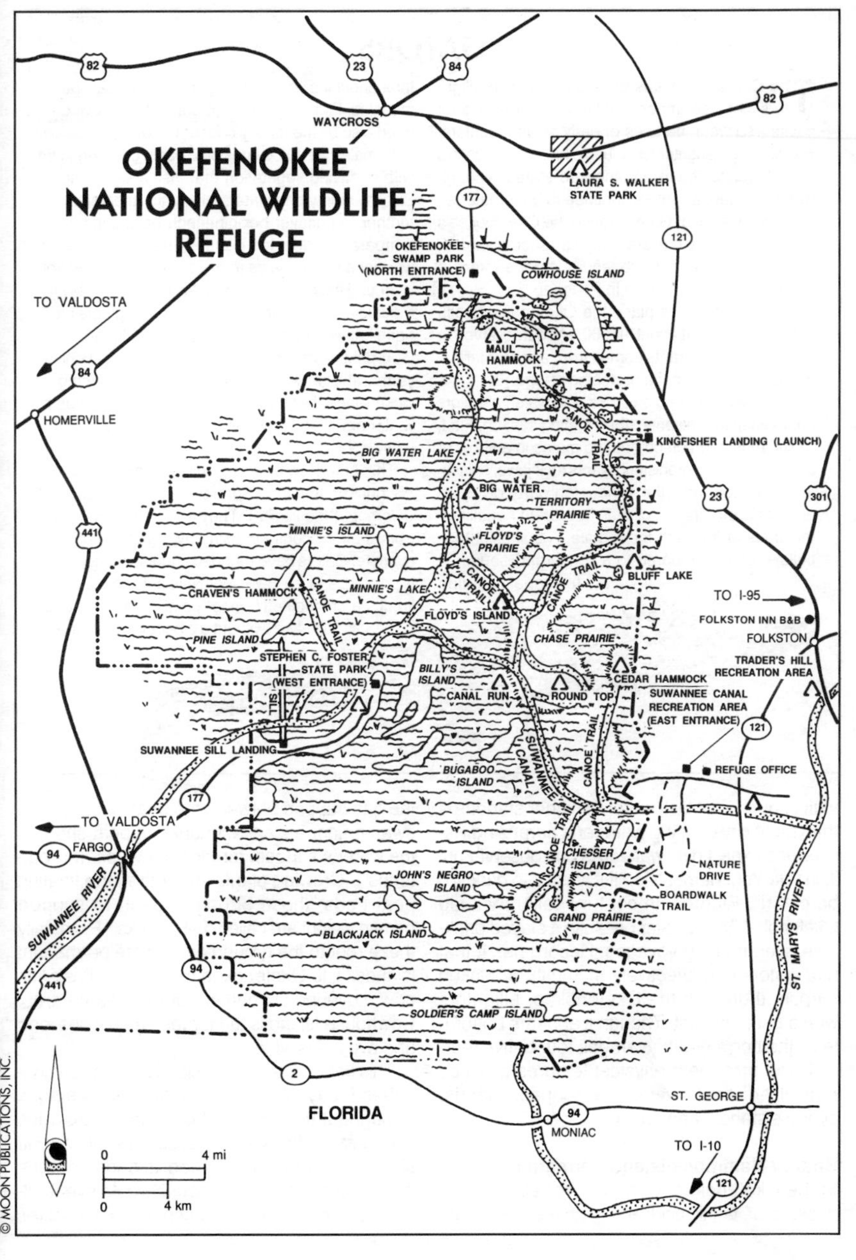
OKEFENOKEE NATIONAL WILDLIFE REFUGE
WAYCROSS
LAURA S. WALKER STATE PARK
OKEFENOKEE SWAMP PARK (NORTH ENTRANCE)
COWHOUSE ISLAND
TO VALDOSTA
MAUL HAMMOCK
HOMERVILLE
CANOE TRAIL
KINGFISHER LANDING (LAUNCH)
BIG WATER LAKE
BIG WATER
TERRITORY PRAIRIE
MINNIE'S ISLAND
FLOYD'S PRAIRIE
CRAVEN'S HAMMOCK
MINNIE'S LAKE
BLUFF LAKE
TO I-95
FLOYD'S ISLAND
FOLKSTON INN B&B
FOLKSTON
PINE ISLAND
CHASE PRAIRIE
STEPHEN C. FOSTER STATE PARK (WEST ENTRANCE)
BILLY'S ISLAND
CANAL RUN
ROUND TOP
CEDAR HAMMOCK
TRADER'S HILL RECREATION AREA
SUWANNEE CANAL RECREATION AREA (EAST ENTRANCE)
SILL
SUWANNEE SILL LANDING
SUWANNEE CANAL
REFUGE OFFICE
BUGABOO ISLAND
TO VALDOSTA
FARGO
CHESSER ISLAND
NATURE DRIVE
JOHN'S NEGRO ISLAND
BOARDWALK TRAIL
SUWANNEE RIVER
GRAND PRAIRIE
ST. MARYS RIVER
BLACKJACK ISLAND
SOLDIER'S CAMP ISLAND
ST. GEORGE
FLORIDA
MONIAC
TO I-10
0 4 mi
0 4 km
MOON
82
23
84
177
121
441
301
94
2

'GATORS

The Okefenokee was once so thick with alligators that a swamper could ford streams on their backs—so went the tales of early swamp settlers. But years of slaughter for valuable hides reduced this abundant species to endangered status. Though now protected, alligators continue to be threatened by illegal poaching. Gates around the Okefenokee's national wildlife refuge are locked up soon after dark to discourage the practice, and bumper stickers in the vicinity proclaim "Turn In Poachers!"

Current estimates place the Okefenokee's alligator population at about 10,000. (Alligator served in some local restaurants comes from alligator farms, not, of course, from the protected refuge.)

Easily seen basking on shore or in water, alligators are most active in spring, their mating season. First, "bulls" must fend off competing males in a show of strength: the two prehistoric giants lock jaws, splash, and roll about until the exhausted party gives up and slinks off. The victor then begins an equally tumultuous ordeal with the female. A bull alligator's bellow (often compared to a lion's roar) sounds a territorial warning throughout the year, but in spring the cry has special meaning. Females follow this sound to the love den, lured also by the musky odor of the bull's emission.

Females lay 40-60 eggs on a bank, covering them with decaying vegetation that insulates the eggs. Sixty to ninety days later, "clucking" cries alert the mother to uncover her nine-inch hatchlings. Nest temperature decides gender: males hatch from warmer spots, females from cooler. The babies frolic around their mother for months in an unusually familial relationship for reptiles (though alligators have been known to eat their young in hard times).

Alligators live almost as long as humans, about 50 years, and grow to 18 feet. They eat anything in close range that moves; their appetite subsides in winter and they hibernate the coolest weeks of the year.

The American alligator, *Alligator mississippiensis,* got its name from Spanish sailors, who called it *el largota* ("the lizard"). They can be distinguished from their crocodile cousins by snout shape and overbite. Gators have rounded snouts, a crocodile's is pointed, and if a lower tooth juts outside the upper lip, it's a crocodile. (A moot point in the Okefenokee, without a crocodile to be seen.)

vative, purifying black water to higher standards than most city drinking water and surprising visitors who expect dirty water. (As one observer put it, in true Yogi Berra style, "If it wasn't so dark, it'd be clear!") Eighteenth-century sailors valued Okefenokee black water because it stayed drinkable even on long voyages. Record has it that bog waters can effectively mummify a sunken corpse, though in the Okefenokee, alligators would get there first. Though it appears bottomless, the bog's depth averages four to five feet.

Three prominent physical features produce radically distinct swamp landscapes: islands, cypress stands, and prairies.

Battery-Hammock-Island Formation

In the Okefenokee, decaying vegetation produces peat, tannic acid, and methane gas. When the gas trapped between the peat layers on the swamp floor escapes, chunks of peat shoot to the water's surface, forming "blowups" (or "batteries"). Growing plants strengthen the floating peat beds; those strong enough to support human weight are called "hammocks." Eventually these root to the ground and create permanent islands. The Okefenokee has about 70 islands now, covering six percent of the swamp area. Cowhouse Island is the largest, nine miles long and two miles wide.

This battery-hammock-island succession continues today. You can see its various stages throughout the swamp, from sudden blowups in waterways (thus the necessity of shallow-draft skiffs) to mature hardwood islands at each swamp entrance. This process would eventually consume the swamp's open areas, if wildfires didn't keep growth in check. Fires in 1954-55 burnt much vegetation clear down to the surface of the water.

Cypress Stands

Dense cypress stands evoke the typical image of a swamp: a tall, dark forest planted underwater and draped with dangling Spanish moss. Eighty feet overhead, the cypress crowns into a thick canopy that cools the interior. Around each base, knobby cone-shaped "knees" protrude above the water like dark wooden stalagmites. Vegetation caught between bases forms a cypress "house" or "head," formations once favored by trappers as campsites. Cypress stands make up around 80% of the swamp, and can be most readily seen on foot at the northern entrance and by boat at the western entrance.

Prairies

A third Okefenokee landscape offers a sharp contrast to the sheltered growth of islands and cypress stands. Large watery fields called "prairies" fill 60,000 swamp acres (15% of the total area) with such wispy vegetation as water lilies, grass, and aquatic sedge. Imagine an acres-wide expanse of pristine white water lilies on green pads. It's a placid scene, until the wind kicks up their purple-veined undersides; set against rippling black water and a thunderous sky, the sight resembles nothing less than a moonscape.

Streams, lakes, and "gator holes" (small ponds clear of vegetation) dot the prairies, though all open-water areas combined make up only 1,000 of the swamp's 438,000 acres.

Climate

Generally mild weather makes the swamp enjoyable most all year long. In spring the swamp fills with colorful wildflowers, loud alligator mating roars, and hungry fish (anglers book overnight excursions quickly). Temperatures are mild, with daytime highs in the 70s and mid-80s (°F), dropping to the 40s and 50s at night. Rain is common. Summer days shoot up to the 90s or higher while nights hover around 70. July and August afternoons can be uncomfortably hot and humid in exposed areas. On these hot lazy summer days, alligators bask on the banks and people head to cool shade under the cypresses. Afternoon thunderstorms bring some cooling relief, along with an average rainfall of 8.5 inches per month; boaters must heed precautions to avoid danger from lightning. Fall brings colorful foliage, active bears, and moderate temperatures once again—daytime highs of 70-80° F and overnight lows of 40-50° F. Winter temperatures can range from 40-80° F during the day (averaging in the 50s and 60s) and may drop to near freezing at night. Winter rains are unlikely, and low water levels may close some canoe trails. But winter brings out otters and thousands of migratory birds.

FLORA

The **cypress** is the granddaddy of swamp flora, occupying four-fifths of the Okefenokee. Though coniferous, the American bald and pond cypress are actually deciduous, shedding their

KAP STANN

Boardwalks allow visitors close-up views of hammocks and cypress stands in the swamp.

needles each fall, and they grow equally well on land or submerged in water. Biologists speculate that the odd root protrusions keep trees stable and aerated; outside the protected refuge, the burly knots are used to make furniture and primitive sculptures. Loggers cut most original-growth cypress earlier this century, so except for a few isolated virgin trees in remote areas of the swamp, everything you see is second growth.

Swamp **pines,** slash and longleaf, forged a turpentine industry around the swamp (look for chevron-shaped cuts on trunks to find a tapped tree). The leaves of **wax myrtle** trees contain a natural insect repellent; old-time swampers and hunters rubbed themselves with leaves or lit candles made from leaves to discourage mosquitoes. **Swamp black gum, red maple,** and **bay** rise above an understory of **bamboo** and several **berry** varieties, while **magnolias** thrive on the perimeter of swamp islands.

Several more unusual botanical specimens also thrive in the swamp. One of these, the **Spanish moss** seen "dripping" off tree branches, is actually not a moss but an epiphyte—a plant that derives its nutrients from air and rain independent of the plant to which it is attached. Another, *Clethra alnifolia,* is a favorite of swamp-boat guides, who enjoy demonstrating the unusual properties of this "poor man's soap"; its leaves lather up into a cleansing white foam. Then there are the "meat-eating" plants. **Pitcher plants,** for example, lure insects into funnel-shaped leaves with the bloom's sweet nectar, then fool the bugs into trying to escape through translucent spots until they die trying. Another indigenous plant was used by the Timucuan natives. They consumed a black drink brewed from holly leaves (*Ilex vomitoria)* as an emetic, repeatedly drinking the highly caffeinated substance and vomiting it up each time, presumably for its stimulating and purifying effects.

Wildflowers fill the swamp in spring, though colorful blooms of many varieties appear during most warm months. **Golden club,** purple **pickerelweed,** and **rose pogonias** (a wild orchid) are a few common types.

FAUNA

As if on an American safari, visitors turning onto Hwy. 177 at the western swamp entrance can expect to stop for families of raccoons and deer, the odd armadillo or snake, and turkey buzzards feasting on road kill. And that's just at the edge in the *daytime*—many species are nocturnal, so the real action starts after dark. What you can't see by moonlight you can hear: gators bellowing, owls screeching, frogs croaking, wings flapping.

The compact and critical habitat pushes animals together, unlike vast secluded terrain in, say, the American West. Every square foot of the swamp teems with wildlife, often in surprising combinations. Egrets skip beside foraging deer, turtles and alligators share pits, bunnies and quail wait together to cross the road—it's like pages from a children's picture book.

Because of a swamper's keen "game eye" (enabling him to spot animals at great distance or in darkness) and hunting prowess, most species made their way into swamp stew. Even now, road kill doesn't go to waste—a bear or "rooter" (feral pig) would likely end up butchered and barbecued on the table of a local who knows wild game is superior to store-bought.

Mammals

Of 49 species now living in or around the swamp, **black bears** (a population estimated around 100), **white-tailed deer, foxes, wild pigs** (descended from pioneer homesteader stock), and **bobcats** are the largest, followed by **possums, otters, armadillos, minks, weasels,** swimming **marsh rabbits** and **raccoons** (the most abundant large mammal). Most of these mammals prowl at night, but many can be seen during the day, particularly early mornings and late afternoons.

The absence of **beavers** lends credibility to a local legend about how the swamp was created. The story goes that the numerous beavers sought revenge against the Seminoles by breaking dams, flooding the area, and leaving the newly created swamp forever.

Early pioneers saw evidence of the **Florida puma** (also called cougar or panther), but this endangered species no longer roams the Okefenokee. With luck, it may return: the Nature Conservancy aims to reintroduce the puma near the southern Okefenokee.

Reptiles and Amphibians

Reptilians give the Okefenokee its exotic primeval feel—bony scaled **alligators,** eight-foot-long **king snakes** (farmers like these helpful creatures around to keep the rodent population down), and 150-pound **alligator snapping turtles** crawl through the Okefenokee.

Local swampers worry less about alligators than some of the nasty turtles. Of the bullies, the mammoth snappers and leathery **Florida softshells** live deeper in; you're more likely to run into the **common snapping turtles,** which can inflict a vicious bite. Some turtles share dens with alligators, so you know they're mean. (But they still have to be *quick*—that loud crunching sound late at night indicates an alligator is having a hard-shelled roommate for dinner. Swampers say that for the human palate, softshell is tastier —not to mention quieter.) A dozen darting species of lizards include the **legless glass lizard** (often mistaken for a snake), the **American chameleon,** and the nifty **ground skink** (which leaves its tail behind if a predator grabs hold).

Thirty-seven snake species inhabit the swamp; five are venomous. The one most closely identified with the swamp is the black **water moccasin,** nicknamed "cottonmouth" for the white lining it reveals when it opens its mouth. Because they closely resemble harmless black water snakes, tales of cottonmouth sightings far outnumber actual encounters. To tell a brightly striped venomous **coral snake** from a similarly banded nonvenomous type, swampers learn the rhyme: "Red and yellow, kill a fellow; red and black, nice to Jack." The largest and deadliest of three rattlesnake species, the **eastern diamondback,** grows to an average of six feet long. The **timber rattler,** once called canebrake because of its preferred habitat, and the **dusky pygmy rattlesnake** should also be avoided.

Frogs and **toads** of 22 varieties are the most numerous amphibians in the swamp.

Though the refuge harbors dangerous animals, it would be wrong to leave the impression that the swamp is a menacing place. Animals rarely bother people unless disturbed, and they live largely in more remote areas. Common sense prevents most dangerous encounters, and chance encounters at a safe distance can be one of the most rewarding aspects of exploring the swamp.

Birds

From the tiny **ruby-throated hummingbird** to the 17-pound **wild turkey,** birds love the swamp. More than 234 species can be seen and heard, different sets for each season. Seventy-five species nest in the swamp, including the rare **osprey, snowy egret, screech owl,** and endangered **red-cockaded woodpecker.** Birds particularly enjoy the prairies—**white egrets, great blue herons,** and graceful **sandhill cranes** (locally called "whooping" cranes because of their piercing cry) are visible here all year long. Spring displays the greatest variety and activity. Winter migration brings more than a dozen species of **ducks** and even an occasional **bald eagle.** Contact the refuge offices in Folkston for a complete list.

Fish

Largemouth bass, black crappie, catfish, and **sunfish** (including bluegill and redbreast) are popular sporting catches of the 39 fish species found in the Okefenokee. Anglers descend on the swamp in spring and late fall, boating out to the Okefenokee's 60 open lakes and small ponds known as

bald eagle

SWAMP FOLK

When the Seminoles broke away from the powerful Creek Confederacy and moved to the swamp (Seminole means "runaway" in the Muskogean Creek language), they became the first of a long line of independents and renegades to inhabit the Okefenokee. The isolated black-water swampland and bizarre "trembling earth" also attracted a reclusive lot, many escaping either injustice or justice.

Swamp island names reflect this colorful past. **Billy's Island** was named for Seminole chief Billy Bowlegs, who resisted ousting when the federal government sent in the Army to evict all Native Americans from the Southeast in 1838 and banish them to Oklahoma. (The Seminoles escaped, fleeing to the sanctuary of Florida's Everglades.) **Floyd's Island** commemorates the ouster himself, General Charles Floyd, whose troops came against Bowlegs. Civil War times inspired **Soldier's Camp,** home to army deserters, and **Cowhouse Island,** where swampers hid cattle from marauding troops. Though **John's Negro Island** is named for a stolen slave, many runaway slaves fled to freedom in the swampland.

By rights, there ought to be an island honoring moonshiners, another outlaw swamp breed. (If there were, the name "Autumn Leaf" would immortalize the 190-proof swamp concoction said to make you change color and fall to the ground.)

Of course, the outlaw mystique tells only part of the story. Many God-fearing homesteaders settled the Okefenokee Swamp, too. Families such as the Chessers, who for several generations raised sugarcane on **Chesser Island.** The Wilkes' family cabin on Cowhouse Island is largely all that remains after most family members were killed in an Indian raid in the 1800s. The Lee family cemetery on Billy's Island dates from the 1850s, when Dan Lee and his bride settled there, to 1937, when the last of their descendants moved off the island to make way for the newly named refuge.

Yet the pioneer swamp spirit lives on around the periphery. Inside, the swamp offers living proof that nature can prevail over human intervention.

Cowhouse Island forms the northern entrance to the swamp, outside of Waycross. You can reach Chesser Island by a short trail from the nature drive at the eastern swamp entrance south of Folkston. Boat trails lead to Billy's Island (day-use only) and Floyd's Island (canoe campers only, wilderness permit required). (Other islands mentioned are not accessible to the general public.) Guided swamp boat tours available at each entrance tell more of the Okefenokee's natural and human history.

"gator holes." Note: Live minnows are prohibited, and trotlines are discouraged because they attract alligators and snakes; use an ice chest to store your catch instead of stringing it alongside your boat.

HISTORY

Early Inhabitants

Ancient "Mound-Builder" tribes, so named for the earthen constructions they raised on landscapes throughout the Southeast, left their mark on the Okefenokee as well. Sixty-five mounds dating back 4,000 years lace the swamp. Excavations of skeletons and relics have led archaeologists to conclude that these mounds served as sacred burial grounds for high-standing members of the community, and anthropologists speculate that tribes held religious rituals at these sites. Two of the most accessible mounds are on Chesser Island (east entrance) and Billy's Island (west entrance).

At the time of earliest European exploration, the Timucuan inhabited the swamp, then the Yuchi, then the Creek. Breaking off from the Creek, the Seminoles lived in the swamp when homesteaders began to settle around 1800.

European Exploration

Two famous European expeditions, that of Spanish explorer Hernando de Soto in 1539 and Quaker naturalist William Bartram in 1773, passed by the swamp but never ventured inside. From skirting its periphery both heard tales of the giant race said to live within (skeletal remains of Timucuan men confirm that they were uncommonly large) and their beautiful sirenlike maidens.

Trappers and traders eager to exploit the fur-rich Okefenokee built a thriving business obtaining pelts and skins from the natives, paving the way for future settlement.

As European settlers throughout colonial Georgia began encroaching on Native American territory, animosities naturally developed. An event well-remembered to this day in the swamp is the Wilkes Family Massacre, in which a large homesteading family was wiped out (save a few children who escaped) by Seminoles in the 1800s. Their restored cabin at Okefenokee Swamp Park tells the story.

Expansionism reached a tragic climax in 1838 when federal troops stormed through Georgia to expel all Native Americans from their ancestral homelands, sending most marching along the Trail of Tears to designated Indian territory in Oklahoma. The Seminoles, however, escaped this fate by fleeing southward.

When General Charles Floyd marched federal troops into the Okefenokee, he met resistance from Seminole chief Billy Bowlegs. Bowlegs managed to lead his people into Florida to safety, where they took refuge in the wilds of another swamp, the Everglades. (Their descendants live there to this day.) Two of the Okefenokee's largest islands, Billy's Island and Floyd's Island, commemorate these two historical characters.

Development

Homesteaders soon replaced the Seminoles, developing a self-sufficient swamper culture that lived off the natural bounty of the swamp. They hunted alligators for the valuable skins, lit their log cabins with pine-knot torches, and made stew from turtles and rattlesnakes. Their isolation in the unusual natural environment fostered unique folk customs whose threads can still be found around the swamp today.

Developers began looking for ways to cash in on the swamp's natural resources. In 1889, the Suwannee Canal Company bought much of the swamp from the state, intending to drain out the water and raise valuable cropland. From the sale price of $62,000 (less than 27 cents an acre), the company ended up spending a million dollars to build 12 miles of the still-standing canal before abandoning the effort. A far larger task than the canal-builders had imagined, the doomed effort led by Atlanta lawyer Henry Jackson was dubbed "Jackson's Folly."

At the turn of the century, the Charles Hebard Cypress Company of Waycross saw a lumber bonanza in the Okefenokee. During its 20 years of operation, the enterprise took nine million board feet of virgin cypress from the swamp. The central headquarters for the logging enterprise was the same Billy's Island from which the Seminoles held off General Floyd.

Looking at the remote island wilderness now, it's hard to imagine Billy's Island was once a boomtown—complete with hotel, school, store, and even a movie theater. At its heyday in the early 1900s, 600 people lived here; workers earned $2.50 per day in company scrip redeemable only at the island store. A railroad built 35 miles into the swamp transported the lumber out.

Fire destroyed most remnants of that time and jungle reclaimed the rest, so now it's hard to tell a rusted pipe from a dead branch. But you'll still stumble upon old steam-engine parts and chimneys, a cast-iron stove, and a washtub or two. (The old Hebard hunting cabin on Floyd's Island now shelters overnight campers.)

Okefenokee National Wildlife Refuge

In 1936, President Roosevelt established the 293,000-acre federal refuge as a result of an appeal by the wife of famed naturalist Francis Harper, a Cornell biologist fascinated by the swamp's natural history. In 1974, the most remote region of the swamp was designated a national wilderness area.

WHERE TO START

Three main entrances provide access to the swamp. The northern entrance, **Okefenokee Swamp Park,** lies 13 miles south of Waycross via US 1/23 and Hwy. 177; the eastern entrance, **Suwannee Canal Recreation Area,** is 11 miles southwest of Folkston off Hwy. 23/121, and the western entrance, **Stephen C. Foster State Park,** is 17 miles northeast of Fargo on Hwy. 177 (see map). For information about towns around the swamp, see the end of this chapter.

Each entrance is managed by a different authority, is situated in distinct terrain, and holds its own natural and recreational attractions. At all three you can find guided boat trips, canoe rentals, boardwalks above the swamp, and wonderful opportunities to see varied Okefenokee wildlife and swamp ecology. Two secondary swamp entrances, **Kingfisher Landing** and the **Suwannee River Sill** provide boat access, but no other services.

For first-timers and experienced boaters alike, the best way to sense the secluded serenity and natural primitive beauty of the Okefenokee is to get out on the water. More than 120 miles of waterways course through the swamp, between islands, around lakes, through the canal and prairies, offering panoramic scenery and glimpses of wildlife in action.

Getting There

Driving to Folkston (eastern entrance) from the nearest major airport (in Jacksonville, Florida) takes an hour and a half; from Savannah, less than two hours; from Atlanta, six hours. Distances around the swamp are considerable: to get from the eastern to western entrance means a detour into Florida and a two-and-a-half-hour ride (see map).

Because the Okefenokee Swamp is such an enclosed wilderness, no drive along its perimeter hints at the richness within. Highway 177 up from Fargo to the state park offers a chance to see swamp animals but not terrain, although its isolation makes this scenic drive impractical for drivers just passing through. To view wildlife, take the 4.5-mile nature drive at the eastern entrance near Folkston, take a hike out on the trails or boardwalks, or best of all, get out on a boat.

What to Bring

The Okefenokee inspires everyone to use binoculars and cameras; if you have them, bring them. In summer, carry insect repellent, sunscreen, and a hat; long pants and long sleeves offer the best protection. Boaters will want to carry drinking water and food, and remember "dry bags" for camera equipment. Campers need to bring all necessary supplies; the few camp stores available carry minimum stock. For extensive outings, carry emergency supplies, including a compass, a flashlight, a first-aid kit, extra food and clothing, and a whistle (three toots sound a distress signal).

Safety

The greatest danger in the swamp is not from the wildlife, as one might fear, but instead from lightning. Electrical storms are common on summer afternoons, and rangers advise that boaters in exposed areas seek shelter under a thick growth of small trees when they see a storm approach. Nevertheless, visitors must use caution and good sense to avoid the rare encounter with dangerous snakes or alligators: watch where you put hands and feet, turn canoes over cautiously, and check under seats. Never disturb animals or nests; no swimming, live bait, or pets (dogs are an alligator delicacy). Adventurers should know first-aid and the signs and prevention of heatstroke (replenish fluids, carry salt tablets) and hypothermia (stay dry, warm, and sheltered).

Insects can be bothersome on humid summer days. Biting deerflies are present at swamp's edge, less prevalent deeper in. Twilight brings the mosquitoes out; insect repellent is a must (other deterrents: campfire smoke, earth-toned clothing, citronella candles, and wax myrtle leaves). Long pants worn tucked into socks or boots are a good precaution against ticks and chiggers. A thorough body check after a wilderness day catches any ticks before they burrow too deeply to be easily removed. Small red chiggers are harder to spot—if an itchy red rash develops, it might be chiggers. Try suffocating them by covering the area with clear nail polish.

Refuge Regulations

The U.S. Fish and Wildlife Service operates the Okefenokee National Wildlife Refuge, and it means business. Uniformed rangers patrol roads and waterways to prevent poaching and ensure compliance with regulations. Wilderness permits are required for overnight canoe camping in the swamp, deep swamp excursions, and trips beyond the Suwannee River sill. Motorboats up to 10 horsepower are permitted; some trails are reserved for canoes only. The speed limit on roads within the refuge is 35 mph in the daytime, dropping to 10 mph after dark (watch carefully for animals). No swimming is allowed. Fishing is permitted; live minnows and trotlines are not. Call the refuge for wilderness permits or information on occasional managed hunting permitted by the Fish and Wildlife Service.

Entrance fees (excepting Okefenokee Swamp Park) are $5 per car per day. Long-term parking requires a permit and is advisable only at secured primary entrances, not at unsecured secondary landings. For more information, call or write the Okefenokee National Wildlife Refuge, Rte. 2 Box 3330, Folkston, GA 31537, tel. (912) 496-7836.

NORTHERN ENTRANCE

The **Okefenokee Swamp Park,** tel. (912) 283-0583, a private day-use attraction 12 miles southeast of **Waycross,** features wildlife shows, swamp ecology exhibits, a serpentorium, and a restored pioneer homestead. But its greatest attraction is simply the swamp itself—rambling boardwalks above the black water lead out to a 90-foot observation tower overlooking the cypress-belt canopy; there are plenty of places to look and linger along the way. (Families with small children must be alert on unfenced walkways.)

Looping fern-lined waterways through the cypress weave past such Disney-worthy sights as an old moonshine still (built on a float to easily evade "revenooers"), a Seminole dugout canoe, and a backward sign that reads correctly only in its black-water reflection.

The admission is $8, $7 for children 5-11 (under five free), or purchase a $12 admission ticket that includes a 25-minute boat trip a mile and a half through the swamp. The boat trips are led by colorful guides full of anecdotes about swampland history and folklore, and are well worth the additional expense. For an additional $16 per person, take a 10-mile guided trip deep into the swamp (by reservation only). Or rent a canoe and wind your own way around. The park is open 9 a.m.-5:30 p.m. year-round every day but Christmas. For camping and lodging nearby, see **Waycross.**

EASTERN ENTRANCE

Twelve miles south of **Folkston,** the **Suwannee Canal Recreation Area** (SCRA) provides access to the swamp's "prairies" and offers the most extensive services for boating excursions (including rental equipment). The SCRA serves as the federal entrance to the Okefenokee National Wildlife Refuge; the **refuge office** is on Rte. 2 (outside the gates), Folkston, GA 31537, tel. (912) 496-7836. Inside the gates, there's a visitors center and the boathouse, operated by private concessionaire. For information about rental equipment, boating services, or guided tours, call the concessionaire at (912) 496-7156. Gates and concession are open 7 a.m.-7:30 p.m. spring and summer, 8 a.m.-6 p.m. fall and winter, closed Christmas. (For nearby camping and lodging, see **Folkston,** below.) The entrance fee is $5 per car.

Typical of the eastern terrain are the prairies, large watery fields of wispy aquatic vegetation spotted with open ponds. Its dominant feature is the 12-mile canal, the remnant of an unsuccessful attempt to drain the swamp at the turn of the century.

Drivers may slowly cruise the 4.5-mile **nature drive** to see local wildlife, or park and get out on the 4,000-foot **boardwalk,** which leads to a 50-foot observation tower overlooking Seagrove Lake and Chesser Prairie. Other short walking trails lead to a restored pioneer homestead and aboriginal mound on Chesser Island; the canal-diggers trail sheds light on the construction of the Suwannee Canal.

The SCRA **visitor center** at the swamp's edge presents an interpretive slide show on swamp ecology, sells books on natural history and Okefenokee lore, and distributes free pamphlets about Okefenokee wildlife.

Boating

Boating is the main event at the swamp, and this entrance has the most complete and extensive boat services available at the swamp. For more information on guided tours or outfitting, call the concessionaire at (800) SWAMP 96 (or 800-792-6796). **Guided tours** on pontoon boats hold a particular appeal for birders, though in general the tours here in federally managed territory are less colorful than at the other entrances. One-hour trips cost $8.50 adults; for two hours, $17. **Night tours** through the swamp are found here only, and the sounds and sights create a lasting impression ($15, by reservation only). Canoes (with paddles) rent for $17 per day, 14-20 foot boats $9.75-12.75, plus $18.75 extra for outboard motor with gas, life vests (required) $1.50 each. Ask for a free water-trails map when you rent your boat.

The straight, wide, 12-mile **Suwannee Canal** creates a highway through the swamp most conducive to motorboating; this scenic arcade of cypress and slash pine ends at 6,000-acre Chase Prairie. Three rest stops (at 2.5, 8, and 12 miles in from the SCRA boat dock) provide shelter and chemical toilets. At **Grand Prairie Lakes,** the clear pools within the thick growth of the prairies are prized fishing spots and secluded areas from which to watch wildlife (travel in 2.2 miles from the dock to the lakes turnoff; follow the trail south four miles to the first set of lakes, or continue two miles to Gannett Lake, the southernmost accessible point in the swamp). In addition to these all-access trails, two **canoe-only trails** leave the noise and wakes of motorboats behind. These trails lead off from the main canal 2.2 miles in from the SCRA boat dock, south to Cooter Lake or north across Mizell Prairie (named for Josiah Mizell, who designed the prototype swamp skiff).

WESTERN ENTRANCE

Stephen C. Foster State Park (SCF), tel. (912) 637-5274, 20 miles from the tiny town of **Fargo** (population 300), sits in the most remote corner of the swamp. This isolated 80-acre enclave has a lot to offer—the only overnight lodging at swamp's edge, access to the historically and ecologically rich Billy's Island, and 25 miles of waterways through some of the most spectacular scenery in the Okefenokee. The park is on Jones Island at the "Pocket," a spit of land jutting out into the swamp, so it's the closest you can get to the heart of the swamp without getting your feet wet. Here the headwaters of the Suwannee River take shape and drain out of the swamp, aiming for the Gulf of Mexico.

Besides the lodging, camping, and boating facilities (see below), the park offers a 1.5-mile boardwalk trail, an interpretive center and programs, and bike rentals. A small store sells fishing licenses and stocks bare necessities (canned food, Kraft macaroni and cheese, matches, ice, and ersatz milk). The nearest supermarket or pharmacy lies a hundred miles away, so bring all you'll need!

The entrance fee is $5 per car. Gates are open 6:30 a.m.-8:30 p.m. spring and summer, 7 a.m.-7 p.m. fall and winter, with office hours 8 a.m.-5 p.m.

Accommodations and Camping

In either a jungle hammock or a roomy air-conditioned cabin, Stephen C. Foster State Park is the place to stay when visiting the swamp. Nine fully equipped two-bedroom cottages rent for $56-76. Camp for $14-17 at 66 campsites, each with water/electric hookups, access to bathhouses and sanitary dump station. During the summer thundershower season, tent campers should bring thick ground cover. For cottage or camping reservations, call (800) 864-PARK (or 800-864-7275).

Boating

Park rangers lead **guided boat tours** of the western Okefenokee three times a day for $8 adults, under 12 years $6, under six free. **Boat rentals** include canoes, johnboats (skiffs), and motorboats. Ask for a free waterways map from the park office.

A free launch is available five miles south of the state park dock at the Suwannee River Sill, but no other services. Two water trails lead from the state park dock to the sill; one is all-access and the other for canoes only.

Billy's Island

Exploring Billy's Island is one of the best boating and hiking adventures in the swamp. Imagine this 3,140-acre island wilderness as home to ancient tribes, the base of operations for Native American resistance to U.S. expansionism, a homestead, a logging boomtown turned bust, and now, once again home only to swamp animals.

Within a half-mile of the dock lie many remnants from these times. The first you'll come across is the old Lee (no relation to Robert E.) family cemetery (descendants of this 1850s homesteading family still come out to the island to pay their respects). Up the trail from the cemetery you'll come upon the old railroad bed from early 1900s logging days; about 300 feet off this rise lies a 4,000-year old aboriginal burial mound. Back on the main trail, the path leads to the old "downtown." Watch for strewn steam boiler parts, chimney foundations, a rusty bed frame, and metal washtubs. As ruins go, these aren't the oldest or rarest, but as a contrast to the prevailing jungle wilderness, the rusty debris of Billy's Island is first-rate.

Stay on marked trails; watch where you reach and step; and pack out what you pack in (no trash containers on the island). The day-use-only island (4.25 miles long and 1.5 miles wide) is accessible to day-boaters only from the state park. Ask at the park office for an island trail map. From the state park boat dock, turn right out of the channel and go east through Billy's Lake 1.8 miles to Billy's Island (motorboats okay). Park boats at the dock or pull up on shore, and head up the trail.

Minnie's Lake/Big Water Lake

The middle fork of the Suwannee River branches off of Billy's Lake. Following the narrow winding channels of water lilies and cypress for five miles, boaters reach Minnie's Lake. From here the stream crosses Big Water Prairie to trail's end at Big Water Lake (12 miles from the SFC state park boat dock). Freestanding wooden platforms at both lakes offer rest stops for boaters; the one at Big Water has a chemical toilet.

Jimmy Walker, director of the Okefenokee Swamp Park and great-grandson of early swamp pioneer Obediah Barber, considers Big Water "the most beautiful place in the swamp." Actually a wide expanse of the contracting-and-expanding Suwannee River, the six-mile-long, 100-foot-wide clearing is surrounded by forest so thick that animal sounds echo around the lake. As dead-center of the swamp, Big Water is the heart of the Okefenokee wilderness.

OVERNIGHT CANOE TRIPS

Canoe campers can experience deep-swamp wilderness on overnight trips ranging in length from a 14-mile two-day loop trip to a 43-mile five-day trip crisscrossing the swamp. A permit is required from the Okefenokee National Wildlife Refuge authority in Folkston; reservations are accepted up to two months in advance by calling the refuge office. A brochure titled ***Wilderness Camping in Okefenokee*** outlines all requirements and lists all 15 designated canoe-trip routes. Write the refuge for a copy (enclose a business-size SASE to speed reply): Okefenokee National Wildlife Refuge, Rte. 2 Box 338, Folkston, GA 31537. Phone (912) 496-3331 Mon.-Fri. 7 a.m.-3:30 p.m. EST.

Call early to reserve your choice of trail; popular trails fill quickly during peak spring months. Have one or two alternative routes in mind if your first choice is taken or the refuge will assign you whatever is available. The refuge charges $10 per person per night; each party must consist of at least two people, no more than 20 people and 10 canoes. Canoeists must make their own arrangements for equipment, supplies, and shuttles to and from put-in and take-out points.

Campers on the Canal Run or Craven's Hammock routes set up tents (freestanding only) on sheltered wooden sleeping platforms measuring 20-by-28-feet (except on Floyd's Island, where campers can stay in an early 1900s wooden hunting cabin); a "jungle hammock" will suffice

KAP STANN

Canoeing in the Okefenokee offers visitors an up-close and unforgettable experience of the swamp.

in place of a tent. Most rest stops provide chemical toilets; nevertheless the refuge requires canoes to carry portable toilets with disposable bags (both available from the refuge concessionaire).

Refuge regulations require canoeists to carry a life vest for each person, a compass, and a flashlight (remember extra batteries). Recommended supplies include drinking water, a first-aid kit, rain gear, litter bags, a whistle, insect repellent, rope (to pull canoe across peat blowups or portage over Floyd's Island), mosquito netting, sleeping bag or jungle hammock, camp stoves and fuel, sunscreen, and a hat.

The refuge concessionaire rents all necessary equipment (canoe with paddles, life vest, tent, sleeping bag, pads, tarp, cookware, ponchos, stove and lantern with gas, portable toilet, and cartop carrier), priced individually. Complete gear rental for two people for two days totals around $100. Call the concessionaire at the Suwannee Canal Recreation Area at (912) 496-7156, about rentals and guided excursions.

Leave cars at secured entrances only; obtain necessary parking permits for the length of your trip. Shuttles are available from Suwannee Canal Recreation Area concessionaire for about a dollar a mile (calculated roundtrip from SCRA).

The St. Simons-based **SouthEast Adventures Outfitters,** organizes day and overnight ecotourist paddling excursions into the swamp.

Three-Day Excursions

The **Green Trail,** a three-day 24-mile trip, runs from one remote corner of the swamp to the other, starting at Kingfisher Landing and ending at Stephen C. Foster State Park. Crossing all three varieties of swamp terrain, the Green Trail features an overnight stop on Floyd's Island. Campers may stay in a turn-of-the-century cypress cabin nestled among magnolias and oaks and explore the four-mile-long, mile-wide island (portage required over the island's narrow tip). For a fitting finale to roughing it in the swamp, reserve a furnished two-bedroom cabin at the trail's terminus, Stephen C. Foster State Park, and cook up some of that fresh-caught bass.

This trail demands the most shuttling around the swamp, a logistical and financial consideration. Since cars are safest at secured entrances, many campers park at the Suwannee Canal Recreation Area when they check in at refuge headquarters and then take a prearranged shuttle to and from their put-in and take-out points. At a dollar a mile (calculated roundtrip from the refuge each way) shuttle fees for the Green Trail add approximately $200 to the cost of your trip. (Fee applies to 1-10 canoes, so the effective price per person decreases with larger groups).

One-Night Excursions

Single-overnight loop trips, available from three starting points, offer short adventurous excursions into the swamp, ideal for weekenders.

From Kingfisher Landing in the northeast, two different roundtrips are available, to either Maul Hammock or Bluff Lake. Both routes explore remote areas of the swamp, including prized fishing lakes.

From Stephen C. Foster State Park's western entrance, one loop trip runs to Craven's Hammock; the other goes to Canal Run, passing Billy's Island. Trips to and from the state park offer the bonus of staying overnight at park cabins or campsites (reservations required).

Of the three single-overnight loop trips starting at the Suwannee Canal Recreation Area's eastern entrance, the narrow winding canoe-only trail is more scenic than the all-access routes through the canal.

One trip crosses the swamp in a single overnight. East-to-west or west-to-east, this trail passes Billy's Island and includes paddling through the 12-mile canal. (Shuttling required.)

BLACK WATER RIVERS

The Okefenokee Swamp's characteristic black color is visible on the two rivers that originate in the swamp. As an alternative to overnight canoe trips in the swamp (say, in spring when swamp trips are booked solid), both offer a taste of blackwater country. Though missing distinct swamp terrain, river trips offer fast currents and a more relaxed ride: you aren't committed to predetermined stops every single day or subject to stringent refuge regulations (for example, the daring can swim in river black water).

The federally designated "Wild and Scenic" **Suwannee River** spills out of the swamp at Stephen C. Foster State Park (western entrance, north of Fargo). It parallels Hwy. 177 for 17 miles to the Hwy. 441 crossing, then ambles another 250 miles through Florida to the Gulf of Mexico. Canoeing its entire length takes about two and a half weeks.

For shorter jaunts, the 106-mile Suwannee River Canoe Trail begins two miles below the refuge at Lem Griffis Fish Camp (private, tel. 912-637-5395, camping available for about $5 per person, more for hookups, long-term parking available for a fee; write the camp at Fargo, GA 31631). At 13 miles is the Hwy. 441 crossing (parking available, walk to restaurants or grocery), then the trail continues south 93 miles into Florida, with camping areas every 20-26 miles. The most popular canoe trip is the two-day cruise from Griffis Camp to Florida SR 6. The river is rated Class I, with the exception of White Water Shoals above White Springs, which even experts should portage. Paddlers may also launch four miles up from Griffis camp at the Suwannee River Sill—this requires a wilderness permit from the refuge, a charge for entrance and parking, and a long-term parking permit.

The **St. Marys River** originates in the southeast corner of the swamp and winds 175 miles to the Atlantic Ocean. The first opportunity to put in is the town of Moniac on Hwy. 94 east of St. George, but the established canoe trail starts about 12 miles downstream at the Hwy. 121 crossing north of Macclenny, Florida. From here the four-day, 66-mile Class I trail crosses Hwy. 94 (restaurant and groceries available) and continues past Trader's Hill county campground south of Folkston to Camp Pickney Park and campground. Camping is also available on white sandbars along the river, surrounded by pine wilderness.

For maps, rental equipment, shuttles, or more information about black-water canoe trips, call the Suwannee Canal Recreation Area concessionaire at (912) 496-7156. **Canoe Outpost** specializes in Suwannee River trips (Rte. 1 Box 98A, Live Oak, FL 32060, tel. 800-428-4147).

WAYCROSS

Distinguishing itself as "the Largest City in the Largest County in the Largest State east of the Mississippi," Waycross arose in 1872 at the intersection of stagecoach roads and pioneer trails. The town quickly built up sawmill, turpentine, and farming industries that were largely destroyed by boll weevils and careless logging earlier this century. As railroads and highways supplanted stage roads, modern industry helped the city grow to its present population of 16,000.

Its true heyday was the 1950s and '60s, when gas was cheap and travelers hadn't yet abandoned the state highways for newly completed interstate freeways. Florida-bound travelers passing through Waycross brought hordes of visitors to the Okefenokee. Some attractions and businesses still evoke that family-station-wagon, road-motel feeling, creating an old-fashioned ambience that adds to the time-warp sense of the swamp itself.

Though locals boast about Waycross natives Burt Reynolds and writer Stanley Booth, the true patron saint of these parts is Ponce de Leon Montgomery County Alabama Georgia Beauregard Possum—better known as "Pogo." The philosophizing critter, the cartoon creation of the late Walt Kelly, is honored at the town's annual **PogoFest** in November. (Wonderful cartoon collections are available year-round at the Okefenokee Swamp Park gift shop.)

Sights

Of course, the greatest attraction around Waycross is the **Okefenokee Swamp Park,** where boat rides and rentals, boardwalks, and wildlife shows display the primeval swamp in all its natural glory. (see **Northern Entrance,** above.)

Obediah's Okefenok, tel. (912) 287-0090, the restoration of the 19th-century homestead of early settler Obediah Barber, features exhibits of pioneer farm life, including farm animals, a gristmill, and period costumes. Admission costs $4.50 adults, $3.50 seniors, $3 children 6-17. In mid-March, the place goes "hog wild" for a good old-fashioned hog-butcherin'. Follow Swamp Rd. 15 miles south of Waycross. It's open daily 10 a.m.-5 p.m.

The **Okefenokee Heritage Center,** 1460 N. Augusta Ave., tel. (912) 285-4260, features exhibits on Native American and pioneer swamp history. It's open Mon.-Sat. 10 a.m.-5 p.m., Sunday 1-5 p.m. Admission is $2 adults, $1 youth (under four free). The adjacent **Southern Forest World** promotes the local logging industry. Admission is $2, $1 seniors. It's open daily.

Walt Kelly's 1948 Pogo *comic strip ran as a daily through the 1970s. Pogo is famous for the statement, "We have met the enemy and he is US."*

Accommodations and Food

More than a half-dozen motels are clustered along Memorial Dr. where Hwy. 82 and Hwy. 84 meet. At this hub, the **Holiday Inn,** tel. (912) 283-4490, is one of the oldest properties and the most venerable hotel and meeting place in town. Room rates are moderate. Among older motels, **Palms Court,** tel. (912) 283-4794, and **Pinecrest,** tel. (912) 283-3580, have budget rates and appear well-kept. Recent additions are the **Jameson Inn,** tel. (912) 283-3800, and **Hampton Inn,** tel. (912) 285-5515, with inexpensive-to-moderate rates.

The **Holiday Inn** is also where locals go for a nice reasonably priced Southern buffet, especially on Sunday (casual is okay most days, but be particularly neat and tidy on Sunday). Fast food choices and supermarket shopping centers surround the Hwy. 82/84 junction.

Information and Services

The **Waycross Tourism and Convention Bureau,** 200 Lee Ave., P.O. Box 137, Waycross, GA 31502, tel. (912) 283-3742, fax (912) 283-0121, distributes city and swamp information; also see www.okeswamp.com.

The closest comprehensive medical services available are at the **Satilla Regional Medical Center,** tel. (912) 283-3030.

Laura S. Walker State Park

Set in the piney South Georgia woods 12 miles east of Waycross, Laura S. Walker State Park, tel. (912) 287-4900, features a 120-acre lake for boating and fishing and an 18-hole golf course. Water-skiing is a popular activity here (10 hp limit except midday); you can also rent canoes and swim in the pool (summers only). A 1.2-mile nature trail winds through the woods.

A small 44-site campground hasn't much privacy, but is nonetheless invitingly set by the lake in a grassy area surrounded by pines ($14 per night, senior discounts, water/electrical hookups, dump station, and laundry facilities available). For camping reservations, call (800) 864-PARK (800-864-7275). The park is open 7 a.m.-10 p.m. (gates lock). The parking fee is $2 per car, free on Wednesday.

OTHER TOWNS AROUND THE SWAMP

Folkston

The sleepy town of Folkston (population 2,300) has traditionally catered to out-of-towners on weeklong fishing or hunting vacations. Lately a new breed of ecotourists have been frequenting the swamp, and you can see the changes it has brought to town.

Bed and breakfast lodging has found its way to Folkston. **The Inn at Folkston,** 509 W. Main St., tel. (912) 496-6256, is in a pretty house a short walk to everything downtown (such as that is). At **Okefenokee Pastimes,** Hwy. 121 S, tel. (912) 496-4472, spirited pioneers operate cabin rentals (from $35), a camping pasture, and an otherworldly Swamp Gas folk art gallery, across from the turn-off to the National Wildlife Refuge. Camping is also available at **Trader's Hill Recreation Area,** tel. (912) 496-3412, alongside the St. Marys River on the site of an 18th-century British fort.

The home-style **Okefenokee Restaurant,** tel. (912) 496-3263, on Main St. at US 1 and Hwy. 301 (east of the tracks), serves three meals daily, specializing in a generous Southern buffet—look for the lines around lunchtime.

The **Folkston Chamber of Commerce,** housed in the old 1903 train depot in the center of town, tel. (912) 496-2536, distributes city and swamp information and maintains a few old railroad exhibits inside. This is also where the town's annual Okefenokee Festival is held the second weekend in October.

St. George

At this one-intersection crossroads 60 miles south of Folkston (en route to Fargo), **Shirley's Cafe** serves decent cheap food (BLT on white $2). It's open Mon.-Thurs. 5 a.m.-3 p.m., till 10 p.m. Friday, open at 5:30 or 6 a.m. on Saturday, closed Sunday.

Fargo

The four-pump town of Fargo has one grocery store, two restaurants, a mini-mart, and the five-room **Gator Motel** (resembling a self-storage unit). Eat at **Carlene's,** open Mon.-Sat. 6 a.m. to 7 or 8 p.m., Sunday 6 a.m.-2 p.m. A ham-and-egg breakfast biscuit is $2, and the daily lunch buffet is around $5 for all you can eat.

THE COAST

INTRODUCTION

Not one but two radically different coasts make up Georgia's Atlantic Seaboard. The mainland coast seeps into tidal marshlands—a solitary miles-wide expanse of tall green reeds. Within sight of the mainland, but a world away, the outer coast is made up of a string of remote barrier islands, where high dunes and white-sand beaches meet the gentle ocean, and the calls of gulls squawk over the distant hum of a trawler's engine. Together the two coasts make up the "low country," a singularly beautiful province with a distinct history and culture shaped by the land.

Only one-tenth of Georgia's 100-mile outer seashore is developed beachfront, attracting vacationers to barefoot cafes, historic lighthouses, and regal island resorts. The rest is largely wild and uninhabited, unless you count feral horses, boar, deer, and sea turtles (historians say the islands have fewer human residents now than at any other time in the last 4,000 years).

The unspoiled marshlands have a quieter appeal. Struggling to define their compelling nature, Pat Conroy writes in *Prince of Tides,* "I would have to take you to the marsh on a spring day, flush the great blue heron from its silent occupation, scatter marsh hens as we sink to our knees in mud, open you an oyster with a pocketknife and feed it to you from the shell and say 'There. That taste.'"

The pristine subtropical coast is dotted with evidence of its human history—ancient shell "middens," the orchards of Spanish friars, the eroded levees of abandoned rice plantations, old Sea Island Cotton fields, and ruins of forts once colonial or Confederate. Seven different nations have left traces of their claim to this land.

From Savannah, a city of exceptional grace and charm, to the bluffs, marshes, and small fishing villages in the rural north coast backcountry, from bustling Golden Isles resorts to remote neighboring islands, Georgia's fascinating coast is packed with treasures.

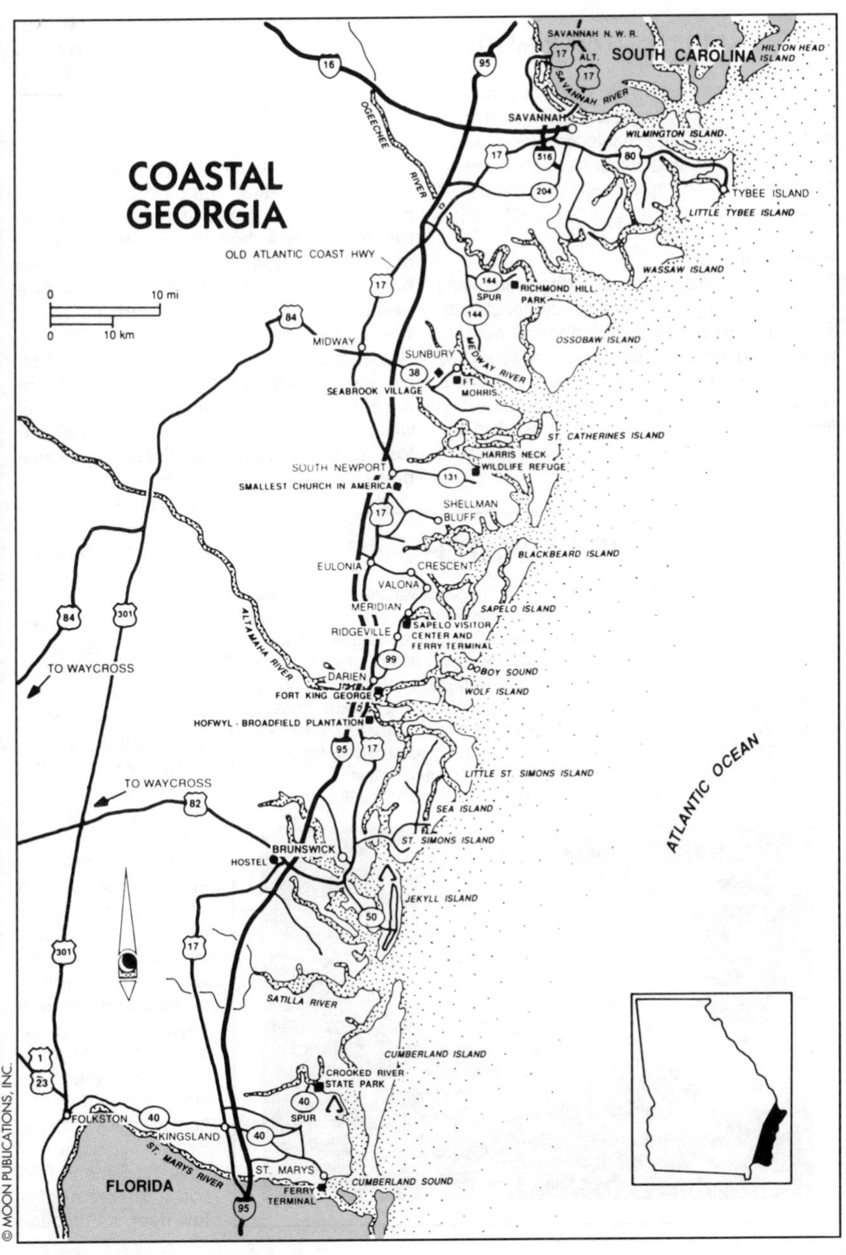
COASTAL GEORGIA
SAVANNAH N.W.R.
SOUTH CAROLINA
HILTON HEAD ISLAND
ALT.
SAVANNAH RIVER
OGEECHEE RIVER
SAVANNAH
WILMINGTON ISLAND
TYBEE ISLAND
LITTLE TYBEE ISLAND
OLD ATLANTIC COAST HWY
WASSAW ISLAND
RICHMOND HILL PARK
SPUR
0 10 mi
0 10 km
MIDWAY
OSSOBAW ISLAND
SUNBURY
MEDWAY RIVER
FT. MORRIS
SEABROOK VILLAGE
ST. CATHERINES ISLAND
HARRIS NECK WILDLIFE REFUGE
SOUTH NEWPORT
SMALLEST CHURCH IN AMERICA
SHELLMAN BLUFF
BLACKBEARD ISLAND
EULONIA
CRESCENT
VALONA
MERIDIAN
SAPELO ISLAND
SAPELO VISITOR CENTER AND FERRY TERMINAL
RIDGEVILLE
ALTAMAHA RIVER
TO WAYCROSS
DARIEN
DOBOY SOUND
FORT KING GEORGE
WOLF ISLAND
HOFWYL - BROADFIELD PLANTATION
ATLANTIC OCEAN
LITTLE ST. SIMONS ISLAND
TO WAYCROSS
SEA ISLAND
BRUNSWICK
ST. SIMONS ISLAND
HOSTEL
JEKYLL ISLAND
SATILLA RIVER
CUMBERLAND ISLAND
CROOKED RIVER STATE PARK
SPUR
FOLKSTON
KINGSLAND
ST. MARYS RIVER
ST. MARYS
FLORIDA
FERRY TERMINAL
CUMBERLAND SOUND
© MOON PUBLICATIONS, INC.

THE NATURAL ENVIRONMENT

Georgia was among the first states to enact legislation permanently protecting tidal marshlands, and many islands are either federal wildlife sanctuaries or restricted parkland. As a result, coastal ecology has been impressively preserved in its near-wild state along most of the coast.

Barrier Islands

The barrier islands are long (north to south) and narrow (east to west), with sandy beaches at eastern shores, tidal marshlands at western shores, and dense vegetation in between. They were formed when the polar ice cap melted, flooding the lowlands to the west and isolating the high sand dunes to the east. Vegetation stabilized the dunes, allowing the eventual growth of thick forests.

As strong offshore winds constantly shift sand from here to there, this island-building process continues. The **transitional maritime forest** starts with wispy **sea oats,** the first plant to set roots in the sand. (Because of their importance to local ecology, it's illegal to pick or trample sea oats in Georgia.) These begin to collect the shifting sands and attract varied vegetation, such as **yuccas, panic grass,** and **prickly pear cactus.** As the ecosystem matures, **live oaks** predominate. Though they weather the salty sea breeze better than most trees, the live oaks are nevertheless shaped by the corrosive spray, which gnarls the limbs into strangely twisted shapes and warps the canopy into a dense slanted crown. Shielded in the delicate substory below are floating strands of **Spanish moss,** vines of wild **muscadine** grapes, fan-shaped **palmettos,** and several varieties of **pines.** Coastal **mulberry** trees fueled early English visions of establishing a silk industry in the new Georgia colony. As you head away from the sea, island woodlands give way to open savannas, old rice and cotton fields, and freshwater ponds, until the land reaches the western tidal marshlands.

The islands shelter wildlife common to the coastal plain. Mammals such as **white-tailed deer, armadillos, opossums, raccoons,** and **squirrels** now run wild with once-domestic species brought to the islands long ago, such as the **feral hogs** and **donkeys** on Ossobaw Island, or the **wild horses** on Cumberland Island (said to descend from the stables of early Spanish missionaries). Little St. Simons harbors a population of **fallow deer,** a European

TURTLE WATCH

Five endangered sea turtle species swim in coastal waters. One of these, the loggerhead sea turtle, nests on Georgia's barrier islands. Weighing an average of 150 pounds (though individuals of the species have been known to reach 300 pounds), a female loggerhead digs a nest onshore, then deposits about 100 eggs the size of ping pong balls. Only the females return to land; after hatching, males spend their entire lives at sea. The **Caretta Project** (*Caretta caretta* is the scientific name for the loggerhead sea turtle) coordinates a "Turtle Watch" program in which volunteers search beaches daily for nests, removing eggs to protect against predators, later returning them to shore to hatch. For more information call the Caretta Project at (912) 355-6705.

KAP STANN

KAP STANN

Georgia's tidal marshlands are the most extensive on the East Coast.

species brought to the island in the 1920s—smaller than the **white-tailed** variety common to the rest of the islands. The once-populous **bobcat** is being reintroduced to the islands, starting with Cumberland. Saint Catherines Island sponsors a captive breeding program for the New York Zoological Society; **zebras, antelope, gazelles,** and other rare and endangered species are found there.

As for birds, Audubon himself had this to say about St. Simons Island in the 1850s: "I was fain to think I had landed on some of those fairy islands said to have existed in the Golden Age." Made up largely of protected refuges, and lying right along the Atlantic flyway, the islands attract more than 200 species of songbirds, shorebirds, and wading birds. One commonly sees—and hears—**Carolina chickadees, bluebirds, northern cardinals, mockingbirds, owls,** dozens of **warblers,** and **wild turkeys.** Of course, the beach attracts **brown pelicans, gulls,** and many varieties of shorebirds. The state's Department of Natural Resources—a big player in coastal management—sponsors a **bald eagle** "hacking" program on the coast, releasing eaglets hatched in captivity.

With no predators besides man, the **eastern diamondback rattlesnake** thrives on the islands, but is usually cautious, well-fed, and inactive in hot temperatures. Other venomous snakes on the islands are **canebrake rattlers** and **cottonmouths.** All visitors and hikers would be wise to stay on trails, watch where you put hands and feet, and stay off dunes (to protect fragile vegetation as well as to avoid sunning snakes).

On the beaches, visitors will find **ghost crabs, horseshoe crabs, sponges,** and such beach-combing trophies as **sand dollars, whelks** (look inside their rattling cases to find miniature whelks), and spit-shined **olive shells.** Delicate coral-like twigs, in varying shades of white, orange, and purple, are called **sea whips.** Collectors should be sure to remove only uninhabited shells, and only a handful at that, and only in areas where such collecting is permitted.

Dolphins and **manatees** swim close to shore and throughout marshland waterways. The rare **right whale,** of which only 350 are estimated to exist worldwide, calves solely off the Georgia coast.

(Also see the special topic **Turtle Watch.**)

Tidal Marshlands

A scenic maze of cordgrass-lined tidal creeks, rivers, and estuaries, Georgia's marshlands stretch from five to 10 miles between the mainland and barrier islands. At 250,000 acres in all, they're the most extensive on the east coast. Marshlands produce more biomass per acre than any other ecosystem.

Spartina alterflora defines the marsh; solid acres of this smooth **cordgrass,** vividly green most of the year, turn golden in the fall. Besides the **great blue heron** and **marsh hen** Conroy wrote of, many other bird species inhabit the marshes: the **snowy egret,** rare **least tern** and

osprey, and dozens of varieties of **ducks** and **geese.** The natural habitat for many varieties of shellfish, marshlands support the **oysters, mussels, clams, blue crabs,** and **shrimp** that fuel the local commercial seafood industry. **Alligators** inhabit shallow waters.

Mainland

The mainland edgewater once produced the greatest wealth for colonial Georgia; here grand rice plantations thrived as early as the 1740s. Today, only **wild rice** flourishes in the shallow ponds between the levees, attracting **ducks** and other marshland birds. Tall **pine** forests—long the mainstay of the state's lumbering, turpentine, and paper and pulpwood industries—stand alongside groves of coastal palms and palmettos.

In 1774, the coastal travels of naturalist William Bartram moved him to file this extravagantly romantic report: "the beautiful woods presented a view of magnificence inexpressibly charming and animated." Today you can retrace his steps on the Bartram Trail, following routes established by early natives or colonists.

Climate

Coastal Georgia's climate is subtropical. Summers are hot and humid with afternoon thundershowers. Temperatures climb above 90° F about 55 days in summertime, mostly in July and August. Fall stretches warm summer days into October, and short, mild winters rarely experience freezing temperatures. Spring is warm and occasionally wet. Though spring and fall are the most temperate, summer is the high season for coast visitors; winter holidays run a close second (though daytime temperatures may not rise above the 50s some days). For saltwater fishing, crabbing, and shrimping, late summer and fall are best.

Along the southeastern coast of the U.S., June through October is "hurricane season," yet tropical cyclones rarely hit the Georgia coast—at least not with the frequency and severity of neighboring states north and south. Yet even storms that stay offshore can bring torrential rains or severe thunderstorms (sailors take warning). Weather radio equipment is a valuable precaution for boaters.

HISTORY

To appreciate the history of the southeastern coast, you need to know a little something about oyster shells. The refuse of every coastal population dependent upon the flourishing food source, oyster shells mark the passage of time. Pre-Columbian shell rings, called "middens," resulted from the natives' practice of discarding shells behind a central campfire. The resulting glistening white heaps created an alkaline environment so hostile to plantlife that only the resistant cedar took root—today stands of tall cedars indicate the location of middens.

The Spanish used the shells to make an adobe-like material called "tabby," from which they constructed forts and missions along the Georgia coast in the mid-1500s. Subsequent inhabitants followed suit, and today you can find tabby ruins left by every nation that has claimed the coast—from French Huguenots and the colonial British, to the fledgling U.S., the Confederacy, and even a short-lived Black Republic in 1865. Tabby is still used as a construction material today, and crushed oyster shells serve as gravel for shell roads and paths.

Colonial Times

Little evidence remains of the French and Spanish, or of the pirates common to that age (though the hidden treasure of famous brigand Edward Teal, for whom Blackbeard Island is named, supposedly lies off the Georgia coast). The British influence, in contrast, is still keenly felt in Savannah, the original settlement of the Georgia colony and the southernmost outpost of the British in America. From Savannah, the British faced off against the Spanish, who also claimed the "Debatable Land" of the Georgia coast.

After founding the city in 1733, British General James Oglethorpe ventured south to establish Fort Frederica on the Spanish-named San Simons, provoking the Spanish into venturing north from their stronghold in Florida. At the Battle of Bloody Marsh in 1742, they waged one of the most decisive battles in the history of the world. Though little more than a skirmish, it decided the fate of the new continent. After being routed in the St. Simons ambush, the retreating Spanish abandoned the goal of continental domination.

KAP STANN

passing the time of day on Sapelo Island

The colonial town of New Inverness, settled by Scottish Highlanders in 1736, remains today as Darien, but most other coastal colonial towns fell victim to severe Revolutionary War fighting or changing fortunes. Only an occasional old fort or church stands today in such "ghost" towns as Ebenezer, Midway, and Sunbury.

The early American coastal economy grew on rice, indigo, and a strain of high quality but temperamental cotton that flourished only on the islands, earning the name "Sea Island Cotton." Huge plantations with hundreds of slaves supported these industries, under subtropical conditions so harsh that most planter families lived elsewhere half the year (facts which came to define the character of the low country, see **The People,** below).

Civil War

At the outbreak of the Civil War, Georgia Governor Joseph Brown ousted federal troops from Fort Pulaski (near Savannah) even before Georgia officially seceded. After Fort Sumter, the federals took it right back again, blockading Savannah and waiting the length of the war for the action to catch up to them. Reportedly, Union troops passed much of that time playing baseball, and to this day historical reenactments at the fort feature ball games played in Yankee costumes.

When Sherman arrived in Savannah in December 1864 after his march through Georgia, the city surrendered without a fuss. From his headquarters in the Green-Meldrim House (today one of Savannah's many antebellum house museums), Sherman sent a telegram to President Lincoln, delivering him the city of Savannah "as a Christmas present."

Sherman's next task was providing for the thousands of liberated slaves his army had attracted on its March to the Sea. After conferring with local black leaders (members of Savannah's 3,000-member free black community), Sherman issued his famous Field Order #15, granting "40 acres and a mule" to former slaves, on a reservation made up of the Sea Islands and the coastal mainland. Blacks established a low-country republic in 1865, naming St. Catherines Island its capital. Yet the agreement proved to be as short-lived as historical treaties with Native Americans—during Reconstruction, the land was taken back by the government and returned to former landowners.

From Plantations to Resorts

The collapse of the plantation system left many estates abandoned; today many plantation houses can be seen in either restorations or ruins. Some estates and islands became occupied by new Northern owners, who sought out the low country as a winter retreat. The most famous of these getaway spots was Jekyll Island, where such early-American industrialists as Rockefeller, Goodyear, and Vanderbilt established an exclusive enclave centered around the regal Jekyll Island Club (still one of the East Coast's most distinguished hotels).

With the construction of bridges to the mainland, four of Georgia's islands became popular resort destinations, and today their local economies depend on tourism as well as an extensive seafood industry. The remaining islands are nearly all protected as natural refuges, and much of the marshland coast—once holding busy colonial seaports and crowded plantations—has reverted to its original natural state, save for a small shrimping fleet here and there.

THE PEOPLE

The land, climate, isolation, and history of Georgia's coast have shaped a character unique to the low country. Visitors emerging from the pine barrens of Georgia's southeastern interior will quickly sense a seaward expansiveness, a Creole flavor, and pick up the distinct drawling coastal accent. But most unusual by far is the fascinating Gullah culture created by the peculiar regional history.

Slaves on coastal plantations had a much different experience than did slaves in other regions. Because slave ships unloaded their human cargo directly at the coast, and because the large coastal plantations used hundreds of slaves, coastal slaves tended to end up working around large numbers of their countrymen. As a result, they avoided much of the culturally destructive assimilation common to slaves sent to interior regions. In addition, the coast's harsh subtropical summer climate drove most white overseers to cooler highlands for nearly half the year, allowing coastal slaves to continue cultural practices banned by plantation owners. Coastal slaves were thus able to hang on to a group identity more than their counterparts elsewhere, and hand down cultural traditions from generation to generation. Over the years, this African heritage melded with their American experience to create the rich amalgamated culture still found in isolated Sea Islander communities.

In Georgia, the Sea Islanders are named "Geechee," after the local Ogeechee River. The broader term for this folk culture and language throughout the low country (which includes South Carolina) is "Gullah," short for Angola, from where slaves were smuggled. The Gullah dialect, spoken today by an estimated 250,000 people, combines African syntax and occasional African words with Southernisms and folk language, producing a unique lexicon with a sound all its own. As an example, the Bible in the Gullah dialect translates the Gospel According to Luke as "De Good Nyews Bout Jedus Christ Wa Luke Write."

Traditional Sea Island music is a rich blend of spirituals, gospel, blues, old slave songs, and work chants that can trace the rhythms back to their African roots.

Today, the inevitable forces of modern life and mainland culture are eroding the viability of traditional Sea Island folkways, carried on largely by rapidly aging communities. As a result, the fate of these communities after the next decade or so is uncertain. In the meantime, traditional Geechee culture is celebrated at the annual **Georgia Sea Island Festival** on St. Simons Island every August, featuring Geechee music and low-country cuisine.

Geechee Folklore and Beliefs

One story tells of a captured Igbo leader who, upon debarkation from a slave ship, led his tribesmen into the water instead of submitting to slavery. The Geechee elevated this story to the mythological tale of the people who "walked back to Africa." Though the historical episode happened on St. Simons Island, every sea island has named its own "Ebo Landing," where the spirits of the dead Africans remain.

Spiritual healers—"conjure doctors"—were important members of the community, able to placate the spirits of the dead that vexed the living and upset the balance of life. Such beliefs sprang from traditional Haitian voodoo (also called "hoodoo"; Haiti was a way station for many slave ships), which combined with traditional African beliefs, Islam, and Afro-Christianity to create the folk mythology of the Geechee. (Some Geechee rituals and beliefs are recounted in John Berendt's bestseller *Midnight in the Garden of Good and Evil.)*

Low-Country Cuisine

After plantation owners abandoned the barrier islands, the remaining slaves of necessity developed self-sustaining communities dependent on

NEITHER LAND NOR SEA

The concave Southern Atlantic coastline, known as the Georgia Bight, creates the exceptionally high tides that shape coastal ecology. Tidewaters accumulate toward the middle of the curve, so Georgia tides can vary as much as 10 feet between high and low tide, compared with three feet at the top or bottom of the bight (see map). Along the Atlantic Seaboard, only Maine has a greater tide differential. At high tide, seawater penetrates as much as 40 miles up some coastal rivers—supporting Georgia's extensive saltmarshes (5-10 miles wide) and the estuaries farther upriver where fresh and salt water meet. This creates a large area neither completely land nor sea, but one or the other depending on the time of the tide. It also means a greater risk to boaters unfamiliar with local tide patterns, who may find themselves stranded or lost on unrecognizably swollen or shallow waterways.

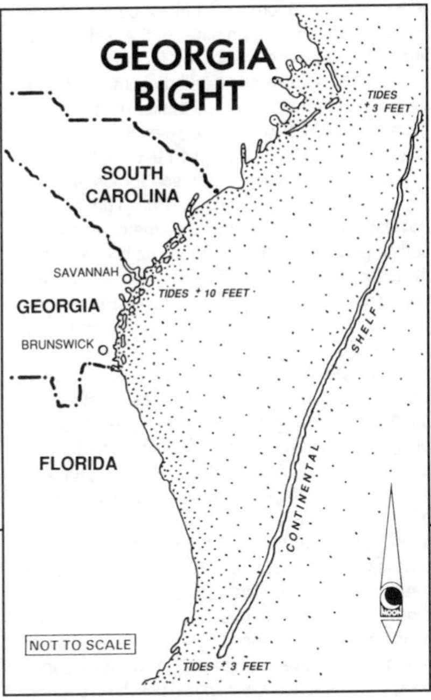

GEORGIA BIGHT
TIDES ± 3 FEET
SOUTH CAROLINA
SAVANNAH
TIDES ± 10 FEET
GEORGIA
BRUNSWICK
FLORIDA
CONTINENTAL SHELF
NOT TO SCALE
TIDES ± 3 FEET

local seafood, vegetables, and rice. Lowcountry cuisine incorporated shellfish into okra soup (okra seeds were brought by slaves from Africa), she-crab soup, and many other dishes seasoned with West Indian spices. Also brought from Africa, benne seeds now accent popular benne wafers.

WATER RECREATION

Not just ocean but every manner of creek, river, delta, estuary, sound, canal, inlet, and harbor defines Georgia's secluded coast—and the best way to experience it is on a boat. Every type of craft cruises coastal waters, from skiffs to yachts. Rent a canoe or sea kayak, join an excursion trip, or charter a boat yourself over to the remote islands—just go!

The Atlantic Coast's **Intracoastal Waterway** weaves through the entire 100-mile length of Georgia's marshlands from South Carolina to the Florida border. Popular en route marinas include Thunderbolt (near Savannah), St. Simons Island, and the historic Jekyll Island Wharf. Mariners can pick up the federal waterway guide for the Georgia region (*United States Coast Pilot,* Southern Atlantic coast edition) at nautical supply shops or government bookstores.

River trips take paddlers down beautiful coastal plain rivers, particularly the Ogeechee, the St. Marys, and the Savannah. The premier paddling guide to the region is Don Otey's *Southern Georgia Canoeing,* available at Savannah's outfitter stores. Short **marshland** jaunts start at any one of scores of boat launches. Watercraft rentals are available in Savannah and the Golden Isles.

Paddlers may legally alight or camp on any island below the high-tide line, but that's a risky proposition. The unusually high tide differential here demands a familiarity with tidal patterns, not only for tide-zone camping but for navigation in general. Even expert paddlers can become stranded or lost as the tide ebbs or flows by as much as 10 feet. This text lists only wide, well-worn paths that should be trouble-free to

ISLAND-HOPPING (NORTH TO SOUTH)

Only four of Georgia's 13 major barrier islands are bridged to the mainland; the rest are defined by their inaccessibility. Yet for those who can expend a little extra effort and do some planning, the rare wilderness you'll encounter once you get there will make it all worthwhile. Here old shell roads, jeep trails, and wide walkable beaches lead you past the nests of loggerhead sea turtles and the tracks of deer and armadillo, and into a dense subtropical woodland of live oak, palmetto, and muscadine grape vines as big around as your arm. On these remote islands you'll find a wilderness strewn with ruins of ancient tribes, European explorers, and Sea Island Cotton plantations far from mainland worries.

On remote islands, transportation is by foot only, so wear comfortable walking shoes (in summer, choose light hiking shoes; for marsh exploration, bring old sneakers). Island roads are ideal for trail biking, and if you charter a boat you could probably take one out with you, but the ferries won't allow bikes. Hikers must bring an adequate supply of food and water (more than the bare minimum). Water sources, if they exist at all, are infrequent and may need to be treated. The remote islands have no stores (though an occasional soda machine or candy-vending machine at docks can be a lifesaver to those who haven't prepared). You may want to bring a swimsuit and towel, or rain poncho in addition to the necessities listed below. You'll need warm hats, scarves, gloves, and jackets in winter.

Tybee Island
Known as "Savannah Beach," this Coney-Island-spirited funky beach town of developed beaches, hotels, and amusements is accessible by car 18 miles east of Savannah (see **Vicinity of Savannah**).

Little Tybee Island
Small and uninhabited, Little Tybee's sandy shores are accessible by boat only but are just a short canoe ride away from Tybee Island (see **Vicinity of Savannah**).

Wassaw Island
A federally owned wildlife refuge accessible only by boat, Wassaw is one of the least-spoiled natural islands on the east coast. Visitors arrange charters through Savannah-area marinas or follow a paddling route from Skidaway Island (see **Vicinity of Savannah**).

Ossabaw Island
State-owned and operated in cooperation with a private organization, Ossabaw Island is open only to educational or artistic groups; boat access only (see **North Coast**).

Saint Catherines Island
The New York Zoological Society operates a captive breeding program for endangered animals on the island, and actively discourages visitation. Accessible by boat only (see **North Coast**).

Blackbeard Island
A federally owned and operated national wildlife refuge, Blackbeard is accessible only by boat. Visitors arrange charters through local marinas or via excursions from Sapelo Island (see **North Coast**).

Sapelo Island
Largely state owned and operated as a marine research center and wildlife preserve, Sapelo is served

paddlers with some experience. But if in doubt, hire a guide or go with a tour.

Excursions and Boat Charters

Several local, regional, and statewide groups lead guided paddling tours down the coast from Savannah, but the premier local outfitter is **SouthEast Adventure Outfitters** based in St. Simons (see **St. Simons Island** or www.gacoast.com/navigator/sea.html.

For most boat-access-only islands, the only way independent travelers can arrange a visit is by chartering a boat. Many such services exist at local marinas along the coast, and prices start from about $50 for a roundtrip charter. For a list of charter services and boat ramps along the Georgia coast, order a copy of the *Coastal Georgia Fishing* brochure from the Regional Development Center, P.O. Box 1917, Brunswick, GA 31523 (enclose a business-sized SASE). The Georgia Conservancy's thorough *Coastal Georgia* guide includes lists of full-service marinas and boat captains; it's available at bookstores along the coast and in Atlanta. The Savannah tourist bureau also distributes lists of charter captains and local marinas.

by a daily ferry, but passage is restricted to public tours organized by McIntosh County or by reservation with an overnight hostelry (see **North Coast**).

Wolf Island
A federally owned and operated national wildlife preserve, Wolf Island lacks the dense and varied habitats of larger barrier islands (see **North Coast**).

Little Saint Simons Island
Privately owned and operated by innkeepers as a rustic (but exclusive) retreat, Little St. Simons is accessible only by boat (for guests only) from St. Simons Island (see **Golden Isles**).

Sea Island
Accessible by car from St. Simons Island, Sea Island holds the five-star Cloister Hotel (see **Golden Isles**) and an exclusive residential community.

Saint Simons Island
Rich history, scenic beauty, and a year-round residential community make St. Simons a nice island town as well as a popular upscale beach resort. Bridged to the mainland and developed since 1736, St. Simons is accessible by car (see **Golden Isles**).

Jekyll Island
Once the exclusive preserve of wealthy tycoons but now open to the public, the state-owned and leased Jekyll Island resort is home to the historic Jekyll Island Club Hotel, as well as an island campground and middle-class beach resort (see **Golden Isles**).

Cumberland Island
Federally owned and operated as a National Seashore, Cumberland is the most readily accessible "hidden" island, and to many the most scenic. Daily ferry service departs from St. Marys, overnight camping permitted. An exclusive private inn offers lodging and private ferry service for guests (see **St. Marys and Cumberland Islands,** below).

Little Cumberland Island
At the north tip of Cumberland Island, Little Cumberland remains largely in private hands as a residential retreat. A ferry runs from Jekyll Island for residents only.

(Note: During winter hunting seasons, remote island preserves may be open to hunters only.)

Subtropical Precautions
Overexposure is the number one medical emergency on the islands, so seek shelter in the forest during the hottest times of day and carry enough water (perhaps also salt tablets). Confine strenuous outdoor activity to early morning or late afternoon, and seek shelter midday. Wear sunscreen, sunglasses, and a hat (for the most protection, dress in lightweight, long-limbed clothing). Carry insect repellent (locals favor "Claubo" or an Avon skin lotion called "Skin-So-Soft," which also seems to do the trick; both are easily available locally). Sand gnats that act up in spring and fall can be a nuisance on still days; if you can't choose a breezy day, see the beach early and retreat to the forest midday. Mosquitoes are most noticeable at dusk in the summer, in heavily wooded areas, or a week after heavy rains. Avoid chiggers and ticks (found in high grass or thick woods) by dousing bare ankles and legs with repellent or tucking long pants into socks. A thorough "tick check" after a wilderness hike can spot ticks; chiggers are harder to detect (if a red spot itches a few hours later, cover the area with clear nail polish).

Encounters with venomous snakes are rare; snakes are nocturnal, naturally cautious, and inactive in cold or hot weather. To be most cautious, stay on cleared trails and watch where you place hands and feet—especially in woods, tall grass, or at the edge of low wet areas. If you plan on doing any serious backcountry hiking, you might consider taking a snakebite kit.

Now for the flip side: Heed precautions but don't let caution overshadow the opportunity to see the wilder coast; spontaneous day-trippers armed with only a pair of shorts, a fanny pack of trail mix, and a sense of adventure might wonder what all the fuss was about. Determine your own measure of safety and margin for error, but remember that there's no backup if you've misjudged. Conserve emergency rescue resources by being adequately prepared.

SAVANNAH

An 18th-century village that lives resolutely in the present, Savannah brings together an exotic history (all the Redcoats, silkworms, Indian chiefs, blockade runners, Sephardim, and utopian ideals you could ask for) and a steamy subtropical nature (tendrils of Spanish moss, wisteria, and wild grapevines drape like tinsel off majestic oaks), then wraps it up in one compact, charming package. Like Taos is to the American Southwest, Savannah is to the Southeast—it's the one city that best encapsulates the regional aesthetic. If you see one city in the American Southeast, make it Savannah.

Rows of European townhouses border cobblestone streets and shady squares full of Grecian fountains, obelisks, and towering magnolias. You'll see gold domes and Corinthian columns, wrought-iron balustrades and sweeping staircases. But in Savannah nothing goes without a touch of whimsy—like dolphin-shaped drainspouts, flowerboxes grown wild, and water fountains for dogs. Residents live comfortably among the griffons, never too far from an auto shop or ramshackle lot fit languidly into what is, after all, a neighborhood.

Yet the sleepy tidewater city has found its repose disturbed as hordes of tourists have descended upon the town following the phenomenal success of John Berendt's account of a Gothic local murder in his 1994 bestseller *Midnight in the Garden of Good and Evil,* known throughout town as simply "The Book." Being Savannahians, they've come to take all the hoopla in stride.

At the Atlantic shore, Tybee Island ("Savannah Beach") adds a sandy stretch of Coney Island-like appeal to Savannah's urbane attractions. Between riverfront and oceanfront, 18 miles of scenic marshlands provide a close-in wilderness.

HISTORY

General James Oglethorpe founded Savannah as the southernmost outpost of England's American colonies in 1733. Choosing a high bluff above the Savannah River 18 miles inland from the Atlantic Ocean, Oglethorpe mapped out a planned city according to 18th-century British specifications, a design preserved to this day. Around the squares and narrow lanes rose Oglethorpe's utopian enterprise—he and the original Trustees of the new Georgia colony envisioned a place without slavery, alcohol, speculation, religious persecution, or oppressive class differences. Not all of those ideals held fast—most notably slavery, as the Trustees succumbed to the colonists' complaints about unfair competition from neighboring slaveholding states. Nevertheless, Savannah became known for its large free black community, composed of African immigrants, freed slaves, and later, Haitians.

Oglethorpe tried to establish silk and wine-making industries in this 13th and final American colony, and though the city's mulberry trees and wild muscadine vines are all that remain of those dashed hopes, what did flourish were crops of cotton, peaches, rice, and tobacco. The town quickly grew into a prosperous seaport and financial center, punctuated only briefly by four years of British occupation during the Revolutionary War. Savannah replaced King George with King Cotton; the cotton gin was invented nearby, and Savannah's Cotton Exchange set cotton prices around the world for nearly a century.

When General William T. Sherman arrived at the end of his infamous March to the Sea in 1864, Savannah surrendered, and by invitation Sherman established himself in the Green-Meldrim House. From here Sherman sent a telegram to President Lincoln: "I beg to present to you as a Christmas gift, the City of Savannah, with 140 heavy guns and plenty of ammunition and also about 25,000 bales of cotton." Sherman also conferred with local black leaders, then issued Field Order #15, which reserved the Sea Islands and "40 acres and a mule" for freed slaves (promises later rescinded).

Nearby, Forts Jackson, Pulaski, Screven, and McAllister testify to Savannah's military history during Spanish skirmishes, the Revolutionary War, the War of 1812, and the Civil War.

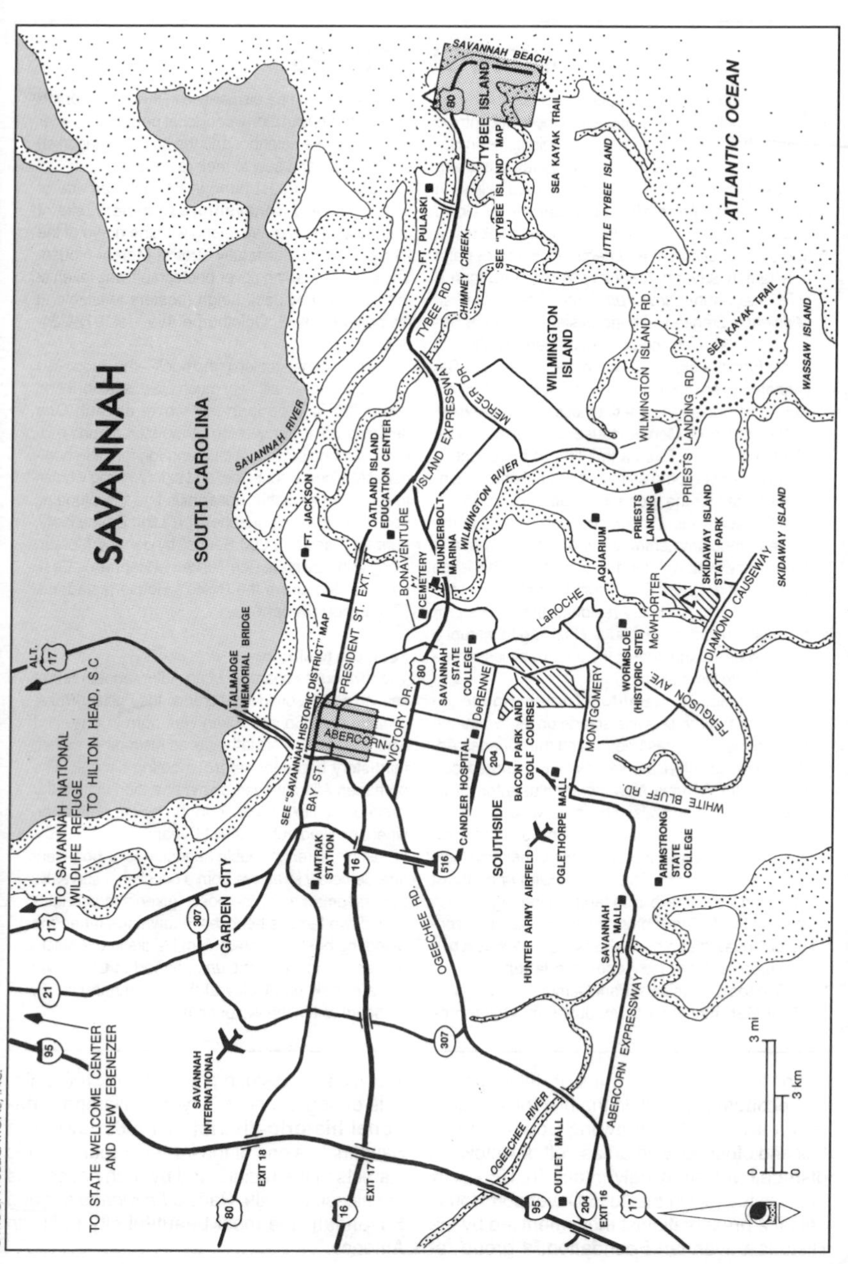
SAVANNAH
SOUTH CAROLINA
SAVANNAH RIVER
TO SAVANNAH NATIONAL WILDLIFE REFUGE
TO HILTON HEAD, S C
ALT. 17
TALMADGE MEMORIAL BRIDGE
SEE "SAVANNAH HISTORIC DISTRICT" MAP
FT. JACKSON
OATLAND ISLAND EDUCATION CENTER
BONAVENTURE CEMETERY
THUNDERBOLT MARINA
FT. PULASKI
TYBEE RD.
CHIMNEY CREEK
SEE "TYBEE ISLAND" MAP
TYBEE ISLAND
SAVANNAH BEACH
SEA KAYAK TRAIL
LITTLE TYBEE ISLAND
ATLANTIC OCEAN
WILMINGTON ISLAND
WILMINGTON RIVER
MERCER DR.
ISLAND EXPRESSWAY
WILMINGTON ISLAND RD.
PRIESTS LANDING RD.
PRIESTS LANDING
WASSAW ISLAND
SKIDAWAY ISLAND STATE PARK
SKIDAWAY ISLAND
DIAMOND CAUSEWAY
AQUARIUM
McWHORTER
LaROCHE
WORMSLOE (HISTORIC SITE)
FERGUSON AVE
MONTGOMERY
WHITE BLUFF RD.
ARMSTRONG STATE COLLEGE
SAVANNAH STATE COLLEGE
PRESIDENT ST. EXT.
VICTORY DR.
ABERCORN
BAY ST.
DeRENNE
CANDLER HOSPITAL
BACON PARK AND GOLF COURSE
OGLETHORPE MALL
SOUTHSIDE
HUNTER ARMY AIRFIELD
AMTRAK STATION
GARDEN CITY
OGEECHEE RD.
SAVANNAH MALL
ABERCORN EXPRESSWAY
OGEECHEE RIVER
OUTLET MALL
SAVANNAH INTERNATIONAL
TO STATE WELCOME CENTER AND NEW EBENEZER
EXIT 18
EXIT 17
EXIT 16
80
16
95
204
17
21
307
516
3 mi
3 km
0

MIDNIGHT TOURS

According to a local voodoo priestess, the difference between good and evil in the lowcountry is a single half-hour, either side of midnight. Yet in Savannah proper the line is less clearly drawn, or that's what author John Berendt would have you believe in his 1994 book ***Midnight in the Garden of Good and Evil.*** Though it reads like fiction, the book tells a true story of decorum and decadence, murder and mayhem in Savannah society. After more than a solid year on the *New York Times* best-seller list, *Midnight* is credited with increasing tourism in Savannah by 50%, as book-in-arm readers flock to visit sights from the story. So welcome to Berendt's Savannah, a "semitropical terrarium, sealed off from a world that suddenly seemed a thousand miles away."

The first stop is **Mercer House,** on azalea-studded Monterey Square. Even without the intrigue associated with murder, the salmon-brick Italianate mansion (named for the great-grandfather of composer Johnny Mercer) is a stunning sight, with its formidable four-column entrance and intricate ironwork balconies woven with tendrils of wisteria. This is the scene of *Midnight's* crime. From its arched second-story windows, its ornery resident (the book's protagonist) once draped a huge Nazi flag to disrupt a movie scene being shot in the square by less-than-considerate filmmakers.

The imposing **Hamilton-Turner House** on Lafayette Square likewise stands on its own architectural merits—it has been called the "Charles Addams House" after the whimsically haunted cartoons of the famous *New Yorker* illustrator for its shipdeck crown and raised-eyebrow window-work—but lovers of Berendt's postmodern Southern gothic tale will know it as the residence of beloved local con man Joe Odom. The ivory-tickling opportunist outraged local sensibilities (and zoning regulations, to boot) by offering impromptu house tours and concerts. Today the notorious house operates as a bed and breakfast inn (see **Accommodations**).

Overlooking Colonial Park Cemetery, the refined **Mary Marshall Row** townhouses on Oglethorpe Ave. were due to be dismantled in the 1960s for the price of the *bricks* alone until local patron Lee Adler (Mercer House neighbor and the book's antagonist) spared them and saw to their restoration.

A short drive east through the palm arcade of Victory Drive is **Bonaventure Cemetery,** site of Johnny Mercer's grave, along with the grave of the 21-year-old hustler fatally shot at Mercer House. The book's beguiling cover photograph was taken at the cemetery by Jack Leigh (posters available at his gallery, 132 E. Oglethorpe Ave., tel. 912-234-6449).

But the scene-stealer in the book—the audacious Lady Chablis—is still very much alive, shakin' it and raking it in with performances over at **Club One Jefferson.** The transvestite shows start around midnight, slowing down just long enough for stiff-shouldered Marines, limber lads, and sturdy young women to reach up and stuff dollar bills into the plunging bodices of the drag queens. You'll find Emma Kelly, dubbed "Lady of 6,000 Songs" by Johnny Mercer, along with jazz great Ben Tucker, at **Hannah's East,** the jazz club above the Pirate's House restaurant. (See **Entertainment.**)

Footnote to Murder

The rowhouses spared by Lee Adler (above) represent an earlier sordid local drama: the Pulitzer-Prize-winning poet Conrad Aiken was born in one, and when he was 11, his father killed his mother in their third-story bedroom before shooting himself. The orphaned Aiken moved away, and then closed the circle of his life by retiring in the house next door, where he lived out his last 11 years.

Aiken's parents' double headstones at Bonaventure Cemetery sit across from a bench that serves as the gravemarker for the poet. (Aiken's memorial is one of two famous benches in town, the other one being the poster perch of Tom Hanks in the blockbuster movie *Forrest Gump,* filmed in Chippewa Square, now on display at the Savannah History Museum within the visitor center).

For many decades, a lull of development and economic activity in the historic city center (in favor of the sprawling Southside district and other outlying areas) left downtown in disrepair yet amazingly intact. In 1957, city plans to tear down the 1815 Davenport House set off a preservationist movement led by the Historic Savannah Foundation, a group responsible for restoring more than 1,100 buildings during the next 30 years. Named a **national historic district** in 1966, downtown Savannah is one of the largest urban historic districts in the nation, and by many accounts the nicest. In 1989, Paris's *Le Monde* dubbed Savannah "the most beautiful city in North America."

Savannah's economic base is secured by its port operations, tourism, and manufacturing (principally pulpwood, paper, and aircraft production). Nearby Fort Stewart is the region's largest single employer. Much of the metropolitan area's population of 251,000 lives in the outlying districts and islands of Chatham County.

GETTING ORIENTED

Savannah is a walker's town—the historic district measures a compact 2.5 square miles, and the original 1732 city grid is quickly evident. From Bull St. in the center, the historic downtown is divided neatly into symmetrical eastern and western sections, bounded by E. Broad and Martin Luther King, Jr., Blvd. respectively. South from the riverfront, the historic district ends at Gaston Street. Here beautiful Forsyth Park and environs, and the annexed historic Victorian district, both hold wonderful sights, yet in general the district south of Gaston St. quickly becomes questionable. In fact, historic district chauvinists are proudly dubbed NOGs, meaning they stay "North Of Gaston."

Wander around squares (each one of 21 has its own distinct character), or visit house museums, the Riverfront, or City Market. If you like, follow self-guided walking-tour maps availabe from the visitors center, or take a guided tour. You can also rent bikes at many outlets around town for easy exploring, though the many cobblestone streets make for bumpy rides.

Savannah Visitors Center and History Museum

The Savannah Visitors Center, tel. (912) 944-0460 or (800) 444-2427, housed in the restored Central of Georgia railroad station at 301 Martin Luther King, Jr., Blvd. (formerly W. Broad St.), provides all you'll need to begin exploring the historic district. Rent audiotape tours or pick up free walking-tour maps, metro-area maps and guides, scores of brochures, and discount coupons for local lodging and attractions.

The **Savannah History Museum,** tel. (912) 238-1779, in the adjacent train shed displays an 1890 locomotive, a "Bird Girl" plaster cast and the story of the artist, the famed Forrest Gump park bench, and historical exhibits largely about rice and shipping—you may prefer to skip the museum and just get on out to the real thing. Admission is $3 adults.

The center and museum are open daily year-round: Mon.-Fri. 8:30 a.m.-5 p.m., Sat.-Sun. 9 a.m.-5 p.m. there is no charge for parking for your first hour, then it's $1 for the second hour, then 50 cents for each additional hour. You can catch many city tours from here or hop on a municipal shuttle to get downtown.

Organized Tours

Climb aboard buses, trolley cars, paddlewheel boats, or horse-drawn carriages, or stay on foot for a wide variety of guided tours that serve as a great introduction to the city. There are historic house tours, ghost story tours, shopping tours, garden tours, and tours devoted to sites in the bestselling book *Midnight in the Garden of Good and Evil* (see the special topic ***Midnight* Tours**). Contact the visitor center for the full selection. Many tours leave from the visitors center or the riverfront, some pick you up at your hotel, and most last around an hour or two.

The most evocative are **Carriage Tours of Savannah,** tel. (912) 236-6756 or (800) 442-5933, that leave from City Market, the Visitors Center, and the Hyatt Regency Riverfront (times vary at each location). Twelve-seat carriages amble about the city at just the right pace ($13-16 adults, $6 children, call for schedule and reservations). The 6 p.m. ride makes a particularly appealing dusky tour through the quieted town—guides tell of legends and ghost stories in drawling coastal accents, horseshoes clatter against cobblestones, and you half expect to see lanternlighters illuminating street lamps in the squares. Intimate private tours on smaller carriages are also available.

The **Black Heritage Trail Tour,** tel. (912) 234-8000, also makes a strong impression, telling history from a seldom-heard African American perspective and incorporating tours of heritage sights (from around $10 adults, around $5 children).

Gray Line, tel. (912) 234-TOUR (912-234-8687), runs trolley tours, including the widest selection of bilingual tours (French, German, Spanish, Dutch, and Japanese), from $14. **Old Town**

ARCHITECTURAL STYLES

FEDERAL

GREEK REVIVAL

ITALIANATE

QUEEN ANNE

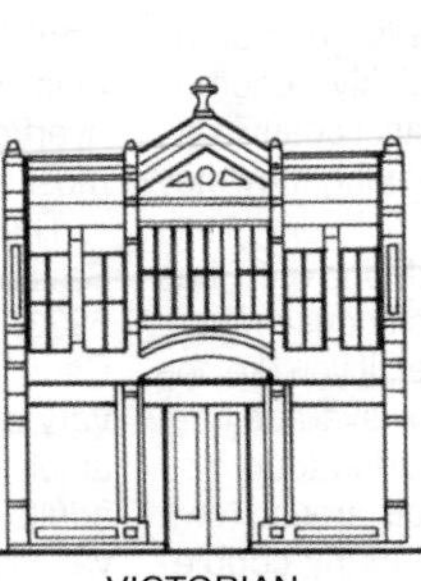

VICTORIAN RENAISSANCE

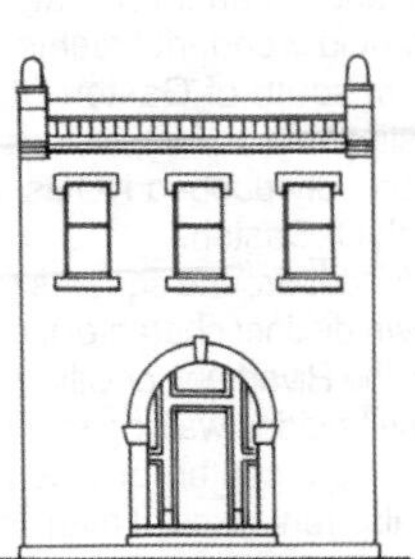

VICTORIAN ROMANESQUE

VICTORIAN GOTHIC

VICTORIAN FUNCTIONAL

SECOND EMPIRE

SAVANNAH'S ARCHITECTURAL HERITAGE

Much of the visual charm of Savannah's historic district comes from impressive 18th- and 19th-century styles of architecture, artfully restored and preserved in mansions, cottages, churches, and public buildings. Even a novice can begin picking out certain details that define a particular style and era.

The grandest example of the earliest **Georgian** period is the 1820 Davenport House. Rows of three- to four-story brick townhouses also date from this period. While resembling the older streets of London, these row houses also reflect a tropical sensibility. Because the upper floors were considered to be "above" the risk of malaria, the ground floors were devoted to offices, and the living spaces were reserved for the second floor and higher, reached by curved staircases ornamented with wrought-iron handrails. Kitchens were typically the back room of the ground floor.

Early brick buildings were constructed from imported brick, often brought over on sailing ships as ballast (the now elegantly restored buildings that line Factors Walk are composed of cruder ballast stone). Later, local kilns produced "Savannah Gray" bricks, named for the distinctive color they derived from local sandy soils.

Savannah's prosperity of the early 1800s coincided with the **Regency** period, and as a result, many fine old houses were built in this style. Grander flourishes were added to Georgian sensibilities—high ceilings, oval rooms, intricately carved moldings and great marble fireplaces were typical of that time. British architect William Jay designed many of Savannah's finest buildings in this style, most notably the Owens-Thomas House and Telfair Academy of Arts.

The following **Greek Revival** period brought the large colonnaded entrances and grand staircases associated most closely with Southern plantation architecture, thanks largely to director Selznick's vision of the fictional Tara in *Gone with the Wind.* Continuing prosperity meant that many homes, and particularly public buildings, conform to this style.

Then the **Victorian** era (1827-1901) revived row houses of a different sort, many still constructed with brick but without the delicate ornamentation of the previous Georgian period. Many wooden-frame houses with gingerbread accents and other elaborate Queen Anne-style homes make up the Victorian district, which lies just outside the main historic district boundary. The Green-Meldrim House reveals a mixture of architectural styles in this period, with its Gothic roof line and intricate French ironwork. The 1886 Cotton Exchange remains as another example of this time.

Equally interesting as these classical architectural motifs are the changes brought about by the different ethnic groups that settled in the city. Wrought-iron balcony rails, typically associated with New Orleans, were brought to Savannah by the French resettling in Savannah after fleeing slave rebellions in Haiti. From Barbados came the side-of-the-house gallery entrances commonly associated with Charleston. Peaked roofs reflect the German Jews and Salzburg Protestants who were among the city's original settlers.

Less prevalent in refined Savannah than elsewhere on the coast but still common is "tabby" construction, a stucco-like mix of oyster shells, sand, lime from burned shells, and water. Used most often for outbuildings in Savannah, and for everything up to grand plantation homes down the coast, the material was also used by the natives. Origins of the term "tabby" are unclear; some theories say it comes from the Spanish *tapia,* others say the African *tabax.* Some say the method of tapping the mixture to settle it became the origins of "tappy," later Southernized to tabby.

Today the black marble floors, skylit rotundas, and majestic staircases give visitors reason to stop and consider the details of Savannah's long architectural history. The Massie Heritage Interpretation Center devotes several exhibits to the city's architectural underpinnings. The center, 207 E. Gordon St., is open Mon.-Fri. 9 a.m.-4 p.m., $1.50 admission; tel. (912) 651-7380. Certain city tours focus primarily on architectural style; inquire at the Welcome Center for more information.

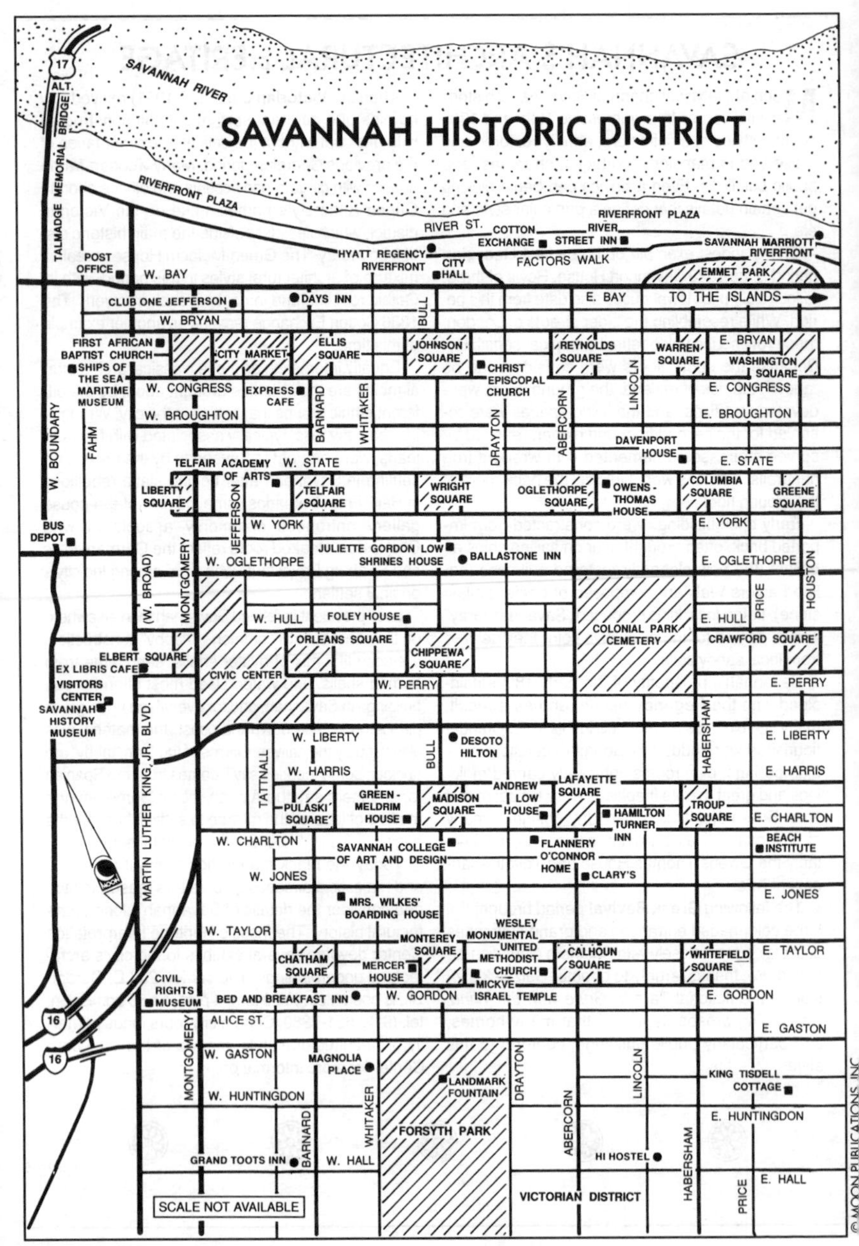

SAVANNAH HISTORIC DISTRICT
SAVANNAH RIVER
17
ALT.
TALMADGE MEMORIAL BRIDGE
RIVERFRONT PLAZA
RIVER ST.
COTTON EXCHANGE
RIVER STREET INN
SAVANNAH MARRIOTT RIVERFRONT
HYATT REGENCY RIVERFRONT
CITY HALL
FACTORS WALK
EMMET PARK
POST OFFICE
W. BAY
E. BAY
TO THE ISLANDS
CLUB ONE JEFFERSON
DAYS INN
W. BRYAN
E. BRYAN
FIRST AFRICAN BAPTIST CHURCH
CITY MARKET
ELLIS SQUARE
JOHNSON SQUARE
REYNOLDS SQUARE
WARREN SQUARE
WASHINGTON SQUARE
SHIPS OF THE SEA MARITIME MUSEUM
CHRIST EPISCOPAL CHURCH
W. CONGRESS
E. CONGRESS
EXPRESS CAFE
W. BROUGHTON
E. BROUGHTON
W. BOUNDARY
FAHM
BARNARD
WHITAKER
BULL
DRAYTON
ABERCORN
LINCOLN
DAVENPORT HOUSE
TELFAIR ACADEMY OF ARTS
W. STATE
E. STATE
LIBERTY SQUARE
JEFFERSON
TELFAIR SQUARE
WRIGHT SQUARE
OGLETHORPE SQUARE
OWENS-THOMAS HOUSE
COLUMBIA SQUARE
GREENE SQUARE
W. YORK
E. YORK
BUS DEPOT
JULIETTE GORDON LOW SHRINES HOUSE
BALLASTONE INN
W. OGLETHORPE
E. OGLETHORPE
MONTGOMERY
(W. BROAD)
HOUSTON
PRICE
W. HULL
FOLEY HOUSE
E. HULL
COLONIAL PARK CEMETERY
ORLEANS SQUARE
CHIPPEWA SQUARE
CRAWFORD SQUARE
ELBERT SQUARE
EX LIBRIS CAFE
CIVIC CENTER
W. PERRY
E. PERRY
VISITORS CENTER
SAVANNAH HISTORY MUSEUM
HABERSHAM
W. LIBERTY
E. LIBERTY
DESOTO HILTON
MARTIN LUTHER KING, JR. BLVD.
TATTNALL
W. HARRIS
E. HARRIS
ANDREW LOW HOUSE
LAFAYETTE SQUARE
PULASKI SQUARE
GREEN-MELDRIM HOUSE
MADISON SQUARE
HAMILTON TURNER INN
TROUP SQUARE
E. CHARLTON
W. CHARLTON
BEACH INSTITUTE
SAVANNAH COLLEGE OF ART AND DESIGN
FLANNERY O'CONNOR HOME
W. JONES
CLARY'S
E. JONES
MOON
MRS. WILKES' BOARDING HOUSE
W. TAYLOR
WESLEY MONUMENTAL UNITED METHODIST CHURCH
MONTEREY SQUARE
CALHOUN SQUARE
WHITEFIELD SQUARE
E. TAYLOR
CHATHAM SQUARE
MERCER HOUSE
MICKVE ISRAEL TEMPLE
CIVIL RIGHTS MUSEUM
BED AND BREAKFAST INN
W. GORDON
E. GORDON
16
ALICE ST.
E. GASTON
W. GASTON
MAGNOLIA PLACE
LANDMARK FOUNTAIN
KING TISDELL COTTAGE
W. HUNTINGDON
E. HUNTINGDON
FORSYTH PARK
GRAND TOOTS INN
W. HALL
HI HOSTEL
E. HALL
VICTORIAN DISTRICT
SCALE NOT AVAILABLE
© MOON PUBLICATIONS, INC.

Trolley Tours, tel. (912) 233-0083, charges $17 adults, $7 children.

Ragtop Tours, 19 E. Perry St., tel. (912) 944-0999, takes a maximum of five passengers around town in a vintage Cadillac convertible from the Kennedy era ($40 for two plus $10 each additional person).

In general, open-air tours are more engaging than being sheltered away from the city's heat, sounds, and scents in an air-conditioned bus.

HISTORIC DISTRICT

Riverfront

Factors Walk, the dignified Bay St. promenade at the top of the bluff named for cotton merchants, parallels the high row of ballast-stone and brick buildings that once served as cotton warehouses. The scenic shaded plaza that surrounds the walk is dotted with majestic oaks, magnolias, and statues of stern soldiers on horseback. The venerable 1887 **Cotton Exchange** here can be reached via one of the many catwalks that cross over the cobblestone lane below. Today, antique stores, a branch library, offices, and the **River Street Inn** occupy the beautifully restored 19th-century buildings.

Walk down through one of the cutaway alleys to the **River Street** side at the base of the bluff for a contrasting scene. Here, eye-level with the busy tugs and barges of the brimming ship channel, you'll find Savannah's lively entertainment and tourist center full of shops, restaurants, pubs, and nightclubs. On weekend nights and during city festivals, River Street turns into one giant block party, with dancing in the streets, seafood stalls, sidewalk margarita stands (plastic containers only), live entertainment inside and out, and rocketing fireworks. By day, you'll find plenty of shops selling local curios, shell ornaments, and the like. Among the most distinctive is the Callaway Gardens store, which stocks Southern foods, treats, and handcrafted gifts (see **Callaway Gardens**).

At the eastern end of River St., the **waving girl statue** honors Florence Martus, a local woman who loyally greeted ships from her youth in 1887 until her death in 1931.

City Market

City Market, a pedestrian arcade along W. St. Julian between Barnard and Montgomery, is a cozy, inviting complex of outdoor cafes, underground clubs, eateries, shops, galleries, and studios exhibiting the in-process works of 35 artists. The original city marketplace here was torn down for a parking lot, outraging local preservationists. This modern version quickly became a magnet for locals hungry for a laid-back alternative to the boisterous River Street scene. But within 10 years City Market has developed into quite a scene itself, with dance clubs and frequent outdoor concerts turning the plaza into another continuous block party each weekend, though with a slightly more local crowd than down at River St.

Historic House Tours

Savannah is blessed with many exquisite historic house museums that lead visitors through period rooms of lush drapery, fine antique furniture, appointed table service, and other decorative arts. Impressive at any time, and always a wonderful step-back-in-time introduction to Savannah, historic homes are at their best when decorated for seasonal tours. The annual **Tour of Homes and Gardens** is the city's all-out three-day house tour extravaganza, held annually in spring since its inception in the 1920s.

The 1820 **Davenport House,** on Columbia Square at 324 E. State St., tel. (912) 236-8097, started the whole local preservation movement in the early 1960s. When the city proposed tearing down the dilapidated old building (see the "before" pictures in the unrestored attic) to build a parking lot, several outraged, preservation-minded women banded together to save the historic structure. Today the Federal-style mansion is magnificently restored to its original splendor, open daily 10 a.m.-4 p.m.; tours run every 30 minutes. Admission is $5 adults.

The elegant 1816 tabby **Owens-Thomas House** on Oglethorpe Square at 124 Abercorn St., tel. (912) 233-9743, is considered among the finest examples of Regency architecture in the U.S. The house tour includes a look at the inventive early plumbing, formal garden, and "haint blue" slave quarters. Forty-five minute guided tours are held daily until 5 p.m. starting at noon on Monday, from 10 a.m. Tues.-Sat., and from 2 p.m. Sunday (closed September and national holidays). Admission is $7 adults, $2-4 for children, students, and seniors. The gift shop sells Gullah baskets from Sapelo Island among many distinctive crafts.

The **Green-Meldrim House** on Madison Square at 1 W. Macon St., tel. (912) 233-3845, served as General Sherman's headquarters during his occupation of Savannah. At that time, it was the home of a wealthy cotton merchant; now it's the parish house for St. John's Episcopal Church next door. The Gothic 1850s house is open Tuesday and Thurs.-Sat. 10 a.m.-4 p.m., closed holidays. Admission is $3 adults, students $1, children under six free.

At the **Juliette Gordon Low Birthplace,** 142 Bull St., tel. (912) 233-4501, Girl Scouts can earn a pin by just showing up; it's the birthplace of the organization's founder. The 1821 Regency-style house is furnished in late-19th-century style; the Victorian garden is also on view. It's open Mon.-Tues. and Thurs.-Sat. 10 a.m.-4 p.m., Sunday 12:30-4:30 p.m. (closed Wednesday). Admission is $5 adults, $4 children ages 6-17 (Girl Scout discount).

After Juliette Gordon's marriage to Andrew Low, the couple resided in the 1848 stuccoed brick **Andrew Low House,** 329 Abercorn St., tel. (912) 233-6854, now also a house museum. It's open for tours Fri.-Wed.; last tour at 3:30 p.m. Admission is $6 adults, $3 children (Girl Scout discount).

The **Flannery O'Connor Home,** on Lafayette Square at 207 E. Charlton St., tel. (912) 233-6014, commemorates the birthplace of one of Georgia's most famous writers. O'Connor (1925-1964) wrote *Wise Blood* and *The Violent Bear It Away,* among other classics of Southern Gothic literature. The modest home with its lovely tiny garden is open Fri.-Sun. 1-4 p.m. A $2 donation is requested. Literary events are held here Oct.-May.

The **King Tisdell Cottage,** 514 E. Huntingdon St., tel. (912) 234-8000, an 1896 Victorian museum dedicated to African-American heritage, houses period furnishings along with African art and exhibits on slave history and the unique Sea Island black culture. It's open by appointment for $3 adults (or seen as part of the Black Heritage Trail Tour; see **Organized Tours** above).

Historic Religious Centers

Savannah's congregations date from the city's founding in 1733, and many fine 19th-century sanctuaries remain in use today. **Christ Episcopal Church,** on the preeminent Johnson Square down from City Hall, was the first church in the colony; its current sanctuary was built in 1838. The 1890 **Wesley Monumental United Methodist Church,** on Calhoun Square at E. Gordon and Abercorn, commemorates John Wesley, who founded Methodism here.

Mickve Israel Temple, on Monterey Square at Bull St. and E. Gordon, founded in 1878, is the third oldest Jewish congregation in the nation, and the oldest in the South. Interestingly, it is housed in a former Christian church.

The **First African Baptist Church,** 23 Montgomery St., and **First Bryan Baptist Church,** 559 W. Bryan St., are two halves of the oldest African-American Baptist congregation in North America, dating from 1773.

Many famous city leaders permanently reside at the **Colonial Park Cemetery** on Abercorn St. and Oglethorpe Avenue, a shady spot to look and linger. (Cemetery fans wouldn't want to miss **Bonaventure Cemetery,** east of town off Hwy. 80.)

MUSEUMS

Telfair Academy of Arts

On Telfair Square, the Telfair Academy, 121 Barnard St., tel. (912) 232-1177, is the oldest art museum in the South. Its collection of Impressionist paintings, along with 18th- and 19th-century American and European furniture, silver, and decorative arts is housed in an 1818 Regency-style mansion built on the site of the original British colonial governor's house, and designed by William Jay, the architect responsible for many of the city's finest buildings. The Octagon Room is considered among the finest period rooms in the country.

Admission is $5 adults, $1 children (no charge on Sunday). It's open daily: Monday noon-5 p.m., Tues.-Sat. 10 a.m.-5 p.m., Sunday 2-5 p.m.

Ships of the Sea Museum

Housed in the striking 1819 Scarborough House, the Ships of the Sea Museum, 41 Martin Luther King, Jr. Blvd., tel. (912) 232-1511, commemo-

KAP STANN

The Telfair Academy of Arts, housed in an 1818 Regency-style former governor's mansion, is notable for its exhibits of 18th- and 19th-century decorative arts.

rates the art of sailing with scrimshaw carvings, maritime antiques, and many ship models (the one of the *Titanic* is among the most popular, though the namesake *Savannah*—first steamship to cross the Atlantic Ocean—is the sentimental favorite). A 50-minute Discovery Channel video documentary airs downstairs. The house and garden are added pleasures. Admission is $5 adults, $4 students. Hours are Tues.-Sun. 10 a.m.-5 p.m.

Ralph Mark Gilbert Civil Rights Museum

Savannah's new civil rights museum, 460 Martin Luther King, Jr. Blvd., tel. (912) 231-8900, traces the history of the era and movement with frank descriptions of local living conditions for blacks in the 1950s. Films, vintage video footage, and 1960s artifacts tell the story of how the local African-American community targeted the white power structure through an economic boycott that lasted 15 months before desegregation was achieved, a year prior to the passage of the Voting Rights Act. The museum adds an important dimension to a well-rounded perspective on city history and should be on the itinerary of at least every non-Southerner and young person visiting Savannah. It's named after the late pastor of First African Baptist Church, leader of Savannah's civil rights movement.

Admission is $4 adults, $2 students. It's open daily: Mon.-Sat. 9 a.m.-5 p.m., Sunday 1-5 p.m. It's a short drive down from the visitor center and parking is easy.

Other Exhibits

The **Massie Heritage Interpretation Center,** 207 E. Gordon St., tel. (912) 651-7022, contains historical design exhibits that can deepen one's appreciation for architectural variety and detail in the historic district. It's open weekdays only: Mon.-Fri. 9 a.m.-4:30 p.m.

The **Beach Institute,** 502 E. Harris St., tel. (912) 234-8000, is an African-American cultural center housed within a historic primary school founded after the Civil War; exhibits tells the school's story and display the wood sculptures of Ulysses Davis.

SCHOOLS

Savannah College of Art and Design (SCAD)

Savannah's renowned art school, headquartered at 516 Abercorn St., tel. (912) 238-2483 or (800) 869-7223 (SCAD), enrolls 4,500 students in programs dedicated to the visual arts, design, building arts, and the history of art and architecture. The school uses the city as its laboratory, transforming neglected buildings into masterpieces of creative and sustainable re-use. The historic district is its gallery, with more than 40 beautiful college buildings, restaurants, cafes, a theater, stores, and even classic old diners bearing the familiar SCAD imprint of forward-looking design and preservation. Many of these enterprises continue to be operated by the college itself, and are therefore havens for SCAD students from throughout the U.S. and abroad, as well as other artists, ecologists, and the avant-garde and intelligentsia in general. Visitors quickly find that not only has SCAD contributed a great deal to local historic preservation efforts, but it's what gives the town its "edge." For information on current exhibits and hours for SCAD's 12 indoor gallery spaces, call (912) 238-2480.

The Preston Hall Library on 342 Bull St. has online computers. Address e-mail inquiries to info@scad.edu; see also www.scad.edu.

University of Georgia System

Two colleges outside the historic district are part of the state university system. As you'll find is common throughout the South, one is historically white—**Armstrong Atlantic State University** in Southside, with 5,700 students—and one is historically black—**Savannah State College** east of town in Thunderbolt, with 3,400 students. Founded in 1890 as Georgia State Industrial College for Colored Youths, Savannah State was the first publicly supported state college for African-Americans in Georgia.

SPORTS AND RECREATION

Besides its historical and urban pleasures, Savannah also has an outstanding natural environment in which to enjoy many recreational pursuits.

Water Sports

Paddlers head out to the many scenic creeks, rivers, and byways of the Savannah River delta region east of downtown. If you're going out on your own, be sure to note the tide tables—novices should start out when the tide is rising.

Sea Kayak Georgia, (912) 786-8732, organizes guided trips. The *Simply Savannah* guide available at the visitors center lists local marinas, charter-boat services, and water-sports equipment rental services.

Fishing, of course, is a favorite activity of both locals and visitors. A one-day freshwater fishing license is available for $3.50, a seven-day license is available for out-of-state visitors only for $7, and a seasonlong freshwater fishing license costs $24 for nonresidents, $9 for residents; saltwater fishing does not require a license. Licenses and regulations are widely available at sporting goods stores and many local marinas.

Golf and Tennis

The 27-hole **Bacon Park Golf Course** on Shorty Cooper Dr., tel. (912) 354-2625, complete with pro shop, carts, and a lighted driving range, is part of a 1,021-acre city park with many other recreational options, such as tennis courts, an archery range, and ball fields. The 18-hole **Henderson Golf Course,** off Hwy. 204, tel. (912) 920-4653, charges $30-38.

Downtown you can find tennis courts at the beautiful **Forsyth Park** at Gaston and Drayton streets, tel. (912) 351-3852, and at **Daffin Park,** 1500 E. Victory Dr., (912) 351-3851.

Jogging, Hiking, and Biking

The flat, compact city center so suitable for walking is also ideal for jogging; ask for a **jogging map** at the visitors center. For wilderness hikes, see **Vicinity of Savannah,** below.

Bicyclists can rent bikes to tour the city or ride out to the forts and beach. **Savannah Bicycle Rentals,** within the City Market parking garage, tel. (912) 232-7900, rents bikes and offers a drop-off/pick-up service upon reservation. It's open daily 10 a.m.-6 p.m. It costs $8 an hour, $20 half-day, $30 all day.

ENTERTAINMENT

A great variety of lively, good-time entertainment is available in Savannah, from high-brow cultural arts supported by the city's elite to melancholy karaoke at bawdy sailors' dives. The free entertainment weekly ***Creative Loafing*** is an indispensable guide to local entertainment; it's distributed free at many spots around town. The Friday edition of the ***Savannah Morning News*** also features an entertainment tabloid.

Performing Arts

The **Savannah Symphony,** 225 Abercorn St., tel. (912) 236-9536, hosts its regular season Sept.-May. During the summer, the Symphony performs free concerts in the squares. Call the

SAVANNAH FESTIVALS AND EVENTS

Savannah loves an excuse to open River Street to a gigantic block party, with live music coming from all directions, food stalls hawking low-country seafood specialties, and fireworks lighting up the waterfront. This is the scene on the **First Saturday** of most months from February to December—Savannah's standing party invitation.

January
Martin Luther King, Jr. Birthday celebrations around Jan. 15 include a parade and Freedom Ball.

February
Founders Day, the first Saturday of February. Savannah celebrates its birthday with a reenactment of Oglethorpe's founding of the new Georgia colony in 1733, complete with sailors in full British regalia kissing the shores.

March
St. Patrick's Day Celebration and Parade, the week of March 17. The second-largest Irish celebration in the U.S. brings upwards of 100,000 revelers to the weeklong festivities, which include live jazz, rock, and blues—as well as traditional Irish music.

April
Tour of Homes, in April or May. An old tradition. Beautifully restored, decorated, and landscaped historic homes and gardens are opened to public view. Four days of varied events include walking tours, candlelight tours, luncheon and cruise tours.

Hidden Gardens Tour, mid-April. This tour reveals lush landscaped walled gardens in full spring bloom, and includes afternoon tea at the antebellum Green-Meldrim mansion.

Siege and Reduction Weekend at Fort Pulaski, early April. The 133rd anniversary of the capture of Fort Pulaski is commemorated by costumed Union and Confederate volunteers.

May
Savannah Seafood Festival, early May. Forget the costumes and drama, this event goes straight for the food, particularly the shrimp and shellfish specialties that make low-country cuisine so delectable.

June
Beach Music Festival on Tybee Island, late June. Top beach-music bands hold a big dance party on the sand.

July
Independence Day Celebration, July 4. The classic American merriment here includes the largest fireworks display in the Southeast. Tybee Island (Beach) also throws a party, with oceanside fireworks.

August
Candle Lantern Tour on Tybee Island, the first and third Fridays of June, July, and August. Local legends and ghost stories enliven this evening tour.

September
Jazz Festival, midmonth. All stripes, all venues, all times are devoted to the city's annual celebration of the native southeastern art form, highlighted by a jazz parade.

October
Greek Festival, late October. St. Paul's Greek Orthodox Church brings out souvlakia, spanakopita, togas, and dancers.

November
Folklife Festival, second Saturday in November. Fifty southeastern artisans demonstrate (and sell) traditional crafts. There's also cane-grinding and folk music, all at the humble Oatland Island Education center on Oatland Island.

December
Christmas Celebrations, all month. Nineteenth-century decorations and festivities dress Savannah up for the holidays, with historic home tours, traditional caroling, the lighting of River Street, and candlelight tours.

New Year's Eve Block Party, Dec. 31. Live music, dancing, and food outdoors at City Market rings in the New Year.

Savannah Ballet Theatre at (912) 236-2894 for a schedule of performances.

City Lights Theatre Company features local productions in a 100-seat theater at 125 E. Broughton, tel. (912) 234-9860. They also present the annual free Shakespeare on the Square performances in early May. The **Savannah Theatre Company,** 222 Bull St., tel. (912) 233-7764, presents seasonal productions of contemporary drama, musicals, and comedy.

The **Savannah Civic Center,** a modern auditorium within the historic district at 301 W. Oglethorpe, tel. (912) 651-6550, hosts big-name performers and groups.

Riverfront Nightlife

Savannah's answer to Bourbon St. in New Orleans, River Street fills with partygoers, couples, and sailors walking along the largely pedestrian promenade and popping into many bars and clubs with live music. Many festivals are also held here, with dancing in the streets and fireworks among the typical festivities, as well as a giant block party the first Saturday of every month from February to December. From east to west, a roundup of River Street's bars would include **Spanky's,** a local hangout, **Huey's** and the **Bayou Cafe** for rockish guitarists (muy *Desperado),* **Cowboy Bill's** for bluegrass, and **Kevin Barry's** for Irish music, predominantly Irish rock. On any given night, the music of the likes of Van Morrison, the Eagles, and the Allman Brothers is surprisingly well represented in River St. clubs. Early in the evening, the crowd includes young tourist families pushing strollers, as the evening wears on it becomes a harder-drinking singles scene—predominantly young, black and white, blue-collar or college-kid heterosexuals. Most grown-up men wear shorts, T-shirts, and baseball caps for a night out on the town, many women wear snug jeans and struggle across cobblestones in heels.

On the bluffside off Bay St., famed bassist Ben Tucker and renowned local jazz singer Emma Kelly, "the Lady of 6,000 Songs," perform at **Hannah's East,** 20 E. Broad St., tel. (912) 233-5757 (above the Pirate's House restaurant), a mainstream jazz bar now attracting a mixed bag of Book followers and Generation X swingers.

City Market Area Nightlife

Within the City Market complex, many local bands perform for free in the central plaza outside **Malone's;** beer is sold at streetside stands and you can help yourself to patio tables for low-key, no pressure cheap thrills. Also within the complex, the **Bar Bar** attracts a thirtysomething crowd of largely white heterosexuals.

Many more bars and clubs are in a compact strip along W. Congress St. beside City Market. From east to west, the **Zoo** attracts a young, thin, pierced, baggy-panted crowd for loud modern dance music; **Velvet Elvis** features the most eclectic alternative crowd for ska, retro, punk, rockabilly, and lounge music; **Savannah Coffee House** features serious folk music and poetry readings; **Whitaker St. Saloon** (a half-block down) is a somewhat wistful strip club for local men in shabby suits; **Conga Club** (in the alley) is a Latin disco that is just about the hottest thing south of the Mason-Dixon line (complete with Virgin of Guadalupe shrines and a disco ball); **The Rail** is a comfortable neighborhood tavern for chess-playing locals and friendly visitors; and **B & B Billiards** draws an intelligent crowd that loiters around the bar, occasionally wandering downstairs for blues music at **Crossroads.**

A block north of City Market, **Club One Jefferson,** 1 Jefferson St., tel. (912) 232-0200, where the notorious Lady Chablis rose to fame (and still performs), continues to feature drag shows in its three-story nightclub, along with dance music on two raucous dance floors. The club draws a compelling crowd of gays and straights, young and old, players, regulars and tourists. The club currently hosts two shows nightly on Wednesday and Fri.-Sun. The cover charge varies (from $5 at last visit, call for current prices), with a premium for shows that feature Lady Chablis herself. See also the special topic ***Midnight* Tours.**

ACCOMMODATIONS

Savannah is a wonderful town in which to splurge on lodging, with many wonderful choices of unique places to stay in fabulous locations throughout the historic district. It would be hard to go wrong; enjoy!

Hostel

A turn-of-the-century Victorian with 14-foot ceilings houses the **Hostelling International**-member dormitory downtown at 304 E. Hall St., tel. (912) 236-7744. Fees run $15 members, $18 not (extra for linens, bring your own sleep sack); guests are expected to heed a curfew and do minor chores. It closes 10 a.m.-5 p.m. and doesn't accept reservations ("not necessary").

Historic Inns

Savannah's many historic inns are a big part of the city's charm as a romantic destination. Dozens of elegant century-old mansions provide overnight guests with a gracious ambience that matches the city itself—among the standard amenities you'll find brandy served in the front parlor, porch swings on wide verandas, lavish period antiques, formal gardens, and of course, plenty of Southern hospitality.

Style and perks set them apart. Some provide fancy breakfasts, liqueurs, and afternoon teas, while others might make bicycles available or throw in a carriage tour—all part of one total price. Some generalizations apply to most of the city's historic inns (including those listed below): period furnishings are augmented by such modern conveniences as phones, TVs, and central air-conditioning and heating, most rooms have private baths, some properties have hot tubs and most all have one or more barrier-free rooms. Several inns request no children under 12 years old (families with young children may prefer more kidproof lodging).

KAP STANN

Savannah's HI Hostel is housed in a turn-of-the-century Victorian home.

Most rooms are in the **expensive** ($85-110) range or higher—but a great value for what you get for the money compared to, say, what you'd get in Atlanta for the same price. A few select finds with shared baths, or fewer amenities, or at the fringe of the historic district, are more **moderate** ($60-85), while the most opulent places charge rates considered **premium** ($110-150) or **luxurious** ($150 and beyond). Inquire about parking fees and in-and-out privileges, about elevators if walk-ups bother you, or about private entrances if you'd rather not be greeted by a concierge at every trip through the door.

What follows is a subjective selection. For a complete list of properties, contact **Savannah Historic Inns and Guesthouses,** 147 Bull St., tel. (800) 262-4667, or the **Savannah Convention and Visitors Bureau,** tel. (912) 944-0456, which operates a toll-free information and reservation line at (800) 444-CHARM (800-444-2427).

Bed and Breakfast Inn, 117 W. Gordon St., tel. (912) 238-0518, is the largest of Savannah's *guesthouses* (small resident-operated establishments that are less expensive than inns) that occupies two 19th-century Federal townhouses overlooking Chatham Square, not far from the visitor center. Rates range from inexpensive for shared bath rooms to moderate (under $80).

Magnolia Place Inn, 503 Whitaker St., tel. (912) 236-7674 or (800) 238-7674 (outside GA), is housed in a regal 1878 mansion with 13 period-furnished guest rooms and wide verandas overlooking Forsyth Park. In the elegant pale-yellow parlor, contemporary artwork blends right in with the brocade; here afternoon tea and evening aperitifs are served. Come morning, guests may elect to have their silver breakfast-set delivered to the porch outside their rooms. Like Savannah, Magnolia Place is never precocious, quaint, or stiff—but charming, comfortable, and gracious. This is John Berendt's old haunt. Rates are expensive to luxury.

River Street Inn, 115 E. River St., tel. (912) 234-6400 or (800) 253-4229, is a beautiful spacious renovation of an 1853 cotton warehouse right at the waterfront. It features 44 rooms that face either the stately Factors Walk promenade atop the bluff or the lively River Street action on the waterfront below. Riverside balconies are coveted places to watch the fireworks displays that usually follow River Street festivals. Rates are expensive to luxury.

The **Foley House Inn,** 14 W. Hull St., tel. (912) 232-6622 or (800) 647-3708, has 19 comfortable rooms carved out of a 1896 three-story mansion, with a nice central location off Bull St. overlooking Chippewa Square (of *Forrest Gump* fame). Rates are premium to luxury.

The **Hamilton-Turner House,** 330 Abercorn St., tel. (912) 233-1833 or (888) 448-8849 (which resembles a house from a Charles Addams *New Yorker* cartoon for its raised eyebrow windows and ironwork crown) is now more notorious to *Midnight* readers and viewers as the party house of Joe Odom. A family now operates the house as an inn, offering spacious, airy rooms and suites with sprightly teenagers helping out. Rates are expensive to premium.

The 1830s **Ballastone Inn** and townhouses, 14 E. Oglethorpe Ave., tel. (912) 236-1484 or (800) 822-4553, have been opulently furnished —near theatrical—with an exacting eye for period authenticity. Cosmopolitan guests in 24 rooms and suites meet in the front parlor or at a full-service bar resembling a bar car on the Orient Express. The private townhouse suites would be pretty hard to leave, with all that tropical breeze wafting through the shuttered French doors. Rates are expensive to luxury.

The **Gastonian,** at 220 E. Gaston St., tel. (912) 232-2869 or (800) 322-6603, adjoins two elegant 19th-century mansions with a winding raised walkway over a manicured garden that has a hot tub tucked under the trellis. Thirteen guest rooms are sparsely furnished with gauzy canopy beds and Persian rugs over hardwood floors; ceiling fans rotate from high ceilings. It draws a genteel clientele. Rates are premium to luxury.

The **Grande Toots Inn,** 212 W. Hall St., tel. (912) 236-2911 or (800) 671-0716, restored by an African-American matriarch and operated by a young couple, recently opened on the fringe of the historic district. It's somewhat unevenly furnished with modern glassy pieces among the antiques, but its newness means its style is less firmly fixed and therefore more fraught with possibilities (besides, staying here spreads the wealth around a little). At rates from $85, it's comparable to other inns but perhaps more expensive than its borderline location might warrant.

More refined historic inns in the expensive class include **Kehoe House** on Columbia Square at 123 Habersham St., tel. (912) 232-1020 or (800) 531-5578, and **Lion's Head Inn,** 120 E. Gaston St., tel. (912) 232-4580 or (800) 355-LION (800-355-5466). Larger, less intimate and more businesslike, but still more personal than most hotels, are such choices as the **East Bay Inn,** 225 E. Bay St., tel. (912) 238-1225 or (800) 553-6533, and **President's Quarters,** 225 E. President St., tel. (912) 233-1600 or (800) 233-1776. Both have expensive rates.

Beyond the historic district in the adjacent Victorian district, **912 Barnard,** 912 Barnard St., tel. (912) 234-9121, is a welcoming bed and breakfast that offers two (soon to be four) suites in an interesting emerging area for $79 year-round. Look for the rainbow flags out front.

Hotels and Motels

Within the historic district, the **Days Inn** occupies a historic brick building in a prime location at 201 W. Bay St., tel. (912) 236-4440 or (800) 325-2525 (pool, suites, 24-hour coffee shop), with moderate-to-expensive rates. The **Hampton Inn,** 201 E. Bay St., tel. (912) 231-9700 or (800) 426-7866, also has a wonderful location and has been designed to blend well with the historic district; rates are expensive.

Like a plantation Big House, the **Hyatt Regency Riverfront Hotel** at 2 W. Bay St., tel. (912) 238-1234 or (800) 233-1234, presides over the waterfront at the head of Bull Street. For a long time this was the city's primary full-service hotel, and it acts as a central hub for much of the local tourist activity. Here you'll find popular riverview lounges and carriage tours, as well as guest rooms with views of the channel. Its location can't be beat, though its dated boxy exterior looms like the *raison d'ètre* of preservationist development restrictions. Rates are in the luxury range beyond $150; pool available.

From the same era, the 250-room **DeSoto Hilton** is centrally located off Bull St. in the middle of the historic district at 15 E. Liberty St., tel. (912) 232-9000 or (800) 426-8483. The Hilton's full-service amenities include a pool and restaurant; room rates range from expensive to premium.

The **Savannah Marriott Riverfront,** occupies the far east side of the waterfront at 100 General McIntosh Blvd., tel. (912) 223-7722 or (800) 228-9290. A 10-story atrium is the centerpiece of this 384-room brick-and-glass hotel that opened in 1994; other features include a T.G.I.Friday's restaurant and lounge with riverside patio dining. Room rates are premium to luxury.

Beyond the historic district, dozens of standard chain motels line a miles-long stretch of Americaan generica along Abercorn St. in the Southside district, a 15-minute drive south of downtown. For beach lodging 18 miles east, see **Tybee Island** under **Vicinity of Savannah,** below.

Camping

The nearest campgrounds to Savannah are at Skidaway Island and Tybee Island. For more about these areas, see **Vicinity of Savannah.**

Skidaway Island State Park, tel. (912) 598-2300, 25 minutes south of the historic district, offers a scenic slice of marshland wilderness close to civilization. The wonderful 88-site campground set at the edge of the marsh includes a pool, water and electric hook-ups, drive-throughs, a disposal station, a nature trail, and boat rentals among its well-maintained amenities. Campsites run $15-17; for reservations call (800) 864-PARK (800-864-7275). The parking fee is $2 per car, free on Wednesday.

Rivers End Campground and R.V. Park, 18 miles from Savannah and three blocks from the beach, holds a 10-acre site on Tybee Island at 915 Polk St., tel. 786-5518 or (800) 786-1016. Tent sites cost $16, full hookups cost $22 a night, more for extra people or cars. The site has a pool, dump station, and small store.

FOOD AND DRINK

Call a restaurant to ask when it's open and expect to hear the perfect Savannah response: "Why, we're open *now!*"

Coffeehouses

Savannah's coffeehouses offer a place to start out, end up, or alight throughout the day for gourmet coffee and baked goods; light meals are also served. You can usually hang out and cool off for the price of a cup of joe; some offer occasional live entertainment too.

Savannah Coffee House, corner of W. Congress and Whitaker, tel. (912) 233-5311, near City Market, is open daily with the longest hours. **Savannah Coffee Roasters,** corner of Bull and Congress streets, tel. (912) 352-2994, is a popular, often crowded spot with a few patio tables in the center of the downtown scene. The Savannah College of Art and Design's (SCAD) **Ex Libris,** 228 Martin Luther King, Jr. Blvd., tel. (912) 238-2427, offers a wonderful coffee bar and corner tables in its fabulous bookstore for a leisurely read. **Huey's** on River St., tel. (912) 234-7385, is a full-service Cajun restaurant, but in the morning you can pop in for just beignets and coffee.

Casual

Two words about **Mrs. Wilkes' Boarding House**—Go There. The lines are long but move quickly, the food is good, cheap, and plentiful, and the style is Southern Classic. Fifteen dishes are served family style (see the special topic **Lunch Menu**) by generations of the Wilkes family, as they've done since the 1940s. Queue up at 107 W. Jones St., tel. (912) 232-5997. Breakfast is served 8-9 a.m., lunch 11:30 a.m.-3 p.m. Prices are under $10 for all you can eat. It's open weekdays only and you can get takeout meals at the back door.

Express Cafe, 39 Barnard St., tel. (912) 233-4683, has some of the best healthy breakfasts and light meals around: Belgian waffles, great soups, salads, and sandwiches with fresh, exotic ingredients all served cafeteria-style in a bright airy place near City Market—a good coffee-and-treat stop too. It's open Wed.-Fri. 7 a.m.-4 p.m., Saturday 8 a.m.-4 p.m., Sunday 8 a.m.-3 p.m. (closed Mon.-Tues.).

SCAD's **Gryphon Tea Room,** 337 Bull St., tel. (912) 238-2481, serves create-your-own deli sandwiches (from $3.25) with a great selection of mix-and-match ingredients, along with soup, salads, and spanakopita for lunch. They also do morning bakery treats and an afternoon tea (4-6 p.m. daily, $12 fixed), all in a busy, casually elegant marble-and-mahogany setting worthy of Zurich's Banhofstrasse or a scene from a Woody Allen movie. Hours are Mon.-Fri. 8:30 a.m.-9:30 p.m., Saturday 10 a.m.-9:30 p.m., Sunday 10 a.m.-6 p.m.

Nita's, 140 Abercorn St., tel. (912) 238-8233, serves "low-country soul food" lunch specials in a cozy six-table storefront across from Colonial Cemetery. A generous vegetable plate with cornbread is $6. It's open Mon.-Sat. 11:45 a.m.-3 p.m.

Cheap back-alley barbecue is the specialty at **Walls Barbecue,** officially on York St. at Price St., yet actually tucked behind York in the dirt alley in a brick red cabin. Hours are Wed. 11 a.m.-6 p.m., Thurs.-Sat. 11 a.m.-9 p.m. (closed Sun.-Tues.).

Clary's Cafe, 404 Abercorn at E. Jones, tel. (912) 233-0402, is a comfortable corner joint for such American specialties as meatloaf, bacon-and-egg sandwiches, and root-beer floats, served inside or alfresco. It's open Mon.-Fri. 6:30 a.m.-4 p.m., Saturday 8 a.m.-4 p.m., Sunday 8 a.m.-2 p.m.

Beyond the historic district, SCAD's **Streamliner,** 102 W. Henry St. at Barnard St., tel. (912) 238-2447 serves $2 breakfasts and standard American lunch choices (burgers, BLTs, grilled cheese) and milkshakes at its marble counter or wooden booths. It's open weekdays only: Mon.-Fri. 8:30 a.m.-5 p.m.

Moderate

Savannah's most unusual restaurant, **Cafe Metropole,** 109 Martin Luther King, Jr. Blvd., tel. (912) 236-0110, opened in 1997. Entering through the back-alley fence, you stumble upon what resembles an old bus depot (which it was) with all the interior walls removed. Tattooed diners are hunched in clumps against supporting beams on the dirt apron; older couples sit at actual tables. They serve a zealous fusion of French and California cuisine, with some southern Vidalias, Italian pesto, and Tunisian couscous thrown in for fun (entrees $11-16)—choice wine selection too. Lunch is more straightforward, with traditional *salade Niçoise,* roast eggplant sandwiches, and even a ham and Swiss. It's open Mon.-Tues. and Thursday 9 a.m.-10 p.m., Fri.-Sat. 9 a.m.-11 p.m., Sunday brunch 11:30 a.m.-4 p.m., dinner 4-9 p.m.

Across from City Market, **Bistro Savannah,** 309 W. Congress St., tel. (912) 233-6266, is the city's most venerable bistro, serving creative twists on Southern coastal cuisine, with such entrees as flounder topped with an apricot shallot glaze. Next door, **Garibaldi's,** tel. (912) 232-7118, is a Northern Italian bistro featuring such daily blackboard specials as veal *murat* with reportedly the best wine selection in town (reservations recommended). Dinner for two with a modest wine starts around $60 at either restaurant, and they're both open Sun.-Thurs. 6-10:30 p.m., Fri.-Sat. 6 p.m.-midnight.

Called "the fanciest barbecue restaurant in Georgia" (if not the world), **Johnny Harris,** 1651 E. Victory Dr., tel. (912) 354-7810, is also Savannah's oldest restaurant, serving pork, beef, and lamb 'cue since 1942. It's open 11:30 a.m.-11 p.m. weekdays, later on weekend nights, closed on Sunday. A Big Band dance livens up the scene on weekends.

Fine Dining

Savannah is famous for upscale dining, and three places in particular reflect this tradition; entrees start around $18 and the setting is resort-formal (men wear jackets). At **Elizabeth on 37th,** 105 E. 37th St., tel. (912) 236-5547, nationally recognized namesake chef Elizabeth Terry invents "gourmet Southern" concoctions with such local ingredients as fresh fish and other seafood. Broiled flounder in a cream, crab, and sherry sauce is a favorite, along with the pecan-almond tart topped with praline ice cream and Gentleman Jack caramel sauce. ("Some of the best food I've ever eaten in America," was what one well-traveled Swiss businessman had to say.) Set elegantly in a turn-of-the-century mansion, Elizabeth's serves dinner Mon.-Sat. 6-10:30 p.m. Call early for prime-time reservations on weekends.

In the same range, **45 South,** at 20 E. Broad St., tel. (912) 233-1881, presents tuna carpaccio and crabcake appetizers among its local seafood specialties. Dinners are served Mon.-Sat. starting at 6 p.m.

17 Hundred 90, 307 E. President St., (912) 236-7122, part of a luxurious 14-room historic inn, serves continental cuisine, seafood, steaks, and a house specialty of rack of lamb Dijon. Lunch is served Mon.-Fri. noon-2 p.m., dinners daily 6-10:30 p.m. Reservations are recommended.

GETTING THERE

By Air

The beautiful **Savannah International Airport,** tel. (912) 964-0514, 16 miles west of downtown (off I-95 north of I-16), is served by seven airlines, including Delta, Continental, United, and USAir, with connecting flights to hubs at Atlanta, New York, Washington, and other major cities. Thirty shuttle flights a day make the 45-minute run between Atlanta and Savannah. There's a visitor center and currency exchange in the terminal.

Taxis charge about $18 for one person going downtown (higher for more people or service to the islands). Limousine service is also available, and many hotels run independent shuttles.

By Train

Amtrak passenger trains make six stops daily at Savannah's terminal four miles west of downtown at an isolated staffed outpost, with direct service to cities up and down the Atlantic Seaboard, including New York, Baltimore, Washington, D.C., Richmond, Charleston, Jacksonville, and Miami. Savannah is one of Amtrak's package tour destinations (one reduced price for combined train fare and lodging); call (800) USA-RAIL (800-872-7245) for more information about rates and schedules.

Taxis charge about $4-6 for one person going downtown

By Bus

From Savannah's **Greyhound-Trailways** bus depot at 610 W. Oglethorpe Ave., tel. (912) 233-7723, passengers can make connections to most cities in the region and beyond. Five buses run daily between Atlanta and Savannah, leaving from 81 International Blvd. at Atlanta's Hartsfield International Airport (about $90 roundtrip). Several charter companies also run this heavily traveled route.

By Boat

The Intracoastal Waterway weaves through Savannah's marshlands and down the Georgia coast, connecting Savannah to cities on the Eastern Seaboard. The Thunderbolt Marina, tel. (912) 352-4931, is a popular stop. See the introduction of this chapter for more boating information.

By Car

I-95, coastal Georgia's major north-south artery, connects Savannah with the rest of the East Coast. I-16 heads west out of Savannah to Macon, where it meets I-75 for the run into Atlanta. Savannah's historic district lies 10 miles east of the intersection of I-95 and I-16 (Southside Savannah destinations are more directly approached from I-95's Hwy. 204 exit).

Savannah to Atlanta is 250 miles; to the Golden Isles resorts 90 miles; to Charleston, SC, 110 miles; to Jacksonville, FL, 140 miles.

GETTING AROUND

By Car, Pedicab, or Bike

Visitors staying downtown wouldn't necessarily need a car, but major car-rental agencies are well represented in town and at the airport, including Avis, Budget, Enterprise, Economy, Thrift, and Savannah Car and Van Rental. Parking meters are enforced weekdays only, 8:30 a.m.-5 p.m.

Taxi fare within the downtown area is 10 cents every twelfth of a mile. For pedicab service, call (912) 232-7900.

Savannah Bicycle Rentals, within the City Market parking garage, tel. (912) 232-7900, rents bikes and offers a drop-off/pick-up service upon reservation. It's open daily 10 a.m.-6 p.m. It costs $8 an hour, $20 half-day, $30 all day. The designated bike route through the historic district is along Habersham St. (walk bikes through squares or ride around them on the inside of the surrounding street).

By Bus or Van

Chatham Area Transit (CAT), tel. (912) 233-5767, runs municipal bus service as well as van shuttle service within the historic district. The shuttle fare is 75 cents one-way or $2 for an all-day pass. Local bus service fare is $1, transfers five cents. All fare machines require exact change but accept dollar bills.

INFORMATION AND SERVICES

Visitor Information

There are several visitor centers. The **Georgia State Welcome Center** near the South Carolina border off I-95 distributes statewide information as well as information and maps for the city and coastal regions. The **airport visitors center** is open daily 10 a.m.-6 p.m. The central **Savannah Visitors Center,** 301 Martin Luther King, Jr. Blvd., tel. (912) 944-0455, is open daily year-round: Mon.-Fri. 8:30 a.m.-5 p.m., weekends and holidays 9 a.m.-5 p.m. A knowledgeable staff, maps and brochures, and a film orient the visitor to the historic district. Many city tours also leave from here.

The **Savannah Convention and Visitors Bureau,** P.O. Box 1628, Savannah, GA 31402-1628, tel. (912) 944-0456 operates a toll-free information and lodging reservations line at (800) 444-2427 and visitor center at their office on the corner of Drayton and Bay Streets (across from the Cotton Exchange). Contact them via e-mail at info@savcvb.com; see also www.savcvb.com.

Internet access is available through **Kinko's,** 7929 Abercorn St., tel. (912) 927-8119, five miles south of the historic district between Montgomery Cross and White Bluff Rds. It costs a pricey $1 a minute, but it's about the only online service available publicly in coastal Georgia.

Consulates and Currency Exchange

Consulate offices in Savannah include Brazil, Denmark, Germany, Italy, Norway, and Sweden.

The **Savannah Visitors Centers** at the airport and on Martin Luther King, Jr. Blvd. exchange international currency, as does **American Express** and **Nationsbank,** with a number of branches in the historic district and throughout the city.

Shopping and Practicalities

A large part of the appeal of Savannah's beautiful walkable historic district is wandering in and out of antique stores, art galleries, and boutiques, and searching for hidden treasure in dusty flea markets and overflowing second-hand shops found throughout the district.

The refined shopping district around **Madison Square** (Bull St. at Harris) is tailor-made for browsing; leaf through local history books at the **E. Shaver** bookstore, 326 Bull St., tel. (912) 234-7257. The Savannah College of Art and Design operates 12 galleries around town worth browsing through.

SCAD's **Ex Libris** Bookstore, 228 Martin Luther King, Jr. Blvd., tel. (912) 238-2427, sells a wonderful collection of gifts, crafts, and other

In 1864 Union Gen. William T. Sherman presented the city of Savannah to President Lincoln as a Christmas gift.

KAP STANN

items in addition to a great selection of books and periodicals in a wonderful setting near the visitors center; there's a cafe here also.

At **Johnson Square,** downtown's stately financial center at the head of Bull St., you'll find several banks with automatic teller machines, along with business services such as **Mail Boxes Etc.,** a national packaging and shipping chain. Though tourists generally avoid the rundown Broughton Street strip through the historic district, several five-and-dimes there conveniently sell necessary sundries.

Shopping malls can be found in the Southside district; take Abercorn St. south from the historic district. The grand **Savannah Mall,** on Hwy. 204 at the Ogeechee River (near I-95), is anchored by the regional Parisian department store. The older **Oglethorpe Mall,** at 7804 Abercorn St., features more than 140 stores, including Sears and JCPenney. An **outlet mall** at 11 Gateway Blvd. discounts name-brand clothing and merchandise.

The most unusual assortment of treasures can be found at **Keller's Flea Market,,** 5901 Ogeechee Rd., tel. (912) 927-4848, "the largest flea market in the coastal empire," one mile east of I-95 exit 16. Hours are Fri.-Sun. 8 a.m.-6 p.m. year-round.

Important Telephone Numbers

In **emergencies** dial 911. The Savannah **police** (nonemergencies) can be reached at (912) 232-4141. You'll find **Candler General Hospital** at 5353 Reynolds St., tel. (912) 354-9211. Savannah's city information line is (912) 236-7284, which includes disabled access information. From out-of-town, call (800) 444-CHARM (800-444-2427) for toll-free tourist information.

VICINITY OF SAVANNAH

As hard as it may be to pull yourself away from historic Savannah, it would be a shame to come to town and not sample the surrounding low country. Within minutes of downtown, you can find yourself in a wild wetland of salty tidal creeks, abandoned rice fields, and silvery oyster beds—as well as the familiar attraction of Georgia's Atlantic beachfront.

NORTH OF SAVANNAH

South Carolina

Directly across the dramatic Talmadge Memorial Bridge (Hwy. 17A), South Carolina occupies the northern shore of the Savannah River. **Hilton Head Island,** about an hour and some from Savannah, is fully developed as an upscale beach resort, with golf courses, tennis clubs, and exclusive beachfront hotels, such as the **Hilton Resort,** tel. (803) 842-8000 and the **Hyatt Regency,** tel. (912) 785-1234 (summer singles start about $120 at either, rates drop Nov.-Feb.).

Savannah National Wildlife Refuge

This refuge, tel. (912) 653-4415, northernmost in a string of federally protected refuges in the low country, has restored abandoned rice fields of 18th-century plantations to wetlands. More than a hundred species of native and migratory birds thrive on the wild rice that now grows between the old levees; alligators, bobcats, and deer are among many other wildlife species sheltered in the refuge. Visitors can cruise through the scenic five-mile **Laurel Hill Nature Drive** at the South Carolina entrance or walk along levees and trails. The **Tupelo-Swamp Walk** is a favorite of birders and photographers; the shorter **Cistern Trail** also reveals much waterfront wildlife.

From Savannah, take Hwy. 17A north across the river, and go about eight miles to where Highways 17 and 17A meet. Turn left and follow Hwy. 17 south toward the airport for two miles to Laurel Hill Wildlife Drive. See the trail guides at the shelter, and note that the refuge closes for hunting seasons and sensitive waterfowl periods.

New Ebenezer

Northwest of Savannah, in thick woods at the river's edge, the few remains of New Ebenezer recall the once-thriving colonial town. Originally founded in 1734 by Salzburg Lutherans escaping religious persecution in Europe, New Ebenezer now houses the oldest public building still standing in Georgia: the 1769 **Jerusalem Lutheran Church** (Sunday services held at 11 a.m.). A small heritage museum is open only on Wednesday and weekends 3-5 p.m. A short nature walk leads visitors around the colonial ruins. From I-95 exit 19, take Hwy. 21 past Rincon to Hwy. 275, follow to the river.

EAST OF SAVANNAH

Highway 80 stretches east of town 18 miles to the Atlantic coast. On the way, drivers pass through small fishing villages and over the high arched bridges spanning the Intracoastal Waterway to the popular beach resort at Tybee Island. Detour often to discover the quiet appeal of the low country—a haunting cemetery here, an egret rookery there, and a creekside crab shack dinner to top it all off.

Fort Jackson

On the Savannah River three miles east of downtown off the President St. extension, Fort Jackson, tel. (912) 232-3945, dates from the War of 1812. Its brick batteries face the water, with a view of the port to the west and the wild marsh to the east. The fort is open daily 9 a.m.-5 p.m. (admission $2.50 adults, $2 children). Each May, the fort hosts the annual **Scottish Games and Highland Gathering,** a traditional plaid-and-bagpipe affair held mid-month. Scuba divers take note: A sunken ironclad rests at the bottom of the channel out from the fort by marker 82A (the water's often too murky to see much; check with Tybee Island dive shops for conditions).

Bonaventure Cemetery

"One of the most impressive assemblages of animal and plant creatures I have ever met," was what naturalist John Muir had to say about this riverside haunt. ". . . Never since I was allowed to walk the woods have I found so impressive a company of trees as the tillandsia-draped oaks of Bonaventure." Muir spent several days in the historic cemetery in 1867, camping out and waiting for money to be sent to him so that he could continue his travels. Today Bonaventure is just as captivating, with folks strolling among the statues and dusty lanes, glancing at Hebrew inscriptions on the graves of Savannah's Jewish founding families and searching for the memorials of such celebrities as Johnny Mercer and Conrad Aiken. (The cemetery figures prominently in the bestselling *Midnight in the Garden of Good and Evil,* though the statuette that appears on the book's cover has since been removed. See special topic ***Midnight* Tours.)**

Turn left off Hwy. 80 onto Mechanics Ave., turn left again onto Bonaventure Rd.; turn right at the stop sign and enter the cemetery through the gate.

Oatland Island Education Center

At the Oatland Island Education Center, 711 Sandtown Rd., tel. (912) 897-3773, 175 acres of different coastal habitats—salt marsh, maritime forest, tidal creeks, and freshwater ponds—shelter such native residents as wolves, panthers, deer, black bears, bobcats, and alligators. Sheep, geese, and mules roam the grounds. Cross self-guided trails across the marsh boardwalk and climb the observation tower overlooking a bluff of sawtooth palmettos to get a feel for low-country ecology. Operated by the local school board, it's open weekdays only; a small donation is requested.

At the center's heritage homesite, 19th-century cabins serve as stage for a **Folklife Festival,** which draws more than 200 artisans demonstrating and selling traditional arts and crafts each November. The center also houses the coastal office of the **Georgia Conservancy,** tel. (912) 897-6462.

To get there from downtown, take the President Street Extension toward Tybee, cross the Wilmington River, and watch for signs to your right.

Fort Pulaski National Monument

The perfectly preserved brick behemoth Fort Pulaski, 15 miles east of Savannah via Hwy. 80, tel. (912) 786-5787, sits placidly behind a moat along green tidal marshlands like a medieval fortress. The irregular pentagon occupies a site at the mouth of the Savannah River that has held forts since 1761. The current structure was painstakingly built over an 18-year period beginning in 1829; earlier ones succumbed to the Revolution or hurricanes. With the advent of rifled cannons in the Civil War—capable of bursting through even Pulaski's eight-foot-thick walls—the era of masonry forts was gone.

Even before Georgia officially seceded in 1861, the state's governor, Joseph E. Brown, defied the Union by expelling federal troops from Fort Pulaski. When the Civil War began, the Yankees promptly took it back. Here Union troops blockaded the Savannah River and waited out the war until Sherman arrived in 1864. Today, the annual **Labor Day Encampment** recaptures garrison life with costumed living-history programs, right down to the ball games that were a popular Yankee pastime during the two-year occupation. The fort is open daily 8:30 a.m.-6:45 p.m. from Memorial Day to Labor Day, to 5:15 p.m. the rest of the year. Admission to the fort is free, but summer admission to the museum is $2 (16 and under free). Set on Cockspur Island in the lush marshlands, the fort makes a scenic side trip from Savannah. Picnic grounds and self-guided trails are also available at the site.

TYBEE ISLAND

Once called "Savannah Beach," Tybee's long sandy stretch attracts vacationers to one of the coast's oldest resorts. Tybee exudes an old-fashioned, Coney Island-type appeal, complete with a rickety-tik amusement park, putt-putt golf, corn dog stands, and clapboard cottages that rent by the week or month. It's a perfect Spring Break kind of town (the whole place smells like Coppertone) except most of the Spring Breakers are now 40 years old and run around mostly after their own toddlers. Tybee offers a lighthouse to climb, video arcades, airbrushed T-shirts, bikes to rent, and a wide white-sand

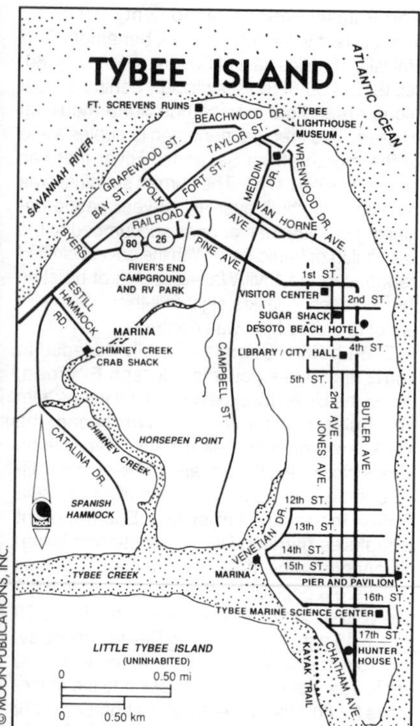

beach. A year-round community of 2,800 steadfast expatriates from the mainland (largely former hippies and retirees) populate the "state of Tybee."

Highway 80 dead-ends at Tybee's South Beach parking area. Most of the action happens where 16th St. meets the main Butler Ave. drag. Here a visitor center can direct you about the island. The new **Tybee Pier** is located on the strand between 15th and Tybrisa Streets.

Attractions

Most people come to Tybee to go to the beach, a miles-wide expanse of white sand with a long shallow shoreline perfect for wading and castle-building. Two public parking lots at each end of the beach charge $5 for all-day use (and for that price you'd hope the restrooms and showers were in better shape than they are). At each far end of the island, the beach narrows and the shoreline drops into deeper swimming holes with smaller crowds, and you might see dolphins nearby. Join the **Beach Bum Parade** in mid-May, the beach party at mid-June's **Beach Music Festival,** and **Fourth of July** antics, culminating with a huge fireworks display over the ocean.

A few easily accessible sights provide a rainy day's distraction. At the northern tip, 150-foot **Tybee Lighthouse** at 30 Meddin Dr., tel. (912) 786-5801, was built in the late 19th century, but a lighthouse has marked this site since 1736. You're welcome to climb it any day during the summer, and watch for **candle lantern tours,** the first and third Fridays of June, July, and August. The museum next door displays artifacts such as old dolls and Indian War weaponry. Adult admission is $3, $1 children. Hours are roughly 10 a.m.-4 or 6 p.m. (open winter weekends afternoons only). The ruins of **Fort Screven's** embattlements lie nearby.

See an aquarium and marine life exhibits at the **Tybee Island Marine Science Center,** on the beach at 16th St., tel. (912) 786-5917, open Mon.-Sat. 9 a.m.-4 p.m., free. At the heart of the beach strip, **Tybee Island Amusement Park,** 16th St. and Butler, tel. (912) 786-8806, gyrates with Ferris wheel rides and a carousel. Tybee Island's **library,** at 405 Butler Ave., tel. (912) 786-7733, occasionally hosts storytelling and video programs.

The **Crimson Monkey Gallery,** 1511½ Butler, tel. (912) 786-5552, showcases local artists' work, and **T.S. Chu & Co.,** 6 16th St., tel. (912) 786-4561, draws shoppers to search the dusty shelves for rare two-bit finds.

Recreation

Visitors rarely venture west of Butler St. to the "Backriver," a neighborhood of year-round residences and modest summer cottages. But here at the small backriver marina you might find someone to shuttle you across the small inlet to four-and-a-half miles of empty beach at uninhabited **Little Tybee Island.** Or you can dart over on your own in a canoe or sea kayak—it's a pretty straightforward run, but be mindful of the tides and currents just the same. Beginners ought to go out with a rising tide; check tide tables in local papers or at the marina. Call **Sea Kayak Georgia,** tel. (912) 786-8732, for guided kayak trips and instruction.

At the **Chimney Creek Fishing Camp,** 48 Estill Hammock Rd., tel. (912) 786-9857, you'll find freshwater or offshore fishing charters, hoists, bait, tackle, gas, ice, and overnight dockage. And if you come back empty-handed, there's a great crab shack nearby (see **Food and Drink,** below).

Accommodations and Camping

Within the widest stretch of the beach, the oceanfront and the main Butler Ave. drag is lined with motels and guesthouses. The **17th Street Inn,** 12 7th St., tel. (912) 786-0607, is an eight-room guesthouse that lets moderately priced rooms. In a great location beyond most of the traffic, **Hunter House,** 1701 Butler Ave., tel. (912) 786-7515, offers bed and breakfast rooms (from $80) in a two-story house surrounded by a veranda with a view—great steak-and-shrimp restaurant too.

Such large modern motels as the **Econo-lodge Beachside,** 404 Butler Ave., tel. (912) 786-4535 or (800) 55-ECONO (800-553-2666), and **Ocean Plaza Beach Resort,** off 15th St. at the oceanfront, tel. (912) 786-7777 or (800) 215-6370, have rates from moderate to expensive in summer (of course, you can expect to find bargains in winter).

Camp in a nicely wooded location three blocks from the beach at the **River's End Campground and RV Park,** 915 Polk St., tel. (912) 786-5518 or (800) 786-1016. Tent sites are $14, full hook-ups cost $20, with additional charges for each guest, extra tents or vehicles. The grounds have a pool, dump station, and small store.

Food and Drink

The **Breakfast Club,** 1500 Butler Ave. (follow the crowds), tel. (912) 786-5937, serves popular plates in a comfortably casual hash-house atmosphere 6 a.m.-1 p.m. (go early or sit at the counter to avoid long lines for tables). Try the "Grill Cleaner's Special"—diced potatoes, Polish sausage, green peppers and onions, scrambled with eggs and topped with two cheeses.

For a milkshake treat, look for the **Sugar Shack** at the corner of Second and Jones, tel. (912) 786-4482, which has been whipping up exotic shakes and basic American lunch fare for more than 25 years. It's open daily 7 a.m.-10 p.m.

For beachfront beers, you can't beat the thatched deck of the 1938 art deco **DeSoto Beach Hotel,** 212 Butler Ave., tel. (912) 786-4542, with live entertainment most nights—classic Tybee summer vacation material.

The **Oar House,** 1311 Butler Ave., tel. (912) 786-5055, serves peel-a-meal steamed shrimp ($7.50 for a half pound) and crab cakes with homemade chutney. Seafood dinner entrees start around $13; early-bird discounts 5-7 p.m.

At the **Chimney Creek Crab Shack** off Estill Hammock Rd., tel. (912) 786-9857, clattering platters of crab, shrimp, oysters and other fresh

KAP STANN

The wide sandy beach is the main attraction of Tybee Island.

seafood are served along with frothy pitchers of beer under the Christmas lights strung between the palms at the creekside deck of its waterfront cabin. Order boiled shellfish by the pound—shrimp, blue crab, rock crab (seafood from $8.50 for a half-pound order), or the Low Country Boil (a spicy mix of sausage, shrimp-in-the-shell, potatoes, and corn-on-the-cob). It's open Mon.-Fri. 5-10 p.m., Sat.-Sun. 1-10 p.m.

THE MARSH ISLANDS

Wilmington Island

This major marsh island between Savannah and Tybee's beach is dominated by exclusive residences and the 200-acre site of an old Spanish-style resort hotel; the adjacent country club operates an 18-hole golf course open to the public.

The Isle of Hope

Across the Skidaway Narrows from Skidaway Island, the Isle of Hope shelters many old estates, one of which dates from the colonial era. The state-operated **Wormsloe** historic site, 7601 Skidaway Rd., tel. (912) 353-3023, retains the tabby ruins of the 1739 estate of Noble Jones, one of Savannah's prominent early leaders. A visitor center exhibits artifacts excavated at the site; a slide show covers the establishment of the 13th and final American colony. Living-history programs throughout the year feature colonial costumes and early-American crafts demonstrations. Wormsloe is open Tues.-Sat. 9 a.m.-5 p.m., Sunday 2-5:30 p.m.; adult admission is $2 adults, $1 children 6-18.

For a scenic approach from Savannah's historic district, drive east on Victory Dr. to Skidaway Rd., turn right and continue south to LaRoche Ave., then turn left and follow LaRoche to the river, where the riverfront is lined with antebellum mansions. Follow the main street south to Wormsloe.

Skidaway Island

Twenty minutes from downtown Savannah, Skidaway Island holds near-wild corners where visitors can see the surrounding marshland habitat close-up. To reach Skidaway Island from Savannah's historic district, take Abercorn St. (Hwy. 204) south to Mall Blvd., turn left, then in short order turn right on Hodgson Memorial Dr., left on Montgomery Crossroads, then right on Whitefield Ave. east to the Diamond Causeway.

On the western shore, Priests Landing provides a put-in point for coastal excursions, including a sea-kayak trail to Wassaw Island. To reach the landing, follow the Diamond Causeway over to Skidaway Island, pass the state park, and head north on McWhorter Road. Turn right at Priest Landing Rd. and continue northwest to the harbor (also see maps). To inquire about rentals or guided trips, pick up a list of local marinas from the Savannah Visitors Center.

Skidaway Island State Park, tel. (912) 598-2300, situated amidst the live oaks, draped Spanish moss, and sandy pines of the maritime forest, makes an ideal getaway close to the city. The 533-acre park has a beautiful low-country campground, pool, boat rentals, and interpretive nature programs. Its mile-long Sandpiper Nature Trail loops through the marshlands of Skidaway Narrows; there's also a three-mile trail. The 88-site campground provides water

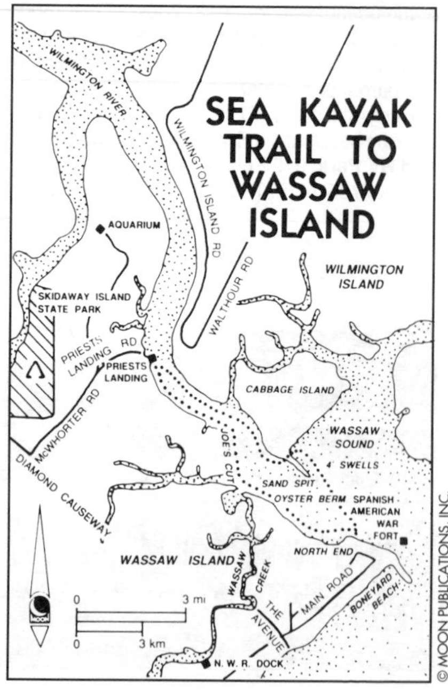

and electric hookups, drive-throughs, a disposal station, and well-maintained bathhouses with laundry facilities. Campsites cost $15-17 a night, call for reservations (800) 864-PARK (800-864-7275). A daily parking pass costs $2, free on Wednesdays. Admission to the pool costs another dollar or so.

At the island's northern tip, the **University of Georgia Marine Extension Aquarium,** tel. (912) 598-2496, houses an up-close collection of sea turtles, sharks, and beautiful tropically colored fish and sealife representing coastal Georgia habitats—more than 200 animals in all. Native American historical exhibits trace the coast's history back thousands of years with pottery, tools, and ample explanation. It's open weekdays 9 a.m.-4 p.m., Saturday noon-5 p.m. Admission is $1 (under six free). The inviting site overlooks a wide stretch of the Wilmington River.

WASSAW ISLAND

One of the least developed barrier islands on the east coast, Wassaw Island preserves the natural subtropical environment of the barrier islands in its pristine shape. Now a national wildlife refuge, and the highlight of a string of federally protected Savannah coastal refuges, Wassaw Island is open to the public for day-use only and is accessible only by boat.

Owned by the Parsons family (originally from Maine) as a family retreat since the 1850s, Wassaw was never heavily farmed, logged, or cleared for cropland, as were most of the other barrier islands. In the mid-1960s, Parsons heirs contacted the Nature Conservancy, who found an anonymous donor to buy the island and transfer title to the U.S. Fish and Wildlife Service to create a wildlife refuge. The Parsons family still maintains a 180-acre "Home Parcel" in the center of the island, and visitors should respect their privacy.

With seven miles of deserted sands and dolphins swimming in warm waters offshore, **Wassaw Beach** attracts visitors for beachcombing, swimming, and hiking. At the northern end, **Boneyard Beach** gets its name from the skeleton-like driftwood—bleached a ghostly white by the sun, sand, and salt—washed up on its shore. Offshore ruins of an 1898 **Spanish-American War fort** testify to the constantly shifting shorelines of the barrier islands; the fort was once hundreds of feet from shore and is today partially covered by each high tide. The Atlantic shore is also the center of coastal Georgia's **Caretta Project** (see the special topic **Turtle Watch**).

Twenty miles of trails—old jeep roads, shell roads, and footpaths—weave through an old-growth maritime forest dominated by live oak, palmetto, and slash pine and traverse freshwater sloughs. Hikers can take loop trips of various lengths; the island is 10 miles tip-to-tip. (Bring insect repellent to hike interior trails in warm months.)

To reach the island, you'll need to either charter a boat or sail out yourself. Lists of marinas and charter-boat services are available at the Savannah Visitors Center, or call the **Savannah Coastal Refuges** office, tel. (912) 652-4415. Paddlers follow a **sea kayak trail** that leads through the Wilmington River from Skidaway Island's eastern shore to the northern tip of Wassaw Island, putting in at Priests Landing; see **Skidaway Island,** above, for directions. Small-craft sailors follow the Intracoastal Waterway to the U.S. Fish and Wildlife Service dock at the southern end of the island.

NORTH COAST

From Savannah, you can hop on I-95 south and blast clear over the Florida border in little more than an hour. Detour once, however, and you'll find yourself drawn into an unfolding Southern landscape of strangely silent marshlands, historical oddities, and the ruins of the road-stop way of life that predates the interstates.

Used to be all that traffic from the Northeast—city folk heading to beaches in Florida—rode the Atlantic Coast Highway through the small towns of the Georgia coast. A crop of roadside businesses sprang up suddenly to cater to the crowds and disappeared just as quickly once the bypass was built. Today, the near-deserted old coast highway (Hwy. 17) makes one of the best routes to explore the buried treasure (and skeletons) of Georgia's fascinating north coast.

Before you head south out of Savannah, gas up and buy picnic supplies just in case. Gas stations are few and far between even around the interstate corridor. Off the interstate, stations are rare and tend to close early (and most everything closes Sunday mornings).

SOUTH OF SAVANNAH

Across the Ogeechee River

The last resistance the Confederates mustered before Sherman took Savannah was from **Fort McAllister** on the Ogeechee River. Considered the best preserved earthwork fortification of the Confederacy, the fort features living-history programs that reenact the fort's "Baptism by Fire" in July, the Labor Day Encampment, and December's "Winter Muster." The site and a small museum displaying Civil War artifacts are open Tues.-Sat. 9 a.m.-5 p.m. and Sunday 2-5:30 p.m.; adult admission costs $2, children 5-18 $1.

The adjacent **Richmond Hill Park,** set on an inviting low bluff overlooking the estuary, provides easy access to the pine-and-palmetto forest and serene coastal marshlands (a nice respite to the urbanity across the river, and a scenic stop for through-travelers). You'll find picnic areas, a 1.3-mile hiking trail, and a 65-site campground ($10 per site). For information and reservations, call (912) 727-2339. The parking fee is $2 per car. Follow signs from Hwy. 17 or I-95.

Farther south (I-95 exit 13), two "ghost towns" reveal just a faint shadow of their distinguished past. The 1792 **Midway Church** and the **Midway Museum** are all that's left of Midway, a town settled by Massachusetts Puritans in 1754. When colonial Georgia failed to send representatives to the first Continental Congress, the outraged ex-New Englanders here sent one of their own, Lyman Hall. Hall and neighbor Button Gwinett became two of Georgia's three signers of the Declaration of Independence. The small museum, tel. (912) 884-5837, tells more about the town's history (admission $2, closed Monday).

Four-and-a-half miles east, **Seabrook Village,** 660 Trade Hill Rd., tel. (912) 884-7008, is a unique living-history museum founded in 1991 and dedicated to the authentic portrayal of African-American history and culture from 1865 to 1930. A historic freedmen's schoolhouse, cottages, and outbuildings exhibit the region's Gullah heritage, while gardens, croplands, and farmyards illustrate lessons in self-sufficiency. You can wander about the quiet 104-acre site on your own (open Tues.-Sat. 10 a.m.-4 p.m.), but what brings the region's rich history to life is a guided tour, available by reservation.

Melon Bluff Preserve, three miles east of I-95 exit 13, tel. (912) 884-5779 or (888) 246-8188, is another unusual venture—a local family, in an effort to turn the tide of coastal development, opened 3,000 acres of their land as a private nature preserve. The preserve is open Tues.-Sun. 9 a.m.-4 p.m. for hiking, mountain biking, and birding; admission is $9 adults, $6 seniors and children. It also offers a nature center and mule wagon rides, and such weekend events as kayak instruction, hayrides, and oyster roasts.

Continue down the road to **Fort Morris,** which once defended Georgia's second busiest port at Sunbury. The earthworks are all that remain of that time, but the small museum tells of the busy town and the Revolutionary War battles fought there against the British. Rebuilt for the War of 1812, the fort is now a state historic site, tel. (912) 884-5999, where costumed battle reenactments are held in February and October, among other colonial events throughout the year. The museum is open Tues.-Sat. 9 a.m.-5 p.m., Sunday 9:30 a.m.-5:30 p.m., and on most Monday holidays. Adult admission costs $2-4. Midway is west of I-95, and Sunbury lies east, off the same exit.

For refreshments, stop by **Ida Mae and Joe's,** tel. (912) 884-3388, on Hwy. 17 south, a classic roadhouse that has outlived both Ida Mae and Joe (open 6 a.m.-8 p.m.). When we were last by they were serving a plate lunch of smoked sausage and red rice, rutabagas, speckled butter beans, and fried squash for $5.65.

The **Harris Neck Wildlife Refuge,** 3,000 acres of saltwater marsh, deciduous woods, croplands, and grasslands, attracts birdwatchers, anglers, crabbers, and anyone else looking for a peaceful and scenic retreat. An arcade of massive live oaks—draped with Spanish moss nearly touching the ground—leads to a loop road through the maritime forest and past a ghostly WW II airstrip. The refuge shelters deer, geese, possums, armadillos, and raccoons; its wetlands harbor more than 225 species of birds. To reach the refuge, take I-95 exit 12, go south on Hwy. 17 for one mile, then drive east on Hwy. 131 for seven miles. At the end of the highway, boaters enter refuge tidewaters or head out to Blackbeard Island from a public boat ramp.

In South Newport you'll find the **"Smallest Church in America"** (or at least in all of Georgia), a 12-seat cabin endowed by the inheritance of a local woman. It's open round the clock for a nice solitary retreat (but as they say in these parts, "You're never alone if the Lord's with you"). Kindly switch down the lights as you leave.

Shellman Bluff

This small backwoods fishing village on the Julienton River offers two of the best home-style seafood restaurants in the state, and two marinas where you can charter boats to remote barrier islands. To reach the bluff, take Hwy. 17 south of South Newport's small church, look for the next turnoff left named Minton Rd. (signs say Shellman Bluff), follow the paved road east to its end, where roadside signs direct you to restaurants and marinas to the left (first-timers may want to head back to main routes before dark to most easily retrace their steps). Sailors wandering off the Intracoastal Waterway follow their noses to the bluffside restaurants, bringing occasional New England Topsider-types to this obscure corner of coastal Georgia.

At **Hunter's Cafe,** tel. (912) 832-5848, let the screen door bang behind you and order great crab stew, broiled stuffed flounder, or one of many other local seafood specialties served with a bluffside view of the salt marsh. The cafe opens Tues.-Sun. at 7 a.m., closes for a 2-5 p.m. siesta, and then opens again from 5 p.m. to about 9 p.m. (closed Monday). Beside its wooden cabin there's a tiny smoky bar playing country music. Or follow signs to **Speed's Kitchen,** down past the Baptist Church, for the best fried seafood on the coast (dinners only), open Thurs.-Sat. 5-10 p.m., Sunday noon-9:30 p.m., tel. (912) 832-4743).

Fisherman's Lodge, tel. (912) 832-4671, and **Kip's Fish Camp,** tel. (912) 832-5162, arrange charters to ferry adventurers out to remote barrier islands for hiking or fishing (or, in season, hunting). You can reach the Blackbeard Island National Wildlife Refuge and wilderness area, Sapelo Island's northern shore, and St. Catherines Island from here (see island descriptions below).

(Coastal trivia: In 1975, U.S. Customs agents seized 12 tons of marijuana at Shellman Bluff.)

The Route 99 Loop

Route 99 (a loop turnoff from Hwy. 17 or I-95's exit 11) takes drivers on a backcountry adventure through the heart of the old coast. From Eulonia to Darien, old fishing villages, nests of summer cottages overlooking the delta, and knots of trailers and shacks with swept yards remain unchanged over decades. This route makes a great bicycling excursion—a small ridge adds variety to the flat coastal plain, and many intriguing side trips can yield discoveries along the way.

Three-and-a-half miles east of Hwy. 17 in **Crescent,** a road swings off the highway a mile and a half to the river, where the **Pelican Point Restaurant** and bar, tel. (912) 832-4295, perches over a scenic panorama of Sapelo Sound. The moderately priced restaurant features "fleet fresh" seafood and live entertainment most weekends. It's open Mon.-Sat. 5:30-10-ish, Sunday noon-10 p.m.

A SENSE OF PLACE

"History . . . is what Darien has the way other communities have rich topsoil, or a wealth of hidden talent, or fine high-school athletics. Coastal people understand history personally, the way religious people do, the way ancient people did. They own history in a way lost to most Americans except in a generic, national sort of way, because the rest of us move around so much, intermarry, adopt new local loyalties, and blur the simple narrative line."

—Melissa Fay Greene, *Praying for Sheetrock*

Four miles farther south of Crescent off Hwy. 99, the boat dock in **Meridian** is the jumping-off point for Sapelo Island tours. Tickets are sold in the new visitors center by the dock, which also contains exhibits on coastal history and ecology (see **Sapelo Island,** below, for more tour information). Meridian, by the way, has a small grocery store and gas station. A couple of miles below Meridian, a historic marker points down a half-mile dirt road to the "Thicket," where **tabby ruins** of an 1816 sugar mill and rum distillery still stand near the marsh.

Ridgeville, locally called "the Ridge," marks the high elevation on the route. Historically, elite families were drawn to this area as an escape from the hotter summer temperatures at the water's edge, and many 19th-century homes and estates remain visible.

DARIEN

To casual visitors, the sleepy coastal town of Darien appears little more than a tidal backwater to speed through on the way to beach resorts farther south—the town's biggest annual event is the blessing of the local shrimp fleet—yet scratch below the surface, and Darien reveals a gold mine of historical riches and intrigue.

History

Darien sits at the mouth of the great Altamaha River, and every nation ever to lay claim to this coast has left its mark. In the 16th century, the Spanish established a presidio here, populating it with missionaries whose aim it was to convert the coastal natives to Christianity. It wasn't long before the natives rebelled, and as a warning to Europeans who might follow, they killed the Spanish and impaled the heads of the priests on tall poles facing the river.

At that time, the Altamaha marked the frontier of what was known as the "Debatable Land" claimed by both England and Spain. In 1721—twelve years before Savannah was settled—the British established **Fort King George** on the site, making Darien the first British outpost in what would become the Georgia colony.

James Oglethorpe, the general responsible for founding the Georgia colony, specifically recruited Scottish Highlanders to populate and defend this frontier, because the Scots were renowned for their military might. The first of the McIntosh clan arrived in 1736 and named the town New Inverness; another boatload arrived six years later. Many residents in Darien today can easily trace their lineage to these original settlers (descendants of the later embarkation are still jibed as "newcomers").

Under the new name of Darien, the town developed into an important seaport, exporting lumber that was cut in the interior and floated downriver to port. Rice and cotton cultivation gave rise to huge antebellum plantations, each of which required hundreds of slaves forced to work under grueling conditions. One plantation owner, Pierce Butler, brought to Darien in 1838 his British wife—an actress named Fanny Kemble. Kemble was appalled to witness first-hand the hardships of slavery, and the record she kept of her observations was published in England as the *Journal of a Residence on a Georgia Plantation.* Kemble's fierce indictment of slavery was considered largely responsible for turning British popular opinion against the South during the Civil War.

Though the Georgia coast was only lightly touched by the Civil War compared to the interior, here again Darien made history. The town was burnt to the ground by none other than the famous all-black regiment, the 54th Massachusetts. Offended that his troops be asked to perform such punitive tasks instead of fighting battles, their commander demanded that they next be sent to the front lines. His wish was granted, and their next assignment, an assault on South Carolina's Fort Wagner, led to the death of the commander along with nearly his entire regiment (a story recounted in the film *Glory.)* The rebuilt town continued to thrive on the lumber trade and developed a shrimping industry.

Then in the late 1950s and 1960s—the heyday of the early highways—Darien was back on the map. The meandering two-lane through town became part of the Atlantic Coast Highway, and was soon congested with truck commerce and Florida-bound travelers. As the saying goes, the locals soon discovered that "a Yankee was worth two bales of cotton, and was a lot easier to pick." Many ways were devised to exploit this new resource, and the town gained notoriety for shady dealing. Admittedly, this was an unsavory time in many parts of the South, and Darien might have slipped through it unnoticed if another historical expose hadn't hit the market in 1991. Melissa Fay Greene tells this story of McIntosh County in *Praying for Sheetrock,* as a compelling allegory of the pre-civil rights South.

Darien bears its historical infamy with pride. Read up before you go to get the most out of your visit.

Sights

The **McIntosh County Welcome Center,** on Hwy. 17 at the bridge, tel. (912) 437-4192, distributes self-guided maps for historical walking tours and driving tours of the area. You can also inquire here about local boat trips and charters.

At **Fort King George,** tel. (912) 437-4770, a reconstructed cypress blockhouse, Native American exhibits and a self-guided tour illustrate the remote spot's turbulent history. On summer weekends, costumed guides deck out in full British regalia, and every now and again boat tours are available. It's open Tues.-Sat. 9 a.m.-5 p.m., Sunday 2-5:30 p.m.; admission is $2-4 adults.

The **Hofwyl-Broadfield Plantation,** five miles south of Darien on Hwy. 17, tel. (912) 264-9263, makes an intriguing stop. The state-operated historical site commemorates Georgia's unusual rice culture, and a modest antebellum house recalls plantation history. Start at the visitor center, where a slide show and exhibits relate stories of the rice fields, then follow a half-mile walk through the quiet maritime forest of live oak and pine to the house and farmyard (the site served as a dairy farm earlier this century). One outbuilding still standing was the one hastily converted to a payroll shed after the Civil War abolished slavery. Nature-lovers will want to detour off the paths to see the rice levees, now thriving wetlands for native and migratory birds. The plantation is open Tues.-Sat. 9 a.m.-5 p.m., Sunday 2-5:30 p.m. (closed Monday except for legal holidays). Admission is $2-4 adults.

A 75-foot brick rice-mill chimney marks the old **Butler Island** rice plantation across the bridge from Darien, where Fanny Kemble wrote her famous journal (see **History,** above). Though now a private residence, its owners allow visitors to walk the rice fields.

Accommodations and Food

Considering that in the author's personal experience the closer you get to town the more odd your experiences tend to get, you might prefer to stay around the interstate gulch at I-95 exit 10. Here a Hampton Inn, Comfort Inn, Holiday Inn Express, and an inexplicably Tyrolean Super 8 have sprung up in the last few years.

A huge factory outlet mall (with a putting green, nice playground, and small picnic area out back) offers a food court that unfortunately hadn't completely gelled yet at the time of our last visit, and the one open stall was wildly crowded. We ended up at the Kentucky Fried Chicken across the street, which serves an okay luncheon buffet with vegetable plates in addition to its standard fast food menu. Several gas stations nearby offer convenient mini-marts for last-minute Sapelo tour supplies.

SAPELO ISLAND

Adventurers often travel to far corners of the globe to discover an isolated subtropical island with a unique culture, language, and history all its own—but few would guess that they could find all that and more on Sapelo Island, U.S.A.

Sapelo is graced with the beauty of all the Sea Islands—powdery shell paths through pine-

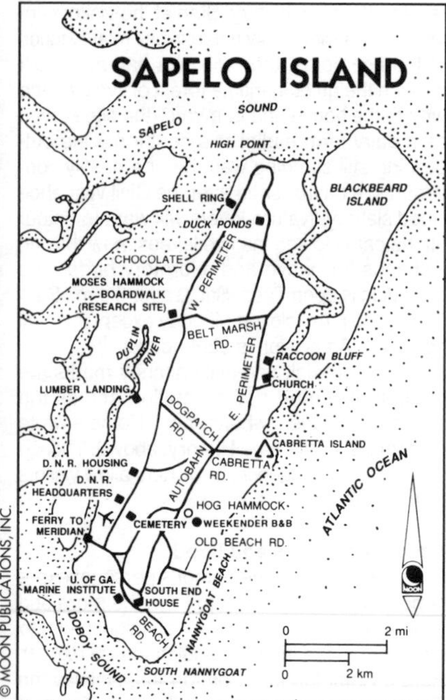

and-palmetto forests, startled herons gliding across abandoned rice fields—yet beyond that, Sapelo is home to a Geechee community largely descended from a single slave. The only other island residents are the scientists who inhabit the marine research institute there.

Access to the island is restricted to protect island ecology, but a daily ferry runs for visitors and guests. Tourists interested in a day-trip can most readily sign up for a guided island tour, although with some planning it is possible to visit the island outside of the packaged tour.

The 30-minute ferry ride to the island is reason enough to travel to Sapelo—the graceful *Sapelo Queen* weaves through still blue-green marshlands, past oyster beds, and alongside schools of dolphins into wide Doboy Sound; the mysterious island looms on the horizon. Then there's the island itself—far removed from civilization, overgrown with thick forests, and with a wide untrammeled beach studded with whelks, sea whips, and olive shells.

History

One of the few Sea Islands that retains its Native American name, Sapelo was called Zapala by the Creek, who hunted and fished here when Europeans arrived. But its native history dates back thousands of years—some of the earliest pottery found in North America was unearthed here. Of the **shell middens** on Sapelo, the largest measures 12 feet high and 300 feet in diameter.

In the 16th century, the Spanish established a mission named **San Jose de Zapala** on the north end of the island. Later a small colony of refugees from the French Revolution founded a community at **Chocolate** nearby. But the greatest change to the island was brought by Thomas Spaulding, who bought the island in 1802 and built a large cotton and sugarcane plantation at the island's south end. The tabby remains of the sugar mill still stand. When the Civil War came, the Spauldings abandoned the island, and their rambling **South End** house, made of tabby walls three feet thick, fell to ruins under the occupation of Federal troops. Former slaves of the Spaulding plantation remained on the island and established their own self-sufficient and self-regulated communities. They lived in such isolation through the generations that they retained many of the West African beliefs and traditions that mainland African-Americans had lost through assimilation and repression.

In 1936, tobacco magnate R.J. Reynolds bought the island, and later established the marine institute and wildlife refuge here. The state now owns most of the island and maintains the institute, refuge, the national estuarine sanctuary offshore (see the special topic **Gray's Reef**), and operates the South End mansion as a conference center.

In the 434-acre private parcel of **Hog Hammock,** descendants of Spaulding slaves (many descended from a single slave, a West African Muslim named Bailli) carry on their unique Geechee heritage. The community today numbers around 70, including several families whose children ferry over to mainland schools each day, but the majority of the residents are of advanced age, as the youth are drawn to wider educational and economic opportunities on the mainland. The future is uncertain for this cultural enclave in the coming decade unless the islanders can solidify an economic base to hang on to its next generation.

Organized Tours

The Official Tour: The Sapelo Island Natural Estuarine Research Reserve, tel. (912) 485-2251, managed by the state, operates half-day bus tours of Sapelo Island. A mainland **visitors center,** tel. (912) 437-3224, near the Meridian dock, takes reservations for the official tour, and tourists need to stop in here to pick up their tickets before heading to the ferry.

The tour schedule is presently as follows: Saturday at 9 a.m. year-round (returns at 1 p.m.), and also Wednesday and Friday at 8:30 a.m. (returns 12:30 p.m.) during the summer. From March to October, an extended daylong tour is offered once a month. The standard half-day tour costs $10 adults.

On the half-day tour, guides bus sightseers around the island while explaining local history and ecology. The bus stops at sugar mill ruins, by the Big House, the marine institute, and out at the beach for leisurely beachcombing or a walk through the maritime forest. The whole party stops at Hog Hammock for a drink. With the combination of the peculiar history, heat, isolation, and such random sights as entangled landscapes, dead armadillo roadkill, subtropical scientists, and a de facto African-American reservation with its lilting Geechee dialects, it makes for an exotic American safari. (Not for everyone—tourists with more mainstream interests are better off sticking to the resort areas farther south, and young children could be miserably uncomfortable on a tour with such uncommon appeal).

The full-day tour takes in North End sights—the plantation ruins at Chocolate, the shell midden left by the Guale Indians, and the long-abandoned First African Baptist Church at Raccoon Bluff.

The Unofficial Tour: You can pretty well pick your own itinerary of sights or leave it up to the Hog Hammock natives if you take one of the tours the residents now offer. Stanley Walker runs visitors around in his ancient VW van with the panel door open for a close-up look at island landscapes; call him at (912) 485-2206. For a slower pace, Maurice Bailey takes visitors around on a three-hour mule-drawn wagon tour; call him at (912) 485-2170. All tour arrangements must be made in advance.

Recreation

Paddling excursions to Sapelo and from Sapelo over to Blackbeard Island are organized by the St. Simon-based outfitter **SouthEast Adventure Outfitters,** tel. (912) 638-6732; call for dates and rates of day kayak and canoe trips and overnight camping excursions.

GRAY'S REEF

East of Sapelo Island 17.5 nautical miles, in ocean waters 50-80 feet deep, lies America's northernmost coral reef. **Gray's Reef National Marine Sanctuary,** one of 10 federally protected marine sanctuaries nationwide, is named for Milton B. Gray, the biologist credited with discovery of the reef in 1981. Here a 17-square-mile area of concentrated limestone outcroppings rise above an otherwise barren seafloor to heights of eight feet, attracting an abundant and colorful collection of unique sealife (not to mention scuba divers and fishing boats).

Tropical atolls of hard corals cover the outcroppings. Soft corals (called octocorals because of their eight tentacles) wave hypnotically, earning such names as sea whips, deadmans fingers, knobby candelabra, and sea feathers. The coral-reef community attracts and shelters anemones, sponges, jellies, worms, mollusks, crabs, lobsters, shrimp, and many temperate and tropical varieties of fish. Schools of barracuda, amberjack, scad, and spadefish move through underwater currents warmed by the Gulf Stream, along with threatened and endangered varieties of sea turtles. The waters surrounding Gray's Reef also contain the only known calving grounds for the most highly endangered of all great whales—the North Atlantic right whale *(Eubalaena glacialis)*—only an estimated 350 individuals exist.

Gray's Reef is one of the most popular recreational dive sites off the Georgia coast, and it's the best known destination for offshore sportfishing.

For more information, contact the Georgia Department of Natural Resources, Coastal Resources Division, One Conservation Way, Brunswick, GA 31523-8600.

Accommodations and Camping

Nancy and Caesar Banks operate the **Weekender,** tel. (912) 485-2277, a modern tabby three-bedroom cabin with private baths and shared kitchens. Linens and cooking utensils are provided, but you'll need to bring all your own food and drink. By island standards, the family has gone to great lengths to make the modest rooms clean and comfortable. The lounge—where old Chevy bench seats constitute the booths, and fawning fan letters and photographs adorn the walls—best reflects the islanders' recycled thrift and Geechee generosity of spirit. Room rates run from $35 single. Bicycles are available for your stay at no charge. Inquire about camping at the Weekender.

Stanley Walker and his mother Cornelia Bailey (the island's unofficial historian), tel. (912) 485-2206, are building a raised wooden cabin for overnight guests; call for rates.

The state authorities open dormitory rooms at the **South End** Reynolds plantation house to groups demonstrating a legitimate naturalist or historical purpose to their visit. The state also maintains the primitive **Cabretta Island** campground (with a bathhouse and platforms for freestanding tents) off the east shore of Sapelo Island, which it reserves for groups under the same conditions. Call (912) 485-2251 for group rates and reservations (up to 11 months in advance).

Food and Drink

George and Lula Walker, tel. (912) 485-2270, operate **Lula's Kitchen,** where they'll make dinner by advance reservation—the likes of Southern fried chicken, or a low-country boil.

If **B.J.'s Confectionery** is not bolted shut (with a broomstick through the door handles), Viola's probably out front weaving baskets. Her handcrafted creations hang from empty cabinets around the old cafe that looks like it served its last meal in the Johnson administration. (Framed photographs of then-Governor Carter's visit to Hog Hammock hang on the walls; a broken jukebox lists hits that weren't "oldies" when they were installed.) The "store" part—a box of instant rice, a bottle of bleach, several individually wrapped rolls of toilet tissue—resembles a store in Nicaragua at the height of the U.S. embargo, but Viola stocks cold drinks (usually offbeat brands: Mr. Pibb, Bubble-Up), some candy, and cooks up 79-cent hot dogs.

Up the road, Cornelia Bailey runs the local watering hole, as well as a small crafts store where she sells baskets and fabric dolls.

Getting There and Around

The state Department of Natural Resources (DNR) operates daily ferry service for residents and guests from the dock in Meridian, 10 miles north of Darien on Rte. 99. The only visitors allowed on the ferry are those on the official tour or those with a resident sponsor. Hog Hammock guests pay the $1 resident rate and your hosts meet you at the dock.

George Walker at Lula's Kitchen rents bikes; call (912) 485-2270.

OUTLYING ISLANDS

To reach any of the four outlying barrier islands on the north coast, visitors need to arrange independent boat charters. Try either of two marinas in the small fishing village of Shellman Bluff, 51 miles south of Savannah off Hwy. 17; see **Shellman Bluff,** above.

Ossabaw Island

Ossabaw Island was protected in 1976 as Georgia's first "Heritage Preserve," and today it's operated by a public-private partnership. Shelters on the island are open only to selected educational or artistic nonprofit groups. Rare wild hogs (introduced to the island 400 years ago) and donkeys (introduced earlier this century) roam at will around Ossabaw, another island that retains its Native American name. A few tabby buildings date from slavery days, and a hunting lodge and helicopter wreck stand as relics of more recent eras. For more information, contact the Department of Natural Resources island manager, P.O. Box 14565, Savannah, GA 31416, tel. (912) 485-2251.

St. Catherines Island

Named capital of nearly every nation and enterprise that ever claimed the Sea Islands, St. Catherines Island has the most fascinating history of all. First, Spanish missionaries estab-

KAP STANN

Tabby ruins are strewn through the islands and coastal mainland.

lished their domain on Georgia's Sea Islands, constructing a string of presidio-missions designed to convert natives to Christianity. The capital of these island settlements was **Santa Catalina de Guale;** its ruins here still attract archaeologists studying Georgia's 16th-century mission system. As for the origins of the word "Guale" (WAL-ee) commonly seen in connection to coastal history, the name was probably a Spanish corruption of the native Muskogean word "wahali," meaning "south."

Then the British settled Savannah in 1773 and what they wanted from the Creek was land. As the British progressively overstepped original territorial agreements made with Creek Chief Tomo-chi-chi, a half-Creek princess named Mary Musgrove Bosomworth took up the cause of her people. She successfully negotiated with the British to retain at least St. Catherines Island as Creek territory.

After her death, a famed local American Revolutionary came into the picture. Button Gwinett, one of Georgia's three signers of the Declaration of Independence, bought the island and moved here with his wife and daughter. Legend has it that after Gwinett was killed in a duel on the mainland in 1777, his spirit returned to inhabit his island home and is seen most often sailing stormy waters in the sound.

The island passed down to a planter, who established a flourishing cotton plantation here before the Civil War, which was abandoned when war broke out. The historic plantation house, cottages, and tabby slave cabins remain in use. In 1864, General Sherman allocated the Sea Islands (and much of the coastal low country) as the exclusive domain of former slaves. The entrepreneurial Tunis Campbell quickly declared himself governor of this new Black Republic, from headquarters here on St. Catherines Island. When Congress repealed Sherman's directive during Reconstruction, returning ownership to the planters, Campbell was removed by federal troops.

Eventually, after changing hands from heir to heir, the island came under the control of a private foundation. This foundation established the Rare Animal Survival Center of the New York Zoological Society on the island in 1974. Because of its captive breeding program, St. Catherines is today off-limits to the general public. Zebras, antelope, lemurs, and gazelles are now among the exotic animals that roam the 14,000-acre subtropical island. For more information, contact the **Georgia Conservancy,** tel. (912) 897-6462.

Blackbeard Island

Named for Edward Teach, the famous "Blackbeard" of swashbuckling fame (legend says his hidden treasure may remain buried off Tybee Island), Blackbeard Island is separated from northeastern Sapelo Island by a thin creek. Originally bought by the U.S. Navy in 1800 as a source of live oak timber for shipbuilding, in 1940 the Interior Department took it over and designated it a national wildlife refuge. In 1975, half of its 5,618 acres were set aside as a national wilderness area.

Hikers use several miles of trails, roadways, and beaches for wildlife (especially birdlife) viewing. From March 15 to October 25, fishing is allowed on two large freshwater ponds; saltwater creeks are open to fishing throughout the year, except during managed hunts in the fall and winter. For more information, call the coastal refuges office at (912) 944-4415. (See **Sapelo Island** for paddling excursions across the creek separating the two islands.)

Wolf Island

Actually, three islands—Wolf, Egg, and Little Egg—make up the Wolf Island National Wildlife Refuge, a low-lying preserve of 4,000 acres of tidal marshlands with only 135 acres of forests. Limited recreational opportunities appeal mostly to fishermen and birdwatchers. For more information, call the coastal refuges office at (912) 944-4415.

THE GOLDEN ISLES

The island resorts of St. Simons, Jekyll, Sea Island, and Little St. Simons, first called the "Golden Isles" by the Spanish (a term happily revived by local promoters), offer visitors easily accessible beach resorts with plenty of recreation, an unusual history, and accommodations that range from camping and a treehouse hostel to five-star resorts and exclusive private islands. Located 72 miles south of Savannah and 290 miles southeast of Atlanta, the largest resort islands, St. Simons and Jekyll, are bridged to the mainland at Brunswick. Sea Island is bridged to St. Simons Island. Little St. Simons Island is accessible only by boat from St. Simons Island.

BRUNSWICK

The city of Brunswick, a major state port, is the jumping-off point for vacationers headed to the Golden Isles. Most people rush through Brunswick on their way to the beach—to judge by the looks of the tacky Hwy. 17 strip you can guess why—yet tucked behind the strip visitors can find the downtown historic district around Union Street, with several impressive old buildings shaded by venerable oaks, and the scenic waterfront, where you can buy fresh shellfish straight off the boats.

The **Golden Isles Welcome Center** 4 Glynn Ave., tel. (912) 265-0620 or (800) 933-2627, can be found on the west side of Hwy. 17 just south of the entrance to the causeway. They offer maps, events calendars, and information about lodging, dining, and recreation on the islands and in Brunswick (and introductory brochures in six languages).

Sights and Recreation

The **Low Country Alligator Farm,** 6543 New Jesup Hwy., tel. (912) 280-0300, offers an impressive display of slithering, writhing, tail-slapping reptilians in tanks, cages, and ponds—from just out of the egg to hungry 14-footers. It's pricey at $7 adults (only $3 children 6-12), but memorable (additional charge for souvenir photos with ornamental snakes or baby alligators). It's open daily Apr.-Nov. 10 a.m.-6 p.m. Find it north of I-95 exit 7B (Hwy. 341).

Kayaking expeditions through the Marshes of Glynn here are led by the St. Simons-based **SouthEast Adventure Outfitters;** see **St. Simons Island,** below, for more information.

Accommodations and Camping

Brunswick motels are less expensive than staying on the islands, yet without the amenities of sand and surf. Newer chains are found out by the interstate, including **Hampton Inn,** tel. (912) 261-0002 (127 rooms, pool, moderate prices), and **Best Western Brunswick Inn,** tel. (912) 264-0144 (143 rooms, pool, inexpensive).

Some of the most distinctive bargain lodging in all of Georgia is found outside of town at the **Hostel in the Forest,** tel. (912) 264-9738, a wooded hideaway down a bumpy dirt road, where peacocks roam the grounds and guests stay in geodesic dome dormitories or tiny treehouses for $13 a night (tent camping for $8). Look for the hostel symbol sign on Hwy. 82 (southwest of Brunswick, a mile west of Hwy. 17, 1.5 miles west of I-95), turn left, and follow the rugged dirt driveway a half mile down.

The **Blythe Island Regional Park** campground, 6616 Blythe Island Hwy., tel. (912) 261-3805 or (800) 343-7855, is geared to fishing folk

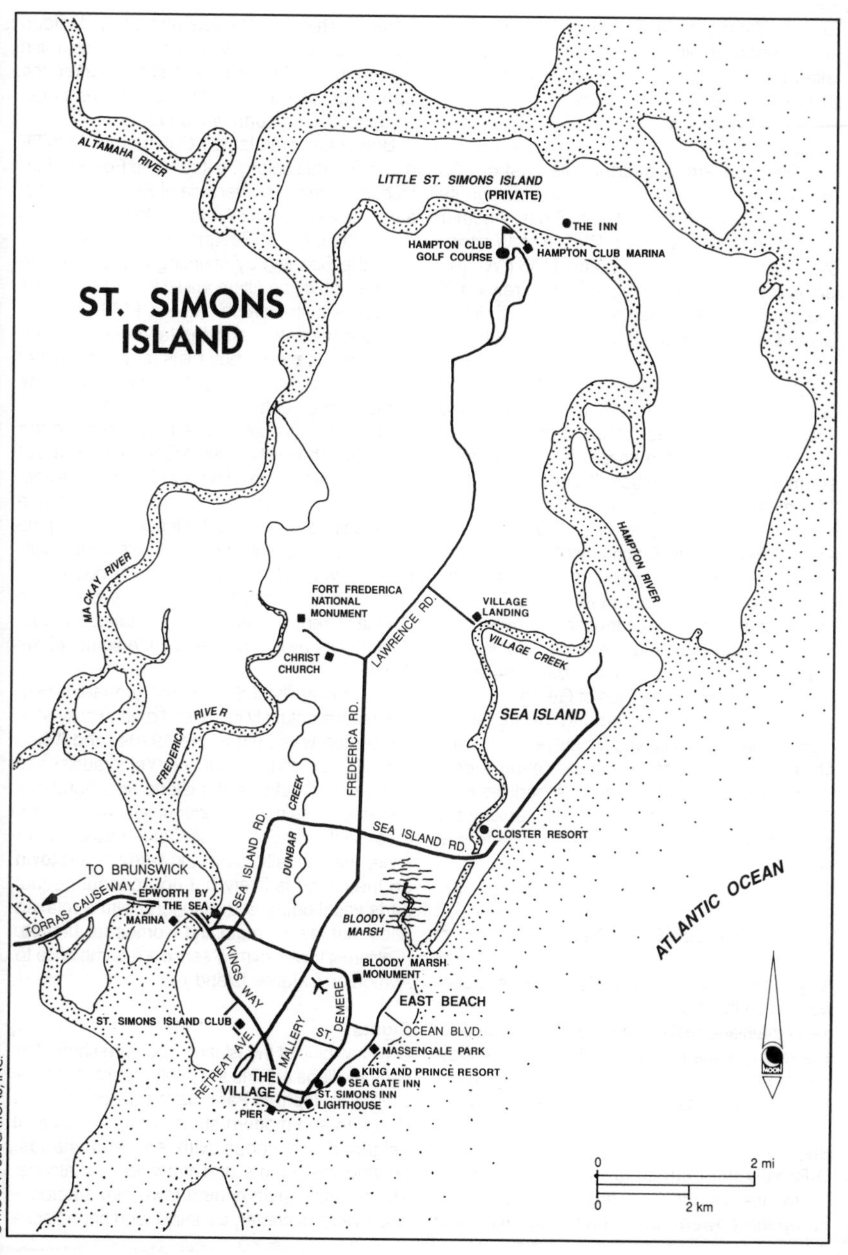
ST. SIMONS ISLAND
ALTAMAHA RIVER
LITTLE ST. SIMONS ISLAND
(PRIVATE)
THE INN
HAMPTON CLUB GOLF COURSE
HAMPTON CLUB MARINA
HAMPTON RIVER
MACKAY RIVER
FORT FREDERICA NATIONAL MONUMENT
VILLAGE LANDING
LAWRENCE RD.
VILLAGE CREEK
CHRIST CHURCH
SEA ISLAND
FREDERICA RIVER
FREDERICA RD.
DUNBAR CREEK
SEA ISLAND RD.
CLOISTER RESORT
TO BRUNSWICK
TORRAS CAUSEWAY
EPWORTH BY THE SEA
MARINA
BLOODY MARSH
ATLANTIC OCEAN
KINGS WAY
BLOODY MARSH MONUMENT
EAST BEACH
ST. SIMONS ISLAND CLUB
MALLERY
ST. DEMERE
OCEAN BLVD.
RETREAT AVE.
MASSENGALE PARK
KING AND PRINCE RESORT
THE VILLAGE
SEA GATE INN
ST. SIMONS INN
LIGHTHOUSE
PIER
MOON
0
2 mi
0
2 km

who use the marina for easy access to tidewater and offshore fishing. They also have a small lakefront swimming beach. Exposed sites cost $10 for tents, $17 with hookups.

Food and Drink

The **Georgia Pig,** a quarter mile east of I-95 exit 6, offers brick-pit barbecue specials in its log cabin; it's open daily 11 a.m.-8 p.m. Another local landmark is **Willie's Wee-nee Wagon,** 3599 Altama Ave., tel. (912) 264-1146 ("We relish your bun"), which offers a $2,000 reward "if you can find a better fried pork chop sandwich in Glynn County." It's open Mon.-Sat. 10 a.m.-10 p.m.

Spanky's, on the water off Hwy. 17, tel. (912) 267-6100, is a perky local hangout for buffalo fingers and loud beach music, but the view is the best thing—watch kayakers come in as a storm rises over the marsh. It's open daily from 11 a.m. to at least 9:30 p.m.

Pam's, Hwy. 17 N, tel. (912) 267-7267, outside the Federal Law Enforcement Training Center, bills itself without contest as "the largest law enforcement dinner club in the world." Inside, the shoulder patches of thousands of the nation's police forces line the walls, brass plate partner memorials cover the bar, and autographed glossies of the likes of George Wallace and Lester Maddox are among the treasured memorabilia. Pam's serves a high-yang selection of red meat-and-potato platters (even Kiddie Copper specials) and frequently schedules Free Beer customer appreciation nights. Look for the decommissioned black-and-white outside that says PAM'S.

ST. SIMONS ISLAND

As you cross the high span of the Torras causeway, everything suddenly changes. You leave dingy mainland reality behind and enter the pristine realm of the jungly islands, with their slow tropical pace, white sands, and serene blue-green marshlands. All this for a 35-cent toll!

History

Originally the hunting grounds of the native Creek, the islands were fought over by major European powers: the French, Spanish, and English. This contest was ultimately decided here on St. Simons Island, where the skirmish called the "Battle of Bloody Marsh" marked the Spaniards' last attempt to expand their continental dominion north of Florida.

British General James Oglethorpe, founder of the Georgia colony, established Fort Frederica here on the backriver side of St. Simons (now a compelling historical site), both to secure his new settlement at Savannah and also to provoke the Spanish by claiming the "Debatable Land" south of the Altamaha River. From here he led troops to the marsh battle in 1736.

In the plantation era, the land grew Sea Island Cotton (a few tabby ruins remain from that time), and, like the rest of the islands, became home to a Geechee community when the islands were occupied by federal troops in the Civil War. The mythologized Geechee folktale of the slaves who "walked back to Africa" has its origins here on St. Simons: upon debarking from a slave ship, a captured Igbo leader from Nigeria led his tribesmen into the ocean rather than submit to slavery. Though the original "Ebo's Landing" is on St. Simons (on private property up Dunbar Creek), in Geechee folktales each island has its own, inhabited by the spirits of the Africans.

The popularity of St. Simons' turn-of-the-century resorts naturally increased dramatically after the bridge was built in the 1920s, and it has steadily increased ever since. Yet in addition to its tourist attractions, the island also houses a year-round residential community, making it the most "well-rounded" of the Golden Isles. As for style, the casually classy, low-key resort town on the island is lively but not raucous, equal parts vacationers and islanders, with a relaxed pace that leaves mainland worries far behind. (California travelers may sense a resemblance to Avalon on Catalina Island.)

Sights

On a low bluff at the island's southern shore, the central village adjoins the public beach and fishing pier at **Neptune Park.** Several blocks of small Victorian and modern storefronts mix practical neighborhood shops with souvenir stands, gourmet restaurants, and margaritaville saloons. The Spanish-style central town plaza holds a small **visitors center,** a library (used paperbacks for sale, cheap), and Casino community center. From here a **trolley tour,** tel. (912) 638-8954, surveys the island ($10 adults, $5 under 10).

The historic **St. Simons Lighthouse** here overlooks the village as well as the panoramic coastline; climb the 129 steps for the best view. The adjacent **Museum of Coastal History,** tel. (912) 638-4666, displays small exhibits and features slide shows on local history. Both are open Mon.-Sat. 10 a.m.-5 p.m. Admission is $2 adults, $1 children.

A short beach walk or drive up Ocean Blvd. will take you to the wide beach where the regal **King and Prince Hotel** dominates the scene. To the north, **Massengale Park** provides public beach access, parking, and showers. Nearby **Coastal Encounters Nature Center,** tel. (912) 638-0221, provides reasonably priced educational ecological children's programs (hello: child care!) as well as free exhibits on local wildlife; it's open daily: Mon.-Sat. 9 a.m.-5 p.m., Sunday 1-5 p.m. Farther north at East Beach, guided hour-long nature walks led by marine experts meet at the rear of the old Coast Guard Station (call 912-638-7652 for times).

At **Fort Frederica National Monument,** ruins of the 1736 fortified village built by General James Oglethorpe sit scenically on a backriver bend, with just a few tabby ruins attesting to the town's former glory. It's open daily 8 a.m.-6 p.m. from May through Labor Day, until 5 p.m. all other times. Self-guided audio tours can be rented from the museum. Admission costs $3 per vehicle, free for seniors or bicyclists. Take Frederica Rd. (or the parallel bike path) a few miles north from the causeway, then follow signs west.

Nearby **Christ Church** served the colonial village and was presided over by the founders of Methodism, John and Charles Wesley. The current sanctuary dates from 1886. The adjacent cemetery has marble statues and stone gravemarkers shrouded by Spanish moss. Across the street, a pretty nature trail loops through the woods.

Looking nearly as it must have when the British pummeled the Spanish, the **Bloody Marsh Battle Site** is as anticlimactic as the skirmish itself, impressive in its humility considering that the outcome decided control of the American continent. The National Park Service

KAP STANN

St. Simons Lighthouse at Neptune Park

opens the gates 8 a.m.-4 p.m. daily, no charge, and no other services besides parking are available.

The restored **Hamilton Island Slave Cabins,** once part of a cotton plantation, recall "slavery time" with period furnishings. One houses the local garden society responsible for the restoration. On the grounds of a retreat center called Epworth by the Sea (on Arthur Moore Dr. at Hamilton, follow signs), the cabins are open to the public only on Wednesday 10 a.m.-2 p.m., but you can always look at the exteriors.

Water Sports

The premier outfitter on the Georgia coast, **SouthEast Adventure Outfitters,** in the village at 313 Mallery St., tel. (912) 638-6732, organizes guided sea kayak and canoe trips, from two-hour rides to multi-day excursions, up and down the coast. Among their most popular local excursions is a three-hour guided sea kayak tour that samples a great variety of coastal ecology as it loops through the marsh, beach, and ocean ($40, $10 off for kids, minimum 120 lbs. to ride independently, tandems also available for ages 6-12). In their store, they stock a great selection of outdoor gear and supplies along with maps and guides that are hard to find elsewhere. See also www.gacoast.com/navigator /sea.html.

The **Golden Isles Marina,** 206 Marina Dr. at the causeway, tel. (912) 634-1128, is a major stop on the Intracoastal Waterway. It's the center for all kinds of water sports, including fishing charters, parasailing rides, and JetSki rentals. The **Island Dive Center** here, tel. (912) 638-6590 or (800) 940-3483, organizes scuba-diving trips to Gray's Reef and other submerged sites. Several marine supply shops stock all matter of navigational resources and marine supplies.

Golf

At the island's exclusive golf courses—the King and Prince Resort's Hampton Club (with an island green), Sea Palms Golf and Tennis Resort, and the Sea Island Golf Club (ruins of an old slave hospital remain visible here)—expect green fees above $50. The public **St. Simons Island Club** charges the lowest rates, yet the most thrifty golfers find equally scenic courses on Jekyll Island for half the price. Note that many island hotels offer golf or tennis vacation packages with unlimited play.

Bicycling

The island's flat terrain and slow pace make it ideal for bicycling. A bike path weaves from the village and beaches north up Frederica Road. Maps are available from the many bike rental outlets, such as **Toler's Amoco,** 533 Ocean Blvd., tel. (912) 638-6775. Detour on shell roads to find secluded interior marshlands, Geechee communities, and old fish camps.

Entertainment

The local theatrical group the **Island Players,** tel. (912) 638-3031, present productions of musicals and drama in Neptune Park during their season from fall through spring.

Nightlife is centered along two blocks of Mallery St. downtown, where several saloons offer live music most summer nights—beach music and classic rock is most popular, but there's also a karaoke place and a blues club. **Murphy's Tavern** at the inland end of the strip is the best local watering hole and pool hall (closed Sunday). The more respectable **St. Simons Brewing Co.** is set off at the marina (nice sunset views).

Accommodations

St. Simons has a nice range of lodging choices from good to luxurious—you can't go wrong. Note that summer rates may be twice as high as Oct.-March off-season rates, weekday rates are generally lower than weekends and holidays, and ocean-view rooms may cost a third more than rooms facing inland.

The Methodist retreat center **Epworth by the Sea,** 100 Arthur Moore Dr., tel. (912) 638-8688, welcomes all vacationers to its quiet motel complex overlooking the serene backriver marsh. Guest rooms are inexpensive (alcohol is prohibited).

The best economical choice is **Queens Court,** 437 Kings Way, tel. (912) 638-8459, a nicely shaded two-story older court motel right in the center of the action, a busy block away from the beach (inexpensive rates, efficiencies available, no pool).

The newer **St. Simons Inn,** 609 Beachview Dr., tel. (912) 638-1101, is a new 34-room motel with a pool, by the lighthouse in a slightly quieter but just as central location (moderate rates). **Sea Gate Inn,** 1014 Ocean Blvd., tel. (912) 638-8661 or (800) 562-8812, is a lovely, older, quiet, two-story oceanfront motel under a half-mile from the village (moderate to expensive rates for view rooms). Several modern chain motels can be found on interior roads, particularly Frederica Rd., a short drive from the beach.

For more than 60 years, the **King and Prince Resort,** tel. (912) 638-3631 or (800) 342-0212, 201 Arnold Rd., has presided over the wide stretch of beach under a mile from the village. The sprawling three-story Mediterranean-style oceanfront hotel features an elegant dining room, a casual bar-and-grill, tennis courts, and pools indoors and out. Standard oceanfront room rates start at $110 during the off-season and go up from there; two- and three-bedroom villas are also available.

Food and Drink

In the village, **Fourth of May Cafe,** at the corner of Mallery St. and Kings Way, tel. (912) 638-5444, offers daily Southern meat-and-two specials (smothered pork chops, pot roast) with cornbread for $6, along with salads, overstuffed deli sandwiches, and a wide selection of cold beers. It's open daily 11 a.m.-9 p.m. More Southern specials are on the menu at **Barbara Jean's** down the way at 214 Mallery St., tel. (912) 634-6500, such as catfish for $9 or a five-veggie plate for $6, as well as burgers and salads. It's open daily 11 a.m.-10 p.m.

At the Methodist retreat center **Epworth by the Sea** along the backriver, an inexpensive cafeteria open to the public serves three hearty meals a day (no alcohol).

In an isolated two-story cabin overlooking the marsh, **Village Creek Landing,** 526 S. Harrington Rd., tel. (912) 634-9054, serves no-frills steamed or fried shrimp, crab, oysters, and combination platters at reasonable prices, accompanied by cold drafts, sweet tea, and if you're lucky, a panoramic sunset. Dinner is served Thurs.-Sun. 6-9 p.m.

Information and Services

A tiny **visitor center** at Neptune Park (next to the library) distributes information on area sights and lodging 9 a.m.-5 p.m. daily. The small commercial center in the village contains a pharmacy, laundromat, mini-mart, and used bookstore. Out Frederica Rd. near the airport you'll find the central business activity: supermarkets, shopping malls, banks, and office centers. The closest medical facility is on the mainland; call the **Southeast Georgia Regional Medical Center,** 3100 Kemble Ave. in Brunswick, at (912) 264-7000.

SEA ISLAND

Separated from St. Simons Island by a small stream, Sea Island protects a tony enclave of imposing residential estates and the preeminent Cloister Hotel. To reach the island, take Sea Island Rd. across St. Simons Island, and cross the bridge over the marshlands.

Cloister Hotel

The world-class Cloister Hotel, a Mobil five-star resort for 22 consecutive years, occupies the southern end of Sea Island, from the marsh beach to miles of ocean sands. Sprawling Spanish-style buildings are surrounded by immaculately landscaped lawns, gardens, ponds, and live oak trees. Blue-blooded families find a comfortably formal style, impeccable service, and five-star amenities. Two pools, four lounges, four restaurants, and a full-service spa serve guests in 262 rooms. A social staff maintains a busy schedule of activities for guests—kayaking, snorkeling, bicycling, food festivals, boat rides, ghost stories, big band dancing . . . the works.

The **Sea Island Golf Club,** tel. (912) 638-5118, offers a total of 54 holes to guests ($90 for 18 holes). The **Cloister Racquet Club** maintains 17 clay courts ("rested and groomed twice every 24 hours"). The **Sea Island Stables** provide horses for beach rides or instruction.

High-season rates at the hotel include three meals a day and start at $334 a night for two people; golf or tennis package rates include unlimited play. Call (800) SEA-ISLAND (800-732-4752) for more information; also see www.seaisland.com.

LITTLE ST. SIMONS ISLAND

Now here's a real jewel. Little St. Simons Island, privately owned by the same family for generations, offers an exclusive retreat for the rich and rustic. The pristine 10,000-acre island harbors a compact combination of habitats: marsh, ocean, woodland, ponds, and a savanna that looks out of Africa. This diversity attracts more than 200 species of birds; experts say it's among the best birdwatching sites on the East Coast. Fallow deer (a European breed, smaller than the common white-tailed deer), old rice levees, shell middens, and seven miles of hard-packed sands are among the island's many other sights.

The island's rice plantation was owned by Pierce Butler, whose famous wife, British actress Fanny Kemble, chronicled antebellum life in her *Journal of a Residence on a Georgia Plantation* (an influential treatise against slavery, see **Darien**).

At the turn of the century, the island was sold to a pencil manufacturer who intended to farm the island's cedars. But the cedar turned out to be too twisted to use, and the owner retained the island as a private retreat—the last family-owned barrier island in Georgia. In 1976, the island's housing was converted to an inn.

Little St. Simons Island Resort

Debbie and Kevin McIntyre, the innkeepers of Little St. Simons Island Resort, can be reached via post at P.O. Box 21078, St. Simons Island, GA 31522, tel. (912) 638-7472, fax (912) 634-1811, or via e-mail at 1lssi@mindspring.com; see also www.pactel.com.au/lssi. What Debbie calls "summer camp for adults" is the island's High Rustic style, an artful spirit of casual camaraderie and private sanctuary.

Staff naturalists and guides maintain a full slate of daily recreational activities: canoe trips, horseback riding, fly fishing, birding, and interpretive programs. The bike barn is always open for leisurely rides along shell-and-sand roads to the beach and remote corners of the island.

Overnight guests choose from two lodge rooms with two twin beds in each, a two-bedroom honeymoon cottage, or two modern four-bedroom cabins, all centrally located near the pool and dock. Guests may book individual rooms in the lodge or the houses, or whole cabins, or for that matter, you can also book the whole island.

Hearty, healthy meals are served family-style in the hunting lodge (brook trout stuffed with wild rice was on the menu at a recent visit). A very civilized cocktail hour before dinner also encourages a rapport with fellow guests. The lodge comes fully stocked with board games, taxidermy, old family photos, and books related to local history and ecology.

Rates include all meals, recreation, and transportation: prices range from $290 double (hunting lodge, low season) to $515 double (cottage, a high season weekend). Discounts for single occupancy, child occupancy (over 6 only in the high season), and weekly rates are available.

The island's captain shuttles guests between Little St. Simons and the Hampton Club Marina at the northern tip of St. Simons Island. Day trips may be available by prior arrangement, definitely a worthwhile prospect to experience a small slice of island life (call for schedule and fees).

JEKYLL ISLAND

State-owned Jekyll Island, a self-contained resort, is like a giant amusement park of beaches, bike paths, boat rides, golf courses, tennis courts, and oceanfront restaurants, all in a magnificent natural and historical setting. Its premier hotel, the Jekyll Island Club Hotel, once served as the exclusive getaway of America's richest tycoons. In 1904, Jekyll Island was considered "the richest, most exclusive, most inaccessible Club in the world." Today, it's among the most "democratic" subtropical islands in the world, as its operators act with near-missionary zeal to bring the former Yankee preserve "to the people."

It's very easy to visit Jekyll Island: you pay a $2 parking fee at the toll booth, and receive a warm welcome and a map of every island road, historic site, commercial enterprise, and special event. Amazingly, for such a well-worn and popular path, secluded corners of the island appear near wild—from deserted "boneyard" beaches and woods full of deer, to haunting tabby ruins strewn with languid Spanish moss, and serene marshlands inhabited only by egrets, herons, and fiddler crabs.

Trade in the car as quickly as possible for bikes, in-line skates, golf carts, a tour tram, or sandy bare feet.

History

Leading industrialists from the Northeast, including Rockefeller, Vanderbilt, and Goodyear, staked out Jekyll as a private getaway resort in the late 19th century. Building the majestic Jekyll Island Club, club members also constructed individual family "cottages" the size of mansions. From 1886 to 1942, they engaged in an opulent lifestyle of lawn parties, croquet, and elaborate feasts. Understandably, as the tycoon era waned, so did Jekyll. When WW II brought threatening German submarines to coastal waters, it was thought unwise to concentrate so much wealth and power on one vulnerable island—it was estimated that winter residents controlled one-sixth of the world's wealth—and the club disbanded.

The island came under state control and was in turn leased to the Jekyll Island Authority to operate as a resort.

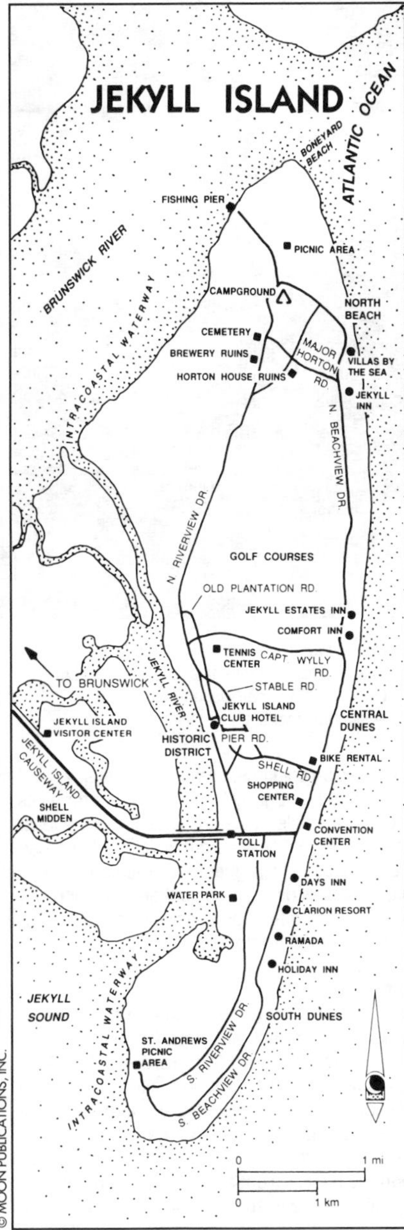

Sights

The rambling four-story **Jekyll Island Club,** built in 1887, elegantly dominates Jekyll's early 20th-century **historic district** (with all those gazebos and turrets, it could fit as well into Nantucket or colonial Malaya). Surrounding it are the restored Club-era (1886-1942) **cottages** of millionaire families and outbuildings now inhabited by small shops selling crafts or candy. The small **Faith Chapel,** open each afternoon 2-4 p.m. for no charge, is ornamented by stained glass windows designed by Louis Comfort Tiffany.

For an interior view of the house restorations and a concise overview of the historic district, take a **tram tour** from the visitor center (housed in the former stables). Tours leave regularly 10 a.m.-2 p.m. daily in summer (adults $10, $6 children 6-18, under six free) and last an hour and a half. Guides relate tales of the rich and famous with a zesty mix of awe and comeuppance.

More historic sites lie north up the backriver from the historic district: tabby ruins of an old brewery, a small family cemetery, and the crumbling remains of the two-story plantation-era Horton House.

For natural attractions, aim for each tip: at the northern end, a **boneyard beach** is strewn with bleached driftwood resembling skeletons (hence the name); at the south end (the island's most remote corner), tiny **St. Andrews Park** makes a particularly scenic picnic spot. Directly behind each tip on the sound side, stiller waters at small sandy beaches seep into backriver marshlands.

Recreation and Entertainment

Go to the beach! The central dunes, where beach parties and events are held, are the widest (but also the most exposed). Sands taper at each wooded end, and shade can be found nearby. The best way to get around is by bicycle; a **bike trail** winds around the island. Rent bikes behind the **miniature golf course** across from the central dunes gazebo, or at hotels, the campground, or the airport.

All **water sports** activity—fishing, scuba diving, dolphin-watch tours, sightseeing cruises, and charter boats—center around the historic wharf at the Jekyll Island Club Hotel, facing the Intracoastal Waterway. There's also a small dock below the bridge and a fishing pier at the north end, out from the picnic area near the campground.

Three 18-hole **golf courses** sit smack dab in the center of the island (the 11th hole on the Pine Lake course abuts an egret rookery), next to 13 clay courts at the **tennis center.** Or try the **fitness center** and the **Summer Waves Water Park.** University of Georgia Marine Extension Service docents lead turtle walks and nature walks year-round; call (912) 635-2232.

Summer theater troupes present performances at the amphitheater, and many special events are scheduled during busy seasons (see **Festivals,** below, and check the information packet you receive at the toll booth).

Accommodations

Jekyll has a wonderful selection of overnight accommodations at its premier hotel, condos, or at many reasonable motels. Expect summer, weekend, and holiday rates to cost more than weekdays or the Oct.-March off-season. And ocean views command a premium. Prices quoted above are for standard rooms in spring and summer. Most places offer package deals for golfers or tennis players.

More than a dozen oceanfront motels are along Beachview Dr., including such chains as the Clarion Resort, Comfort Inn, and Holiday Inn. All properties are well-maintained and offer comparably high amenities, with fairly comparable rates from around $75 in the high summer season. The Days Inn, tel. (912) 635-3319 or (800) 325-2525, and Ramada Inn, tel. (912) 635-2111 or (800) 835-2110, offer high season rates starting around $50. A bargain independent is **Jekyll Estates Inn,** tel. (912) 635-2256, with high season rates from $52.

At the secluded north end, **Villas by the Sea,** tel. (912) 635-2521, rents suites, "mini-suites," and two-bedroom townhouses in a beautifully wooded setting from $84 in the high season.

The magnificent **Jekyll Island Club Hotel,** 371 Riverview Dr., tel. (912) 635-2600 or (800) 535-9547, remains one of the most grand coastal hotels in the East. A four-story rambling Victorian structure garnished with flagged turrets, balconies, pool, indoor tennis courts, and croquet greensward, the hotel faces the scenic backriver marsh. Inside, an appointed and refined decor has been restored to 19th-century elegance, with Grecian columns, arched doorways, leaded glass, and mahogany furnishings. Yet for all its sophisticated elegance, the Club is not the least bit stiff or formal; visitors are welcome to peruse the grounds or join guests for meals or drinks in the candlelit dining room, bakery cafe, or piano lounge. They offer high season rates from $89-119 for a standard double.

KAP STANN

Until WW II, the Jekyll Island Club Hotel was an exclusive retreat for the Rockefellers, Goodyears, Vanderbilts, and other aristocratic families.

Camping

The best spot for car-camping on the coast is under the live oaks and Spanish moss at the 200-site **Jekyll Island Campground,** tel. (912) 635-3021. Only the periphery sites have much privacy, but in the rarefied island atmosphere it doesn't seem to matter. A small store open 8 a.m.-8 p.m. rents bikes and sells slightly more than the basics. Tent sites are $12 a night, $17 for full hookups (disposal station also available);

there's a 14-day limit. Put up here as long as they'll let you, get on a bike, and go fishin'.

Food and Drink

The **Grand Dining Room** at the Jekyll Island Club Hotel, tel. (912) 635-2600, is open daily for three meals during the week and lavish brunches on Sunday. Prices are surprisingly reasonable, considering the refined setting and service, but the cuisine is unspectacular. The hotel's **Wharf Restaurant** has a casual "raw bar" for fresh seafood. The best bet may be **Cafe Solterra,** a casual deli-cafe around back, for healthy soups, salads, sandwiches, snacks, and bakery treats.

Outside of the Club, you're left to family seafood restaurants and very ordinary hotel restaurants. For the record, **Crackers** at Villas by the Sea packs a generous takeout sandwich, **Huddle House** stays open 24 hours, and really, the chicken stir-fry at **Denny's** isn't half bad. Or bring a fishing pole, seine net, or crab trap, and catch your own seafood dinner.

Information and Services

The **Jekyll Island Welcome Center,** P.O. Box 13186, Jekyll Island, GA 31527, tel. (800) 841-6586, distributes comprehensive brochures listing all island facilities and prices. See also www.jekyllisland.com.

A small shopping center at the end of the entrance road sells groceries and supplies. A **summer day camp** for kids aged 4-12 operates weekdays from June through late August at the convention center; call (912) 635-2232.

GOLDEN ISLES FESTIVALS

For complete lists of all events held throughout the year on St. Simons Island, Jekyll Island, and in Brunswick, contact the Brunswick/Golden Isles Visitors Bureau (see **Brunswick,** above).

Summer: In June, the **Country-by-the-Sea** festival brings nationally known country-western musicians and thousands of barefoot fans to Jekyll Island's beach party. Independence Day **fireworks** cap a three-day festival at St. Simons' Neptune Beach; Jekyll Island has its own July Fourth celebrations and fireworks. In August, Jekyll's annual **Beach Music Festival** rocks the volleyball crowd. Also in August, the **Georgia Sea Island Festival** on St. Simons celebrates one of the country's rarest folk cultures, the "Geechee" Sea Islanders (see **People** in this chapter), whose distinctive music, language, and low-country cuisine can be sampled at the weeklong festival.

Fall: Brunswick's **Stews and Blues Festival** in October celebrates the namesake Georgia barbecue staple, Brunswick stew, and down-home Southern blues.

Winter: Jekyll hosts a **Bluegrass Festival** in December. Also in December, historic homes, specially draped in Christmas decor, open for public tours.

ST. MARYS AND CUMBERLAND ISLAND

The premier attraction of the southern Atlantic coast is Cumberland Island, a pristine barrier island protected and managed by the national park system. To preserve the natural environment and wilderness experience, only a limited number of visitors are allowed over to the national seashore each day. You can camp and backpack, or explore the trails, beach, and history of Georgia's largest and southernmost barrier islands.

St. Marys is the jumping-off point for Cumberland Island, overlooking the scenic sound and looming wilderness of Cumberland across the marsh. Crooked River State Park makes a handy base of operations for campers, attracting anglers and boaters to its deserted bluffs. To reach downtown St. Marys, take I-95 to Hwy. 40, follow it east until you hit the water.

ST. MARYS

St. Marys has three oddly juxtaposed major industries: not only is it the point of departure for one of the Atlantic Seaboard's most pristine ecological marvels, but it is also home to the **Kings Bay Naval Submarine Base,** where nuclear-powered subs are made, and the site of a huge odoriferous paper and pulpwood mill. To kill time, watch people pass, and pick out which one of these three things drew them to town. You can't miss.

The town started out as a Timucuan Indian village, visited by French Huguenots in 1562 and settled by the Spanish a few years later. The Spanish occupation lasted about a hundred years, until the British forced their retreat into Florida. In the mid-1700s, a band of exiled Acadians ended up settling here after they were denied refuge in Savannah (the British there feared the Cajuns would act as spies for the marauding French or Spanish). Before long, the Cajuns picked up and moved again, this time to the French colony of Santa Domingo (Haiti). The slave rebellion there displaced them once more, and some of those families returned to St. Marys. You can still make out the French names on gravemarkers in the historic Oak Grove Cemetery.

The Waterfront at the foot of Osborne St. is the center of action. Here you can see the bobbing *Cumberland Queen* ferryboat at its dock, the latticework gazebo on the pier, and the small historic strip of houses and shops that comprise downtown St. Marys. Historical markers with Braille translations cite points of interest along the main street.

The three-story Greek Revival mansion called **Orange Hall** at Osborne and Conyers is now an antebellum house museum, tel. (912) 882-4000 (tours $2). It also houses the **St. Marys Welcome Center** around back (open Mon.-Sat. 9 a.m.-5 p.m. and Sunday 1-5 p.m.).

Accommodations

The 1916 **Riverview Hotel** at 105 Osborne St., tel. (912) 882-3242, anchors the waterfront. Enter through the spacious lobby, across the checkerboard linoleum, and sally up to the worn wooden counter; the massive staircase to the right leads up to second-story guest rooms. Flocked white-on-white wallpaper lines the hall, and the cozy simple rooms open up to a wide wraparound veranda with a view of the docks and Cumberland Island. Rates are moderate.

Two bed and breakfast inns down the block offer period-furnished guest rooms starting at about $75 a night: the **Goodbread House,** 209 Osborne St., tel. (912) 882-7490, or **Spencer House Inn,** 101 E. Bryant St., tel. (912) 882-1872.

A dozen chain motels can be found on Hwy. 40 around I-95 exit 2 in Kingsland, including Best Western, Comfort Inn, Days Inn, Econo-lodge, Hampton Inn, Super 8, and Jameson Inn.

Food and Provisions

Across from the Cumberland Ferry dock, **Trolley's Bar and Grill,** is a cheery tavern for jalapeno poppers, peel-and-eat shrimp, burgers, and kid food. It opens at 11 a.m. (closed Sun.). The sweet shop **Sweet Magnolia** in the Cumberland Post complex next door serves breakfast weekdays 8-10:30 a.m. and also

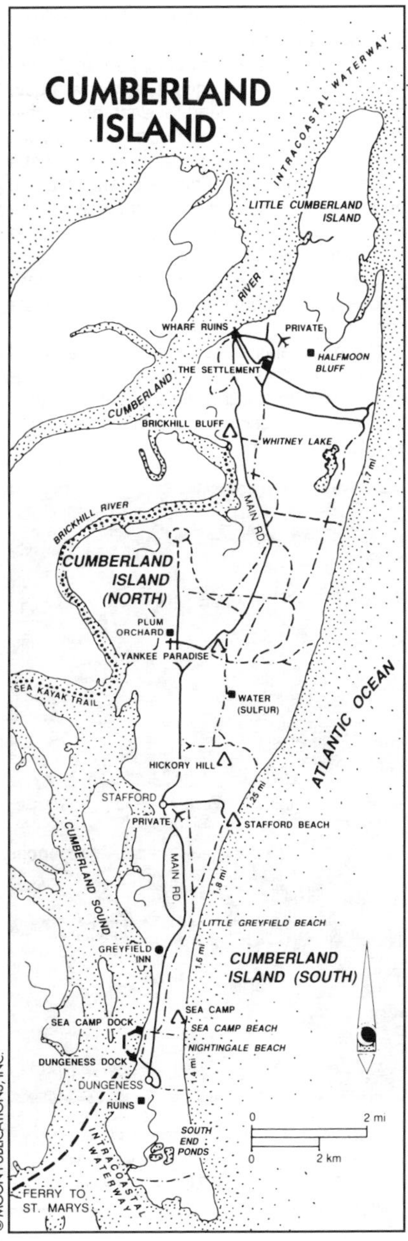

makes box lunches—handy for Cumberland visitors. At the Riverview Hotel, **Seagle's Restaurant and Lounge** serves basic American fare and local seafood for dinner only.

The few small shops downtown should have any sunscreen or insect repellent you might have forgotten; for a supermarket you'll need to go back up to the Piggly Wiggly or Food Lion shopping center at the intersection of Osborne and Crooked River.

Crooked River State Park

Crooked River State Park, tel. (912) 882-5256, sits on a secluded bluff overlooking the beautiful sound and marshlands. A pool, boat launch, and 1.5-mile nature trail are scattered around the 500-acre park, and you can rent fully equipped cottages ($60-80 a night for two bedrooms) or camp in coastal woods ($14 a night). The parking fee is $2 per car, free on Wednesday.

The park lies on a seven-mile dead end of Spur 40, so stock up on provisions before you arrive. There's a large shopping center off Rte. 40 on the way to town. (Note also the tabby ruins of an old sugar mill across from the nuclear submarine base.) The St. Simons-based **South-East Adventure Outfitters** runs kayaking excursions from the boat landing at the foot of Spur 40 to the less-traveled northern end of Cumberland Island; see **St. Simons Island** for more information.

CUMBERLAND ISLAND

So you've been along the Georgia coast, maybe to Savannah, acquiring a sense for the history, the heat, and the subtropical nature of it all. Say you've arrived at land's end, at the mouth of the St. Marys River, the very boundary of the American South (Florida barely counts). And here you are, at the dock, looking across the sound at the prize.

The largest of Georgia's barrier islands, Cumberland offers a long, lean stretch of subtropical paradise sealed off from the outside world. Gleaming shell-gravel paths lead through lusty jungles of gnarly oaks, draping vines and Spanish moss, and stumpy palmettos waving their broad circular fronds like fans. Wild horses—

wild horses!—languidly lower hooves into the surf; bobcat tracks closely follow armadillo tracks on the dune, then disappear. Giant nesting sea turtles take their chances.

Then, in one of those juxtapositions so startling about the South, you emerge from your long hike through nothing but wilderness, up onto a clearing. Down an arcade appears a three-story mansion, where a handsome couple on the second-story veranda sport evening clothes and toast the sunset over the marsh.

Welcome to Cumberland.

History

The Timucuan natives inhabited Cumberland Island for more than 3,000 years. A tribe distinct from the Creek of the northern islands, the Timucuans lived similarly, depending on oysters as a primary food source and discarding the shells in huge mounds (middens), typically found near cedar groves. (Cedar is one of the few plants able to root in the high alkaline soil produced by eroding shells; look for cedars at the marsh fringes of Cumberland's forests to find middens.)

In the late 1500s, Spanish soldiers and priests built forts and missions on the islands, though the only remnants of their hundred-year occupation are the wild horses on the island—believed to have descended from Spanish herds. Native rebellions, pirates, and threats from the hovering French and English finally persuaded the missionaries to abandon attempts to convert the Timucuans to Christianity, and the island returned to Timucuan control.

In 1736, General James Oglethorpe, extending his domain south after founding the new Georgia colony at Savannah, built two forts on the island and a hunting lodge he called Dungeness at its southern end. Skirmishes were fought with the Spanish, but the island remained essentially uninhabited until Revolutionary War General Nathaniel Greene bought the island, logged the live oaks for the navy's sailing ships, and built a house he called Dungeness as well. Fire destroyed the house a hundred years later, and his heirs abandoned the island.

In 1881, Thomas Carnegie (brother of Andrew Carnegie) bought much of the island and built yet another house at the former Greene homesite. Carnegie's mansion burned down in 1959, but the ruins are still visible today, surrounded by the old stables, carriage houses, and other outbuildings. His widow, Lucy, built homes on the island for each of her children, and of these, **Plum Orchard** is now vacant and under consideration as an artist's colony. Another, **Greyfield,** is operated as an exclusive lodge by Carnegie heirs (see below), and two other homes remain in use on pockets of private property. The northern tip of the island, once the slave quarters for island plantations, is now home to a small Sea Islander community.

The park service bought most of the island in 1972 to establish the Cumberland Island National Seashore, and in 1982 the northern part of the island was designated a wilderness area.

Sights and Trails

KAP STANN

A dirt road on Cumberland Island can lead to anywhere: a remote Sea Island community, the aristocratic Greyfield Inn, or miles and miles of wilderness.

CUMBERLAND ISLAND FERRY SCHEDULE

Leave St. Marys: 9:00 a.m., 11:45 a.m.
Leave Cumberland Island: 10:15 a.m., 4:45 p.m.

From March 1 to September 30, ferries operate daily. From October 1 to February 28, ferries run Thurs.-Mon. only (no ferries run Tues.-Wed. in winter). Reserve by phone (912) 882-4335 (Mon.-Fri. 10 a.m.-2 p.m. EST) or by fax (912) 673-7747.

Fares: Adults $9.50, seniors $7.50, children 12 years and under (including infants) $5.65, plus tax. Add to that a day-use fee of $4 per person per day. Boats leave from the dock at St. Marys (from I-95, take exit 2, go east on Hwy. 40). Arrive at the dock 30 minutes before departure to assure your seat (standby tickets available depending on no-shows). Trips take 45 minutes.

The first ferry stop docks near the Dungeness historical site. Here a small museum (the old icehouse) tells the story of the Native American islanders, European exploration and settlement, Sea Island Cotton, and of the families who lived here in the high-style plantation era. Most historic sites lie along the short walk between the west-side dock and the east-side beach.

The beach is exceptionally long and wide, with a very gradual slope by the surf and high dunes banking the forest. You might want to loop around from the Dungeness stop through the historic sites, out to the beach and north along the sand, then back by way of the Sea Camp dock. (You could reverse the direction, but signs in to the Dungeness dock are less readily seen than the other way.) It's always best to give yourself ample time to get back to the dock; if you miss the ferry you'll have to charter a boat back for $60.

A network of trails (dirt roads, shell roads, and footpaths) laces through the island's varied natural environments. Many are on the northern part of the island, too far to be practical unless you're staying overnight. For day-trippers, the following trails are the most practical: the loop trail described above, a marsh trail at the southern tip of the island (disembark at Dungeness, walk out to the beach and turn right), and the trails through the forest between the two docks (the River Trail or Nightingale Trail).

Rangers offer guided history walks, nature walks, seine netting workshops, and short videos or movies among their daily programs.

Camping

Visitors may camp overnight at the Sea Camp campground ($4 a night) or at primitive back-country sites ($2), for a maximum of seven nights; advance reservations are required. Upon arrival, campers disembark at the second island stop (Sea Camp); where sites are assigned. It's a short quarter-mile walk to the campground. Some wooden "pony" carts are available to haul gear, but these can be very awkward unless you're a pony. If you can rig something with a strong-wheeled luggage carrier that'll transport a packed ice chest over a shell road, so much the better.

The Sea Camp campground, sheltered by a 15-foot-high dune and a thick canopy of stunted oaks, is carved out of the dense palmetto substory. Well-secluded sites round out like little nests, each with a picnic table, a small latched food locker (string up or secure the rest of your food), and ample space to set up one or more tents. Two group camps accommodate 12 people maximum at each site. The bathhouse has toilets and cold-water showers.

Backpackers must register at the visitor center after disembarking to obtain backcountry permits and sign up for one of four primitive camping areas. Each has a well nearby, but you must treat the water before drinking.

Greyfield Inn

The aristocratic Greyfield Inn operates out of a turn-of-the-century mansion, once a winter retreat for the Carnegie family. Still in family hands, the beautiful period-furnished (right down to the original family china) house sits on a 1,300-acre private compound in the midst of the national parklands. The house's library, porch swings, honor bar, bicycles, marsh shore, and easy access to the beach complement 17 elegant guest rooms with private baths. Rates start about $300 a night for two and include breakfast, picnic lunches, and elegant formal dinners—jackets are required for men. (The innkeeper tells the story of a sparky camping couple who made dinner reservations, hauled a white dinner jacket and heels along with their camping gear, and enjoyed an elegant dinner around the table with the inn guests before heading back to camp!)

A ferry for guests runs from Fernandina Beach, Florida. Call the inn's Fernandina Beach office, tel. (904) 261-6408, for information or reservations.

Getting There

A private concessionaire operates a passenger ferry (no cars, bikes, or pets) from St. Marys to Cumberland Island (see schedule). Though not required, reservations are highly recommended and are accepted up to six months in advance. Cumberland allows only 300 people a day, a limit quickly reached on certain days in popular seasons. The island is closed to visitors during five annual deer hunts in winter.

Once you have reservations, arrive at the St. Marys dock 30 minutes before departure with adequate food, water, and supplies for a day's outing; a tiny concession on the boat sells sodas and some packaged snacks. Passengers receive a trail map and ranger orientation before departure.

Day-trippers can choose to get off at either at the **Dungeness** or **Sea Camp** dock. All overnighters disembark at Sea Camp. Drinking water and restrooms are available at both docks, with more in the campground and historical area.

Private boats may dock at Sea Camp, near the ranger station, for day-use only—first-come, first-served. Call ahead and let them know of your arrival. Beware if approaching from the north—the rangers say St. Andrews Sound is the third most dangerous inlet on the East Coast.

Little Cumberland Island

At the northern tip of Cumberland Island, Little Cumberland Island holds a privately owned residential community; a ferry operates from Jekyll Island for residents.

SCOTT TEEPLE

peaches

BOOKLIST

DESCRIPTION AND TRAVEL

American Automobile Association. *Georgia, North Carolina, South Carolina Tour Book.* Published annually. Capsule descriptions of the more popular tourist areas, including up-to-date hotel, motel, and restaurant information.

Georgia Conservancy. *The Georgia Conservancy's Guide to the North Georgia Mountains.* Atlanta: The Georgia Conservancy, 1990 (distributed by Longstreet Press, 2150 Newmarket Pkwy. #102, Marietta, GA 30067). A yard-by-yard guide to the natural areas of North Georgia, thoroughly describing local terrain, flora, and fauna.

Georgia Conservancy. *A Guide to the Georgia Coast.* Savannah, GA: The Georgia Conservancy (711 Sandtown Rd., Savannah, GA 31410). A detailed guide to coastal Georgia's natural areas, including appendices of marinas and boat captains.

Georgia Department of Industry, Trade, and Tourism. *Georgia On My Mind.* Published annually; 176 pages. Magazine-format compendium of state sights, including lodging and dining information (no prices). Though the organization of the state's tourist bureau districts can sometimes be hard to follow, the guide is nevertheless a resource, particularly for places the auto club doesn't mention. Each edition contains a full-size highway map pullout. Order from P.O. Box 1776, Atlanta, GA 30301-1776.

CULTURE

Cherokee Publications, P.O. Box 256, Cherokee, NC 28719. The eastern band of Cherokee Indians distributes dozens of publications—covering everything from culture, history, and folktales, to cuisine and children's books—from its North Carolina reservation.

Grizzard, Lewis. *Aim Low Boys, They're Riding Shetland Ponies. Don't Bend over in the Garden, Granny; Them 'Taters Got Eyes.* The titles of these collections of essays hint at this late native son's humorous take on life in the South.

Harper, Francis and Delma E. Presley. *Okefinokee Album.* Athens: University of Georgia Press, 1981. A large-format collection of old-time photographs, stories, and profiles of the Okefenokee Swamp region, and a "swamp talk" glossary that's worth a look alone.

Mickler, Ernest Matthew. *White Trash Cooking.* Berkeley: Ten Speed Press, 1986. A collection of recipes and cooking methods that unveils the secrets of Southern low cuisine.

Pope, Trey. *Barbecue On My Mind.* Atlanta: Cherokee Press, 1992. Thirty of the state's finest 'cue establishments are rated by an esteemed aficionado.

Wigginton, Eliot, ed. *The Foxfire Book and Foxfire 2 through 9.* Garden City: Anchor Press/Doubleday, 1972-86. The hands-on student-written guide to the heritage, handicrafts, and folklore of the Southern Highlanders.

HISTORY

Branch, Taylor. *Parting the Waters: America in the King Years: 1954-1963.* New York: Simon & Schuster, 1988. Branch, focusing on Dr. Martin Luther King, Jr., offers a look at the nation during the American civil rights movement, from the early Eisenhower years to the Kennedy assassination.

Carter, Jimmy. *Turning Point.* New York: Times Books, 1992. Carter deciphers the early days of the civil rights movement in Georgia that shaped his political career.

Coleman, Kenneth. *A History of Georgia.* Athens, GA: University of Georgia Press, 1990. A comprehensive European history of Georgia, from Spanish exploration up through the 1980s.

Davis, Burke. *Sherman's March.* New York: Random House, 1980. The mile-by-mile account of Sherman's devastating crusade through Georgia in 1864.

Hudson, Charles. *Southeastern Indians.* Knoxville, TN: University of Tennessee Press, 1976. The comprehensive resource work on southeastern Indian nations, including history, mythology, and culture.

Kemble, Fanny. *Journal of a Residence on a Georgian Plantation in 1838-39.* Athens: University of Georgia Press, 1984 (reprint). The personal account of a sojourning British actress, whose scathing indictment of slavery was thought to sway British public opinion against the South during the Civil War.

RECREATION AND RESOURCES

Georgia Atlas and Gazeteer. Yarmouth, ME: DeLorme Publishers, 1998. A handy tabloid-sized atlas ideal for recreation and getting around rural regions. See also www.delorme.com.

Pfitzer, Donald. *The Hiker's Guide to Georgia.* Helena, MT: Falcon Press, 1993; 294 pages. Covers 74 trails, including lengths, elevations, difficulty, water availability, etc.

Sehlinger, Bob, and Don Otey. *Northern Georgia Canoeing* and *Southern Georgia Canoeing.* Birmingham, AL: Menasha Press, 1980. Two guides to Georgia's waterways, roughly divided at the fall line.

GOOD READING

Berendt, John. *Midnight in the Garden of Good and Evil.* New York: Random House, 1994. A sordid murder story spiced with scandal and eccentricity among Savannah society, a factual account that reads like fiction.

Conroy, Pat. *The Prince of Tides.* Boston: Houghton Mifflin, 1986. A story of a traumatized tidewater family that lovingly describes the low country (also a film by the same name).

Dickey, James. *Deliverance.* Boston: Houghton Mifflin, 1970. Maverick canoeists meet mountain men in this haunting tale set in North Georgia (also a film by the same name).

Greene, Melissa Fay. *Praying for Sheetrock.* New York: Addison-Wesley, 1991. A poignant true tale of corruption in a rural town in the pre-civil rights South.

Harris, Joel Chandler. *Uncle Remus Tales.* Marietta, GA: Cherokee Press, 1981 (reprint, original publication 1880). African-American folktales as told to the author as a young boy (inspiration for Disney's animated film *Song of the South*).

Mitchell, Margaret. *Gone with the Wind.* New York: Macmillan, 1936. Full-bore plantation mythology in all its glory, fastest selling novel in U.S. history (also a classic MGM film).

O'Connor, Flannery. *The Complete Stories.* New York: Farrar, Straus, and Giroux, 1946. Stunningly gothic vignettes of the rural South.

Walker, Alice. *The Color Purple.* New York: Simon & Schuster, 1982. The Pulitzer prize-winning tale of a black woman's struggle in the Georgia heartland.

White, Bailey. *Mama Makes Up Her Mind.* New York: Addison-Wesley, 1993. Slice-of-life stories of South Georgia, as featured on National Public Radio.

Wolfe, Tom. *A Man in Full.* New York: Farrar, Straus, and Giroux, 1998. Portrays Atlanta society's attempt to cover up a white woman's date-rape charge against an African-American football star at Georgia Tech.

INDEX

B

C

CAMPGROUNDS/RV PARKS

CIVIL WAR

D

G

GARDENS

HIKING AND BACKPACKING

I

J

N

NATIVE AMERICAN HERITAGE

NATURE AND CONSERVATION AREAS

O

SCHOOLS, COLLEGES, AND UNIVERSITIES

STATE PARKS

T

U

UNUSUAL CLAIMS TO FAME

V

W

XYZ

ABOUT THE AUTHOR

A travel writer specializing in the southeastern U.S., Kap Stann has written guides to nearly every state below the Mason-Dixon line. Though she has traveled to remote corners of Central America, South America, and Southeast Asia, Kap maintains that the American South is the most "unexpectedly exotic" place she has ever seen. Originally from New York, Kap now lives in Berkeley, California, with her daughter Cory.

ANGELA GENNINO

MEXICO

"These books will delight the armchair traveler, aid the undecided person in selecting a destination, and guide the seasoned road warrior looking for lesser-known hideaways."

—*Mexican Meanderings* Newsletter

"From tourist traps to off-the-beaten track hideaways, these guides offer consistent, accurate details without pretension."

—*Foreign Service Journal*

Archaeological Mexico Andrew Coe	**$19.95** 420 pages, 27 maps
Baja Handbook Joe Cummings	**$16.95** 540 pages, 46 maps
Cabo Handbook Joe Cummings	**$14.95** 270 pages, 17 maps
Cancún Handbook Chicki Mallan	**$14.95** 240 pages, 25 maps
Colonial Mexico Chicki Mallan	**$18.95** 400 pages, 38 maps
Mexico Handbook Joe Cummings and Chicki Mallan	**$21.95** 1,200 pages, 201 maps
Northern Mexico Handbook Joe Cummings	**$17.95** 610 pages, 69 maps
Pacific Mexico Handbook Bruce Whipperman	**$17.95** 580 pages, 68 maps
Puerto Vallarta Handbook Bruce Whipperman	**$14.95** 330 pages, 36 maps
Yucatán Handbook Chicki Mallan	**$16.95** 400 pages, 52 maps

"Beyond question, the most comprehensive Mexican resources available for those who prefer deep travel to shallow tourism. But don't worry, the fiesta-fun stuff's all here too."

—*New York Daily News*

LATIN AMERICA AND THE CARIBBEAN

"Solidly packed with practical information and full of significant cultural asides that will enlighten you on the whys and wherefores of things you might easily see but not easily grasp."

—Boston Globe

Belize Handbook	**$15.95**
Chicki Mallan and Patti Lange	390 pages, 45 maps
Caribbean Vacations	**$18.95**
Karl Luntta	910 pages, 64 maps
Costa Rica Handbook	**$19.95**
Christopher P. Baker	780 pages, 73 maps
Cuba Handbook	**$19.95**
Christopher P. Baker	740 pages, 70 maps
Dominican Republic Handbook	**$15.95**
Gaylord Dold	420 pages, 24 maps
Ecuador Handbook	**$16.95**
Julian Smith	450 pages, 43 maps
Honduras Handbook	**$15.95**
Chris Humphrey	330 pages, 40 maps
Jamaica Handbook	**$15.95**
Karl Luntta	330 pages, 17 maps
Virgin Islands Handbook	**$13.95**
Karl Luntta	220 pages, 19 maps

NORTH AMERICA AND HAWAII

"These domestic guides convey the same sense of exoticism that their foreign counterparts do, making home-country travel seem like far-flung adventure."

—Sierra Magazine

Alaska-Yukon Handbook	**$17.95**
Deke Castleman and Don Pitcher	530 pages, 92 maps
Alberta and the Northwest Territories Handbook	**$18.95**
Andrew Hempstead	520 pages, 79 maps
Arizona Handbook	**$18.95**
Bill Weir	600 pages, 36 maps
Atlantic Canada Handbook	**$18.95**
Mark Morris	490 pages, 60 maps
Big Island of Hawaii Handbook	**$15.95**
J.D. Bisignani	390 pages, 25 maps
Boston Handbook	**$13.95**
Jeff Perk	200 pages, 20 maps
British Columbia Handbook	**$16.95**
Jane King and Andrew Hempstead	430 pages, 69 maps

Canadian Rockies Handbook	**$14.95**
Andrew Hempstead	220 pages, 22 maps
Colorado Handbook	**$17.95**
Stephen Metzger	480 pages, 46 maps
Georgia Handbook	**$17.95**
Kap Stann	380 pages, 44 maps
Grand Canyon Handbook	**$14.95**
Bill Weir	220 pages, 10 maps
Hawaii Handbook	**$19.95**
J.D. Bisignani	1,030 pages, 88 maps
Honolulu-Waikiki Handbook	**$14.95**
J.D. Bisignani	360 pages, 20 maps
Idaho Handbook	**$18.95**
Don Root	610 pages, 42 maps
Kauai Handbook	**$15.95**
J.D. Bisignani	320 pages, 23 maps
Los Angeles Handbook	**$16.95**
Kim Weir	370 pages, 15 maps
Maine Handbook	**$18.95**
Kathleen M. Brandes	660 pages, 27 maps
Massachusetts Handbook	**$18.95**
Jeff Perk	600 pages, 23 maps
Maui Handbook	**$15.95**
J.D. Bisignani	450 pages, 37 maps
Michigan Handbook	**$15.95**
Tina Lassen	360 pages, 32 maps
Montana Handbook	**$17.95**
Judy Jewell and W.C. McRae	490 pages, 52 maps
Nevada Handbook	**$18.95**
Deke Castleman	530 pages, 40 maps
New Hampshire Handbook	**$18.95**
Steve Lantos	500 pages, 18 maps
New Mexico Handbook	**$15.95**
Stephen Metzger	360 pages, 47 maps
New York Handbook	**$19.95**
Christiane Bird	780 pages, 95 maps
New York City Handbook	**$13.95**
Christiane Bird	300 pages, 20 maps
North Carolina Handbook	**$14.95**
Rob Hirtz and Jenny Daughtry Hirtz	320 pages, 27 maps
Northern California Handbook	**$19.95**
Kim Weir	800 pages, 50 maps
Ohio Handbook	**$15.95**
David K. Wright	340 pages, 18 maps
Oregon Handbook	**$17.95**
Stuart Warren and Ted Long Ishikawa	590 pages, 34 maps

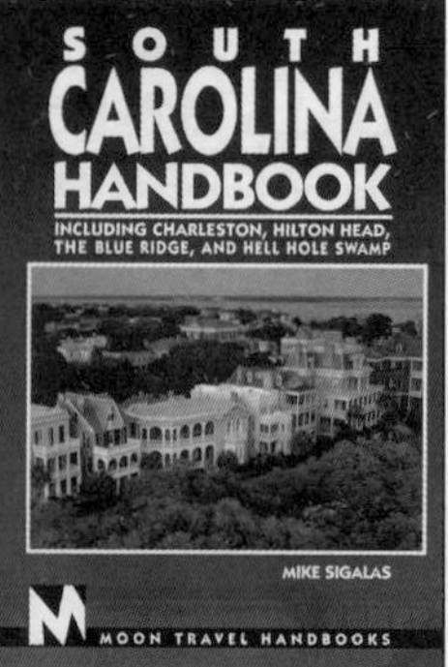

Pennsylvania Handbook	**$18.95**
Joanne Miller	448 pages, 40 maps
Road Trip USA	**$24.00**
Jamie Jensen	940 pages, 175 maps
Road Trip USA Getaways: Chicago	**$9.95**
	60 pages, 1 map
Road Trip USA Getaways: Seattle	**$9.95**
	60 pages, 1 map
Santa Fe-Taos Handbook	**$13.95**
Stephen Metzger	160 pages, 13 maps
South Carolina Handbook	**$16.95**
Mike Sigalas	400 pages, 20 maps
Southern California Handbook	**$19.95**
Kim Weir	720 pages, 26 maps
Tennessee Handbook	**$17.95**
Jeff Bradley	530 pages, 42 maps
Texas Handbook	**$18.95**
Joe Cummings	690 pages, 70 maps
Utah Handbook	**$17.95**
Bill Weir and W.C. McRae	490 pages, 40 maps
Virginia Handbook	**$15.95**
Julian Smith	410 pages, 37 maps
Washington Handbook	**$19.95**
Don Pitcher	840 pages, 111 maps
Wisconsin Handbook	**$18.95**
Thomas Huhti	590 pages, 69 maps
Wyoming Handbook	**$17.95**
Don Pitcher	610 pages, 80 maps

ASIA AND THE PACIFIC

"Scores of maps, detailed practical info down to business hours of small-town libraries. You can't beat the Asian titles for sheer heft. (The) series is sort of an American Lonely Planet, with better writing but fewer titles. (The) individual voice of researchers comes through."

—Travel & Leisure

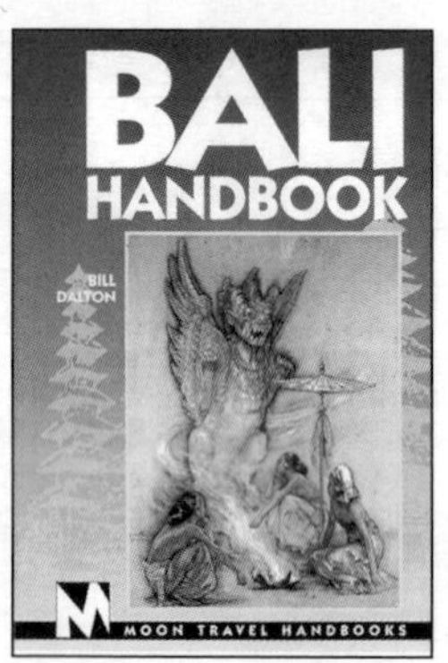

Australia Handbook	**$21.95**
Marael Johnson, Andrew Hempstead, and Nadina Purdon	940 pages, 141 maps
Bali Handbook	**$19.95**
Bill Dalton	750 pages, 54 maps
Fiji Islands Handbook	**$14.95**
David Stanley	350 pages, 42 maps
Hong Kong Handbook	**$16.95**
Kerry Moran	378 pages, 49 maps

Indonesia Handbook	**$25.00**
Bill Dalton	1,380 pages, 249 maps
Micronesia Handbook	**$16.95**
Neil M. Levy	340 pages, 70 maps
Nepal Handbook	**$18.95**
Kerry Moran	490 pages, 51 maps
New Zealand Handbook	**$19.95**
Jane King	620 pages, 81 maps
Outback Australia Handbook	**$18.95**
Marael Johnson	450 pages, 57 maps
Philippines Handbook	**$17.95**
Peter Harper and Laurie Fullerton	670 pages, 116 maps
Singapore Handbook	**$15.95**
Carl Parkes	350 pages, 29 maps
South Korea Handbook	**$19.95**
Robert Nilsen	820 pages, 141 maps
South Pacific Handbook	**$24.00**
David Stanley	920 pages, 147 maps
Southeast Asia Handbook	**$21.95**
Carl Parkes	1,080 pages, 204 maps
Tahiti Handbook	**$15.95**
David Stanley	450 pages, 51 maps
Thailand Handbook	**$19.95**
Carl Parkes	860 pages, 142 maps
Vietnam, Cambodia & Laos Handbook	**$18.95**
Michael Buckley	760 pages, 116 maps

OTHER GREAT TITLES FROM MOON

"For hardy wanderers, few guides come more highly recommended than the Handbooks. They include good maps, steer clear of fluff and flackery, and offer plenty of money-saving tips. They also give you the kind of information that visitors to strange lands—on any budget—need to survive."

—US News & World Report

Moon Handbook	**$10.00**
Carl Koppeschaar	150 pages, 8 maps
The Practical Nomad: How to Travel Around the World	**$17.95**
Edward Hasbrouck	580 pages
Staying Healthy in Asia, Africa, and Latin America	**$11.95**
Dirk Schroeder	230 pages, 4 maps

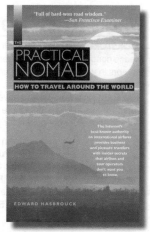

WHERE TO BUY MOON TRAVEL HANDBOOKS

BOOKSTORES AND LIBRARIES: Moon Travel Handbooks are distributed worldwide. Please contact our sales manager at info@moon.com for a list of wholesalers and distributors in your area.

TRAVELERS: We would like to have Moon Travel Handbooks available throughout the world. Please ask your bookstore to contact us for ordering information. If your bookstore will not order our guides for you, please contact us for a free catalog.

Moon Travel Handbooks
c/o Publishers Group West
Attn: Order Department
1700 Fourth Street
Berkeley, CA 94710
fax: (510) 528-3444

IMPORTANT ORDERING INFORMATION

PRICES: All prices are subject to change. We always ship the most current edition. We will let you know if there is a price increase on the book you order.

SHIPPING AND HANDLING OPTIONS: Domestic UPS or USPS priority mail (allow 10 working days for delivery): $6.00 for the first item, $1.00 for each additional item.

UPS 2nd Day Air or Printed Airmail requires a special quote.

International Surface Bookrate 8-12 weeks delivery: $5.00 for the first item, $1.00 for each additional item. Note: We cannot guarantee international surface bookrate shipping. We recommend sending international orders via air mail, which requires a special quote.

FOREIGN ORDERS: Orders that originate outside the U.S.A. must be paid for with an international money order, a check in U.S. currency drawn on a major U.S. bank based in the U.S.A., or Visa, MasterCard, or American Express.

INTERNET ORDERS: Visit our site at: www.moon.com

ORDER FORM

Prices are subject to change without notice. Please check our Web site at **www.moon.com** for current prices and editions.
(See important ordering information on preceding page.)

Name: ____________________ Date: ____________________

Street: ____

City: ____________________ Daytime Phone: ____________________

State or Country: ____________________ Zip Code: ____________________

QUANTITY	TITLE	PRICE

Taxable Total ________

Sales Tax in CA and NY ________

Shipping & Handling ________

TOTAL ________

Ship: ☐ UPS (no P.O. Boxes) ☐ Priority mail ☐ International surface mail

Ship to: ☐ address above ☐ other ____________________

____

____

Make checks payable to: **PUBLISHERS GROUP WEST**, Attn: Order Department, 1700 Fourth St., Berkeley, CA 94710, or fax to (510) 528-3444. We accept Visa, MasterCard, or American Express.

To Order: Call in your Visa, MasterCard, or American Express number, or send a written order with your Visa, MasterCard, or American Express number and expiration date clearly written.

Card Number: ☐ **Visa** ☐ **MasterCard** ☐ **American Express**

☐☐☐☐ ☐☐☐☐ ☐☐☐☐ ☐☐☐☐

Exact Name on Card: ____________________

Expiration date: ____________________

Signature: ____________________

Daytime Phone: ____________________

U.S.~METRIC CONVERSION

1 inch = 2.54 centimeters (cm)
1 foot = .304 meters (m)
1 yard = 0.914 meters
1 mile = 1.6093 kilometers (km)
1 km = .6214 miles
1 fathom = 1.8288 m
1 chain = 20.1168 m
1 furlong = 201.168 m
1 acre = .4047 hectares
1 sq km = 100 hectares
1 sq mile = 2.59 square km
1 ounce = 28.35 grams
1 pound = .4536 kilograms
1 short ton = .90718 metric ton
1 short ton = 2000 pounds
1 long ton = 1.016 metric tons
1 long ton = 2240 pounds
1 metric ton = 1000 kilograms
1 quart = .94635 liters
1 US gallon = 3.7854 liters
1 Imperial gallon = 4.5459 liters
1 nautical mile = 1.852 km

To compute celsius temperatures, subtract 32 from Fahrenheit and divide by 1.8. To go the other way, multiply celsius by 1.8 and add 32.

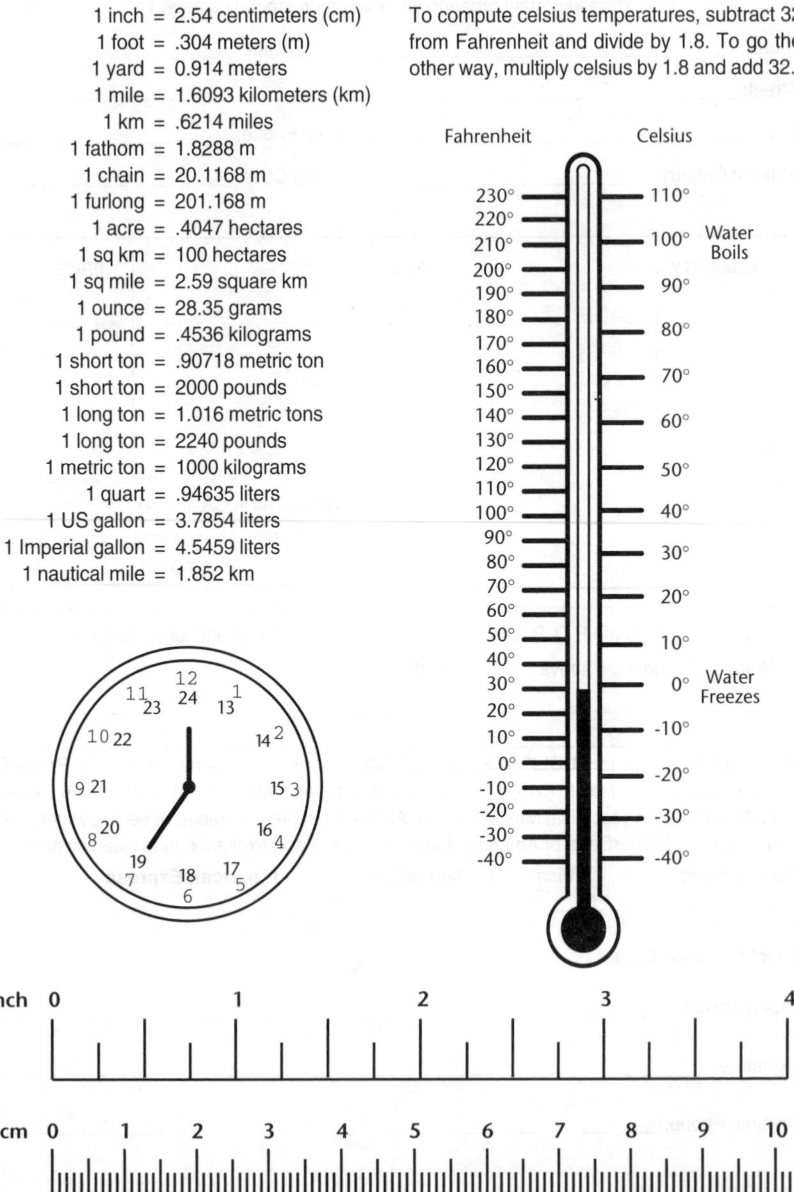

NOTES

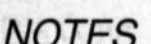

NOTES

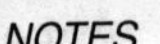